Developments in Macro-Finance Yield Curve Modelling

Changes in the shape of the yield curve have traditionally been one of the key macroeconomic indicators of a likely change in economic outlook. However, the recent financial crises have created a challenge to the management of monetary policy, demanding a revision in the way that policymakers model expected changes in the economy. This volume brings together central bank economists and leading academic monetary economists to propose new methods for modelling the behaviour of interest rates. Topics covered include: the analysis and extraction of expectations of future monetary policy and inflation; the analysis of the short-term dynamics of money market interest rates; the reliability of existing models in periods of extreme market volatility and how to adjust them accordingly; the role of government debt and deficits in affecting sovereign bond yields and spreads. This book will interest financial researchers and practitioners as well as academic and central bank economists.

JAGJIT S. CHADHA is Professor of Economics at the University of Kent and is on the Advisory Board of the Centre of International Macroeconomics and Finance at the University of Cambridge. His research involves incorporating financial factors in macroeconomic models and he has acted as an adviser to many central banks throughout the world.

ALAIN C. J. DURRÉ is Principal Economist in the Financial Research Division of the Directorate General Research of the European Central Bank and is Associate Professor of Finance at IÉSEG-School of Management at Lille Catholic University. He has published various papers on monetary and financial economics in many leading academic journals and he has acted as Monetary Policy Adviser for the International Monetary Fund.

MICHAEL A. S. JOYCE is an Adviser in the Macro Financial Analysis Division of the Bank of England and has over twenty years' experience working at the Bank of England in various economics roles. His recent research has focused on modelling the term structure of interest rates and on analysing the effects of the UK's quantitative easing policy.

LUCIO SARNO is a Professor of Finance, Deputy Dean and Head of the Finance Faculty at Cass Business School, City University London. His main research interests are in international finance, and he is a leading expert on exchange rates, a subject on which he writes prolifically and on which he is routinely called for advice by governments, international organisations, and financial companies around the world.

Macroeconomic Policy Making

Series editors

Professor JAGJIT S. CHADHA University of Kent, Canterbury
Professor SEAN HOLLY University of Cambridge

The 2007–2010 financial crisis has asked some very hard questions of modern macroeconomics. The consensus that grew up during 'the Great Moderation' has proved to be an incomplete explanation for how to conduct monetary policy in the face of financial shocks. This series brings together leading macroeconomic researchers and central bank economists to analyse the tools and methods necessary to meet the challenges of the post- financial crisis world.

Published titles:
Chadha and Holly *Interest Rates, Prices and Liquidity: Lessons from the Financial Crisis*
Coffman, Leonard and Neal *Questioning Credible Commitment: Perspectives on the Rise of Financial Capitalism*

Developments in Macro-Finance Yield Curve Modelling

Edited by

Jagjit S. Chadha
Alain C. J. Durré
Michael A. S. Joyce
Lucio Sarno

CAMBRIDGE
UNIVERSITY PRESS

University Printing House, Cambridge CB2 8BS, United Kingdom

Cambridge University Press is part of the University of Cambridge.

It furthers the University's mission by disseminating knowledge in the pursuit of education, learning and research at the highest international levels of excellence.

www.cambridge.org
Information on this title: www.cambridge.org/9781316623169

© Cambridge University Press 2014

First published 2014
First paperback edition 2016

A catalogue record for this publication is available from the British Library

ISBN 978-1-107-04455-5 Hardback
ISBN 978-1-316-62316-9 Paperback

Contents

Part V Default risk

Figures

Tables

Contributors

MORTEN BECH Bank for International Settlements

ANDREA BURASCHI University of Chicago

PRISCILLA BURITY Pontifical Catholic University of Rio de Janeiro

ANDREA CARNELLI Imperial College London

JAGJIT S. CHADHA University of Kent and CIMF, University of Cambridge

MICHAEL DEMPSTER University of Cambridge

HANS DEWACHTER National Bank of Belgium and University of Leuven

ALAIN C. J. DURRÉ European Central Bank and IÉSEG-School of management

PATRIK EDSPARR Visiting Fellow, Bank of England

JACK EVANS evalueFE

PAUL FISHER Bank of England

JEAN-SÉBASTIEN FONTAINE Bank of Canada

JUAN ANGEL GARCÍA European Central Bank

LEONARDO IANIA Louvain School of Management, National Bank of Belgium and KU Leuven

MICHAEL A. S. JOYCE Bank of England

ELIZABETH KLEE Federal Reserve Board

YVAN LENGWILER University of Basel

CARLOS LENZ Swiss National Bank

MARCO LYRIO Insper Institute for Education and Research

LUIGI MARATTIN University of Bologna

MARCELO MEDEIROS Pontifical Catholic University of Rio de Janeiro

ELENA MEDOVA Cambridge Systems

ALAIN MONFORT CREST

JEAN-PAUL RENNE Banque de France

PAOLO PAESANI University of Rome, Tor Vergata

MARCELLO PERICOLI Bank of Italy

SIMONE SALOTTI Oxford Brookes University

LUCIO SARNO City University London

FRANK SMETS European Central Bank and KU Leuven

VIKTORS STEBUNOVS Federal Reserve Board

JAMES STEELEY Aston Business School

DANIEL THORNTON The Federal Reserve Bank of St Louis

PHILIP TURNER Bank for International Settlements

LUCIANO VEREDA Universidade Federal Fluminense

THOMAS WERNER European Central Bank

PAUL WHELAN Imperial College London

Foreword

Macroeconomics and finance are often housed within separate faculties in universities, and within separate divisions in central banks. In the real world, however, the two are intimately related. Savers, borrowers and investors meet through financial markets and institutions. Insurance markets support the pooling, distribution and diversification of risks. Money markets underpin the most basic plumbing of modern economies: the payment systems through which we pay for goods and services, in different currencies, anywhere in the world. Banks combine the provision of credit, payments and liquidity-insurance services. Finance matters to macro, and vice versa!

Finance theory has made real progress over the past couple of decades in modelling yield curves. Armed with, admittedly strong, 'no arbitrage' assumptions that risk is priced consistently across the bond market at all times, this allowed a measure of the markets' beliefs about the path of short-term interest rates to be derived from the term structure of forward interest rates. Together with similar information from index-linked government debt, this unlocked the extraction of estimates of inflation expectations at different horizons - vitally important for monetary policy makers, and also for legislators and the public in holding independent central banks accountable for the price-stability goal they have set us.

Although no-arbitrage provides a means of deriving risk premia, measuring *and explaining* the various risk premia priced into different financial contracts remains one of the biggest challenges for macro-finance. This is not only a technical question for finance. Macroeconomic policymakers need to understand the real economy counterparts to identified shifts in risk premia. For example, does a fall in long-term rates driven by a compression in term premia have the same implications for investment prospects as a fall driven by lower expected future central bank interest rates?

The importance of questions of that kind has been underlined by central banks' use of quantitative easing given that our short-term policy interest rates are at, or around, their lower bound. Separately from any signals that QE might give about the likely path of the policy rate, policymakers have purchased longer-term bonds in order to influence term premia directly and, through portfolio-balance effects, the price of other assets. We have therefore needed rich models in order to understand those features of the real world - preferred habitats, imperfect arbitrage, and the associated balance sheet constraints amongst intermediaries - that make this possible, and to identify and forecast the effects of a given stock of asset purchases.

The effect of the size and composition of central bank balance sheets on asset prices touches on old debates about the overlap between debt management operations and monetary conditions. A 1998 Bank of England conference[1] concluded that, though changes in debt management policy were unlikely at the margin to have first-order effects, it was 'less clear that large changes in the quantity or composition of debt [would] not have implications for monetary conditions'. Fifteen years on, the influence of quantitative easing on long-term interest rates looks to have over-turned previous scepticism about the effectiveness of the kind of operations employed in the Federal Reserve's 'Operation Twist' in the early 1960s.

There is an accumulating body of evidence that central banks' influence over risk-premia extends beyond unconventional monetary policy instruments such as quantitative easing. The prevailing level and expected path of the risk-free interest-rate matters too. Movements in long-term (forward) interest rates following changes in central bank policy rates appear consistent with a risk channel of conventional monetary policy, with cuts in short-term interest rates bringing about a compression in term premia as investors adjust their portfolios in a search for yield.[2] Monetary policymakers need to be alive and open to the possibility that their actions may well have a bearing on risk-taking in financial markets. That need not imply that monetary policy must routinely be adjusted actively to meet a financial stability objective. Where risks to financial stability emerge, financial policy tools - the regulation of banks and other institutions - can be used to address the problem more directly.

Incorporating a role for changes in risk premia in macroeconomic fluctuations is, I believe, vital to a deeper understanding of the drivers and implications of developments within financial markets. In addition to

---

[1] See Crystal (1999), 'Government Debt Structure and Monetary Conditions' for a record of the conference proceedings.

[2] See Hanson and Stein (2012), 'Monetary Policy and Long-Term Real Rates', Harvard Business School Working Paper, No. 13-008, and Tucker (2012), 'National Balance sheets and macro policies: lessons from the past'.

accounting for term premia, we need macro-models that properly incorporate credit risk, including the non-linearities associated with default. At its core, default is a boundary condition where debtors are unable, or simply unwilling, to service their outstanding obligations given the value of their assets, including their prospective future incomes. A realistic model of credit risk needs to be able to capture the sharp pick up in credit losses that can occur when asset values are sufficiently depressed, and trace through the effects on intermediaries' net worth. Models where different agents' financing costs vary with net worth, but without any prospect of default, are probably not worth much. Moreover, we probably need models with heterogeneity in levels of indebtedness across households, firms and, possibly, also intermediaries.

Real progress also requires macro-finance to re-engage with banking. "Money and banking" used to be at the core of university courses in macroeconomics but, even before the so-called 'Great Stability', came to be regarded as old fashioned. Sadly, the same was true in parts of central banking. The costs of the crisis and the difficulties in generating recovery have put beyond doubt, once again, the importance of banks and other key financial intermediaries to market liquidity, asset prices, the allocation of resources to productive ends, and household and firms' behaviour. It is very important that UK-based researchers should be active in this field, and this conference engaged with a number of the issues. With short-term interest rates close to their effective lower bound, understanding central banks' ability to influence aggregate demand by acting through a broader range of instruments is crucial to underpinning economic recovery. Further ahead, richer models of the connections amongst banking (including shadow banking), risk premia and macro-economic fluctuations would help to avoid similar crises in the future. This timely conference volume addresses issues that are central both to the research agenda for macroeconomics and finance and to the decisions that policymakers will face as we emerge from the crisis.

Paul Tucker, former Deputy
Governor of the Bank of England

Preface

The monetary transmission mechanism relies heavily on the impact of the current level and expected path of policy rates on longer term interest rates paid on government liabilities and a wide constellation of retail and wholesale borrowings. It is mostly this transmission of interest rates along the maturity and risk spectrum that gives monetary policy its traction on the wider economy. And yet much of this transmission was assumed away in many macroeconomic models used prior to the economic crisis: often, even those who modelled the links did not necessarily develop models in which longer term interest rates reflected liquidity or default risk. The problems of this assumption emerged with some force as the evolving financial and sovereign debt crisis in the euro area brought to the fore the intimate relationship between the macroeconomic economy and the financial system. In turn, policymakers have had, in turn, to rethink many assumptions that have been made about the relationship between the state, monetary policy and the financial sector. The extensive and persistent use of near zero interest rates at the short end of the term structure has significantly reawakened research and policy interest in the link between the yield curve and the macro economy.

The development of extraordinary policies such as quantitative and credit easing, as well as extended open market operations such as Operation Twist, have been designed to alleviate premia in longer term interest rates. And yet we remain at some distance from understanding the impact of signalling and purchases on many key interest rates. The conference we held at Clare College Cambridge in September 2011 brought together many economists in academia, financial markets and central banks to look afresh at these relationships and we are pleased to sponsor the publication of the contributions, which have benefitted from the comments of the conference discussants and also many anonymous referees.

JAGJIT S. CHADHA AND SEAN HOLLY

1   Editors' introductory chapter and overview

*J. S. Chadha, A. C. J. Durré, M. A. S. Joyce
and L. Sarno*

The on-going financial crisis continues to expose the limits of our collective knowledge and thereby motivate new avenues of research for academics, practitioners and policymakers and perhaps none more so than those that lie at the intersection of monetary and financial economics. As has been well documented, the origins of the crisis go back to problems in the US sub-prime market that became increasingly clear in the early part of 2007 and culminated in the announcement by BNP Paribas on 9 August 2007 of the suspension of a number of funds as it was no longer possible to value their assets. The BNP Paribas statement was a reflection of the fact that by that summer liquidity had all but evaporated in many securitised lending markets. But the statement itself triggered a further collapse in liquidity in many other markets and also a break-down in interbank lending markets. And what started as a liquidity crisis soon became a credit crisis as it became increasingly apparent that risk in many capital markets had been underpriced and that consequently much of the private sector was carrying too much debt, with many parts of the financial sector leveraged to an untenable degree. Subsequently, at various points in the crisis the very financial network itself seemed threatened with extinction, most notably after the collapse of Lehman Brothers in September 2008. Eventually, the interaction between banking and sovereign risk led to increasing spreads on government debt in many countries and full-blown sovereign debt crises in a number of euro area countries.

The crisis led to governments and central banks having to provide considerable levels of liquidity and capital to the financial sector, and ultimately to a fundamental rethink of many of our working assumptions about the appropriate degree and scale of interaction between the state and the financial sector. As well as providing direct support to the financial sector, policymakers found that they had to adopt extraordinary accommodative policies to help smooth the adjustment of private sector balance-sheets. These policies included the adoption of near-zero policy interest rates, various forms of extended open market operations, known as credit or quantitative easing, and running large and persistent fiscal deficits. Under these conditions, it is perhaps no surprise that the considerable progress that had been made in linking yield curve models to the state of the macroeconomy was going to be put under a great deal of scrutiny. As the chapters in this volume show, it turned out that many of the models developed in the preceding decade or so could not really address many of the key issues that needed to be accounted for in order to price bonds accurately. For example, the limited attention paid to credit and liquidity risk premia and our scant understanding of the implications of heightened uncertainty or disagreement about the macroeconomy or, indeed, policy was thrown into sharp relief; and meant that the specific impact of liquidity risk and portfolio reallocation on bond yields was hard to gauge and the importance of credit and sovereign risk was poorly understood.

Against this background, it was clear that when we planned a Modern Macroeconomic Policymaking conference on money and bond markets there would be considerable interest from the research community. But the quality of the papers we received and also of the extent to which the conference itself promoted a sustained and constructive dialogue greatly exceeded our expectations.[1] We are therefore pleased to be able to publish the papers presented at that conference, which have been thoroughly revised following the comments of the discussants, referees and editors. In this introductory chapter we provide a short summary of each chapter in the book and conclude with what we consider to be the main themes that emerged, which could usefully form the basis of a future research agenda.

The first four substantive chapters represent the keynote addresses given at the conference. In Chapter 2, Philip Turner (Bank for International Settlements) provides a wide-ranging discussion of the nature of the long-term interest rate, asking whether it is a policy victim, a policy variable or a policy lodestar. Turner begins by documenting the decline in long-term interest rates in the major international centres over the last couple of decades, which he suggests cannot be easily explained by the normal determinants of long rates. Turner argues that the long rate has become a policy victim to the extent that it has been affected by a number of different official policies that have all had the effect of increasing the demand for government bonds. This includes: the impact of the

---

[1] This conference was jointly organised by the Centre for International Macroeconomics and Finance (University of Cambridge), the IÉSEG-School of Management (Lille Catholic University) and the Money, Macro Finance Group. The conference papers can be found at www.econ.cam.ac.uk/MMPM/YieldCurve.html.

'saving glut' and the associated choice by Asian countries to accumulate large foreign exchange reserves and invest them in US Treasuries; the impact of regulatory policies on insurance companies and the banking industry; and changes in the valuation of pension funds, which have all led to these institutions increasing their demand for government securities. The consequence of these official policies has been to lower long rates and also to make them more sensitive to the business cycle, insofar as institutional investors have been given greater incentives to increase their government bond holdings when economic prospects deteriorate and to reduce them when growth prospects improve. The long-term interest rate has also become a policy variable in the current crisis. Central banks through their balance sheet policies and governments through their debt management policies have both tried to influence long-term rates. Turner argues there is nothing new in the idea that policy can influence bond yields, with Keynes the best known advocate. The key issue is the degree of imperfect substitutability across the yield curve, which will depend on uncertainty about the future path of interest rates. High government debt and deficits are likely to increase this uncertainty, but they also make the yield curve vulnerable to excess volatility, which reduces the ability of central banks to steer long-term rates for any length of time. Lastly, Turner asks whether the long-term interest rate should be used as a lodestar to guide policy. While the yield curve is often used to measure expectations of inflation and growth and can be central to many microeconomic policies because of its influence on the discount rate, Turner argues that great caution is required in drawing policy implications from its current level. This is because we do not know the extent to which it has been distorted by the effects of government and other policies, nor how persistent these effects will be. Overall large fiscal deficits and high levels of government debt mean that there is a significant risk of instability in bond markets, which may pose threats to financial stability because of the sharply leveraged position of financial firms and create awkward tensions for monetary policy in setting short rates and deciding the extent of central bank holdings of government bonds.

In Chapter 3, Alain Durré (European Central Bank and IÉSEG-School of management) and Frank Smets (European Central Bank and KU Leuvan) pick up the theme of the interaction between fiscal policy and monetary policy, with an emphasis on developments in the euro area. They begin by reviewing the theoretical and institutional framework that existed before the recent financial crisis. From a theoretical perspective, they show why the pursuit of price stability requires fiscal policy to be sustainable. This leads to the desirability of an 'active monetary and passive fiscal policy' framework that avoids the risk of fiscal dominance, i.e. the risk that unchecked fiscal policy and rising government debt endangers the ability of the central bank to maintain price stability. They suggest that institutional fiscal and monetary policy arrangements in the euro area were designed to ensure such a stability-oriented framework in a monetary union with many national fiscal authorities. They go on to review fiscal developments during the recent crisis and show how the interaction between banking and sovereign risks has led to increasing spreads on government debt and a sovereign debt crisis in a number of euro area countries. They also discuss the ECB's policy response, which has included (in addition to the standard easing of policy rates) the use of non-standard policy measures geared at addressing malfunctioning financial markets and repairing the monetary transmission process. As a result of its role as a market maker of last resort, the ECB's balance sheet has increased in size, which has brought with it increased risks. The authors argue that the interaction between financial stability, fiscal sustainability and monetary policy seen during the European sovereign debt crisis make it clear that the EMU framework needs to be deepened and extended.

In Chapter 4, Dan Thornton (Federal Reserve Bank of St Louis) turns to the unconventional monetary policy actions taken by the Federal Reserve in response to the crisis, providing a critical review of where he believes these actions were appropriate and where they were not, and offering his own views of what policies should have been implemented. In the pre-Lehman's phase of the crisis, the Fed brought about a large reduction in the funds rate target and a large expansion of lending, mainly through the Term Auction Facility (TAF). Thornton believes the former was appropriate but largely ineffective, given the weakness of the interest rate and credit channels of monetary policy. The latter was rendered ineffective because the lending was sterilised by the Fed selling equivalent amounts of Treasuries, ensuring that the volume of credit did not rise overall. The Fed did this, Thornton believes, because Chairman Bernanke believed that the composition of its balance sheet was more important than its size. The Fed was apparently trying to undo an inefficient allocation of credit by lending to the institutions it deemed to be in most need of liquidity. Thornton views this as a major policy error and in his assessment the policy produced no noticeable effects. Instead he believes the Fed should have engineered a large expansion in the monetary base. This is indeed what happened after the collapse of Lehman's, when Thornton notes there was an explosion of primary credit borrowing and TAF lending, which the Fed did not attempt to sterilise, possibly because its holdings of Treasuries were too low. Thornton believes that, whatever the rationale, this action was appropriate and successful in reducing risk spreads. He is critical, however, of the Fed's use of so-called forward guidance that began at the end of 2008 and its quantitative easing (QE) or large-scale asset purchases policy. He argues that the former is based on the expectations hypothesis, which is strongly rejected in the data and he cites evidence suggesting there is no evidence that forward guidance improves central banks' control over longer-term rates. He also argues that the Fed's QE policy was ineffective in reducing long-term interest rates and stimulating aggregate demand, while at the same time unnecessary. Although not disputing the event study evidence that asset purchases affected yields, he argues that these effects were short-lived and not visible in the monthly data. He also notes that to the extent that larger effects on yields reflect greater segmentation then pass-through to the rest of the economy is likely to have been smaller. In his view, by March 2009 when the Fed decided to expand its large-scale asset purchases to include longer term Treasuries, as well as increased amounts of MBS and agency debt, there were already signs that financial markets had stabilised and economic recovery was underway, something he attributes to the earlier expansion of credit. The further expansion of the Fed's balance sheet was therefore unnecessary and likely to have been counterproductive.

In Chapter 5, Patrik Edsparr and Paul Fisher (Bank of England) take a different look at what has been learned from the crisis, by focusing on the design of financial contracts from a financial stability perspective. In particular, they look at contracts which fail to take into account how the financial system as a whole operates, which leads to the true value of a contract being different than expected for at least one of the counter-parties in stressed conditions. They discuss and give practical examples of two ways this can happen and consider what lessons can be drawn. The problem arises in the first category of contracts because the correlation structure may be very different for tail events, so that the insurance provider is not in a position to pay out at the time the investor wants to exercise the contract. Examples of this kind of contract include where a bank hedges its corporate lending by purchasing offsetting CDS protection on a portfolio of loans from another leveraged market participant. In this case, the bank needs to take into account the correlation between the risk profile of the corporate borrower and the provider of CDS protection, which can be very different in stressed conditions. Moreover, if all big banks follow similar strategies, they will all end up with similar portfolios of risk. In such an interconnected financial system, a big shock affecting one bank will affect all banks. The second category of contracts considered is where the perceived payoff in the tail event is offset by unforeseen costs. This occurs where a market participant may choose not to enforce a contract because the repercussions for its reputation of doing so will cause more damage than will be gained by enforcing the contract. The problem this creates is that it is hard to determine *ex ante* what such contracts are worth. The authors cite many examples, including banks accepting responsibility for the distressed assets of the off-balance-sheet Structured Investment Vehicles (SIVs) they had set up, banks not enforcing 'break clauses' in derivative contracts which would entitle them to earlier payment, and money market funds making up losses to avoid 'breaking the buck'. If the reputational and signalling implications of exercising a contract are too damaging in cases of extreme stress, this is something regulators need to take into account when determining the risk profile of an institution and its appropriate capital buffer. They draw two main lessons from their analysis. The first is that there is a need to critically evaluate contingent exposures with proper stress tests that capture tail events. The second is that contract design features that are exclusively reliant on extreme tail events are best avoided, as such features, which do not normally matter, end up being treated as if they never matter. They also argue that it would be worthwhile to assess where these tail risks should be held, as leveraged financial institutions pose larger systemic risks than more traditional unlevered investor categories, though such considerations need to be carefully weighed against other investor protection concerns.

A number of chapters consider methodological or technical innovations to term structure or credit models. The financial crisis has provided considerable momentum to the development of new techniques and results that will take researchers and practitioners some years to absorb. A common theme was the need to move away from linear models. An example is explored by Jean-Sébastien Fontaine (Bank of Canada) in Chapter 9, who shows how moving to a more accurate description of central bank operating procedures – treating them as lumpy rather than continuous – leads to a significantly better characterisation of the yield curve.

Most central banks, he argues, effect changes to their target or policy rate in discrete increments (e.g., multiples of 0.25 percentage points) following public announcements on scheduled dates. Yet most researchers rely on the assumption that policy rates change linearly and do not distinguish between dates with and without scheduled announcements. This assumption, it turns out, is not innocuous when estimating the policy rule at a daily frequencies. He examines a daily sample from 1994 to 2011 and finds that accounting for discrete changes, as opposed to the Gaussian alternative, in an otherwise standard term structure model leads to significantly different estimates of the price of macroeconomic risk. Only the model based on discrete changes depicts a picture that is consistent with the evidence of the response of the term structure to monetary policy announcements and the recent behaviour at the lower zero bound, including liquidity and open market operations.

James Steeley (Aston Business School) in Chapter 7 reminds us that prior to the sharp reduction in the UK Bank Rate between October 2008 and March 2009, cubic spline and Nelson–Siegel models were equally adept at fitting the cross section of gilt yields. Subsequent to the unprecedented level of rates after March 2009, both models required a substantially increased number of parameters to achieve comparable levels of fit and smoothness; as much as a six-fold increase in the case of the Nelson–Siegel model. While the smoothness of the yield curve does not seem to respond to market events associated with quantitative easing (QE), it turns out that the estimation errors are significantly greater on days featuring gilt purchases. Enhanced undulations in the forward curve can be thought of as a fourth factor corresponding to changes in curvature. These event days point to the need for more flexibility in yield curve modelling, and foreshadow the results of principal components analysis that finds a significant increase in the explanatory power of the fourth principal component since the encroachment of the lower zero bound. Finally, based on his analysis of average forward curves estimated on QE auction days and non-auction days, Steeley finds that there does not seen to be any obvious relationship between the maturity of the bonds purchased by the Bank of England and the response of yields, which he suggests may indicate that QE may have difficulty working through a portfolio rebalancing channel. He finds, however, that after the Bank extended the range of maturities it purchased in August 2009, auctions generally tilted the long end downwards, possibly consistent with a change in inflation expectations because the differences do not show obvious differences with the bonds being purchased this may indicate that QE may work more through the signalling channels than through portfolio rebalancing. Furthermore, he argues that the effects coincide with the extension of the maturity ranges in August 2009 after which the auctions generally tilted the long end downwards.

In Chapter 6, Alain Monfort (CREST) and Jean-Paul Renne (Banque de France) outline a discrete-time modelling framework for defaultable-bond yields. They show that a compound autoregressive (Car) process makes it possible to account for sophisticated dynamics of yields and spreads, under both the risk-neutral and the historical dynamics. This framework is applied to bonds in the euro area and both credit and liquidity premia are estimated.

In Chapter 8, Yvan Lengwiler (Basel) and Carlos Lenz (Swiss National Bank) apply the intelligible factors decomposition of the yield curve to data from 1999 to 2010 for the USA, UK and Germany in order to identify some common stylised facts. This decomposition relies on an orthogonality identification scheme for each of the three factor's innovations and gives profoundly different loadings at each horizon when compared to the standard level, slope and curvature factors found in the standard literature on factor models. The resulting stylised facts present something of a puzzle for the standard view that the central bank determines the short end of the curve and thereby exercises some leverage over long-term rates. The authors find that the long-term factor interacts little with the other factors and seems related to international drivers and that the dominant factor in yield curve movements is the medium-term, or business cycle factor, which also plays a dominant role in explaining the variance of shorter-term rates. The results are shown to maintain their stability over the recent financial crisis.

In Chapter 10, Michael Dempster (University of Cambridge), Jack Evans (evalueFE) and Elena Medova (Cambridge Systems) outline some of the problems with various approaches to yield curve modelling, which leads them to implement a model of the term structure based on an idea from Fisher Black. This idea asserts that interest rates generally come with a 'stuff it under the mattress' option in which investors just keep their money when faced with a negative interest rate. This means that we can model interest rates as options on some more fundamental, but possibly hard to observe, shadow rates which guarantee positive rates or set minimum rates. The original idea is described, but not implemented, in Fischer Black's last (posthumously) published paper. The corresponding yield curve model has been implemented a number of times before, often with Japanese interest rates in mind. But all previous examples have used two factors; the authors here develop a three-factor version in which forward rates are a non-linear function of the state space related to the option value of the short rate. The model is simulated and shown to match the required stylised facts of any yield curve model.

As stressed by Philip Turner (Chapter 2), the yield curve can be a useful tool to extract inflation and growth expectations, at least in normal times. But the current financial crisis has highlighted that many of the necessary conditions for extracting these expectations accurately may not always be met over time. The purpose of the analysis reported in the next two chapters is therefore to quantify empirically the main driving forces behind the evolution of the yield curve before and during the financial crisis in both the United States and some European countries, focusing on the implementation of the monetary policy at the short end of the yield curve (or the agents' expectations about what might drive the monetary policy decisions).

In Chapter 11, Morten Bech (Bank for International Settlements), Elizabeth Klee and Viktors Stebunovs (Federal Reserve Board) examine the relationship between various segments of the US overnight money market before and during the financial crisis. More specifically, they analyse the transmission of the US monetary policy stance from the overnight federal funds market to overnight US Treasury general collateral repurchase agreements. These segments of the money market play a key role in the first stage of the monetary policy transmission chain. From the viewpoint of central banks, transmission of monetary policy decisions between the unsecured and secured segments of the money market allows monetary policy to influence the long end of the yield curve, possibly aligning expectations with the desired policy stance. Bech, Klee and Stebunovs discuss the implications of relying on larger-than-normal repo operations to inject liquidity into the federal funds market and analyse the effectiveness of monetary policy transmission with three main tools: (i) a mean-reversion process – namely the speed of adjustment to the long-term relationship between the overnight federal funds rate and the repo rate; (ii) the width of spread between both interest rates; and (iii) the sensitivity of both interest rates to liquidity provided by the US Federal Reserve. They find that the pass-through from the federal funds rate to the repo rate fractured from the onset of the financial crisis in August 2007. Although both rates stayed together during the first stage of the crisis, the speed of adjustment to their long-run relationships slowed considerably with respect to the period before the crisis. The authors argue that growing credit risk concerns, capital limitations of banks and changes in the demand for reserve balances may explain why some arbitrage opportunities were left unexploited during the crisis period. In the later stage of the crisis, the two rates actually appear to have decoupled. The authors conclude that non-conventional measures are justified because the effectiveness of traditional monetary policy has weakened during the crisis.

In Chapter 12, Andrea Buraschi (University of Chicago), Andrea Carnelli and Paul Whelan (Imperial College, London) analyse the perceptions of economic agents of US monetary policy from 1986 to 2011. Within a Taylor-rule setting, they wonder whether economic agents really believe the US Federal Reserve follows a given policy function. This is an important question as the results may, for instance, help us understand the power of announcements by the central banks on financial asset prices. By deriving implied consensus and individual measures of output and inflation – based on forecasts relying on surveys of professional economists from leading financial institutions – this chapter disentangles the three main sources of uncertainty about the future path of the policy rate, namely: the expected path of state variables, the parameter values of the rule and the functional form of the rule itself. First the authors find substantial differences in the value of the estimated coefficients between traditional Taylor rules in the literature and those using survey measures. Second, there exists time-dependent variation in the policy parameters implied by agents' expectations based on survey forecasts. Third, from estimating the degree of dispersion around the parameters of the Taylor rule, agents' perceptions also appears heterogeneous. They show in particular that the cross-sectional dispersion in the perceived parameters of the policy model is highly correlated with the average individual uncertainty about the parameters. Two possible interpretations are of relevance from a policy viewpoint. On the one hand, their evidence suggests that agents' expectations of the monetary policy stance of the US Federal Reserve have evolved over time on account of increased non-linearities and state dependence, e.g. expecting more aggressive tightening decisions when inflation is high and more accommodative decisions when the output gap is negative. On the other hand, standard results obtained under the rational expectations framework may differ substantially from those obtained with subjective response functions, since individuals may disagree about the expected path of parameters in the rule and the functional form of the rule. Among the possible implications for the conduct of monetary policy, these results may encourage central banks to use market participants' views to help formulate better strategies for the communication of their policies.

The next three chapters focus more specifically on term structure models and their role in the context of central banks' operating procedures. In Chapter 14, Hans Dewachter, Leonardo Iania (National Bank of Beliguim and KU Leuven) and Marco Lyrio (Insper Institute for Education and Research) revisit the common practice of using yield spreads to forecast inflation, which has been popular in the academic literature as well as with central banks and practitioners. They address two main issues. First, they assess the importance of decomposing yield spreads into an expectations component and a term premium component in order to predict inflation. Secondly, they quantify the impact of financial shocks on the dynamics of each of these components. The yield spread decomposition is achieved through the use of a no-arbitrage macro-finance model that incorporates both macroeconomic and financial factors. The model is estimated using data for the US economy with Bayesian techniques. The results reveal that the yield spread decomposition is crucial to forecasting inflation over a variety of forecasting horizons and that financial shocks are of substantive importance for the dynamics of bond yields. In particular, they show that macroeconomic factors alone are not able to capture much of the variation in yield spreads and attribute an important role to financial factors, mainly via liquidity and risk premium shocks, during the period 2004–2012. This includes the period in which the behaviour of world bond markets was described by the former Federal Reserve Chairman Alan Greenspan as a 'conundrum', and the current financial crisis. The decomposition into expectations and term premia is important since the dynamics of long-term yields are heavily influenced by term premia movements, which occur mainly due to financial shocks.

Using a similar conceptual framework, in Chapter 15 Marcello Pericoli (Banca D'Italia) employs the no-arbitrage affine Gaussian term structure model to analyse the impact of macroeconomic surprises on the nominal and the real-term structures, in the euro area and in the US. He finds that nominal rates are sensitive to surprises in economic growth, the labour market and the economic outlook in the US and mostly to surprises in inflation in the euro area. In the US, forward inflation risk premia became sizable around the start of the late-2000s financial crisis and increased considerably just before the adoption of the unconventional monetary policy measures introduced in March 2009. By contrast, in the euro area forward inflation risk premia remained unchanged even after the adoption of the unconventional monetary policy measures in October 2008 and in May 2010. The author documents that in both the US and the euro area expected long-term inflation expectations have been well anchored over the past few years, confirming the ability of the respective central banks to control inflation expectations even during the most severe periods of the ongoing crisis.

Chapter 13 by Juan García and Thomas Werner (European Central Bank) focuses on the extraction of reliable indicators of breakeven inflation (BEI) rates in the euro area and the modelling challenges posed by the financial crisis. Their analysis shows that pricing distortions in BEI rates became considerable during the financial crisis and were mainly related to the rising liquidity premium in both nominal and inflation-linked bonds. They find that the term structures of euro area BEI rates and inflation risk premia have been predominantly upward sloping. Since the start of the financial turbulence in mid-2007 and in particular following its intensification in the autumn of 2008, inflation compensation became more volatile. The euro area BEI rate curve was inverted for most of 2008 before steepening strongly in 2009, reflecting the volatility of realised inflation and the revisions to short-term expected inflation during the crisis. The authors' affine model decomposes BEI rates into the inflation expectations and risk premia components and shows that the term structure of inflation risk premia in the euro area also exhibits a predominantly upward slope but the spread across maturities is also quite compressed: on average the inflation risk premium was between 5 and 10 basis points up to two year maturity and about 25 basis points at the five year maturity, becoming then very tiny at the longest maturities. The authors' estimates of inflation expectations embodied in bond yields, in line with the evidence from survey data, suggest a strong anchoring of inflation expectations at medium-to-long maturities. From a monetary policy perspective, the results are important in that they suggest short horizon BEI rates are more volatile than longer-term ones, and most of the volatility reflects movements in short-term inflation expectations, with inflation risk premia playing a limited role. In contrast, the volatility of inflation compensation at longer horizons is almost wholly driven by inflation risk premia, while the limited contribution of long-term inflation expectations reflects a strong anchoring of euro area inflation expectations.

The final two chapters, 16 and 17, question the role of fiscal fundamentals in the fluctuations at the longer end of the yield curve. In Chapter 16, Priscilla Burity, Marcelo Medeiros (Pontifical Catholic University of Rio de Janeiro) and Luciano Vereda (Universidade Federal Fluminense) attempt to distinguish the contribution of fiscal shocks (in terms of both deficit and debt) from the influence of other macroeconomic variables in the fluctuations of sovereign bond yields. They study the bond yields of the three main euro area countries that have been subject to some market pressures *vis-à-vis* German bond yields: Greece, Spain and Italy. The authors use an arbitrage-free affine term structure framework to model the spreads between the yield to maturity of sovereign bonds and maturity-equivalent German bonds, allowing them to decompose the driving forces into three main categories of variable: own and German fiscal variables; a market stress indicator; and macroeconomic variables. Interestingly, they find that the main driving forces diverge substantially from one country to another. In particular, changes in Greek spreads seem to be mostly explained by local fiscal stance whereas other macroeconomic variables and a market stress indicator play a stronger explanatory role in the case of Spanish and Italian spreads. More surprisingly, the authors find that German fiscal variables play a key role in the widening of spreads in Spain and Italy, with the indicator of market stress also playing a significant role.

In Chapter 17, Luigi Marattin (University of Bologna), Paolo Paesani (University of Rome, Tor Vergata) and Simone Salotti (Oxford Brookes University) offer a theoretical and empirical analysis of the relationship between debt accumulation and financial asset prices, real long-term interest rates in particular. Although economists agree in general that increasing real interest rates may at some point render the public debt unsustainable at a given economic growth rate, such agreement seems to be questioned by the current debate about the wisdom of fiscal consolidation and the need for binding fiscal rules. The results in this chapter provide some interesting new evidence that may help clarify the issues. Using a simple dynamic model that allows for interaction between government bond issuance and interest rates with imperfect asset substitutability, the authors estimate the linkages between debt accumulation, refinancing rates and the reaction of financial markets for three countries with large and relatively liquid sovereign debt bond markets, namely the United States, Germany and Italy. Their findings suggest that fiscal shocks play an essential role in the behaviour of interest rates, both in terms of the level of real long-term interest rates and in terms of the slope of the term structure. Although this conclusion applies to all three countries under investigation, there is a clear distinction between the US and the two euro area countries. For both Germany and Italy, real long-term interest rates increase and the yield slope rises. By contrast, for the US there is almost no reaction of the slope of the yield curve and a decrease of the real long-term interest rate. They argue that their results for the US mostly reflect the flight-to-quality phenomenon and possibly the impact of liquidity effects. By contrast, in the case of the two euro area countries, they stress that specific events may have a similar impact on the fiscal stance (e.g. debt deterioration in the pre-EMU period and fiscal consolidation with loss of autonomous monetary policy in the EMU period have led to similar patterns in the dynamics of interest rates). In the light of this evidence, Marattin, Paesani and Salotti point to two main policy implications. On the one hand, fundamentals matter and must receive careful attention when understanding the dynamics of the yield curve. In particular, a clear distinction between structural and cyclical debt accumulation must be made to anticipate possible impacts on real long-term interest rates, and hence on debt sustainability. In this regard, this conclusion clearly supports binding fiscal rules and multilateral monitoring of public finances in countries suffering from structural imbalances. On the other hand, their results also tend to suggest that government bond interest rates react inversely to the size and the international integration of the bond market.

Concluding remarks

In our view the chapters in this book highlight three main themes. *The first theme* concerns the impact of policymakers' behaviour on the yield curve especially in relation to the conventional and non-conventional measures implemented by governments, fiscal authorities and central banks around the world. Regarding central banks, a large academic literature has built up on the success or otherwise of recent non-conventional measures, and in particular LSAPs or QE, in loosening monetary conditions at the zero lower bound through the lens of the portfolio balance theory. Accordingly, when assets held in private sector portfolios are not perfect substitutes for one another, changes in the central bank's portfolio of asset holdings and/or the structure of its liabilities can induce changes in the yield curve, which may in turn influence private spending, saving and investment decisions and thus macroeconomic outcomes. The consequent changes in the central bank's balance sheet may be accompanied by an increase of its size or not (when assets substitutions are sterilised). Of course, the theoretical underpinnings of portfolio balance theory are a matter of considerable controversy, and some authors emphasise effects through policy signalling and other channels, or question whether central bank asset purchases have had material effects. Without diminishing the importance of asset purchases, it could also be argued that the recent crisis has emphasised the need for the central bank to intervene directly when markets become dysfunctional. This new development in the behaviour of central banks is discussed in the chapters of Thornton (Chapter 4) and Bech et al. (Chapter 11). Beyond the quantitative impact of central bank operations on the yield curve, the ability of monetary policy makers to influence the markets' expectations through appropriate communication (and hence the yield curve ultimately through qualitative tools) should not be denied, as shown by Buraschi et al. in Chapter 12. Regarding the government, while recent experience has shown its ability to affect the yield curve through stimulus packages and rescue measures to support the financial soundness of banks, debt accumulation has clearly influenced market expectations of the sustainability of public finances and level of the long-term real interest rates, although the transmission channels are not univocal and not necessarily stable over time. At the same time, the balance of power between the government and the central bank has also changed with respect to the theoretical approach that emerged in the early 1980s, with the so-called Kydland–Prescott–Barro–Gordon paradigm. The attempt to disentangle the importance of these elements which clearly play a role in the evolution of the yield curve can be found in the analysis of Turner

(Chapter 2), Durré and Smets (Chapter 3), Burity et al. (Chapter 16) and Marattin et al. (Chapter 17).

A second theme that emerges questions the reliability of existing models to estimate accurately the yield curve in the crisis environment we have observed since August 2007. By the same token, it requires us to wonder what may and should have changed in modelling a world with highly volatile excess returns and risk premia in a zero lower bound environment. These issues are addressed in the analysis provided by Fontaine (Chapter 9), Steeley (Chapter 7), Monfort and Renne (Chapter 6) and Dempster et al. (Chapter 10). In fact Lengwiler and Lenz (Chapter 8) go as far to suggest a different decomposition of latent factors, which would place much more weight on the curvature than has been typical until now. The bottom line of these analyses is to point out the technical challenges implied by the current crisis environment, which calls for taking more account of non-linearity in the estimation with respect to previous modelling techniques. Ultimately, the discussion contained in these chapters calls for more caution in modelling and more careful interpretation of the results from models that do not take into account the implications of the crisis.

The third theme relates to our ability to extract accurate macroeconomic information from the yield curve when the latter is affected by the above-mentioned phenomena caused by the crisis environment. In all circumstances policymakers need, not only to check whether their behaviour is well understood by market participants, but also to extract from the yield curve market expectations of future inflation and economic growth. This is one of the main reasons why policymakers in general and the central bank in particular attach so much importance to the estimation of the yield curve. The technical challenges implied by the crisis environment thus obliges modellers and policymakers to question the reliability of their models and to anticipate possible break points before structural models have the possibility of capturing them. This is clearly an ambitious task, for which the empirical evidence reported in Dewachter et al. (Chapter 14), Pericoli (Chapter 15) and García and Werner (Chapter 13) is highly relevant. Ultimately, our need to extract the expectations of market participants may well also provide some impetus to the development of new financial instruments, with Edsparr and Fisher (Chapter 5) providing a useful pointer.

The financial crisis has produced many hardships for ordinary people and, as economists, we have an intellectual duty to use these events to understand the limitations of our tools. It is, for instance, now abundantly clear that the small, linearised, micro-founded models that were developed in the long expansion from the early 1990s to 2007 were simply not rich enough. Models that ticked over nicely in moderate times were almost entirely unsuited to help us understand market conditions and the scope for policy responses during the crisis. Some of the chapters show how these models can be extended to allow for various features of the crisis but much work remains to be done, as most of the other chapters make clear. We hope this book provides some basis for a future research agenda that will develop models that are likely to be more robust in both good and bad times, and therefore of more use to policymakers and practitioners.

Part I

Keynote addresses

2 Is the long-term interest rate a policy victim, a policy variable or a policy lodestar?

Philip Turner

2.1 Introduction

It is an excellent idea to focus a conference about 'what have we learnt from the 2007–2010 financial crisis' on the yield curve. It is an excellent idea because one end of that curve – the long-term rate of interest – has fallen so low that serious questions about monetary policy frameworks and financial stability risks are inescapable.

Because it is a *lodestar* for the financial industry and for many government policies, it would be reassuring to imagine that the real long-term interest rate is determined by the market. We would like to think that fundamentals such as the underlying saving and investment propensities of the private sector (and the corresponding 'habitat' preferences of investors) play the dominant role. All appearances suggest a vibrant market: interest rates markets are among those most heavily traded and prices are indeed very responsive to changes in economic conditions.

Yet there is a major difficulty: the aggregate impact of many official policies – taking quite different forms – has been to increase the demand for government bonds, particularly those in key international currencies. The long-term interest rate can then become a *victim* of such policies. How far this reflects a motivation for such policies is an open question; but governments with massive debts to finance obviously welcome low long-term rates.

In any event, the long-term rate has become a *policy variable* during this crisis. Central banks through their balance sheet policies and governments through their debt management policies have sought to directly influence the long-term interest rate. Although such policies have been

Views expressed are my own, not necessarily those of the BIS. I am very grateful to Hervé Hannoun for several suggestions and for encouragement. Stephen Cecchetti, Mike Joyce, M. S. Mohanty and Anthony Turner helped sharpen the analysis in a number of points. Clare Batts, Gabriele Gasperini, Branimir Gruic, Denis Pêtre and Jhuvesh Sobrun provided valuable help in preparing the chapter.

billed as exceptional, it should not be forgotten that Keynes regarded the long-term interest rate as a key policy variable.

Hence my question: is the long-term interest rate a policy victim, a policy variable or a policy lodestar?

2.2   Real long-term interest rates

2.2.1   *Historical overview*

The decline in long-term interest rates in the major centres over the past decade has been remarkable. The real long-term interest rate on global risk-free assets – as measured by 10-year US index-linked Treasuries (TIPs) – has averaged 1.9% since 2002 (see Figure 2.1; the UK inflation-linked averaged 1.5% over the same period). The very steep decline since early 2010 – by May 2012, the real rate had become negative – presumably reflected the post-crisis flight to safe assets as the euro area crisis deepened. But this downward trend predated the crisis. It persisted

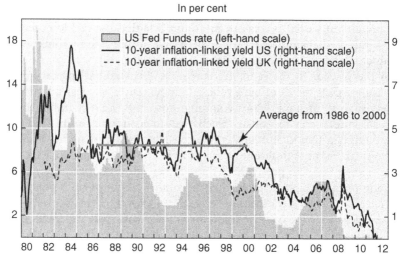

Figure 2.1 Real long-term Treasury yields
Ten-year Treasury Inflation Indexed zero coupon yields (TIPS); prior to 1999, return on ten-year zero coupon bond deflated by centred 3-year moving average of core PCE inflation. The horizontal line indicates the 1986–2000 average of the 10-year US real rate (4.26%). The average of the Fed Funds rate over that period was 5.82%, shown on the left-hand scale.
Source: National data; BIS calculations.

through both the expansion and the contraction phases of the unusually sharp global cycle over the past decade. This suggests important non-cyclical influences on the long-term rate.

There has been much debate among economists about the 'normal' long-term interest rate. Hicks (1958) found that the yield on UK consols over 200 years had, in normal peacetime, been in the 3 to 3.5% range. After examining the yield on consols from 1750 to 2006, Mills and Wood (2009) noted the remarkable stability of the real long-term interest rate in the UK – at about 2.9%. (The only exception was between 1915 and 1964, when it was about 1% lower.) Amato's (2005) estimate was that the long-run real natural interest rate in the US was around 3% over the period 1965 to 2001 and that it varied between about 2.5% and 3.5%.

The low real long-term rate over the past decade – well below these historical averages – is perplexing on both macroeconomic and microeconomic grounds. One macroeconomic puzzle is that its pre-crisis decline took place in the face of an apparent rise in the potential growth rate of the global economy (mainly due to high rates of fixed investment in the emerging economies). In principle, the natural rate of interest should increase with higher potential growth. In practice, measurement of potential growth is subject to a wide margin of error. And potential growth may have fallen after the crisis. In addition, variable liquidity premia – which were high in the early years of TIPs – make real interest rates hard to measure.

Is there an obvious microeconomic explanation for the decline in bond yields? One possible explanation is that bonds have become a more stable investment in recent decades. Before the subprime crisis, for example, it was sometimes argued that the Great Moderation (that is, low inflation, no sharp recession, more credible macroeconomic policy frameworks, etc.) made investing in government bonds safer. But the problem with this explanation is that bond yields have become more, not less, volatile. The (surprising) increase in the variability of long-term interest rate changes that Mark Watson noted in 1999 has actually persisted (Table 2.1). He took as the basis of his comparison the period January 1965 to September 1978.[1] As might be expected, the standard deviation of interest rate changes over that period fell along the maturity curve – from 0.45 for the Federal funds rate to 0.19 for the 10-year yield. But in recent periods this difference has vanished: the variability of

---

[1] This period was one of great macroeconomic turbulence: the Bretton Woods system of fixed exchange rates broke down, inflation surged and there was a severe global recession.

Table 2.1 *Standard deviations of interest rate changes*[1]

		In percentage points			
Fed funds	3-month T-bill	10-year nominal yield	10-year real yield	Yield curve slope[2]	Yield curve slope average
1965.1 to 1978.9	0.45	0.37	0.19	na	0.33	0.85
1986.1 to 1998.12	0.24	0.20	0.25	0.25	0.23	1.94
1999.1 to 2012.7	0.20	0.21	0.23	0.20	0.28	2.08
Memorandum:						
1999.1 to 2006.12	0.20	0.19	0.22	0.16	0.27	1.77
2007.1 to 2012.7	0.19	0.22	0.25	0.24	0.30	2.51

[1] Standard deviation of the first differences (i.e. $R_t - R_{t-1}$) of the monthly averages of daily observations of interest rates measured in percentage points. [2] 10-year nominal yield *less* 3-month Treasury bill rate.
Sources: DataStream; National data; BIS calculations.

short rates has actually fallen but that of long rates has risen. The standard deviation of monthly changes in 10-year yields was 23 basis points over the period from January 1999 to July 2012. Separating this period into a stable subperiod (January 1999 to December 2006) and an unstable subperiod (January 2007 to the current period) does not alter this observation: see the memorandum item of Table 2.1.

Another possible explanation of the greater willingness of investors to hold bonds is a sharp increase in the term premium. In principle, measuring this requires a quantification of interest rate expectations; but one simple proxy over a long period is the average of the yield curve slope. This has risen to about 200 basis points over the last 25 years – from less than 100 basis points during the period 1965 to 1978 (last column of Table 2.1). Unlike the long-term yield, the yield curve slope has *not* become more volatile in recent years. This combination of a steeper but not more volatile yield slope may have enhanced the attractions of borrowing short and lending long. (The issue of the link between interest rate exposures and volatility is explored further using measures of implied volatility in Section 2.2.2 below.)

2.2.2   Consequences of low long-term rates

The persistence of a very low long-term real rate of interest has several consequences.

As a percentage of GDP

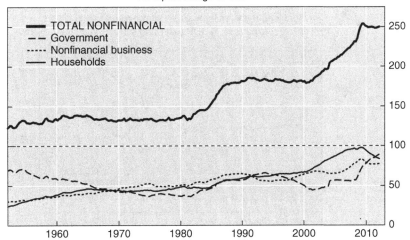

Figure 2.2 Outstanding debt of domestic US non-financial borrowers
Federal plus State and Local.
Source: Board of Governors of the Federal Reserve.

(i)   *Cheaper leverage*

The first is that it has reduced the real interest cost of servicing higher
debt/GDP ratios. Figure 2.2 charts the aggregate debt of domestic US
non-financial borrowers – governments, corporations and households –
as a percentage of GDP. From the mid-1950s to the early 1980s, this
aggregate was remarkably stable – at about 130% of GDP. It was even
described as the great constant of the US financial system. The sub-
components moved about quite a bit – for instance, with lower public
sector debt being compensated by higher private debt. But the aggregate
itself seemed very stable. During the 1980s, however, this stability broke
down. Aggregate debt rose to a new plateau of about 180% of GDP in
the United States. At the time, this led to consternation in some policy circles about the burden of too much debt. It is now about 240% of
GDP. Leverage thus measured – that is, as a ratio of debt to income –
has increased. Many observers worry about this.[2]

Whatever the worries, lower rates do make leveraged positions easier
to finance. Once account has been taken of lower real interest rates, debt

---

[2] For an international analysis of aggregate indebtedness see Cecchetti, Mohanty and
Zampolli (2011). They identify the thresholds beyond which the burden of debt lowers
growth.

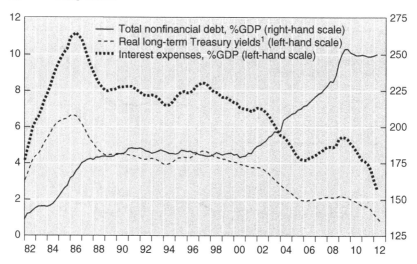

Figure 2.3 Lightening the interest expense of heavy debt
[1] Four-year moving average, shown at end.
Source: Board of Governors of the Federal Reserve.

servicing costs currently are actually rather modest: Figure 2.3 illustrates this point. On this (hypothetical) calculation, the real interest expense of servicing this debt (the thick dotted line) has been below 5% of GDP since 2003 – much lower than in earlier decades. This explains why the household debt service ratio is now below where it was (the dashed line in Figure 2.4) in the early 1990s – even though debt is much higher.

Stocks of assets have also risen. The combination of good quality assets and high levels of debt is not necessarily problematic. Note that lower long-term interest rates also have valuation effects – boosting the market price of bonds and probably other assets too. This also makes the asset/liability balances look better (the nominal value of bonds held as assets rise but debtors do not owe more).

(ii)   Increased tolerance for fiscal deficits

Another, related, consequence is that large budget deficits have been easier to finance. The fiscal accounts of the US federal government provide an illuminating example. During much of the 1980s, nominal government interest payments were between 8 and 10% of outstanding debt (see Figure 2.4). Part of this reflected inflation expectations during that decade. Historically, it has been the burden of interest payments – and not the size of the primary deficit – that has triggered corrective fiscal

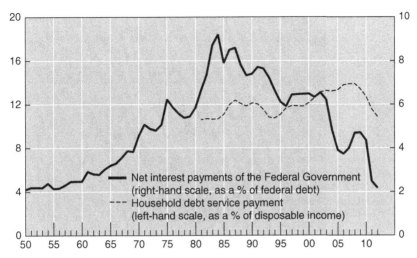

Figure 2.4 Net interest payments and household debt service ratio
Sources: Economic Report of the President; Federal Reserve.

action (Sims, 2008). Currently, net interest payments in the US amount to only a little over 2% of government debt ... one has to go back to the 1950s to find a lower debt service rate. So, if Sims is correct, another consequence of low long-term rates may be to delay fiscal correction. (The lowering of long-term interest rates in peripheral euro area countries following the adoption of the common currency had a comparable effect.)

(iii)   Increased interest rate exposures

The third consequence of low long-term rates is that interest rate exposures in the private sector have risen. Massive public sector debt financed at ever lower real long-term rates implies an increased stock of private sector assets locked into very low real returns. With a term spread of around 300–400 basis points over the period between late 2001 and mid-2004 (Figure 2.5), banks and others had an incentive to assume maturity exposures. The decline in the term spread to zero by mid-2006 forced banks and others to reassess, and probably cut, their maturity exposures well before the subprime crisis broke.

Expansionary monetary policies pursued from late 2007 in the wake of the crisis-induced fall in real demand restored the term spread. With yield curves again upward sloping, banks and other financial firms were encouraged to increase their maturity exposures. Not only was the term

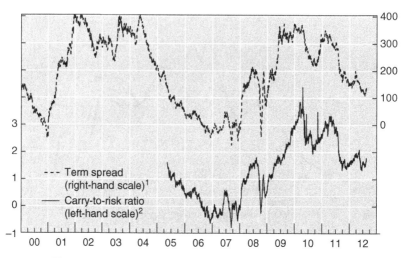

Figure 2.5 Incentives for interest rate carry trades
[1] 10-year swap rate minus 3-month money market rate, in basis points.
[2] Defined as the differential between 10-year swap rate and 3-month money market rate divided by the 3-month/10-year swaption implied volatility.
Sources: Bloomberg; BIS calculations.

spread high (sometimes over 300 basis points), but volatility in interest rate derivatives markets was quite low. Hence using options to limit potential losses from borrowing short and lending long was rather cheap: as an illustration of this, Figure 2.5 uses a measure of the volatility of 3-month/10-year swaps. With a carry-to-risk ratio above 2 from mid-2009 to late 2011, interest rate carry trades in many guises have been encouraged.

The greater their leverage in interest rate exposures, the more attentive investors must be to the interest rate environment. When interest rate expectations change, attempts by investors to close or to hedge their positions can lead to unusually brutal market movements. Many non-linearities can come into play – particularly when prices cross key thresholds that trigger further sales in a market that is already falling.

2.3   Is the long-term interest rate a policy victim?

2.3.1   *Macroeconomic factors: US monetary policy or the global saving rate*

The idea that many years of low *real* long-term rates – or indeed any real variable exhibiting such persistence over time – can be attributed to monetary policy (as conventionally understood) is implausible. But it would be true that the more central banks get involved in 'forward guidance' about their future policy rate, the stronger the link could become.[3]

Statistically, the long-term rate has not been closely correlated with the contemporaneous short-term policy rate. Time series of the short-term rate and the long-term rate have been shown to have quite different statistical properties. But there is, of course, some correlation. A simple regression result using annual data would suggest, on average over the past 30 years, a 100 basis point rise in the Federal funds rate has been associated with a 24 basis points rise in the real 10-year yield on US Treasuries in that year.[4] Other studies have reported a similar average relationship. Nevertheless, such simple equations are probably mis-specified because the link between the two interest rates is unlikely to be constant over time as investors' expectations and their assessment of term risk change as circumstances alter. The coefficient should be time-variant. There have been many periods when there has been no apparent relationship. For instance, during the first 18 months of the pre-crisis period of monetary policy tightening (i.e. from mid-2004 to end-2005) the US government bond yield did not rise – the famous Greenspan conundrum.[5]

---

[3] The role of overly easy monetary policy in driving down long-term rates, inflating asset prices and causing the financial crisis has been much debated. Shigehara and Atkinson (2011) provide a good review of this question and analyse how far the major international institutions argued for global monetary tightening during the years before the crisis.

[4] The regression using annual data from 1981 to 2011 is:

$$RL = 7.61 + 0.24FF - 0.08Y - 0.31(S/Y)_{-1} + 0.51RL_{-1}$$
$$\quad\;(2.1)\quad(5.9)\quad\;(0.8)\quad\;(2.0)\quad\quad\;(4.8)$$

$$\text{Adj } R^2 = 0.84; F = 40.0; DW = 2.05;$$

where
RL = Real 10-year yield on US Treasuries (measured from TIPs)
FF = Federal funds rate
Y = Growth of world GDP
S/Y = World saving rate
subscripts −1 refer to the previous period

A higher world saving rate seems to reduce the real interest rate but the world growth rate has no effect. Comparable US variables for savings and for growth were not significant.

[5] But there was a more subtle link between the stance of monetary policy and the long-term rate on this occasion. The 'measured pace' policy of Federal Reserve tightening deliberately nurtured in markets a sense of interest rate predictability. The Federal Reserve was anxious to avoid a bond market collapse similar to the one that took place around the early 1994 tightening. The knowledge that short-term rates would be kept low made banks and others more willing to borrow short to finance bond holdings – and so kept long-term rates lower than would have been the case otherwise.

As a percentage of GDP

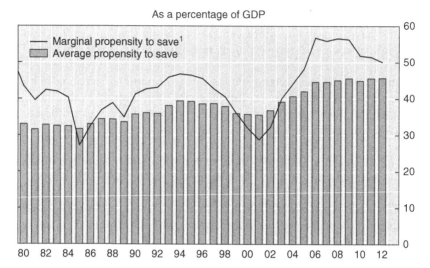

Figure 2.6 Propensity to save in developing Asia
[1] Calculated over 7 years.
Sources: IMF World Economic Outlook; World Bank World Development Indicators.

Perhaps the most widely accepted macroeconomic explanation of low long-term rates is the global 'saving glut' thesis of Bernanke. The rise in the global propensity to save since 2002 has indeed been remarkable. This rise was almost entirely due to a rise in the marginal propensity to save in developing Asia. Figure 2.6 shows that the marginal propensity to save in developing Asia has been above 40% for almost a decade. In the years before the subprime crisis, it rose to 55%. This is unprecedented for such a large area. Investment ratios in Asia also rose but by less. The aggregate current account surplus of emerging Asia therefore widened.

Because Asia was such an attractive place for foreigners to invest in, this surplus was supplemented by substantial capital inflows. Gross capital inflows into developing Asia (i.e. the sum of portfolio investment, direct investment and bank lending) amounted to almost $1 trillion in 2010. Given policies of resisting currency appreciation in many Asian countries, current account surpluses and strong gross capital flows have created a surplus for governments to invest in foreign financial assets. Their heavy investment in US securities has driven down long-term yields in US dollar bonds. Warnock and Warnock (2009) estimate that foreign purchases lowered US Treasury yields by 90 basis points in 2005.

2.3.2 'Habitat' choices of investors: hunger for AAA-rated paper

Macroeconomic factors, however, are not the end of the story. It is the 'habitat' choices of investors – that is, assets in which they choose to invest their surpluses – that shape the precise impact of fundamental macroeconomic forces on financial markets.

The governments, central banks and sovereign wealth funds in Asia are typically conservative in their foreign investment strategies. Their proclivity for highly liquid, AAA-rated assets of government (or quasi-government) bonds issued in the main financial centres – especially those denominated in dollars – is well known.

In addition, the insurance and bank regulators in the developed world have in recent years reinforced the global appetite for all such AAA-rated assets. Government paper has been especially favoured. Insurance regulators tend to give all local currency government bonds a zero risk weight. Local currency government bonds held by banks also carry a zero risk weight in most – but not all – jurisdictions. But it is important to underline that current international regulations do allow leeway in this matter. Although the zero risk weight is envisaged under the standardised approach of Basel II (which was carried over into Basel III), the internal ratings-based (IRB) approach requires banks to allocate capital according to their own assessment of a country's credit risk. But it seems that few (if any) major international banks actually departed from the zero risk weight. Hannoun (2011) argues that large and sophisticated banks are meant to follow the IRB, and not the standardised approach.[6]

The use of the government bond yield to discount the future liabilities of pension funds, etc. – often at the behest of those who frame accounting rules – also pushed those managing investment funds on behalf of others to purchase government bonds of a similar duration as their liabilities.

Non-government AAA-rated paper has also been nurtured. The low risk weight for AAA-rated assets under the standardised approach of Basel II, for example, provided an unintended invitation to banks and others to 'manufacture' new AAA-rated asset-backed securities on the

---

[6] He concludes that the accumulation of sovereign risk on the balance sheets of banks up to 2009 was the result of 'market participants' complacent pricing'. He points out short-comings in both the European Union and the United States. The European Union's Capital Requirements Directives, which had introduced a generalised zero risk weight for all EU central government debt denominated and funded in domestic currency, are not in line with the spirit of Basel II. The United States has not yet implemented Basel II (it is still applying the OECD/non-OECD distinction of Basel I).

back of risks that were anything but AAA. (This was corrected by the Basel Committee in July 2009, with implementation due by end-2011).

2.3.3   An elastic supply of 'new' AAA-rated paper

These strong and growing demands for AAA-rated paper swamped the volume of bonds issued by AAA governments and official international institutions in the years before the crisis. It was sovereign paper that had dominated global issuance of AAA-rated debt securities until the early 1990s. But it was then overtaken by the issuance of asset-backed securities or ABS (that is, including mortgaged-backed securities and covered bonds). ABS issuance of AAA-rated securities rose from about $80 billion in 1993 to almost $1 trillion by 2001, and to a peak of $2.8 trillion in 2006 (Figure 2.7).[7] During these years, non-financial corporate AAA issuance tended to decline as the population of AAA corporations shrank. Issuance in these five segments of AAA-rated paper, however, have different impacts on the long-term rate. This is because the floating-rate share of ABS and financial institution issuance is much higher

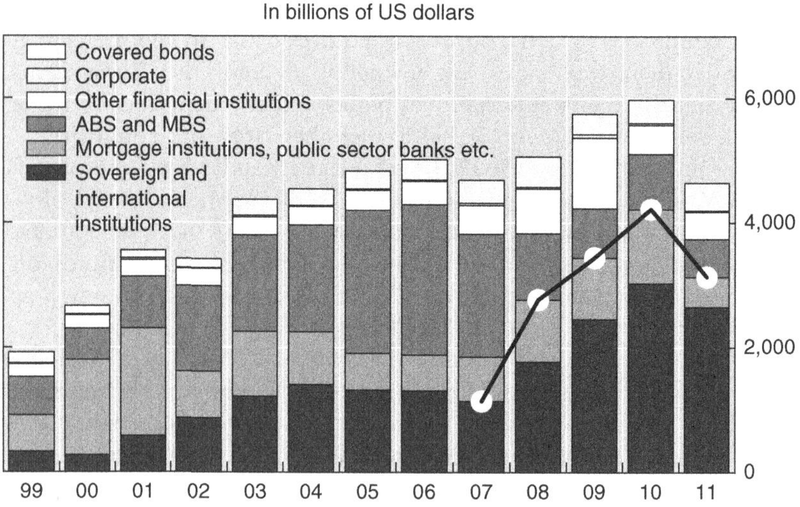

In billions of US dollars

Figure 2.7 Issuance of AAA-rated securities
Note: Categories are defined in the order stacked; that is, covered bonds, corporate, other financial institutions, etc.
Sources: Dealogic; BIS calculations.

---

[7] Note that this phenomenon (i.e. the replacement of sovereign debt by ABS paper) applied only to AAA-rated paper. It did not happen for AA-rated securities.

Table 2.2 *Floating rate issuance of AAA-rated securities by sector*

	As a % of total AAA issuance				
	Sovereign[1]	ABS[2]	Mortgage institutions[3]	Other financial firms	Non-financial corporations
2000	0	38	4	30	4
2005	1	59	9	21	22
2010	2	37	16	21	4
2011	3	35	16	23	11

[1] Includes international institutions. [2] Asset-backed securities including MBS and covered bonds. [3] Mainly the US agencies – Fannie Mae, Freddie Mac and the Federal Home Loan banks.
Sources: Dealogic, BIS calculations.

In billions of US dollars

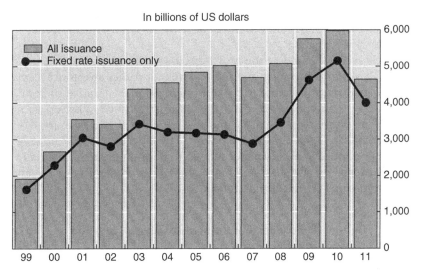

Figure 2.8 Issuance of AAA-rated securities: fixed-rate
Sources: Dealogic; BIS calculations.

than that of sovereign bonds (Table 2.2). Hence sovereign issuance continued to dominate the supply of AAA-rated fixed-rate issuance – and thus presumably the long-term rate – even in the heyday of ABS issuance. Aggregate fixed-rate issuance actually fell from 2003 to 2007 (Figure 2.8) – and this perhaps helped to hold down long-term rates.

After the financial crisis broke, the deflation of securitised debt structures based on subprime mortgages and other doubtful debts led to a dramatic shrinkage in ABS and MBS issuance from $2119 billion in 2006 to $608 billion in 2011 (Figure 2.7). Yet the crisis itself also paradoxically favoured alternative AAA-rated paper. Because banks found it harder to issue unsecured debt in capital markets, they increased their issuance of covered bonds (generally backed by their mortgage loans) from $329 billion in 2006 to $447 billion in 2011. Confidence in the viability of Fannie Mae and Freddie Mac was shaken during the crisis. They were nationalised in September 2008 – which had the short-term benefit of greatly reassuring those who held their bonds. The spreads on their bonds over US Treasuries fell from 84 bp on the Friday before the announcement of nationalisation to 56 bp on the Monday after. By end-2010, the aggregate issuance of US mortgage agencies had doubled, reaching just under $1.2 trillion.[8] Adding the issuance of these agencies to pure sovereign issuance from the year the mortgage agencies were nationalised (the black line with white circles shown in Figure 2.7) shows a very steep rise in the issuance of what are in effect AAA-rated public sector obligations – from just over $1 trillion in 2007 to over $4 trillion in 2010. In 2011, however, issuance by the US mortgage agencies fell below $500 billion.

All this seems to support the much-discussed 'shortage of safe assets' thesis. This argument is that, in times of stress or panic, investors accept very low real rates on long-term government bonds as a price of security. During many phases of the (still unfinished) 2007–20xx crisis, a flight of investors to core bond markets has indeed been observed – even in the face of such massive issuance. Huge government borrowing and the continued size of issuance related to housing finance (especially the US mortgage agencies which are still under Federal government conservatorship) are not benign forces.

2.4   High government debt and asset substitutability across maturities

When sovereign debts are so large, and fiscal prospects very uncertain, the risk of large movements in bond prices is surely greater than when fiscal positions are stronger.[9] Many would argue that heavily indebted governments have historically either defaulted or inflated.

---

[8] Issuance of AAA-rated paper of the US mortgage agencies were (annual rate, in $ billion):

2000–05	2006	2008	2009	2010	2011
1057	567	997	985	1190	481

Note that the Federal Reserve became a large purchaser of these bonds during the crisis. Source: Dealogic.

[9] The rest of this chapter draws on Turner (2011), where the issues are set out more fully.

From their examination of earlier periods of high indebtedness, for instance, Reinhart and Sbrancia (2011) conclude that financial repression (that is, regulation to ensure favoured access to credit for the government) in combination with inflation has historically played an important role in reducing government debts. They suggest that similar policies may be used to deal with the current high debt levels but 'in the guise of prudential regulation rather than under the politically incorrect label of financial repression'. Much recent commentary in the financial press goes in a similar direction.[10] So the links between government deficits, debt and the long-term interest rate deserve a closer look. Section 2.5 will look at regulatory policies.

Large and persistent budget deficits in the advanced economies have increased government debt. According to BIS estimates of global aggregates, government bonds outstanding amounted to almost $45 trillion by end-2011, compared with less than $15 trillion at the start of 2000. There is a huge uncertainty about future budget deficits and their financing. Economists disagree about how quickly deficits should be reduced: some would stress deflation risks and others inflation risks. It is nevertheless certain that government debt/GDP ratios in major countries will continue to rise over the next few years. Even the optimistic G20 pronouncements do not envisage debt/GDP ratios in the advanced countries stabilising before 2016.

There is no consensus among economists about the impact of high government debt/GDP ratios on the level of long-term interest rates.[11] Most policymakers believe that the need to finance a large increase in public deficits and debt would, in a closed economy, drive up the long-term interest rate and crowd out private borrowers. Some economists would challenge this. If the private sector response were Ricardian, they would argue, high government debt would have no effect on the long-term rate of interest as the private sector would increase saving to meet future tax liabilities. Another complication is the nature of the central bank's policy response. One characterisation of this that has excited much debate is 'fiscal dominance' versus 'monetary dominance'. Do the needs of financing very large government budget deficits force the central bank to keep interest rates low? Or does the central bank, committed to low inflation, drive up interest rates and so force the government to reduce its borrowing? In any case, as Woodford and others have shown, the problem is more complex than simple fiscal versus monetary

---

[10] See, e.g. Milne (2011), who argues that risky assets do not cause crises, but rather it is those perceived as safe that do.

[11] The discussion in this paragraph focuses on local currency debt. In the case of foreign currency debt, however, the markets enforce much lower debt/GDP ratios.

dominance. Even faithful adherence by the central bank to an anti-inflation monetary rule (e.g. a Taylor rule) may not by itself be sufficient to ensure price stability when budget deficits are large – because government policy frameworks may engender fiscal expectations that are inconsistent with stable prices (Leeper and Walker, 2011).

How and when high government debt affects some equilibrium long-term interest rate will also depend on market dynamics. Market movements will depend in part on the initial balance sheet positions of investors, of debtors and of financial intermediaries when expectations change.

The probability of destabilising dynamics once expectations change will be higher when interest rate exposures are leveraged. Economy-wide leverage – of households and non-financial companies as well as of financial intermediaries – is key. For instance, households with short-term or variable rate mortgages would rush to lengthen the maturity of their mortgages when they expect interest rates to rise. This would force their lenders to cover their new interest rate exposures. This would set off price movements in interest rate markets. Financial intermediaries with leveraged exposures would be forced to respond. Wholesale investors in the markets for bonds and interest rate derivatives (such as banks, pension funds, hedge funds and so on) can act very quickly and on a large scale. When expectations about yields change, efforts by these intermediaries to cut interest rate exposures can magnify the movement of market yields. Lower bond prices can in turn trigger yet further sales. The increased volatility of prices (historic or implied from options prices) would itself raise the measure of market risk used by banks. Households and firms would react further as interest rates change. Such mutually reinforcing feedbacks can further destabilise markets even in the absence of a new macroeconomic shock. Several past episodes of government bond market crisis have demonstrated that such leverage-dependent effects can move market interest rates much more than seems warranted by fundamentals.

For all these reasons, a long period of high government debt/GDP ratios may unsettle expectations about the future path of interest rates, both real and nominal. There are grounds for thinking that unquantifiable uncertainty (in the Knightian sense) could increase. It is impossible to know how Ricardian households will be in the face of a global fiscal crisis. And doubts about the nature of the policy response will increase uncertainty about inflation and, perhaps, about future growth. Many believe that macroeconomic tail risks – inherently difficult to quantify – have risen in the global economy.

A related aspect is stability or instability in the process of expectations formation. Changes in policy regime can be very important because they can engender instability in expectations. For instance, the financial crisis has probably weakened the credibility of fiscal and monetary policy frameworks in the advanced countries. A loss of credibility would change the expectations formation process – markets might, for instance, attach greater weight to unfavourable news.

Uncertainty about future interest rates is important because it determines whether investors regard short-term and long-term paper as close substitutes. In a world of perfect certainty about future short-term rates, the maturity mix of debt would have no consequences because debt of different terms would be perfect substitutes for one another. There would be no term premium for longer-dated paper. A high degree of asset substitutability and well-anchored expectations would also support the pre-crisis monetary policy orthodoxy that control of the overnight interest rate (combined with credible communication about the likely path of the policy rate over a near-term horizon) is sufficient for central banks to shape macroeconomic developments. Changes in the overnight rate and expected future overnight rates feed through quickly to at least the near end of the yield curve. Transmission of policy rate changes to the whole structure of interest rates is thus effective.

But uncertainty about the path of future interest rates will make debt of different maturities imperfect substitutes.[12] As uncertainty increases, term premia would rise and become less stable. Because of this, changes in the mix of short-term and long-term bonds offered by the government will change relative prices and thus influence the shape of the yield curve. At the same time, monetary policy based on setting the policy rate becomes less effective: the lower the degree of asset substitutability, the weaker the transmission of changes in the overnight rate to other interest rates. Hence government debt management policies (or central bank purchases of bonds) become more effective in influencing longer-term rates in circumstances of market instability or uncertainty – exactly when classic monetary policy reliant on the overnight rate works less well in influencing the yield curve.

2.5   Increased regulatory demands to hold government bonds: financial repression?

The global financial crisis has not only given governments massive debts to finance but has also led to (or reinforced) rules requiring regulated financial firms to hold more government bonds. Although such rules are

---

[12] In their analysis of the effects of quantitative easing, Joyce and Tong (2012) find evidence of local supply and duration risk effects that are consistent with imperfect substitution in bond markets.

part of post-crisis efforts to make the financial system safer, there are concerns of financial repression.

Institutional investors such as insurance companies and pension funds have liabilities that extend far into the future, and their business models have been hard-hit by a prolonged period of low long-term interest rates. Such firms use some variant of a long-term interest rate to discount their future liabilities in the instruments they sell. Many insurance companies have liabilities from products (sold in earlier years) that offer guaranteed minimum returns that are now above the current level of interest rates on government bonds. Those meeting the commitments of defined-benefit pensions made at a time when long-term rates were higher face a similar problem.

The new European supervisory framework for insurers, Solvency II, is one instance of recent (or proposed) regulation that is likely to affect the market for government bonds. First, it contains several provisions that will induce insurance companies to increase their holdings of government bonds. Peter Praet's recent report throws much useful light on this (Bank for International Settlements, 2011c). All European government bonds in domestic currency – even euro area periphery debt – are classified as risk-free and thus carry a zero capital requirement. Capital requirements for other bonds are calculated by multiplying the rating-based risk factor by the duration of the bonds – thus penalising such long-term paper.[13]

Secondly, insurers' demand for government bonds may be made more procyclical. For example, a sharp decline in the value of total assets coming from a decline in prices of the risk assets of an insurance company (for instance, equities and corporate bonds) will reduce the solvency ratio of the company. If the firm cannot raise new capital, it could be forced to sell its equities (which carry a significant risk weight and thus capital requirement) and buy government bonds (which carry zero capital requirement). Such rebalancing could destabilise markets by reinforcing downward pressure on equity prices and upward pressure on bond prices.[14] A sharp rise in equity prices would have the opposite effect, and encourage firms to sell low-yielding government bonds when economic prospects improve and equity prices rise.

---

[13] The regulatory treatment of AAA-rated covered bonds appears more lenient than that of corporate bonds, which effectively attract a capital charge similar to that of equities.

[14] Institutional investors are often procyclical without any official encouragement. Keynes criticised the procyclical behaviour of pension funds in the 1930s. He resigned as Chairman of the National Mutual over their sales of US equities after the 1937 recession (Tily, 2010).

Thirdly, Solvency II will require insurers to use the government bond yield to calculate the present discounted value (PDV) of their liabilities. This means that the simplest way to minimise the volatility of the gap between the market value of assets and the PDV of liabilities is to hold as assets those bonds used to define the discount rate. A similar logic is increasingly applied to pension funds, trustee-managed accounts and so on. Some accounting rules and regulators impose the government bond yield as the discount rate to be applied. For those subject to such accounting rules, holding government bonds can represent the line of least resistance. Many pension fund consultants advise this, calling it 'liability-driven' investment strategy. But such rules are unlikely to represent the true interest of the end investor.[15]

The choice of the government bond yield to calculate the PDV of future liabilities is arbitrary. And regulators have in the past been willing to relax the rules in difficult market circumstances – when rigid maintenance of the rules would have forced sales and aggravated market instability.[16]

Regulators are also requiring banks to increase their holdings of liquid assets. There is much debate as to what form such assets should take. One dimension of this is the choice between short-dated bills and long-term bonds. Traditionally, liquidity rules have required banks to hold *short-dated* government bills to meet liquid asset ratios. The UK imposed such ratios up until the 1970s, and long-term government bonds did not qualify. The practice in some other countries, and that envisaged under Basel III, is to allow government bonds of all maturities as liquid assets in meeting the Liquidity Coverage Ratio.[17] If banks hold long-term bonds, they are exposed to maturity mismatches and interest rate risks. On the other hand, if banks hold short-term government bills, it

---

[15] A long-term investor, for instance, could choose bonds, equities, gold or houses. Views differ on what to choose. The choice depends on expectations and the investor's appetite for risk. Each investment class would have its own expected mean, variance and vulnerability to tail risk. Rational investors have to assess all three components of the distribution of future returns. There is no reason why they should only wish to minimise the variance of their expected returns and (for diversification of risk) the correlation between the returns on different asset classes. And even if these accounting rules did make sense from the microeconomic perspective of an individual, the aggregate impact for the economy as a whole may be suboptimal.

[16] Gyntelberg et al. (2011) point out that the Danish FSA in October 2008 temporarily allowed pension funds to replace the government bond yield by the (higher) mortgage bond yield to compute the market value of future liabilities – to bring it more in line with the valuation of assets. In some euro area countries, insurance regulators recently relaxed the rules on recognising the full impact of falling government bond prices.

[17] That is, those issued in domestic currency by the sovereign or the central bank in the country. Note that Basel III does *not* designate government securities as the only qualifying liquid assets. See Hannoun (2011).

is the government that faces comparable refunding risks. A key issue, then, is whether the banks or the government is best placed to bear such risks.

The second choice is between private sector and public sector paper. The Bank of England's preference in its discount operations for commercial bills – and not government bonds – in the nineteenth century lasted well into the 1920s. Nowadays the preference is for public sector paper. Allowing banks to meet liquidity rules by holding short-term debt securities issued by other banks would probably increase systemic risk by magnifying bank-to-bank contagion. But it is always worth exploring how greater use could be made of *reliable* private sector paper. For instance, the greater acceptance of high-quality private sector debt products issued by non-financial firms or households (e.g. credit card debt) could help securitisation markets recover. Securitised products that are based on liabilities that are due to mature over approximately the next 12 months would have the attractive self-liquidating properties that exchange bills had in the nineteenth century. The accuracy of credit ratings assigned to such short-term paper could be regularly tested as maturing paper falls due within short intervals – quite unlike the ratings on very long-term debt!

A final dimension that could be of great systemic importance is that forcing banks and other financial firms to increase their holdings of bonds issued by their own governments will accentuate interconnections between banks and sovereign risk. Fabio Panetta's recent report (Bank for International Settlements, 2011b) analyses the many ways that increased sovereign risk can undermine local banks. The balance sheets of banks are weakened when the value of the government bonds they hold falls or becomes more volatile. The value of such bonds as collateral for wholesale borrowing from other banks can be severely eroded.[18] This report shows how important these contagion links have been in the current euro area crisis. When fiscal trajectories are unsustainable, therefore, the authorities will need to watch potentially dangerous interaction between heightened sovereign risk and regulatory policies that induce banks to hold large stocks of government debt.[19]

It is clear from this brief overview that a number of policies (of regulators, of accountants, of trusteeship rules) led regulated firms to increase

---

[18] Davies and Ng (2011) note that the share of European repo transactions collateralised by Greek, Irish or Portuguese bonds fell by more than half from the second half of 2009 to the second half of 2010.

[19] When fiscal trajectories are unsustainable, this report argues that 'the preferential treatment given to government debt (particularly that which is lower-rated) relative to private debt may be less justified'.

their holdings of government bonds. Viewed from the microeconomic perspective of an individual firm, these rules or practices may be rational. But their aggregate impact could be harmful. One major drawback is that such regulations may inadvertently reinforce the procyclical behaviour of investors: the appetite for safer assets such as government bonds tends to rise in pessimistic phases of financial market cycles. A related aspect is that increased holdings of government bonds by leveraged and large investors such as banks could increase bond market volatility in periods when expectations become unstable. As Hannoun (2011) has pointed out, these herding effects are not inevitable: the internal ratings-based approach of Basel II *did* encourage banks to apply their own judgement in discriminating between countries of different creditworthiness. They were not meant to apply a uniform zero risk weight for all sovereigns.

2.6   The long-term rate as a policy variable?

2.6.1   *Monetary policy and the long-term interest rate*

Recent central bank operations in government debt markets have in effect made the long-term interest rate a policy variable. This is usually presented as wholly exceptional – justified because of the zero lower bound (ZLB) constraint on further monetary easing once the policy rate is close to zero. The argument is that policies that shorten the maturity of debt held by the public (i.e. selling Treasury bills and buying government bonds) may lower long-term yields without raising short-term yields, which are glued close to zero at the ZLB.

Yet the case for central bank purchases or sales of government debt is actually much more general and depends on the strength of portfolio rebalancing effects. How large such effects are depends on the degree of asset substitutability across the yield curve. As argued above, it is uncertain or unstable expectations about the path of future interest rates that makes debt of different maturities imperfect substitutes.

How such uncertainty influences actual market prices depends in part on the supply of interest rate arbitrage. If the bond yield is too high relative to average expected future short-term yields, an arbitrageur has an expected gain by buying the bond and borrowing short-term. But this arbitrage trade could face losses if short yields rise beyond expectations. Wider dispersion of expectations (greater riskiness) about future short-term rates (or greater Knightian uncertainty) would increase such risks. If arbitrageurs are risk averse, they reduce their trading as risk or uncertainty rises. In addition, the risk appetite of arbitrageurs – mainly banks – is variable (typically declining in a financial crisis) and subject to capital constraints (which also tighten in a crisis).

(i)   *Keynes and the National Debt Enquiry*

The general argument that central banks could be more effective by acting directly in bond markets is a very old one. Keynes was probably the most famous proponent. Open market operations in long-term government debt were central to his analysis in *Treatise on Money* of how central banks could combat slumps.[20] Keynes argued for what he called 'open market operations to the point of saturation':

> My remedy in the event of the obstinate persistence of a slump would consist, therefore, in the purchase of securities by the central bank until the long-term market rate of interest has been brought down to the limiting point.[21]

He felt that central banks had 'always been too nervous hitherto' about such policies, perhaps because under the 'influence of crude versions of the quantity theory [of money]'. He repeated this analysis in *The General Theory*:

> The monetary authority often tends in practice to concentrate upon short-term debts and to leave the price of long-term debts to be influenced by belated and imperfect reactions from the price of short-term debts – though . . . there is no reason why they need do so.[22]

Contrary to popular myth, he did not believe that there had been a liquidity trap in the 1930s: it was a theoretical possibility that had not been tested 'owing to the unwillingness of most monetary authorities to deal boldly in debts of long term'.

He went on to suggest that the 'most important practical improvement which can be made in technique of monetary management' would be to replace 'the single Bank rate for short-term bills' by 'a complex offer by the central bank to buy and sell at stated prices gilt-edged bonds of all maturities'.

---

[20] The focus of his analysis was on the asset side of the central bank's balance sheet and thus mirrors the Federal Reserve's rationale for its recent quantitative easing. Unlike Hawtrey (for instance), he did not focus on the liability side – that is the impact on commercial bank deposits.

[21] Keynes (1930), pp. 331–2. One constraint he saw was that a central bank acting alone would simply induce capital outflows: he felt the newly established BIS could encourage internationally coordinated central bank efforts to reduce long-term interest rates. Per Jacobsson, Economic Adviser at the BIS at the time, also strongly supported policies aimed at reducing long-term rates.

[22] Keynes (1936), page 206.

It is true that there was a massive conversion of government debt to a lower coupon in 1932, which Keynes hailed as a 'great achievement' for the Treasury and the Bank of England. Short-term rates were cut sharply, and the authorities deliberately nurtured expectations that short-term interest rates would be kept down in the future.[23] But his more general advice for aggressive central bank purchases of debt (or the equivalent change in issuance) went unheeded. The average maturity of government debt actually lengthened as a result of this debt conversion. In the mid-1930s, only 3% of bonds had a maturity of less than 5 years and 86% of bonds had a maturity in excess of 15 years. Susan Howson's (1975) study of British monetary policy in the 1930s found that this limited the effectiveness of the cheap money policy instituted once Britain had left the gold standard: debt management policy ran counter to the monetary policy intent of low short-term rates.[24]

During World War II, low interest rates became a key ingredient of wartime finance. In the closing months of World War II, with the UK facing huge government debts, Keynes, an influential member (with Meade and Robbins) in the UK Treasury's National Debt Enquiry (NDE), argued against the 'dogma' of financing debt at long maturities. Governments should not 'fetter themselves . . . to a counter-liquidity preference' but should accommodate the preferences of the public for different maturities.

In the NDE, Keynes won the argument he had lost in the 1930s. The Permanent Secretary to the Treasury, who summarised the Enquiry's conclusions, made a point of noting that the Enquiry had taken as given Keynes's view that the long-term rate of interest could be controlled by determined official action. This view, he noted, 'would now command a wide measure of agreement among economists'. The proposed 'programme of initial procedure', as he put it – the idea was to adapt this policy in the light of experience – was: 'the Treasury bill rate to be brought down to $1/2\%$ and 5-year bonds to be issued at $1^1/2\%$ and 10-year bonds at 2% to be issued on tap, a new series to be started annually' (Tily, 2010).

But Keynes did not want the long-term rate to go to zero. It was, he said, 'socially desirable' that rentiers should get some return on their

---

[23] Bank rate was cut progressively from 6% in early 1932 to 2% on 30 June 1932, the day the debt conversion was announced. It remained at 2% until August 1939. Howson (1975, p. 89) observes that creating the expectations of low rates was not difficult 'because the public had been expecting a period of lower interest rates ever since the New York stock market crash of 1929'. This did not conflict with external policy objectives because policy was to keep the pound down to help exporters.

[24] See Allen (2012) for an interesting analysis of the ebb and flow of the link between monetary policy and government debt management since 1919.

capital.[25] He argued that this was necessary for viable pension provision for unsophisticated, small investors (widows and orphans was his phrase) and for university endowments (dear to his heart).

This line of reasoning has found significant echoes in some recent work. In his analysis of maturity transformation by financial intermediaries which have (uncertain) long-term liabilities, Tirole has developed this Keynesian tradition further. In the presence of macroeconomic shocks that affect everybody simultaneously, he argues, private sector assets are not useful. Instead what is needed is an external risk-free store of value such as government bonds. A prolonged period of low rates of interest on government bonds can make some pension products offered by such firms unviable. Tirole (2008) therefore argues that:

> liquidity premia [on] risk-free assets [are] a useful guide for the issuing of government securities both [in total] and in structure (choice of maturities) ... a very low long rate signals social gains to issuing long-term Treasury securities. A case in point is the issuing by HM Treasury of long-term bonds in reaction to the low rates triggered by the 2005 reform of pension funds requirements.

In arguing for an elastic supply of 10-year bonds at 2% in 1945, the NDE had made a similar point: this would allow insurance companies to offer 'annuities on joint lives, calculated on the basis of a low rate of interest' and so encourage 'the habit of thrift' on the part of households.[26]

(ii)   The Radcliffe Report

The Radcliffe Report (Committee on the Working of the Monetary System, 1959) strongly reiterated Keynes's view that policy should consciously influence the long-term rate of interest. But it did so because of worries about an inadequate central bank response to inflation, not deflation.

As HM Treasury made quite clear in its evidence to Radcliffe, the authorities cared more about maintaining stability in the bond market than about macroeconomic control:

---

[25] Meade, who believed that investment was more interest rate sensitive than Keynes did, disagreed. His view was that the long-term rate of interest could be reduced to near zero to counter depression but should rise to meet any inflationary threat. His diary entry for 26 February 1945 reads: 'in my mind the real social revolution is to be brought about by the most radical reduction in interest rates which is necessary to prevent general deflation'. See Meade (1990), page 46.

[26] The post-war context explains this mention of thrift. An important policy objective was to sustain (voluntary) household saving as the forced saving schemes enacted during the war would be dismantled. Some opposed the policy of low interest rates on the grounds that savings would be discouraged.

No attempt is made to use official purchases and sales in the market for the specific purpose of raising or lowering the level of medium and long-term interest rates... [because this] would create market uncertainty and so impair the prospects of continuing official sales of securities... Such operations would involve a serious risk of damage to confidence and to the Government's credit.

Many of the economists who gave evidence to Radcliffe disagreed with this policy orientation. Several argued that a main effect of monetary policy on aggregate demand worked through the long-term interest rate. R. F. Kahn reiterated the view that both Keynes and Meade had expressed in the NDE, namely that the:

authorities... including the Bank of England... and those responsible for managing the national debt... are capable, within very broad limits, of achieving any desired structure of interest rates... provided they are not worried about the quantity of money.

The Radcliffe Report sided with the economists – and against the Treasury. A key conclusion was that 'the structure of interest rates rather than the supply of money [was] the centre piece of the monetary mechanism'. In this, government debt management was to play a central role. The Report concluded with five main points. Among them a clear – and all-too-often overlooked – statement of the importance of the long-term interest rate as an objective of monetary policy:

There is no doubt that... monetary policy... can... influence the structure of interest rates through the management of the National Debt which, if burdensome to the financial authorities in other respects [i.e. increasing debt servicing costs], affords in this respect an instrument of single potency. In our view debt management has become the fundamental domestic task of the central bank. It is not open to the monetary authorities to be neutral in their handling of this task. They must have and must consciously exercise a positive policy about interest rates, long as well as short.

The Report argued that policy reliance on short rates alone had proved ineffective. It noted that, in one tightening phase in the early 1950s, higher short rates were followed by higher long rates only after a long lag. This lag made the eventual movement in long rates procyclical, rising when the downturn was already underway. It would have been better to have directly encouraged the rise in long rates right at the beginning of the tightening phase. Moving all rates up improves the chances of timing countercyclical monetary policy correctly.

The Report explicitly countered the Treasury view on the need to support the bond market by arguing that greater efforts 'to foster greater understanding outside official circles... of the intentions of the authorities would reduce the risk of perverse reactions in the market [from bond sales]'.

Their recommendation for greater activism in moving long-term rates, however, fell on deaf ears. With government debt around 130% of GDP, it is perhaps not surprising the authorities were reluctant to countenance any rise in debt servicing costs.

(iii)   Tobin and Friedman

It was Tobin (1963) who developed the theoretical models of how central bank operations in long-term debt markets work. He stressed the importance of the policies of government debt finance for the long-term rate of interest. Central banks in effect issue the shortest duration official debt in their operations to implement monetary policy. From the perspective of portfolio choice, government issuance of short-term debt is like monetary expansion. Tobin puts this point well:

> There is no neat way to distinguish monetary policy from debt management, [both] the Federal Reserve and the Treasury ... are engaged in debt management in the broadest sense, and both have powers to influence the whole spectrum of debt. But monetary policy refers particularly to determination of the supply of demand debt, and debt management to determination of the amounts in the long and nonmarketable categories. In between, the quantity of short debt is determined as a residuum.

Milton Friedman had made exactly the same point in 1959: he devoted the third chapter of his *A Program for Monetary Stability* to debt management, saying that 'open market operations and debt management are different names for the same monetary tool'. For him, central bank purchase of bonds could be the 'major weapon' in a crisis to lower long-term yields relative to the expected path of short-term rates. See Nelson (2011).

Tobin went on to argue for the use of debt management (i.e. shifting between short-dated and long-dated paper) as a countercyclical policy to influence private capital formation, and thus real output. His conclusion was:

> The Federal Reserve cannot make rational decisions of monetary policy without knowing what kind of debt the Treasury intends to issue. The Treasury cannot rationally determine the maturity structure of the interest-bearing debt without knowing how much debt the Federal Reserve intends to monetise.[27]

---

[27] His suggestion was that full responsibility for Federal government debt management be assigned to the Federal Reserve, not the US Treasury.

His analysis was that of portfolio choice under uncertainty (which he had used in his famous interpretation of Keynes's liquidity preference theory). Official sales of debt trigger portfolio rebalancing effects that can take many forms.

Few dispute the logic or importance of such portfolio rebalancing effects.[28] But there is much controversy about magnitudes. This is probably because the degree of substitutability across asset classes is not stable but rather depends on macroeconomic and financial conditions. This makes empirical estimation very hard.

2.6.2 Government debt management and the long-term interest rate

Imperfect substitutability between assets of different maturities means that government debt management choices matter for the long-term interest rate. In principle, such choices could be made independently of macroeconomic or monetary developments. In practice, they are probably not.

(i) Macroeconomic responses of government debt managers

The average maturity of issuance of US government debt, for instance, has shown quite wide variation over the years. In recent years, the underlying policy objective has been to lengthen the (comparatively short) maturity of US government debts: see Figure 2.9. Whether pursuit of this objective has been justified by lower (*ex post*) borrowing costs is doubtful. The discussion of the average slope of the yield curve in Section 2.2 (larger in recent decades and no more unstable than in the 1960s and 1970s) suggests that, in general, shorter-dated financing would have been cheaper. For the purpose of this chapter, however, it is the link with the macroeconomic policy stance that is of most interest. There is statistical evidence that, over the past 30 years, the maturity of outstanding US government debt has tended to be shortened when the Federal funds rate is low.[29] This may reflect the fact that debt managers deliberately take advantage of unusually low near-term market rates when the central bank's policy stance is accommodating.

---

[28] Such effects are deemed irrelevant in the New Keynesian framework only on some strong assumptions (including full information about the future). See Zampolli (2012) for a review.

[29] The evidence is set out in Turner (2011), pp. 30–31.

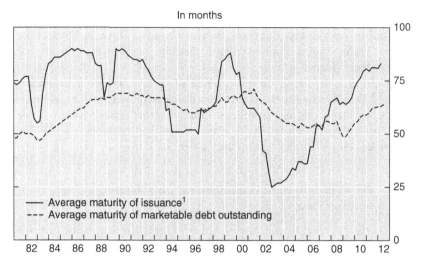

Figure 2.9 Maturity of US government bonds
[1]One-year moving average; shown at the end.
Sources: Datastream; US Treasury.

Shortening the maturity of debt issuance and lowering the policy rate are both expansionary: in this sense, policies work in the same direction.[30]

There is also evidence that larger fiscal deficits tend to lead to a lengthening of maturities in the following year. Debt managers often say that longer maturities are indeed needed to spread out higher debt over longer time periods. The academic literature on this link has focused on the role of debt management in providing fiscal insurance (Missale, 2012). Faced with a deterioration in its fiscal position (according to reasoning based on an intertemporal budget constraint), a government seeks to reduce the market value of its debt. It can drive up the long-term rate by lengthening the maturity of its issuance. At the limit, it could overfund its budget deficit – issuing long-dated paper on a massive scale and buying short-term assets from the private sector. Faraglia et al. (2008) have shown this is not what happens. Their explanation is that potential private buyers of government debt would face credit constraints and that the government would have to hold risky private assets. The assumption of market completeness is therefore not satisfied.

---

[30] This assumes that the central bank effectively controls short-term yields through expectations about its policy rate over the relevant horizon. In some circumstances, however, the interest rate offered by the government on Treasury bills could move short-term yields away from the central bank's policy rate. There have been instances of such divergence in some emerging market economies; in some jurisdictions, government issuance of Treasury bills is subject to central bank agreement.

Whatever the reasons, debt management choices do seem to have responded to the stance of both monetary policy and fiscal policy. But endogeneity does not reflect a conscious view that debt management policies could be deliberately adjusted to serve fiscal or monetary policy objectives.

How large the macroeconomic impacts of more activist debt-management policies would be depends on the strength of portfolio-balancing and the substitutability between short-term and long-term debts. For the reasons discussed above, such substitutability will not be uniform either across countries or over time. The experience of one country will not necessarily be a good guide to what would happen in another country. What works in one episode will not necessarily work in another. Nevertheless, it is not difficult to imagine circumstances in which such policies can be highly effective. In times of crisis, for instance, a large (but temporary) decline in asset substitutability (because of greater macroeconomic uncertainty, banks with weakened balance sheets less able to take interest rate risks, etc.) will make activist debt management policies more effective in influencing the yield curve. (How far private borrowers benefit from the lower rates paid by government depends on many other factors.)

(ii)   Coordination between central banks and debt managers

It is clear that activism motivated by macroeconomic objectives in both debt management policies by the Treasury (or DMO) and central bank balance sheet policies would create coordination problems. A central bank could not take optimal decisions in response to macroeconomic developments if it did not take account of how the Treasury would respond. How any policy towards the long-term rate is made operational would matter. A target range could be set for the rate itself (as Keynes advocated): in this case, the central bank balance sheet/government debt issuance becomes endogenous. Or the authorities could set quantity targets for sales or purchases (as in the recent policies of quantitative easing) leaving the market to determine the rate. Different coordination mechanisms would be applied according to which mode of operation is selected.

Without mechanisms to ensure the consistency of different policies, QE operations decided by the central banks could well be contradicted by Treasury financing decisions. Remember that the government's balance sheet is much larger in normal times than that of the central bank. The central bank's balance sheet is more elastic perhaps – because it can create liabilities on a very large scale to finance assets. But if its policies just induce the opposite reaction of the debt manager (taking advantage of an unusual configuration of interest rates), its theoretical elasticity will have less practical effect. Recall the famous 'Operation Twist'.[31] When the Federal Reserve used open market operations to flatten the yield curve by shortening the average maturity of Treasury debt in the early 1960s, the US Treasury in effect worked against this policy by ultimately lengthening the maturity of issuance.

What about the recent QE policies in the United States? QE cannot be analysed without taking account of changes in Treasury debt management policies. The US Treasury has been lengthening the average maturity of its outstanding debt in recent years. This is difficult to square with QE, which aims to shorten the maturity of bonds held by the public. One simple approach is to examine elements of the consolidated balance sheet of the Treasury and the central bank. The first table in Tobin's 1963 classic paper – which summarised the structure of Federal government debt in the hands of the public – is a good place to start. (But it is, of course, a highly stylised characterisation of the monetary impulse of changes in debt maturity.)

With the adoption of QE after the crisis, reliance on short-term debt and Federal Reserve obligations were increased. Between the end of FY2007 and the end of FY2009, currency and Federal Reserve obligations more than doubled (Table 2.3). Short-term marketable securities outstanding also doubled with an almost $2 trillion expansion in money and short-dated paper, this clearly represented a very significant easing of policy. What might be called 'monetary financing' in the first two years of the crisis went from 34% to 43%.

But in the third year of the crisis, the maturity of Treasury debt issuance changed in a restrictive direction. Monetary financing actually declined from 43% at end-September 2009 to 35.5% at end-September 2010. In the most recent period, QE was partly offset by longer-dated Treasury issuance.

Table 2.4 provides further data on maturity choices. It shows that the Federal Reserve's portfolio of US Treasuries with a maturity of two years or more rose by $759 billion; US Treasury issuance was $1303 billion. Hence Federal Reserve policies reduced the volume of new long-dated paper to be sold to the public, which tended to lower bond yields. But note, however, that Treasury issuance was of longer maturity than

---

[31] See Swanson (2011), who explains that it began as a joint FRB–Treasury programme – unlike the later programmes. Chadha and Holly (2011) estimate that the Federal Reserve's purchases of $8.8 billion under this programme are the equivalent of $225 billion when scaled at today's GDP.

Table 2.3 *Composition of marketable US Federal government debt held by the public*

	$ billion				
	Marketable securities		Currency & Federal Reserve obligations	Total	Money, Federal Reserve obligations and short-term debt
End of fiscal year (Sept)	(≤ 1 year) (a)	(> 1 year) (b)	(c)	(d)	=(a + c) as % of d
1st 2 years of crisis					
2007	955	3474	834	5263	34%
2009	1986	5002	1780	8768	42.9%
	+1031		**+946**		
3rd year of crisis					
2010	1784	6692	1896	10372	35.5%
	−202		**+163**		

Sources: This is an update of that in Tobin (1963); US Treasury Bulletin and Federal Reserve Flow-of-Funds.

Table 2.4 *Activity in US Treasuries*

Change from 11 November 2010 to 30 June 2011

	$ billion	Average maturity (years)
Federal Reserve's net purchases	759	6.9
Stock of Treasury issuance	1303	7.2
Treasury issuance *minus* Fed's net purchases	544	7.8

Note: This is a summary of issuance of bonds with maturities of two-years or more.
Source: FRBNY and US Treasury.

Federal Reserve purchases.[32] The average maturity of new issuance *placed with the public* rose to about 7.5–8 years – as the average maturity of Federal Reserve purchases was a little below that of gross Treasury issuance. This compares with an average maturity of new issuance of four years in 2006 – the year before the crisis. Hence the maturity of

---

[32] Note that this changed in late 2011 when the Federal Reserve lengthened the maturities of their purchases under their Maturity Extension Program ('Operation Twist 2'). Ehlers (2012) estimates that, without Operation Twist 2, investors would have had to absorb Treasuries with an average maturity of 7.7 years in the fourth quarter of 2011. Operation Twist 2 reduced this to only 5.5 years.

government debt held by the public has risen substantially during the recession – notwithstanding Federal Reserve purchases.

Somewhat different issues arise in the euro area, which does not have a single fiscal authority. Hoogduin et al. (2010) point out that the Maastricht Treaty did not constrain national debt managers in the euro area – even though their local decisions (for example, to issue short-dated paper) could have monetary implications. They show that, in the euro area, a steepening of the yield curve had led national debt managers to shorten the duration of their issuance.

More work is needed on the complex interaction between monetary policy and debt management policy. Paul Fisher's recent report (Bank for International Settlements, 2011a) on potential interactions between sovereign debt management and central banks provides an authoritative account of (difficult) coordination issues. This report analyses how circumstances can alter the nature of policy spillovers involved. It considers practical steps to ensure effective coordination.

2.7   Conclusion

Policy victim, policy variable or policy lodestar – what best describes the long-term interest rate? This question was prompted by the observation of a strong, apparently secular, decline in benchmark long-term interest rates in major currencies to very low levels. This decline has generated capital gains for bond investors. In this sense, it has helped the balance sheets of banks, pension funds and other investors in such securities. This decline in yields is paradoxical given the extraordinary expansion in the issuance of AAA-rated fixed-rate paper during the 2000s. Huge fiscal deficits and heavy issuance by the US mortgage agencies (which have been in effect nationalised) have been the main drivers.

Has the long-term interest rate become the victim of government policies? The aggregate impact of many quite distinct policies – the investment of foreign exchange reserves, the regulation of the insurance and banking industry, valuation rules for pension funds and so on – on the long-term interest rate has become more marked than a decade or so ago. These policies have contributed to a lowering of the real risk-free long-term interest rate – and this has been largely unintended. By how much we do not know – so we cannot compute where the long-term rate would be in the absence of such policies. Such policies may also have made the long-term interest rate more procyclical – falling more when economic prospects weaken and rising more sharply when growth recovers.

How powerful such effects have been is an empirical question. There are, of course, several countervailing forces. The IRB approach under Basel II did try to encourage large and sophisticated banks to be more discriminating in their sovereign exposures. All regulated investors should have their own risk management policies. Another countervailing force is that non-regulated investors can exploit any mispricing caused by regulation. Greater financial market depth creates arbitrage opportunities that can be used to circumvent regulation. The integration of global capital markets tends to weaken the impact of one country's regulations.

Have the crisis responses of central banks in many advanced countries made the long-term interest rate a policy variable? Perhaps this is purely temporary and exceptional, motivated by a wish to implement further monetary easing when short-term rates are already at or close to zero. But there is nothing new in the view that central banks can be more effective when they intervene directly in bond markets. Keynes was perhaps the best known advocate. Milton Friedman shared his opinion that central banks, in a crisis, should purchase government bonds to drive down long-term yields. Regarding the long-term rate as a policy variable would inevitably focus more attention on the macroeconomic and financial consequences of government debt management policies. As Goodhart (2010) has argued, these policies will no longer be regarded as the exclusive domain of debt managers constrained by technical benchmarks.

The fundamental issue is the degree of asset substituitability across the yield curve: uncertainty about the path of future interest rates makes debt of different maturities imperfect substitutes. A prolonged period of high government debt/GDP seems likely to increase such uncertainty. If so, the long-term rate may come to be regarded as a policy variable for some considerable time. It is not difficult to envisage many, quite different scenarios. The euro area crisis has concentrated attention on sovereign risk. Another scenario centres around inflation risk. For example, a sharp upward hike in bond yields triggered by an inflation scare that is regarded as unwarranted in official circles might lead to calls for direct central bank or government action in the bond market. The purported rationale could be to counter the consequences of "excessive market volatility", not to provide government direction to a market price. But central banks will naturally be wary about unwarranted optimism about their ability to steer long-term rates for any length of time when budget deficits and government debt are very high.

Should the long-term interest rate still be taken as a key market signal to guide policy? It is widely used as a policy lodestar. It is important for guiding *macroeconomic policies* because it can be used to measure expectations of inflation and growth. Such expectations about an uncertain future can weigh heavily in deliberations about macroeconomic policies. DeLong and Summers (2012) have recently argued that low long-term interest rates signal the need for increased government investment spending.

It can be central to many *microeconomic policies* because of its influence on the discount rate. Public sector investment decisions depend on the discount rate applied to future costs and benefits. Ramaswamy (2012) has shown how sensitive choices about pension provisions are to the long-term rate of interest.

This chapter argues that great caution is needed in drawing policy implications based on the real long-term interest rate currently prevailing in markets. This interest rate has moved in a wide range over the past 20 years. At present, it is clearly well below longstanding historical norms. Several explanations come to mind. But not enough is known about how far the long-term rate has been contaminated by government and other policies. Nor is the persistence of such effects clear. And the various policies will have impacted different parts of the yield curve in ways that are hard to quantify.

The concluding note of caution is this: beware of the consequences of sudden movements in yields when long-term rates are very low. Accounting and regulatory changes may well have made bond markets more cyclical. There is no evidence that bond yields have become less volatile in recent years. Indeed, data over the last decade or so mirror Mark Watson's (1999) well-known finding that the variability of the long-term rate in the 1990s was actually greater than it had been in the 1965–78 period. A change of about 50 basis points in one month (i.e. not so unlikely since only twice the standard deviation shown in Table 2.1) would have a larger impact when yields are 2% than when they are 6%.

With government debt/GDP ratios set to be very high for years, there is a significant risk of instability in bond markets. Greater volatility in long-term rates may create awkward dilemmas in the setting of short-term rates and decisions on central bank holdings of government bonds. Because interest rate positions of financial firms are leveraged, sharp movements could also threaten financial stability.

References

Allen, W. A. (2012). Government debt management and monetary policy in Britain since 1919, in BIS (2012), pp. 15–50.

Amato, J. (2005). The role of the natural interest rate in monetary policy. BIS Working Paper no. 171. March.

Bank for International Settlements (2011a). Interactions of sovereign debt management with monetary conditions and financial stability. CGFS Papers no. **42**. May. www.bis.org/publ/cgfs42.htm

Bank for International Settlements (2011b). The impact of sovereign credit risk on bank funding conditions. CGFS Papers no. **43**. July. www.bis.org/publ/cgfs43.htm

Bank for International Settlements (2011c). Fixed-income strategies of insurance companies and pension funds. CGFS Papers no. **44**. July. www.bis. org/publ/cgfs44.htm

Bank for International Settlements (2012). Threat of fiscal dominance? BIS Papers no. **65**. May. www.bis.org/publ/bppdf/bispap65.htm

Cecchetti, S. G., Mohanty, M. S. and Zampolli, F. (2011). The real effect of debt. Symposium sponsored by the Federal Reserve Bank of Kansas City, Jackson Hole, Wyoming, 25–27 August. BIS Working Paper no. 352.

Chadha, J. S. and Holly, S. (2011). New instruments of monetary policy, in *Interest Rates, Prices and Liquidity – Lessons from the Financial Crisis* (J. S. Chadha and S. Holly, eds.), Cambridge University Press.

Committee on the Working of the Monetary System (1959). *Radcliffe Report*, Cmnd 827, London HMSO.

Davies, M. and Ng, T. (2011). The rise of sovereign credit risk: implications for financial stability. *BIS Quarterly Review*. September. www.bis.org/publ/qtrpdf/r_qt1109.htm

DeLong, J. and Summers, L. H. (2012). Fiscal policy in a depressed economy. *Brookings Papers on Economic Activity*. 22 March. www.brookings.edu/economics/bpea/Latest-Conference/delongsummers.aspx

Ehlers, T. (2012). The effectiveness of the Federal Reserve's Maturity Extension Program – Operation Twist 2, in BIS (2012), pp. 245–55.

Faraglia, E., Marcet, A. and Scott, A. (2008). Fiscal insurance and debt management in OECD economies. *Economic Journal*, **118**. March. pp. 363–86.

Friedman, M. (1959). *A Program of Monetary Stability*. New York: Fordham University Press.

Goodhart, C. (2010). The changing role of central banks. BIS Working Papers no. 326. www.bis.org/list/wpapers/index.htm

Gyntelberg, J., Kjeldsen, K. and Persson, M. (2011). The 2008 financial crisis and the Danish mortgage market, in *Global Housing Markets* (A. Bardhan, R. Edelstein and C. Kroll, eds.). City: John Wiley & Sons.

Hannoun, H. (2011). Sovereign risk in bank regulation and supervision: where do we stand?. FSI presentation at Abu Dhabi, 26 October. www.bis.org/speeches/sp111026.htm?ql=1

Hicks, J. (1958). The yield on consols, Paper read to the Manchester Statistical Society in March 1958 and submitted in evidence to the Radcliffe Committee. Revised and reprinted in *Critical Essays in Monetary Theory*, Oxford University Press, 1967.

Hoogduin, L., Öztürk, B. and Wierts, P. (2010). Public debt manager's behaviour: interactions with macro policies. Banque de France and BETA workshop: New Challenges for Public Debt in Advanced Economics, Strasbourg, September. Reprinted as DNB Working Paper no. 273.

Howson, S. (1975). Domestic monetary management in Britain 1919–38. University of Cambridge. Department of Applied Economics. Occasional Paper 48.

Joyce, M. and Tong, M. (2012). QE and the gilt market: a disaggregated analysis, *The Economic Journal*, **122**(564) F345–384.

Keynes, J. M. (1936). *The General Theory of Employment Interest and Money*. Volume VII, Collected writings of John Maynard Keynes. Macmillan for the Royal Economic Society.

Keynes, J. M. (1930). *A Treatise on Money Vol. 2*, Volume VI, Collected writings of John Maynard Keynes. Macmillan for the Royal Economic Society.

Leeper, E. M. and Walker, D. B. (2011). Perceptions and misperceptions of fiscal inflation. BIS Working Paper no. 364. December. www.bis.org/publ/work364.htm

Meade, J. (1990). *The Collected Papers of James Meade*, Volume IV: *The Cabinet Office Diary 1944–46* (S. Howson and D. Moggridge, eds.). London, Unwin Hyman.

Mills, T. and Wood G. E. (2009). Two and half centuries of British interest rates, monetary regimes and inflation. Mimeo. October.

Milne, R. (2011). Beware of safe havens when seeking the next financial crisis. *Financial Times*, 28 June.

Missale, A. (2012). Sovereign debt management and fiscal vulnerabilities, in BIS (2012), pp. 157–76.

Nelson, E. (2011). Friedman's monetary economics in practice. Finance and Economics Discussion Series. 2011–26. Federal Reserve Board. April.

Ramaswamy, S. (2012). The sustainability of pension schemes. BIS Working Paper no. 368. January. www.bis.org/publ/work368.htm

Reinhart, C. and Sbrancia, B. (2011). The liquidation of government debt. NBER Working Paper no. 16893. March. (BIS Working Paper no. 363).

Shigehara, K. and Atkinson, P. (2011). Surveillance by international institutions: lessons from the global financial and economic crisis. OECD Economics Department Working Paper no 860. May.

Sims, C. A. (2008). Stepping on a rake: the role of fiscal policy in the inflation of the 1970s. Mimeo. October.

Swanson, E. (2011). Let's Twist again: a high-frequency event-study analysis of Operation Twist and its implications for QE2. *Brookings Papers on Economic Activity*. Spring, pp. 151–88.

Tily, G. (2010). *Keynes Betrayed: the General Theory, the Rate of Interest and 'Keynesian' Economics*. Palgrave Macmillan.

Tirole, J. (2008). Liquidity shortages: theoretical underpinnings. *Banque de France Financial Stability Review*. February.

Tobin, J. (1963). An essay on the principles of debt management, in *Fiscal and Debt Management Policies*, Prentice-Hall. Reprinted in James Tobin, *Essays in Economics: Volume 1* (1971). Chicago: Markham Publishing Company.

Turner, P. (2011). Fiscal dominance and the long-term interest rate. Financial Markets Group, London School of Economics. Special Paper No 199. March. www2.lse.ac.uk/fmg/workingPapers/specialPapers/PDF/SP199.pdf

Warnock, F. and Warnock, V. (2009). International capital flows and US interest rates, *Journal of International Money and Finance*, **28**, 903–19.

Watson, M. W. (1999). Explaining the increased variability of long-term interest rates. Federal Reserve Bank of Richmond. *Economic Quarterly*. **85/4**.

Zampolli, F. (2012). Sovereign debt management as an instrument of monetary policy: an overview, in BIS (2012), pp. 97–118.

3 Sovereign debt and monetary policy in the euro area

Alain C. J. Durré and Frank Smets

3.1 Introduction

On average public debt in the advanced economies has exceeded 100% of GDP in 2012, levels that are unprecedented in peace time. The rise in government debt raises concerns about the sustainability of public finances and the implications for growth and inflation. For example, taking into account the large and rising fiscal costs related to an ageing population, Cecchetti et al. (2010) conclude that the path pursued by fiscal authorities in a number of industrial countries is unsustainable. Reinhart and Rogoff (2010), Cecchetti et al. (2011) and Baum et al. (2013) have documented that historically public debt ratios of more than 80–90% typically are associated with a long subsequent period of low growth. Smets and Trabandt (2012) review the implications of rising government debt for inflation and monetary policy. First, they argue that high government debt constrains an active use of fiscal policy (as was for example the case within the euro area for Belgium and Italy going into the financial crisis of 2008) and therefore puts a larger burden on monetary policy to stabilise the economy. This may not be straightforward if standard monetary policy is constrained by the zero lower bound on nominal short-term interest rates. Second, to the extent that long-term government debt is issued in nominal terms it increases the pressure to reduce the real value of the debt by unexpected inflation. High government debt may also increase the pressure to rely on alternative sources of government finance such as central bank seignorage. These pressures risk undermining the credibility and the independence of the central bank to maintain price stability and may thereby give rise to higher inflation expectations. Finally, the increasing riskiness of government debt may undermine the proper functioning of financial markets

The views expressed are our own and should not be attributed to the European Central Bank. Thanks are due to Mathias Trabandt for contributions to earlier collaborations.

and the transmission process of monetary policy. For example, by reducing the value and quantity of safe collateral it may increase the price of risk and liquidity premia. Moreover, to the extent that government interest rates set a floor for the cost of financing of private firms and households in the country, it increases the cost of finance and complicates the transmission of monetary policy. Finally, a reduction in the value of government bonds will reduce the capital ratio of banks holding these government bonds and may thereby lead to a credit crunch as those banks try to adjust and deleverage.

Against this background, the need for fiscal consolidation has quickly become one of the top priority policy challenges in many countries. Moreover, in a number of euro area countries the rapidly growing government debt has led to rising interest rate spreads, setting in motion a self-fulfilling negative spiral whereby rising spreads increase the interest rate burden, thereby reinforcing the increase in debt and justifying a further rise in spreads, in turn creating systemic risks in the euro area as a whole.

In this chapter we review the interaction between public debt and monetary policy from a conceptual, institutional and empirical perspective with an emphasis on developments in the euro area. In Section 3.2, we review the theoretical and institutional framework that existed before the recent financial crisis. From a theoretical perspective the main objective of an 'active monetary and passive fiscal policy' framework is to avoid the risk of fiscal dominance, i.e. the risk that unchecked fiscal policy and rising government debt endangers the ability of the central bank to maintain price stability. As discussed in Section 3.2.2, the institutional fiscal and monetary policy arrangements in the euro area are geared at ensuring such a stability-oriented framework in a monetary union with many national fiscal authorities. In Section 3.3, we then review actual fiscal developments during the most recent crisis and show how the interaction between banking and sovereign risks has led to increasing spreads on government debt and a sovereign debt crisis in a number of euro area countries. In this section we also discuss the ECB's policy response. In addition to the standard easing of policy rates, the ECB has increasingly deployed non-standard policy measures geared at addressing malfunctioning financial markets and repairing the monetary transmission process. As a result of this role as a market maker of last resort, both the size of the balance sheet and the associated risks have increased significantly. Finally, in Section 3.4, we review some of the lessons learned. The banking and sovereign debt crisis has brought to the fore the important role of central banks in addressing liquidity problems in malfunctioning financial markets. At the same time, central banks cannot address solvency problems either in the banking sector or of the government and it is not always clear where the boundary between liquidity and solvency lies. In order to alleviate the risk of fiscal and financial dominance in such circumstances, the economic and financial governance framework of the Economic and Monetary Union (EMU) needs to be strengthened. First, it is necessary to re-establish sufficient buffers in government finance to reduce the risk of unsustainable government debt dynamics. This requires a strengthening of the fiscal framework as adopted in the so-called six pack and the Fiscal Compact at the end of 2011. Second, as one source of implicit government liabilities has been excessive creation of private domestic and external debt, there is a need to strengthen the surveillance of growing imbalances within the monetary union. This has led to the establishment of an Excessive Imbalances Procedure and the European Systemic Risk Board (ESRB). Third, in order to break the link between national sovereign and banking risks, mend the fragmentation of the financial market in the euro area and avoid free-rider problems in addressing weak banking systems, it is important to strengthen the financial union. This involves further integration of financial supervision of, in particular, cross-border banks, combined with a common deposit guarantee scheme and a bank restructuring and resolution mechanism. Finally, to ringfence solvent government and avoid contagion, it is important to establish a sufficiently large, permanent and flexible support mechanism. The establishment of the temporary European Financial Stability Facility (EFSF) and the permanent European Stabilisation Mechanism (ESM) should contribute to increasing investors' confidence in the ability of the euro area to preserve its stability as a whole by offering temporary and conditional financial support to euro area members in need.

3.2   The interplay between fiscal and monetary policies

3.2.1   *General theoretical considerations and potential risks*[1]

The notion that the central bank's ability to achieve price stability depends on a credible debt-stability-oriented fiscal policy has long been recognised. There are two basic approaches that explain the link between unsustainable fiscal policy and inflation. The traditional and most well-known argument relies on the Sargent–Wallace framework of the so-called 'unpleasant monetary arithmetic' whereby an increase in government debt, if not fully backed by future real primary surpluses,

---

[1] This section is based on Smets and Trabandt (2012).

will increase concerns about the monetisation of public debt. In this case, seignorage is seen as an alternative source of finance. As emphasised by Buiter (2007) and Durré and Pill (2010), the central bank's exceptional credibility for maintaining price stability ultimately depends on its fiscal backing. When this fiscal backing is no longer sufficient, then also the central bank's credibility will be undermined. This will raise inflation expectations and thereby increase long-term interest rates, which, in turn, will reduce money demand and push up the price level even without a contemporaneous increase in money supply. It is, however, worth noting that seignorage is a relatively limited source of government revenue and is also subject to a Laffer curve which determines the maximum amount of revenues that the government can collect. As inflation rises, the demand for money (the tax base) will fall, reducing overall seignorage income.

The second approach corresponds to the Fiscal Theory of the Price Level (FTPL). Leeper and Walker (2011) recently summarised the research on the FTPL and clarified perceptions and misperceptions of fiscal inflation. Using a simple infinitely lived representative household model with a constant endowment and a government that issues nominal debt and raises lump-sum taxes to finance transfers, they describe two possible regimes. Following the terminology of Leeper (1991), an active monetary/passive fiscal policy regime is characterised by monetary policy which focuses on maintaining price stability and fiscal policy that adjusts the primary surplus in order to back up the value of debt. In this case, if the central bank responds aggressively to inflation and debt above target generates expectations of higher taxes or lower transfers, the unique bounded solution for inflation is the inflation target and debt is expected to return to steady state following a shock. Passive tax policy implies that fiscal adjustment must occur regardless of the reason why debt increases such as economic downturns, changes in household portfolio preferences, or central bank open-market operations.

In the other regime with passive monetary policy (e.g. a constant interest rate set by the central bank) and active fiscal policy (e.g. a constant tax rate set by the fiscal authorities) on the other hand, the price level will be determined by fiscal policy. The real value of the nominal debt has to be equal to the expected future primary surpluses. In this environment changes in debt do not elicit any changes in expected taxes. As a result, at initial prices households feel wealthier and they try to shift their consumption patterns. Higher demand for goods drives up the price level and continues to do so until the wealth effect dissipates and households are content with their initial consumption plan. In other words, in this regime the price level is the factor that equilibrates the nominal value of future discounted primary surpluses and the nominal value of public debt. This regime is sometimes called one of fiscal dominance.

In this regime, the impact of monetary policy changes dramatically. When the central bank chooses a higher interest rate, the effect is to raise inflation in the next period. The higher interest rate payments increase income, consumption and the price level. As discussed in Leeper and Walker (2011), more realistic adjustment patterns may take place if government debt is long-term. In that case, the maturity composition of existing government debt may determine the pattern of inflation following a fiscal shock. However, also in this case the value of the long-term government bond will necessarily go down. Interestingly, Cochrane (2011) shows that in such a case, buying long-term debt for short-term debt will increase inflation now relative to later.

In sum, in both approaches unsustainable fiscal policies will result in rising inflation expectations and falling nominal bond prices. As mentioned before, in a number of euro area countries the rapidly growing government debt has led to rising interest rate spreads. However, in the major advanced economies like the United States, the United Kingdom and Germany, long-term bond yields are currently still very low and medium- to long-term inflation expectations are stable. This raises the question of under what circumstances fiscal policy may undermine monetary control of inflation. One such scenario is a renewed weakening of economic activity, which could lead to a still higher fiscal deficit and an unsustainable accumulation of government debt, while at the same time keeping short-term nominal interest rates stuck at levels close to zero. If such a situation leads to a perceived probability of a switch to an active fiscal policy/passive monetary policy regime, this by itself will have an impact on inflation and inflation expectations. Leeper and Walker (2011) show that in this case, the economy will not exhibit Ricardian equivalence, but the quantitative effects will depend on how large the shock to public finances and the fiscal space is. In such a situation, higher expected deficits may start reducing the value of debt because they reduce the backing and therefore the value of government liabilities and monetary policy may lose control of inflation. The current relatively benign long-term interest rates in the largest advanced economies may not be of much comfort to the extent that the switch to an active fiscal/passive monetary policy regime may occur quite abruptly, as shown in Bi, Leeper and Leith (2011). In order to preserve the central bank's ability to maintain price stability, it is therefore very important that fiscal consolidation preserves the sustainability of government debt.[2]

---

[2] See also the discussion in Davig et al. (2011) and Sims (2011).

In a monetary union with a limited federal budget and different national fiscal policies, an additional reason for having fiscal rules that stabilise government debt is that the national fiscal authorities may not internalise the impact they have on area-wide inflation and interest rates. For example, in the model of Chari and Kehoe (2007) it is shown that the national fiscal authority takes account of the cost of the induced inflation on its own residents, but ignores the costs on other member states. This free-rider problem leads to too much government debt and inflation. Imposing constraints on the amount of debt that each fiscal authority is allowed to issue makes all member states better off.[3]

3.2.2   The institutional arrangements of EMU

It is worth recalling that history contains a series of striking examples where the central bank, fuelled, independently or not, the inflation process through measures aiming at counteracting rising constraints on public finances – namely the simultaneous impossibility to raise taxes and to cut public expenditures further. The most famous example is certainly the case of the German hyperinflation in 1923 where rising public budget deficits in conjunction with the government's failure to raise tax revenues induced monetary accommodation which eventually fuelled the inflation process.[4] A more recent example outside Europe also points to the United States.[5]

These experiences show that having a clear separation of responsibilities between the central bank and the public sector ensuring, a three-dimensional (operational, financial and institutional) independence[6]

---

[3] Uhlig (2002) also emphasises the free-rider problem in a monetary union and studies it a conventional New Keynesian model.

[4] In particular, Webb (1985) emphasises the role of increased inflation expectations due to adverse fiscal news – among others the breakdowns in reparations negotiations – in the acceleration of debt monetisation by the Reichsbank. In the same vein, Dornbusch (1985) underlines the role of foreign exchange market intervention by the Reichsbank in order to stabilise the exchange rate in early 1923. While confirming the results of Dornbusch (1985), Burdekin and Burkett (1992) also demonstrate convincingly that the 'fiscal news' pushed up the expected inflation, which in turn led to rising wage claims and increases in private credit demand leading ultimately to an acceleration of Germany's inflation.

[5] Hetzel and Leach (2001) recall the confrontation between the Federal Reserve and the US Treasury in the aftermath of World War II which resulted in a peak of annual inflation at 21 per cent in March 1951, reflecting the implications of the obligation for the Federal Reserve to target an interest rate on the US government debt.

[6] The concept of 'operational independence' is defined here as the absence of interference from the Treasury (or more broadly the public sector's bodies) on the performance of the central bank's tasks and/or on the choice of monetary policy instruments. 'Financial independence' assumes that the central bank must generate sufficient

of the central bank may not be a sufficient condition to ensure an autonomous and powerful conduct of the monetary policy solely focused on pursuing the central bank's objective.[7] Against this background (including the possible negative spillovers emerging from a non-cooperative interference between central bank's and public sector's activities as described in the previous section),[8] there has been a growing tendency across (advanced and emerging) countries, first, to limit by law the direct support by the central bank of, the activities of the public sector in a broad sense (i.e. including the Treasury, the general and local governments and all entities belonging to the public sector) and second, to constrain fiscal policy to ensure sustainable government debt.[9]

In the specific case of Economic and Monetary Union (EMU), the institutional design reflects the view according to which monetary financing by EU central banks must be avoided for three interrelated reasons: (a) to ensure 'monetary dominance' over the price level, hence guaranteeing in turn the integrity of central bank's balance sheet; (b) to strengthen the credibility of central bank as regards its monetary policy objective and its stability-orientation, hence underpinning the operational, financial and institutional independence of the central bank; and (c) to increase financial discipline imposed on the public sector, hence serving fiscal responsibility.[10]

Accordingly, the Treaty establishing the Functioning of the European Union (TFEU, hereafter 'the Treaty') has created a structure within which an independent central bank with responsibility for monetary policy (namely the ECB) – where its decisions are executed by independent national central banks (namely the National Central Banks, NCBs) – is assigned the primary (and thus overriding) objective of maintaining price stability.[11] In addition, a (legally binding) prohibition of monetary

---

financial resources to conduct monetary policy and that the public sector bodies are not limiting (or reducing) financial resources of the central bank. 'Institutional independence' means that a third party cannot exercise any direct or indirect influence on the central bank's decisions which would reduce its ability to fulfil its mandate.

[7] To be a sufficient condition, it would then be implicitly necessary that: (i) the budget of the state has little influence on inflation; and (ii) the monetary policy has marginal effects on the fiscal budget. However, history has shown little evidence for both assumptions.

[8] See also Chadha (2011).

[9] See for instance Arnone et al. (2007).

[10] This last element is also seen as necessary to reinforce the incentives of euro area countries to comply with the Stability and Growth Pact (SGP). This appears especially relevant in the absence of fiscal union in the euro area.

[11] Articles 127 and 130 of TFEU also repeated into Articles 2 and 7 of the Statute of the European System of Central Banks (ESCB) and of the European Central Bank (ECB).

financing[12] and privileged access[13] is imposed on EU central banks (including the ECB) in order to avoid any complacency with regard to the public sector.

More specifically, under Article 123 of the Treaty (which prohibits monetary financing), the ECB and the NCBs are prohibited from providing direct lending[14] (in the form of overdraft facilities or any other type of credit facility) to, and/or from purchasing debt instruments directly (i.e. debt instruments issued in the primary market) from, public sector entities and bodies at large.[15] In this regard, recital one of the Council Regulation (EC) No. 3603/93 specifies that: 'For the purposes of Article [123] of the Treaty: *(a) 'overdraft facilities' means any provision of funds to the public sector resulting or likely to result in a debit balance; (b) 'other type of credit facility' means: [...]; (ii) any financing of the public sector's obligations vis-à-vis third parties; [...]'*. Accordingly, the legal interpretation is that liquidity support to illiquid but solvent credit institutions is a central bank task (hence compatible with the prohibition stated in Article 123 of the Treaty) whereas solvency support by the ECB and NCBs would constitute monetary financing as it would assume the state's obligations *vis-à-vis* third parties.[16] By contrast, the acquisition in the secondary market by NCBs or the ECB of debt instruments issued by public sector entities and bodies is, in principle, allowed. However, in accordance with recital seven of Council Regulation (EC) 3603/93, such purchases must not be used to circumvent the objective of

---

[12] As referred to in Article 123 of TFEU and the associated provisions of Council Regulation (EC) No. 3603/93 of 13 December 1993 specifying definitions for the application of the monetary financing prohibition.

[13] As referred to in Article 124 of TFEU and the associated provisions of Council Regulation (EC) No. 3604/93 of 13 December 1993 specifying definitions for the application of the privileged access prohibition.

[14] Only intra-day credits that 'assist the smooth operation of payment systems' are, as specified in Recital 10 of the Council Regulation 3603/93, 'compatible with the objectives of Article 101 [now Article 123] of the Treaty, provided that no extension to the following day is possible'. This naturally implies that inter-day credit is not compatible with the prohibition of monetary financing.

[15] This qualification includes the following categories of public sector entities and bodies (or assimilated): (1) European Union institutions or bodies, (2) central governments, (3) regional, local or other public authorities, (4) other bodies governed by public law, (5) public undertakings of Member States or (6) undertakings in which it is demonstrated that a Member State has a dominant influence on the decision-making process.

[16] See, for instance, ECB Opinion on State guarantee covering credit extended by the Nationale Bank van België/Banque Nationale de Belgique in the context of its contribution to financial stability (CON/2008/46), at www.ecb.europa.eu/ecb/legal/opinions/html/index.en.html.

Article 123 of the Treaty.[17] Indeed, the danger exists that central banks may be subjected to political pressure to circumvent the prohibition by significant purchases of public sector debt in the secondary market.[18]

Under Article 124 of the Treaty, financial institutions (including the EU central banks)[19] are also prohibited from adopting any measure – not based on prudential considerations – which would result in establishing privileged access by public sector entities and bodies. By warranting an equal treatment between the public and private sector entities, this prohibition aims at forming an essential element of the submission of the public sector in its financing operations to the discipline of the market mechanism.[20] This is in turn in line with the obligation for Member States and the Community institutions to act with due regard for the principle of an open market economy in which there is free competition in accordance with Article 3 of the Treaty on the European Union.

In principle, the prohibition contained in Articles 123 and 124 of the Treaty should also help avoid wars of attrition between permissive fiscal policies and a restrictive monetary policy stance which would, in the extreme case where central bank and governments would strictly not cooperate, lead to a situation where the level of public debt, self-sustained by growing interest payments, becomes unsustainable in the long run. In this non-cooperative context, a strict interpretation of the

---

[17] This also applies to marketable debt instruments issued by all EU institutions or bodies.

[18] Under Article 270(d) of TFEU, the ECB is entrusted with the task of ensuring the fulfilment by NCBs of their obligations with respect to the provisions of the Treaty. Consequently, the ECB is conducting an annual monitoring exercise with regard to its own and NCBs' compliance with the monetary financing and privileged access prohibitions. In the context of this monitoring exercise, the ECB also monitors secondary purchases of public debt instruments by central banks. Indeed, the view is that some limitation of secondary market purchases of public sector debt by central banks should be required. Therefore, the Governing Council of the ECB has adopted over time thresholds for assessing secondary market purchases by EU central banks of public debt instruments. In case of secondary market purchases in excess of thresholds, this triggers additional information to ensure that secondary market purchases by central banks of public debt instruments are not used to circumvent the objective of the monetary financing prohibition in accordance with recital seven of Council Regulation (EC) 3603/93.

[19] To some extent it could be argued that the objective of the privileged access prohibition enhances the compliance of EU Member States with Article 126 of TFEU and the Stability and Growth Pact (SGP). It is worth mentioning that the prohibition of both monetary financing and privileged access (as referred to in Articles 123 and 124 of TFEU) applies to all EU central banks and not only to those sharing the single currency. No exemption has been accepted, contrary to some other Treaty provisions where the in/out options may apply for few non-euro area countries (and thus their respective national central banks).

[20] See, for further details, the Council Regulation (EC) No. 3604/93 of 13 December 1993 specifying definitions for the application of the privileged access prohibition.

legal framework prohibiting direct credits and indirect credits to governments ensures that the central bank is never legally compelled to satisfy the inter-temporal budget constraint of the public sector at the expense of its price stability objective. As argued in Durré and Pill (2010), such legally enforceable constraints may appear even more necessary in a monetary union with decentralised fiscal policies like in the euro area.

The implicit philosophy of both prohibitions is to enforce public sector bodies at large (and governments in particular) to maintain their budget in order.[21] However, as market discipline may not be sufficient to ensure budgetary discipline, the Treaty also requires sustainable public finances in the long run by forcing compliance of EU Member States with the Stability and Growth Pact (SGP) in conjunction with the prohibition of excessive deficits.[22] According to Article 126 of TFEU, it is stated that *'governments shall avoid excessive government deficits and that the Commission shall monitor the development of the budgetary situation* [...]'.

Overall, the logic of this framework is to ensure an active monetary policy and a passive fiscal policy regime within the EMU, in which governments ensure debt sustainability and the central bank focuses on maintaining price stability over the medium term.

3.3 The case of the 2010–2012 sovereign debt crisis in the euro area

3.3.1 Interaction between sovereign debt crisis and banks' funding

The financial crisis that intensified after the collapse of Lehman Brothers (Figure 3.1) and the subsequent worldwide recession in 2008–2009 triggered a rapid response of monetary and fiscal authorities across the world. On the fiscal policy side, the deterioration of the economic outlook, discretionary fiscal stimulus programmes and to a lesser extent support to the financial sector resulted in an initial sharp increase in the general government budget deficit and a rapid rise in public debt. Figure 3.2 compares the deterioration in public finances across the euro area, Japan, the United Kingdom and the United States. Both the total and the structural government deficit have increased by less in the euro area than in the other countries. As a result, government debt rose more

---

[21] The idea was also to aim at an optimal allocation of resources in financial markets, as explained in von der Groeben et al. (1997). See also the introduction of the Council Regulation (EC) No. 3604/93 of 13 December 1993 specifying definitions for the application of the privileged access prohibition.

[22] The prohibition of excessive deficits is referred to in Article 126 of TFEU.

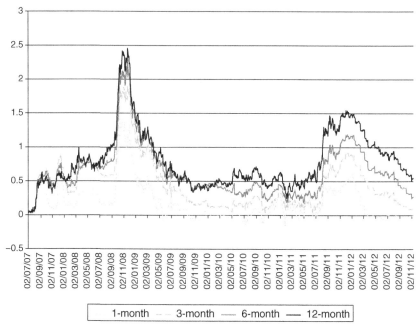

Figure 3.1 Money market spreads at various maturities in the euro area

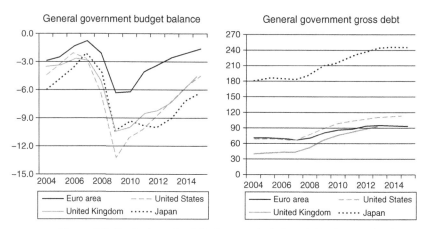

Figure 3.2 Evolution of public finances in industrialised countries from 2005 (% of GDP)

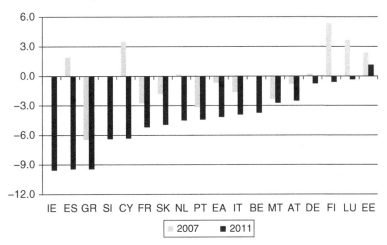

Figure 3.3 General government deficit within the euro area (% of GDP)

rapidly in the latter countries and surpassed the net debt to GDP ratio in the euro area in 2011.

This overall picture masks, however, quite diverse fiscal developments within the euro area. Figures 3.3 and 3.4 illustrate the cross-country variation in debt and deficits (where DE stands for Germany, FR for France, and so on). The bursting of a credit and/or house price bubble in a number of euro area countries such as Ireland, Spain, Portugal and Greece and the sudden stop in private capital inflows led to a deep recession, sharply rising unemployment, and an exposed and fragile banking sector. As a result, the government finances in those countries quickly deteriorated.[23] Figure 3.3 shows that in Ireland and Spain a small surplus in 2007 rapidly turned into a large deficit of more than 10% of GDP in 2011. As a result, the government debt to GDP ratio has skyrocketed over the past four years and has reached more than 100% of GDP in Ireland, Portugal and Greece. In Spain the government debt almost doubled over the same period (Figure 3.4). Although the current level of debt contains the direct government support to the banking sector (in the form of capital injections, purchases of assets and/or direct loans), it does not contain the potential future liabilities coming from the state's guarantees provided to banks.[24]

---

[23] See Smets (2012) for a more detailed description of the growing imbalances within the euro area and their unwinding.

[24] In fact, the fees paid by the financial institutions benefiting from state's guarantees are considered as revenues in the public budget while the underlying financial risk for

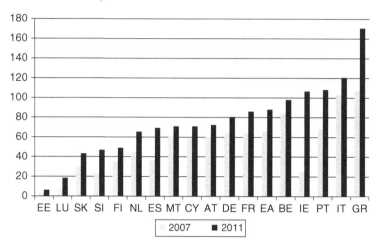

Figure 3.4 General government gross debt within the euro area (% of GDP)

Triggered by fiscal profligacy in Greece and the news that the Greek fiscal deficit and debt were much larger than originally announced, the rapidly rising government debt as well as the uncertainty regarding implicit government liabilities from guaranteeing the banking sector led to a confidence crisis in government finances and rising sovereign spreads (Figure 3.5) and corresponding credit default swap premia in a number of the periphery countries. This set in motion a mutually reinforcing negative spiral between sovereign and banking risks all over the euro area. On the one hand, weak banking sectors in a number of countries undermined the credibility of planned consolidation programmes, in particular in those countries with weak fiscal fundamentals. On the other hand, uncertainty about the involvement of the private sector in a possible restructuring of the Greek debt and the exposure of European banks to the sovereign risks led to rising costs of bank finance and banking risks across Europe. This tight link between sovereign and banking risks has been reflected in a large positive correlation between sovereign and bank bond premia in the euro area. The consequent financial fragmentation in the euro area illustrated by a significant reduction of cross-border interbank lending and an increasing concentration of recourse to Eurosystem liquidity operations in some countries

governments does not affect public finances as long as the government is not bound to honour the guarantee. See the 9 July 2009 decision of Eurostat on deficit and debt: the statistical recording of public interventions to support financial institutions and financial markets during the financial crisis.

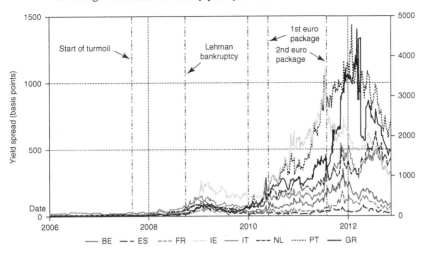

Figure 3.5 10-year government bond spreads against German Bunds

(reflecting a sudden stop in banks' funding in distressed countries) further reinforced the cross-country heterogeneity in macroeconomic outcomes.[25]

The self-fulfilling nature of the twin funding problems of the banking sector and the government became particularly acute towards the end of 2011, when it became obvious that both governments and banks were facing large refinancing needs in 2012. Against the background of an already weakened financial sector following the Lehman collapse, confidence in the banking sector evaporated as, for example, indicated by the widely used EURIBOR-OIS spread indicator, a measure of the perceived credit risk in the banking sector. By the end of 2011, the 3-month EURIBOR-OIS spread reached again 100 basis points, a level not seen since the heat of the banking crisis following the Lehman collapse in early 2009 (Figure 3.1). While the stress in the banking sector following the collapse of Lehman Brothers on 15 September 2008 was mostly related to the exposure of banks to the subprime crisis and toxic assets in the United States, the epicentre had moved to Europe in the summer of 2011 as uncertainty regarding the exposure to European sovereign risks dominated. The systemic character of the sovereign debt crisis can also be seen in Figure 3.6, which shows the Composite Index of Systemic Stress (CISS) indicator developed by Holló et al. (2012). The CISS covers stress in five different European financial markets and in

[25] For instance, the share of cross-border interbank lending in the overnight market in September 2012 was less than 40% of total transactions, down from 60% in mid-2011.

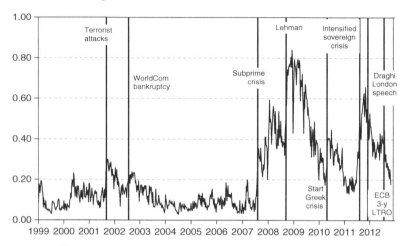

Figure 3.6 Composite Index of Systemic Stress (CISS) indicator

contrast to many other indicators also takes into account the degree of correlation between those five markets, making it a particularly useful indicator of systemic stress. Also, from this indicator it is clear that the systemic stress in European financial markets breached its crisis threshold of 0.35 in early summer of 2010 as the Greek debt crisis intensified and reached a new high towards the end of 2011.

A number of empirical papers (e.g. Arghyrou and Kontonikas (2011), Ejsing et al. (2011) and De Grauwe and Ji (2011)) have documented a regime change in the determinants of sovereign bond spreads before and after the financial crisis. Before 2007 sovereign bond spreads were only weakly related to fiscal fundamentals. In contrast, after 2008 both sovereign bond and CDS spreads became increasingly, and possibly excessively, sensitive to large changes in government debt. Following the work of Calvo (1988) and Cole and Kehoe (2000) and the small literature on speculative attacks on government debt applied to the case of Italy in the 1990s (Alesina et al. (1992) and Giavazzi and Pagano (1992)), a number of authors have interpreted this shift as evidence of self-fulfilling speculative dynamics in the government bond market, akin to what may happen in a bank run.[26] In practice, it is, however, very difficult to distinguish between the role of fundamentals and a self-fulfilling confidence crisis. Both empirical evidence and theoretical analysis suggest that fundamentals determine the likelihood of being subject to a speculative attack. For example, Alesina et al. (1992) find that fiscal sustainability and the likelihood of a speculative attack depend

---

[26] See, for example, Krugman (2011) and De Grauwe (2011).

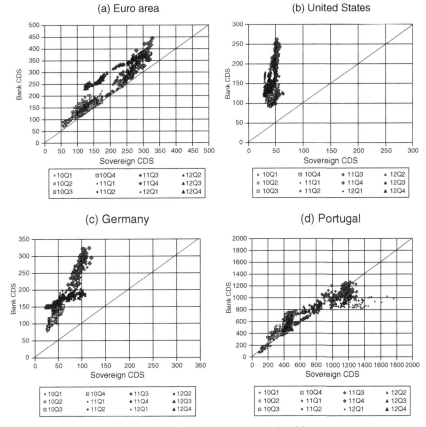

Figure 3.7 Contagion from government to banking sector

on the initial debt and deficit levels, the interest and growth differential, the maturity structure of debt and the state of the economy. Corsetti and Dedola (2012) provide a model in which sovereign risk premia are driven by both fundamentals and confidence factors. Such models may provide a rationale for putting a ceiling on interest rates (possibly at a penalty rate) as a strategy to coordinate market expectations on fundamentals. However, such a strategy may also reduce the incentives of fiscal authorities to consolidate and stay away from the region in which weak fundamentals may give rise to multiple equilibria.[27] As with the

---

[27] However, as Corsetti and Dedola (2012) point out, once one is in a regime with a positive probability of a self-fulfilling default, a backstop policy may strengthen rather than weaken the social incentives to implement reforms and budget corrections in crisis countries, because it increases the return of the reforms.

traditional lender of last resort function to financial institutions, central banks may therefore face a trade-off between reducing the probability of costly speculative attacks and maintaining market discipline for sustainable fiscal policies.

There was also increasing evidence of contagion both among government bond markets in the euro area (e.g. De Santis (2012)) and between the sovereign and the banking sector, as reported in Figure 3.7 (e.g. Corsetti et al. (2011)). The nature of contagion took many forms. Part of it is associated with macroeconomic feedback mechanisms, such as cross-country exposure to the sovereign risks. Another part of the contagion may come from coordination failures and the self-fulfilling dynamics described above.

3.3.2   ECB actions

The challenges posed by the 2007–2012 financial crisis have forced the ECB to intervene more than in normal times. While its actions have remained focused on achieving and maintaining price stability in the medium term, at the same time it has been necessary to counteract financial market malfunctioning and to help restore normal trading conditions in order to preserve the transmission mechanism of the monetary policy stance decided by the Governing Council of the ECB. This has been reflected in a distinction between standard monetary policy, i.e. interest rate decisions taken to maintain price stability (the determination of the monetary policy stance) and non-standard measures such as extended liquidity refinancing operations and other direct financial market interventions such as the Covered Bond Purchases Programmes (CBPP) or the Security Markets Programme (SMP), which aim at contributing to the efficient functioning of financial markets in stress periods and a properly working transmission mechanism.

Against this backdrop, the nature and the intensity of the ECB's policy actions since the onset of the crisis have reflected the changing outlook for price stability and the state of functioning of financial markets. Three main phases can be distinguished: (i) the turmoil period (from 9 August 2007 to 15 September 2008); (ii) the financial crisis (from 15 September 2008 to 10 May 2010); and (iii) the sovereign debt crisis (from 10 May 2010 to the present).

The most striking feature of the 2007–2012 financial crisis is that in each of the phases the liquidity position of financial institutions and the functioning of the inter-bank money market have been affected, thereby endangering financial stability and the transmission of the monetary

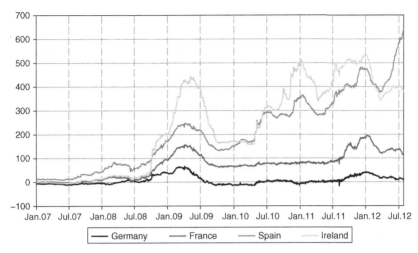

Figure 3.8 Covered bond spreads against 5-year swap rate (daily, basis points)

policy stance along the yield curve. Although tensions and volatile (mis-)pricing during the first two phases directly affected the various segments of the money market – originally rooted in the seizing up of the unsecured (deposit) transactions in phase I to gradually contaminate the secured (repo) transactions and the activity in the covered bond market in phase II (Figures 3.1 and 3.8) – the third phase has affected the liquidity position of financial institutions through a more indirect and complex channel.[28] Given the purpose of the analysis, the description of the ECB actions in the remainder of the paper essentially focuses on the developments during the third phase.[29]

---

[28] With the benefit of hindsight, it is now recognised that the main concern in the first phase was essentially related to the risk of a liquidity shortage of financial institutions whereas in the second phase it was mostly related to the risk of default of counterparties following the collapse of the company Lehman Brothers Ltd on 15 September 2008, both concerns having potential implications in terms of pricing and credit supply in retail banking activities. The prominent role played by liquidity risk perceptions in the determination of the EURIBOR-/LIBOR-OIS spreads until September 2008 is indeed demonstrated, for instance, in McAndrews, Sarkar and Wang (2008) or Sarkar (2009) for the US market and in Schwarz (2010) for the European context. Similarly, findings in Beirne (2012) suggest that credit risk does not significantly alter the EONIA spread before the collapse of Lehman Brothers while its sensitivity to liquidity risk increases significantly in the first phase.

[29] The description of the ECB actions in the first two phases has been widely documented. See in particular Cassola et al. (2008), Cassola et al. (2011), Lenza et al. (2010), Pill and Smets (2011), Fahr et al. (2011) and Drudi et al. (2012) among others.

In this third (and current) phase – the so-called 'sovereign debt crisis' period (from 10 May 2010 to the present) – the ECB faced a mutation of financial distress towards the sovereign debt market in the euro area. Although the situation in the cash segments of the money market and in the covered bond market were stabilising, latent tensions in the sovereign debt markets started to become obvious as of October 2009 in the aftermath of elections in Greece when the audit of public finances ordered by the newly elected government led to huge revisions of fiscal budget data going back to the adoption of the euro in 2002. Although Greece became a focal point, investors' suspicion about the sustainability of public finances spread to other euro area countries (Ireland, Portugal, Spain and Italy in the first place). It is fair to say that such a suspicion took its roots in the combination of very accommodative fiscal crisis measures and already fragile pre-crisis fiscal position amid weak economic fundamentals.[30]

In the light of the risks of contagion and self-fulfilling speculative dynamics (as spelt out in the previous section), the ECB decided to extend its outright purchases of securities to government bond markets in some countries that threatened to seize up. Consequently, both the size and the composition of the ECB's balance sheet continued to change, as was already the case in phase II (Figure 3.9).

The main concern of the ECB at that time was that transmission mechanisms be impaired again, given the central role played by sovereign debt in financial markets – namely both as source of collateral for repo operations and a basis for pricing other securities – and the existence of a potential negative feedback loop between government bond yields and banks' funding (as discussed in the previous section). In addition, the stabilisation in the money market was also endangered since tensions in the sovereign bond market weakened the liquidity position of financial institutions.

---

[30] Like other industrialised countries, many euro area fiscal authorities took a number of crisis measures in the aftermath of the Lehman bankruptcy. These measures included discretionary fiscal stimulus to support economic activity and/or a number of measures to help revive ailing financial markets or banking systems in the form of public guarantees and/or outright injection of public funds into financial institutions (in the form of recapitalisation and/or direct loans). The impact of these measures on the public finances was potentially important. Note for instance that it was estimated that the gross impact (aggregated for 2008–2010) of bank support via capital injections and asset purchases on euro area government debt was almost 6% of 2010 GDP whereas the guarantees granted (off-balance contingent liabilities) were 7.4% of 2010 GDP, while the ceiling of potential guarantees was estimated to be at least 19% of 2010 GDP. In a deteriorating economic environment (hence reducing further government revenues), the sustainability of the fiscal position in various countries was consequently put into question.

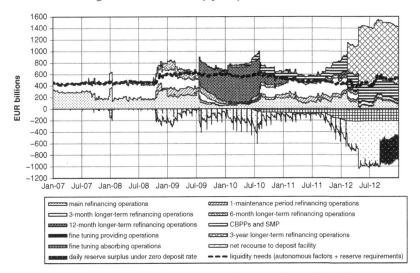

Figure 3.9 Outstanding open market operations of the Eurosystem (in EUR billions)

In this respect, a number of observations can be made from Figures 3.10 to 3.13. First, the initial jump in spreads (i.e. on 9 August 2007) during the first crisis phase appears relatively modest and only valid for the unsecured segment of the money market (Figure 3.10 vs Figure 3.11). Spreads between unsecured and secured segments (Figure 3.1) continued to increase until the freeze of the money market (i.e. on 30 September 2008) after which they fell back on the account of the combined effect of the FRFA tender procedure and the cumulative cut of 325 basis points of the policy rate (by 14 May 2009). While the additional non-standard measures continued to move down the spreads (e.g. on 10 May 2010), the intensification of tensions in the sovereign debt market (i.e. on 5 October 2011) led to an increase of spreads at a level between the peak reached at the time of the Lehman Brothers bankruptcy and their levels on 14 May 2009, thereby eroding significantly the outcome of October 2008 decisions by the ECB. Interestingly, although spreads in the secured segments had appeared relatively immune so far, the increased tensions in the sovereign debt markets (i.e. on 5 October 2011) more than tripled their level across various maturities.[31] To put it differently, as of phase III the existence

---

[31] Note that the slightly negative spreads in the repo market until 2011 (i.e. repo rates lower than their corresponding OIS rates) is mainly explained by the usual convenience yield resulting from the benefit from physically holding the collateral prior to the maturity of the term contract which is not obtained from holding OIS contract.

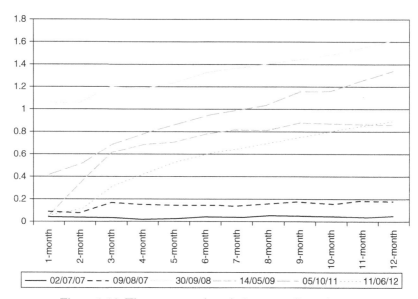

Figure 3.10 The euro area deposit (unsecured) market: yield curve of spreads against OIS

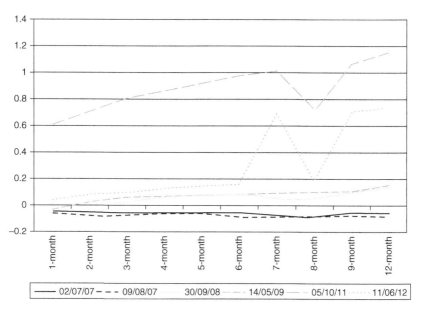

Figure 3.11 The euro area repo (secured) market: yield curve of spreads against OIS

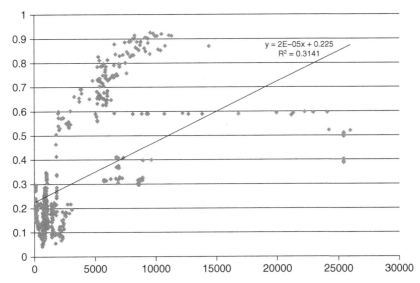

Figure 3.12 Tensions on sovereign debt and money market: link between Greece's CDS premium (5-year) and the 3-month EURIBOR-OIS spreads

of collateral (mostly government bonds) no longer appears sufficient to guarantee the liquidity of repo transactions.[32] Similarly, we also observed a positive correlation between fluctuations of the CDS premium for countries under EU/IMF programmes (i.e. Greece, Ireland and Portugal) and the 3-month EURIBOR-OIS spread (Figures 3.12 and 3.13). As reported by Figures 3.12 and 3.13, adverse fiscal news (with a consequent impact on the corresponding bond yields) tended to increase the EURIBOR-OIS spreads despite the then prevailing accommodative impact from other non-standard measures.

In this situation, the ECB decided to strengthen its non-standard measures. First, the Securities Markets Programme (SMP) was launched as of 10 May 2010 which amounted at the time of writing (June 2012) to

[32] From the outset of the crisis, the list of eligible collateral for private repo transactions shrunk towards preference for government bonds. However, in the aftermath of adverse fiscal news for Greece (i.e. in October 2009), a double risk was rejected by counterparts (e.g. a bank from one euro area country pledging a government bond of the same country) while Greek government bonds became no longer eligible. The contagion of sovereign budget concerns to other euro area countries than Greece has substantially reduced the probability of being able to sell government bonds issued by several countries in a liquid market. As a result, the bonds of these countries used as collateral in the repo market have lost the protection they should have in the case of counterpart's default as of October 2009.

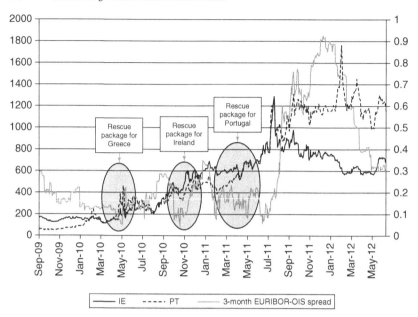

Figure 3.13 CDS premium of Portugal (PT) and Ireland (IE) and 3-month EURIBOR-OIS spreads

a total of EUR 212bn of purchased securities (see also Figure 3.9).[33] Preliminary analyses tend to suggest that the ECB's purchases of bonds have had a negative impact on the corresponding bond yields (both in levels and volatility).[34] Second, temporary liquidity swap arrangements with other central banks were reactivated, with the result that US dollar liquidity-providing operations with a fixed rate full allotment procedure against eligible collateral were resumed. Third, the ECB decided in various meetings to maintain the fixed rate/full allotment (FRFA)[35] tender procedure in all of its refinancing operations (now lasting at the time

[33] See ECB (2010) for further details. A key distinguishing feature of asset purchases made under the SMP is that their liquidity impact has been sterilised through the conduct of weekly liquidity absorbing operations. Therefore, there has been no net injection of central bank liquidity to the market as a consequence of these operations.

[34] For instance, Eser and Schwaab (2012) find that the yield effects of the SMP accumulate to a reduction relative to the counterfactual of non-intervention. In the same vein, Ghysels et al. (2012) find that the most striking and robust effects of the programme is to address market malfunctioning by reducing the volatility of sovereign yields.

[35] The implementation of the FRFA tender procedure was only officially implemented as of 13 October 2008 although it took place before on an ad-hoc basis for some operations in practice (e.g. the overnight liquidity-providing fine-tuning operation on 9 August 2007).

of writing until at least the end of 2012) while reintroducing one supplementary 6-month refinancing operations on 11 August 2011 at the same
price and tender conditions as other operations. Last but not least, the
ECB also decided in the second half of 2011 to activate further standard and non-standard measures amid tightened financial conditions
and decreasing economic confidence. In particular, high financial market
uncertainty (mainly driven by increasing concerns about public finances
in several euro area countries and by the prospects of a restructuring of
Greek sovereign debt) together with banks' balance sheet deleveraging
contributed to reducing money and credit growth further towards the
end of 2011. Similarly, rising spreads on government yields and bank
funding costs started to affect the outlook for economic activity and
price stability as the cost of finance of non-financial sectors increased
and credit standards tightened (Figures 3.14 and 3.15). In this environment the ECB cut interest rates on two occasions (3 November 2011
and 8 December 2011) by a total of 50 basis points[36] while introducing

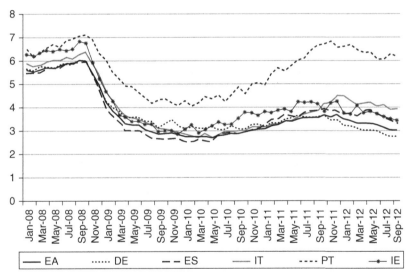

Figure 3.14 Composite bank lending rate for non-financial
corporations (% per annum)

[36] In the light of weak economic growth prospects and contained inflationary pressures,
the ECB decided to cut its key interest rates by a further 25 basis points on 5 July
2012, setting the interest rate on the main refinancing operations at 0.75% (with the
rate on the marginal lending facility and on the deposit facility at respectively 1.50%
and 0.00%).

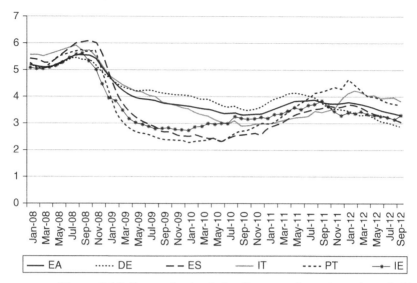

Figure 3.15 Composite bank lending rate for private households (% per annum)
Source: ECB calculations.
Note: The composite indicator weights short and long-term lending rates to households for house purchase. The short-term lending rate to households is a lending rate on a loan of up to one year maturity. Long-term lending rates to households are interest rates on loans with a maturity of more than one year. Short and long-term lending rates are then weighted using a 24-month moving sum of new business volumes.

additional non-standard measures.[37] Indeed, the escalation of financial tensions had the potential to cut off market funding of a significant portion of the banking sector in the euro area. The magnitude of the difficult balance sheet situation of euro area banks was reflected in the high volumes of liquidity allotted at the 3-year refinancing operations totalling together around EUR 1 trillion (Figure 3.9). It is also reflected

---

[37] More specifically, six non-standard measures were also introduced, while the fixed rate tender procedure with full allotment was maintained for all refinancing operations. First, on 6 October 2011 two longer-term refinancing operations of, respectively, 12 months and 13 months were announced, as was a second covered bond purchase programme (CBPP2) for an intended amount of EUR 40 billion. Second, on 8 December 2011 the following were announced: two 3-year longer-term refinancing operations (settled in December 2011 and February 2012) with the option of early repayment after one year; the enlargement of the collateral list (via a reduction of the rating threshold for certain asset-backed securities and the acceptance of bank loans); the reduction of the reserve ratio from 2% to 1%; and the discontinuation of the fine-tuning operations carried out on the last day of each maintenance period.

in the magnitude of capital flows within the euro area where claims on the banking system of programme countries (but also in Spain and Italy) have decreased significantly while cross-border claims in countries perceived as less risky (Germany in first place) have risen sharply.[38]

As reflected in Figures 3.10 and 3.11, the various measures of the ECB have led to a decrease of spreads in the various segments of the money market (i.e. both for the EURIBOR-OIS (unsecured transactions) spreads and the REPO-OIS (secured transactions) spreads) from the peak reached on 30 September 2008 in the aftermath of the Lehman bankruptcy when the money market segments seized up in the euro area. However, it is also worth noticing that the situation remains fragile since any news with the potential to weaken the liquidity position of banks tends to move the level of spreads back up, hence reducing considerably the benefits of past ECB interventions. Despite the magnitude of non-standard measures implemented as of the second half of 2011, the decline in spreads may be seen as relatively modest (in both the unsecured and secured segments by looking for instance at their levels on 11 June 2012). In the same vein, it cannot be totally ruled out that upward pressures on spreads materialise when the supplementary long-term refinancing operations mature if investors' confidence in the sustainability of public finances is not restored (since government bonds have been used as collateral). Indeed, the renewed tensions during the summer of 2012 – leading to further severe malfunctioning in the price formation process in the bond markets of euro area countries – have motivated the ECB's decision to stand ready to undertake outright open market transactions (OMT) under strict conditions.[39] Historically high and volatile risk premia observed in government bond prices in several countries together

---

[38] In the euro area jargon, these cross-border movements in payments are known as TARGET2 balances. For further detailed explanation, see Bindseil, Cour-Thimann and König in CESifo forum 2012, at www.cesifo-group.de/portal/pls/portal/docs/1/1213646.PDF.

[39] On 6 September 2012, the ECB detailed the framework of the OMT and in particular the strict conditionality attached to these operations. To be considered as eligible public debt instruments for the OMT, the issuer country must be enrolled in an appropriate European Financial Stability Facility/European Stability Mechanism (EFSF/ESM) programme (either in the form of a full EFSF/ESM macroeconomic adjustment programme or a precautionary programme (Enhanced Conditions Credit Line) and must fully respect the programme conditionality. In addition, the corresponding purchases will be focused on sovereign bonds with a maturity of between one and three years without setting *ex ante* quantitative limits. On the same day, the ECB also decided to preserve collateral availability. See details at www.ecb.europa.eu/press/pr/date/2012/html/pr120906_1.en.html.

with financial fragmentation clearly hindered the effective working of monetary policy.[40]

Although the situation is still fragile in many respects, it appears so far that the ECB's actions have alleviated funding conditions in the banking sector. However, there are by definition natural limitations to the impact of central bank's interventions since their sole purpose is to address the liquidity shortage of financial institutions and not the structural problems (of banks and or governments). In this regard, using a theoretical model, Cassola et al. (2011) argue that, while credit risk and liquidity risk are clearly interlinked, the central bank mostly has an impact on the liquidity risk component contained in money market spreads. This seems to be supported by the empirical evidence in the case of the ECB.

3.4   Lessons learned

The interaction between financial stability, fiscal sustainability and monetary policy witnessed during the third phase of the financial crisis in the euro area has made it crystal clear that the EMU framework that we discussed in Section 3.2.2 above needs to be deepened and extended.

Historical examples show that financial crises require prompt and rapid policy responses from the authorities in order to preserve macroeconomic and financial stability. Given its unique role as a market maker and lender of last resort, it is natural to expect the central bank to play an essential role, especially if the crisis is caused by market distortions which ultimately create a liquidity shortage of financial institutions at the aggregate and/or individual level. Central banks are indeed uniquely well placed to provide the necessary liquidity by issuing their own monetary liabilities and can thereby avoid a significant drop in the money stock which would in turn negatively affect output. The fact that central banks can react faster than other institutions (probably accentuated over time by the shift towards central bank independence) and therefore play a specific and predominant role in crisis management also holds, however, a risk, if it leads to excessive expectations by the public of the role of the central bank and an underestimation of the responsibilities of other players in the government in the crisis resolution.

---

[40] As mentioned by the ECB President Draghi himself, '*risk premia that are related to fears of the reversibility of the euro are unacceptable, and they need to be addressed in a fundamental manner*'. It thus appeared necessary to counteract the irreversibility of the euro through secondary market purchases of government bonds in possibly unlimited amounts. See details at www.ecb.europa.eu/press/pressconf/2012/html/is120802.en.html.

From this perspective, a crucial distinction needs to be made between liquidity and solvency support. Given its ability to provide an elastic supply of liquidity, the central bank can deal with liquidity problems. By contrast, given the primacy attached to the price stability objective, it is not the central bank's responsibility to address solvency problems which would entail assuming fiscal responsibilities. As spelt out in Section 3.2.2, this view is supported by the legal framework governing the EMU. Bailing out failing institutions and/or governments is not legally permitted in the case of the ECB, as it is seen as being in direct conflict with the primary mandate of ensuring price stability over time.

The experience during the financial crisis has, however, revealed two complications in the implementation of this framework. First, it is often not easy to distinguish between liquidity and solvency problems either in the banking sector or in government finance. Often the source of liquidity problems is the existence of underlying fundamental weaknesses, which can only be addressed through recapitalisation and structural and fiscal reforms, the responsibility for which lies with the fiscal authorities. In such circumstances, liquidity support may buy some time to address the underlying weaknesses, but may backfire if it leads to a delay in the structural adjustment. Second, neither is it easy to distinguish between sovereign and banking risks. As described in Section 3.3.1 above, banking risks may turn into sovereign risks when the fiscal authorities are called upon to back up bank liabilities (e.g. in the case of deposit insurance), while sovereign risks have the potential of mutating into banking problems (e.g. through the banks' holdings of government bonds), creating a so-called 'diabolic' loop between sovereign and banking risks.

Against this background, a key question is about the possible limitations of central bank interventions (and more specifically of ECB interventions) in either banking or government bond markets. Let us first take the case of intervention in the government bond market. What if some governments, as suggested by recent research, are subject to self-fulfilling speculative dynamics in the bond market which leads to an overreaction of bond yields to changes in the level of debt and endangers macroeconomic and financial stability? Given the role played by government yields in the monetary policy transmission mechanism, the central bank cannot ignore such developments which may impair its control over the price level. On the other hand, central bank interventions in the bond market, if too great over a too long period of time, may endanger the integrity of its balance sheet (by excessively increasing risk's exposure beyond reasonable standards), and hence its credibility and reputation. In the specific case of the euro area, the framework organising the responsibilities of institutions within the EMU provide sufficient leeway for the ECB to intervene since secondary market purchases are allowed, provided that they are not used to circumvent the prohibition of monetary financing and privileged access. It is within this specific institutional architecture that the SMP has been launched as of 10 May 2010. The SMP has helped avoid the sovereign debt crisis turning into a full-blown systemic financial crisis, while making clear that such non-standard measures are temporary in nature and conditional on government ensuring the sustainability of public finance. This conditionality was made explicit in the OMT programme, which was announced on 6 September 2012 and geared at reducing the tail risks associated with fears of the reversibility of the euro. As discussed below, in this context there is a need to strengthen the fiscal governance framework in the EMU, not only to build up sufficient buffers to reduce the probability of speculative attacks, but also to reduce the risks of free-riding given the decentralisation of fiscal policies.

The intertwining of sovereign and banking risks, however, also raises questions about the limits of the central bank's refinancing operations with the banking sector. In this case, the distinction between liquidity and solvency support is in principle ensured by, on the one hand, the collateral policies of the central bank which ensure that lending only happens against adequate collateral and, on the other hand, the eligibility requirements for a monetary and financial institution to be a central bank counterparty, which ensure that lending occurs only to solvent banks. In a financial crisis, the valuation and availability of collateral may, however, be distorted, making the appropriate pricing of collateral less clear cut and making it necessary to enlarge the available collateral set, as was also the case in the euro area as discussed above. This again complicates making the distinction between liquidity and solvency and underlines the appropriateness of a solid risk management framework at the central bank. As the collateral also includes government bonds, collateral policy with respect to those bonds will have an indirect impact on government bond markets, making the distinction from direct government bond market interventions less clear cut. Moreover, in the EMU financial supervision is still a national competency, complicating the information sharing on the viability of financial institutions. In this context there is a need to strengthen the integration of the supervisory framework not only to cut the link between national banking systems and governments, but also to reduce the risks of free-riding in addressing the solvency problems and the need for recapitalisation in the banking sector.

In summary, a more durable solution must build upon four pillars. First, it is essential to rebuild the confidence in sovereign bond markets by appropriate fiscal consolidation establishing sufficient fiscal buffers and strengthening the fiscal governance framework. In this respect, the recent establishment of a 'fiscal compact' – which still needs be ratified – aims at responding to these concerns. In practice, this compact contains two main elements: a mandatory introduction of a balanced budget rule with a correction mechanism for deviations from balanced budgets at the national level; and a strengthening of the excessive deficit procedure within the Stability and Growth Pact.[41]

Second, it is also necessary to strengthen the surveillance of private sector imbalances within the monetary union. The introduction of the so-called 'six-pack' secondary EU law in 2011 meets that concern by establishing macroeconomic surveillance under a new Macroeconomic Imbalance Procedure.[42] In parallel, a new macroprudential supervisory framework has been put in place for the European Union as a whole with the establishment the European Systemic Risk Board (ESRB), which may issue warnings and macroprudential recommendations whenever necessary.[43]

Third, it is also of utmost importance to establish a sufficiently large, permanent and flexible mechanism to ringfence solvent governments and avoid contagion. In this regard, the establishment of the temporary European Financial Stability Facility (EFSF) and the permanent European Stabilisation Mechanism (ESM) should help to increase investors' confidence in the ability of the euro area to preserve its stability as a whole by offering temporary and conditional financial support to euro area members in need. The main functions of the ESM will be to (a)

[41] The so-called 'Fiscal Compact' referred to in the fiscal part of the Treaty on Stability, Coordination and Governance (TSCG). More specifically, it requires contracting parties to respect/ensure convergence towards the country-specific medium-term objective (MTO), as defined in the Stability and Growth Pact (SGP), with a lower limit of a structural deficit (cyclical effects and one-off measures are not taken into account) of 0.5% of GDP; (1.0% of GDP for Member States with a debt ratio significantly below 60% of GDP). Correction mechanisms should ensure automatic action to be undertaken in case of deviation from the MTO or the adjustment path towards it, with escape clauses for exceptional circumstances. Compliance with the rule should be monitored by independent institutions. Note that TSCG also includes a part on economic governance in the euro area, e.g.: Euro Summits at least twice a year; reinforced economic cooperation.

[42] The so-called 'six-pack' regulation reinforces both the preventive and the corrective arm of the SGP, i.e. the Excessive Deficit Procedure (EDP). As regards its link with the 'Fiscal Compact' (included in TSCG) two observations can be made. On the one hand, a couple of provisions included in the TSCG are mirroring concepts existing in the Stability and Growth Pact as reformed by the six-pack (e.g. medium-term objectives (MTOs), significant deviation, exceptional circumstances). On the other hand, some provisions of the TSCG are more stringent than the six-pack. See the website of the European Commission for further details at ec.europa.eu/economy_finance/articles/governance/2012-03-14_six_pack_en.htm.

[43] Further details can be found at ec.europa.eu/internal_market/finances/committees/index_en.htm.

issue bonds or other debt instruments on the market to raise the funds needed to provide loans to countries in financial difficulties; (b) intervene in the primary and secondary debt markets; (c) act on the basis of a precautionary programme; (d) finance recapitalisations of financial institutions through loans to governments including in non-programme countries. All financial assistance to Member States is linked to appropriate conditionality.[44] With an effective lending capacity of EUR 500 billion (for a total subscribed capital of EUR 700 billion, out of which EUR 80 billion is in the form of paid-in capital provided by the euro area Member States), the ESM will be the main instrument to finance new programmes as from July 2012, whereas the EFSF will only remain active in financing programmes that have started before that date.

Fourth, in order to break the link between national sovereign and banking risks, mend the fragmentation of the financial market in the euro area and avoid free-rider problems in addressing weak banking systems, it is important to strengthen the financial union. This should in particular cover three areas: (i) a strengthening of prudential supervision of, at a minimum, the systematically relevant institutions in the euro area; (ii) the introduction of a crisis resolution scheme which, in conjunction with the previous surveillance, should make it possible simultaneously to prevent (or at least to diminish) the occurrence of failing institutions and to close non-viable and insolvent banks when necessary; (iii) the establishment of a euro area deposit insurance scheme to protect deposits within the monetary union.

Apart from certainly contributing to reduce moral hazard among the banking community, such a banking union would also increase, at the same time, protection of the central bank balance sheet while reducing the risks of governments becoming trapped in a vicious spiral of twin funding problems where financial weaknesses of banks decreases sustainability of public finances and vice versa. The implementation of such a financial union is clearly the next step of consolidation to be made in the euro area financial architecture.

References

Alesina, A., De Broek, M., Prati, A. and Tabellini, G. (1992). Default risk on government debt in OECD countries, *Economic Policy*, **15**(7), 427–463.
Arghyrou, M. and Kontonikas, A. (2011). The EMU sovereign debt crisis: fundamentals, expectations and contagion, European Commission, Economic Paper, no. 463.

---

[44] For further details, please consult the European Council Conclusions of 25 March 2011 www.consilium.europa.eu/uedocs/cms_data/docs/pressdata/en/ec/120296.pdf.

Arnone, M., Laurens, B., Segalotto, J. F. and Sommer, M. (2007). Central bank autonomy: lessons from global trends, IMF Working Paper, No. 07/88.

Baum A., Checherita-Westphal, C. and Rother, P. (2013). Debt and growth: new evidence for the euro area, *Journal of International Money and Finance*, **32**, 809–821.

Beirne, J. (2012). The EONIA spread before and during the crisis of 2007–2009: the role of liquidity and credit risk, *Journal of International Money and Finance*, **31**(3), 534–551.

Bi, H., Leeper, E. and Leith, C. (2011). Uncertain fiscal consolidations, Mimeo, University of Indiana.

Buiter, W. (2007). Seignorage, *E-conomics*, 2007–10.

Burdekin, R. C. K. and Burkett, P. (1992). Money, credit, and wages in hyper-inflation: post-World War I Germany, *Economic Inquiry*, **30** (July), 470–495.

Calvo, G. (1988). Servicing the public debt: the role of expectations, *American Economic Review*, **78**(4), 647–661.

Cassola, N., Durré, A. and Holthausen, C. (2011). Implementing monetary policy in crisis times: the case of the ECB, in *Approaches to Monetary Policy Revisited – Lessons from the Crisis* (M. Jarocinski, F. Smets and C. Thimann, eds.), Session 5, European Central Bank, pp. 280–321.

Cassola, N., Holthausen, C. and Würtz, F. (2008). Liquidity management under market turmoil: experience of the European Central Bank in the first year of the 2007–2008 financial market crisis, in *The First Credit Market Turmoil of the 21ˢᵗ Century* (D. Evanoff, P. Hartmann and G. E. Kaufman, eds.), World Scientific Studies in International Economics 10, New Jersey: World Scientific, 195–228.

Cecchetti, S., Mohanty, M. S. and Zampolli, F. (2010). The future of public debt: prospects and implications, BIS Working Paper, No. 300.

Cecchetti, S., Mohanty, M. S. and Zampolli, F. (2011). The real effects of debt, BIS Working Paper, No. 352.

Chadha, J. S. (2011). Policy rules under the monetary and the fiscal theories of the price-level, *Macroeconomics and Finance in Emerging Market Economies*, **4**(2), 189–212.

Chari, V. V. and Kehoe, P. J. (2007). On the need for fiscal constraints in a monetary union, *Journal of Monetary Economics*, **54**(8), 2399–2408.

Cochrane, J. H. (2011). Understanding policy in the great recession: some unpleasant fiscal arithmetic, *European Economic Review*, **55**(1), 2–30.

Cole, H. and Kehoe, T. (2000). Self-fulfilling debt crises, *Review of Economic Studies*, **67**, 91–116.

Corsetti, G. and Dedola, L. (2011). Fiscal crises, confidence and default: a bare-bones model with lessons for the euro area, Mimeo, ECB.

Corsetti, G., Kuester, K., Meier, A. and Müller, G. (2011). Sovereign risk and the effects of fiscal retrenchment in deep recessions, FRB of Philadelphia Working Paper, No. 11–43, September.

Davig, T., Leeper, E. M. and Walker, T. D. (2011). Inflation and the fiscal limit, *European Economic Review*, **55**(1), 31–47.

De Grauwe, P. (2011). The ECB as a lender of last resort, *VOXEU*, 18 August.

De Grauwe, P. and Ji, Y. (2011). Mispricing of sovereign risk and multiple equilibria in the eurozone, Mimeo, University of Leuven.

De Santis, R. A. (2012). The Euro area sovereign debt crisis: safe haven, credit rating agencies and the spread of the fever from Greece, Ireland and Portugal, ECB Working Paper Series, No. 1419.

Dornbusch, R. (1985). Stopping hyperinflation: lessons from the German inflation experience of the 1920s, NBER Working Paper Series, No. 1675.

Drudi, F., Durré, A. and Mongelli, F. P. (2012). The interplay of economic reforms and monetary policy: the case of the euro area, *Journal of Common Market Studies*, **50**(6).

Durré, A. and Pill, H. (2010). Non-standard monetary policy measures, monetary financing and the price level, ECB conference on *Monetary and Fiscal Policy Challenges in Times of Financial Stress*.

ECB (2010). The ECB's response to the financial crisis, *ECB Monthly Bulletin*, October, 59–74.

Ejsing, J., Lemke, W. and Margaritov, E. (2011). Sovereign bond spreads and fiscal fundamentals – a real-time, mixed-frequency approach, Mimeo, ECB.

Eser, F. and Schwaab, B. (2012). The yield impact of the securities markets programme, Mimeo.

Fahr, S., Motto, R., Rostagno, M., Smets, F. and Tristani, O. (2011). Lessons for monetary policy strategies from the recent past, in *Approaches to Monetary Policy Revisited – Lessons from the Crisis* (M. Jarocinski, F. Smets and C. Thimann, eds.), Session 1, European Central Bank, pp. 26–66.

Ghysels, E., Idier, J., Vergote, O. and Manganelli, S. (2012). A high-frequency assessment of the ECB Securities Markets Programme, Mimeo.

Giavazzi, F. and Pagano, M. (1990). Confidence crisis and public debt management, in *Capital Markets and Debt Management* (M. Draghi and R. Dornbusch, eds.), Cambridge University Press.

Hetzel, R. L. and Leach, R. F. (2001). The Treasury-Fed accord: a new narrative account, *Federal Reserve Bank of Richmond Economic Quarterly*, **87**(1), 33–55.

Holló, D., Kremer, M. and Lo Duca, M. (2012). CISS – a composite indicator of systemic stress in the financial system, ECB Working Paper, No. 1426.

Krugman, P. (2011). A self-fulfilling euro crisis? The conscience of a liberal, *New York Times*, August 7.

Leeper, E. M. (1991). Equilibria under 'Active' and 'Passive' monetary and fiscal policies, *Journal of Monetary Economics*, **27**(1), 129–147.

Leeper, E. and Walker, T. B. (2011). Perceptions and misperceptions of fiscal inflation, Mimeo, Indiana University.

Lenza, M., Pill, H. and Reichlin, L. (2010). Monetary policy in exceptional times, *Economic Policy*, **62**, 295–339.

McAndrews, J., Sarkar, A. and Wang, Z. (2008). The effect of the term auction facility on the London inter-bank offered rate, Federal Reserve Bank of New York Staff Reports, No. 335.

Pill, H. and Smets, F. (2011). Monetary policy frameworks after the great financial crisis, Mimeo, ECB.

Reinhart, C. and Rogoff, K. (2010). Growth in time of debt, *American Economic Review Papers & Proceedings*, **100**, 573–8.

Sarkar, A. (2009). Liquidity risk, credit risk, and the Federal Reserve's responses to the crisis, *Financial Markets and Portfolio Management*, **23**(4), 335–348.

Schwarz, K. (2010). Mind the gap: disentangling credit and liquidity in risk spreads, Mimeo.

Sims, C. (2011). Stepping on a rake: the role of fiscal policy in the inflation of the 1970s, *European Economic Review*, 55(1), 48–56.

Smets, F. (2012). Imbalances in the euro area and the ECB's response, in *Governance for the Eurozone: Integration or Disintegration?* (F. Allen, E. Carletti and S. Simonelli, eds.), Florence: FIC Press and University of Pennsylvania, Philadelphia: Wharton Financial Institutions Center, pp. 43–62.

Smets, F. and Trabandt, M. (2012). Sovereign debt overhang and monetary policy, *Second International Research Conference of the Reserve Bank of India on Monetary Policy, Sovereign Debt and Financial Stability: The New Trilemma*.

Uhlig, H. (2002). One money, but many fiscal policies in Europe: what are the consequences?, CEPR Discussion Paper, No. 3296.

von der Groeben, H., Thiesing, J. and Ehlermann, C. D. (eds.), (1997). *Kommentar zum EU-/EG-Vertrag*, 5th edition, Brussels: Nomos, 65–68.

Webb, S. B. (1985). Government debt and inflationary expectations as determinants of the money supply in Germany 1919–1923, *Journal of Money, Credit and Banking*, November, 479–492.

4 The Federal Reserve's response to the financial crisis: what it did and what it should have done

Daniel L. Thornton

4.1 Introduction

The financial crisis began on August 9, 2007, when BNP Paribas, France's largest bank, halted redemption of three investment funds. The federal funds rate spiked about 13 basis points on the day only to fall by nearly 75 basis points the next. The Fed's initial response was anemic: on August 10, the Fed announced that the discount window was "open for business"; on August 17, the primary credit rate (the discount rate) was cut by 50 basis points. As evidence mounted that difficulties in financial markets were intensifying, the Fed took bolder steps. The Federal Open Market Committee (FOMC) decreased the federal funds rate from 5.25 percent to 2 percent in a series of seven moves between September 18, 2007, and April 30, 2008; the primary lending rate was reduced to 25 basis points on December 11; and Term Auction Facility (TAF) was introduced on December 12.[1] The Fed's next major policy actions did not occur until Lehman Brothers filed for bankruptcy protection on September 15, 2008. The Fed responded by injecting massive amounts of credit into the market, mostly through its lending facilities. Between September 15, 2008 and January 2009 the monetary base doubled. In mid-March 2009 the FOMC initiated what is commonly referred to as quantitative easing 1 (QE1), announcing that

The views expressed here are the author's and do not necessarily represent the views of the Board of Governors of the Federal Reserve or the Federal Reserve Bank of St. Louis. I would like to thank two anonymous referees for their comments and suggestions and Sean Grover for helpful research assistance.

[1] The Term Securities Lending Facility (TSLF) on March 11, 2008; the Primary Dealer Credit Facility (PDCF) on March 16, 2008; and lending in support of the acquisition of Bear Stearns by JPMorgan Chase on March 24, 2008; and authorizing lending to Freddie Mac and Fannie Mae on July 13, 2008. A complete time line of the financial crisis can be found at http://timeline.stlouisfed.org/.

it would purchase up to \$1.75 trillion in mortgage-backed securities, agency debt, and longer-dated Treasuries. QE1 was followed by QE2, the purchase of an additional \$600 billion in longer-term Treasuries, and Operation Twist, the purchase of \$400 billion in longer-term Treasuries while simultaneously selling the same amount of short-term Treasuries.[2] These actions were intended to stimulate aggregate demand by reducing longer-term yields.

I discuss which of the Fed's primary monetary policy actions were appropriate and which were not. I also discuss what the Fed should have done, along with reasons why the economic recovery would have been stronger had the FOMC followed these suggestions. Indeed, Lehman might not have failed, and even if the output response would not have been stronger, the FOMC would at least not be mired in a Japanese-style zero interest rate policy.

My analysis begins with a discussion of "conventional" versus "unconventional" monetary policy. I then discuss the Fed's pre-Lehman monetary policy, followed by a discussion of its post-Lehman monetary policy. I present my analysis of how the Fed should have responded to the financial crisis and the reasons why my approach would have likely resulted in better financial market and economic outcomes. I conclude with some thoughts about the direction that policy should now take.

4.2   Conventional versus unconventional monetary policy

At a fundamental level, the Fed has done one thing historically: it has expanded or contracted its balance sheet through its lending and investing activities. These activities increase or decrease the monetary base and the supply of credit. Given the structure of the banking system and reserve requirements, changes in the monetary base are linked to changes in the supply of money. Indeed, the effect on the money supply is thought to be the reason that Fed actions affect interest rates: the demand for money is a function of interest rates so that an increase in the supply of money causes interest rates to decline via the so-called *liquidity effect*. I have noted elsewhere (Thornton, 2012a), however, that monetary policy actions can affect interest rates even if the money demand was not a function of the interest rate. The reason is that the Fed's lending and investing activities affect the supply of credit. This would be true even if the demand for money were independent of the interest rate, or if, as Woodford (2000) has suggested might happen, money

---

[2] Operation Twist was tried previously in 1961 and determined to be unsuccessful (Modigliani and Sutch, 1996). For some new evidence on the 1961 experiment see Swanson (2011).

did not exist. Until the 1990s, it was believed that the Fed controlled the federal funds rate by adjusting the supply of reserves (credit) in the funds market through daily open market operations – increase the monetary base and the federal funds rate falls; decrease the base and the federal funds rate rises.[3] Indeed, this mechanism continues to appear in textbook descriptions of how the Fed controls the federal funds rate. However, since at least the mid-1990s, the Fed has controlled the federal funds rate though open mouth operations; the FOMC simply announces its target and the federal funds rate immediately adjusts to the new target level. This mechanism works because the market believes that the Fed has the power and willingness to achieve and maintain the new target level. Elsewhere (Thornton, 2010d) I show that greater control over the federal funds rate has been accompanied by a marked deterioration in the relationship between the federal funds rate and longer-term Treasury yields.

The important point is that any action the Fed takes to change the supply of credit – either by making loans or purchasing assets – is conventional monetary policy. The Federal Reserve Act gives the Fed the authority to purchase a wide variety of assets, other than those which it has purchased historically (Thornton, 2009, p. 18).[4] Hence, quantitative easing *per se* is not unconventional. What is unconventional is the magnitude of the purchases and the reason for doing so.

The Federal Reserve Act limits who the Fed can lend to under normal circumstances. However, Section 13(c) of the Act gives the Federal Reserve Board the authority to make loans and provide financial assistance to whomever in "unusual and exigent" circumstances. Hence, loans made to any institution other than depository institutions are unconventional in the sense that "unusual and exigent" circumstances arise very infrequently.[5]

What are the FOMC's truly unconventional policies? There are two: (1) the use of forward guidance, whereby the FOMC attempted to reduce longer-term interest rates by publicly committing to keep the policy rate at zero for an extended period of time; and (2) Operation Twist, whereby the FOMC attempted to reduce longer-term rates by

---

[3] It is interesting to note that despite the widespread belief in this mechanism, evidence of the "liquidity effect" in the federal funds market has been remarkably difficult to find, see Hamilton (1997), Thornton (2001a, 2004, 2007, 2010a), and Carpenter and Demiralp (2006, 2008).

[4] The average annual increase in the monetary base over the period 1980–2007 was just $25 billion, nearly all of which was required to accommodate the increase in the currency component of the money supply over the period.

[5] See Mehra (2010) for a discussion of the legality of the Fed's operations under Section 13(3) of the Federal Reserve Act.

purchasing long-term securities and simultaneously selling an equivalent quantity of short-term securities, thereby leaving the total supply of credit unchanged.

4.3   Pre-Lehman monetary policy

There were just two major policy actions prior to Lehman: the 325-basis-point reduction in the federal funds rate target between September 18, 2007 and April 30, 2008, and the Fed's lending primarily through the TAF. The reduction of the federal funds rate target was appropriate but largely ineffective. For one thing, the *interest rate channel of monetary policy* is relatively weak and has long been considered so for a variety of reasons (Bernanke and Gertler, 1995; Thornton, 2010c). The interest rate channel will be particularly ineffective during economic crises because the expected return on capital spending is typically marked down so low that investment is unattractive at virtually any interest rate. This is particularly true for residential and commercial investment in the current economic crisis because of the enormous overhang in residential and commercial real estate capital. Finally, the ability of Central Banks to affect longer-term rates that matter for economic activity is thought to be limited (Bernanke and Gertler, 1995; Greenspan, 1993; Thornton, 2012a,b).

The consensus that the interest rate channel of monetary policy is relatively ineffective was the primary motivation for the *credit channel of monetary policy*. However, the credit channel is also of questionable strength. Bernanke and Gertler (1995) point out that the credit channel has two distinct parts – the *net worth channel* and the *bank lending channel*. Thornton (1994) shows that the ability of banks to obtain funds for lending in the certificate of deposit (CD) market significantly mitigates the effectiveness of the bank lending channel and presents evidence that this channel is weak at best.

The net worth channel is based on the idea that the larger the net worth of the borrower, the more likely the borrower will have access to external finance. This provides a mechanism whereby changes in interest rates can affect borrower's net worth. There are two possibilities. First, a rise in interest rates will increase a borrower's interest expense to the extent that the borrower has short-term debt on the balance sheet. This will reduce the cash flow and the ability to secure credit. Second, rising interest rates may cause a decline in asset prices, which reduces the borrower's net worth and, thereby, collateral. These effects are second order and would vary considerably depending on the structure of the balance sheet of individual borrowers. Moreover, the direct effect on a borrower's net worth should be large only if the borrower was holding relatively long-dated assets and then only if the change in the overnight policy rate was accompanied by a change in longer-term rates; this is very doubtful, at least since the late 1980s (Thornton, 2010d). In any event, the empirical support of the credit channel is weak (Kashyap and Stein, 2000; Carpenter and Petersen, 2002; Ashcraft, 2006; Holod and Peek, 2007; Bernanke, 2007).

4.3.1   *Sterilized lending*

During a financial crisis, risk premiums rise and credit markets freeze up because of uncertainty and the corresponding increase in credit risk. Considerable uncertainty arose this time because financial institutions were holding large quantities of mortgage-backed securities (MBS). The quality of most of these MBS was largely unknown even to the financial institutions holding them. The existence of large quantities of these so-called *toxic* assets made it difficult to assess the creditworthiness of borrowers. Financial institutions were forced to spend considerable time and resources to determine the quality of their MBS portfolios. In such an environment, the Fed could have facilitated the adjustment process by massively increasing the supply of credit through open market operations and direct lending (Allen and Gale, 2008).

The Fed made significant loans to depository institutions, primarily through the TAF. However, the Fed sterilized the effect of its lending activities on the supply of credit (i.e., the monetary base) by selling an equivalent quantity of government securities. Sterilized lending is not unconventional. The Fed has historically sterilized discount window lending. Indeed, it has an incentive to do so when it is attempting to control either the federal funds rate or the money supply (Thornton 2001b).[6]

The volume of lending during the pre-Lehman period was sufficiently large that, had it not been sterilized, the FOMC would have had to reduce the federal funds rate target significantly more than it did. This does not appear to be the reason the FOMC sterilized its pre-Lehman lending, however. The apparent motive for sterilizing the lending was unconventional. Chairman Bernanke (2009) argued that it is the composition of the balance sheet that matters, not its size, pointing out that the Fed's approach was different from quantitative easing where the "focus

---

[6] This approach is consistent with Bernanke and Blinder's (1988) analysis of the special role of banks, i.e., monetary policy will matter even in a liquidity trap. For a good discussion of this and other emergent theoretical issues associated with the financial crisis, see Chadha and Holly (2011).

of policy is the quantity of bank reserves, which are liabilities of the central bank; the composition of loans and securities on the asset side of the central bank's balance sheet is incidental." He went on to state that "the Fed's approach focuses on the mix of loans and securities that it holds and on how this composition of assets affects credit conditions for households and businesses." Bernanke (2008b) motivated this approach, saying "recent research by Allen and Gale (2007) confirms that, in principle at least, 'fire sales' forced by sharp increases in investors' liquidity preference can drive asset prices below their fundamental value, at a significant cost to the financial system and the economy ... A central bank may be able to eliminate, or at least attenuate, adverse outcomes by making cash loans secured by borrowers' illiquid but sound assets." Apparently, the idea was to undo the inefficient allocation by the credit market by essentially making the market lend to financial institutions the Fed deemed most in need of liquidity.[7] This is unconventional. Historically the Fed has argued that it is the size and not the composition of the balance sheet that matters: the Fed's job is to supply credit; the market's job is to allocate the credit to its most efficient use. Before Lehman, the Fed apparently believed that the market's ability to allocate credit efficiently was impaired, so it took on the job of reallocating credit (Thornton, 2009).

I view the Fed's decision to reallocate the existing quantity of credit to particular financial institutions as a major policy error. Friedman and Schwartz (1963) argued convincingly that the Fed made a major policy error at the start of the Great Depression by contracting the monetary base. The FOMC did not contract the supply of credit as it did at the outset of the Great Depression, but it did not increase it as it should have.

Temporarily increasing the monetary base to better enable the normal adjustment process would have been the appropriate action. Indeed, this is what the Fed did in advance of Y2K and immediately following

---

[7] Goodfriend (2011) mentions that sterilized lending through the TAF – which he calls credit policy – was a mistake. However, his suggestion that TAF lending exposed taxpayers to excessive risk of loss because "central bank lending that is collateralized fully exposes taxpayers to losses if the borrower fails subsequently" is an overstatement. Also, his definition of monetary policy – "open market operations that expand or contract high-powered money (bank reserves plus currency) by buying or selling *Treasury securities*" is too narrow. Actions which increase the size of the adjusted monetary base are monetary policy actions, regardless of their intent. Moreover, this definition would seem to apply only if the Fed were constrained to have zero default risk. However, the Federal Reserve Act allows the Fed to purchase a wide range of assets. Hence, it imposes no such requirement. The desire to be self-sustaining motivates the Fed to minimize default risk on its balance sheet. The Fed accomplishes this by only purchasing high-grade securities and by making highly collateralized loans. Hence, I agree with Goodfriend (2011) that the Fed's decision to add $29 billion in "toxic assets" to its balance sheet, in order to rescue Bear Stearns, was a mistake for this reason.

the 9/11 terrorist attacks. In expectation that there would be a marked increase in the need for liquidity (credit) in the financial market at the turn of the century because of a large number of computer failures, the Fed significantly increased the monetary base. Concern about Y2K turned out to be unwarranted and the additional funds were withdrawn quickly so that the monetary base returned to its pre-easing level. The Fed also significantly increased the monetary base immediately following the 9/11 terrorist attacks. Given these actions, I find it puzzling that the Fed decided not to increase the monetary base even though it was increasingly clear that the difficulties in the financial markets and the economy were intensifying and financial markets were in need of additional credit. Increasing the monetary base would not have been a panacea, but increasing the availability of credit to the market would have facilitated the adjustment process significantly. In any event, not increasing the supply of credit by sterilizing the effect of the Fed's lending on the monetary base produced no noticeable results. Financial market and economic conditions continued to deteriorate, risk spreads remained high, and on March 14, 2008, the Fed participated in a bailout of Bear Stearns.

4.4   Post-Lehman monetary policy

Immediately following Lehman's announcement, primary credit borrowing and TAF lending – which had increased significantly during the months prior to Lehman's announcement – exploded. The Fed ceased sterilizing lending. Was this a shift in monetary policy philosophy or merely something that happened because the Fed lacked the ability to sterilize such lending? By the time of Lehman's bankruptcy announcement, the Fed's holdings of Treasuries had shrunk to about $475 billion, of which about $200 billion was pledged under the Fed's Term Securities Lending Facility (TSLF) which was introduced on March 11, 2008. Consequently, the Fed's ability to continue its sterilization policy was significantly impaired.

Whatever the rationale, the action was appropriate. The effectiveness of this action is reflected in risk spreads. Figure 4.1 shows the 1-month Libor/OIS and CD/Treasury spreads over the period January 3, 2006 through April 23, 2012. These spreads, which had increased markedly with the onset of the financial crisis, and more dramatically following Lehman's announcement, had fallen below their post-financial-crisis/pre-Lehman levels by early 2009. Longer-term and private security spreads, shown in Figure 4.2, also declined markedly but remained at their post-financial-crisis/pre-Lehman levels.

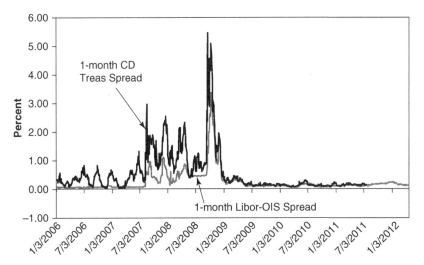

Figure 4.1 The 1-month Libor-OIS and CD-Treasury spreads
Source: Federal Reserve Board/Haver Analytics, British Bankers Association/Haver Analytics.

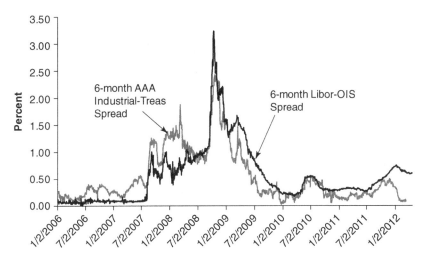

Figure 4.2 The 6-month Libor-OIS and AAA industrial-Treasury spreads
Source: Federal Reserve Board/Haver Analytics, British Bankers Association/Haver Analytics, Bloomberg.

4.4.1   *The federal funds rate target and forward guidance*

Figure 4.3, which plots the monetary base, the federal funds rate, and the FOMC's federal funds rate target weekly over the period January 2006 through April 2012, shows that the massive increase in the monetary base was accompanied by a decline in the federal funds rate to near zero long before the FOMC reduced its federal funds rate target to that level. Indeed, the last three reductions in the FOMC's federal funds rate target were the endogenous responses of the FOMC to a supply-induced decline in the federal funds rate. This is illustrated in Figure 4.4 which shows the effective federal funds rate, the federal funds rate target, and the 1-month OIS rate daily from January 2, 2007 through February 28, 2009. The vertical line denotes September 15, 2008. Prior to that date, the federal funds rate declined immediately on the announcement of a target change – reflecting the open mouth operations discussed in Section 4.2. Moreover, the 1-month OIS rate declined ahead of the target change, reflecting the fact that target changes were anticipated somewhat before they occurred. After Lehman, however, the federal funds rate declined in advance of target changes and the OIS rate lagged rather than led changes in the federal funds rate. This reflects the fact, as suggested in Section 4.3.1, that a massive increase in the supply of credit by the Fed would cause the federal funds rate to decline significantly. The fact that the FOMC did not immediately reduce the target to zero indicates that the FOMC did not appreciate this fact. This suggests that the decision to sterilize its pre-Lehman lending was not because the FOMC

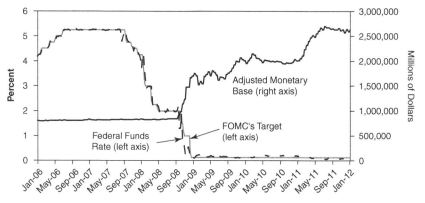

Figure 4.3 The monetary base, the federal funds rate, and the funds rate target
Source: Federal Reserve Board/Haver Analytics.

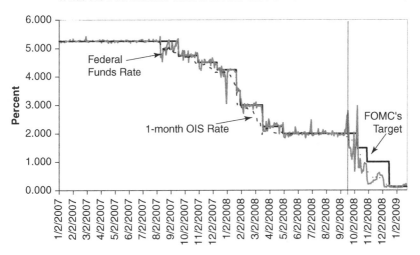

Figure 4.4 The federal funds rate, funds rate target, and 1-month OIS rate

believed it would be unable to maintain its federal funds rate target had it not sterilized its lending, but rather because it was pursuing a credit reallocation policy as Bernanke's (2008a,b, 2009) statements suggest.

The decision to reduce the federal funds rate target to between zero and 25 basis points was accompanied by the adoption of forward guidance. The FOMC had briefly experimented with forward guidance between 2003 and 2005 (Kool and Thornton, 2012). The first attempt at forward guidance was likely motivated by a January 2003 FOMC discussion of Woodford's (1999, 2001, 2003) suggestion that the efficacy of Central Banks' interest rate policy could be increased if the Central Bank committed to keep its policy rate at a given level for a longer period of time. Governor Bernanke noted "I'm very interested in this basic point that the Fed should be more predictable in order to use the short-term rate to influence long-term rates ..." Following up on a suggestion that the Fed's behavior was not inertial, Bernanke suggested the Fed's behavior should be more inertial "in order to get more effect on long-term rates." In any event, after reducing the federal funds rate target to the then historically low level of 1 percent in June 2003, the FOMC announced that it "believes that policy accommodation can be maintained for a considerable period." When it began increasing the target in June 2004, the Committee announced "that policy accommodation can be removed at a pace that is likely to be measured."

After reducing the federal funds rate target to between zero and 25 basis points in December 2007, the FOMC noted that it "anticipates that weak economic conditions are likely to warrant exceptionally low levels of the federal funds rate for some time." The Committee became more aggressive in its use of forward guidance at the August 2011 meeting by announcing that it "anticipates that economic conditions ... are likely to warrant exceptionally low levels for the federal funds rate at least through mid-2013." The period of forward guidance was lengthened to "late 2014" at the January 2012 meeting.

The theoretical justification for forward guidance is the expectations hypothesis (EH) of the term structure on interest rates. The EH asserts that a rate on a long-term security with maturity n at time t is equal the average of the time-t expectation for the rate on an otherwise equivalent security with maturity m ($m < n$) plus a constant term premium. The EH has been massively rejected (e.g., Sarno et al., 2007, and the references therein) using a wide variety of interest rates, sample periods, and monetary policy regimes. While a variety of explanations for the failure of the EH have been advanced, Guidolin and Thornton (2012) show that a likely reason is that short-term interest rates are essentially unpredictable beyond their current level.[8] In any event, there is little evidence that forward guidance improves Central Banks' control over longer-term rates (Andersson and Hoffmann, 2010; Goodhart and Lim, 2011; Kool and Thornton, 2012).

The massive empirical failure of the EH and the lack of empirical support for the effectiveness of forward guidance policies generally suggest that the FOMC's forward guidance policy may have been unsuccessful. This conclusion is intensified by the lack of support for the interest rate channel of monetary policy. The interest rate channel of policy is likely to be particularly weak during economic crises. Hence, it seems particularly unlikely that the FOMC's current forward guidance policy will be effective in facilitating an economic recovery.[9]

4.4.2   Quantitative easing

Quantitative easing (QE) is a policy of purchasing a large quantity of longer-term assets and maintaining a very large portfolio of government and private debt. The objective of QE and forward guidance is the same – to reduce longer-term yields and thereby increase the efficacy of monetary policy. I have noted elsewhere (Thornton, 2010c, 2012b)

---

[8] The failure of the EH is frequently attributed to a time-varying risk (term) premium. However, that is simply an alternative way of saying that the EH fails: if EH held, the risk premium would be constant.

[9] Fuhrer (1996) has suggested that the EH survives because alternatives to replace it are "weak".

that the simultaneous pursuit of QE and forward guidance is confusing because their theoretical justifications conflict.[10]

While not termed QE, the Fed's first LSAP occurred when the Fed announced on November 25, 2008, that it would purchase up to $100 billion in agency debt and up to $500 billion in MBS to "support housing markets and foster improved conditions in financial markets more generally." The announcement made no mention of reducing longer-term rates. However, in a speech on December 1, 2008, Chairman Bernanke (2008b) pointed out that even though the FOMC's policy rate was effectively zero, "the Fed could purchase longer-term Treasury or agency securities on the open market in substantial quantities. This approach might influence the yields on these securities, thus helping to spur aggregate demand." This was the first hint that the Fed might consider a QE policy. The possibility of QE actions was reinforced in the FOMC statements of December 16, 2008 and January 28, 2009, when the FOMC indicated that it "stands ready" to increase its purchases of securities "as conditions warrant."

QE1 occurred on March 18, 2009, when the FOMC announced that "to provide greater support to mortgage lending and housing markets" it decided to expand its large-scale asset purchases program by purchasing an additional $1.25 trillion in MBS, agency debt, and longer-term Treasuries over the next six months. On August 10, 2010, the FOMC announced that it would maintain its balance sheet at its current level by reinvesting principal payments on MBS and agency debt in longer-dated Treasuries. A second program of quantitative easing (QE2) was announced on November 3, 2010, when the FOMC announced its decision to purchase an additional $600 billion of longer-term Treasury securities at the pace of about $75 billion per month.

I believe the FOMC's decision to increase the size of the Fed's balance sheet to unprecedented levels and to maintain it at those levels was unnecessary and largely, if not completely, ineffective in reducing longer-term real rates and stimulating aggregate demand. QE was unnecessary because financial markets had already stabilized significantly; as I noted above, prior to March 18, 2009, risk spreads declined significantly; in some cases, they were below their pre-financial-crisis levels. Moreover,

---

[10] Several economists have suggested to me privately that the market might not be characterized by perfect substitutability or by market segmentation, suggesting that somehow forward guidance and QE could have the desired effects on longer-term rates. While I don't know for sure that this is impossible, it seems unlikely because there is considerable evidence suggesting that financial markets are very efficient. In any event, given the theoretical conflict between the two policies, the FOMC could increase transparency and improve the public's understanding by simply telling us why they are pursuing what appear to be contradictory strategies.

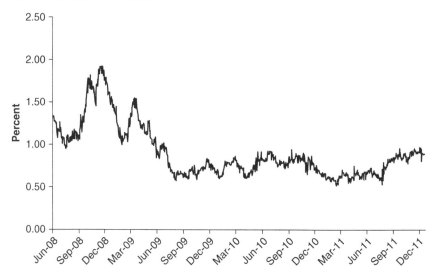

Figure 4.5 The spread between 10-year AAA industrials and Treasuries

other financial stress indices, such as the St. Louis Financial Stress Index, had declined significantly from their post-Lehman peak.

Primary credit borrowing had also declined from a peak of $112 billion to $63.5 billion by the week ending March 12, 2009, TAF auctions were under-subscribed, and the demand for TAF loans peaked at the February 12, 2009 auction. There were other signs of economic recovery. Default risk spreads, such as the spread between the yields on AAA-rated corporate industrial bonds and 10-year Treasuries, shown in Figure 4.5, had declined considerably. This credit risk spread increased dramatically following Lehman's announcement from about 110 basis points to a peak of about 195 basis points, but had fallen to its pre-Lehman level by early February 2009. From February 6, 2009 through March 3, 2009, the spread averaged 108 basis points. The spread increased again beginning in early March; however, 24 basis points of the 25-basis point net change in the spread from March 3 to March 17 occurred on three days when there were announcements that could have increased credit spreads.[11] The spread increased by 7 basis points on

[11] On March 3, 2009, the Treasury and the Fed announced the Term Asset-Backed Securities Loan Facility; on March 6, the Treasury announced that it had purchased $284.7 billion in preferred stock from 22 banks; and on March 13 the Treasury announced that it had purchased an additional $1.45 billion in preferred stock from 19 banks.

the March 18 announcement. Particularly noteworthy is the fact that the recession, which intensified up to and especially following Lehman's announcement, ended just three months after QE1 (i.e., June 2009). Of course, it could be that the recovery began in June because of the FOMC's decision to purchase large amounts of longer-term securities. However, as discussed below, this would appear to be inconsistent with the fact that long-term yields had risen significantly above their March 18 level. A more likely explanation is that the recovery was facilitated by what I would call conventional monetary policy, i.e., the massive injection of credit following Lehman's announcement.

There are several reasons for believing that the LSAP programs had little, if any, effect on longer-term rates. For one thing, most of the evidence supporting the effectiveness of LSAP in reducing interest rates comes from event studies (Gagnon et al., 2011; Krishnamurthy and Vissing-Jorgensen, 2011; Neely, 2012; and Joyce et al., 2010) which show that there was an unusually large decline in longer-term yields on the days of certain LSAP announcements – i.e., there was an announcement effect. But, to be convincing, the announcement effect should be persistent. However, Wright (2011) shows that these announcement effects were short-lived.

More generally, it is virtually impossible to infer a causal relationship between announcement effects and more persistent or permanent movements in longer-term yields that matter for spending decisions. Figure 4.6 shows the daily 10-year Treasury yield over the period from June 13, 2008 (the peak in the 10-year Treasury yield prior to Lehman) to December 30, 2011. The seven vertical lines denote seven important LSAP announcement dates: November 25, December 1, and December 16, 2008, January 28 and March 18, 2009, and August 10 and November 3, 2010, respectively. The three 2008 announcements were associated with drops in the 10-year Treasury yield of 24, 21, and 16 basis points, respectively. The 10-year yield began trending down in mid-to-late October. Consequently, it is difficult to know how much of these responses are due to the announcement and how much is a continuation of the trend that began earlier. For example, over the three days, November 18, 19, and 20, 2008, the 10-year Treasury yield declined 58 basis points, with no monetary policy announcements.[12]

[12] One way to investigate this possibility is to see whether there is a significant change in the trend following key announcements. Because interest rates are highly persistent, this can be done by regressing the change in the 10-year yield on a constant term and dummy variable that takes the value of one after an announcement and zero before the announcement and testing the hypothesis that the coefficient on the dummy variable is zero. The coefficient on the constant term reflects the average daily change in the rate over the period, called the drift. If the coefficient dummy variable is not negative

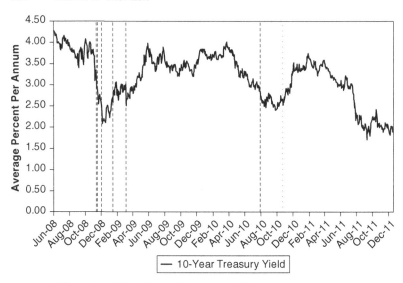

Figure 4.6 The 10-year Treasury yield
Source: Federal Reserve Board/Haver Analytics.

The second FOMC announcement on January 28, 2009, had no effect. The QE1 announcement effect was very large (51 basis points), but short-lived. The yield had recovered 30 basis points of the decline by March 25 and all of it by April 24, 2009. Hence, the March 18, 2009, announcement appears to have only resulted in a pause in the upward trend of 10-year yield, which began in late December 2008. The 2010 announcements had no significant announcement effect. It is sometimes suggested that these two announcements produced no effect because they were expected. However, if this is true, the Treasury yield should have declined in advance of the announcement. There was no such decline. The yield began trending down in early April 2010, well in advance of the October 10 announcement, and was relatively flat

and statistically significant from zero, there is no significant change in the drift. This would suggest that the announcements had no additional effect on the 10-year yield apart from what would have occurred otherwise. For the sample period October 14, 2008 through December 30, 2008, the coefficient on the dummy variable is -0.011 with a t-statistic of -0.40 and -0.002 with a t-statistic of -0.07 using November 24, 2008 and December 1, 2008 as the key announcement dates, suggesting no statistically significant change in the drift following either of these dates. However, the estimates of $\bar{R}^2$ are very small, so this does not constitute strong evidence against the hypothesis that these announcements had an effect beyond the drift which had began earlier, but there is no evidence that these announcements had a separate effect either.

in the weeks before the announcement. The 10-year yield was trending up prior to the QE2 announcement and continued to do so for a significant period after. This very simple analysis suggests that these announcements had little or no lasting effect on yields. More generally, statistically significant announcement effects do not provide compelling evidence that LSAP caused longer-term interest rates to decline secularly.

More compelling evidence of a lack of an effect of QE on longer-term yields is the fact that there is no evidence that the LSAPs were effective using lower-frequency, monthly, data. Elsewhere (Thornton, 2012b), I show that the strongest evidence supporting the portfolio balance channel using monthly data (Gagnon et al., 2011) is due entirely to a common trend in the data used.[13] When the trend is accounted for the evidence of an effect of QE on longer-term rates vanishes. Furthermore, there is no evidence that QE reduced long-term yields or term premiums using a variety of debt measures that are hypothesized to generate a portfolio balance effect on longer-term yields.

Even if QE caused a significant decline in Treasury yields, the effect on economic activity should have been relatively modest. The reason is the effectiveness of QE and Operation Twist on long-term Treasury yields can only occur if the market is segmented. However, if the market for longer-term Treasury debt is segmented from the rest of the credit market, the effect of QE or Operation Twist on Treasury yields cannot spill over to private security yields, which matter for economic activity. Hence, the more effective QE and Operation Twist are in reducing longer-term Treasury yields, the less effective they will be in stimulating aggregate demand; the more segmented the long-term Treasury market, the smaller the effect these actions on private long-term yields.

Given the massive failure of the EH and the weak theoretical underpinnings and empirical evidence of the portfolio balance channel, I believe that neither forward guidance nor QE accounts for a significant amount of the recent decline in longer-term yields. Consistent with the classical theory of interest (Thornton, 2010d), the decline in longer-term yields since early 2011 most likely reflects weakening expectations for economic growth in the US and globally and, in the case of Treasuries, a flight to safety in response to the sovereign debt crisis.[14]

---

[13] I also discuss the theoretical foundations for the effectiveness of LSAP and suggest several reasons for skepticism.

[14] See Thornton (2010d) for a discussion of the EH versus the classical theory of interest and evidence supporting the classical theory. Also see Swanson and Williams (2012) for some additional evidence consistent with the classical theory.

4.4.3   *Are QE and Operation Twist counterproductive?*

Proponents of QE frequently suggest that even if it has little or no effect on longer-term yields, it should be done because it does no harm. I question this belief. Had the FOMC not pursued QE, the Fed's balance sheet would look pretty normal today and the federal funds rate would be closer to a rate consistent with a positive real rate of interest and the FOMC's 2 percent inflation objective, i.e., closer to the 4 percent natural rate that is characteristic of a standard Taylor rule. Had the FOMC pursued this path, I believe economic growth and employment would be higher than they are currently.

How could the FOMC's aggressive balance sheet and zero interest rate policy make things worse? My one-word answer is "expectations". It is sometimes said that if you ask 10 economists a question you will get 11 opinions. There is one area where there has been a convergence of views; the importance of expectations for economic activity. Most economists agree that if important policymakers were to tell the public that we could be facing the next Great Depression, consumption would fall like a rock, pushing the economy closer to another Depression. In a similar vein, I believe an "extreme" policy stance, such as the one the FOMC has pursued since late 2008 and indicates that it will continue until late 2014, generates expectations that the economy is much worse than it might otherwise appear. This expectations effect will be particularly important when the actions are taken at a time when there are significant signs that financial markets are stabilizing and the economy is improving. This adverse expectations effect of QE is extremely difficult to document. Nevertheless, it is possible, even likely, the Fed's extreme policies have worked against the goal they were intended to achieve.

This possibility is supported by Thornton's (2011a) finding that the marked increase in Christensen et al.'s (2009) Libor factor, following the Fed's TAF announcement and the simultaneous announcements of other Central Banks that additional actions were being undertaken to mitigate the effects of the financial crisis, is almost completely accounted for by credit risk spreads. The marked increase in credit risk is consistent with the hypothesis that announcements signaled that policymakers believe the crisis was intensifying. Hence, rather than having the beneficial effect of reducing liquidity premiums, as Christensen et al. (2009) contend, these announcements had the detrimental effect of increasing credit risk.

The FOMC's balance sheet and zero interest rate policies are so extreme that it is virtually impossible for anyone to believe that the economy has returned or is returning to "normal" while such policies are in place. A variety of financial and economic facts deny the need for such extreme policies, e.g., risk spreads are relatively low and stable, and the economy fully recovered its previous level of output in the third quarter of 2011. The extreme policy stance causes consumers and investors to be more cautious than they might be otherwise. Savers are finding it difficult to get a reasonable return, and incomes of the retired have declined drastically. Such an environment is not conducive to rational economic decision making and, consequently, economic growth.

There are other adverse effects of the FOMC's policy. Principal among these is the fact that the Fed's massive balance sheet and the FOMC's concomitant low interest rate policy enables the government to avoid dealing with its deficit/debt problem. The FOMC's zero interest rate policy has reduced the burden of the debt – the average interest rate paid on interest-bearing public debt declined from 4.2 percent in September 2008 to 2.7 percent in April 2012. The Fed's revenue from its massive portfolio has also reduced the debt burden. For reasons that I have discussed elsewhere (Thornton, 2010b, 1984), I don't believe that the FOMC is monetizing the debt *per se*. Nevertheless, the Fed's balance sheet of $2.8 trillion – more than three times its pre-Lehman level – makes it easier for the government to finance the debt.

What are the benefits from maintaining such an easy policy for such a long period of time? To answer this question it is useful to evaluate monetary policy since January 1990. The stance of monetary policy is measured by the difference between the FOMC's target for the federal funds rate and the natural rate of interest, i.e., the interest rate consistent with the long-run real rate of interest and the FOMC's inflation objective. I assume the natural rate of interest is 4 percent, consisting of a 2 percent real interest rate and the FOMC's 2 percent inflation target. Figure 4.7 shows the difference between the FOMC's federal funds rate target and the 4 percent natural rate from January 1990 through 2014. Monetary policy was somewhat restrictive by this measure from January 1990 through June 2001. In contrast, policy has been relatively easy since June 2001 and is expected to remain so until late 2014.

What was the effect of these markedly different long-run policies? Table 4.1 shows the average rate of inflation, output growth, and unemployment over two periods. The first data column for each period presents the average of these variables for the entire period. The second data column shows the averages when recession months or quarters are removed. The third data column, which applies only to the second period, shows the averages for the period ending June 2007 to remove the effect of the financial crisis. These markedly different monetary policies had little effect on the average inflation rates over the two periods.

Table 4.1 *Average annual rates of inflation, output growth, and unemployment*

	Full sample	Less recessions	Less financial crisis
	January 1990 – June 2001		
Headline PCE inflation	2.40	2.30	–
Growth rate of real GDP	3.20	3.70	–
Unemployment rate	5.54	5.54	–
	July 2001 – March 2012		
Headline PCE inflation	2.21	2.47	2.36
Growth rate of real GDP	1.65	2.66	2.50
Unemployment rate	6.50	6.54	5.31

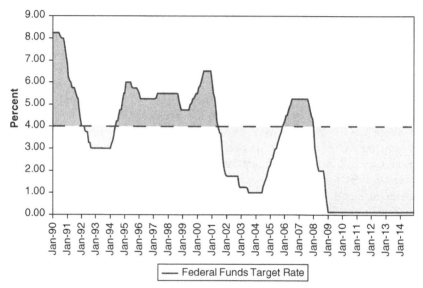

Figure 4.7 The federal funds rate target
Source: Federal Reserve Board/Haver Analytics.

The average rates of inflation are very similar over both periods whether or not the recession months are removed or if the second period ends in June 2007.

There are differences in the average rate of economic growth and the unemployment rate, but not in the way that one might expect given the relative stance of monetary policy. Output growth was twice as high during the period when monetary policy was tight than when it was easy. Some of this difference is due to the fact that the 2007–2009 recession was much more severe and protracted than the 1990–1991 and 2001 recessions. When the recessions are accounted for, the difference is much smaller. The difference is not improved, however, if the period of the financial crisis is removed. The unemployment rate is higher during the easy monetary policy period, but all of the difference is attributed to the financial crisis and its aftermath. The average unemployment rates for 1990–2001 and 2001–2007 are essentially the same. This simple analysis suggests that monetary policy appears to have had little effect on output growth or the unemployment rate. This is consistent with the idea that monetary policy is neutral in the long run and evidence that the interest rate channel of monetary policy is weak. Whatever the explanation, these very different monetary policies appear to have little or no effect on real variables over the two decades.

Why was the stance of policy so different over these decades? A simple analysis suggests it was because the FOMC was responding to inflation and unemployment during the first period, but only unemployment during the second. It is well known that policymakers care about both inflation and output growth. This basic fact is reflected in monetary policy rules, such as the Taylor rule. While there is no evidence that the FOMC has ever followed a policy rule, it is useful to see how the stance of policy is related to inflation and output growth. This is done by estimating a simple policy reaction function of the form

$$ps_t = \alpha + \beta gap^{ur}_{t-1} + \delta gap^{inf}_{t-1} + \varepsilon_t,$$

where ps denotes the stance of monetary policy given by the difference between the FOMC's federal funds rate target and 4 percent, gap^{ur} denotes the unemployment rate gap measured by the difference between the unemployment rate and 5.5 percent, and gap^{inf} denotes the inflation gap measured by the difference between headline PCE inflation and 2 percent. The unemployment rate is used rather than output because output is available only quarterly. The equation is estimated over the periods January 1990 through June 2001 and July 2001 through December 2008.[15]

The results are presented in Table 4.2. For the first period, either gap^{ur} or gap^{inf} alone is highly statistically significant; each accounts for about 20 percent of the variation in the stance of policy. However, when both are included in the regression, each remains highly statistically significant and together they account for nearly 75 percent of the variation in the stance of policy. Both coefficients are near unity and the point estimate

[15] The qualitative conclusions are the same if the equation is estimated over the period July 2001–March 2012; however, there is no variation in the dependent variable after December 2007.

Table 4.2 *Estimates of the equation* $ps_t = \alpha + \beta gap^{\text{ur}}_{t-1} + \delta gap^{\text{inf}}_{t-1} + \varepsilon_t$

	January 1990 – June 2001			July 2001 – December 2008		
α	1.222	0.953	0.807	−1.714	−1.477	−1.741
	(0.000)	(0.000)	(0.000)	(0.000)	(0.000)	(0.000)
β	−0.590		−0.959	−2.502		−2.474
	(0.000)		(0.000)	(0.000)		(0.000)
δ		0.564	1.024		0.540	0.069
		(0.000)	(0.000)		(0.045)	(0.573)
$\overline{R}^2$	0.258	0.170	0.736	0.846	0.073	0.845

of δ is slightly higher than 1.0, suggesting that the FOMC followed the Taylor/Friedman principle.

For the second period, gap^{inf} alone is marginally statistically significant and accounts for only 7 percent of the variation in the stance of policy. In contrast, gap^{ur} alone is highly statistically significant and accounts for nearly 85 percent of the variation in the stance of policy. When both variables are included, gap^{inf} is not statistically significant, and the estimate of $\overline{R}^2$ is the same as with gap^{ur} alone.

The reaction function estimates indicate that the FOMC was attempting to stabilize both inflation and unemployment in the first period, but only the unemployment rate in the second. The focus on the real side of the economy since mid-2001 is likely a consequence of inflation being controlled by inflation expectations during the second period. With inflation expectations well anchored, the FOMC focused its attention on the real economy. Given the theoretical and empirical evidence that monetary policy has little-to-no effect on real variables in the long run and evidence that the interest rate channel of policy is weak more generally, it is reasonable to question the wisdom of such a policy and the FOMC's commitment to maintaining such an uncharacteristically easy policy for such a long period of time.

4.5 How the Fed should have responded to the financial crisis

Having been critical of the Fed's monetary policy response to the financial crisis, I need to suggest how the Fed should have responded. Like many economists, I was not that concerned on August 9, 2007.[16]

---

[16] I have not discussed the issue of the Fed's role in the financial crisis and what if anything the Fed should have done to help prevent it. My view is that the financial crisis is the consequence of home prices getting too far from their fundamental value. The causes

However, as more information became available it was clear that an immediate problem was that most mortgage lending was securitized based on general characteristics of the borrowers and the loans. This meant that financial institutions did not know the real value of their MBS portfolios. Consequently, lenders would be understandably concerned about making loans to institutions with large MBS portfolios, i.e., risk premiums would increase significantly.

It was also clear that the 5 percentage-point increase in home ownership that occurred between 1994 and 2006 was likely to be unsustainable and that home prices would continue to fall, causing a further deterioration in financial markets and the economy more generally. More importantly, the bursting of the home-price bubble was going to be considerably more serious than the bursting of the dot-com bubble in the 2001 recession. The reason is that few, if any, physical assets were created during the dot-com bubble. This would not be the case for the home-price bubble. The bursting of the home-price bubble would be accompanied by a large overhang of residential real estate. There was also going to be significant overhang in commercial real estate. The equilibrating process associated with the dot-com bubble was relatively painless and quick because there was no excess of physical capital – only flows needed to adjust. As a consequence, the recession was relatively mild and short-lived. Economic theory shows that stock-flow adjustments are more difficult and take much longer. Hence, this recession would be much larger and more protracted. Equilibrium would require a very large reduction in the real value of the stock of housing. This would require very large reductions in house prices since the physical quantity of houses can change only slowly. Moreover, the wealth effect on consumption would be large.

The appropriate monetary policy in this circumstance is to significantly increase the monetary base, i.e., the supply of credit, to facilitate the adjustments required to achieve a new equilibrium. Consequently, I advocated that the Fed purchase large quantities of securities to increase the supply of credit. There is no formula to know exactly how much the monetary base should be increased in such a circumstance.

are many, but much of the blame must be placed on governmental policies to encourage home ownership by extending home ownership to those who would not qualify for it under conventional lending standards. The Fed policy undoubtedly contributed to the problem during the period between 2002 and early 2005 by keeping the federal funds rate far below the rate consistent with existing economic circumstances (output grew at a 3 percent rate and inflation averaged 2.2 percent). It is difficult, if not impossible, to determine the degree to which the FOMC's federal funds rate policy contributed to the financial crisis. However, I am inclined to believe that only a very restrictive interest rate policy would have had a significant effect in curbing the home-price bubble.

I recommended $600 billion, but suggested that more should be done if markets did not stabilize sufficiently. When asked by colleagues whether the Fed should restrict its purchases to Treasuries, I responded that what the Fed purchased was less important than the amount purchased. The only requirements were: (a) high-quality securities are purchased in order to minimize the Fed's credit risk, and (b) the public be informed that the increase in the monetary base is temporary and that the composition of the Fed's balance sheet and the size of the monetary base would be returned to normal as financial markets and economic activity began to normalize.

By this time, the Fed had already been supplying funds to banks via the TAF. The TAF was a good idea, but the fact that TAF loans were made at subsidized rates was troublesome. The big mistake, however, was the decision to sterilize the lending. It would have been a better course of action to announce that the FOMC would suspend targeting the federal funds rate and significantly increase the supply of credit to the market by making loans and purchasing assets. I would have announced that the additional funds would be removed and the FOMC would return to federal funds rate targeting as soon as financial markets began to stabilize. Announcing that the actions are temporary is necessary to allay concerns that the FOMC might renege on its commitment to long-run price stability.

I would have taken these actions and given them time to work. Only if it was clear that providing additional credit to the market was not helping the market would I have considered taking more extreme actions. Moreover, I would have pursued more extreme actions only if there was strong theoretical or empirical evidence (say from the experiences of other countries) supporting the effectiveness of such actions.

I thought it dangerous to translate experiences from previous US financial crises to the current one. Financial markets today are just too different from those of the late 1800s or early 1900s. My working hypothesis was that information gleaned from those financial crises may not be useful for understanding or solving the current one.

I would have steadfastly declined to engage in activities that might significantly impair the Fed's independence, such as participating in the bailout of Bear Sterns, or providing credit to particular segments of the market at the expense of others. It is Congress' prerogative to decide if a firm is too-big-to-fail, not the Fed's. The Fed should supply the liquidity, i.e., short-term credit, the government should provide capital if it deems it necessary to do so. If the administration or Congress wants to prevent the failure of a large "systemically significant" financial institution, for whatever reason, it must justify the action to the public and determine how to finance it. The Fed's decision to purchase $29 billion of Bear Sterns assets of questionable quality was a huge mistake – one of many subsequent actions that may have seriously compromised the Fed's independence.[17]

Of course, it is impossible to prove that my approach would have resulted in a better outcome than the actions the Fed has taken. We don't get to construct controlled experiments in economics. Moreover, there is no model of the economy sufficiently good to construct useful simulations of alternative policy actions. Hence, the usefulness of my approach must be evaluated based on existing theory and empirical evidence.

Nevertheless, I believe that providing massive amounts of credit is effective only during the early stages of a financial crisis, when financial market turmoil and uncertainty are high. When financial markets have stabilized considerably, supplying additional credit is relatively ineffective. This was the experience in Japan. The Bank of Japan provided no additional liquidity at the outset of its recession. It did, however, reduce its policy rate to zero and massively increase the monetary base in early 2001. The effectiveness of these actions appears to have been weak and highly uncertain (Spiegel, 2006; Bowman et al., 2011). Moreover, financial markets (and other markets) were largely controlled by the Japanese government. Indeed, the extent of the government's interference in the economy significantly reduced the likelihood that monetary policy actions would have a significant effect.

There is some evidence that the course of action I have outlined would have produced a more favorable outcome. After Lehman, the Fed took a course of action similar to what I had recommended. The size of the monetary base doubled between August and December of 2008. While Lehman's announcement was catastrophic for financial markets and economic activity, there was a significant improvement in financial markets by early 2009 and the recession ended in June 2009. Of course, these improvements could have been due to the Economic Stimulus Act of 2008, which was signed into law on February 13, 2008, or the Troubled Asset Relief Program (TARP), which was signed on October 3, 2008. Consequently, it is impossible to know the extent to which the FOMC's response to Lehman alone was responsible for the marked improvement in financial markets and the economy.

It appears that the Fed's actions prior to Lehman did little to improve financial markets or the economy. The unemployment rate rose to 6.1 percent by August 2008 and the industrial production index declined

---

[17] See John Cochrane's blog, The Grumpy Economist, "Fed Independence 2025," for a discussion of other Fed actions that may have compromised its independence.

from 100.7 in December 2007 to 96.2 in August 2008. Moreover, the continued deterioration in financial and economic conditions led first to the failure of Bear Stearns and eventually Lehman. Much of the FOMC's actions since Lehman have been motivated by a macro-finance term structure nexus that appears to be flawed and has little empirical support. The FOMC's zero interest rate policy is motivated by the EH, which has been repeatedly rejected on an empirical basis. The theoretical basis for QE or Operation Twist is questionable and there is little evidence that these policies have reduced longer-term yields significantly. The evidence using lower frequency data is weak at best and the magnitude, statistical significance, and permanence of the high-frequency effects on longer-terms yields is far from compelling. Nor is there compelling evidence that Central Bank forward guidance policies have had a significant or lasting effect on longer-term yields.

Evidence that these policies have increased economic growth and employment is essentially non-existent; the public's perception of the FOMC's ineffectiveness is growing (*Wall Street Journal*, 2012). My own research (Thornton, 2010d, 2012c) suggests that the FOMC's low interest rate policies of the last decade have had little effect on longer-term Treasury yields or economic activity. With banks holding nearly $1.5 trillion in excess reserves, businesses with massive holdings of cash, and long-term rates significantly below any reasonable estimate of the natural rate, it is difficult to see how additional Central Bank asset purchases could have a significant impact on economic activity or employment.

It is also important to note that the goal of these policies is to affect economic decisions by distorting asset prices. Such distortions can have effects that hinder growth and create potential problems in the future. For example, the FOMC's zero interest rate policy has dramatically reduced the incomes of retirees and others who are dependent on their prior saving for current income. Moreover, the inability to generate reasonable income on safe short-term assets provides an incentive for both individuals and pension funds to take on more risk in their portfolios. There is evidence that the FOMC's low interest rate policy may be inflating commodity prices (Thornton, 2011b) and contributed to the housing bubble.

Given these facts, I suggest it is time for the FOMC to turn the page in its monetary-policy playbook. My recommendation is that the FOMC announce that a continuation of the zero interest rate and unconventional policies will promote excessive risk taking and are likely to impede economic growth. Moreover, a persistent zero nominal interest rate policy is inconsistent with a positive long-run real rate of interest and the FOMC's 2 percent inflation objective. To bring interest rates more in line with the natural rate of interest, the Fed should shrink its balance sheet close to its pre-financial-crisis level. This can be accomplished through outright sales, with the pace of the sales being determined, in part, by the market's ability to absorb the securities. When the balance sheet has shrunk sufficiently, the federal funds rate target will be increased to a level that is more consistent with the long-run natural rate of interest. The FOMC anticipates that the net effect of moving the stance of monetary policy back to "normal" will be beneficial: investor outlook will improve, interest income will increase, and the distortionary effects of a prolonged zero interest rate on asset prices and risk taking will be eliminated.

If done carefully, with proper communication and strong leadership I believe the new policy can be implemented with no significant effects on economic activity or financial markets. My policy recommendation stems from a number of facts: the zero interest rate, QE, and Operation Twist policies are based on the EH (a theory of the term structure that is virtually without empirical support); evidence (Thornton, 2010d) that increased control over very short-term rates by the Federal Reserve, the Bank of England, and Reserve Bank of New Zealand resulted in a significant breakdown of the relationship between the long-term sovereign debt yields and the rate that Central Banks targeted; evidence from that same research that the classical theory of interest rates (which hypothesizes that long-term yields are driven by economic fundamentals and short-term rates linked to long-term yields by arbitrage) appears to be a better description of the behavior of interest rates along the term structure than the EH; the fact that existing evidence on Central Bank forward guidance policy shows no increased ability of such policies to affect longer-term yields in a manner consistent with the EH; the fact that a persistent zero nominal interest rate is inconsistent with a positive real rate of interest and a 2 percent inflation objective – such a policy will achieve one or the other but not both; my belief that it is essentially impossible to have both significant positive economic growth and a long-term real rate of interest that is zero or negative; and the fact that there is no evidence of a statistically significant or economically meaningful liquidity effect.[18]

4.6   Conclusions

I have argued that the Fed didn't massively increase the monetary base in early 2008 when it should have but did following Lehman Brothers' bankruptcy announcement because it had no choice, and also took

---

[18] Moreover, the evidence of a statistically significant liquidity effect was subsequently shown to be the consequence of the endogenous behavior of the Fed or idiosyncrasy of the federal funds market (Thornton 2001a,b).

steps to maintain the monetary base at the post-Lehman level rather than allowing the monetary base to decline passively as it should have as financial market stabilized and the recession ended. Faced with unacceptably high unemployment and anemic economic growth, the FOMC tried to stimulate aggregate demand by attempting to reduce longer-term rates using forward guidance, QE, and Operation Twist. The FOMC's behavior was motivated by policymakers' nearly religious faith in the EH, the fact that the Fed only make loans and investments or controls the federal funds rate either through open mouth operations or by engaging in large-scale open market operations, and the increased emphasis on "financial market frictions" to account for what some see as the apparent historical effectiveness of monetary policy. The last of these helps explain the FOMC's failure to significantly increase the monetary base in early 2008. The first two account for the zero interest rate policy, QE, and Operation Twist. The Fed's response to the financial crisis would have been much better had policymakers taken the massive empirical rejections of the EH seriously, considered the fact that long-term Treasury yields were unresponsive to the 425 basis point increase in the federal funds rate target from June 2004 through June 2006, and believed, as I do, that real long-term rates are largely driven by economic fundamentals, such as the rate of economic growth, and are therefore effectively independent of countercyclical monetary policy. Moreover, policymakers should take the Fisher equation seriously. If they did, they would realize that a zero nominal interest rate policy is inconsistent with 2 percent inflation and positive economic growth, i.e., a positive real long-run interest rate. While a zero nominal policy rate might be defensible for a relatively short period of time, it is totally indefensible as a long-run policy.

Finally, I believe that the FOMC's extreme actions likely reflect Friedman's (1970) suggestion of a Central Bank's version of "the natural human tendency to say 'For God's sake, let's do something,' when faced by unpleasant developments. The action is its own reward, even if it has consequences that make the developments still more unpleasant."[19] Unfortunately, extreme actions can have negative consequences for growth and longer-run economic and financial market stability. The long-run economic consequences of such a policy are difficult to predict. However, such policies can have long-run consequences for the Federal Reserve monetary policy; namely, the loss of credibility and influence as the increasingly extreme policy actions generate smaller and perhaps worse outcomes (*Wall Street Journal*, 2012; Bank for International Settlements, 2012).

---

[19] Friedman (1970), p. 18.

References

Allen, F. and Gale, D. (2007). *Understanding Financial Crises*, Clarendon Lectures in Finance. Oxford: Oxford University Press.

Allen, F. and Gale, D. (2008). Understanding financial crises, in *Financial Crisis*, the International Library of Critical Writings in Economics, **218**, Northampton, MA: Edward Elgar Publishing Ltd., 233–272.

Andersson, M. and Hofmann, B. (2010). Gauging the effectiveness of central bank forward guidance, in D. Cobham, Ø. Eitrheim, S. Gerlach and J. Qvigstad (eds.), *Twenty Years of Inflation Targeting: Lessons Learned and Future Prospects*, New York: Cambridge University Press, 368–97.

Ashcraft, A. B. (2006). New evidence on the lending channel, *Journal of Money, Credit, and Banking*, **38**(3), 751–75.

Bank for International Settlements. (2012). *BIS Annual Report 2011/2012*, Chapter IV, The limits of monetary policy, June 24, 2012.

Bernanke, B. S. (2007). The financial accelerator and the credit channel. Credit Channel of Monetary Policy in the Twenty-First Century Conference, Federal Reserve Bank of Atlanta, June 15, 2007, www.federalreserve.gov/newsevents/speech/bernanke20070615a.htm.

Bernanke, B. S. (2008a). Liquidity provision by the Federal Reserve. Federal Reserve Bank of Atlanta Financial Markets Conference, Sea Island, Georgia, May 13, 2008.

Bernanke, B. S. (2008b). Federal reserve policies in the financial crisis, Greater Austin Chamber of Commerce, Austin, TX, December 1, 2008.

Bernanke, B. S. (2009). The crisis and the policy response, Stamp Lecture, London School of Economics, London, England, January 13, 2009.

Bernanke, B. S. and Blinder, A. S. (1988). Credit, money, and aggregate demand, *American Economic Review*, **78**(2), 435–39.

Bernanke, B. S. and Gertler, M. (1995). Inside the black box: the credit channel of monetary policy transmission, *Journal of Economic Perspectives*, **9**(4), 27–48.

Bowman, D., Cai, F., Davies, S., and Kamin, S. (2011). Quantitative easing and bank lending: evidence from Japan, Board of Governors of the Federal Reserve System, International Finance Discussion Papers, No. 1018.

Carpenter, S. and Demiralp, S. (2006). The liquidity effect in the federal funds market: evidence from daily open market operations, *Journal of Money, Credit, and Banking*, **38**(4), 900–920.

Carpenter, S. and Demiralp, S. (2008). The liquidity effect in the federal funds market: evidence at the monthly frequency, *Journal of Money, Credit, and Banking*, **40**(1), 1–24.

Carpenter, R. E. and Petersen, B. C. (2002). Is the growth of small firms constrained by internal finance? *Review of Economics and Statistics*, **84**(2), 298–309.

Chadha, J. S. and Holly, S. (2011). New instruments of monetary policy, in J. S. Chadha and S. Holly (eds.), *Interest Rates, Prices, and Liquidity: Lessons from the Financial Crisis*, Cambridge, UK: Cambridge University Press.

Christensen, J. H. E., Lopez, J. A. and Rudebusch, G. D. (2009). Do central bank liquidity facilities affect interbank lending rates? Working Paper, No.

2009-13, Federal Reserve Bank of San Francisco, June 2009; www.frbsf. org/publications/economics/papers/2009/wp09-13bk.pdf.

Friedman, M. (1970). Controls on interest rates paid by banks, *Journal of Money, Credit, and Banking*, 2(1), 15–32.

Friedman, M. and Schwartz, A. J. (1963). A monetary history of the United States, 1867–1960, Princeton, NJ: Princeton University Press.

Fuhrer, J. C. (1996). Monetary policy shifts and long-term interest rates, *Quarterly Journal of Economics*, 111(4), 1183–1209.

Gagnon, J., Raskin, M., Remache, J. and Sack, B. (2011). The financial market effects of the Federal Reserve's large-scale asset purchases, *International Journal of Central Banking*, 7(1), 3–43.

Greenspan, A. (1993). Testimony of Alan Greenspan, Chairman, Federal Reserve Board, in *Monetary Policy Objectives: Midyear Review of the Federal Reserve Board*. Washington, DC: Federal Reserve, July 20, 3–13.

Goodfriend, M. (2011). Central banking in the credit turmoil: an assessment of federal reserve practice, *Journal of Monetary Economics*, 58(1), 1–12.

Goodhart, C. A. E. and Lim, W. B. (2011). Interest rate forecasts: a pathology, *International Journal of Central Banking*, 7(2), 135–171.

Guidolin, M. and Thornton, D. L. (2012). Predictions of short-term rates and the expectations hypothesis, Federal Reserve Bank of St. Louis Working Paper 2010-013B, revised 2012.

Hamilton, J. D. (1997). Measuring the liquidity effect, *American Economic Review*, 87(1), 80–97.

Holod, D. and Peek, J. (2007). Asymmetric information and liquidity constraints: a new test, *Journal of Banking & Finance*, 31(8), 2425–2451.

Joyce, M., Lasaosa, A., Stevens, I., and Tong, M. (2010). The financial market impact of quantitative easing, Bank of England Working Paper, No. 393.

Kashyap, A. K. and Stein, J. C. (2000). What do a million observations on banks say about the transmission of monetary policy? *American Economic Review*, 90(3), 407–428.

Kool, C. J. M. and Thornton, D. L. (2012). How effective is central bank forward guidance? Utrecht School of Economics Discussion Paper Series 12-05.

Krishnamurthy, A. and Vissing-Jorgensen, A. (2011). The effects of quantitative easing on interest rates: channels and implications for policy, *Brookings Papers on Economic Activity*, Fall, 215–265.

Mehra, A. (2010). Legal authority in unusual and exigent circumstances: the Federal Reserve and the financial crisis, *University of Pennsylvania Journal of Business Law*, 13(1), 221–274.

Modigliani, F. and Sutch, R. (1966). Innovations in interest rate policy, *American Economic Review*, 56(1/2), 178–197.

Neely, C. J. (2012). The large-scale asset purchases had large international effects, Federal Reserve Bank of St. Louis Working Paper, No. 2010-018D, revised April 2012.

Sarno, L., Thornton, D. L. and Valente, G. (2007). The empirical failure of the expectations hypothesis of the term structure of bond yields, *Journal of Financial and Quantitative Analysis*, 42(1), 81–100.

Spiegel, M. M. (2006). Did quantitative easing by the Bank of Japan "work"? Federal Reserve Bank of San Francisco Economic Letter, No. 2006-28.

Swanson, E. T. (2011). Let's Twist again: a high-frequency event-study analysis of Operation Twist and its implications for QE2, *Brookings Papers on Economic Activity*, Spring, 151–188.

Swanson, E. T. and Williams, J. C. (2012). Measuring the effect of the zero lower bound on medium- and longer-term interest rates. Federal Reserve Bank of San Francisco Working Paper Series, No. 2012-02.

Thornton, D. L. (1984). Monetizing the debt, *Federal Reserve Bank of St. Louis Review*, **66**(10), 30–43.

Thornton, D. L. (1994). Financial innovation, deregulation and the "credit view" of monetary policy, *Federal Reserve Bank of St. Louis Review*, **76**(1), 31–49.

Thornton, D. L. (2001a). Identifying the liquidity effect at the daily frequency, *Federal Reserve Bank of St. Louis Review*, **83**(4), 59–78.

Thornton, D. L. (2001b). The Federal Reserve's operating procedure, non-borrowed reserves, borrowed reserves and the liquidity effect, *Journal of Banking and Finance*, **25**(9), 1717–1739.

Thornton, D. L. (2004). The Fed and short-term interest rates: is it open market operations, open mouth operations or interest rate smoothing? *Journal of Banking and Finance*, **28**(3), 475–498.

Thornton, D. L. (2007). Open market operations and the federal funds rate, *Federal Reserve Bank of St. Louis Review*, **89**(6), 549–70. Also in D. G. Mayes and J. Toporowski (eds.), *Open Market Operations and Financial Markets*, London: Routledge International Studies in Money and Banking, 2007, 178–202.

Thornton, D. L. (2009). The Fed, liquidity, and credit allocation, *Federal Reserve Bank of St. Louis Review*, **91**(1), 13–21.

Thornton, D. L. (2010a). The relationship between the daily and policy-relevant liquidity effects, *Federal Reserve Bank of St. Louis Review*, **92**(1), 73–87.

Thornton, D. L. (2010b). Monetizing the debt, Federal Reserve Bank of St. Louis Economic Synopses, No. 14.

Thornton, D. L. (2010c). Monetary policy and longer-term rates: an opportunity for greater transparency, Federal Reserve Bank of St. Louis Economic Synopses, no. 36.

Thornton, D. L. (2010d). The unusual behavior of the federal funds rate and treasury yields: a conundrum or an instance of Goodhart's law? Federal Reserve Bank of St. Louis Working Paper, No. 2007-039C, revised June 2012.

Thornton, D. L. (2011a). The effectiveness of unconventional monetary policy: the term auction facility, *Federal Reserve Bank of St. Louis Review*, **93**(6), 439–453.

Thornton, D. L. (2011b). Is the FOMC's policy inflating asset prices? Federal Reserve Bank of St. Louis Economic Synopses, No. 18.

Thornton, D. L. (2012a). Monetary policy: why money matters and interest rates don't, Federal Reserve Bank of St. Louis Working Paper, No. 2012-020A, revised July 2012.

Thornton, D. L. (2012b). Evidence on the portfolio balance channel of quantitative easing, Federal Reserve Bank of St. Louis Working Paper, No. 2012-015A.

Thornton, D. L. (2012c). The efficacy of monetary policy: a tale from two decades, Federal Reserve Bank of St. Louis Economic Synopses, no. 18.

Wall Street Journal. (2012). The music men, August 1.

Woodford, M. (1999). Optimal monetary policy inertia, *The Manchester School Supplement 1999*, **67**, 1–35.

Woodford, M. (2000). Monetary policy in a world without money, *International Finance*, **3**(2), 229–260.

Woodford, M. (2001). Monetary policy in the information economy, Symposium on Economic Policy and the Information Economy, Federal Reserve Bank of Kansas City, Jackson Hole, Wyoming, August–September 2001, 297–370.

Woodford, M. (2003). *Interest and Prices: Foundations of a Theory of Monetary Policy*, Princeton: Princeton University Press.

Wright, J. H. (2011). What does monetary policy do to long-term interest rates at the zero lower bound? National Bureau of Economic Research Working Paper, No. 17154.

5 Tail risks and contract design from a financial stability perspective

Patrik Edsparr and Paul Fisher

5.1 Introduction

The wider theme of this book is about what we have learned from the recent crisis. There have been many lessons. Some are not new but just a re-learning of old lore: 'banks need to hold adequate capital'; 'real-estate prices can fall dramatically'; 'financial institutions need to avoid excessive risk taking'. The authorities are pursuing a long list of regulatory initiatives to address the externalities arising from risks in banks and markets, including Dodd–Frank in the US, the European Market Infrastructure Regulation (EMIR) in Europe, the report of the Independent Commission on Banking (ICB) in the United Kingdom and the various Basel capital and liquidity rules internationally. And the Financial Stability Board has taken on a role in coordinating much of the other international effort. Academic research also has a large part to play in this process, in both identifying the issues and proposing or evaluating policy responses.

A lot of discussion is taking place around disentangling different forms of complexity in the market place. For example, regulators are promoting more transparency around funding and legal entity structure within complex financial institutions. And there is also a growing body of work that is exploring clearing houses and exchanges as important structural vehicles to mitigate the increased inter-connectedness driven by the growth of derivatives.[1]

The approach taken in this chapter is to look at some of the details of how risk-taking is executed and the underlying market structures. These

The authors would like to thank Ravi Mattu (PIMCO, Newport Beach), Morten Hviid (UEA) and colleagues at the Bank of England for their comments on a draft of this chapter. The views represented in this chapter are those of the authors and should not be taken as the policy of the Bank of England or to represent the views of any other person at the Bank.

[1] Squam Lake Working Group (2010) for example.

micro-foundations can have a profound impact on systemic stability beyond the normal consideration of formal regulations. In particular, we focus on one aspect of market structure: contracts where, because of a failure to take into account how the financial system as a whole operates, the true value of the contract is different from what it was intended to be – by at least one of the counterparties who struck the contract. This can arise either because in states of the world in which a particular contract is designed to have value there is high correlation with other events or where, in that state of the world, full adherence to the legal structure would cause large unintended consequences in terms of signalling or reputational damage.

5.2   Tail risks with counterparty risk correlation

The first category of contracts falls under the broad headline of 'wrong-way' risk in tail events, and is purely statistical in nature. The particular issue is focused on contracts that can be perceived of as providing insurance, yet, in a stress scenario, when the contract is sufficiently in the money to be worth calling, there is a significant conditional probability that the insurance provider is no longer in business to pay out. In what follows, we look how such problems arise using practical examples and consider what lessons should be drawn.

When investor 'A' decides to buy protection from bank 'B' on exposure to a third company 'X', she may or may not explicitly take into account that in the event of default by X, B may in fact also be in trouble. Whether or not she does so would depend on the reason for the trade. If A wants default protection then that default correlation certainly should be taken into account.[2] But if, for example, the goal is just to offset the price volatility of holdings of a certain corporate bond issued by X, this default correlation may not be seen as that relevant.

As a practical example, take the case of **a pension fund managing its corporate bond portfolio**. Suppose the pension fund owns a large amount of a particular corporate bond and wants to reduce this holding, but the liquidity for outright sales is limited. The fund may take a view that it will have less price impact by gradually selling the bond in the cash market over a period of a few months but, at the same time, it would prefer to take off the market risk immediately. If that is the case, the fund may take out a standardised Credit Default Swap (CDS) contract with a bank, probably written on a basket of bonds issued by the same corporate. There would be basis risk from any mismatch in the bonds,

---

[2] When the Bank of England takes collateral, it is solely to guard against the risk of default and so all correlations in that state of the world are relevant to what collateral is taken and the haircuts applied. See Breeden and Whisker (2010).

so the CDS is not an exact hedge, but in most scenarios, holding the bond and the CDS contract together will ensure a substantial reduction in the net value of the market position, compared with holding the bond alone. The fund could then unwind the CDS contract simultaneously with slowly selling the cash bond. In short, the superior liquidity of the more homogeneous CDS market (which benefits from relatively elastic gross supply) enables the pension fund to reduce the execution costs of its portfolio management whilst not sacrificing its nimbleness in terms of market risk management.

In this example, the strategy seems reasonable. The probability that the corporate defaults in the few months the strategy takes to execute is probably pretty low, and the joint probability of the corporate and bank defaulting is even less. In essence, the CDS protection is not really being used to insure against default but to reduce market price volatility.

Let us now turn to a second example of **a bank hedging its corporate lending**. Banks lend to a broad range of companies. In many cases they would be expected to hold these loans on their books until maturity (as opposed to selling them off to other investors). In order to reduce its measured outstanding credit risk, a bank may choose to purchase offsetting CDS protection, probably on a portfolio of loans. By so doing, the bank can make greater use of its internal credit risk limits and may get regulatory capital relief. In most cases, another leveraged market participant (bank or hedge fund) would write the CDS. (In some cases the insurance provider may be an unlevered institution, for which most of the concerns below would be reduced.)

In the first example, the pension fund was concerned about short-term price swings. In this second example, the bank should be concerned to protect itself against clusters of defaults. But if the risk management of the ensuing portfolio of loans and CDS is not done with serious attention paid to the joint risk profile of the corporate borrowers and the providers of the CDS protection, the true net risk position might be worse than it appears. That could fool regulators as well as the bank's own risk management function. Any risk management framework that is driven by the correlation structure of short-term moves alone would most likely be proven too rosy in the event of clusters of defaults. The issue is that the correlation structure locally may be very different from that in the tail of the distribution. Of course, there are many practical problems in analysing what could happen statistically in the tails, since these scenarios are, by definition, rare and the payoffs may be non-linear.[3]

---

[3] See Haldane and Webber (2008) for a wider discussion of the problems in pricing tail risk and Gennaioli et al. (2012) for the possible consequences.

Taking this second example a little further, assume that most big banks follow similar strategies. Most banks will then end up with a more diversified credit portfolio than if each bank was only holding the loans it originated itself, but they may also end up with similar portfolios of risk. In such a scenario, the system can easily absorb small shocks, but because of the diversification, a really big shock may threaten to bring down all of them instead of just the ones that happened to have originated the most problematic loans. In a very inter-connected financial system, it can be almost self-fulfilling that when the market starts to think some of the banks are in trouble, in fact all of them are.[4]

A third example in this section is the dynamic hedging strategy of a bank's credit risk arising from its derivatives portfolio (**Credit/ Counterparty Valuation Adjustment: CVA hedging**). This normally refers to the credit risk of a counterparty that is not directly offset by some form of collateral.[5] Suppose a corporate has issued a fixed rate bond because investor preference makes that the best value, but really it wants to have a floating rate liability. A bank will accommodate this by providing an interest rate swap. If interest rates go up, that swap may generate a net value owing to the bank. Receiving that value depends on the corporate not defaulting and so the bank will have a credit exposure to the corporate. But the corporate cannot be expected to post collateral – it will just regard its debt as having been converted to floating rate (and typically it won't hold any collateral it could post anyway). A bank that is active in these interest rate swaps will end up with a large number of such mark-to-market exposures. Collectively, the resulting exposures constitute a credit portfolio which changes with the mark-to-market values of the underlying derivatives contracts. To manage the credit risks embedded in this so-called CVA portfolio, most banks will hedge dynamically in the CDS market. This is usually a very effective risk management technique during periods when CDS markets function normally. But it is worth emphasising that the embedded 'jump to default' risks in credit products, coupled with liquidity issues during times of extreme stress, can make it very difficult to execute a dynamic hedging strategy in stressed conditions.

In addition, and as already noted, CVA hedging is likely to be undertaken by buying CDS from another bank or a hedge fund. In this example we have tail-risk correlation not just with corporate and counterparty risk but with CDS market liquidity. If proper consideration is not given to the correlation structure, the danger is clearly that the

---

[4] See for example Haldane (2009) for a discussion on the inter-connectedness of the financial system.

[5] Bank of England (2010).

realised outcome in extreme scenarios would look very different from what was expected by senior management, regulators, etc., based on local analysis. Much of this risk can now be mitigated by collateralising the mark-to-market value of the CDS: that doesn't reduce the overall amount of risk but it can spread crystallisation of the risk over time. And there remains a 'gap risk' in the event of an actual default by the counterparty.

A fourth example from the recent crisis was the **'super senior' credit exposure from pools of US mortgage loans** reinsured with monoline insurance companies (MBIA, FGIC, AMBAC, etc.) or other insurers such as AIG. Banks and other originators of leveraged credit risk (either in cash form of CDOs or CLOs, or in its synthetic forms) needed to warehouse excess 'super-senior' tranches, which were considered virtually risk free, to support the origination business. After the volatility experienced in 2005, banks started to worry about controlling the mark-to-market volatility, even though the fundamental risk initially continued to be considered negligible. The idea came to lay off a significant portion of this negligible economic risk to reduce the short- and medium-term price volatility. Similar risk reduction processes largely worked for traditional corporate credit risk, but proved disastrous in the case of super-senior risk backed by US subprime mortgages. Insurance by the monolines proved practically worthless as they successively failed. And reinsurance with AIG would have proved worthless if AIG had not been rescued by the US government. The problems affected other securities in unexpected ways – at one point, US municipal debt wrapped by monolines was trading at a discount to the same debt without a wrap.

Once a default event has occurred, the correlation problems with such contracts become obvious. The question is why they are not apparent *ex ante*. The normal motivation for insurance is risk aversion to large losses arising through tail events. If such an insurance contract is worth having, one must be able to envision the tail event happening and what the circumstances might be. Why was it so hard to anticipate what would happen if there were losses on large numbers of bonds insured by monoline insurers which had relatively small amounts of capital?

One reason why such risks may not be appreciated *ex ante* is overreliance on local risk measures such as VaR (value at risk) or other historical average correlations, and not enough on severe stress tests over different horizons. For example, in the United States it was widely believed that house prices would not fall significantly nationally (it had never happened since the Great Depression in the 1930s). We assert that, if one had stressed bank capital in the US with the explicit assumption that national residential real estate prices could go down 30 to 40%, and in some local markets more, most of the losses for US banks could have been correctly predicted (at least if the complexities of structured credit products were properly assessed[6]). The collapse of functioning inter-bank money markets and other 'run-on-the-bank' phenomena obviously added further costs, but the first-order effect was caused by residential house prices falling. The key, however, was to correctly predict what that kind of price drop would do to other market participants, and market structures, as well as to the individual firm. Extreme stress tests have served a crucial purpose after the crisis to re-establish confidence in banks, and might usefully play a wider role in more aspects of on-going bank oversight.

An additional concern is that many of the transactions suffering from this risk may have been entered into for portfolio management reasons (such as the pension fund example) or regulatory capital relief and other 'window dressing' purposes rather than genuinely to protect against default. Net exposure numbers quoted on earnings calls, or stress losses reported to regulators, can all be made to look more palatable if the insurance is apparently in place, while the true risks in the event of default may not have changed much.

These issues raise general questions for market structure with trade-offs that are far from trivial. Is it beneficial for, say, banks to lay off sovereign risk with other banks and other leveraged financial institutions such as hedge funds, or does the ensuing web of contingent exposures across leveraged institutions *increase* the systemic risks? It seems that many of these arrangements increase diversification in the case of small- and medium-size stress scenarios, but may actually exacerbate the systemic implications in the case of very large shocks.[7] These arrangements also highlight the delicacy of the appropriate regulatory structure. In many instances, subject to sufficient diversification, tail risks might be better borne by so-called 'real money' investors, i.e. insurance companies, pension funds and traditional long-only bond and equity funds, as these investor categories operate with little or no leverage. In case of massive shocks, these investors could be better suited to absorb the losses, as there is limited leverage to trigger further spillovers through defaults or panic driven asset sales. Many of these investor groups are, however, subject to an extensive regulatory framework, making them unable to hold such risks in their portfolios, in many cases even as a

---

[6] This caveat might seem an important element of hindsight. But one reason why the complexities were not addressed was the assumption – based on local correlations – that the fundamental risk was negligible.

[7] A general idea explored by Acharya (2009) in a somewhat different context. See also Haldane (2009) and Nier et al. (2008).

very small fraction of total assets. There is a potentially difficult trade-off here between public policy objectives of appropriate investor protection and systemic stability considerations that probably deserves to be debated more fully. It is clear, however, that highly leveraged institutions such as banks and hedge funds are not really suited to be the ultimate repositories of extreme tail risk.[8]

What does all of the above tell us? The answer may seem trivial *ex post* but if these issues had been highlighted and subjected to more transparency, we believe that the ultimate outcome could have been different. A lot of the surprise seemed to come from the fact that virtually all risk management had been done within a 'local' framework, rather than genuinely extreme stress tests. If regulators, rating agencies or, for that matter, bond and equity investors had demanded analysis based on extreme stress tests, many of the repercussions in the system could have been identified. The main point is that a stress test has to be internally consistent. As an example, if you stress test a 30–40% fall in US residential real estate prices and that shows your institution would be in trouble, you need to make consistent assumptions about the deteriorating credit conditions of your counterparties, anyone that provides reinsurance and general market conditions.

At some level, there is always a stress scenario that forces bankruptcy. Perhaps the greatest sin in the years preceding the financial crisis was blatantly ignoring what really would happen if the 'unthinkable' drop in US house prices actually happened.[9] Some major institutions seemed to have had no grasp of how risky their exposures really were, despite spending millions of dollars on risk management and while being inspected by regulators on an on-going basis. By addressing these issues, the stress tests implemented by the Federal Reserve in the United States, and by the European Banking Authority in Europe, could eventually play a key role in re-establishing confidence in the banking system.[10]

---

[8] Nor, of course, should the public sector be expected to socialise losses from tail events!

[9] Since the crisis, many firms are now considering the previously unthinkable, e.g. the sustainability of sovereign debt, liquidity in core markets, etc.

[10] The recently announced 'Comprehensive Capital Analysis and Review 2012' seems to contain a lot of the features we have highlighted, as the Federal Reserve is continuing its efforts to re-establish market confidence in the most systemically important banks (firms with assets above $50 bn) in the United States with the help of stress tests. In particular, it is worth noting that the supervisory stress scenario is far from benign, but in fact assumes a further drop in the National House Price Index from 136.9 in Q3 2011 to a trough of 108.1 in Q1 2014, a peak in the unemployment rate at 13% in 2013, and a real GDP decline of more than 4% in the next year. This scenario is clearly not what anyone expects, but simply an exercise to force banks and others to analyse contingency plans under an extreme set of circumstances, and thus ensure credibility. See Federal Reserve System (2012).

5.3   Reputational risks in tail events

The second category of contracts we want to examine can be put into more of a game theoretic framework, where the perceived payoff in the tail event is offset by 'unforeseen' costs. In this section, we are focusing on behaviour that, at first glance, may seem irrational, but is best understood as being driven by classic time inconsistency. In particular a market participant may voluntarily choose not to enforce a contract that is 'in the money', if the reputational repercussions are perceived to cause more damage than whatever could be gained financially by enforcement.

During the crisis, banks moved a significant amount of their mortgage-based assets off-balance sheet into **structured investment vehicles (SIVs)**. Most of the funding for these SIVs came from publicly sold asset-backed commercial paper (ABCP) and other medium-term notes (MTN). There was a small amount of equity in the form of a junior 'capital note', which split the excess return with the asset manager. From their invention by Citigroup in 1988 until the crisis, there was sufficient spread between the assets and the funding to generate a reasonable return to attract investors to buy the capital notes. In addition, there was typically a partial backstop liquidity facility provided by the originating bank. When all the capital notes had been sold, there was no economic risk retained by the originating bank except the backstop facility, and only a management fee continued to accrue to the asset manager (typically, the originating bank).

When the crisis hit in autumn 2007, one of the first casualties was the closure of the ABCP markets and funding for the SIVs dried up. Beyond the liquidity lines, banks generally had very limited legal obligations to the SIVs (e.g. for credit losses on the assets) but most decided to accept responsibility for the assets and absorb them back on balance sheet or at least fund them directly. This was obviously done for reputational reasons and was viewed as less costly to the franchise than walking away.

Part of the explanation for banks' behaviour was that these structures were not necessarily designed to be profit centres, but rather to enhance capital efficiency for the bank. There was essentially a massive maturity mismatch between the banks' underlying assets and their funding. And the SIV structure effectively enabled the bank to isolate that mismatch and hence support its other businesses with the embedded lending in the assets that were being put into the SIVs.

The perception was that the quality of the underlying assets was so good that the risk of a real loss (as opposed to some shorter-term mark-to-market fluctuations) was negligible, and that the returns accruing to the capital note holders and the asset manager were largely due to the funding arbitrage. Another way of explaining it would be that, because of the difference in liquidity, the 'buffers' in the structure, the capital notes and the liquidity back-stop provider were effectively earning a risk premium for absorbing this liquidity mismatch between assets and liabilities. This view of the world made most of the capital note holders believe that the risk of any loss was very limited.

We now know all of that changed when subprime mortgage assets had become a significant portion of the assets in a typical SIV. The US housing market had started to slide and the lax underwriting standards started to show their impact on recovery rates. Suddenly, investors in the ABCP market came to realise that the risk of actual loss was very real and that a game of 'musical chairs' was unfolding in the roll-over process of the short-term debt. At this juncture, one would think that the optimal economic behaviour for the banks with outstanding SIVs would be to let the SIVs unwind according to the legal construct in place, rather than accept responsibility. In fact, all the banks except one decided to collapse the structures and repurchase the securities.[11]

From an investor protection standpoint, one may have drawn a sigh of relief, as any potential issues about misrepresented risk profile disappeared, but from a financial stability perspective, it was obviously disturbing. In a short space of time, billions of assets showed up on already over-extended bank balance sheets.

One may think it somewhat surprising that (almost) all the banks decided to absorb their SIVs, especially since it must have seemed likely that the SIV structure would not come back quickly as a viable funding structure. We believe that the main reason for doing this was that *not* doing so would have sent a distress signal to the market. In other words, if a bank chose not to absorb this problem, the perception would be that they simply could not afford to do it, thus telling the market that they were in even worse shape than previously feared. There may also have been an element of 'repeat game'. If one lets investors take the pain, then they may not return for future transactions.

It seems plausible that if the SIV crisis had transpired during a time when most other markets had remained functioning, the decision making process might have been very different. 'Signalling' is at its most powerful when the level of uncertainty in the system is highest.[12]

---

[11] The one notable exception was Standard Chartered, which let its 'Whistlejacket' SIV unwind.

[12] The issues arising from ABCP conduits were similar, although the structures were slightly different. The key difference from SIVs was that the underlying assets were largely purchased from third-parties and not necessarily in securities form.

We now want to turn to an example of a structure that did at least partially survive the crisis: **UK RMBS master trusts**. These are versatile structures that allow an issuer to transform a portfolio of assets into a very different investment product. In principle, the master trust purchases mortgages from the bank and issues tailored bullet-maturity securities. The assets and the liabilities can be very different, e.g. the demand for the securities may be stronger in US dollars than in sterling, so an FX swap converts the cash-flows into dollars. Or most of the mortgages may be floating rate, whereas investor demand is stronger for fixed-rate product, and an interest rate swap(s) converts the cash flows accordingly. Mortgages typically pay down somewhat randomly and relatively quickly, whereas investors prefer straight-bullet maturities. The master trust can accommodate this by allowing on-going reinvestments of the pay downs and conversely allowing the trust to put assets back to the bank if the cash-flows are not sufficient to make a particular principal repayment. The downside is clearly that the on-going linkages between the issuer and the trust remain very strong, and it is thus hard to identify where economic risks ultimately reside.

RMBS master trust securitisations are designed to be called on their bullet maturity date and that is how they were priced and traded. In one case that didn't happen: in November 2008 it was announced that the £40bn 'Granite' master trust had failed a non-asset trigger[13] which meant that Northern Rock would no longer provide new mortgages to the structure and it went into pass-through mode (early amortisation). Instead of owning bullet securities, the investors ended up holding potentially long-dated pass-through notes. Trading in the securities effectively ceased and, because of the maturity extension, the securities issued by Granite fell precipitously in price – even though there had been no material credit losses.[14] The subordinated securities would only be paid off after enough cash had come in to first pay off the senior bonds. As Northern Rock had already been nationalised, the dynamic around the decision to run-off Granite was obviously quite different from what other banks were grappling with at the time. This event clearly 'burnt' a number of investors, many of whom have indicated that they will not return to purchase any master trust structure in future. In pure economic terms, it might have paid other banks also to not call RMBS when

---

[13] After the 'current seller share' had fallen below its minimum on two successive distribution dates – the company's own investment in the vehicle had not been maintained at a high enough level. See Northern Rock (2008).

[14] By the end of 2008, the price of Granite's AAA and AA tranches had fallen by around 30% and 40% respectively.

funding pressures were at their highest. But this would have destroyed the market and damaged relations with investors, possibly beyond repair.

Another example is the existence of **break clauses in derivatives contracts**. These clauses enable either counterparty to a derivatives trade to call for cash settlement of the mark-to-market of their contract at a particular future date. The main reason for this 'break clause' is that it reduces the contingent credit exposure. Think in terms of a simple fixed-for-floating swap for 10 years. (This transaction could be to convert a company's fixed-rate bond issue into a floating-rate liability, for example.) The bank pays a fixed rate in exchange for receiving a floating rate (say, LIBOR) from the corporate that issued the bond. If no break clause exists, the bank's credit department would price the contingent credit exposure to the corporate over the full life of the contract. This could be very high: a substantial rise in short-term interest rates would make the bank effectively owed a significant amount of money by the corporate. The bank needs to factor in that with this 'gain' there is an associated risk of default of the corporate. In reality, one can think of all these contingent credit exposures as the modern derivatives book's 'loan portfolio'. It is equivalent to a traditional loan book, except that it dynamically changes in line with market prices. The credit risk is obviously bigger when the creditworthiness of a company is lower and when the maturity is longer.

The bank's credit department will therefore calculate a credit spread that it will charge on top of the 'risk free' swap level (that would be charged between financial institutions that fully collateralise any mark-to-market swings). For a longer-dated swap, this charge may be very large. Introducing a break clause allowing either counterparty to terminate the contract effectively shortens the maturity of the swap, since the bank (or the company, in case it is owed money and the bank's credit appears more shaky) can contractually demand payment at that time. In reality, most corporates do not expect such a break clause ever to be exercised.

The concern would be that, if the corporate expects the bank to ignore the break clause regardless of the circumstances, exercising the clause would be a surprise for which the firm may not have put appropriate contingencies in place – perhaps even making default more likely. Or that the market may start to interpret the enforcement of 'break clauses' as a sign of weakness on the bank's part. In other words, such behaviour could be seen as so antagonising to customers that a bank would only do it if it is absolutely desperate. Yet if the bank cannot in fact enforce the break clause, its credit pricing and risk management has been faulty.

Another example, comprising elements of the break clause and the SIV problem, is the behaviour of managers of money market funds when faced with the prospect of **'breaking the buck'**.

A money market fund calculates its net asset value (NAV) on a daily basis. The NAV is its price per share, which reflects the total value of the fund's investment holdings. Traditional money market funds seek to maintain a constant NAV (CNAV funds), i.e. they invest with the explicit goal of maintaining a stable NAV of $1.00 per share. Investors like this because it avoids any market price fluctuations in their investments.

A CNAV money market fund is said to 'break the buck' when its NAV falls below $1.00 per share (or the equivalent in a fund's respective currency). This is a rare event. Prior to the crisis, it had not happened to a US money market fund since the Community Bankers US Government Fund broke the buck in 1994.[15] The conventional perception was that the principal should be 'safe'. When money funds came under pressure during the crisis, more than 60 asset managers (among others, Wachovia and Legg Mason) unilaterally made up more than $12 billion of losses.[16]

On 16 September 2008, the Prime Reserve Fund, the oldest US money market fund, wrote off 3 cents of losses on Lehman Brothers. Not being able to make up the losses, the fund was left with a NAV of $0.97, triggering a 'run' in the money markets. On 19 September 2008, the US Treasury announced the establishment of a temporary one-year guarantee programme to protect investors in money market funds. The funds that were eligible had to pay a fee to participate in the programme, and any fund that had already 'broken the buck' could not participate.

This example raises several interesting issues. In keeping with previous examples, it illustrates the extreme non-contractual lengths some of the asset managers were willing to go to in order to protect their reputations. It also shows how the equivalent of a 'bank run' can happen in the shadow banking system. And it shows the potential importance of public sector support – another complicating factor that makes the true risks in a tail event difficult to assess.

As a final example in this section, we have Deutsche Bank's decision in December 2008 *not* **to call a lower tier 2 subordinated debt issue** (a € 1bn 2004/2014 bond with a call date of 16 January 2009), despite the fact that it was customary for banks to call such bonds at the first possible date. The reason that this is interesting is that it was actually economically rational in isolation for Deutsche Bank not to call, and it

---

[15] In Japan, money market funds lost much of their appeal after principal losses due to Enron-related investments, and investors largely returned to bank deposits.

[16] See Brewster and Chung (2008) and the *Financial Times* and Moody's Investor Service August 9, 2010.

was fully within its right not to do so, but still there was a very adverse short-term reaction,[17] with some investors threatening to end all dealings with the firm. Subsequently the decision appeared justified since it was followed by similar non-calls by other institutions and Deutsche Bank was able to keep market access and to successfully issue further capital instruments in the months thereafter.

The theme we have encountered in these examples is that many of the decisions taken during times of extreme pressure seem to be affected by (apparent) considerations outside of the immediate financial contract – at least, rejecting options which were perceived to be acceptable when the original contract was struck. Or that the financial consequences of particular decisions were more adverse for the decision maker (or more generally the markets) than anticipated. In that sense they are classic examples of time inconsistency. We have tried to illustrate how acting narrowly rationally when it is perceived to be outside the realm of 'what is normally done' can carry massive risks. The problem that this creates is that, when we are dealing with tail events and disaster insurance, it is hard to determine *ex ante* what such insurance contracts (or options delivering insurance) are worth. How should investors and regulators evaluate these contracts? If the reputation and signalling implications of exercising are too damaging in the case of extreme stress, it would be naive to attribute full value to them when determining the risk profile and hence the appropriate capital buffer. It is also worrying from a financial stability perspective if these considerations force possible systemic implications to be more extreme rather than less.

5.4   Stress tests and contract design considerations

So what have we learned? The first set of examples above highlighted the need to critically evaluate contingent exposures: without true stress correlations, tail events will not be captured properly. We believe more emphasis should be put on this by investors, analysts and regulators alike.

Inevitably that means severe stress tests involving 'jump to default' risk and the need to consider counterparty and market liquidity risks, not just issuer risks in these circumstances. Some banks have told us that they think they should not be required to hold capital and liquidity to deal with such extreme tail events – leaving the public sector to be the capital provider of last resort. But that leads directly to moral hazard and excessive risk-taking. Tail events seem to happen far more often

---

[17] Indicative calculations show that, by April 2009, the price of Deutsche Bank's callable debt relative to its non-callable debt had fallen by around 20%. See chart 3.23 in Bank of England (2011).

than people assume[18] and if the risks were properly acknowledged at the outset, many structures would be avoided or risks re-structured so as to limit losses in the event of tail risks. That has obvious implications for financial stability.

A crucial component of this analysis is the proper design of stress tests. Obviously, scenarios have to be rather draconian in order to serve the purpose of challenging the 'unthinkable', but at the same time there are difficult decisions to be made, for example, in deciding how much bank capital (contingent or not) banks should hold – and what the probability is of it being wiped out. We believe that it is better to have a collection of *ex ante* determined stress scenarios that illustrate banks' potential weaknesses publicly, even if the actual regulatory capital is not sufficient in all those scenarios. In other words, stress tests should not always be a checklist 'pass' or 'fail' (after all, to make a bank fail or pass a stress test is just a question of scaling the test). Comparable, tail event stress tests could be an important piece in the information set that investors and regulators analyse to determine the relative value and risk profile of the institution.

The second set of examples above illustrated that contract design features which are exclusively relevant in the extreme tails are perhaps best avoided. The reason is simply that such features, which do not seem to matter in most states of the world, end up being treated as if they will never matter. In other words, market participants need to make sure that an exercise of an option is seen as just that, a normal exercise of an option. No more and no less. Sophisticated market participants should not be genuinely surprised (or feign surprise) when another market participant tries to optimise its behaviour consistent with a contract. The implications of a contract should be clear and the structures should be as transparent as possible.

As the debate about adequate capital levels for banks rages on, we feel that it is important to keep these lessons in mind. Whatever is decided in terms of capital requirements, the numbers should be calculated with tail event analysis in mind.

5.5   A new example: contingent capital securities

One present issue is that, given banks will need to hold much more capital in future, how could that best be achieved? Some have called for very high levels of equity capital in banks;[19] others have been focusing on requirements to raise new equity before it is too late, e.g. mandatory

---

[18] How many 'once-in-a-lifetime' events happen to us every year?
[19] See Admati *et al.* (2010).

rights issues.[20] We find contingent capital securities – so-called co-cos – to be a potentially attractive proposition for a number of reasons.

One has to evaluate contingent capital on how it would perform in a crisis. First, the funding for extra capital is already in place. In other words, no one has to scramble to execute a contingency plan, or convince someone to come up with new cash in a difficult situation. Obviously, conversion is consistent with a bank being under stress, but if conversion was always automatic, not discretionary, that could help to avoid signalling even wider problems.

Second, and related to the examples in this chapter, because the contingent conversion feature is explicit, no investor should be able to say that 'equity conversion' could never have been anticipated. As new mechanisms are being explored, we believe that it is crucial that investors correctly assess and price the probability of conversion into common equity.

Third, sufficient level of contingent capital should enable a well-run bank to still operate with significant leverage and thus earn a healthy return. In the more extreme suggestions for the amount of contingent capital, one would very substantially change the return profile of common equity for banks, perhaps creating an entirely new investor category.

There are two lessons from this chapter which should be applied to contingent capital instruments. First it has been suggested to us by market contacts that the trigger point in existing contingent instruments is such that many investors have bought them on the assumption that these contingent capital securities never will be called (or worse, that there will be official support before that point). If that were to be the foundation for this market, we believe that the very purpose of contingent capital may be subverted, creating a risk to financial stability in a crisis situation. The whole point of contingent capital securities should be that the recapitalisation is triggered without any grand repercussions, making it easier than raising fresh capital in the market. If triggering the conversion were to cause the sort of damage reported in our examples above, then the market could be severely disrupted just when it was most needed. The contract design must therefore reflect a need for the trigger to be as smooth as possible.

One potential mitigant would be to have a range of trigger levels, so no single level becomes a focal point for indicating severe distress. It would be helpful if actual conversions happened reasonably frequently and not only in a rare crisis, demystifying the whole process. One would also need

---

[20] See Duffie (2010).

to make sure that the maturity profile was such that no dominant amount of contingent capital was rolled at any one point in time. There could be an on-going process of monitoring, rather than particular trigger dates that may cause a focus for a 'run' during times of stress.

Stress tests could also be one of the tools to force conversion of contingent capital securities by bank regulators. In addition to the accounting based capital trigger, capital requirements could be expressed in terms of what scenarios a bank has to be able to withstand, with capital securities triggered when the existing common equity is not sufficient.

One argument that has been raised against contingent capital has been the lack of a natural investor base, reflecting market segmentation between 'credit', 'rates' and 'equity' investors. We believe strongly that market segmentation is an inefficiency which should not be taken as a given; there are already regular convertible debt securities with an investor base. New market segments can be created if the risk-return trade-off is appropriate. The new issues (Credit Suisse and Rabobank), have so far been very well received and we are aware of plans for funds being created to invest in these instruments. We see every reason to believe that new vehicles for owning contingent capital instruments can be created and existing mandates modified to allow them, as long as the market sees these securities as an asset class that will develop and reach critical scale, and subject to the normal market discipline of risk and return.

This plays into a second lesson from the crisis. It is obviously crucial from a financial stability standpoint that contingent capital securities do not end up largely in the hands of other highly leveraged financial institutions, where losses could cause further spillovers and thus generate financial instability. We believe that regulators could play a constructive role in allowing a broad range of 'real money' investors to own sensible amounts of this systemic risk.

5.6   Conclusion

In this chapter, we have given a number of examples taken from the financial crisis, where financial contracts undertaken for hedging purposes, or with optional features designed to protect the issuer or the investor, have not had the value expected at precisely the time when they needed to. These now look like classic time inconsistency problems coupled with partial equilibrium analysis. To avoid these pitfalls, a more extensive use of extreme and holistic stress tests could be used to assess individual counterparties as well as systemic risks. It would also be worthwhile to debate further where these tail risks should be held, as leveraged financial institutions pose larger systemic risks than more traditional unlevered investor categories. Such considerations need to be carefully weighed against other investor protection concerns. We believe that a properly designed stress testing framework could provide a basis for a balanced discussion around future risk concentrations and systemic vulnerabilities.

References

Acharya, V. (2009). A theory of systemic risk and design of prudential bank regulation, *Journal of Financial Stability*.

Admati, A. R., DeMarzo, P. M., Hellwig, M. F., and Pfleiderer, P. (2010). Fallacies, irrelevant facts and myths in the discussion of capital regulation: why bank equity is not expensive, Stanford GSB Research Paper No. 2065.

Breeden, S. and Whisker, R. (2010). Collateral risk management at the Bank of England, Bank of England *Quarterly Bulletin*, Q2, 94–103.

Bank of England (2010). *Quarterly Bulletin*, Q2, **50**, 81.

Bank of England (2011). *Financial Stability Report*, December.

Brewster, D. and Chung, J. (2008). Fear of monetary market funds 'breaking the buck'. *Financial Times*. 17 September.

Duffie, D. (2010). Contractual methods for out-of-court restructuring of systemically important financial institutions, in Scott K. E., Schulz, G. P. and Taylor, J. B. (eds.), *Ending Government Bailouts as We Know Them*. Stanford: Hoover Institution Press.

Federal Reserve System (2012). *Comprehensive Capital Analysis and Review*. http://www.federalreserve.gov/newsevents/press/bcreg/bcreg20120313a1.pdf

The *Financial Times* and Moody's Investor Service (August 9, 2010). *Sponsor Support Key to Money Market Funds*.

Gennaioli, N., Schleifer, A. and Vishny, R. W. (2012). Neglected risks, financial innovation and financial fragility, *Journal of Financial Economics*, **104**(3), 452–468.

Haldane, A. (2009). Re-thinking the financial network. Financial Student Association, Amsterdam. www.bankofengland.co.uk/publications/Documents/speeches/2009/speech386.pdf.

Haldane, A. and Webber, L. (2008). Risk reallocation, *Risk*. July, 51–53.

Nier, E. W., Yang, J., Yorulmazer, T. and Alentorn A. (2008). Network models and financial stability, Bank of England Working Paper No. 346.

Northern Rock (2008). *Annual Report and Accounts*, 25–6.

Squam Lake Working Group on Financial Regulation (July 2009). *Credit Default Swaps, Clearing Houses, and Exchanges*. http://i.cfr.org/content/publications/attachments/squam_lake_working_paper5.pdf

Part II

New techniques

6 Compound autoregressive processes and defaultable bond pricing

Alain Monfort and Jean-Paul Renne

6.1 Introduction

Various yield spreads have attracted a lot of attention since the onset of the current financial crisis. For instance, (a) the spreads between interbank unsecured rates and the overnight index swaps – the so-called LIBOR-OIS spreads – gauging market concerns regarding banks' solvency and liquidity, (b) the spreads between corporate bonds and their Treasuries counterparts and, more recently, (c) sovereign spreads can all be seen as thermometers for the intensity of the crisis developments.[1] These spreads reflect market-participants' assessment of the risks ahead and therefore contain information that is key for both policymakers and investors. In particular, meaningful information is embedded in the *term-structure* of those spreads and in its dynamics. In order to optimally extract this information, one has to rely on term-structure models. In several respect, the ongoing financial crisis has highlighted the limits of many dynamic term-structure models, notably those that are not able to accommodate non-linearities, stochastic volatilities or switching regimes.

The aim of the present chapter is to propose a general and tractable strategy to model the dynamics of the term structure of defaultable-bond yields. To achieve this, we rely on the properties of compound autoregressive (Car) processes. The usefulness of these processes in the building of risk-free (non-defaultable) bond pricing models is now well documented (see Darolles, Gouriéroux and Jasiak, 2006, Gouriéroux and Monfort, 2007, Monfort and Pegoraro, 2007 or Le, Singleton and

We are grateful to Alain Durré and to an anonymous referee for helpful comments and suggestions. The views expressed in this chapter are ours and do not necessarily reflect the views of the Banque de France.

[1] For the LIBOR-OIS spread, see e.g. Taylor and Williams (2009) or Sengupta and Tam (2008); for corporate credit spreads, see e.g. Gilchrist and Zakrajšek (2011); for sovereign spreads see e.g. Borgy et al. (2011), Longstaff et al. (2011) or Monfort and Renne (2012).

142 *Alain Monfort and Jean-Paul Renne*

Da, 2011). On the contrary, the number of papers using Car processes in defaultable-bond pricing models is small.[2]

Beyond the search for a good fit to the data, our approach is aimed at exploring potential credit-risk premia present in bond yields. Such risk premia are likely to enter bond prices as soon as the underlying credit risk – that reflects the risk that the issuer defaults – can not be diversified away and is correlated with investors' utility. Because of risk premia, extracting so-called 'market expectations' from asset prices under the assumption that investors are risk neutral is misleading. As regards risk-free bond yields, risk premia account for the failure of the expectations hypothesis (EH). Under the latter, long-term yields should be equal to the expectation of future short-term ones (till bond maturity). Most empirical studies, however, suggest that this assumption does not hold (see e.g. Campbell and Shiller, 1991) and the difference between observed long-term bonds and the yields that would prevail under the EH are attributed to risk premia that are called *term premia*. The same kind of hypothesis tends to be rejected in the case of credit spreads: for instance, Huang and Huang (2002) show that only a small part of average credit spreads can be accounted for by expectations of default-related loss rates, pointing to the existence of risk premia associated with credit risk.

Our framework is consistent with the existence of such *credit risk premia* in credit spreads and further, it allows us to study the dynamics of these. These risk premia stem from the specification of a stochastic discount factor (sdf). In that context, the physical and the risk-neutral dynamics of the pricing factors – and notably the default process – do not coincide. The risk-neutral dynamics is the dynamics of the pricing factors that would be consistent with observed prices under the (potentially false) assumption that investors are risk-neutral. In our framework, we can assess the size of the (potential) errors that are implied by assuming that the historical and the risk-neutral dynamics coincide. A typical example lies in the computation of market-based probabilities of default (PDs). To get these, the vast majority of practitioners or market analysts resort to approaches ending up with risk-neutral PDs.[3] While risk-neutral PDs are relevant for pricing purposes, historical ones are

---

[2] See Gouriéroux, Monfort and Polimenis (2006), Monfort and Renne (2012) and (2013), Gouriéroux et al. (2012).

[3] Most of these methodologies build on Litterman and Iben (1991), see e.g. (amongst many others) Bank of England (2012), CMA Datavision (2011) and O'Kane and Turnbull (2003). Studies resorting to these methods are usually silent about this caveat. Notable recent exceptions include Blundell-Wignall and Slovik (2010), in an OECD study, who note: 'In the real world, actual defaults are fewer than market-driven default probability calculations would indicate. That is because market participants demand

needed (a) if one wants to extract real-world investors' perception of the credit quality of the issuer, (b) for the sake of forecasting or more generally (c) for risk management purposes. Regarding the latter point, note for instance that value-at-risk measures (VaR) should be based on the real-world measure and not on the risk-neutral one (see Gouriéroux and Jasiak, 2009).

Being able to identify risk premia is important from a policy perspective. In particular, in the context of the on-going financial crisis, Longstaff et al. (2011) stress the key importance of a better understanding of the so-called sovereign risk. To that respect, Borri and Verdelhan (2011) develop a theoretical model that highlights the central place of risk premia in the derivation of optimal borrowing and default decisions by sovereign entities. Exploiting the properties of Car processes, Monfort and Renne (2012) show that the present framework is appropriate to model the joint dynamics of euro-area sovereign spreads. Their results point to the importance of the risk premia to account for the dynamics of these spreads. In particular, during stress periods, these premia translate into wide deviations between risk-neutral and physical probabilities of default. In the present chapter, an empirical section supports Monfort and Renne's (2012) result by presenting an estimated model of Spanish sovereign spreads (versus Germany). Such findings are of significant interest in the current context where regulators want banks to model the *actual* default risk of even high-rated government bonds.[4]

In order to emphasise the fact that the appealing properties of the Car processes are needed in the risk-neutral world, but not necessarily in the historical world, we adopt a back modelling approach (see Bertholon, Monfort and Pegoraro, 2008), in which the risk-neutral dynamics and the short rate are specified in the first place, and where the historical dynamics is obtained through the specification of the stochastic discount factor. We show that we can obtain quasi-explicit formulas for the bond prices and therefore for the yields, even if the whole state vector is not Car in the risk-neutral world. Only the subvector appearing in the specification of the short rate and of the default intensities has to be Car. In particular, if we assume that these variables are not directly impacted by the individual default events, we obtain appealing linear formulas for the risky yields, both in the cases of zero and non-zero recovery rates.

[4] Regulators' views are expressed e.g. by Hannoun (2011) or Nouy (2011). As stressed by Carver (2012), these changes in regulation reveal the practitioners' lack of tools to extract actual default probabilities from market prices.

Once this modelling of the risk-neutral dynamics and of the short rate is done, and once possible internal consistency conditions are taken into account, the modelling of the historical dynamics through the stochastic discount rate is completely free and, hence, very flexible. In such a context, one can fully benefit from the discrete-time framework to ensure a good fitting of the data and to model potential interactions between the pricing factors. Modelling interactions between pricing factors is easier in discrete time than in continuous time since discrete-time models are much more flexible than continuous-time models (see e.g. Le et al., 2010 or Gouriéroux et al., 2006). Working with discrete-time models necessitates choosing a time unit adapted to the objective of the model and to the data. A specification for a given time unit implies a dynamics for all the time units which are multiples of the basic time unit, but not for the other time units, in particular those which are smaller than the basic one, contrary to the continuous-time specification. However, the implicit assumption of the continuous-time approach, namely that the dynamics corresponding to all time units (from the minute to the year, for instance) can be derived from a unique specification, is highly questionable. Moreover, the discrete versions of the continuous-time models are in general intractable, except in simple cases without practical interest, and are replaced by approximations for which the time consistency is lost. Finally, the discrete-time models obtained from a discretisation of a continuous-time model are often poor compared to those which can be introduced directly, like the ones proposed in this chapter.

The remainder of this chapter is organised as follows. Section 6.2 gives the definition of compound autoregressive processes and develops a recursive algorithm to compute multi-horizon Laplace transforms of the processes (which is key to deriving the term structure of yields). Section 6.3 details the risk-neutral dynamics and its pricing implications. After having introduced the stochastic discount factor, Section 6.4 derives the implied historical dynamics of the processes. Section 6.5 provides examples of Car processes. Section 6.6 presents possible estimation strategies. Section 6.7 proposes an application to the modelling of the term structure of Spanish sovereign spreads and Section 6.8 concludes.

6.2   Compound autoregressive processes

6.2.1   Definition

Let us define the compound autoregressive (Car) processes. An n-dimensional process w_t is called Car(p) if its conditional log-Laplace transform $\psi_{t-1}(u) = \ln E_{t-1} e^{u'w_t}$ is of the form

$$\psi_{t-1}(u) = a_1(u)'w_{t-1} + \cdots + a_p(u)'w_{t-p} + b(u), \qquad u \in \mathbb{R}^n,$$

where the a_i and b are some $\mathbb{R}$-valued functions and where E_{t-1} denotes the conditional expectation, given the past values of w_t: $\{w_{t-1}, w_{t-2}, \ldots, w_1\}$. It is straightforward to show that if w_t is Car(p), then $(w_t', \ldots, w_{t-p+1}')'$ is Car(1). Therefore, without loss of generality, we will focus on Car(1) processes in the following.

As will be shown below (Section 6.5), this class includes a large number of processes, e.g. Markov-switching Gaussian vector autoregressive, autoregressive gamma processes or quadratic functions of Gaussian processes. The reason why Car processes are central in termstructure modelling is that there exist quasi-explicit formulas to compute multi-horizon Laplace transforms. These formulas are provided in the following subsection.

6.2.2 *Multi-horizon Laplace transform*

Let us consider a multivariate Car(1) process w_t and its conditional Laplace transform given by $u \mapsto \exp\left[a'(u)w_{t-1} + b(u)\right]$. Let us further denote by $L_{t,h}(U_h)$ its multi-horizon Laplace transform given by

$$L_{t,h}(U_h) = E_t\left[\exp\left(u_h'w_{t+1} + \cdots + u_1'w_{t+h}\right)\right], \quad t = 1, \ldots, T,$$

where $U_h = (u_1', \ldots, u_h')$ is a given sequence of vectors.

Proposition 6.1 *We have, for any t,*

$$L_{t,h}(U_h) = \exp\left(A_h'w_t + B_h\right),$$

where the sequences A_h, B_h are obtained recursively by

$$A_h = a(u_h + A_{h-1}),$$
$$B_h = b(u_h + A_{h-1}) + B_{h-1},$$

with the initial conditions $A_0 = 0$ and $B_0 = 0$.

Proof It is straightforward to show that the formula is true for $h = 1$. If it is true for $h - 1$, we get:

$$\begin{aligned} L_{t,h}(U_h) &= E_t\left[\exp\left(u_h'w_{t+1}\right) E_{t+1}\left(\exp\left(u_{h-1}'w_{t+2} + \cdots + u_1'w_{t+h}\right)\right)\right] \\ &= E_t\left[\exp\left(u_h'w_{t+1}\right) L_{t+1,h-1}(U_{h-1})\right] \\ &= \exp\left[a(u_h + A_{h-1})'w_t + b(u_h + A_{h-1}) + B_{h-1}\right] \end{aligned}$$

and the result follows. $\qquad\qquad\qquad\qquad\qquad\qquad\qquad\qquad\qquad\square$

6.3   Risk-neutral modelling

6.3.1   *Assumptions*

The global new information in the economy at date t is $w_{G,t} = (w'_{c,t}, w'_{s,t}, d'_t)'$, where $w_{c,t}$ is a vector of common factors (for instance macroeconomic variables), $w_{s,t}$ is a vector $\left(w^{1'}_{s,t}, \ldots w^{n'}_{s,t}, \ldots w^{N'}_{s,t}\right)$ of specific variables, $w^n_{s,t}$ being associated with debtor n (for instance a firm or a country), and $d_t = \left(d^1_t, \ldots d^n_t, \ldots d^N_t\right)'$ is a vector of binary variables, d^n_t indicating whether entity n is in default ($d^n_t = 1$) or not ($d^n_t = 0$) at time t.

We assume that $\left(w'_{s,t}, d'_t\right)'$ does not Granger-cause $w_{c,t}$ in the risk-neutral ($\mathbb{Q}$) dynamics, that d_t does not Granger-$\mathbb{Q}$-cause $\left(w'_{c,t}, w'_{s,t}\right)'$ and that the $\left(w^{n'}_{s,t}, d^n_t\right)'$, $n = 1, \ldots, N$ are independent conditionally on $(w_{c,t}, \underline{w}_{G,t-1})$.

We introduce the notations $w_t = \left(w'_{c,t}, w'_{s,t}\right)'$ and $w^n_t = \left(w'_{c,t}, w^{n'}_{s,t}\right)'$. Further, we assume that, for any n, w^n_t is $\mathbb{Q}$-Car(1), which implies that w_t is also $\mathbb{Q}$-Car(1), and which includes the case where w_t is Car(p) as mentioned in Section 6.2. Therefore we have

$$E^{\mathbb{Q}}\left(\exp\left(u'w_t\right) \middle| \underline{w}_{G,t-1}\right) = E^{\mathbb{Q}}\left(\exp\left(u'w_t\right) \middle| \underline{w}_{t-1}\right)$$
$$= \exp\left(a^{\mathbb{Q}}(u)'w_{t-1} + b^{\mathbb{Q}}(u)\right). \quad (6.1)$$

We also assume that

$$\mathbb{Q}\left(d^n_t = 0 \middle| d^n_{t-1} = 0, \underline{w}_t\right) = \exp\left(-\lambda^{\mathbb{Q}}_{n,t}\right), \quad (6.2)$$

where

$$\lambda^{\mathbb{Q}}_{n,t} = \alpha_{0,n} + \alpha'_{1,n}w^n_t. \quad (6.3)$$

The risk-neutral default intensity $\lambda^{\mathbb{Q}}_{n,t}$ is close to the conditional default probability $\mathbb{Q}\left(d^n_t = 1 \middle| d^n_{t-1} = 0, \underline{w}_t\right)$ if it is small. We also assume that the default state is absorbing.

Finally, we assume that the risk-free short-term rate between t and $t+1$, which is known at t, only depends on $w_{c,t}$ and is given by

$$r_t = \beta_0 + \beta'_1 w_{c,t}. \quad (6.4)$$

6.3.2 Computation of the defaultable bond prices

Assuming first that the recovery rate is zero, the price at time t of a zero-coupon bond issued by entity n, with a residual maturity (at t) of h, is

$$B_n(t,h) = E_t^\mathbb{Q}\left(\exp\left(-r_t - \cdots - r_{t+h-1}\right)(1 - d_{t+h}^n)\right). \quad (6.5)$$

We have assumed that w_t is $\mathbb{Q}$-Car(1). However, it is easily seen that $\left(w_t', d_t^n\right)'$ is not $\mathbb{Q}$-Car.[5] Nevertheless, the causality structure described above implies that the computation of $B_n(t,h)$, for any h, boils down to the computation of a multi-horizon Laplace transform of w_t in which the coefficients are ordered backward and is therefore easily obtained (see Proposition 6.1 above).

Proposition 6.2 $B_n(t,h)$ *is obtained, for any h, from a multi-horizon $\mathbb{Q}$-Laplace transform of $w_{t+1}, \ldots, w_{t+h}$ in which the coefficients are ordered backward.*

Proof We proceed under the assumption that entity n is alive at date t, i.e. $d_t^n = 0$. We have

$$B_n(t,h) = E_t^\mathbb{Q}\left(\exp\left(-r_t - \cdots - r_{t+h-1}\right)(1 - d_{t+h}^n)\right)$$

$$= \exp\left(-r_t\right) E_t^\mathbb{Q}\left(\exp\left(-r_{t+1} - \cdots - r_{t+h-1}\right)(1 - d_{t+h}^n)\right).$$

Conditioning with respect to $\underline{w}_{t+h}$, we get

$$B_n(t,h) = \exp\left(-r_t\right) E_t^\mathbb{Q}\left(\exp\left(-r_{t+1} - \cdots - r_{t+h-1}\right)\right.$$

$$\left. \times \prod_{j=1}^{h} \mathbb{Q}\left(d_{t+j}^n = 0 \middle| d_{t+j-1}^n = 0, \underline{w}_{t+h}\right)\right).$$

Since d_t does not Granger-$\mathbb{Q}$-cause w_t and Granger non-causality is equivalent to Sims non-causality, we can replace $\underline{w}_{t+h}$ by $\underline{w}_{t+j}$ in the generic term of the product above and we get

$$B_n(t,h)$$

$$= \exp\left(-r_t\right) E_t^\mathbb{Q}\left(\exp\left(-r_{t+1} - \cdots - r_{t+h-1} - \lambda_{n,t+1}^\mathbb{Q} - \cdots - \lambda_{n,t+h}^\mathbb{Q}\right)\right)$$

$$= \exp\left(-h(\beta_0 + \alpha_{0,n}) - \tilde{\beta}_1' w_t^n\right) E_t^\mathbb{Q}\left(\exp\left(-(\tilde{\beta}_1 + \alpha_{1,n})' w_{t+1}^n - \cdots\right.\right.$$

$$\left.\left. -(\tilde{\beta}_1 + \alpha_{1,n})' w_{t+h-1}^n - \alpha_{1,n}' w_{t+h}^n\right)\right), \quad (6.6)$$

---

[5] See Monfort and Renne (2013).

where $\tilde{\beta}_1 = (\beta_1', 0)'$. So the expectation term in the previous equation is a multi-horizon Laplace transform of $w_{t+1}^n, \ldots, w_{t+h}^n$, with a sequence of coefficients $U_h = \{u_1, \ldots, u_h\}$ (see Proposition 6.1 for the definition of the u_i) defined by

$$u_1 = -\alpha_{1,n}, \quad u_j = -(\tilde{\beta}_1 + \alpha_{1,n}), \quad \forall j \geq 2. \tag{6.7}$$

$\square$

Given Proposition 6.1, the previous proposition implies that the yield $R_n(t, h)$ of a zero-coupon bond issued by debtor n with a residual maturity of h is of the form

$$R_n(t, h) = -\frac{1}{h} \log B_n(t, h)$$
$$= c_n(h)' w_t^n + f_n(h), \tag{6.8}$$

where the $c_n(h), f_n(h), h = 1, \ldots, H$ are computed from a unique recursive scheme.[6] We get an affine term structure of interest rates. It is important to stress that the $c_n(h)$ and the $f_n(h)$ have to be computed only once (they do not depend on t). Since these pricing formulas do not require the use of time-demanding simulations, this framework turns out to be very tractable and, hence, amenable to empirical estimation.

In that framework, it is easily seen that credit spreads, i.e. yields differentials between defaultable bonds and their risk-free counterpart (of the same maturity), are also affine functions of the factors w_t^n. Specifically, let us denote by $R^*(t, h)$ the yield of the risk-free bond with a residual maturity of h. By definition, the risk-free issuer is characterised by zero default intensity, that is, $\alpha_0^* = 0$ and $\alpha_1^* = 0$. Using the recursive algorithm, we get $c^*(h)$ and $f^*(h)$ coefficients that are such that

$$R^*(t, h) = c^*(h)' w_t^n + f^*(h),$$

where only the components of $c^*(h)$ that correspond to $w_{c,t}$ are non-zero. Thus, the credit spreads associated with entity n are simply given by

$$R_n(t, h) - R^*(t, h) = \left[c_n(h) - c^*(h) \right]' w_t^n + \left[f_n(h) - f^*(h) \right]. \tag{6.9}$$

6.3.3   Non-zero recovery rate

Building on the so-called recovery of market value assumption introduced by Duffie and Singleton (1999), Monfort and Renne (2013) show that, when the recovery rate is non-zero, the previous pricing machinery

---

[6] By 'unique' recursive scheme, we mean that only H recursions are needed to compute the $c_n(h)$ and the $f_n(h)$ for any $h \leq H$. This is obtained thanks to the fact that the sequence U_h defined by (6.7) corresponds to the beginning of a longer sequence.

is still valid if λ_t^n is replaced by a recovery-adjusted default intensity $\tilde{\lambda}_t^n$. Specifically, the recovery of market value assumption can be stated in the following manner: if the issuer defaults between the dates $t-1$ and t, the recovery payoff is equal to a fraction $\zeta_{n,t}$ – that can be a function of w_t^n – of the price that would have prevailed, absent the default of the issuer. In this context, the recovery adjusted default intensity is given by[7]

$$\exp(-\tilde{\lambda}_t^n) = \exp(-\lambda_{n,t}^{\mathbb{Q}}) + \left(1 - \exp(-\lambda_{n,t}^{\mathbb{Q}})\right)\zeta_{n,t}. \qquad (6.10)$$

Obviously, if $\zeta_{n,t} \equiv 0$, the recovery-adjusted intensity is equal to the default intensity and if $\zeta_{n,t} \equiv 1$, the bond turns out to be equivalent to a risk-free bond.

6.3.4   Internal-consistency conditions

The general framework of Section 6.3.1 contains the particular situation in which some components of w_t^n are yields $R_n(t, h_i)$, $i = 1, \ldots, I$. In this case, the coefficients $c_n(h)$ and $f_n(h)$ appearing in formula (6.8) must satisfy the conditions

$$c_n(h_i) = e_i, \; f_n(h_i) = 0,$$

where e_i is the selection vector picking the entry of w_t^n that correspond to $R_n(t, h_i)$.

6.4   Back to the historical world

6.4.1 $\mathbb{Q}$-dynamics, $\mathbb{P}$-dynamics, sdf and the short rate

The historical and risk-neutral conditional distributions of $w_{\mathrm{G},t}$ given $\underline{w}_{\mathrm{G},t-1}$ have probability density functions (pdf) with respect to a same measure, these pdfs are denoted respectively by $f^{\mathbb{P}}(w_{\mathrm{G},t} \mid \underline{w}_{\mathrm{G},t-1})$ and $f^{\mathbb{Q}}(w_{\mathrm{G},t} \mid \underline{w}_{\mathrm{G},t-1})$. Denoting by $M_{t-1,t}(\underline{w}_{\mathrm{G},t})$ the stochastic discount factor between $t-1$ and t, and by $r_{t-1}(\underline{w}_{\mathrm{G},t-1})$ the risk-free short rate between $t-1$ and t, we know that the four mathematical objects $f^{\mathbb{P}}$, $f^{\mathbb{Q}}$, $M_{t-1,t}$, r_{t-1} are linked by the relation[8]

---

[7] See Monfort and Renne (2013) for the proof.

[8] The existence, the unicity and the positivity of the sdf are consequences of the assumptions of existence, linearity and continuity of the pricing function and of the assumption of absence of arbitrage opportunity (see Bertholon, Monfort and Pegoraro, 2007). In the particular case where $w_{\mathrm{G},t}$ is a vector of prices of basic assets, this implies that the other prices are functions of the basic prices. This can be viewed as a completeness property. However, as usual in discrete-time models where the reallocation of portfolios is only allowed at discrete dates, exact replicating portfolios do not exist in general.

$$f^{\mathbb{Q}}(w_{\mathrm{G},t}|\underline{w}_{\mathrm{G},t-1}) = f^{\mathbb{P}}(w_{\mathrm{G},t}|\underline{w}_{\mathrm{G},t-1})M_{t-1,t}(\underline{w}_{\mathrm{G},t})\exp(r_{t-1}(\underline{w}_{\mathrm{G},t-1})), \tag{6.11}$$

Since $f^{\mathbb{Q}}(w_{\mathrm{G},t}|\underline{w}_{\mathrm{G},t-1})$ integrates to one, we have

$$E_{t-1}^{\mathbb{P}}(M_{t-1,t}) = \exp(-r_{t-1}(\underline{w}_{\mathrm{G},t-1})), \tag{6.12}$$

Equation (6.11) can also be written

$$f^{\mathbb{P}}(w_{\mathrm{G},t}|\underline{w}_{\mathrm{G},t-1}) = f^{\mathbb{Q}}(w_{\mathrm{G},t}|\underline{w}_{\mathrm{G},t-1})M_{t-1,t}^{-1}(\underline{w}_{\mathrm{G},t})\exp(-r_{t-1}(\underline{w}_{\mathrm{G},t-1})), \tag{6.13}$$

which implies

$$E_{t-1}^{\mathbb{Q}}M_{t-1,t}^{-1}(\underline{w}_{\mathrm{G},t}) = \exp(r_{t-1}(\underline{w}_{\mathrm{G},t-1})) \tag{6.14}$$

or

$$M_{t-1,t}(\underline{w}_{\mathrm{G},t}) = \frac{f^{\mathbb{Q}}(w_{\mathrm{G},t}|\underline{w}_{\mathrm{G},t-1})}{f^{\mathbb{P}}(w_{\mathrm{G},t}|\underline{w}_{\mathrm{G},t-1})}\exp(-r_{t-1}(\underline{w}_{\mathrm{G},t-1})). \tag{6.15}$$

In particular, (6.15) shows that once $f^{\mathbb{Q}}$ and r_{t-1} are specified, as we did above, $f^{\mathbb{P}}$ can be chosen arbitrarily and (6.15) gives the stochastic discount factor.

In this chapter, we assume that the sdf $M_{t-1,t}$ only depends on the common variables $\underline{w}_{\mathrm{c},t}$ or, equivalently, that the specific variables $\underline{w}_{\mathrm{s},t}$ and the individual default variables d_t have no direct impact on $M_{t-1,t}$. In this case $f^{\mathbb{P}}$ given by (6.13) is no longer arbitrary. More precisely, since we have assumed that $f^{\mathbb{Q}}(w_{\mathrm{G},t}|\underline{w}_{\mathrm{G},t-1})$ can be factorised as

$$f^{\mathbb{Q}}(w_{\mathrm{c},t}, w_{\mathrm{s},t}, d_t|\underline{w}_{\mathrm{G},t-1}) = f_{\mathrm{c}}^{\mathbb{Q}}(w_{\mathrm{c},t}|\underline{w}_{\mathrm{c},t-1})f_{\mathrm{sd}}^{\mathbb{Q}}(w_{\mathrm{s},t}, d_t|w_{\mathrm{c},t}, \underline{w}_{\mathrm{G},t-1}). \tag{6.16}$$

We see, by integrating both sides of (6.13) with respect to $(w_{\mathrm{s},t}, d_t)$ that

$$f_{\mathrm{c}}^{\mathbb{P}}(w_{\mathrm{c},t}|\underline{w}_{\mathrm{G},t-1}) = f_{\mathrm{c}}^{\mathbb{Q}}(w_{\mathrm{c},t}|\underline{w}_{\mathrm{c},t-1})M_{t-1,t}^{-1}(\underline{w}_{\mathrm{c},t})\exp(-r_{t-1}(\underline{w}_{\mathrm{c},t-1})). \tag{6.17}$$

Therefore, $(w_{\mathrm{s},t}, d_t)$ does not cause $w_{\mathrm{c},t}$ in the historical world and, moreover,

$$\begin{aligned} f_{\mathrm{sd}}^{\mathbb{P}}(w_{\mathrm{s},t}, d_t|\underline{w}_{\mathrm{c},t}, \underline{w}_{\mathrm{G},t-1}) &= \frac{f^{\mathbb{P}}(w_{\mathrm{c},t}, w_{\mathrm{s},t}, d_t|\underline{w}_{\mathrm{G},t-1})}{f_{\mathrm{c}}^{\mathbb{P}}(w_{\mathrm{c},t}|\underline{w}_{\mathrm{G},t-1})} \\ &= f_{\mathrm{sd}}^{\mathbb{Q}}(w_{\mathrm{s},t}, d_t|\underline{w}_{\mathrm{c},t}, \underline{w}_{\mathrm{G},t-1}). \end{aligned}$$

Hence the following proposition.

Proposition 6.3 *Under the causality assumptions defined in Section 6.3.1, and if $M_{t-1,t}$ only depends on the common variables $\underline{w}_{\mathrm{c},t}$:*

- $(w_{s,t}, d_t)$ *does not cause* $w_{c,t}$ *in the historical world;*
- *the conditional distribution of* $(w_{s,t}, d_t)$ *given* $(w_{c,t}, \underline{w}_{G,t-1})$ *are the same in both worlds.*

The assumptions made in Section 6.3.1 and the second part of the previous proposition imply that the historical conditional distribution of $w_{s,t}$ given $(w_{c,t}, \underline{w}_{G,t-1})$ is the same as in the risk-neutral world and that the functional forms of the risk-neutral default intensities given in (6.2) and (6.3) are also valid in the historical world:

$$\lambda_{n,t}^{\mathbb{P}} = \lambda_{n,t}^{\mathbb{Q}} = \alpha_{0,n} + \alpha'_{1,n} w_t^n. \tag{6.18}$$

However, it is important to stress that the risk-neutral and the historical dynamics of $\lambda_{n,t}^{\mathbb{P}}$ (and $\lambda_{n,t}^{\mathbb{Q}}$) are different because those of w_t are different. The fact that $\lambda_{n,t}^{\mathbb{P}} = \lambda_{n,t}^{\mathbb{Q}}$ is very important. Indeed, it means that we can compute historical – or real-world – default probabilities as soon as we know the historical dynamics of w_t and the parameterisations of the vectors $\alpha_{0,n}$ and $\alpha_{1,n}$. Given that (a) we observe the historical dynamics of the yields $R_n(t, h)$ and that (b) these yields are related to the factors w_t through the coefficients $c_n(h)$ and $f_n(h)$ that depend themselves on the $\alpha_{i,n}$s, it is possible to estimate the vectors $\alpha_{0,n}$ and $\alpha_{1,n}$ and the historical dynamics of the factors w_t (inference will be discussed in Section 6.6). This is exploited by Borgy et al. (2011) and Monfort and Renne (2012), who derive historical term structures of probabilities of default after having estimated some affine-term structure models.

6.4.2   Specification of the sdf

From formula (6.17) we see that once the risk-neutral dynamics of the common factors $w_{c,t}$ is specified as well as the function $r_{t-1}(w_{c,t-1})$, we can choose the historical dynamics of $w_{c,t}$ completely freely, and the sdf $M_{t-1,t}(\underline{w}_{c,t})$ is obtained as a by-product. However, in order to have a specification of $M_{t-1,t}(\underline{w}_{c,t})$ which is easily interpretable, it is usual to choose a particular form, for instance the exponential affine form:[9]

$$M_{t-1,t}(\underline{w}_{c,t}) = \exp\left(-r_{t-1}(\underline{w}_{c,t-1}) + \gamma(\underline{w}_{c,t-1})' w_{c,t} + \Psi_{t-1}^{\mathbb{Q}}(-\gamma(\underline{w}_{c,t-1}))\right),$$
$$\tag{6.19}$$

where $\Psi_{t-1}^{\mathbb{Q}}(u)$ is the risk-neutral conditional log-Laplace transform of $w_{c,t}$ defined by

$$\Psi_{t-1}^{\mathbb{Q}}(u) = \ln E_{t-1}^{\mathbb{Q}}\left[\exp\left(u' w_{c,t}\right)\right].$$

[9] See Monfort and Pegoraro (2012) for a generalisation to the exponential quadratic case.

Note that condition (6.14) is automatically satisfied by this specification.

The coefficients $\gamma(\underline{w}_{c,t-1})$, also denoted by γ_{t-1}, are interpreted as the risk sensitivities associated with the risk factors, i.e. the components of $w_{c,t}$.

In this case, the historical conditional log-Laplace transform of $w_{c,t}$ is

$$
\begin{aligned}
\Psi^{\mathbb{P}}_{t-1}(u) &= \log E^{\mathbb{P}}_{t-1}\left[\exp\left(u'w_{c,t}\right)\right] \\
&= \log E^{\mathbb{Q}}_{t-1}\left[M^{-1}_{t-1,t}(\underline{w}_{G,t})\exp(-r_t(\underline{w}_{G,t-1}))\exp\left(u'w_{c,t}\right)\right] \\
&= \log E^{\mathbb{Q}}_{t-1}\left[\exp\left((u-\gamma_{t-1})'w_{c,t}-\Psi^{\mathbb{Q}}_{t-1}(-\gamma_{t-1})\right)\right] \\
&= \Psi^{\mathbb{Q}}_{t-1}(u-\gamma_{t-1})-\Psi^{\mathbb{Q}}_{t-1}(-\gamma_{t-1}).
\end{aligned} \tag{6.20}
$$

Hence the following proposition.

Proposition 6.4 *If the sdf has the exponential affine form (6.19), the historical dynamics of $w_{c,t}$ is easily deduced from the risk-neutral one, by the formula*

$$
\Psi^{\mathbb{P}}_{t-1}(u) = \Psi^{\mathbb{Q}}_{t-1}(u-\gamma_{t-1})-\Psi^{\mathbb{Q}}_{t-1}(-\gamma_{t-1}).
$$

Also note that setting $u = \gamma_{t-1}$ in (6.20) results in $\Psi^{\mathbb{P}}_{t-1}(\gamma_{t-1}) = -\Psi^{\mathbb{Q}}_{t-1}(-\gamma_{t-1})$ and replacing u by $u+\gamma_{t-1}$, we get the reverse relation:

$$
\Psi^{\mathbb{Q}}_{t-1}(u) = \Psi^{\mathbb{P}}_{t-1}(u+\gamma_{t-1})-\Psi^{\mathbb{P}}_{t-1}(\gamma_{t-1}). \tag{6.21}
$$

In Section 6.2.2, we have assumed that $w_t = (w'_{c,t}, w'_{s,t})'$ is Car(1). Therefore, its log-Laplace transform is of the form (6.1):

$$
\begin{aligned}
& E^{\mathbb{Q}}_{t-1}\left[\exp\left(u'w_{c,t}+v'w_{s,t}\right)\right] \\
& = \exp\left[a^{\mathbb{Q}}_1(u,v)'w_{c,t-1}+a^{\mathbb{Q}}_2(u,v)'w_{s,t-1}+b^{\mathbb{Q}}(u,v)\right]. \tag{6.22}
\end{aligned}
$$

Since $w_{s,t}$ does not cause $w_{c,t}$, it turns out that $w_{c,t}$ is also Car(1). Indeed, the conditional Laplace transform of $w_{c,t}$ given $\underline{w}_{t-1} = (\underline{w}'_{c,t}, \underline{w}'_{s,t})'$ is obtained by putting $v = 0$ in (6.22), and since the result does not depend on $w_{s,t-1}$, we have $a^{\mathbb{Q}}_2(u,0) = 0$ and finally

$$
\begin{aligned}
E^{\mathbb{Q}}_{t-1}\left[\exp\left(u'w_{c,t}\right)\right] &= \exp\left[a^{\mathbb{Q}}_1(u,0)'w_{c,t-1}+b^{\mathbb{Q}}(u,0)\right] \\
&= \exp\left[a^{\mathbb{Q}}_c(u)'w_{c,t-1}+b^{\mathbb{Q}}_c(u)\right], \quad \text{(say)}.
\end{aligned}
$$

Therefore, $\Psi^{\mathbb{Q}}_{t-1}(u) = a^{\mathbb{Q}}_c(u)'w_{c,t}+b^{\mathbb{Q}}_c(u)$ and

$$
\Psi^{\mathbb{P}}_{t-1}(u) = \left[a^{\mathbb{Q}}_c(u-\gamma_{t-1})-a^{\mathbb{Q}}_c(-\gamma_{t-1})\right]'w_{c,t-1}+b^{\mathbb{Q}}_c(u-\gamma_{t-1})-b^{\mathbb{Q}}_c(-\gamma_{t-1}).
$$

This shows that, in general, the historical dynamics of $w_{c,t}$ is not Car, except when the previous function is affine in $w_{c,t-1}$. A sufficient but not necessary condition is that γ_{t-1} is constant.

6.5   Examples

6.5.1   Autoregressive gamma latent factors

Autoregressive gamma processes are investigated by Gouriéroux and Jasiak (2006). A process y_t that follows an autoregressive gamma process of order one, or ARG(1), can be defined in the following way:

$$\frac{y_t}{\mu_y}\bigg|\tilde{y}_t \sim \gamma(\nu_y + \tilde{y}_t), \quad \nu_y > 0,$$
$$\tilde{y}_t | y_{t-1} \sim \mathcal{P}(\rho_y y_{t-1}/\mu_y), \quad \rho_y > 0, \mu_y > 0,$$

where γ and $\mathcal{P}$ denote respectively the gamma and the Poisson distributions, μ_y is the scale parameter, ν_y is the degree of freedom, ρ_y is the correlation parameter and $\tilde{y}_t$ is the mixing variable. As shown by Gouriéroux and Jasiak (2006), the ARG(1) process is the discrete-time equivalent of the square-root (CIR) diffusion process. It can be shown that

$$y_t = \nu_y \mu_y + \rho_y y_{t-1} + \eta_{y,t},$$

where $\eta_{y,t}$ is a martingale difference sequence whose conditional variance (at date $t-1$) is given by $\nu_y \mu_y^2 + 2\rho_y \mu_y y_{t-1}$. Figure 6.1 (upper right plot) shows the simulated path of an ARG(1) process.

Let us assume that $w_{c,t}$ is a univariate $\mathbb{Q}$ autoregressive gamma (ARG(1)), as well as $w_{s,t}^n$ ($n = 1,\ldots,N$), and that they are $\mathbb{Q}$ (and therefore $\mathbb{P}$) independent. The extension to the multivariate case is straightforward. The conditional log-Laplace transforms of $w_{c,t}$ and $w_{s,t}^n$ in the risk-neutral world are respectively:

$$\frac{\rho_c u}{1-u\mu_c} w_{c,t-1} - \nu_c \log(1 - u\mu_c),$$
$$\frac{\rho_s^n u}{1-u\mu_s^n} w_{s,t-1}^n - \nu_s^n \log(1 - u\mu_s^n).$$

If $w_{c,t}$ and $w_{s,t}$ are latent, we can assume that the scale parameters μ_c and μ_s^n are equal to one. It is well-known (see Gouriéroux and Jasiak, 2006) that these processes are positive and that ρ_c (respectively ρ_s^n) is a (positive) correlation parameter whereas ν_c (respectively ν_s^n) is a shape parameter. Further, we assume that:

$$\lambda_{n,t} = \alpha_{0,n} + \alpha_{1,n}^c w_{c,t} + \alpha_{1,n}^s w_{s,t}^n,$$
$$r_t = \beta_0 + \beta_1' w_{c,t-1}.$$

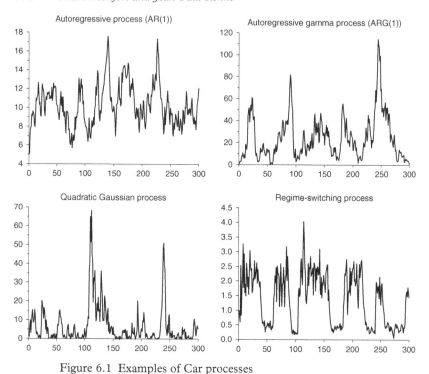

Figure 6.1 Examples of Car processes
The upper left panel shows a simulation of a Gaussian process parameterised by $\varphi = 1$, $\phi = 0.9$ and $\Sigma = 1$ (see Section 6.5.2). The upper right panel displays the simulated path of an autoregressive gamma process with $\mu = 1$, $\rho = 0.95$, and $\nu = 1$ (see Section 6.5.1). The lower left panel shows the square of a Gaussian AR process (therefore a quadratic Gaussian process), with $\varphi = 0$, $\phi = 0.9$ and $\Sigma = 1$ (see Section 6.5.3). The lower right panel displays the simulated path of a switching Gaussian AR process: there are two regimes, the probability of staying in each of these two regimes being 95% (i.e. the $\pi_{i,i}$s are equal to 0.95), $\varphi(z) = [0.1 \quad 1]z$, $\Phi(z) = [0.7 \quad 0.5]z$ and $\Sigma(z) = [0.01 \quad 0.25]z$

Since $(w_{c,t}, w_{s,t}^n)$ is obviously $\mathbb{Q}$-Car(1), we can easily obtain the yields $R_n(t, h)$ as affine functions of $w_{c,t}$ and $w_{s,t}^n$ (using the results of Section 6.3.2 and applying the recursive algorithm proposed in Section 6.2.2). We know, given the independence of $w_{c,t}$ and $w_{s,t}^n$ and the assumption on $M_{t-1,t}$, that the historical dynamics of $w_{s,t}^n$ is the same as the risk-neutral one (Proposition 6.3), and that, if we adopt an exponential affine sdf, the historical conditional log-Laplace transform of $w_{c,t}$ is (using Equation (6.20))

$$\rho_c \left(\frac{u - \gamma_{t-1}}{1 - u + \gamma_{t-1}} + \frac{\gamma_{t-1}}{1 + \gamma_{t-1}} \right) w_{c,t-1} - v_c \left\{ \log(1 - (u - \gamma_{t-1})) \right.$$

$$\left. - \log(1 + \gamma_{t-1}) \right\} = \frac{\rho_{t-1} u}{1 - u\mu_{t-1}} w_{c,t-1} - v_c \log(1 - u\mu_{t-1})$$

with $\rho_{t-1} = \frac{\rho_c}{(1+\gamma_{t-1})^2}$ and $\mu_{t-1} = \frac{1}{1+\gamma_{t-1}}$.

Therefore, if γ_{t-1} is constant, the historical dynamics of $w_{c,t}$ is also ARG(1) with modified parameters $\rho_c^* = \frac{\rho_c}{(1+\gamma)^2}$, $\mu_c^* = \frac{1}{1+\gamma}$, $v_c^* = v_c$. It is important to note that since the processes $w_{c,t}$ and $w_{s,t}$ are positive, the same is true for r_t and λ_t if we take positive coefficients. Moreover, since

$$B_n(t, h) = E_t^{\mathbb{Q}}[-r_{t+1} - \cdots - r_{t+h} - \lambda_{t+1} - \cdots - \lambda_{t+h}],$$

the function under the expectation is always smaller than one and, therefore, all the yields $R_n(t, h) = -1/h \log B_n(t, h)$ are positive. The ability of the ARG processes to model positive yields and spreads is a substantial advantage of these processes.

6.5.2   *Gaussian VAR factors and affine term structures*

We assume that the risk-neutral dynamics of $(w_{c,t}', w_{s,t}')'$ is defined by

$$w_{c,t} = \varphi_c + \Phi_c w_{c,t-1} + \varepsilon_{c,t},$$
$$w_{s,t}^n = \varphi_s^n + \Phi_{sc}^n w_{c,t-1} + \Phi_s^n w_{s,t-1}^n + \varepsilon_{s,t}^n,$$

where $\varepsilon_{c,t}$ and the $\varepsilon_{s,t}^n$s are independent zero-mean Gaussian white noises, with respective variance–covariance matrices Σ_c and Σ_s^n.

This implies that the vectors $(w_{c,t}', w_{s,t}^{n'})'$ and $(w_{c,t}', w_{s,t}')'$ are Gaussian VAR(1). Again, assuming that r_t is an affine function of $w_{c,t}$ and that $\lambda_{n,t}$ is an affine function of $w_{c,t}$ and $w_{s,t}^n$, the yields $R_n(t, h)$ are affine functions of $w_{c,t}$ and $w_{s,t}^n$.

Let us use an sdf of the form

$$M_{t-1,t} = \exp\left(-r_{t-1} + v_{t-1}' \varepsilon_{c,t} + \frac{1}{2} v_{t-1}' \Sigma_c v_{t-1} \right)$$

with $v_{t-1} = v_0(z_{t-1}) + v_1(z_{t-1}) w_{c,t-1}$. This sdf is obviously exponential affine in $w_{c,t}$ and satisfies conditions (6.14), i.e. $E_{t-1}^{\mathbb{Q}}(M_{t-1,t}^{-1}) = \exp(r_{t-1})$.

The conditional risk-neutral log-Laplace transform of $\varepsilon_{c,t}$ is

$$\psi_{t-1}^{\mathbb{Q}} = \frac{1}{2} u' \Sigma_c u.$$

Using (6.20), it is easily seen that the conditional historical log-Laplace transform of $\varepsilon_{c,t}$ is

$$\Psi_{t-1}^{\mathbb{P}}(u) = \frac{1}{2}(u - v_{t-1})'\Sigma_c(u - v_{t-1}) - \frac{1}{2}v_{t-1}'\Sigma_c v_{t-1}$$

$$= -v_{t-1}'\Sigma_c u + \frac{1}{2}u'\Sigma_c u.$$

Therefore, the conditional historical distribution of $\varepsilon_{c,t}$ is $\mathcal{N}(-\Sigma_c v_{t-1},$ $\Sigma_c)$ or, in other words, $\varepsilon_{c,t}$ is equal to $-\Sigma_c v_{t-1} + \eta_{c,t}$, where $\eta_{c,t}$ is a white noise $\mathcal{N}(0, \Sigma_c)$ in the historical world and we get:

$$w_{c,t} = \varphi_c + \Phi_c w_{c,t-1} - \Sigma_c v_{t-1} + \eta_{c,t}$$

$$= (\varphi_c - \Sigma_c v_0) + (\Phi_c - \Sigma_c v_1)w_{c,t-1} + \eta_{c,t}.$$

So, with the specification of $M_{t-1,t}$ chosen above, $w_{c,t}$ is also a Gaussian VAR(1) in the historical world, with arbitrarily modified vector of constants and autoregressive matrix but with the same conditional variance–covariance matrix. This model has been extensively used in the affine term-structure literature.[10]

6.5.3   *Gaussian VAR factors and quadratic term-structures*

Let us consider the same risk-neutral dynamics of $w_t = (w_{c,t}', w_{s,t}')'$ and the same sdf as in the previous subsection. The historical dynamics of w_t is also the same as before. Let us now assume that the short rate r_t and the default intensities are some quadratic functions of the factors

$$r_t = \beta_0 + \beta_1' w_{c,t} + w_{c,t}' \beta_2 w_{c,t},$$
$$\lambda_{n,t} = \alpha_{0,n} + \alpha_{1,n} w_t^n + w_t^{n'} \alpha_{2,n} w_t^n$$

with $w_t^n = (w_{c,t}', w_{s,t}^n{}')'$. It will prove convenient to rewrite r_t in the following way:

$$r_t = \beta_0 + \tilde{\beta}_1' w_t^n + w_t^{n'} \tilde{\beta}_2 w_t^n,$$

where $\tilde{\beta}_1 = (\beta_1', 0)'$ and $\tilde{\beta}_2 = \begin{pmatrix} \beta_2 & 0 \\ 0 & 0 \end{pmatrix}$. Indeed, r_t and the $\lambda_{n,t}$s are then both quadratic forms in w_t^n and they can also be written

$$r_t = \beta_0 + \beta_1' w_{c,t} + \mathrm{Trace}(\beta_2 w_{c,t} w_{c,t}'),$$
$$\lambda_{n,t} = \alpha_{0,n} + \alpha_{1,n} w_t^n + \mathrm{Trace}(\alpha_{2,n} w_t^n w_t^{n'}).$$

Since w_t^n follows a Gaussian VAR(1), it can be shown that $(w_t^{n'},$ $\mathrm{vech}(w_t^n w_t^{n'}))'$ is a Car(1) process (see Gouriéroux and Sufana, 2011),

---

[10] Notably by Ang and Piazzesi (2003) and Joslin, Singleton and Zhu (2011).

therefore any yield $R_n(t, h)$ will be easily computed recursively as an affine function of $(w_t^{n'}, \text{vech}(w_t^n w_t^{n'}))'$, that is to say as a quadratic form in w_t^n.[11]

6.5.4 Switching Gaussian VAR factors

We now introduce a Markov chain z_t valued in $(e_1, \ldots, e_{\mathcal{J}})$, where e_i is the $\mathcal{J}$-vector whose entries are equal to zero, except the ith one, which is equal to one. We assume that, under $\mathbb{Q}$, z_t has a transition matrix $\Pi = \{\pi_{i,j}\}_{i,j \in \{1, \ldots, \mathcal{J}\}}$, where $\pi_{i,j} = \mathbb{Q}(z_t = e_j | z_{t-1} = e_i)$.[12] We also assume that

$$w_{c,t} = \varphi_c(z_{t-1}) + \Phi_c w_{c,t-1} + \varepsilon_{c,t},$$
$$w_{s,t}^n = \varphi_c^n(z_{t-1}) + \Phi_{s,c}^n w_{c,t} + \Phi_s^n w_{s,t-1}^n + \varepsilon_{s,t}^n, \quad (6.23)$$

where, conditionally to the past, $\varepsilon_{c,t}$ and $\varepsilon_{s,t}^n$ are independent zero-mean Gaussian with respective variance–covariance matrices $\Sigma_c(z_{t-1})$ and $\Sigma_s^n(z_{t-1})$ in the risk-neutral world. (For the sake of illustration, Figure 6.1 (bottom-right plot) shows the simulated path of an AR(1) switching process.)

We can see this new model as an augmented common factor model with $\tilde{w}_{c,t} = (w_{c,t}', z_t')'$. It is easily checked that $\tilde{w}_{c,t}$ and $\tilde{w}_t^n = (\tilde{w}_{c,t}', w_{s,t}^{n'})'$ are $\mathbb{Q}$-Car(1) and that $R_n(t, h)$ is affine in $(w_{c,t}', z_t', w_{s,t}^{n'})'$. Let us consider an exponential affine sdf:

$$M_{t-1,t} = \exp\left(-r_{t-1} + v_{t-1}'\varepsilon_{c,t} + \frac{1}{2}v_{t-1}'\Sigma_c(z_{t-1})v_{t-1} + \delta_{t-1}'z_t\right),$$

where $v_{t-1} = v_0(z_{t-1}) + v_1(z_{t-1})w_{c,t-1}$ and δ_{t-1} is the function of $w_{c,t-1}$ and z_{t-1} whose jth component is equal to $\log(\pi_{i,j}/\tilde{\pi}_{i,j,t})$ when $z_{t-1} = e_i$, where the $\tilde{\pi}_{i,j,t}$s are functions of $w_{c,t-1}$ satisfying $\Sigma_j \tilde{\pi}_{i,j,t} = 1$ for any i and any $w_{c,t-1}$. Note that $M_{t-1,t}$ automatically satisfies condition (6.14), i.e. $E_{t-1}^{\mathbb{Q}}(M_{t-1,t}^{-1}) = \exp(r_{t-1})$.

If $z_{t-1} = e_i$, the risk-neutral conditional Laplace transform of $(\varepsilon_{c,t}, z_t)$ is

$$E_{t-1}^{\mathbb{Q}}\left(\exp(u'\varepsilon_{c,t} + v'z_t)\right) = \exp\left(\frac{1}{2}u'\Sigma_c(e_i)u\right) \cdot \sum_{j=1}^{\mathcal{J}} \pi_{i,j} \exp(v_j).$$

---

[11] For any matrix M of dimension $q \times q$, the half-vectorisation of M, denoted by $\text{vech}(M)$, is the $q(q+1)/2 \times 1$ column vector obtained by vectorising only the lower triangular part of M.

[12] Therefore, the rows of Π sum to one.

Therefore, for any z_{t-1}, the conditional log-Laplace transform of $(\varepsilon_{c,t}, z_t)$ is

$$\Psi^{\mathbb{Q}}_{t-1}(u, v) = \frac{1}{2} u' \Sigma_c(z_{t-1}) u + \left[A_1^{\mathbb{Q}}(v), \dots, A_{\mathcal{J}}^{\mathbb{Q}}(v) \right] z_{t-1}$$

with $A_i^{\mathbb{Q}}(v) = \ln \left(\sum_{j=1}^{\mathcal{J}} \pi_{i,j} \exp(v_j) \right)$.

Using the results of Proposition 6.4, the historical conditional log-Laplace transform of $(\varepsilon_{c,t}, z_t)$ is

$$\begin{aligned}
\Psi^{\mathbb{P}}_{t-1}(u, v) &= \Psi^{\mathbb{Q}}_{t-1}(u - v_{t-1}, v - \delta_{t-1}) - \Psi^{\mathbb{Q}}_{t-1}(-v_{t-1}, -\delta_{t-1}) \\
&= \frac{1}{2}(u - v_{t-1})' \Sigma_c(z_{t-1})(u - v_{t-1}) - \frac{1}{2} v'_{t-1} \Sigma_c(z_{t-1}) v_{t-1} \\
&\quad + \frac{1}{2} \Big[A_1^{\mathbb{Q}}(v - \delta_{t-1}) - A_1^{\mathbb{Q}}(-\delta_{t-1}), \ \dots, \ A_{\mathcal{J}}^{\mathbb{Q}}(v - \delta_{t-1}) \\
&\quad - A_{\mathcal{J}}^{\mathbb{Q}}(-\delta_{t-1}) \Big] z_{t-1}.
\end{aligned}$$

It is straightforward to show that

$$A_i^{\mathbb{Q}}(v - \delta_{t-1}) - A_i^{\mathbb{Q}}(-\delta_{t-1}) = \ln \left(\sum_{j=1}^{\mathcal{J}} \pi_{i,j,t} \exp(v_j) \right)$$

$$= A_i^{\mathbb{P}}(v) \quad \text{(say)},$$

which leads to

$$\begin{aligned}
\Psi^{\mathbb{P}}_{t-1}(u, v) &= -v'_{t-1} \Sigma_c(z_{t-1}) u + \frac{1}{2} u' \Sigma_c(z_{t-1}) u \\
&\quad + \left[A_1^{\mathbb{P}}(v), \dots, A_{\mathcal{J}}^{\mathbb{P}}(v) \right] z_{t-1}.
\end{aligned}$$

Therefore, in the historical world, $\varepsilon_{c,t}$ and z_t are conditionally independent, the marginal distribution of $\varepsilon_{c,t}$ is $\mathcal{N}(-\Sigma_c(z_{t-1}) v_{t-1}, \Sigma_c(z_{t-1}))$ and the distribution of z_t is defined by the mass points $\pi_{i,j,t}, j = 1, \dots, \mathcal{J}$ if $z_{t-1} = e_i$.

Using the form of $v_{t-1} = v_0(z_{t-1}) + v_1(z_{t-1}) w_{c,t-1}$, we conclude that the historical distribution of $(w_{c,t}, z_t)$ is given by

$$w_{c,t} = [\varphi_c(z_{t-1}) - \Sigma_c(z_{t-1}) v_0(z_{t-1})] + [\Phi_c - \Sigma_c(z_{t-1}) v_1(z_{t-1})] \, w_{c,t-1} + \eta_{c,t},$$

where the historical conditional distribution of $\eta_{c,t}$ is $\mathcal{N}(0, \Sigma_c(z_{t-1}))$ and z_t is the non-homogeneous Markov chain with transition probabilities $\pi_{i,j,t}$ which may be functions of $w_{c,t-1}$.

The previous equation also shows that, in the historical world, the autoregressive matrix may also depend on the regime z_{t-1}. Finally, as mentioned in Proposition 6.3, the historical conditional distribution of

$w_{s,t}^n$ given $\left(\tilde{w}_{c,t}, \underline{\tilde{w}}_{t-1}^n\right)$ is the same as the risk-neutral one and is given by the second equation of (6.23).

6.6   Inference

The various mathematical objects introduced above are specified parametrically and the parameters must be estimated. The estimation method crucially depends on the observability of the components of $w_t = (w_{c,t}', w_{s,t}')'$. Regarding the yields, we usually observe several of them: $R_n(t, h_i), i = 1, \ldots, I_n, n = 1, \ldots, N, t = 1, \ldots, T$, which are affine functions of the factors w_t. Various kinds of interest-rate term structures can be thought of: sovereign, supra-national, agency, corporate bonds' yields or swap yields.[13]

If the w_ts are observable we can, adding measurement error terms in Equations (6.8), compute the likelihood of the observations $\{w_t, R_n(t, h_i), i = 1, \ldots, I_n, n = 1, \ldots, N\}$ for $t = 1, \ldots, T$ and derive the maximum likelihood estimator (MLE) of the unknown parameters.[14] Note that analytical formulas are readily available to compute the likelihood associated with the processes presented in Section 6.5.

If some components of w_t are latent, some filters have to be applied to compute the likelihood. For instance, if some of the components of w_t are unobserved Gaussian autoregressive processes, the Kalman filter is the appropriate tool (see de Jong, 2000, among many others). When the specifications of the intensities include quadratic functions of Gaussian autoregressive factors (as in Section 6.5.3), the yields are quadratic functions of the factors. In that case, the standard Kalman filter has to be replaced by its extended or unscented versions (see respectively Kim and Singleton, 2012 or Chen et al., 2008), or by the particle filter (see Andreasen and Meldrum, 2011). The next section also shows how inversion techniques *à la* Chen and Scott (1993) can be resorted to in that case. If the unobserved components of w_t follow Markov-switching Gaussian VAR (as in Section 6.5.4), the Kitagawa–Hamilton filter can be applied (see Monfort and Pegoraro, 2007). When the latent factors follow Markov-switching VAR processes, one can use Kim's (1994) filter (see Monfort and Renne, 2012). Besides, Monfort and Renne (2013) show how inversion techniques can be

---

[13] Using approaches consistent with the present framework, Monfort and Renne (2012) and Borgy et al. (2011) model the term structures of euro-area sovereign bond yields. Monfort and Renne (2013) and Mueller (2008) model the term structures of yields associated with different credit-rating classes.

[14] The error terms are usually supposed to be mutually and serially independent and identically normally distributed.

mixed with other techniques, notably the Kitagawa–Hamilton filter, to simultaneously handle different forms of latency in the dynamics of the pricing factors. This methodology is applied by Renne (2012).

6.7   Application: credit-risk premia in Italian and Spanish sovereign yields

6.7.1   Outline

In this section, we use our framework to investigate the dynamics of sovereign spreads. Specifically, we model the term-structure of spreads between Spanish government bond yields and their German counterpart. As in many studies on European sovereign bonds, we consider German bonds (the so-called Bunds) as risk-free benchmarks. We make use of the quadratic framework (see Section 6.5.3), the pricing factors w_t are latent and the model is estimated using maximum likelihood techniques. Once we have estimated both the historical and the risk-neutral dynamics, we compute credit-risk premia. Our results indicate that an important share of the spreads are accounted for by credit-risk premia, which is consistent with the existence of an undiversifiable sovereign risk (see e.g. Longstaff et al., 2011). As in Monfort and Renne (2012), we finally assess the influence of these risk premia on the deviation between risk-neutral and physical probabilities of default.

6.7.2   Model

Since we consider a single country, we drop the n index in the following. In order to keep this illustration simple, as e.g. Pan and Singleton (2008), Longstaff et al. (2011) or Monfort and Renne (2012), we assume that the short-term rate is exogenous. In that context, taking into account non-zero recovery rates (see Section 6.3.3) and using Equation (6.6), it is easily shown that

$$B(t, h) = \exp(-hR^*(t, h))E_t^{\mathbb{Q}}\left(\exp\left(-\tilde{\lambda}_{t+1} - \cdots - \tilde{\lambda}_{t+h}\right)\right)$$

(where $R^*(t, h)$ is the risk-free yield of maturity h and $\tilde{\lambda}_t$ is the recovery-adjusted default intensity), which leads to

$$R^*(t, h) - R(t, h) = -\frac{1}{h}\log E_t^{\mathbb{Q}}\left(\exp\left(-\tilde{\lambda}_{t+1} - \cdots - \tilde{\lambda}_{t+h}\right)\right). \quad (6.24)$$

So, the spread versus the risk-free yield depends on the risk-neutral dynamics of the default intensities only. Therefore, we do not have to specify the dynamics of the risk-free short-term rate. The recovery-adjusted default intensity is given by

$$\tilde{\lambda}_t = \alpha_0 + w_t' \alpha_2 w_t,$$

where w_t is a 2×1 vector of (latent) variables. An important advantage of this setting is that one can easily ensure that the intensity remains positive (which is consistent with its interpretation in terms of probabilities, see Equation (6.2)). For instance, this is obtained if α_2 is a positive-definite matrix and if $\alpha_0 > 0$.

The historical and risk-neutral dynamics of the pricing factors w_t respectively read

$$w_t = \Phi w_{t-1} + \varepsilon_t, \quad \text{where } \varepsilon_t \sim \mathcal{N}^{\mathbb{P}}(0, I),$$
$$w_t = \varphi^* + \Phi^* w_{t-1} + \varepsilon_t^*, \quad \text{where } \varepsilon_t^* \sim \mathcal{N}^{\mathbb{Q}}(0, I).$$

Let us denote by S_t the $k \times 1$ vectors of modelled spreads (for k different maturities). In Section 6.5.3, it is shown that in this framework, the spreads are quadratic functions of the factors. Considering the kth spread, that we denote by $S_{k,t}$, we have

$$\underbrace{S_{k,t}}_{\text{observed spread}} = \underbrace{f_k + c_k w_t + w_t' C_k w_t}_{\text{modelled spread}} + \underbrace{\eta_{k,t}}_{\text{pricing error}},$$

where the $\eta_{k,t}$s are Gaussian iid error terms.

6.7.3   Estimation

As mentioned in Section 6.6, different filtering techniques can be implemented in order to estimate the model by MLE when the w_ts are latent. Here, we resort to inversion techniques *à la* Chen and Scott (1993). If the model features M (say) latent variables, this technique consists of assuming that M of the observed yields (spreads) or, more generally, that M combinations of observed yields (or spreads), are priced without error by the model. Then, using the M corresponding pricing formula, one can solve for the M latent variables from the M perfectly priced yields. The remaining yields are then priced with error (the $\eta_{k,t}$s). Appendix A details the computation of the log-likelihood.

The data are weekly and cover the period July 2008–October 2012 (224 dates). The upper plots of Figure 6.2 show the fit of the model. Obviously, because of the estimation approach, two spreads are perfectly modelled (the 2-year and the 10-year spreads). Regarding the other two spreads that are used in the estimation – the 3-year and the 5-year spreads – pricing errors are relatively small (with a standard deviation

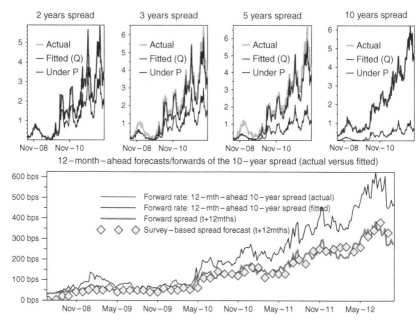

Figure 6.2 Modelling the term-structure of sovereign spreads (Spain vs Germany): model fit and credit risk premia

The four upper plots show the model fit and also illustrate the influence of credit-risk premia. Indeed, the plots report three kinds of spread: the actual (observed) ones, the (model-based) fitted ones (under $\mathbb{Q}$) and the 'physical' ones (under $\mathbb{P}$). The fitted ones are obtained by applying Equation (6.24). The physical ones are the ones that would be observed if the investor were risk-neutral; they are computed in the same way as the fitted ($\mathbb{Q}$) ones, except that the expectation $E^{\mathbb{Q}}$ appearing in Equation (6.24) is replaced by $E^{\mathbb{P}}$ (this amounts to setting the risk sensitivities to zero). The deviation between fitted and physical spreads corresponds to credit risk premia. The lower plot compares 12-month-ahead forwards of the 10-year spread with 12-month-ahead expectation of the 10-year spread (under $\mathbb{P}$). Two kinds of ($\mathbb{P}$) expectation are reported: the model-based ones (solid line) and survey-based ones (diamonds).

of about 20 basis points). The upper plots in Figure 6.2 also illustrate the influence of credit-risk premia. These are discussed in the next subsection.

6.7.4 Credit-risk premia

Credit-risk premia are defined as the deviation between actual spreads and the ones that would prevail if the investor were risk neutral, that is, if the risk sensitivities were nil (see Section 6.4.2 for a formal definition of the risk sensitivities). The upper plots in Figure 6.2 show that these risk premia are sizeable, especially for the longest maturities. This has various important implications in terms of spread analysis.

First, the fact that the historical and the risk-neutral dynamics of the pricing factors w_t are not the same implies that credit-spread forwards cannot be interpreted as market forecasts of future spreads.[15] This is illustrated by the lower plot of Figure 6.2. This plot displays 12-month ahead survey-based forecasts of the Spanish–German spread (source: *Consensus Forecasts*) together with 1-year-forward spreads between Spanish and German 10-year yields.[16] The deviation between the two series is substantial. This suggests that using forwards of spreads to assess market expectations regarding the evolution of future spreads is misleading. In addition, the same plot illustrates the ability of the model to capture this phenomenon. Indeed, it shows that the model-implied 12-month-ahead forecast of the spread (thick solid line) is able to reproduce the level and the main fluctuations in the survey-based forecasts.

Second, the existence of credit-risk premia implies that risk-neutral probabilities of default – for instance those that are backed out from CDS quotes following e.g. O'Kane and Turnbull (2003) – do not coincide with the real-world PDs. Formally, it is easily shown that, in our framework, risk-neutral and historical probabilities of default are given by (see Monfort and Renne, 2012)

$$\mathbb{Q}\left(d_{t+h} = 1 \,\middle|\, d_t = 0, \underline{w_t}\right) = 1 - E^{\mathbb{Q}}\left[\exp\left(-\lambda_{t+1} - ... - \lambda_{t+h}\right)\middle|\, \underline{w_t}\right],$$
$$\mathbb{P}\left(d_{t+h} = 1 \,\middle|\, d_t = 0, \underline{w_t}\right) = 1 - E^{\mathbb{P}}\left[\exp\left(-\lambda_{t+1} - ... - \lambda_{t+h}\right)\middle|\, \underline{w_t}\right].$$
$$(6.25)$$

The linearization of Equation (6.10) leads to $\lambda_t \approx \tilde{\lambda}_t/(1 - \zeta_t)$. Then, assuming that the recovery rate is constant and equal to ζ, the previous probabilities are easily computed using Proposition 6.1 (the expectation terms in Equation (6.25) being multi-horizon Laplace transforms of w_t). Based on a constant recovery rate of 50%, Figure 6.3 compares both kinds of default probability.[17] These computations suggest that real-world probabilities of default are far lower than their risk-neutral counterpart, consistently with the findings of Monfort and Renne (2012).

---

[15] See e.g. Cochrane and Piazzesi (2005) for an investigation of this phenomenon in the non-defaultable case.

[16] This forward rate (in continuously compounded terms) is simply given by $(11S(t, 11) - S(t, 1))/10$.

[17] This recovery rate roughly corresponds to the average of the recovery rates observed for sovereign defaults over the last decade (see Moody's, 2010).

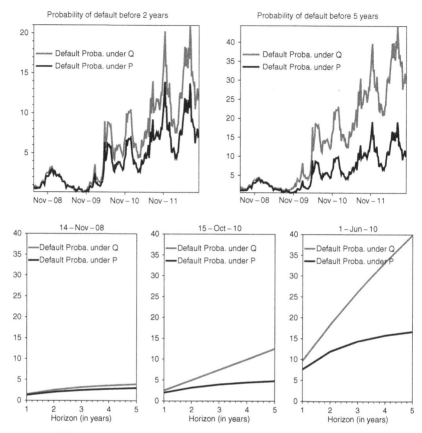

Figure 6.3 Historical vs risk-neutral probabilities of default
The upper plots present estimates of (market-perceived) probabilities of a Spanish-government default. Risk-neutral probabilities (solid lines) are compared with physical ones (dotted lines). The lower plots present, for three differed dates, the term-structures of risk-neutral and physical probabilities of default (example: for maturity m, the plots show the probability of a Spanish-government default before m years).

6.8   Conclusion

In this chapter, we investigated the potential of Car processes to model the dynamics of defaultable-bond prices in a no-arbitrage framework. We showed that these processes make it possible to account for sophisticated dynamics of yields and spreads while remaining tractable. In this intensity-based framework, bond prices and yields are obtained in a quasi-explicit form, thanks to a simple recursive algorithm. This ensures that the models building on this framework are amenable to empirical estimation. Several examples of Car processes were provided (regime-switching, autoregressive gamma and quadratic Gaussian processes). These processes can reproduce various key features of observed yields such as non-linearities or stochastic volatilities. In addition, some of these processes can ensure positivity of yields (and/or spreads), which is crucial in the (current) context of extremely low short-term rates.

As an illustration, we exploited our framework to investigate the dynamics of the term structure of Spanish sovereign spreads (vs Germany). After having estimated the model, we exhibited credit-risk premia, that are defined as those differences between observed credit spreads and the ones that would prevail if the investor were risk neutral. The results suggest that these risk premia are sizeable. This has important implications. Notably, it results in the fact that risk-neutral probabilities of defaults (backed out from spreads under the assumptions that investors are risk-neutral) overestimate physical, or real-world, probabilities of default.

Appendix A   Computation of the likelihood (model presented in Section 6.7)

Let $S_{1,t}$ be a 2×1 subvector of S_t which is modelled without pricing error and let $S_{2,t}$ be the vector of the remaining spreads in S_t. In other terms, $\eta_{k,t}$ is equal to 0 if k is one of the two maturities corresponding to $S_{1,t}$ and an iid Gaussian pricing error otherwise. The two equations associated with $S_{1,t}$ can be inverted in order to recover the two latent factors w_t.[18] Let us denote by $q_\theta(w_t, \theta)$ the function that assigns to the latent variables w_t the perfectly priced spreads $S_{1,t}$. The general term of the likelihood function is the conditional distribution of S_t given $\underline{S}_{t-1}$, which is

$$
\begin{aligned}
f_S\left(S_t \mid \underline{S}_{t-1}\right) &= \left| \det \frac{\partial q_\theta^{-1}(S_{1,t})}{\partial S_{1,t}} \right| f_{S_2, w}\left(S_{2,t}, w_t \mid \underline{S}_{t-1}\right) \\
&= \left| \det \frac{\partial q_\theta^{-1}(S_{1,t})}{\partial S_{1,t}} \right| f_{S_2}\left(S_{2,t} \mid w_t, \underline{S}_{t-1}\right) f_w\left(w_t \mid \underline{S}_{t-1}\right) \\
&= \left| \det \frac{\partial q_\theta(w_t)}{\partial w_t} \right|^{-1} f_{S_2}\left(S_{2,t} \mid w_t\right) f_w\left(w_t \mid w_{t-1}\right).
\end{aligned} \tag{6A.1}
$$

[18] At each iteration (new date t), the numerical procedure uses the previously obtained (date $t-1$) factors as initial conditions. This rules out the possibility of obtaining some jumps in the estimated factors that would be due to the existence of several solutions to this system of equations.

The computation of the three terms of the right-hand side of Equation (6A.1) is straightforward. The last two are Gaussian distributions. The first one is the inverse of the determinant of a multivariate quadratic function.

Appendix B   Estimated model

Parameter estimates are obtained by maximising the log-likelihood computed as detailed in Appendix A. The model is estimated in two steps. In the first step, all parameters in α_0, α_2, Φ, φ^* and Φ^* are estimated. Then, the statistical significance of the parameters is assessed. Those parameters that are not statistically different from zero are then set to zero and excluded from the second step of estimation. The resulting estimated model reads

$$
\lambda_t = 10^{-4} \left(\underset{(0.44)}{4.83} + w_t' \begin{bmatrix} \underset{(0.022)}{4.71} & \underset{(0.012)}{3.65} \\ \underset{(0.012)}{3.65} & \underset{(0.014)}{2.83} \end{bmatrix} w_t \right),
$$

$$
w_t = \begin{bmatrix} \underset{(0.0001)}{0.995} & \underset{(-)}{0} \\ \underset{(-)}{0} & \underset{(0.0000)}{0.992} \end{bmatrix} w_{t-1} + \varepsilon_t, \quad \varepsilon_t \sim \mathcal{N}^{\mathbb{P}}(0, I),
$$

$$
w_t = \begin{bmatrix} \underset{(-)}{0} \\ \underset{(0.0001)}{-0.028} \end{bmatrix} + \begin{bmatrix} \underset{(0.0000)}{1.0} & \underset{(0.00005)}{-0.007} \\ 0 & \underset{(0.00001)}{0.995} \\ & \underset{(-)}{} \end{bmatrix} w_{t-1} + \varepsilon_t^*, \quad \varepsilon_t^* \sim \mathcal{N}^{\mathbb{Q}}(0, I).
$$

The standard deviations of the parameter estimates are reported in parentheses. The standard-deviation estimates are based on the outer-product estimate of the Fisher information matrix.

References

Andreasen, M. and Meldrum, A. (2011). Likelihood inference in non-linear term structure models: The importance of the zero lower bound. Bank of England, mimeo.

Ang, A. and Piazzesi, M. (2003). A no-arbitrage vector autoregression of term structure dynamics with macroeconomic and latent variables. *Journal of Monetary Economics*, **50**(4), 745–787.

Bank of England (2012). Financial stability report, issue no. 31. Technical report, Bank of England.

Bertholon, H., Monfort, A. and Pegoraro, F. (2008). Econometric asset pricing modelling. *Journal of Financial Econometrics*, **6**(4), 407–456.

Blundell-Wignall, A. and Slovik, P. (2010). A market perspective on the European sovereign debt and banking crisis. *OECD Journal: Financial Market Trends*, No. 2, 9–36.

Borgy, V., Laubach, T., Mesonnier, J.-S. and Renne, J.-P. (2011). Fiscal sustainability, default risk and euro area sovereign bond spreads markets. Working Paper Series No. 350, Banque de France.

Borri, N. and Verdelhan, A. (2011). Sovereign risk premia. AFA 2010 Atlanta Meetings Paper.

Campbell, J. Y. and Shiller, R. J. (1991). Yield spreads and interest rate movements: a bird's eye view. *Review of Economic Studies*, **58**(3), 495–514.

Carver, L. (2012). Irksome irc. *Risk Magazine*, **25**(6), 17–20.

Chen, R.-R. and Scott, L. (1993). Maximum likelihood estimation for a multifactor equilibrium model of the term structure of interest rates. *Journal of Fixed Income*, **3**, 14–31.

Chen, R.-R., Cheng, X., Fabozzi, F. J. and Liu, B. (2008). An explicit, multifactor credit default swap pricing model with correlated factors. *Journal of Financial and Quantitative Analysis*, **43**(1), 123–160.

CMA Datavision (2011). CMA global sovereign debt credit risk report, 1st Quarter 2011. Technical report.

Cochrane, J. H. and Piazzesi, M. (2005). Bond risk premia. *American Economic Review*, **95**(1), 138–160.

Darolles, S., Gouriéroux, C. and Jasiak, J. (2006). Structural Laplace transform and compound autoregressive models. *Journal of Time Series Analysis*, **27**(4), 477–503.

de Jong, F. (2000). Time series and cross-section information in affine term-structure models. *Journal of Business & Economic Statistics*, **18**(3), 300–314.

Duffie, D. and Singleton, K. J. (1999). Modeling term structures of defaultable bonds. *Review of Financial Studies*, **12**(4), 687–720.

Gilchrist, S. and Zakrajšek, E. (2011). Credit spreads and business cycle fluctuations. Working Paper 17021, National Bureau of Economic Research.

Gouriéroux, C. and Jasiak, J. (2006). Autoregressive gamma processes. *Journal of Forecasting*, **25**, 129–152.

Gouriéroux, C. and Jasiak, J. (2009). Value at risk. In *Handbook of Financial Econometrics* (Y. Ait-Sahalia and L. P. Hansen, eds.), 553–609. Amsterdam, The Netherlands: Elsevier.

Gouriéroux, C. and Monfort, A. (2007). Econometric specification of stochastic discount factor models. *Journal of Econometrics*, **136**(2), 509–530.

Gouriéroux, C. and Sufana, R. (2011). Discrete time Wishart term structure models. *Journal of Economic Dynamics and Control*, **35**(6), 815–824.

Gouriéroux, C., Monfort, A. and Polimenis, V. (2006). Affine models for credit risk analysis. *Journal of Financial Econometrics*, **4**(3), 494–530.

Gouriéroux, C., Monfort, A., Pegoraro, F. and Renne, J.-P. (2012). Regime-switching and bond pricing. Journal of Financial Econometrics lecture, Sofia annual meeting.

Hannoun, H. (2011). Sovereign risk in bank regulation and supervision: where do we stand? Speech by the BIS Deputy general manager at the Financial Stability Institute high-level meeting, Abu Dhabi, 26 October 2011, Bank for International Settlements.

Huang, J. Z. and Huang, M. (2003). How much of the corporate treasury yield spread is due to credit risk? Working Paper, Penn State and Stanford Universities.

Joslin, S., Singleton, K. J., and Zhu, H. (2011). A new perspective on Gaussian dynamic term structure models. *Review of Financial Studies*, 24(3), 926–970.

Kim, C.-J. (1994). Dynamic linear models with Markov-switching. *Journal of Econometrics*, **60**(1-2), 1–22.

Kim, D. H. and Singleton, K. J. (2012). Term structure models and the zero-lower bound: an empirical investigation of Japanese yields. Journal of Econometrics, Vol. 170, 32–49.

Le, A., Singleton, K. J. and Dai, Q. (2010). Discrete-time affine-q term structure models with generalized market prices of risk. *Review of Financial Studies*, **23**(5), 2184–2227.

Litterman, R. and Iben, T. (1991). Corporate bond valuation and the term structure of credit spreads. *Journal of Portfolio Management*, pp. 52–64.

Longstaff, F., Pan, J., Pedersen, L. and Singleton, K. (2011). How sovereign is sovereign credit risk? *Amercian Economic Journal: Macroeconomics*, **3**, 75–103.

Monfort, A. and Pegoraro, F. (2007). Switching Varma term structure models. *Journal of Financial Econometrics*, **5**(1), 105–153.

Monfort, A. and Pegoraro, F. (2012). Asset pricing with second order Esscher transforms. *Journal of Banking and Finance*, **36**(6), 1678–1687.

Monfort, A. and Renne, J.-P. (2012). Decomposing euro-area sovereign spreads: credit and liquidity risks. c.r.e.d.i.t. conference.

Monfort, A. and Renne, J.-P. (2013). Default, liquidity and crises: an econometric framework. *Journal of Financial Econometrics*, **11**(2).

Moody's (2010). Sovereign default and recovery rates, 1983–2009. Global credit policy, Moody's Investors Service.

Mueller, P. (2008). Credit spread and real activity. Technical report, Columbia Business School.

Nouy, D. (2011). Is sovereign risk properly addressed by financial regulation? *Financial Stability Review*, **16**, 95–106.

O'Kane, D. and Turnbull, S. (2003). Valuation of credit default swaps. Fixed Income – Quantitative credit research, Lehman Brothers.

Pan, J. and Singleton, K. (2008). Default and recovery implicit in the term structure of sovereign CDS spreads. *Journal of Finance*, **63**(5), 2345–2384.

Renne, J.-P. (2012). A model of the euro-area yield curve with discrete policy rates. Working Paper Series No. 395, Banque de France.

Sengupta, R. and Tam, Y. M. (2008). The LIBOR-OIS spread as a summary indicator. *Monetary Trends*, November.

Taylor, J. B. and Williams, J. C. (2009). A black swan in the money market. *American Economic Journal: Macroeconomics*, **1**(1), 58–83.

7 Yield curve dimensionality when short rates are near the zero lower bound

James M. Steeley

7.1 Introduction

The yield curve represents the relationship between the discount rates on a collection of default-free future cash flows, such as the coupon and redemption payments on UK government bonds, which differ only by their due date. By providing a spectrum of interest rates across future time horizons, the yield curve contains information regarding the whole market's expectations of future events, which is valuable for macroeconomic policymakers. In the UK government bond market, as in all bond markets, the cash flows to bondholders are made at regular but infrequent intervals. For a policymaker interested in a particular future date that does not happen to coincide with a cash flow date of a bond, there will be no directly observable discount rate. As a result, techniques have been developed to estimate the whole yield curve from the set of available bonds.

It is typical in bond markets for the set of future cash flow dates to far exceed the number of bonds, so giving rise to an under-identification problem when attempting to estimate the yield curve, as there are fewer known bond prices than unknown discount rates. The solution, first suggested by McCulloch (1971), is to approximate the yield curve with a low-dimensional function of maturity (the due date of the cash flow), which depends on a small number of parameters. By fixing a functional form for the yield curve, it also becomes possible to interpolate between observed maturities to obtain an estimate of the entire continuum of yields. The fewer the parameters in the function (the lower the dimensions of the yield curve), the more rigid will be the estimated curve. The

I would like to acknowledge the insights of two anonymous referees that have led to revisions in the chapter that make the original results more robust and enable the macroeconomic policy implications to be drawn out. I also thank co-editor Lucio Sarno for orchestrating this process, and the CIMF-IESEG conference organisers, Jag Chadha, Alain Durré and Sean Holly, for facilitating my earlier participation.

greater the number of parameters in the function, the more the curve will be able to reflect the potential richness of the relationship between cash flows due at different maturities. While the maximum dimensionality is restricted only by the number of bonds available, the focus in choosing appropriate functional forms has always been on parsimony. There is, however, a trade-off to be made between achieving a better fit, by adding dimensions, and over-smoothing the curve, by adding too few. We explain how this trade-off can be appropriately balanced using two estimation error metrics, and how this then identifies the dimensionality of the curve.

This chapter is concerned with this trade-off and, in particular, how the reduction in UK base interest rates between 8 October 2008 and 5 March 2009 from 5 per cent to 0.5 per cent may have impacted upon it, so changing the dimensions of the curve. The reduction in base rates has had a dramatic effect on the shape of the yield curve for UK government bonds, creating for the first time in many years a very steeply upward sloping curve, see Figure 7.1. It would be surprising if this drop in base rates had not also impacted upon the ability of proven functional forms for the yield curve to both fit well and capture the rich structure of the yield curve's shape.

There is another facet of dimensionality in modelling the yield curve and that concerns the time series of the whole yield curve, as opposed to the cross section of yields (the yield curve on a given date). One of

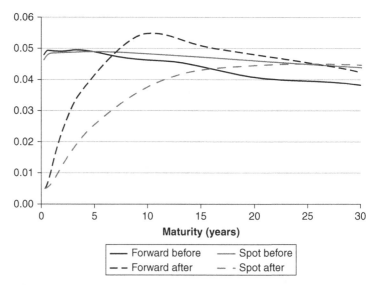

Figure 7.1 Average spot and forward yield curves

the reasons for parsimonious functional forms being used to estimate the yield curve has been the observation that the most of the time series variation in the yield curve can be captured by the variation in a small number of underlying factors. Principal components decompositions of the correlation matrix of yield curve movements are now common-place and indicate that the first three components can often capture more than 99 per cent of the movements in the yield curve.[1] The orthogonality of the principal components imbues these three determining 'factors' with separate shape-based influences on the yield curve, representing changes in level, slope and curvature. This study will examine also whether the change in shape of the yield curve has changed the number of underlying factors driving the yield curve over time and whether these factors have changed their influence on the shape of the yield curve.

The rest of the chapter is structured as follows. Section 7.2 describes the yield curve models that will be used to estimate the cross section of yields and explains how they can be used to assess the dimensions of the yield curve. This section also describes how the time series of estimated yield curves can be analysed using principal components analysis to assess the number of dynamic dimensions (factors) influencing the evolution of the curve. Section 7.3 describes the data base of UK bond yields that is used for the estimation and presents results. The first sets of results identify the dimensions of the cross section of yields (the yield curve), both before and after the reduction in short interest rates and examines the stability of the dimensions across the whole sample. This is followed by an examination of the effects on dimensionality of various aspects of the quantitative easing introduced once interest rates had fallen to 0.5 percent. The final component of the results presents the principal components analysis of the yield curve that distinguishes the periods before and after the fall in the short interest rate. Section 7.4 summarises the main results and offers some conclusions.

7.2   The dimensionality of UK government bond yields

7.2.1   Estimating the term structure of UK government bond yields

When term structure estimation methods are developed they are usually framed within one of the three alternative representations: the discount function (zero-coupon bond prices), $d(\tau)$, the zero-coupon (spot)

---

[1] See, for example, Steeley (1990), Litterman and Scheinkman (1991) and Dybvig (1996) as early examples of the use of this technique.

yield curve, $y(\tau) = -\ln(d(\tau))/\tau$, or the implied forward rate function, $f(\tau) = d'(\tau)/d(\tau)$, which measures the marginal return at maturity τ of extending one's investment.

Following the introduction of the gilt STRIP facility for UK government bonds in December 1997, which permitted the separate trading of the cash flows of a selection of conventional (coupon-bearing) gilts, direct observation of a set of zero-coupon yields, $y(t)$, became possible. The yield to maturity on a stripped cash flow, which is its per-period average rate of return until maturity, defines the unique default-free interest rate for that maturity. Steeley (2008) has shown that using zero-coupon yield data permits a focus on the relative abilities of different yield curve functional forms to fit to observed yields. Given that observations on zero-coupon bond yields are available, this study will examine the dimensionality of models fitted directly to the yield curve.[2]

Since the pioneering work of McCulloch (1971, 1975), a huge literature has grown up devoted to both innovating and comparing alternative approximation functions.[3] Most of these studies of alternative yield curve estimation models have compared the models as originally developed. Since these models may not necessarily have the same number of free parameters (dimensions), such comparisons may neither be fair nor informative. Steeley (2008) undertook a comparison of a variety of alternative functional forms but adapted them to provide comparisons at equal levels of dimensionality. The results suggest that, once the number of parameters has been chosen, there is little to choose between alternative functional forms, but that low dimensional models, such as Nelson and Siegel (1987) can benefit from additional degrees of freedom.

In this study, we focus on the two functional forms that were shown in Steeley (2008) to best fit the UK yield curve for a given number of free parameters: the cubic spline model of McCulloch (1975) and an extended version (having increased dimensions) of the Nelson–Siegel (1987) model. Although these models provided as good a fit across the full range of yields as each other, a difference was found in the ability to fit locally to particular ranges of yields. In particular, the cubic spline was better able to capture the short maturity end of the yield curve, but fluctuated excessively at longer maturities. By contrast, the Nelson–Siegel model could be too smooth at the short end, but provided stability at the longer end of the curve. These differences are likely to become

---

[2] See Steeley (2008) for further discussion of the quality of this data set.

[3] Applications and comparative studies include Anderson (1994), Deacon and Derry (1994), Anderson and Sleath (2001), Bliss (1997), Ferguson and Raymar (1998), Ioannides (2003) and Steeley (2008).

important now that the shorter end of the yield curve has changed shape so dramatically, and so this study will see how these two functional forms cope with this new environment.

Spline function approximation was introduced by McCulloch (1971) to alleviate the numerical problems arising from using polynomials to approximate unknown functions.[4] Spline approximation fits a separate polynomial within successive segments of the maturity span. Intuitively, this reduces the chances of any one polynomial diverging to unbounded values. The divisions between the segments of the interval are called 'knots', and the polynomials are constrained to be continuous and smooth around each knot point. A cubic spline model applied directly to the yield curve is where the zero-coupon yield (spot interest rate), $y(\tau)$, for maturity τ, can be represented by

$$y(\tau) = \sum_{k=0}^{3} \alpha_k \tau^k + \sum_{p=1}^{n-1} \beta_p \left(\tau - \lambda_p\right)^3 D_p, \qquad (7.1)$$

where n is the number of segments of the maturity span, and where $D_p = 1$ if $\tau \geq \lambda_p$ and $D_p = 0$ otherwise. The spline function in (7.1) comprises a cubic polynomial in maturity, τ, with parameters α_k, $k = 0, 1, 2, 3$, to be estimated, and a set of $n - 1$ truncated cubic functions of maturity, with parameters β_p, $p = 1, 2, \ldots, n - 1$, to be estimated. The truncated functions are zero when maturity is less than the 'knot' point divisions, λ_p, between the segments of the maturity span.

The Nelson and Siegel (1987) parameterisation assumes that the zero-coupon yield, $y(\tau)$, for maturity τ, can be represented by

$$y(\tau) = \beta_0 + \beta_1 \left(\frac{1 - e^{-\lambda\tau}}{\lambda\tau}\right) + \beta_2 \left(\frac{1 - e^{-\lambda\tau}}{\lambda\tau} - e^{-\lambda\tau}\right), \qquad (7.2)$$

where $\beta_0, \beta_1, \beta_2$ and λ are the parameters to be estimated. Figure 7.2 shows graphs of the three function-of-maturity components of the Nelson–Siegel model, where it can be seen that they comprise separate level, slope and curvature influences on the shape of the yield curve.

The models in equations (7.1) and (7.2) differ markedly in their dimensions. The dimensions of the cubic spline model depend on the number of knot points, λ_p, and can be increased by adding additional knots. By contrast, the Nelson–Siegel model has just four free parameters. This can restrict its ability to represent the richness in shape of the yield curve. In particular, as maturity increases so the constant (level)

---

[4] Since that time, cubic splines have been applied, for example, by Shea (1984) and Kikugawa and Singleton (1994) to estimating the yield curve for Japanese bonds, by Mastronikola (1991) and Steeley (1991) to the UK government bond market, and by Rumsey (1994) to Canadian government bonds.

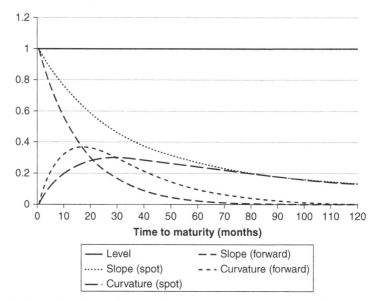

Figure 7.2 Level, slope and curvature components of Nelson and Siegel spot and forward curves

term β_0 will eventually dominate the slope and curvature terms giving rise to asymptotically flat forward curves. This does not well reflect the pronounced downwards slope in forward curves at longer maturities. The forward curves in Figure 7.1 display this characteristic.[5]

To lessen the limitations of the Nelson–Siegel model, extensions have been proposed by Svensson (1995), Bjork and Christensen (1999), De Pooter (2007) and Christensen et al. (2009, 2011). Svensson's model incorporated an additional curvature term, providing two additional dimensions, while Bjork and Christensen and De Pooter added just one dimension by restricting the additional non-linear parameter to be double the value of the existing Nelson–Siegel non-linear parameter. De Pooter's additional term was also a curvature term, while Bjork and Christensen added an additional slope term. Even with these extensions, however, the flexibility of these models in cross section is still constrained relative to the spline function, especially if the non-linear parameter(s), λ, are pre-set to permit linear estimation, which is becoming common

---

[5] This characteristic is a result of Jensen's inequality. Even if interest rates follow a random walk, and expectations of future rates are constant, the convex relationship between bond prices and yields generates a Jensen's inequality bias downwards in forward rates, which is proportional to maturity.

practice.[6] However, as shown in Steeley (2008) it is a simple exercise to extend the Nelson and Siegel model by adding more slope and curvature terms. In principle, it is possible to add either slope or curvature terms rather than corresponding pairs. However, adding pairs of slope and curvature terms maintains consistency with recent developments with dynamic versions of the Nelson–Siegel model, developed by Diebold and Li (2006) and Christensen, Diebold and Rudebusch (2009, 2011).[7]

By pre-specifying the non-linear parameters, λ, in the extended Nelson–Siegel models and using zero-coupon yield data, it is possible to estimate both this and the spline model using linear methods.[8] In all cases, a least squares criterion is used, so the estimated parameters are those that minimise the squared errors between the observed zero-coupon yields and fitted zero-coupon yields, that is,

$$\min{}_{\vartheta}\left((y(\tau) - y(\tau : \vartheta))'\,(y(\tau) - y(\tau : \vartheta))\right), \qquad (7.3)$$

where ϑ is the vector of parameters to be estimated.

Prior to estimation, the non-linear parameters of the Nelson–Siegel model, λ, and the knot points of the cubic spline model, λ_p, must be pre-set. The number of these parameters and knot points will determine the dimensions of the functions. For the spline function, the dimension of the function is four plus the number of knot points. For the Nelson–Siegel model, the dimension is equal to one plus twice the number of non-linear parameters. Since McCulloch (1975), it has become standard practice to set the knot points for a spline function to equalise the degrees of freedom in each segment of the maturity range. Thus if there is one knot within the maturity range, this is located at the maturity of the bond with the median maturity in the sample. For three knots, the settings are the maturity quartiles. For nine knots, the knot settings are the maturity

---

[6] See Diebold and Rudebusch (2013) for a survey of applications of the Nelson–Siegel model.

[7] Christensen et al. (2009, 2011) develop arbitrage free dynamic versions of the Nelson–Siegel model of the yield curve. Maintaining no arbitrage when extending their three factor model required the addition of both an extra slope and an extra curvature term. Steeley (2011) has shown that the time-independent function of maturity that distinguishes the arbitrage-free dynamic Nelson–Siegel model from the (not arbitrage-free) dynamic Nelson and Siegel model of Diebold and Li (2006) is equivalent to adding extra pairs of slope and curvature terms into the original Nelson–Siegel cross section model of the yield curve.

[8] Parameter instability and convergence problems in non-linear estimation are well-known problems in the Nelson and Siegel class of models; see, for example, Anderson and Sleath (2001), and so extending the flexibility of the Nelson and Seigel model through the addition of terms having unknown linear parameters is likely to be more fruitful. See also Diebold and Rudebusch (2011, p. 30).

deciles. In the Nelson and Siegel model, the non-linear parameter on each successive pair of slope and curvature terms is the analogue of a knot in the spline model. As these non-linear parameters are being pre-set to permit linear estimation, the same maturity quantiles are used to set these parameters. Specifically, the non-linear parameter is set equal to the inverse of the maturity quantile. This reflects the fact that the non-linear parameter is equal to the inverse of the maturity at which the curvature component reaches its maximum (see Figure 7.2). It is, of course, possible in both classes of model to improve the fit of the models by undertaking grid searches for the best knot points or best non-linear parameters, but this is not the focus here.[9]

In order to compare the models and determine the impact of the change in the shape of the yield curve, two statistics are calculated: the mean absolute yield error and a smoothness measure based upon the Durbin–Watson statistic. McCulloch and Kochin (2000) observed that the autocorrelation of the fitting errors along a discount function or yield curve can provide guidance as to whether or not the function is sufficiently smooth. If the autocorrelation is significantly positive, then the curve may be too stiff, while if the autocorrelation is significantly negative, then the curve may be too flexible, such that neighbouring errors alternate in sign too frequently to be consistent with chance. To measure smoothness, we first compute the Durbin–Watson autocorrelation statistic for the errors along the yield curve on a given day. This provides a measure of the excess roughness along the curve: the higher the statistic the rougher the curve. Adopting a parsimony criterion, we define a curve to be no longer too smooth when the Durbin–Watson statistic is no longer statistically significant, that is, below the 5% d_L value.[10] We compute p-values for the statistic using a non-linear approximation to make a small sample adjustment to the asymptotic 5% d_L table, as shown in Cummins and Hall (1999, p. 241).

We estimate each yield curve model for a range of dimensions and compute the fitting errors and their autocorrelations. As the focus of this chapter is on the impact of the change in yield curve shape brought about by the near zero interest rate environment, we distinguish the period prior to the sustained reduction in UK base rates, December 8, 1997 to October 7, 2008, from the period during and after the reduction in base rates, October 8, 2008 to April 27, 2011.

[9] The fit of the Nelson–Siegel model is remarkably robust to alternative positioning of the non-linear parameters; see, for example, Diebold and Rudebusch (2013), while Steeley (2008) shows that the fit of a spline model depends much more on the dimensions of the function than on the position of the knot points.

[10] Anderson and Sleath (2001) discuss the dangers of over-smoothing a yield curve.

7.2.2 Principal components analysis of the UK yield curve

The outputs from the yield curve estimation procedures are estimates of the yield curve across the full maturity span. Thus, while the input yields correspond to payment dates that are always drawing nearer with the passage of time, the output yield curves provide estimates of yields for fixed maturity lengths into the future. The time series of these fixed maturity yields can be used to examine the dimensions of the evolution of the yield curve, using the technique of principal components.

There is a direct link between the dimensions of the function used to estimate the cross section of yields and the dimensions of the evolution of the curve. The latter cannot exceed the former. What principal components does, however, is to measure the relative importance of each dimension for the evolution of the yield curve. It is typically found that even though the cross section of yields may have a high number of dimensions, most of the variation in the yield curve over time can be explained by a small number of dimensions.

Principal components analysis decomposes the variance–covariance matrix of yields into $Q\Lambda Q'$, where the diagonal elements of the matrix Λ are the eigenvalues of the variance–covariance matrix and the columns of the matrix Q are the associated eigenvectors. If the largest four eigenvalues are denoted $\gamma_1, \gamma_2, \gamma_3$ and γ_4, and the associated eigenvectors $q_1(\tau), q_2(\tau), q_3(\tau)$ and $q_4(\tau)$, then the first four principal components are defined by $x_{1,t} = q_t(\tau)'y_t(\tau)$, $i = 1, 2, 3, 4$, where $y(\tau)$ is the matrix comprising the vectors of time series of the yields for each of the maturities included in the set of yields. Each successive component offers the highest possible explanation of the variation in the yield curves while being orthogonal to each other. Each eigenvalue provides the proportion (an R^2) of the yield curve's movements that can be explained by the corresponding principal component, while the eigenvectors show how each point along the yield curve responds to movements in each component.

7.3   Data and results

The data used in this study are daily closing prices (GEMMA reference prices) of all UK government bond coupon strips over the period from the beginning of strips trading on December 8, 1997 to April 27, 2011. This provides a total of 3380 trading days of data. During the sample period the number of coupon strips fell in the range 47 to 161, and the maturities spanned ranged from up to 23 years to up to 50 years; the changes being caused by coupons reaching their payment date, and longer maturity strippable bonds being issued. Each of the models are fitted every day using all available coupon strips on that day.

7.3.1   The dimensions of the cross section of yields before and after 2008

Table 7.1 provides measures of goodness of fit for the two yield curve models for the period each side of the change in shape of the yield curve. As the number of free parameters in each function is increased, so both the mean absolute yield error and the over-smoothness, measured by significant error autocorrelation, decreases. In the period prior to the reduction in the base rate, once either the cubic spline model or the Nelson–Siegel model has seven free parameters, the change in yield error is less than one basis point and the level is less than three basis points. This level is well within empirical estimates of dealing costs in UK government bonds; see, for example, Proudman (1995) and Vitale (1998). Moreover, at this dimensionality, the positive autocorrelation in the errors is no longer statistically significant. As each model is estimated each day across the sub-sample period, the reported statistics are averages of each day's actual statistic. So, on average, across the sample period, yield curve functions with seven free parameters cannot be regarded as too smooth. For the cubic spline model this corresponds to using three knots within the range of maturities, while for the Nelson–Siegel model this corresponds to the addition of two pairs of slope and curvature terms beyond the pair in the original formulation.

The results for the sample prior to the reduction in the base rate show that there is little to choose between the two alternative functional forms for estimating the yield curve. Either is a good choice. This result is consistent with the findings reported in Steeley (2008). By contrast, the period after the reduction in the base rate reveals distinct differences between the two models' abilities to capture the change in shape of the curve. For the cubic spline model, thirteen free parameters (corresponding to nine knot points) are required to deliver a mean absolute yield error equivalent to that observed in the earlier sample, but seventeen free parameters (thirteen knot points) are required to provide a yield curve that is no longer significantly too smooth. By contrast, the extended Nelson–Siegel model requires 43 free parameters to generate both the same level of yield errors and a yield curve that is no longer too smooth.[11] This is a dramatic result. While both models indicate that the change in shape of the yield curve requires an increased dimensioned fitted yield curve, it is clear that the Nelson–Siegel model has some

---

[11] A similar result was obtained when a grid search was used to set the non-linear parameters in the extended Nelson–Siegel model and so this result is not an artefact of using pre-set values of λ. Indeed, a grid search could also be used to improve the fit of the spline model further.

Table 7.1 *Fit and smoothness of yield curves of increasing dimensionality*

| | Dec 8, 1997 to October 7, 2008 | | | | October 8, 2008 to April 27, 2011 | | | |
| | Cubic spline | | Nelson–Siegel | | Cubic spline | | Nelson–Siegel | |
Dim.	MAYE	DWp	MAYE	DWp	MAYE	DWp	MAYE	DWp
2	0.1098	<0.0001			0.5860	<0.0001		
3	0.0714	<0.0001	0.0617	0.0001	0.2824	<0.0001	0.1508	0.0000
4	0.0474	0.0005			0.1079	<0.0001		
5	0.0357	0.0066	0.0311	0.0128	0.0508	<0.0001	0.0509	0.0000
6	0.0271	0.0210			0.0481	<0.0001		
7	**0.0229**	**0.0620**	**0.0227**	**0.0879**	0.0378	<0.0001	0.0383	0.0001
8	0.0204	0.1088			0.0300	0.0007		
9	0.0181	0.1888	0.0215	0.1316	0.0277	0.0024	0.0347	0.0011
10	0.0165	0.2752			0.0269	0.0030		
11	0.0150	0.3917	0.0200	0.1905	0.0261	0.0059	0.0311	0.0022
12	0.0143	0.4438			0.0254	0.0097		
13	0.0133	0.5428	0.0189	0.2627	0.0233	0.0113	0.0310	0.0032
14	0.0125	0.6068			0.0196	0.0163		
15	0.0118	0.6621	0.0184	0.3088	0.0163	0.0275	0.0304	0.0040
16	0.0110	0.7354			0.0158	0.0267		
17	0.0107	0.7714	0.0179	0.3651	**0.0135**	**0.1067**	0.0294	0.0061
18	0.0099	0.8154			0.0126	0.1626		
19			0.0175	0.4135			0.0291	0.0063
21			0.0172	0.4677			0.0276	0.0079
23			0.0171	0.5032			0.0274	0.0116
25			0.0165	0.5519			0.0264	0.0137
27			0.0163	0.5974			0.0253	0.0181
29			0.0159	0.6362			0.0250	0.0202
31			0.0154	0.6780			0.0247	0.0225
33			0.0153	0.7052			0.0251	0.0261
35			0.0152	0.7317			0.0252	0.0300
37			0.0151	0.7492			0.0242	0.0313
39			0.0147	0.7700			0.0235	0.0364
41			0.0142	0.7860			0.0231	0.0422
43			0.0137	0.8067			**0.0212**	**0.0542**

This table reports statistics on fit (MAYE) and smoothness (DWp) for the two yield curve functions (cubic spline and extended Nelson–Siegel), fitted to the cross section of yields to maturity of UK coupon strips for each day (separately) between December 8, 1997 and April 27, 2011. The MAYE statistic is the average (across the indicated sub-sample period) mean (across the curve) absolute yield error (MAYE). The probability values (DWp) are for a Durbin–Watson statistic that measures the correlation of adjacent yield errors along the fitted curve. The p-values are calculated using a non-linear approximation to make a small sample adjustment to the asymptotic 5% d_L table, see Cummins and Hall (1999, p. 241). The reported value is the average of this statistic across the indicated sub-sample period. Each row contains the two statistics for the specified number of free parameters in the yield curve function, which is the dimension of the fitted yield curve (Dim.). The cubic spline model reduces to a polynomial for four or fewer parameters. The statistics in bold typeface are from the yield curves estimated using the minimum number of parameters to generate a yield curve that is not statistically significantly too smooth.

greater difficulty in fitting to the shape of the new curve. This is consistent with its known relative weakness to fit to the short end of the yield curve.

7.3.2   The stability of yield curve dimensions before 2008

While the dimensions of both yield curve models have increased during the more recent sample period, this sample has only 646 observations compared to the 2735 observations in the sample prior to the reduction in base rates. Perhaps the longer sample size in this prior period is disguising instability in the number of dimensions in shorter samples, causing the recent sample to reflect the smaller sample size rather than a genuine change in dimensions. To check this possibility, we partition the earlier sample into four sub-samples each of around 684 observations and average the MAYE and DW p-values across these shorter sample periods. Table 7.2 clearly shows that the dimensions sufficient to generate not over-smoothed curves in these shorter samples are remarkably stable. There is some indication that in the sub-sample closest to the start of the drop in base rates (30/1/06 to 7/10/08) the required dimensions began to increase. Indeed, if we also isolate out of the post October 2008 sample the first 6 month period (8/10/08 to 09/03/09) during which the base rate fell from 5 per cent to 0.5 per cent, we can see that the required dimensions are similar to those found for the final sub-sample of the early sample. There is little to suggest, therefore, that the change in dimensions required since the drop in base rates to obtain a yield curve that is not over-smoothed reflects a typical instability in required dimensions. Indeed, dimensionality appears otherwise remarkably stable. By contrast, the change in dimensions observed in Table 7.1 for the periods before and after October 2008 represents an extreme change in dimensions.

7.3.3   Yield curve dimensions and the effects
of quantitative easing

The result regarding stability prompts a more detailed search for the potential causes of the increase in required dimensions to obtain a yield curve that is not too smooth. Accompanying the period of near zero base rates has been a period of further monetary expansion through a process known as quantitative easing (QE). This was effected through a sequence of purchase auctions of government bonds between March 11, 2009 and January 26, 2010. A total of 662 purchase auctions were undertaken

Dim.	8/12/97 – 7/10/08		8/12/97 – 24/8/00		25/8/00 – 15/5/03		16/5/03 – 27/1/06		30/1/06 – 7/10/08		8/10/08 – 4/03/09	
	MAYE	DWp	MAYE	DWp	MAYE	DWp	MAYE	DWp	MAYE	DWp	MAYE	DWp
					Cubic spline							
5	0.0357	0.0066	0.0390	0.0238	0.0355	0.0013	0.0303	0.0012	0.0382	0.0000	0.0818	0.0000
6	0.0271	0.0210	**0.0269**	**0.0711**	0.0265	0.0106	0.0264	0.0018	0.0286	0.0003	0.0741	0.0000
7	**0.0229**	**0.0620**	0.0223	0.1823	**0.0208**	**0.0541**	0.0214	0.0103	0.0274	0.0012	0.0428	0.0000
8	0.0204	0.1088	0.0192	0.3235	0.0189	0.0777	0.0192	0.0249	0.0242	0.0086	0.0438	0.0043
9	0.0181	0.1888	0.0176	0.4404	0.0160	0.2149	**0.0174**	**0.0892**	0.0215	0.0101	0.0409	0.0141
10	0.0165	0.2752	0.0158	0.5684	0.0148	0.3190	0.0157	0.1946	0.0198	0.0178	0.0387	0.0161
11	0.0150	0.3917	0.0142	0.6899	0.0130	0.5288	0.0144	0.2912	**0.0182**	**0.0553**	0.0363	0.0302
12	0.0143	0.4438	0.0136	0.6992	0.0121	0.6920	0.0138	0.3262	0.0176	0.0560	**0.0332**	**0.0527**
13	0.0133	0.5428	0.0122	0.8572	0.0115	0.7531	0.0130	0.4064	0.0165	0.1527	0.0318	0.0593
					Nelson–Siegel							
5	0.0311	0.0128	0.0290	0.0463	0.0303	0.0033	0.0284	0.0013	0.0368	0.0000	0.0761	0.0000
7	**0.0227**	**0.0879**	**0.0208**	**0.2503**	**0.0207**	**0.0689**	0.0209	0.0303	0.0284	0.0020	0.0485	0.0003
9	0.0215	0.1316	0.0199	0.3342	0.0194	0.1185	**0.0201**	**0.0700**	0.0268	0.0034	0.0481	0.0063
11	0.0200	0.1905	0.0187	0.4313	0.0180	0.2117	0.0193	0.1100	0.0240	0.0082	0.0437	0.0124
13	0.0189	0.2627	0.0175	0.5245	0.0164	0.3245	0.0183	0.1821	0.0233	0.0189	0.0417	0.0177
15	0.0184	0.3088	0.0168	0.5999	0.0159	0.3935	0.0180	0.2187	0.0229	0.0219	0.0408	0.0221
17	0.0179	0.3651	0.0163	0.6699	0.0154	0.4791	0.0175	0.2723	0.0226	0.0377	0.0407	0.0341
19	0.0175	0.4135	0.0160	0.7212	0.0148	0.5493	0.0169	0.3339	0.0225	0.0480	0.0406	0.0327
21	0.0172	0.4677	0.0155	0.7838	0.0146	0.6197	0.0167	0.3953	**0.0221**	**0.0703**	0.0383	0.0417
23	0.0171	0.5032	0.0154	0.8221	0.0145	0.6908	0.0168	0.4030	0.0216	0.0951	**0.0374**	**0.0602**
25	0.0165	0.5519	0.0149	0.8642	0.0139	0.7397	0.0161	0.4693	0.0212	0.1326	0.0360	0.0674

This table reports statistics on fit (MAYE) and smoothness (DWp) for the two yield curve functions (cubic spline and extended Nelson–Siegel), fitted to the cross section of yields to maturity of UK coupon strips for each day (separately) between December 8, 1997 and April 27, 2011. The MAYE statistic is the average (across the indicated sub-sample period) mean (across the curve) absolute yield error (MAYE). The probability values (DWp) are for a Durbin–Watson statistic that measures the correlation of adjacent yield errors along the fitted curve. The p-values are calculated using a non-linear approximation to make a small sample adjustment to the asymptotic 5% d_L table, see Cummins and Hall (1999, p. 241). The reported value is the average of this statistic across the indicated sub-sample period. Each row contains the two statistics for the specified number of free parameters in the yield curve function, which is the dimension of the fitted yield curve (Dim.). The cubic spline model reduces to a polynomial for four or fewer parameters. The statistics in bold typeface are from the yield curves estimated using the minimum number of parameters to generate a yield curve that is not statistically significantly too smooth.

on 92 days, during the 46 week period.[12] The key QE announcements relating to the government bond market are summarized in Table 7.3. Perhaps either these announcements or the gilt purchases themselves affected the yield curve in such a way as to make them more difficult to fit and to avoid over-smoothing on announcement or auction days.[13] To examine this question, we examine the fit and smoothness of the yield curves for the period from the announcement of the start of QE on March 5, 2009, with and without the days of QE announcements or gilt purchase auctions. As with the comparison of the periods before and after the drop in base rates, we fit the yield curves using increasing dimensions to compare fit and smoothness as the parameterisation increases.

The results in Table 7.4 show that dimensions of the yield curve model required to ensure that the fitted yield curve is not too smooth do not seem to change when days of either QE announcements or gilt purchases are removed from the sample. In the case of the cubic spline model, the required dimensions remain at 17. At this level, the fitted curve is not statistically significantly too smooth, and the fit is equivalent whether or not QE announcement days or auction days are excluded. Comparing theses results to those in Table 7.1, it can also be seen that excluding the period between October 8, 2008 and March 4, 2009, during which interest rates were falling towards their near zero level, actually improves the fit of the yield curve for a given parameterisation level. For the Nelson–Siegel model, a further increase in dimension is required to ensure that the curve is not over-smoothed during the period following the introduction of QE, but this is also unaffected by the exclusion of QE announcement or gilt purchase auction days.

In Table 7.4, there is some suggestion that the fit of the yield curve is improved when the announcement days and gilt purchase auction auction days are excluded. To examine this issue more rigorously, we compare the fitting errors for the yield curve on event days to the errors on non-event days. We examine both the cubic spline model and the Nelson–Siegel model, using the dimensions suggested in Table 7.1 that provide not over-smoothed curves. To provide some benchmarks, we add days of MPC meetings and base rates changes to our set of event days that already includes QE announcements and gilt auction purchase

---

[12] Although 662 auctions were held, bonds were purchased in only 576 of these auctions. While there were auctions of around seven different bonds on any auction day, on 36 of the 92 auction days, one or more of the auctioned bonds were not purchased. There were no auction days on which no bonds were purchased.

[13] See Daines, Joyce and Tong (2012) for a comprehensive analysis of the effects of QE announcements and gilt market purchase auctions on individual gilts.

Table 7.3 *Key QE announcements relating to UK government bonds*

Announcement date	Decision on QE	Other decisions
19 January 2009	The Chancellor of the Exchequer announces that the Bank of England will set up an asset purchase programme.	
30 January 2009	Asset Purchase Facility Fund established. Exchange of letters between the Chancellor of the Exchequer and the Governor on 29 January 2009.	
11 February 2009	Bank of England's February *Inflation Report* and the associated press conference give strong indication that QE asset purchases are likely.	
5 March 2009	The MPC announces it will purchase £75 billion of assets over three months funded by central bank money. Conventional bonds are likely to constitute the majority of purchases, restricted to bonds with residual maturity between 5 and 25 years.	Base rate reduced from 1% to 0.5%.
11 March 2009	First purchases of UK government bonds (gilts).	
7 May 2009	The MPC announces that the amount of QE asset purchases will be extended by a further £50 billion to £125 billion.	
6 August 2009	The MPC announces that QE asset purchases will be extended to £175 billion and that the buying range will be extended to gilts with a residual maturity greater than three years.	The Bank announces a gilt lending programme, which allows counterparties to borrow gilts from the APF's portfolio via the DMO in return for a fee and alternative gilts as collateral.
5 November 2009	The MPC announced that the amount of QE asset purchases would be extended to £200 billion.	
4 February 2010	The MPC announced that the amount of QE asset purchases would be maintained at £200 billion.	The MPC's press statement said that the committee would continue to monitor the appropriate scale of the asset purchase programme and that further purchases would be made should the outlook warrant them.

Source: Joyce et al. (2012) and Daines et al. (2012).

Table 7.4 *Effects of QE on the smoothness of yield curves of increasing dimensionality*

| | Cubic spline | | | | | | | Nelson–Siegel | | | | | |
| | QE period from 5 March 2009 | | QE period excluding days of gilt purchases | | QE period excluding days of gilt purchases and QE announcements | | | QE period from 5 March 2009 | | QE period excluding days of gilt purchases | | QE period excluding days of gilt purchases and QE announcements | |
Dim.	MAYE	DWp	MAYE	DWp	MAYE	DWp	Dim.	MAYE	DWp	MAYE	DWp	MAYE	DWp
13	0.0217	0.0021	0.0189	0.0025	0.0188	0.0025	43	0.0195	0.0292	0.0178	0.0289	0.0176	0.0277
14	0.0178	0.0047	0.0159	0.0055	0.0158	0.0050	45	0.0195	0.0360	0.0178	0.0352	0.0176	0.0340
15	0.0143	0.0149	0.0130	0.0148	0.0129	0.0138	47	0.0195	0.0435	0.0178	0.0421	0.0177	0.0408
16	0.0140	0.0094	0.0126	0.0097	0.0125	0.0089	49	**0.0193**	**0.0518**	**0.0176**	**0.0491**	0.0174	0.0477
17	**0.0118**	**0.0927**	**0.0109**	**0.0747**	**0.0108**	**0.0725**	51	0.0190	0.0588	**0.0172**	**0.0559**	**0.0171**	**0.0538**
18	0.0112	0.1023	0.0101	0.0853	0.0101	0.0831	53	0.0190	0.0692	0.0172	0.0651	0.0171	0.0629

This table reports statistics on fit (MAYE) and smoothness (DWp) for the two yield curve functions (cubic spline and extended Nelson–Siegel), fitted to the cross section of yields to maturity of UK coupon strips for each day (separately) between March 5, 2009 and April 27, 2011. The MAYE statistic is the average (across the indicated sub-sample period) mean (across the curve) absolute yield error (MAYE). The probability values (DWp) are for a Durbin–Watson statistic that measures the correlation of adjacent yield errors along the fitted curve. The p-values are calculated using a non-linear approximation to make a small sample adjustment to the asymptotic 5% d_L table, see Cummins and Hall (1999, p. 241). The reported value is the average of this statistic across the indicated sub-sample period. Each row contains the two statistics for the specified number of free parameters in the yield curve function, which is the dimension of the fitted yield curve (Dim.). The cubic spline model reduces to a polynomial for four or fewer parameters. The statistics in bold typeface are from the yield curves estimated using the minimum number of parameters to generate a yield curve that is not statistically significantly too smooth.

Table 7.5 *Gilt purchases and the fit of the yield curve*

Event	Cubic spline (7)		Nelson–Siegel (7)		Cubic spline (17)		Nelson–Siegel (43)	
	MAYE	DWp	MAYE	DWp	MAYE	DWp	MAYE	DWp
	Dec 8, 1997 to October 7, 2008							
ΔBase Rate	0.0276	0.0726	0.0269	0.0872	0.0115	0.7503	0.0146	0.7785
\	0.0229	0.0619	0.0227	0.0880	0.0107	0.7717	0.0137	0.8071
p-value	0.2789	0.3513	0.3053	0.4918	0.3897	0.3626	0.3994	0.3359
MPC meeting	0.0261	0.0527	0.0262	0.0712	0.0122	0.8032	0.0154	0.8025
\	0.0228	0.0625	0.0226	0.0888	0.0106	0.7698	0.0136	0.8069
p-value	0.1580	0.2256	0.1484	0.1252	0.1585	0.1194	0.1757	0.4475
	March 5, 2009 to April 27, 2011							
MPC meeting	0.0362	0.0000	0.0359	0.0000	0.0121	0.0670	0.0203	0.0266
\	0.0369	0.0000	0.0364	0.0000	0.0117	0.0940	0.0195	0.0293
p-value	0.4088	0.2191	0.4395	0.1377	0.3938	0.2231	0.3495	0.4593
QE Announce	0.0487	0.0000	0.0498	0.0000	0.0179	0.2311	0.0287	0.1108
\	0.0336	0.0000	0.0325	0.0000	0.0108	0.0725	0.0176	0.0277
p-value	**0.0448**	0.1939	**0.0271**	0.1378	**0.0410**	0.1311	**0.0146**	0.2421
Gilt Purchase	0.0525	0.0000	0.0543	0.0000	0.0161	0.1806	0.0280	0.0306
\	0.0336	0.0000	0.0325	0.0000	0.0108	0.0725	0.0176	0.0277
p-value	**0.0000**	0.1427	**0.0000**	0.1377	**0.0000**	**0.0003**	**0.0000**	0.3897

This table reports statistics on fit (MAYE) and smoothness (DWp) for the two yield curve functions (cubic spline and extended Nelson–Siegel), fitted to the cross section of yields to maturity of UK coupon strips for each day (separately) between December 8, 1997 and April 27, 2011. The MAYE statistic is the average (across the indicated sub-sample period) mean (across the curve) absolute yield error (MAYE). The probability values (DWp) are for a Durbin–Watson statistic that measures the correlation of adjacent yield errors along the fitted curve. The p-values are calculated using a non-linear approximation to make a small sample adjustment to the asymptotic 5% d_L table, see Cummins and Hall (1999, p. 241). The reported value is the average of this statistic across the indicated sub-sample period. Each row contains the two statistics for the specified number of free parameters in the yield curve function, which is the dimension of the fitted yield curve (Dim.). The cubic spline model reduces to a polynomial for four or fewer parameters. The statistics in bold typeface are from the yield curves estimated using the minimum number of parameters to generate a yield curve that is not statistically significantly too smooth. This table reports comparative statistics for events that could influence the fit (MAYE) and smoothness (DWp) of the fitted yield curve. These events are days featuring changes in the base interest rate, a meeting of the Monetary Policy Committee (MPC), an announcement regarding QE, or the occurrence of gilt purchase auctions. For a given sample period, each set of three rows reports the MAYE and DWp for the subset of event days (first row), the subset of days not featuring that specific event (second row), and the p-value of a *t*-test (thrid row) of the significance of the difference between the statistics in the two rows above.

days, and examine events prior to the drop in base rates as well as subsequent to this. If the yield curve is always more difficult to fit on MPC meeting days, for example, then it is less notable that it is difficult to fit on a gilt purchase auction day. Table 7.5 contains the results of this exercise. In the upper panel, the impact of base rate changes and MPC meeting announcements in the period prior to the drop in base rates (8/12/97 to 7/10/08) is examined. The average MAYE and average DWp (smoothness) statistics are reported for announcement days and non-announcement days. We use a two-sample *t*-test to determine whether these averages are different between the announcement day sample and the non-announcement day sample. The p-values of these statistics, reported in Table 7.5, clearly show that none of these event days presented any challenges in fitting the yield curve, regardless of the dimensions of the curve employed. When we turn to the period following the drop in interest rates to 0.5% (5/3/09 to 27/4/11), we again see that MPC announcements do not affect the fit of the yield curve. By contrast, both QE announcements and gilt purchase auction days appear to make the fit of the yield curve significantly worse for a given parameterisation of the curve. The effect is stronger for gilt purchase auction days than for QE announcements and for more parsimonious models of the curve. The curves with increased dimensions absorb the event days more easily.

If the yield curve is having difficulty in fitting the curve on QE related event days then it may be possible to see this in the fitted curves themselves. Since the yield curve represents average rates to maturity, whereas the corresponding forward curves represent the marginal rate at a given maturity, it is more natural to examine the forward curves to expose the impact of events. To make this examination as conservative as possible, we will examine the forward curves of the most heavily parameterised model of the four that were examined in Table 7.5, the extended Nelson–Siegel model with 21 pairs of slope and curvature terms. The forward curve corresponding to the Nelson Siegel model in Equation (7.2) is

$$f(\tau) = \beta_0 + \beta_1 e^{-\lambda\tau} + \beta_2 \lambda\tau e^{-\lambda\tau}, \qquad (7.4)$$

where the three right hand side components also represent level, slope and curvature, see Figure 7.2. Thus the addition of slope and curvature terms into the yield curve will be mirrored by the addition of additional slope and curvature terms in the forward curve.

As the gilt purchase auctions comprise large purchases of bonds at particular points along the yield curve, it may be possible to see the effects at particular locations across the curve. The maturities of gilts available for QE purchases changed over time, as explained in Table 7.3. In the beginning, in March 2009, only maturities of between 5 and 25 years were included. In August 2009, maturities of between 3 and 5 years and greater than 25 years were added. The pattern of auctions

between March 2009 and August 2009 saw the set of bonds being purchased alternating between maturities of 5 to 10 years and maturities
of 10 to 25 years. This structure provides some natural break points to
define different maturity 'buckets' along the yield curve. Short maturities will be defined as 3 to 5 years, medium maturities as 5 to 10
years, long maturities as 10 to 25 years and extra long maturities as
those beyond 25 years. After August 2009 auctions tended to feature
bonds from more than one maturity bucket, although not always were
all buckets used. To look at the effect of the auctions on the shape of
the forward curve, we first estimate the average forward curve for the
days during the active auction period (March 11, 2009 to January 26,
2010) that did not have any gilt purchase auctions. Figures 7.3 and 7.4
provide this curve together with standard deviation bounds to give an
indication of the variability of the curve across the set of non-auction
days. In Figure 7.3, we examine the single bucket auctions, the set of
medium and long maturity auctions that took place between March
2009 and August 2009, and the extra long maturity auctions that took
place after August 2009. It can be seen that the medium and long-term
maturity auctions both pushed the forward curve down in the medium
maturity range and upwards in the long maturity range, but that these
moves are within one standard deviation of the average curve on non-
auction days. By contrast, the extra long maturity auctions lower the
forward curve at long and extra long maturities, but raise it slightly at

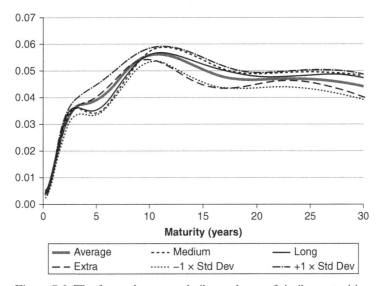

Figure 7.3 The forward curve and gilt purchases of similar maturities

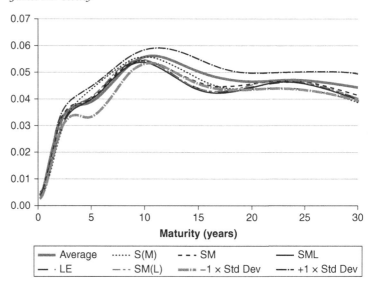

Figure 7.4 The forward curve and gilt purchases across a range of maturities

medium maturities. In Figure 7.4, we examine the purchase auctions of gilts across multiple maturity buckets. In this case, all the auctions appear to reduce the long and extra long-term forward rates and increase the medium term forward rates. The movement in longer term forward rates is greater than that seen with the single maturity bucket auctions.

How then do these forward curve effects inform our analysis of the causes of the increased dimensionality of the yield curve in recent times? It is clear that auction days do coincide with a distinct shape change in the forward curve – relative to the average forward curve. This shape change appears to exaggerate the undulations in the curve; this is particularly noticeable at 5 years to maturity. These increased undulations may require further dimensions to adequately fit the yield curve and avoid smoothing them away. However, there does not seem to be any obvious relationship between the maturity of the bonds being issued and the effects on that maturity region of the curve. If anything, the differing effects seem to coincide with the extension of the maturity ranges in August 2009. Before that time point, the auctions generally tilted the long end of the forward curve upwards, whereas after this point the auctions generally tilted the long end downwards. This could easily be explained by the further expansion of QE in August putting downward pressure on longer term interest rate expectations.

These two contrasting results on the effects of gilt purchases on the shape of the forward curve have important implications for the effectiveness of QE as a macroeconomic policy instrument. Joyce et al. (2011) identify three possible channels through which QE may affect the economy: improved confidence arising from perceptions that the monetary authorities are willing to take bold actions; increased bank lending in response to the boost in commercial bank reserves; and higher asset prices in response to the asset purchases which lead to increased wealth and on to reduced borrowing costs. For the asset prices to respond to asset purchases, there must be an imperfect substitutability among them, so that portfolio rebalancing has material effects. In the context of the bond market, theories of market segmentation such as Modigliani and Sutch's (1966) preferred habitat hypothesis provide a foundation for possible effects from portfolio rebalancing, although the empirical evidence for habitat behaviour is mixed.[14] The evidence provided here that there do not seem to be specific maturity related effects suggests that QE may have difficulty working through a portfolio rebalancing channel. Eggertsson and Woodford (2003) have argued that imperfect substitutability is insufficient on its own to generate portfolio balance effects in standard New Keynesian macroeconomic models. In these models, QE needs also to change agents' beliefs about the future path of inflation. The change in the response of the forward curve to purchases after August 2009 is certainly consistent with a change in inflation expectations; but whether this was caused by the change in the maturities available for asset purchases or is coincidental to it is not possible to determine from yield curve data alone.

Overall, it has been seen that the dimensionality of the yield curve has increased during the period following the move to near zero short rates. There is evidence to suggest that the curve is more difficult to fit on days of QE announcements and on days of gilt purchase auctions, and evidence that the forward curve displays more undulations on such days. Together these offer a potential explanation of why increased yield curves require increased parameterisation to achieve the same levels of fit and smoothness as was possible prior to the reduction in base rates.

7.3.4 *The dimensions of the evolution of the yield curve*

A principal components decomposition of the set of time series of yields is performed for each of the four different functional forms for the yield

---

[14] The earliest systematic empirical study of traditional term structure theories is Dobson, Sutch and Vanderford (1976). A more recent example of a test of a habitat model is Greenwood and Vayanos (2010).

curve. Each functional form is one that requires the minimum number of free parameters to obtain a yield curve that is, on average across time and maturity, not too smooth, as defined in Section 7.3.1. Thus we created the time series of yield curves from the seven parameter cubic spline and extended Nelson–Siegel models, which were the most parsimonious models in the period December 8, 1997 to October 7, 2008, and a 17 parameter cubic spline and a 43 parameter extended Nelson–Siegel model, which were the most parsimonious models in the period October 8, 2008 to April 27, 2011. Each model is run over both subsamples to separate the effects of the different time period from those of the different functional form. As the maximum maturity at some points in the early sample is around 23 years, we use a set of yields for the principal components analysis that have a maximum maturity of 20 years. We use 3 month maturity intervals until 10 years maturity and 6 month maturity intervals until 20 years.

Table 7.6 provides the proportion of the variation of the yield curve that is explained by each of the first four principal components. The pattern is remarkably stable across yield curve functional forms. Most of the variation can be explained by the first three principal components, with the first component accounting for between 81 and 84 per cent of the variation, the second component accounting for around 11 per cent of the variation and the third component accounting for between 2 and 5 per cent of the variation. There is, however, a noticeable difference between the proportion of variation explained by each of the components across the two sub-samples. After the change in shape of the yield curve, the proportion of the yield curve explained by the first factor falls from around 84 percent to around 81 percent. The proportion explained by the second component hardly changes at all, but the proportions explained by both the third and fourth components increase substantially. The third component's explanatory power increases from around 3 per cent to around 4 per cent, while the fourth component that has an R^2 of less than 1 per cent before the reduction in short rates experiences a rise in R^2 to over 2 per cent.

To determine whether these changes in the proportions of the yield curve movements explained by the first four principal components are significant, we use the property of the eigenvectors that the sum of the squares of their elements equals the R^2 of the principal component to construct a t-test of the difference between R^2 values. The R^2 (the eigenvalue) is, therefore, an average of the proportion of the curve at each separate maturity point that is explained by that component. A t-test for the difference between two means can then be used to determine if the changes observed in the eigenvalues are statistically significant.

The p-values of these tests are also shown in Table 7.6. Only the fourth principal component is statistically more important than it was prior to the reduction in base rates. This is true within three of the four yield curve models. Only in the yield curves generated from the more parsimonious version of the Nelson–Siegel model does the fourth eigenvalue not increase by a statistically significant amount. Of more importance, however, are the tests between the models as they change to reflect the need for increased cross sectional dimensions after the reduction in base rates. Here, for both the cubic spline model and the Nelson–Siegel model, the increase in the fourth eigenvalue is statistically significant. These results are, intuitively at least, somewhat intriguing as it is the

Table 7.6 *Variation is the yield curve explained by the first four principal components*

	December 8, 1997 to October 7, 2008				October 8, 2008 to April 27, 2011			
	PC1	PC2	PC3	PC4	PC1	PC2	PC3	PC4
	Cubic spline (7 free parameters)							
R^2	**0.8411**	**0.1196**	**0.0333**	**0.0052**	0.8126	0.1163	0.0413	0.0233
Within model p-values					0.5772	0.9273	0.4661	0.0002
	Cubic spline (17 free parameters)							
R^2	0.8427	0.1197	0.0290	0.0057	**0.8126**	**0.1163**	**0.0413**	**0.0233**
Within model p-values					0.2304	0.8654	0.2073	0.0002
Between model p-values					0.2499	0.8720	0.4554	<0.0001
	Nelson–Siegel (7 free parameters)							
R^2	**0.8413**	**0.1200**	**0.0310**	**0.0065**	0.8291	0.1184	0.0397	0.0125
Within model p-values					0.9301	0.9987	0.8810	0.2959
	Nelson–Siegel (43 free parameters)							
R^2	0.8435	0.1200	0.0293	0.0039	**0.8149**	**0.1164**	**0.0404**	**0.0229**
Within model p-values					0.5549	0.9149	0.9339	0.0155
Between model p-values					0.2893	0.8608	0.3747	<0.0001

The R^2 are the proportion of the variation of the yield curve explained by the principal components of the covariance matrix of fixed maturity yields estimated from the yield curve model indicated. Daily observations on fixed maturities at 3 month intervals until 10 years and 6 month intervals until 20 years are used. The R^2 are equal to the eigenvalues of the matrix divided by the number of yield series. The R^2 in bold typeface are from the yield curves estimated using the minimum number of parameters to generate a yield curve that is not statistically significantly too smooth. Those in regular typeface are for comparison to show the stability of the results across alternative functional forms for the cross section of zero-coupon yields. Within model p-values refer to tests of the difference between the R^2 (eigenvalues) across the two sub-samples for a given yield curve estimation model. Between model p-values test the difference between the R^2 (eigenvalues) in bold typeface.

change in the slope of the yield curve that is the dominant visual change from the early sub-sample to the later sub-sample, see Figure 7.1.

However, the influence of the visual change in slope on the underlying factor structure becomes clearer when we examine the loadings on the principal components, which are the eigenvectors of the covariance matrix of yields. Figures 7.5 to 7.8 show the impact of between minus two and plus two standard deviation shocks to each of the first four principal components on the average yield curve, for each of the sub-samples. In Figure 7.5, it can be seen that the level factor affects the yield curve in the same way after the reduction in base rates as it did beforehand. By contrast, in Figures 7.6, 7.7 and 7.8 it can be seen that the slope factor now has a bigger effect at the short end of the curve than it did before the reduction in base rates, whereas the curvature and fourth factor now have a bigger influence on the longer end of the yield curve.

So, in summary, although the evolution of yield curve remains dominated by three dynamic factors representing level, slope and curvature, the influence of curvature has increased overall, the slope factor now has a bigger impact at shorter yields, and a fourth factor is statistically more important than has hitherto been the case. The increased importance of the fourth principal component has also been detected in the US yield curve, see for example Cochrane and Piazzesi (2005), suggesting that this is not a result unique to the UK yield curve. In terms of the UK yield curve, the forward curves in Figures 7.3 and 7.4 indicated that the gilt purchase auctions undertaken during the QE period were clearly influencing the curvature in the yield curve, making the forward curve undulations much more pronounced. The principal components tend to deliver eigenvectors with successively increasing 'difference' effects on the shape of the yield curve, that is, the second eigenvector represents slope, which is the change in level, while the third eigenvector represents curvature, which is the change in slope. This means that the fourth eigenvector represents a change in curvature. The fourth principal component may therefore be detecting the shocks to curvature occurring when gilt purchase auctions are taking place.

7.4   Conclusions

The main findings of this study, and the implications for market practitioners and policymakers, are as follows. Prior to the reduction in base interest rates, the cross section of zero-coupon yields can be well represented by either cubic spline or Nelson–Siegel functional forms having seven free parameters. Subsequently, the number of free parameters required in either functional form to deliver estimated yield curves that

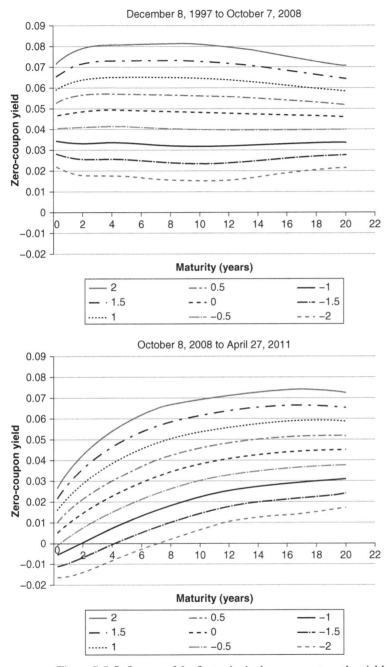

Figure 7.5 Influence of the first principal component on the yield curve

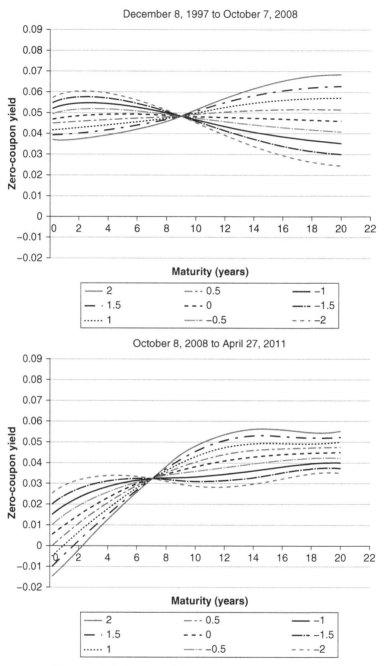

Figure 7.6 Influence of the second principal component on the yield curve

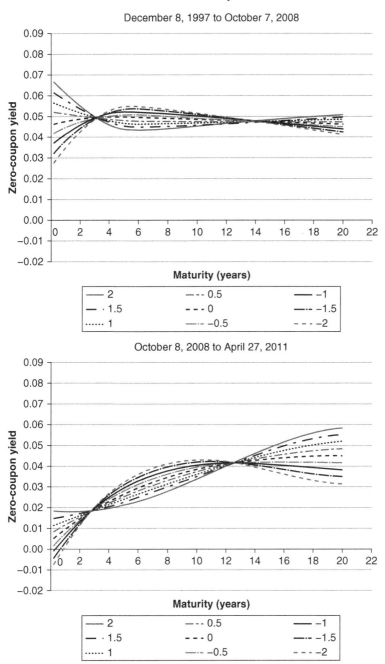

Figure 7.7 Influence of the third principal component on the yield curve

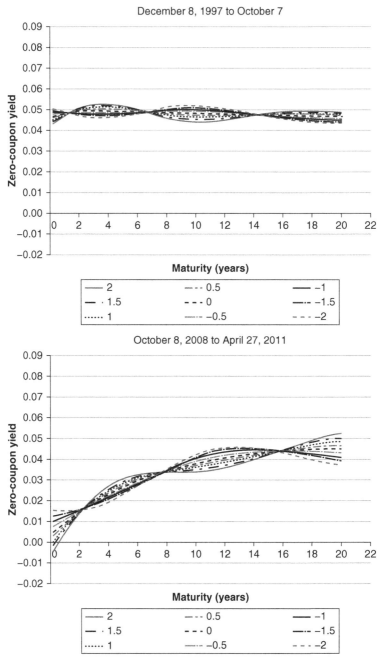

Figure 7.8 Influence of the fourth principal component on the yield curve

fit as well, are not over-smoothed, or both, has increased markedly. A cubic spline requires the addition of a further 10 free parameters, while the Nelson and Siegel model would require a further 36 free parameters. This result is more striking given the general stability in the required number of free parameters that we find prior to the drop in base rates. The increase in the required number of parameters suggests caution in using low dimensional functional forms for estimating yield curves after October 2008, but merit possibly in over-parameterising the yield curve and then constraining back the roughness, as in, for example, Fisher et al. (1995).

As the recent period of low short-term interest rates has been accompanied by a process of quantitative easing, we investigated whether announcements relating to quantitative easing or the gilt purchase auctions that were used to effect it led to the increased yield curve dimensionality. While the smoothness of the curve per se did not seem to be responding to the events, there was evidence that the estimation errors when fitting the curve were significantly larger on event days. We also found that on these same days, the estimated forward curve seemed to display increased undulations relative to the curve on non-event days. Taken together these two observations indicate that more flexibility is desirable when fitting the yield curve in the recent environment of low short-term interest rates.

The principal components analysis also provides further support for a need for enhanced flexibility. While the influence of the first three components on the yield curve did not display a significant change as a result of the drop in base rates, the fourth component experienced a significant increase in explanatory power, albeit that its overall contribution is relatively small. Since each successive principal component represents, intuitively at least, the effects of changes in the previous one, the fourth component can be thought of as representing changes in curvature. The increase in significance of the fourth principal component could well be responding to the increased undulations seen in the yield curve, and more especially in the forward curve, in the more recent period.

The impacts of QE observed on the estimated forward curves provide some evidence that QE may struggle to operate through a portfolio rebalancing channel, but that changing the bonds available for purchase by the Bank of England may have resulted in a change in inflation expectations. Investigating this issue further is left for future research.

References

Anderson, N. (1994). Testing models of the yield curve. Bank of England Mimeo.

Anderson, N. and Sleath, J. (2001). New estimates of the UK real and nominal yield curves. Bank of England Working Paper, no. 126.

Bjork, T. and Christensen, B. J. (1999). Interest rate dynamics and consistent forward rate curves. *Mathematical Finance*, **9**, 323–348.

Bliss, R. R. (1997). Testing term structure estimation methods. *Advances in Futures and Options Research*, **9**, 197–231.

Christensen, J. H. E., Diebold, F. X., and Rudebusch, G. D. (2009). An arbitrage-free generalized Nelson–Siegel term structure model. *Econometrics Journal*, **12**, C33–C64.

Christensen, J. H. E., Diebold, F. X., and Rudebusch, G. D. (2011). The affine arbitrage-free class of Nelson–Siegel term structure models. *Journal of Econometrics*, **164**, 4–20.

Cochrane, J. and Piazzesi, M. (2005). Bond risk premia. *American Economic Review*, **95**, 138–160.

Cummins, C. and Hall, B. (1999). *TSP4.5 Reference Manual*. Stanford: TSP International.

Daines, M., Joyce, M. A. S. and Tong, M. (2012). QE and the gilt market: a disaggregated analysis. Bank of England Working Paper, no. 466.

De Pooter, M. (2007). Examining the Nelson–Siegel class of term structure models: in-sample fit versus out-of-sample forecasting. Discussion paper 2007-043/4. Tinbergen Institute, Erasmus University.

Deacon, M. and Derry, A. (1994). Estimating the term structure of interest rates. Bank of England Working Paper, no. 23.

Diebold, F. X. and Li, C. (2006). Forecasting the term structure of government bond yields. *Journal of Econometrics*, **130**, 337–364.

Diebold, F. X. and Rudebusch, G. D. (2011). *The Dynamic Nelson–Siegel Approach to Yield Curve Modelling and Forecasting*. Princeton, NJ: Princeton University Press.

Dobson, S., Sutch, R. and Vanderford, D. (1976). An evaluation of alternative empirical models of the term structure of interest rates, *Journal of Finance*, **31**, 1035–1066.

Dybvig, P. H. (1996). Bond and bond option pricing based on the current term structure, in *Mathematics of Derivative Securities* (M. A. H. Dempster and S. Pliska, eds.), Cambridge: Cambridge University Press.

Eggertsson, G. and Woodford, M. (2003). The zero bound on interest rates and optimal monetary policy, *Brookings Papers on Economic Activity*, **34**, 139–211.

Ferguson, R. and Raymar, S. (1998). A comparative analysis of several popular term structure estimation models. *Journal of Fixed Income*, March, 17–33.

Fisher, M., Nychka, D. and Zervos, D. (1995). Fitting the term structure of interest rates with smoothing splines. Federal Reserve Board, Finance and Economics Discussion Paper, 95–1.

Greenwood, R. and Vayanos, D. (2010). Bond supply and excess bond returns. NBER Working Paper.

Ioannides, M. (2003). A comparison of yield curve estimation techniques using UK data. *Journal of Banking and Finance*, **27**, 1–26.

Joyce, M. A. S., Tong, M. and Woods, R. (2011). The United Kingdom's quantitative easing policy: design, operation and impact. *Bank of England Quarterly Bulletin*, **51**, 200–212.

Kikugawa, T. and Singleton, K. J. (1994). Modeling the term structure of interest rates in Japan. *Journal of Fixed Income*, Sept., 6–16.

Litterman, R. and Scheinkman, J. (1991). Common factors affecting bond returns. *Journal of Fixed Income*, **1**, 77–85.

Mastronikola, K. (1991). Yield curves for gilt-edged stocks: a new model. Bank of England Discussion Paper (Technical Series) 49.

McCulloch, J. H. (1971). Measuring the term structure of interest rates. *Journal of Business*, **44**, 19–31.

McCulloch, J. H. (1975). The tax adjusted yield curve. *Journal of Finance*, **30**, 811–829.

McCulloch, J. H. and Kochin, L. A. (2000). The inflation premium in the US real and nominal term structures of interest rates. Ohio State University Economics Department Working Paper #98–12.

Modigliani, F. and Sutch, R. C. (1966). Innovations in interest rate policy, *American Economic Review*, **56**, 178–197.

Nelson, C. R. and Siegel, A. F. (1987). Parsimonious modelling of yield curves. *Journal of Business*, **60**, 473–489.

Proudman, J. (1995). The microstructure of the UK gilt market. Bank of England Working Paper, no. 38.

Rumsey, J. (1996). Comparison of tax rates inferred from zero-coupon yield curves. *Journal of Fixed Income*, March, 75–81.

Shea, G. S. (1984). Pitfalls in smoothing interest rate term structure data: equilibrium models and spline approximations. *Journal of Financial and Quantitative Analysis*, **19**, 253–269.

Steeley, J. M. (1990). Modelling the dynamics of the term structure of interest rates, *Economic and Social Review* Symposium on Finance, **21**, 337–362.

Steeley, J. M. (1991). Estimating the gilt-edged term structure: basis splines and confidence intervals. *Journal of Business Finance and Accounting*, **18**, 513–529.

Steeley, J. M. (2008). Testing term structure estimation methods: evidence from the UK STRIPS market. *Journal of Money, Credit and Banking*, **40**, 1489–1512.

Steeley, J. M. (2011). A shape-based decomposition of the yield adjustment term in the arbitrage-free Nelson and Siegel (AFNS) model of the yield curve, unpublished manuscript, Aston University.

Svensson, L. E. O. (1995). Estimating forward interest rates with the extended Nelson–Siegel method. *Sveriges Riksbank Quarterly Review*, **3**, 13–26.

Vitale, P. (1998). Two months in the life of several gilt-edged market makers on the London Stock Exchange. *Journal of International Financial Markets, Institutions and Money*, **8**, 299–324.

8 The intelligible factor model: international comparison and stylized facts

Yvan Lengwiler and Carlos Lenz

8.1 Introduction

Factor models of yield curve dynamics pursue different objectives. Among other things they are used for forecasting, to study the effects of different types of economic shocks, or to reduce complexity while capturing the main features of changes in the shape of the yield curve. Depending on their purpose the models may vary along different dimensions, but their common denominator is a dynamic specification for a small number of factors and a mapping relating the factors to the yield curve.

In this chapter we use a factor model to identify a set of stylized facts of yield curve dynamics across countries. The model is designed to capture the joint movement of yield curve factors. It aims at exploring the impact of a shock to a single factor over the entire yield curve. Our approach therefore provides an answer to questions like "How does a shock to the long-term interest rate propagate over time over the entire maturity range?"

The model separates the cross-sectional and the intertemporal relationships of the yield curve into factors on the one hand, and a dynamic equation for the development of the factors on the other hand. The innovations that drive the factors are serially uncorrelated, independent random variables and are therefore genuine, clean shocks.

Using data for the USA, the UK, and Germany, we find a set of stylized facts that are robust across countries and relevant enough to warrant a deeper economic analysis. For example, we find that shocks originating in the medium maturity spectrum are the main driver of yield

We thank participants of the CIMF-IESEG conference at Cambridge University for useful comments, in particular Hans Dewachter, Petra Geraats, and Rodrigo Guimarães. We also thank Jacob Gyntelberg for helpful discussions. The views expressed in this chapter are those of the authors and do not necessarily represent those of the Swiss National Bank.

curve dynamics. This might be bothersome if one thinks that a Central Bank influencing the short end of the yield curve has some leverage over long-term rates.

In this contribution, we do not dig deeper into such issues, however. Our analysis is purely descriptive and does not attempt to identify the economic sources or particular events behind movements in the yield curve. Therefore, this chapter constitutes a first step towards a more structural type of analysis. Different directions are possible, depending on the questions of interest. One type of question might relate our identified drivers of the yield curve to particular events. Another type could deal with the choice of monetary policy instruments to influence different segments of the yield curve.

8.2   Short review of the model

We apply the model that we recently developed in Lengwiler and Lenz (2010). Let $r_t(m)$ denote the interest rate for a zero bond at time t which matures at time $t + m$. The cross-section of interest rates is described by three factors,

$$r_t(m) = k_1(m)\phi_{1,t} + k_2(m)\phi_{2,t} + k_3(m)\phi_{3,t} + \epsilon_t(m). \qquad (8.1)$$

ϕ are time-varying factors, and k are their loadings. ϕ and k are constructed together so that they have certain advantageous properties.

First, the components of k assume clear interpretations, as can be seen from Figure 8.1. The first factor is the only one that loads on the very long end of the maturity spectrum, so we call ϕ_1 the *long factor*. The second factor is the only one that loads on the very short end of the maturity spectrum, so we call ϕ_2 the *short factor*. The third factor has zero loading at the short and the long end of the maturity spectrum, but it is normalized in such a way that it achieves unit loading somewhere in the middle, $\max k_3(m) = 1$. We call this the *curvature factor*.[1]

Second, the dynamics of the factors ϕ is described by a *structural* VAR,

$$\phi_t = D_0 + D_1\phi_{t-1} + \cdots + D_p\phi_{t-p} + u_t. \qquad (8.2)$$

We set p large enough so that the factor innovations u_t becomes serially uncorrelated. As described in Lengwiler and Lenz (2010), the

---

[1] Note that these loadings differ from the more common loadings "level", "slope", and "curvature", which have become customary in applications of principal component analysis (Litterman and Scheinkman, 1991) or in the specification of Nelson and Siegel (1987).

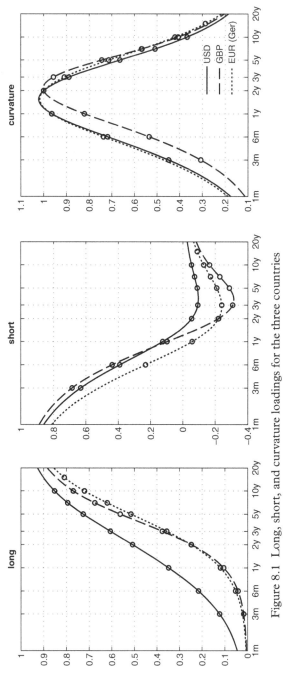

Figure 8.1 Long, short, and curvature loadings for the three countries

$\phi - k$-system is designed in such a way that the covariance matrix of u becomes diagonal.

The result of this procedure is a set of loadings that describes the long end, the short end, and the curvature of the yield curve. The dynamics of these factors are described by a structural VAR model, meaning that the factor innovations are orthogonal to each other and serially uncorrelated. We call such factors *intelligible*.

The decomposition of the yield curve into these three particular factors obviously lacks a theoretical foundation. It is a purely statistical method designed to disentangle aspects of the dynamics of the yield curve. It is designed to identify stylized facts that may go unnoticed otherwise.

8.3   Relations to recent literature

It is almost impossible to keep track of the theoretical and empirical literature on the term structure of interest rates. In the following, we focus on recent contributions that use a factor model to describe the cross-section of interest rates, and a VAR model to analyze the dynamics of the factors. This combination has proved to be empirically successful in modeling the yield curve and its dynamics through time. We discuss the contributions in chronological order.

Dewachter and Lyrio (2006) simultaneously estimate inflation dynamics, the output gap, and an essentially affine term structure model. Their objective is to relate the yield curve to macroeconomic factors. Projecting key macroeconomic variables onto their estimated latent factors allows them to relate the level factor almost exclusively to inflation expectations; the slope factor seems most related to business cycle variables (in their case the output gap and inflation shocks). The curvature factor, in turn is most related to independent real interest rate shocks, which they label an "independent monetary policy stance" factor.

Diebold and Li (2006) use the parsimonious model of Nelson and Siegel (1987) to describe the cross-section of interest rates, and then model the dynamics of these factors with a univariate AR(1) processes. Their aim is to forecast future yield curves.

The contribution of Diebold et al. (2008) is most closely related to ours. It applies the approach presented in Diebold and Li (2006) to an international setting. The authors use a simplified version of the Nelson–Siegel model and yield data from several countries. Within this setting, they identify global and country-specific slope and level factors. They find that global factors are economically important as they explain a substantial share of variation in country yields. In addition, the slope and level factors reflect the major developments in global real activity and inflation. The authors therefore conclude that global macroeconomic factors are an important driver of yield curves of individual countries.

Bianchi et al. (2009) also follow Diebold and Li (2006) in using the Nelson–Siegel factors to describe the cross-section of interest rates. However, they use a FAVAR with time-varying coefficients to describe the dynamics of the Nelson–Siegel factors as well as some macroeconomic variables. They use UK interest rates in their study and are interested in the effects of monetary policy shocks on the yield curve. One of their main conclusions is that the response of the level factor to monetary policy shocks changes from positive to negative in 1992 with the introduction of inflation targeting. Thus, it appears that the monetary policy strategy that a Central Bank pursues affects the makeup of the dynamics of the yield curve and of the connection between the yield curve and other macroeconomic variables.

Mönch (2010) follows the method proposed by Diebold and Li (2006) and also uses the Nelson–Siegel specification to describe the cross-section of interest rates. He combines the resulting three factors with other key macroeconomic time series, and describes the joint dynamics with a VAR. He finds that curvature innovations are very informative about future evolution of the term structure. Positive curvature innovations signal a flattening of the term structure over time and indicate a coming recession.

8.4   Data and results

8.4.1   The data

We use daily data on zero coupon government bond yields from the USA, the UK, and Germany.[2] The common sample is from January 1, 1999 to December 31, 2010 (more than 3000 business days), and thus covers the great moderation and the first years of the financial crisis. For the US and UK data, we use maturities of three and six months, and one, two, three, five, seven, and ten years. In the German case, the three-month maturity is not available. We add the 15-year maturity, which is the longest that is available from the Bundesbank.

---

[2] The data for the USA are taken from the US Treasury and are available for download either from their website of from the FRED database of the Federal Reserve Bank of St. Louis. The UK data are from Datastream. The German data are taken from the website of the Bundesbank. All three data sets represent zero-coupon yield curves that are derived from secondary market prices of coupon-bearing government debt.

For each data set, the lag length of the VAR must be chosen separately. We aim for uncorrelated innovations, so we use the Q-statistic to guide our choice. For simplicity, we choose the same lag length for the three data sets. We have found that a length of 30 days is sufficient to make the innovations serially uncorrelated in all three data sets. This is, of course, a very large number of lags, but we still have many degrees of freedom due to the large sample.

8.4.2   Common stylized facts

The factor loadings for the three data sets are similar, as can be inspected from Figure 8.1 above. In particular, the curvatures assume a maximum at a maturity between one and a half and two years in all three cases.

The dynamics among the factors is also very similar. This is revealed by the impulse-response function, see Figure 8.2.[3] For all three countries we find essentially the same pattern. Long and short innovations (u_1 and u_2, respectively) largely affect only their own factors (ϕ_1 and ϕ_2, respectively).

The long factor is also more or less unaffected by innovations into the short or curvature factors. Thus, the long factor does not affect the other two factors, and is also itself not affected by them. It lives a life of its own. This is our first stylized fact.

Stylized fact 8.1 *The long factor interacts very little with the other two factors describing the yield curve.*

Curvature innovations (u_3) are different: of course they drive the development of the curvature factor (ϕ_3), but they affect the short factor (ϕ_2) almost equally strongly. Thus, the common movements of the short and curvature factors that we see in Figure 8.4 are largely driven by innovations into the curvature factor. This is our second key stylized fact.

Stylized fact 8.2 *Curvature innovations are the most important driver of term structure dynamics. In particular, curvature innovations are the main driver of the short factor.*

This fact is also verified by plotting the term structure of the variance of interest rates, together with the parts of the variance that can be attributed to the three factor innovations (Figure 8.3). Note that the

---

[3] There is one exception to this general pattern: for the GBP data we find that the short factor innovations (u_2) affect the curvature factor (ϕ_3) just barely significantly. The impulse-response functions are reported with 95% confidence bands and separately for each data set in Figure 8.5 in the appendix.

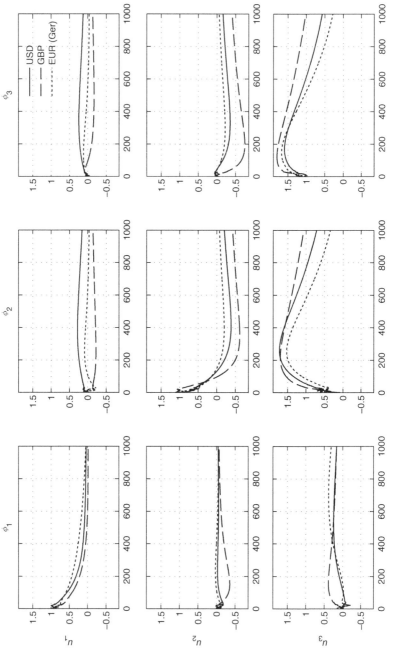

Figure 8.2 Impulse-response functions

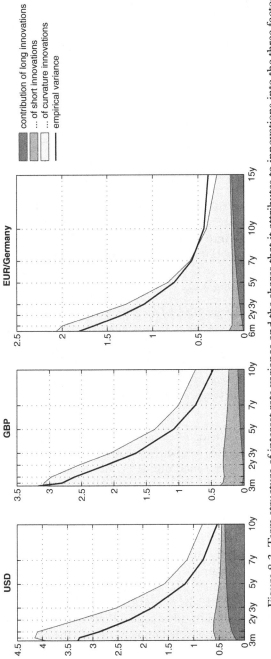

Figure 8.3 Term structure of interest rate variance and the shares that it attributes to innovations into the three factors

model captures the variance structure very well, for all three countries considered. Note further that the lion's share of movements at short and medium maturities is due to curvature innovations. Only for longer maturities do the innovations into the long factor become more important, but even there curvature innovations still contribute substantially to the fluctuations.

8.4.3   Common international trends

Figure 8.4 depicts the three factors for the three currencies. Comparing the middle and the right panel reveals that the short and curvature factors are highly correlated. Remember, though, that the innovations into these processes are by design independent. So why are these two factors relatively closely correlated? This is explained by fact 8.2: most of the movements of the short factor are *not* due to short factor innovations, but rather to innovations into the curvature factor, which then trickle down the yield curve (through the VAR dynamics) to affect shorter maturities and thus the short factor over time. We may sharpen the statement of this fact in the following way.

Stylized fact 8.3 *A large share of the variance of the short rate is explained by shocks that have their origin in the medium maturity spectrum.*

The left panel of Figure 8.4 also reveals another interesting aspect.

Stylized fact 8.4 *There appears to be a common international long factor. In contrast, the curvature and the short factors are internationally more heterogeneous.*

In particular, the USD data seem to lead the two European economies in the second half of the sample. Also, the GBP and the German EUR data appear to be more synchronous in the second half of the sample compared to the first half.

8.5   Why not a simpler alternative?

Before concluding this comparison, it may be necessary to also discuss alternative, and possibly more straightforward, ways of describing the yield curve and its dynamics. Of course, there are many possible ways one can decompose panel data such as the term structure of interest rates. We believe that the decomposition developed in Lengwiler and Lenz (2010) has significant advantages. First of all, the description of the data is simple to interpret; it simply partitions the maturity spectrum into three areas, the long end, the short end, and something in between.

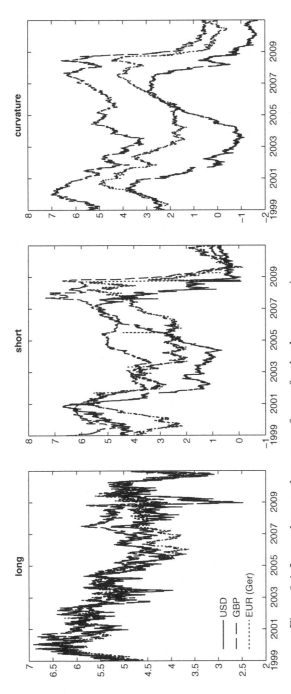

Figure 8.4 Long, short, and curvature factors for the three countries

Secondly, the factors are constructed in such a way that any shock or innovation that happens to one of them is statistically unrelated to the other two factors. Thus, the connections that undoubtedly exist between different maturities are all packed into the dynamics of the VAR, but are kept away from the shocks themselves. We believe that this feature makes the factors indeed "intelligible."

However, the model also has drawbacks. The most serious is certainly that this decomposition together with the dynamics does not insure absence of arbitrage opportunities. We fully acknowledge this shortcoming, but still believe that the model is helpful for describing the data in a meaningful way and uncovering stylized facts. Yet, there are alternatives.

8.5.1 Key rates

Factor models are popular in particular because they reduce the dimensionality of the data. The intelligible factors decompose the yield curve into three factors. With principal components (Litterman and Scheinkman, 1991), we typically also consider only three factors because additional components explain only a very small amount of the variance of the data. Likewise, the popular Nelson and Siegel (1987) specification also uses three factors. But there is an even simpler alternative: one can reduce the dimensionality of the panel by considering only a few (say

Table 8.1 *Correlation coefficients of factor innovations (u) and first differences of yields of particular maturities*

USD	3m	6m	1y	1y	3y	5y	7y	10y
u_1	0.21	0.28	0.44	0.65	0.74	0.86	0.92	0.94
u_2	0.81	0.54	0.23	−0.08	−0.10	−0.09	−0.08	−0.07
u_3	0.34	0.62	0.77	0.70	0.61	0.43	0.31	0.22

GBP	3m	6m	1y	2y	3y	5y	7y	10y
u_1	0.12	0.01	0.02	0.34	0.43	0.65	0.77	0.87
u_2	0.79	0.57	0.16	−0.24	−0.30	−0.26	−0.21	−0.15
u_3	0.31	0.66	0.87	0.86	0.80	0.66	0.55	0.40

EUR	6m	1y	2y	3y	5y	7y	10y	15y
u_1	0.08	0.16	0.27	0.36	0.57	0.73	0.87	0.92
u_2	0.52	−0.07	−0.43	−0.49	−0.46	−0.38	−0.27	−0.15
u_3	0.77	0.90	0.82	0.75	0.62	0.49	0.34	0.23

three) "key rates". In fact, comparing our factor innovations with the first differences of the yields reveals a strong connection, see Table 8.1.

Given this information, one may be tempted to use, say, only the 3-month rate, the 1-year rate, and the 10-year rate as a description of the yield curve.[4] This is also a way of reducing the dimensionality to just three. We can then estimate a VAR[5] on this restricted data set, without going through a factor model to reduce the dimensionality. Pursuing this strategy, however, does not produce innovations that are orthogonal, no matter how many lags are chosen for the VAR. In fact, the innovations of this VAR-on-yields is almost independent of the number of lags. In the USD data set, the correlation matrix of the innovations of this VAR remains almost constant if we vary the number of lags between 1 and 100 days. The correlation coefficient between the innovations into the 3-month rate and the 1-year rate remains in a narrow band of $[0.57, 0.60]$. Likewise, the correlation between 3-month and 10-year innovations is contained in $[0.21, 0.23]$. And finally, the correlation between 1-year and 10-year innovations is contained in the very narrow interval $[0.619, 0.624]$. For the other two data sets, the correlations of the innovations are different, but also independent of the lag length and clearly non-zero.

We conclude that if we want to have a VAR with orthogonal innovations, we do need to go beyond simple yields. This is what sets our method apart: we extract "genuine shocks" that are the independent ultimate drivers of the yields, and we relegate all the dynamic interaction between the yields to the VAR model.

8.5.2   Principal components and Nelson–Siegel

Principal components analysis has the advantage over the intelligible factors decomposition in that it explains the maximum amount of the variation of the data given the number of factors. So, the fit of the three first principal components must be better than the fit of the three intelligible factors. Moreover, the principal components are by construction orthogonal.

Another well-established descriptive factor model is Nelson and Siegel (1987), which captures the typical loadings of the principal components found in term structures with a parametric specification. So why not

---

[4] According to Table 8.1, at these maturities we find a high correlation between the innovations and the first differences of the yields. Moreover, the loading of the curvature factor reaches its maximum around two years, see Figure 8.1.

[5] One could also use a more sophisticated process, such as a multivariate GARCH.

use principal components (PC) or the Nelson–Siegel (NS) specification instead?

The drawback of any ordinary factor model (such as principal components or Nelson–Siegel) for time series analysis is that it does not capture the dynamics: for each observation day, we get a number of factors describing the cross-section, but there is no dynamic model linking the factors over time. The principal components and the Nelson–Siegel factors are serially correlated, so to describe the dynamics of the yield curve, we must somehow model these factors as a stochastic process. If we add a dynamic model of the factors, nothing guarantees that the innovations driving the dynamics are orthogonal. Besides the restrictions we impose on the shape of the loadings, this is the second defining property of the intelligible factors: the factors themselves are not orthogonal, but the shocks that drive them are.

The empirical question is whether the correlation among the shocks that drive the principal components or the three Nelson–Siegel factors are quantitatively important. In fact, Diebold and Li (2006) have combined the Nelson–Siegel decomposition with a VAR of the factors. Actually, they find that using a univariate AR-model yields better forecasting properties. They use monthly data on US government debt yields.

Pursuing this strategy with the daily observations is not successful, though. The resulting innovations of the AR or VAR processes are highly correlated. Estimating a VAR on the Nelson–Siegel factors produces innovations into the level factor and the slope factor that have a correlation coefficient of 0.73 for the USD data. For the GBP and EUR data sets, the corresponding numbers are 0.79 and 0.76, respectively. Level and slope shocks tend to happen simultaneously. In words, that means that when the yield curve shifts upwards, it typically also becomes steeper. Or the other way around, when the yield curve becomes flatter, the level of the yield curve typically declines. We find the same behavior when using principal components instead. Here, the innovations into the first ("level") and the second ("slope") principal component are correlated with a coefficient of 0.64 for the USD data, and 0.63 and 0.57 for the GBP and EUR data, respectively. This is not surprising as the loadings and the factors are similar to the Nelson–Siegel specification.

Stylized fact 8.5 *In all three currencies we study, we find a strong positive correlation between level and slope shocks using the Nelson–Siegel specification or principal components. The nature of the yield curve seems to be such that these factors are not independent.*

There are no independent level or slope shocks. It seems that there is some truth to the preferred habitat hypothesis. Maybe this is the reason why it is more useful to decompose the yield curve into three components that each address different parts of the maturity spectrum. In fact, instead of calling our factors "short," "curvature," and "long," we might just as well have called them "money market," "notes market," and "bond market."

8.6   Conclusions

We used the intelligible factor model to analyze the yield curve dynamics in the USA, the UK, and Germany between 1999 and 2010. This allowed us to study the effects of independent innovations into a long, short, and curvature factor on the entire yield curve. We summarized the empirical results in a set of stylized facts about the yield curve which are quite robust across countries.

Two general conclusions can be drawn. First, innovations into the curvature factor are the most important driver of yield curve dynamics. Changes in the curvature factor precede those in the short factor. In addition, curvature innovations explain most by far of the variance in all three factors.

Second, the "long–short–curvature" categorization is useful because the dynamics of such factors can be made orthogonal. This is empirically not possible for the traditional "level–slope–curvature" categorization. Level and slope shocks are highly correlated for the three countries we consider. Orthogonality of the shocks is important, though, because it allows us to map observable events to shocks at different segments of the yield curve.

The analysis in this chapter can be extended in different directions. First, large measured innovations are amenable to event studies. For instance, in the USD data set, the absolutely largest long factor innovation was measured on March 18, 2009, the day the Federal Reserve announced that it would massively expand its "large scale asset purchase program" (see the FOMC statement of that day). The largest absolute short factor innovation is observed on September 17, 2008, the day AIG was bailed out. Finally, the largest curvature factor innovation happened on September 13, 2001, the day the market reopened after the terrorist attacks. Second, it may be possible to relate the factors to other macroeconomic variables and thus create an economically meaningful explanation of the stylized facts. Third, we could set up an international yield curve model with at least one factor common for all countries. Our analysis suggests that the long factor is the prime candidate for capturing the international co-movement of the yield curve.

Appendix: Impulse-response functions

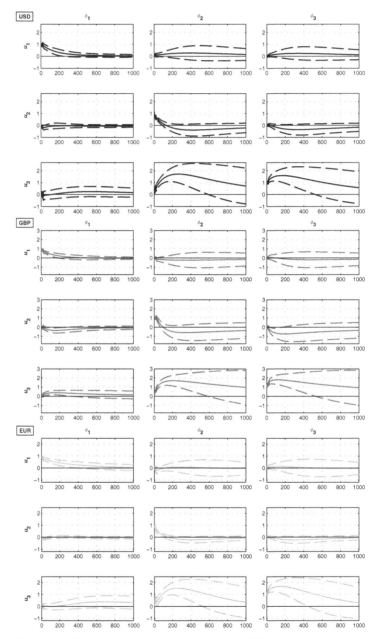

Figure 8.5 Impulse-response functions with 95% confidence bands for the three data sets

References

Bianchi, F., Mumtaz, H., and Surico, P. (2009). The great moderation of the term structure of UK interest rates. *Journal of Monetary Economics*, **56**, 856–871.

Dewachter, H. and Lyrio, M. (2006). Macro factors and the term structure of interest rates. *Journal of Money, Credit, and Banking*, **38**, 119–140.

Diebold, F. X. and Li, C. (2006). Forecasting the term structure of government bond yields. *Journal of Econometrics*, **130**, 337–364.

Diebold, F. X., Li, C., and Yue, V. Z. (2008). Global yield curve dynamics and interactions: a dynamic Nelson–Siegel approach. *Journal of Econometrics*, **146**, 351–363.

Lengwiler, Y. and Lenz, C. (2010). Intelligible factors for the yield curve. *Journal of Econometrics*, **157**, 481–491.

Litterman, R. and Scheinkman, J. (1991). Common factors affecting bond returns. *Journal of Fixed Income*, **1**, 54–61.

Mönch, E. (2010). Term structure surprises: the predictive content of curvature, level, and slope. *Journal of Applied Econometrics*, doi:10.1002/jae.1220.

Nelson, C. R. and Siegel, A. F. (1987). Parsimonious modeling of yield curves. *Journal of Business*, **60**, 473–489.

9 Estimating the policy rule from money market rates when target rate changes are lumpy

Jean-Sébastien Fontaine

9.1 Introduction

Many Central Banks change their target (or policy) rates via discrete increments, typically multiples of 0.25%. Moreover, these changes almost always occur following scheduled meetings and the schedule of meetings is known well in advance to market participants. The intent behind this operational procedure is, or is understood to be, to increase the transparency of the Central Bank's actions and to reduce unnecessary variations in interest rates. Presumably, transparency increases the predictability of future policy rates, tightens the relationship of short-term yields to policy decisions and enhances the effectiveness of the monetary policy transmission mechanism. Indeed, a large literature has shown that short-term interest rates and, in the case of the US, Fed funds futures rates, provide the best forecasts of future target rates and can be used to estimate monetary policy shocks.

An accurate description of expectations as measured from short-term interest rates is crucial for policymakers and market participants. In the following, I compare dynamic term structure models for short-term interest rates that take into account the known schedule of policy meetings. One set of models is based on a discrete support, consistent with the fact that target changes take discrete increments, and another set of models is based on the standard Gaussian approximation.[1] The sample is daily and runs until the end of 2011. A second set of results analyzes

I thank Greg Bauer, Jagjit Chadha, Hans Dewachter, Antonio Diez, Bruno Feunou, Rodrigo Guimarães, James Hamilton, Scott Hendry, Sean Holly, Glenn Rudebusch, Peter Smith, and participants at the CIMF/IESEG conference "The Yield Curve and New Developments in Macro-finance" for their comments and suggestions.
[1] Neglecting the schedule of meetings leads to grossly mis-specified models. I do not discuss this case.

the information content of futures rates throughout the period where the target reached its lower bound in the US.[2]

Specifically, I ask the following questions. First, does using a Gaussian approximation to discrete changes affect policy rule estimates? The answer is yes. Maximum likelihood estimates based on the discrete distribution are substantially different from quasi-maximum likelihood estimates based on the Gaussian distribution. Target rate innovations are far from normal, and in particular, exhibit significant conditional skewness. Second, does the Gaussian approximation affect the estimation of the term structure model? Again, the answer is yes. Unsurprisingly, using futures data alters the estimates of the policy rule substantially for each model. More importantly, the estimates from the discrete-support model are consistent with others found in the literature (e.g., Clarida, Galí, and Gertler, 2000). The discrete-support model implies substantially more mean-reversion in the target rate than estimates from the Gaussian model. The role of the lagged target rate for future target rates is less important and, consequently, the role of the other variables is more important in the discrete-support model. Moreover, consistent with theory and existing evidence, the discrete-support model produces estimates of the price of macro risk that remain positive and evolve smoothly over time. In contrast, using a Gaussian approximation yields unreasonable risk premium variations.

In a third exercise, I measure and summarize the effect of monetary policy announcements (e.g., press releases following FOMC meetings) between the end of 2008, where the target rate reached its lower bound, until the end of 2011. The model is estimated using *daily* data and we can measure the same-day effect of policy on interest rates. I find that every announcement led to a decline in the macro factor. In the model, this translates to a lower risk premium and lower expected future rates. However, the proximity to the lower bound causes variations in the futures rates to be subdued. This introduces an asymmetry in the information content of the macro factor. It still captures improvements in perceived economic conditions but does not capture further deteriorations.

Each model takes into account the known meeting schedule. Each uses the current target rate and a latent macro indicator to drive policy decisions. In each case, the policy rule is linear and variance parameters are constant, with different parameters for days with and without a scheduled policy meeting. In fact the different specifications are identical except for one aspect: the distribution of target rate innovations. The

---

[2] The lower bound is typically considered to be zero but the effective lower bound has been 0.25% so far in the US.

benchmark uses the Gaussian distribution to model target changes. In the alternative models, target rate changes have a discrete distribution, as in the data. In particular, the discrete distribution has fat tails and time-varying skewness. In a final estimation, I impose that the price of risk associated with unexpected target changes is zero. Otherwise, a non-Gaussian model has more flexibility to fit futures data relative to a Gaussian model. I also estimate a variant of the model where the (constant) price of target rate risk is unrestricted. This parameter is significant statistically and economically. Economically, the constant price of target risk induces substantial risk premium variations as well as time-varying volatility in yields. This chapter ends with a discussion of ongoing developments in the literature to address the challenge of the lower bound for existing models of short-term interest rates.

The existing asset pricing literature focuses on long-term yields or has mostly ignored the facts that target changes take discrete increments and typically occur on known dates.[3] A substantial econometric literature has studied federal funds futures and documented their ability to predict future target changes.[4] However, the evidence suggests that the risk premium in Fed funds futures rates exhibits significant variations.[5] This calls for a dynamic term structure model that combines the information in the cross-section of interest rates and sweeps away the effect of risk premium variations on measures of expectations.

Although it is not the objective of this chapter, a target rate specification that accounts for the schedule of policy meetings and for the lumpy changes is applicable in the context of a structural VAR. In particular, one can use the occurrence of policy meetings to obtain a high-frequency identification scheme of monetary policy shocks (Cochrane and Piazzesi, 2002). In addition, one can also use the difference in variance between days with and without meetings to identify the structural shocks (Sentana and Fiorentini 2001, Rigobon 2003). The common identification assumption that monetary policy shocks do not affect macroeconomic variables contemporaneously can be implemented easily. I discuss these issues briefly.

Section 9.2 introduces the model of the target rate. Section 9.3 introduces the corresponding models of the term structure. Section 9.4

---

[3] Notable exceptions include Rudebusch (1995), Balduzzi et al. (1997), Hamilton and Jordà (2002), Piazzesi (2005a) and, recently, Fontaine (2011), Feunou and Fontaine (2012) and Renne (2012).

[4] See Krueger and Kuttner (1996), Cochrane and Piazzesi (2002), Gürkaynak et al. (2007), Ferrero and Nobili (2008), and Hamilton (2009). See also Bhundia and Chadha (1998) for the UK.

[5] See Sack (2004), Piazzesi and Swanson (2006), and Hamilton and Okimoto (2010).

discusses the data and the estimation method. Section 9.5 presents the estimation results. Section 9.6 studies the futures market from the end of 2008 until the end of 2011. Section 9.7 concludes.

9.2 Modeling short-term interest rates

9.2.1 Policy rules in practice

The policy rule followed by the monetary authority to set its target interest rate, r_t, can be generically defined by

$$r_{t+1} = r_t + \delta_r(r_t - \bar{r}) + \delta'_z(z_{t+1} - \bar{z}) + \epsilon^r_{t+1}, \qquad (9.1)$$

for a given set of state variables, z_t, where $\bar{r}$ is interpreted as the natural interest rate, and where $\epsilon^r_{t+1} = r_{t+1} - E_t[r_{t+1}]$. The expectation is taken using the information set of market participants or that of the econometrician so that ϵ^r_{t+1} is the unanticipated target change. Equation (9.1) is often interpreted as the representation of an abstract policy rule. For instance, the celebrated Taylor rule (Taylor, 1993) relates the target federal funds rate in the US to deviations of inflation and real GDP from some targets. This is not to say that actual policy decisions follow Equation (9.1). In Taylor's own words, we should "preserve the concept of a policy rule even in an environment where it is practically impossible to follow mechanically the algebraic formulas economists write down to describe their preferred policy rules." Indeed, the typical Central Bank does not change its target policy rate mechanically with every change in the state of the economy. Most Central Banks have instead elected to change their targets only infrequently and then to use a coarse grid when choosing a new target (i.e. with intervals of 25 bps). Figure 9.1 contrasts the evolution of the target overnight federal funds rate and the 6-month federal funds futures rate. Changes to the target rate are lumped together and the evolution of the target rate follows a step function. These properties of target changes have significant implications for the distribution of ϵ^r_{t+1}, which we discuss in the next section.[6]

A central assumption of a typical interest rate model is that the short rate, and yields, evolve smoothly over a continuous support. Therefore, most policy rules studied in the literature do not describe the evolution of the actual policy instrument – the step function in Figure 9.1 – but

---

[6] The European Central Bank, the Bank of Canada, the Bank of England, the Bank of Japan, the Federal Reserve, the Reserve Bank of Australia, the Reserve Bank of New Zealand, among others, all use an overnight rate as policy instrument. In each case, changes are multiples of 25 bps (including 0), and are announced publicly on scheduled announcement dates or follow scheduled policy meetings.

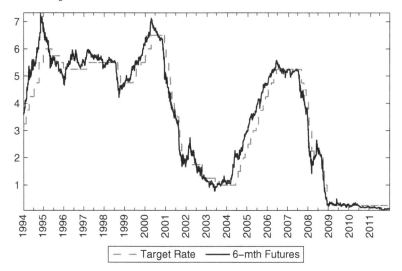

Figure 9.1 The target federal funds rate and the 6-month ahead federal funds futures rates. Daily data 1994–2011

instead use a smoother interest rate with a longer maturity. Yields on instruments with very short maturities are often neglected altogether.[7]

The target rate may be a pure jump process but, nonetheless, the evolution of the futures rate appears smooth to our eyes.[8] But the data say otherwise: changes in yields are are much larger – not as smooth – on days with a policy meeting (see the Appendix). The Gaussian approximation may be sufficiently accurate for many research questions related to the evolution of long-term yields. But it is costly in other applications. The approximation affects estimation of the monetary policy rule and of monetary shocks from short-term money-market instruments (Rudebusch, 1995; Cochrane and Piazzesi, 2002; Hamilton and Jordà, 2002). In turn, different policy rule estimates lead to different measures of the risk premium.[9] More generally, the standard linear Gaussian approximation creates a tension between capturing the evolution of long-term yields and estimating the policy rule at relatively high frequency (i.e., daily). Indeed, models estimated on yields with long maturities perform poorly for yields with short maturities and imply non-realistic dynamics for the policy rate (see Piazzesi, 2005a).

[7] Liquidity effects are also often cited when excluding short-term Treasury bills from estimation (see e.g., Duffee, 1996).

[8] See the Appendix. Futures and interest rates correspond to risk-neutral expectations over all possible realizations of futures target rates. The probability associated with any of these possible realizations and, a fortiori, the corresponding expectation can evolve smoothly as new information arrives.

[9] See Equation (9.24) in the Appendix.

9.2.2 Target rate models

This section introduces a representation of the policy rule based on the distribution of policy shocks and the timing of policy decisions to address the empirical features of target rate changes. I consider a discrete-time model where the sampling frequency (e.g., daily or weekly), is faster than the frequency of scheduled meetings. The target for the overnight rate is given by

$$r_{t+1} - r_t \mid r_t, z_{t+1}, I_{t+1} \sim \mathcal{D}\left(\mu(r_t, z_{t+1}, I_{t+1}), \ \sigma^2(r_t, z_{t+1}, I_{t+1})\right) \quad (9.2)$$

for some parametric distribution family, $\mathcal{D}$, conditional on the state variable z_{t+1}. The indicator function I_{t+1} is equal to 1 if a policy meeting is scheduled to occur at date $t+1$ and zero otherwise. Therefore, the conditional mean and conditional variance $\mu(\cdot)$ and $\sigma(\cdot)$ can depend on calendar time via the schedule of policy meetings. The policy rate is driven by its own shocks, ϵ_{t+1}^r, and by the state variables, z_{t+1}. In the following, I contrast models based where the support of the distribution, $\mathcal{D}$, is continuous, $n_t \in \mathbb{R}$, or discrete, $n_t \in (\ldots, -2, -1, 0, 1, 2, \ldots)$.

Model I: Normal

The standard linear-Gaussian policy rule approximation is nested in Equation (9.2) but where the mean function, $\mu(\cdot)$, does not depend on calendar time and where the variance is constant. I consider the more general alternative where the schedule of policy meetings affects the distribution of policy shocks. Specifically, the specification of the conditional mean $\mu(\cdot)$ is different for days that are followed by a scheduled meeting (i.e., $I_{t+1} = 1$) than for days that are not followed by a scheduled meeting (i.e., $I_{t+1} = 0$). Hence, we have two cases:

$$r_{t+1} - r_t \mid r_t, z_{t+1}, (I_{t+1} = 0) \sim \mathcal{N}\left(0, \sigma_0^2\right),$$

$$r_{t+1} - r_t \mid r_t, z_{t+1}, (I_{t+1} = 1) \sim \mathcal{N}\left(\delta_r(r_t - \bar{r}) + \delta_z'(z_{t+1} - \bar{z}), \sigma_1^2\right). \quad (9.3)$$

Following Piazzesi (2005a) and Fontaine (2011), the expected target change is state-dependent on days with a scheduled policy meeting but zero otherwise. The variance differs between days with and without a scheduled meeting but it is constant otherwise.

Model II: Skellam

Next, I follow Fontaine (2011), which uses the Skellam distribution (Skellam, 1946) to confine target rate changes to a discrete support. Heuristically, this distribution corresponds to the difference between two Poisson random variables. If n_{t+1}^u and n_{t+1}^d have independent conditional Poisson distributions with parameters $\lambda^u(r_t, z_{t+1}, I_{t+1})$ and $\lambda^d(r_t, z_{t+1}, I_{t+1})$, respectively, then $n_{t+1} = n_{t+1}^u - n_{t+1}^d$ has a Skellam distribution, $\mathcal{SK}$. Then, discrete target changes can be written as

$$r_{t+1} - r_t = \Delta n_{t+1} = \Delta(n_{t+1}^u - n_{t+1}^d),$$

where $\Delta = 0.25\%$ is known. I assume that the intensity parameters on days without a scheduled meeting are given by

$$\lambda^u(r_t, z_{t+1}, 0) = \lambda_0, \qquad \lambda^d(r_t, z_{t+1}, 0) = \lambda_0, \tag{9.4}$$

to allow for target rate change following unscheduled FOMC meetings, and by

$$\lambda^u(r_t, z_{t+1}, 1) = \lambda_1 + \lambda_r(r_t - \bar{r}) + \lambda_z(z_{t+1} - \bar{z}),$$
$$\lambda^d(r_t, z_{t+1}, 1) = \lambda_1 + \lambda_r(r_t - \bar{r}) + \lambda_z(z_{t+1} - \bar{z}), \tag{9.5}$$

when there is a meeting. Then, target changes are characterized by

$$r_{t+1} - r_t | r_t, z_{t+1}, (I_{t+1} = 0) \sim \mathcal{SK}\left(0, \sigma_0^2\right),$$
$$r_{t+1} - r_t | r_t, z_{t+1}, (I_{t+1} = 1) \sim \mathcal{SK}\left(\delta_r(r_t - \bar{r}) + \delta_z(z_{t+1} - \bar{z}), \sigma_1^2\right), \tag{9.6}$$

with

$$\sigma_0^2 = 2\lambda_0\Delta^2, \ \sigma_1^2 = 2\lambda_1\Delta^2,$$
$$\delta_r = 2\lambda_r\Delta, \quad \delta_z = 2\lambda_z\Delta. \tag{9.7}$$

Model I and Model II have linear mean function, constant variance, the same number of parameters and can be compared directly. The only difference between Equations (9.3) and (9.6) is the distribution of policy innovations. The Skellam distribution imposes a probability of zero for target changes that are not a multiple of 0.25%. Moreover, this distribution inherits features of the Poisson distribution. Importantly, it allows for time-varying asymmetry (i.e., skewness) in policy innovations, given by

$$\text{Skew}[r_{t+1} - r_t | r_t, z_{t+1}, (I_{t+1} = 1)] = \frac{1}{\sigma_1}\left(\delta_r(r_t - \bar{r}) + \delta_z(z_{t+1} - \bar{z})\right). \tag{9.8}$$

In other words, the asymmetry in the distribution of policy innovations is proportional to the mean. For instance, following an increase in the expected target changes, the probability of specific target hikes (e.g., 0.25%, 0.50%) increases more than the probability of the corresponding target cuts with the same magnitude (e.g., −0.25%, −0.50%).

The Skellam distribution also has fat tails. Its excess kurtosis is inversely proportional to the variance,

$$\text{Kurt}[r_{t+1} - r_t] = 3 + \frac{\Delta^2}{\sigma^2}. \tag{9.9}$$

9.3   Term structure models

This section specifies the dynamics of z_t and of the pricing kernel to complete the term structure models. These additional assumptions are identical across short-rate specifications and remain unchanged throughout the empirical investigation below. Note that all the models considered below belong to the family of 2-factor dynamic affine term structure models (Piazzesi, 2005b).

9.3.1   State variables

In the spirit of standard macro-finance models, I assume that the state-vector, z_{t+1}, has a stationary auto-regressive representation,

$$z_{t+1} - \bar{z} = \phi(z_t - \bar{z}) + \epsilon_{t+1}, \tag{9.10}$$

where $\epsilon_{t+1} \sim N(0, \sigma_z^2)$. As in Piazzesi (2005a) and Fontaine (2011), this latent process is intended to capture variations in the economy relevant to the FOMC. Next, I introduce the spread between the target overnight rate and the effective market rate, $s_t = \tilde{r}_t - r_t$. The effective spread is included for completeness since observed yields and federal funds futures depend on the realization of the market overnight rate (see below). In practice, however, s_t plays no significant role (Balduzzi et al., 1997) since it exhibits little persistence. In addition, it does not affect the evolution of r_t or other macro variables.[10] The target spread s_t follows a leptokurtic process,

$$s_{t+1} - \bar{s} = \phi_s(s_t - \bar{s}) + \epsilon_{t+1}^s + \mathcal{J}_{t+1}^s, \tag{9.11}$$

where ϵ_t^s is iid with distribution $N(0, \sigma_s)$ and $\mathcal{J}_{t+1}^s$ is iid compound Poisson with number of jumps $n_{t+1}^s \sim P(\lambda_s^{\mathcal{J}})$ and jump size $v_{t+1}^s \sim N(v_s, \omega_s^2)$, conditional on the number of jumps. The asymmetry and fat tails of the target spread are well documented and large shocks typically occur

---

[10] The evidence of a liquidity effect between reserves and macro variables is weak and subject to controversial identification assumptions (Hamilton, 1997). Thornton (2006) discusses the relation between reserve (supply) management operations by the Fed, reserve (demand) forecast errors by the Fed, and the effective overnight federal funds rate.

around the maintenance period for required reserve (e.g., Hamilton 1996, Piazzesi 2005a).

To summarize, the state vector $X_t = [r_t \ z_t \ s_t]$ combines the target rate, a latent macro factor and the effective spread. Equations (9.10) and (9.11) can be combined with any of the short-rate specifications above into an auto-regressive representation for X_t (i.e., the mean functions are all linear),

$$X_{t+1} - \bar{X} = \phi(I_{t+1})(X_t - \bar{X}) + \eta_{t+1}, \qquad (9.12)$$

where the innovations η_{t+1} are independent through time, and $E_t[\eta_{t+1}] = 0$. The parameters corresponding to the short-rate rule – the first line of the matrix $\Phi(\cdot)$ – change with I_{t+1}. Equation (9.12) corresponds to the state equation in the state-space system below.

The auto-regressive representation implies that the policy response function is applicable in the context of a structural VAR. In particular, one can use the occurrence of policy meetings to obtain a high-frequency identification scheme of monetary policy shocks (Cochrane and Piazzesi, 2002). In addition, one can also use the difference in variance between days with and without meetings to identify the structural shocks (Sentana and Fiorentini 2001, Rigobon 2003). A common assumption to identify the structural shock is that monetary policy shocks do not affect macro-economic variables contemporaneously. This can be easily implemented here. Moreover, innovations in any of the state variables affect r_{t+1} on FMOC days only via the policy rule parameters.[11]

9.3.2   Pricing kernel

I consider a standard exponential-affine kernel, M_{t+1},

$$M_{t+1} = \frac{\exp(\lambda_s \epsilon_{t+1}^s + \lambda_{t,z} \epsilon_{t+1}^z)}{E_t \left[\exp \left(\lambda_s \epsilon_{t+1}^s + \lambda_{t,z} \epsilon_{t+1}^z \right) \right]}, \qquad (9.13)$$

where λ_s is the price of risk associated with innovation in the effective spread s_t and $\lambda_{t,z}$ is the price of risk associated with innovation in the macro factor z_t. Following Duffee (2002), the price of macro risk is linear,

---

[11] Another way to see the implicit structural restriction is by approximating η_{t+1} with $\Sigma(I_{t+1})u_{t+1}$, where u_{t+1} are uncorrelated white noises, the matrix $\Sigma(I_{t+1})$ is of the form

$$\Sigma(I_{t+1}) = \begin{bmatrix} \sigma_r^2(I_{t+1}) & \sigma_{r,Y}(I_{t+1}) \\ 0 & \Sigma_z \end{bmatrix},$$

and $\sigma_{r,Y}(I_{t+1})$ depends on primitive parameters of λ_t^u and λ_{t+1}^d.

$$\lambda_{t,z} = \lambda_0 + \lambda_{z,r} r_t + \lambda_{z,z} z_t. \tag{9.14}$$

This specification embodies several restrictions on the prices of risk. First, and most importantly, the price of risk associated with innovations to z_{t+1} varies with the latent economic indicator, z_t, and with the current target rate, r_t. This allows business cycle variations in the risk premium implicit in futures rates that has been documented by Piazzesi and Swanson (2006). There is no other source of risk premium variations. Second, the price of target rate risk is zero. This implies that the policy rule is the same under the risk-neutral and the historical probability measures.[12] It also maintains the comparability between different models. Otherwise, the effect of risk on the auto-regressive matrix would not be the same whether the short rate is Gaussian or Skellam. I relax this assumption in Section 9.5.3. Finally, the price of risk associated with ϵ_{t+1}^s is constant and induces a constant risk premium. The effective spread is highly volatile and shows no persistence and it makes little sense to allow the risk premium to vary accordingly. Overall, these restrictions on the price of risk parameters simplify the interpretation of risk premium variations. Moreover, affine models with unrestricted prices of risk tend to over-fit the data and often produce astronomically high Sharpe ratios (Duffee, 2009).

9.4 Estimation

9.4.1 Data

I use a daily sample from February 4, 1994 until the end of 2011. This period covers 144 scheduled meetings. The FOMC effected changes to its target rate following 53 of these scheduled meetings and, also, following seven unscheduled meetings.[13] The data include the target and effective overnight funds rates, available from the Federal Board of Governors, and Fed funds futures data, available from the CME. I use contracts with horizons from 1 to 6 months. Contracts with longer horizons are illiquid for most of the sample – days with no transactions on the exchange are a common occurrence. Table 9.1(a) presents summary statistics of the futures rates. The average term structure of futures rates is upward sloping. Table 9.1(b) presents summary statistics of target rate

---

[12] Fontaine (2011) discusses the parameter shifts between the historical and the risk-neutral measures.

[13] The Fed changed its operational policy starting with the February 1994 meeting and has since announced any target changes following its policy meeting. The history of target rate changes is available at www.newyorkfed.org/markets/statistics/dlyrates/fedrate.html.

Table 9.1 *Summary statistics*

(a) Futures rates

Horizon	1	2	3	4	5	6
μ	3.40	3.41	3.44	3.46	3.50	3.53
σ	2.17	2.18	2.19	2.20	2.20	2.21

(b) Overnight rate and effective spread

	μ	σ	skew	kurt	$\rho(1)$
$r_t - r_{t-1}$	0	22.5	-0.5	5.2	0.55
s_t	1.7	18.0	0.8	32.6	0.51

Panel (a) provides the averages and standard deviations of futures rates for horizons from 1 to 6 months. Panel (b) provides summary statistics for target rate changes following scheduled FOMC meetings and for the spread s_t between the effective overnight rate and the target rate (for all days). Statistics include the average, μ, standard deviation, σ, skewness, kurtosis and auto-correlation of order 1, $\rho(1)$. Annualized basis points. Daily data from Jan. 3, 1994 to Dec. 30, 2011.

changes following schedule FOMC meetings as well as for the effective spread s_t on all days. Target changes averaged zero with standard deviation close to 25 bps in this sample. There is also some evidence of negative skewness and of kurtosis in the distribution of target rate change – consistent with a specification based on the Skellam distribution. The effective spread exhibits a distribution skewed to the right and with substantial fat tails. The estimate of its kurtosis is 32.6!

9.4.2   Measurement equations

The measurement equation includes the target rate, which is observed without error. The corresponding conditional log-likelihood is based on one of the Gaussian density or the Skellam probability mass function,

$$r_t | r_{t-1}, z_t \sim \mathcal{N}\left(\mu_{I_t}(r_{t-1}, z_t), \sigma_{I_t}^2\right) \tag{9.15}$$

or

$$r_t | r_{t-1}, z_t \sim \mathcal{SK}\left(\mu_{I_t}(r_{t-1}, z_t), \sigma_{I_t}^2\right). \tag{9.16}$$

Next, the measurement vector includes futures rates, stacked in the vector F_t.[14] I assume that futures rates are measured with errors,

[14] The quoted price of this contract, $P(t, n)$, is given by $P(t, n) = 100 - F(t, n) \times 3600$. Due to weekends or holidays, the settlement date may not coincide with the last day

$F(t, n) = F(X_t, n) + v_t$, where $F(X_t, n)$ is the model-implied futures rate and v_t is a vector of iid zero-mean uncorrelated Gaussian measurement errors with variance given by

$$\xi(T_n)^2 = (\xi_0 + \xi_1 T_n)^2, \tag{9.17}$$

where $T_n > 0$ is the number of days until the end of the reference contract. Hence the log-likelihood of the futures rates is based on the Gaussian density,

$$F_t | X_t \sim \mathcal{N}\left(F(X_t), \xi^2\right).$$

The model-implied formula for futures rate can be derived from its payoff. With no loss of generality, I standardize the notional of the contract to 1. A futures contract settles at the end of a reference calendar month, n. The federal funds futures contract is essentially a swap between a variable rate and a fixed rate. The variable leg is the average overnight Fed funds rate in the reference calendar month, $\bar{r}_n$. With no cash exchange at inception, the fixed rate of the contract, $F(t, n)$, must be equal to the expectation of average overnight rate under the risk-neutral measure,

$$F(t, n) = E_t\left[M_{t,t+T_n}\bar{r}_n\right] = E_t\left[M_{t,t+T_n}D_n^{-1} \sum_{i=T_n-D_n}^{T_n} r_{t+i}\right]$$

$$= D_n^{-1} \sum_{i=T_n-D_n}^{T_n} E_t\left[M_{t,t+T}r_{t+i}\right]$$

$$= D_n^{-1} \sum_{i=T_n-D_n}^{T_n} f(t, i, T_n), \tag{9.18}$$

where T_n is the number of days between t and the end of the reference month and D_n is the number of days in that month. In turn, the rate on a singleton futures contract, $f(t, h, T)$, for the reference day $t + h$ and settling at date $t + T$, with $0 \leq h \leq T$, is given by

$$f(t, h, T) = \exp\left(d_0(t + h, T - h) + c_0\left(u^*, t, h\right) + c\left(u^*, t, h\right)' X_t\right)$$
$$\times \left[c_0'\left(u^*, t, h\right) C_r + X_t' c'\left(u^*, t, h\right) C_r\right], \tag{9.19}$$

of the month. For simplicity, this possibility is not visible in Equation (9.18) but I use CME's "Following Business Days" convention in the following.

where $u^* = d(t + h, T - h)$ and $C_r = [1 \; 0 \; 0]'$. Note that the coefficient recursions have two dimensions. They depend on the maturity, h, and also on calendar time, t, via the schedule of policy meetings. See Fontaine (2011) for the derivation of futures rates and the computation of the corresponding coefficient recursions.

9.4.3   Filter and likelihood

Equation (9.12) provides the transition equation of the state-space system. However, z_t is not observed and must be filtered from the data. I use the unscented Kalman filter [UKF] since the measurement equation of futures rates is not linear in X_t (see Equation (9.19)). The UKF is an approximate filter that matches the first two moments of the state distribution. A QML estimator is feasible but the variance in the log-likelihood of the F_t and r_t must be adjusted for the uncertainty associated with the filter for z_t.[15] Conditional on values of the latent state variables, the joint (quasi) log-likelihood is given by

$$L(\Theta; Y) = \sum_{t=1}^{T} \log \left(f_t \left(\tilde{Y}_t | \tilde{Y}_{t-1}, I_t; \theta \right) \right)$$

$$= \sum_{t=1}^{T} \log \left(f(Y_t | \tilde{Y}_{t-1}, r_t, s_t, I_t) f(r_t | \tilde{Y}_{t-1}, I_t) f(s_t | s_{t-1}) \right),$$

where all model parameters are grouped in the vector Θ, and $\tilde{Y}_t$ summarizes the history of observable variables for $t = 1, \ldots, t$. The conditional likelihood of Y_t depends on t through the deterministic FOMC schedule. I use the following assumptions to identify the location, the scale, and the sign of the latent factor, $z_t : \bar{z} = 0$, $\sigma_z = 1/360$ bps, and $\delta_z \geq 0$. These are standard in the term structure. In practice, these assumptions imply that the latent indicator is centered around zero, that it has the same unit as a daily interest rate, and that an increase in z_t is associated with an increase of the expected target rate and improving economic conditions. Finally, we have that $|\phi_z| < 1$ and $-2 < |\delta_r| < 0$ so that z_t and the target rate are stationary.

---

[15] This adjustment is standard in linear models and exact when the density is Gaussian (see e.g. Hamilton, 1994). However, the measurement equation is not linear (but Gaussian) in the case of futures and it is not Gaussian (but linear) in the case of the target rate. See Fontaine (2011) for details.

9.5 Results

9.5.1 Effective spread

The restrictions above imply the separation of the marginal likelihood of s_t and, therefore, its dynamics can be estimated separately. Table 9.2 presents maximum likelihood estimates of Equation (9.11). Panel (a) presents the estimates based on data until Dec. 15, 2008 when the FOMC set the interest rates on required reserve balances and on excess balances at 25 basis points. I present results based on the earlier sample separately to document the change in the behavior of the effective spread since the Fed scaled up its liquidity intervention and started paying interest on reserves in the fall of 2008 to implement its policy rate target. Bech and Klee (2009) discuss the changes to the Federal Reserve's operation framework. Figure 9.2 makes evident the change in behavior in 2008. Persistent downward pressures on the effective spread started early in the fall of 2008. The Fed started paying interest on reserves in early October 2008. The results are similar for different starting dates. Panel (b) presents the estimates based on all the data until Dec. 30, 2011.

Table 9.2 *Effective spread parameters*

(a) 1994–2008 sample

μ_s	ϕ_s	σ_s	ν_s	ω_s	$\lambda_s^{\mathcal{J}}$
−0.003	0.23	0.051	0.019	0.305	0.248
(0.00008)	(0.002)	(0.0005)	(0.0027)	(0.0012)	(0.0028)

(b) 1994–2011 sample

μ_s	ϕ_s	σ_s	ν_s	ω_s	$\lambda_s^{\mathcal{J}}$
−0.0138	0.56	0.052	0.031	0.280	0.222
(0.0004)	(0.011)	(0.002)	(0.002)	(0.07)	(0.011)

Maximum likelihood estimates of dynamics of the effective spread, $s_t = \bar{r}_t - r_t$,

$$s_{t+1} = \mu_s + \phi_s s_t + \epsilon_{t+1}^s + \mathcal{J}_{t+1}^s,$$

where s_t is in annualized percentage, ϵ_t^s is iid with distribution $N(0, \sigma_s)$ and $\mathcal{J}_{t+1}^s$ is iid. compound Poisson with number of jumps $n_{t+1}^s \sim P(\lambda_s^{\mathcal{J}})$ and jump size $\nu_{t+1}^s \sim N(\nu_s, \omega_s^2)$, conditional on the number of jumps. Panel (a) displays the estimates in a daily sample from Feb. 3, 1994 to Dec. 15, 2008. Panel (b) displays the estimates in a daily sample from Feb. 3, 1994 to Dec. 30, 2011.

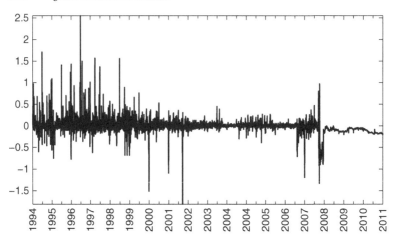

Figure 9.2 The spread between the effective overnight Fed funds rate and the Fed's target rate. Daily data 1994–2011

All parameters are precisely estimated. The effective spread exhibits little persistence and its unconditional mean is close to zero in the first sample. This reflects the Fed's ability to counteract predictable deviation of the market rate from its target. The innovations to the effective spread have an asymmetric distribution with fat tails. The estimate of the jump intensity parameter, $\lambda_s^{\mathcal{J}}$, is 0.25. Innovations to the effective spread mix two Gaussian distributions on average one day out of four. When no jump occurs, the distribution is Gaussian with zero mean and with a volatility of 5 bps. Otherwise, the distribution is mixed with another Gaussian distribution with a mean of 2 bps and a much wider volatility of 30 bps. When we include data after 2008, the innovation distribution remains broadly, but deviations of the market rate are more negative and more persistent. This reflects the Fed's emphasis on the provision of liquidity and, later, the effect of quantitative easing (Bech and Klee, 2009).

9.5.2   Policy rules

This section estimates the policy rule equation based on target rate data *only* – excluding futures rates data. I compare policy rule estimates based on different distributional assumptions for the policy shocks (i.e., Equations (9.3) and (9.6)). Importantly, the Gaussian policy rule and the discrete policy rule have the same linear conditional mean specification, the same number of parameters and a constant variance. The Gaussian policy rule approximates the distribution of target

Table 9.3 *Policy rule parameters*

(a) Gaussian innovations

δ_r	δ_z	σ_1	QML
−0.014	0.031	0.161	1504.5
(0.006)	(0.003)	(0.013)	

(b) Discrete innovations

δ_r	δ_z	σ_1	ML
-2×10^{-12}	0.006	0.208	1533.3
(1×10^{-4})	(0.0018)	(0.015)	

Maximum likelihood (or quasi-maximum likelihood) estimates of the policy rule,

$$r_{t+1} - r_t |\; r_t, z_{t+1}, I_{t+1} = 1 \sim \mathcal{D}\left(\delta_r(r_t - \bar{r}) + \delta_z(z_{t+1} - \bar{z}), \sigma_1^2\right),$$

using target rate observations only, excluding futures rates data, on days with FOMC meetings (i.e., $I_{t+1} = 1$) where r_t is the target rate, z_t is a latent economic indicator, and $\mathcal{D}(\cdot, \cdot)$ is the distribution of the policy rate target innovations, *eta$_t$*. Panel (a) displays results based on a Gaussian (continuous) distribution for the policy innovation and Panel (b) displays results based on a Skellam (discrete) distribution. The estimate of σ_1 for each model is reported in annualized basis point units. The persistence of z_t is fixed at $\phi_z = 0.995$ in each case. Daily data from Feb. 3, 1994 to Dec. 30, 2011. Standard errors in parentheses.

rate changes with a continuous support over the real line. In contrast, the discrete distribution imposes that the target rate can only take discrete values (i.e., multiples of 0.25%). The results show that changing the distribution affects the estimates of policy rule coefficients significantly.

Table 9.3 presents results for each model. Using a discrete distribution yields a higher likelihood value than using a continuous distribution (1533.3 vs 1504.5). Clearly, these models are not nested and a standard likelihood ratio test is not applicable. Nonetheless, ranking the log-likelihoods remains a consistent basis for model selection (Sin and White, 1996) and, therefore, I conclude that the data favor the Skellam distribution.[16]

---

[16] A poorly specified model with discrete support could be rejected in favor of a model with a continuous support.

Each model attributes a different role to z_t. The estimates of the coefficient δ_z is 0.03 in the Gaussian model and 0.006 in the Skellam model. Both estimates are significant (they are non-negative by construction). Moreover, in the case of the Gaussian model, the target rate plays a significant role in its own mean-reversion, $\hat{\delta}_r = -0.014$, but it is insignificant in the discrete model. In fact, the point estimate is trivially small (i.e., -2×10^{-12}). Therefore, a specification where the lag target rate plays no role,

$$r_{t+1} - r_t \mid r_t, z_{t+1}, I_{t+1} = 1 \sim \mathcal{SK}\left(\delta_z(z_{t+1} - \bar{z}), \sigma_1^2\right),$$

cannot be rejected on the basis of target rate data only when we use the Skellam distribution but not otherwise. In other words, variations in z_t are sufficient. But why are the estimates different? The answer must follow from the only difference between the two models.[17] In the discrete-support model, the asymmetry in the distribution of target changes is proportional to its mean. Since the coefficients are positive, improving economic conditions implies that the *likelihood* of a target hike increases by more than the decrease in the *likelihood* of a target cut with the same magnitude. In contrast, the likelihood changes are symmetric in the Gaussian case. Then, one way to shift the distribution function is to also include the target rate as a conditioning variable. In this case, similar economic conditions, as measured by z_t, will be associated with different distributions of future target changes depending on the current value of the target rate.

Finally, target innovations have a relatively large standard deviation in both models. This is not surprising since these simple policy rules do not use any conditioning variable beyond the current target rate and the filtered value of the latent factor, z_t. In turn, the latent factor is filtered only based on past target rate changes. The objective of this section is not to provide a good fit of target rate changes but to highlight the potential consequences of different distributional assumptions on the coefficient estimates. The following section uses term structure data as conditioning data.

9.5.3   Term structure models

This section presents estimation results for the full dynamic term structure model in Section 9.3 using futures rates and the target rate data, jointly. Parameters of the effective spread dynamics are fixed at their

---

[17] There is no reason why these estimates should be equal in a finite sample. In addition, the convergence of the QML estimator based on the Gaussian distribution to the parameters of interest only holds asymptotically and if the distribution is symmetric.

values estimated in the entire sample (see Section 9.5.1 above). I first compare term structure models based on the Gaussian or the Skellam distribution but where target rate risk is not priced (Model I vs Model II). These models have identical parametric specifications and the same number of parameters. The only difference is the distribution of the policy shocks. Clearly, the results below differ from those in Table 9.3 since a much richer information set is used here. The term structure of futures rates brings forward-looking information about the path of future target rates and helps estimate the policy rule reliably.

Pricing errors

Table 9.4 compares the root mean squared pricing error (RMSE), as well as the estimates of standard deviations, $\xi(n)$. All are reported in annualized basis points. Panel (a) and Panel (b) display results for the Gaussian model and the discrete model, respectively. Each model provides a good fit of futures rates.[18] Moreover, these models cannot be distinguished on the basis of the RMSEs.

Table 9.4 *Pricing errors*

(a) Pricing errors – Gaussian model

	Maturity					
	1	2	3	4	5	6
RMSE	4.38	6.67	4.99	3.53	2.29	4.04
$\xi(n)$	5.33	4.99	4.65	4.31	3.97	3.63

(b) Pricing errors – discrete model

	Maturity					
	1	2	3	4	5	6
RMSE	4.43	6.65	4.92	3.58	2.26	4.12
$\xi(n)$	5.28	5.06	4.84	4.62	4.40	4.18

Root mean squared pricing errors (RMSE) and standard deviations of measurement errors $\xi(T_n)$ for futures rates with one to six months to maturity in annualized basis points. Panel (a) presents results for the Gaussian model. Panel (b) presents results for the discrete model. Daily data from Feb. 3, 1994 to Dec. 30, 2011.

[18] Piazzesi (2005a) obtains average absolute pricing errors above 7 bps for LIBOR rates with comparable maturities, Feldhütter and Lando (2008) obtains an RMSE of 22 bps for 3-month LIBOR rates. These authors fit a broader set of maturities and of instruments.

Parameter estimates

Tables 9.5 and 9.6 display parameter estimates for the Gaussian and discrete models, respectively. Unsurprisingly, both sets of results imply that the daily evolution of the target rate is very persistent. But the models differ in how they build the persistence into the target rate equation.

Estimates of policy rule parameters from the Gaussian model are $\hat{\delta}_r \sim 0$ and $\hat{\phi}_z = 0.9948$. In contrast, the estimates from the discrete model are $\hat{\delta}_r = 0.30$ and $\hat{\phi}_z = 0.9999$. The two point estimates have very different forecasting implications. At a 6-month horizon we have $0.9948^{180} = 0.40$ and $0.9999^{180} = 0.98$ (the frequency is daily). Hence, in the Gaussian model, 60% of z_t innovations dissipate within six months relative to only 2% in the model based on the Skellam distribution. Therefore, the effect of current innovations in z_t on future target rate changes is much smaller in the Gaussian model since estimates of the z_t coefficients δ_z are similar (0.016 vs 0.023).

Table 9.5 *Gaussian term structure model*

(a) Policy rule

σ_0	σ_1	δ_r	δ_z	ϕ_z
3.09	5×10^{-5}	1.84×10^{-4}	0.023	0.995
(0.04)	(0.04)	(0.36)	(0.0004)	(0.0001)

(b) Prices of risk

λ_s	$\lambda_{0,z}$	$\lambda_{z,r}$	$\lambda_{z,z}$
8.20×10^4	1.81×10^3	-1.01×10^7	-1.82×10^6
(0.31×10^4)	(0.15×10^3)	(0.04×10^7)	(0.08×10^6)

Parameter estimates for the Gaussian term structure model. Panel (a) reports estimates of the policy rule,

$$r_{t+1} - r_t \mid r_t, z_{t+1}, (I_{t+1} = 1) \sim \mathcal{D}\left(\delta_r(r_t - \bar{r}) + \delta_z(z_{t+1} - \bar{z}), \sigma_1^2\right),$$

(i.e., $I_{t+1} = 1$), where r_t is the target rate, z_t is a latent economic indicator, and $\mathcal{D}(\cdot, \cdot)$ is the distribution of the policy rate target innovations. It also reports the estimate of ϕ_z. Panel (b) displays the estimates of the price of risk coefficients (see Equations (9.13) and (9.14)). Estimation uses daily data including the target rate, the effective spread and futures rates, from Feb. 4, 1994 to Dec. 30, 2011.

Table 9.6 *Discrete term structure model*

(a) Policy rule

σ_0	σ_1	δ_r	δ_z	ϕ_z
1.39	96.33	−0.30	0.016	0.999
(0.10)	(3.70)	(0.006)	(0.0002)	(0.0001)

(b) Prices of risk

λ_s	$\lambda_{0,z}$	$\lambda_{z,r}$	$\lambda_{z,r}$
-1.54×10^3	2.61×10^3	-4.11×10^7	1.73×10^6
(0.79×10^3)	(0.05×10^3)	(0.51×10^7)	(0.24×10^6)

Parameter estimates for the Skellam term structure model.
Panel (a) reports estimates of the policy rule,

$$r_{t+1} - r_t \mid r_t, z_{t+1}, (I_{t+1} = 1) \sim \mathcal{D}\left(\delta_r(r_t - \bar{r}) + \delta_z(z_{t+1} - \bar{z}), \sigma_1^2\right),$$

where r_t is the target rate, z_t is a latent economic indicator, and
$\mathcal{D}(\cdot, \cdot)$ is the distribution of the policy rate target innovations. It
also reports the estimate of ϕ_z. Panel (b) displays the estimates of
the price of risk coefficients (see Equations (9.13) and (9.14)).
Estimation uses daily data including the target rate, the effective
spread and futures rates, from Feb. 4, 1994 to Dec. 30, 2011.
Standard errors in parentheses.

Next, consider the estimate of δ_r. This measures the degree of mean-
reversion in the target rate.[19] The target is nearly a unit root in the
Gaussian model. There is no significant mean-reversion when $z_t = \bar{z}$. In
contrast, the discrete-support model imparts substantial mean-reversion
to the target rate. If the macro factor is held at its mean ($z_t = \bar{z}$)
then the target rate is expected to retrace 30% of the path toward its
unconditional mean at each scheduled meeting. Clarida et al. (2000)
find estimates of the auto-correlation coefficient on the lag short rate
between 0.73 and 0.88 in the post-Volcker era. For comparison, the corresponding coefficient estimate obtained here is $\hat{\rho} = 1 - 0.30 = 0.70$.
These estimates are not directly comparable since they were obtained
from a different sample period and using different instruments. Moreover, the estimates from Clarida et al. (2000) correspond to quarterly
dynamics while the estimates obtained here correspond to the frequency

[19] The stationarity of r_t demands that $\delta_r < 0$ and that $|\phi_z| < 1$ (if $\delta_z \neq 0$). The stationarity
of z_t only demands the second condition.

of scheduled meetings. Nonetheless, this rough comparison suggests that the level of mean-reversion estimated from the Gaussian model is inconsistent with the data (biased) while the estimate from the model based on the Skellam distribution offers a consistent picture.

Looking back at Section 9.5.2, we see that estimates of δ_r and δ_z in Table 9.3 differ substantially from those obtained here. Again, estimates from the full no-arbitrage model use forward-looking information from futures rates. Using futures data changes the description of the policy rule drawn by each model. Moreover, the more realistic model, based on a discrete distribution, appears consistent with existing results and with economic intuition. Estimates from the discrete support model allow for a rapid reversion of the policy rate when economic conditions return to a normal state. On the other hand, estimates from the Gaussian model imply fast mean-reversion of economic conditions but a very persistent process for the target rate.

Is target rate risk priced?

This section relaxes the restriction that target rate innovations are not priced. Instead of Equation (9.13), the pricing kernel is now given by

$$
M_{t+1} = \frac{\exp(\lambda_r \eta_{t+1} + \lambda_s \epsilon^s_{t+1} + \lambda_{t,z} \epsilon^z_{t+1})}{E_t \left[\exp\left(\lambda_r \eta_{t+1} + \lambda_s \epsilon^s_{t+1} + \lambda_{t,z} \epsilon^z_{t+1}\right)\right]}, \tag{9.20}
$$

where λ_r is the constant price of target risk. Table 9.7 reports pricing error RMSE and parameter estimates. Adding a single parameter increases the log-likelihood by 494. In other words, the statistical evidence is overwhelmingly in favor of allowing target rate innovations to be priced. This addition also leads to small decreases in the pricing error RMSEs and the standard deviation estimates.

More importantly, changes in the parameter estimates are economically significant. Introducing a constant price of target rate risk introduces risk premium variations. In contrast, a constant price of risk only contributes a constant to the risk premium in the Gaussian case. Fontaine (2011) shows that the intensity parameters of the Skellam distribution (see Equation (9.5)) are shifted as follows:

$$
\lambda^Q_{u,r} = \lambda_r e^{\lambda_r \Delta}, \qquad \lambda^Q_{d,r} = \lambda_r e^{-\lambda_r \Delta},
$$
$$
\lambda^Q_{u,z} = \lambda_z e^{\lambda_r \Delta}, \qquad \lambda^Q_{d,z} = \lambda_z e^{-\lambda_r \Delta} \Delta, \tag{9.21}
$$

where, as before, $\Delta = 0.25\%$. In particular, the loadings of $\lambda^u(r_t, z_{t+1}, I_{t+1})$ and $\lambda^d(r_t, z_{t+1}, I_{t+1})$ on r_t and z_{t+1} are the same under

Table 9.7 *Discrete support model – priced target risk*

(a) Pricing errors

	Maturity					
	1	2	3	4	5	6
RMSE	4.36	6.57	4.87	3.49	2.25	4.01
$\xi(n)$	5.22	4.89	4.56	4.24	3.91	3.59

(b) Policy rule

σ_0	σ_1	δ_r	δ_z	ϕ_z
0.68	20.98	−0.07	0.0032	0.999
(0.03)	(1.05)	(0.004)	(0.0002)	(0.0002)

(c) Prices of risk

λ_r	λ_s	$\lambda_{0,z}$	$\lambda_{z,r}$	$\lambda_{z,z}$
3.27×10^5	-1.62×10^3	6.76×10^3	-7.06×10^7	3.04×10^6
(0.09×10^5)	(0.08×10^3)	(0.39×10^3)	(0.21×10^7)	(0.24×10^6)

Parameters estimates for the Skellam term structure model with priced target rate risk. Panel (a) reports pricing RMSE for each maturity and the corresponding estimated standard deviation parameters. Panel (b) reports estimates of the policy rule, σ_0 and

$$r_{t+1} - r_t \mid r_t, z_{t+1}, (I_{t+1} = 1) \sim \mathcal{D}\left(\delta_r(r_t - \bar{r}) + \delta_z(z_{t+1} - \bar{z}), \sigma_1^2\right),$$

(i.e., $I_{t+1} = 1$) where r_t is the target rate, z_t is a latent economic indicator, and $\mathcal{D}(\cdot, \cdot)$ is the distribution of the policy rate target innovations. It also reports the estimate of ϕ_z. Panel (c) displays the estimates of the price of risk coefficients (see Equations (9.13) and (9.14)) including the estimate of the (constant) price of target rate risk. Estimation uses daily data including the target rate, the effective spread and futures rates, from Feb. 4, 1994 to Dec. 30, 2011. Standard errors in parentheses.

the historical probability but they are not the same under $\mathbb{Q}$. The corresponding policy rule parameters for the distribution of the target rate are given by (compare with Equation (9.7))

$$\delta_r^{\mathbb{Q}} = (\lambda_{u,r}^{\mathbb{Q}} + \lambda_{d,r}^{\mathbb{Q}})\Delta = \lambda_r(e^{\lambda_r \Delta} + e^{-\lambda_r \Delta})\Delta,$$

$$\delta_z^{\mathbb{Q}} = (\lambda_{u,z}^{\mathbb{Q}} + \lambda_{d,z}^{\mathbb{Q}})\Delta = \lambda_z(e^{\lambda_r \Delta} + e^{-\lambda_r \Delta})\Delta. \tag{9.22}$$

The parameters δ_r and δ_z determine the policy rate dynamics under the historical measure and are used to compute the likelihood of observed policy rate changes. In contrast, the parameters $\delta_r^{\mathbb{Q}}$ and $\delta_z^{\mathbb{Q}}$ determine expected target changes under $\mathbb{Q}$ and are used to compute futures rates. If $\lambda_r = 0$, then these parameters are the same. Therefore, the price of target rate risk introduces a time-varying risk premium in the dynamics of the target rate,

$$E_t^Q[r_{t+1} - r_t] - E_t[r_{t+1} - r_t] = (\delta_r^Q - \delta_r)(r_t - \bar{r}) + (\delta_z^Q - \delta_z)E_t[z_{t+1}]$$
$$+ \delta_z^Q(E_t^Q[z_{t+1}] - E_t[z_{t+1}]), \quad (9.23)$$

where the last term is standard and due to variation in the price of Gaussian macro risk (see below). The estimate of the price of target risk is positive and significant. Unexpected increases in the target rate are considered risky – they are associated with bad states of the economy from the point view of participants in the futures markets. The implied parameter shift is substantial – $e^{\hat{\lambda}_r \Delta} + e^{-\hat{\lambda}_r \Delta} = 9.79$. Under the historical measure, the policy rule coefficient estimates are $\hat{\delta}_r = -0.07$ and $\hat{\delta}_z = 0.0032$. Both are significantly lower than the previous estimates. However, under the risk-neutral measure, the corresponding parameters are $\hat{\delta}_r^Q = -0.33$ and $\hat{\delta}_z^Q = 0.015$. These are almost identical to the estimates of δ_r and δ_z above in Table 9.6. Hence, allowing for the price of target risk makes the target rate less sensitive to economic conditions and with less mean-reversion under $\mathbb{P}$ than under $\mathbb{Q}$. This implies that the risk premium for target rate risk, $E_t^Q[r_{t+1} - r_t] - E_t[r_{t+1} - r_t]$, is higher when economic conditions improve – bond returns become left-skewed – and when the target rate is high.

The market price of macro risk

Figure 9.3 displays estimates of $\lambda_{z,t}$ for both models. The correlation is significant: 0.84. However, there are important differences. The price of risk is typically positive, varies smoothly in the discrete model, and mostly at the monthly frequency. Moreover, the price of risk from the discrete model essentially settles around a constant when the target rate reached its lower bound. In contrast, estimates from the Gaussian model still exhibit important variations after the end of 2008.

The results are also consistent with the fact that innovations in the macro factors should be associated with lower marginal rates of substitution and improved economic conditions for investors. In contrast, the estimates of price of risk from the Gaussian model sometimes swing deeply in the negative territory. Moreover, the distortions are significant for policy purposes. Estimates of the price of risk in the Gaussian model reach large negative values when the target rate declines faster than expected, or when the target rate is close to its lower bound. Therefore, large negative risk premia imply estimates of target rates expectations that are biased upward in periods where the Fed's intent

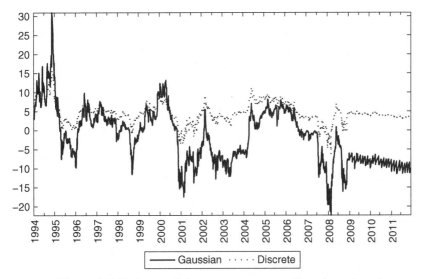

Figure 9.3 Estimate of the parameter controlling the price of macro risk, $\lambda_{z,t}$, from the Gaussian model and the discrete model, respectively. Daily data 1994–2011

is to loosen monetary conditions. Overall, the evidence suggests that the mis-specification of the target rate distribution induces an economically significant bias in the estimates of the prices of macro risk.

9.6   Unconventional policy and the challenges ahead

This section shows that the filtered values of the latent macro factor can be interpreted as changes in economic conditions implicit in Fed funds futures rates. I then use the macro factor to evaluate the effect of different policy announcements. I conclude with a discussion of recent modeling efforts to address the challenges raised by unconventional policy at the zero lower bound.

9.6.1   Link with economic conditions

The Philadelphia Fed publishes the Aruoba–Diebold–Scotti (ADS) index of US real activity. The index summarizes the information content from releases of real economic variables. It does not contain information from asset prices or other nominal variables. The index is published daily and is "designed to track real business conditions at high frequency.[20]

---

[20]   A similar high-frequency index of inflation is not available.

The underlying economic variables blend high- and low-frequency information and stock and flow data (weekly initial jobless claims; monthly payroll employment, industrial production, personal income less transfer payments, manufacturing and trade sales; and quarterly real GDP)."

Figure 9.4 draws the correlations between the current ADS index and the lagged macro factor, with daily lags from zero up to six months. It also draws the converse – the correlations between current macro factor and the lagged index. The highest lag corresponds to the longest futures maturity used to filter the macro factor. The results show that the predictive content of the macro factor for the future values ADS index is substantial. The correlations increase smoothly from 0.4 at low horizons to nearly 0.6 at horizons around six months. In contrast, the predictive content of the ADS index decays smoothly to just above 0.1.

Figure 9.5 compares the filtered values of the latent factor, z_t with the ADS index. The relationship between z_t and the index is visually apparent. These two proxies for economic conditions are closely related. Of course, they do not overlap since futures rates combine information from a broader information set perceived by market participants to be relevant for FOMC decisions. High realizations of the macro factor are associated

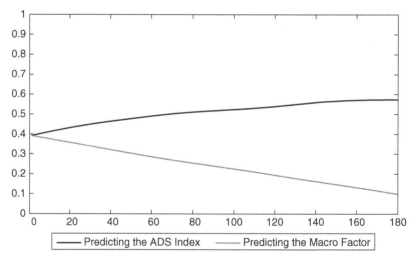

Figure 9.4 Sample correlations between the ADS index and lagged values of the the macro factor (predicting the ADS index), and correlation between the macro factor and lagged values of the ADS index (predicting the macro factor). Correlations are computed for daily lags from 0 to 180. ADS index data from the Federal Reserve of Philadelphia. Daily data (1994–2011)

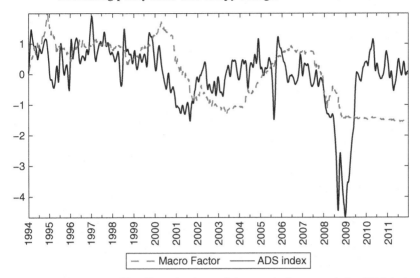

Figure 9.5 The filtered values of the macro factor and the ADS index from the Federal Reserve of Philadelphia. Daily data (1994–2011)

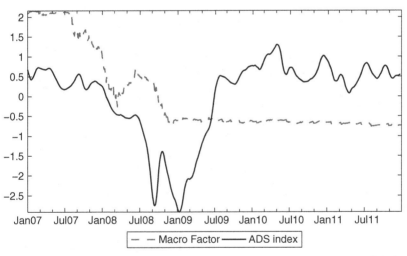

Figure 9.6 The filtered values of the macro factor and the ADS index from the Federal Reserve of Philadelphia. Daily data (2007–2011)

with high values of the ADS index in the future. Figure 9.5 also reveals the relationship between economic activity, as measured by the ADS index, and the macro factor, measured from futures rates changes toward the end of 2008. Figure 9.6 provides a close-up of this period. In fact,

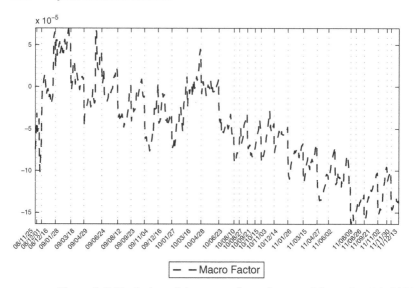

Figure 9.7 Evolution of the macro factor between November 24, 2008 and December 30, 2011. Dashed lines represent dates of key speeches or policy announcements from the Fed (See Table 9.8)
Note: The dates at the foot are in the order year/month/day.

the macro factor appears to be bounded from below. This is a reflection of the Fed's decision, in December 2008, to lower its target to 0.25%, which is effectively the lower bound. The ADS index continued to deteriorate in the recession of 2009 but rates could not be lowered further.

On the other hand, the futures curve still measures improvements of economic conditions. On June 9, 2009, the US Labor Department reported a lower number of job losses than expected. This corresponds to the largest spike in the macro factor in Figure 9.7. Nonetheless, persistently low inflation eventually led the Fed to implement quantitative easing policy and, in addition, to implement a commitment to keep the target rate unchanged until the end of 2013. There is no lower bound in a linear model. Therefore, implementation of a linear filter through a time series of a futures rates that remains relatively unchanged leads to relatively unchanged estimates of the macro factor.

9.6.2 Policy announcements at the lower bound

We can use the macro factor to measure the of impact of policy announcements on the expectations of participants in the futures market. Table 9.8 lists major monetary policy announcements by the Federal

Table 9.8 *Policy announcements 2008–2011*

Date (month/date/year)	Nature of the announcement
11/25/2008	Fed announces purchases of MBS and agency bonds
12/1/2008	Bernanke states Treasuries may be purchased
12/16/2008	Scheduled FOMC meeting
1/28/2009	Scheduled FOMC meeting
3/18/2009	Scheduled FOMC meeting
4/29/2009	Scheduled FOMC meeting
6/24/2009	Scheduled FOMC meeting
8/12/2009	Scheduled FOMC meeting
9/23/2009	Scheduled FOMC meeting
11/4/2009	Scheduled FOMC meeting
12/16/2009	Scheduled FOMC meeting
1/27/2010	Scheduled FOMC meeting
3/16/2010	Scheduled FOMC meeting
4/28/2010	Scheduled FOMC meeting
6/23/2010	Scheduled FOMC meeting
8/10/2010	Scheduled FOMC meeting
8/27/2010	Bernanke speech at Jackson Hole
9/21/2010	Scheduled FOMC meeting
10/15/2010	Bernanke speech at Boston Fed
11/3/2010	Scheduled FOMC meeting
12/14/2010	Scheduled FOMC meeting
1/26/2011	Scheduled FOMC meeting
3/15/2011	Scheduled FOMC meeting
4/27/2011	Scheduled FOMC meeting
6/2/2011	Scheduled FOMC meeting
8/9/2011	Scheduled FOMC meeting
8/26/2011	Bernanke speech at Jackson Hole
9/21/2011	Scheduled FOMC meeting
11/2/2011	Scheduled FOMC meeting
11/30/2011	Coordinated Central Bank announcements
12/13/2011	Scheduled FOMC meeting

Dates of major policy announcements by the Federal Reserve between November 2008 and December 2011. Dates until August 2009 are from Wright (2012).

Reserve since November 2008. It builds from and extends the list in Wright (2012) until the end of 2011. It includes the date of every FOMC meeting, key speeches by Fed Chairman Bernanke, and one coordinated announcement by different Central Banks. We can measure the effect of an announcement on the state of economy, as perceived from market participants, from changes in futures rates.

Figure 9.7 draws the evolution of the macro factor from 2008 until the end of 2011 with vertical lines that indicate the announcement dates listed in Table 9.8. Almost every policy announcement corresponds to a decline in the macro factor. This is consistent with the Federal Reserve signaling that the target rate would remain constant for a longer horizon. This arose either because the Fed's statement related directly to the horizon, or indirectly, as a consequence of other policy decisions (e.g., quantitative easing). These declines in the macro factor are large. The mean response is close in magnitude to the standard deviation of all shocks in this period. However, the shocks show little persistence and the cumulative change of the macro factor is small.

Nonetheless, this measured effect was low by historical standards given that the target rate is bounded below.

9.6.3   The challenges ahead

The lower bound on nominal interest rates is the current frontier for policymakers and researchers studying the term structure of interest rates. Several alternative solutions exist in the literature. First, the seminal work of Cox et al. (1985) is based on "square-root" processes and maintains the positivity of yields as well as computational tractability. But note that most existing empirical applications enforce the Feller conditions. This approach is often criticized on the grounds that zero becomes a reflecting boundary – the short rate bounces off zero and never reaches it. Following this observation, Black (1995) formulated the short rate as an option,

$$r_t = \max(0, \tilde{r}_t),$$

where $\tilde{r}_t$ is the "shadow" policy rate. This allows for more flexibility in the specification of $\tilde{r}_t$ but the analyst must resort to numerical solutions for yields and other asset prices. Finally, a quadratic short rate is always positive,

$$r_t = x_t' \Upsilon x_t,$$

and analytical results are available when x_t is Gaussian. This leads to quadratic-Gaussian term structure models (Ahn et al. 2002 and Leippold and Wu (2003)) where the solution for yields is a linear-quadratic function of x_t.

Kim and Singleton (2012) provide an empirical study of nominal yields in Japan between 1995 and 2008. They show that the behavior of yields is qualitatively different in this period. Empirically, they compare multi-factor square-root, shadow-rate and quadratic-Gaussian term structure models. They focus on long-maturity yields (the shortest maturity in their sample is 6 months) and find that the shadow-rate and quadratic-Gaussian models capture important stylized features of long-term interest rates in Japan. The same is not true for the square-root model.

These formulations are targeted at yields with relatively long maturity and toward relatively low sampling frequencies. They ignore the fact that changes in the target rate are lumpy and occur only rarely. As evidenced above, this omission affects estimation results if one focuses on yields with short maturities at a relatively high frequency. Hence, the pervasive, and sometimes persistent, occurrences of very low policy rates nowadays calls for the development of term structure models that meet the empirical features of the target rate while also enforcing the positivity of yields.

Some recent work seeks to reach this goal. Feunou and Fontaine (2012) introduce the family of discrete choice dynamics term structure models. They define the policy response function as an ordered discrete choice problem (McFadden, 1984). These models are flexible and allow for rich non-linearities in the relationship between yields and the underlying economic variables, including the zero bound. An ordered choice representation of the policy rule has been proposed before (Hamilton and Jordà, 2002) but implications for the term structure of yields have been ignored. Renne (2012) provides an alternative specification based on regime-switching techniques. Although the number of regimes is large, this family of models leads to a tractable affine representation of yields. Empirically, Renne (2012) applies this model to the euro area in a daily sample between 1999 and 2012. Finally, the approach in Black (1995) is also applicable if the shadow rate has a discrete support, as in this chapter.

9.7   Conclusion

This chapter shows that different modeling assumptions yield different interpretations of the term structure of yields. It provides a specification of the term structure that is consistent with the operational policy of modern Central Banks. Policy rate changes occur infrequently, typically on scheduled dates, and they are lumpy (i.e., multiples of 0.25%). The target rate in the US has been fixed to its lower bound since the end of 2008. The positivity constraint has been addressed in the literature in the context of long-term maturities but still poses a challenge when combined with the requirement that the target rate has a discrete support. Moreover, the lower bound does not imply that the Central Bank takes no further action to meet its mandates. Liquidity facilities, credit easing, quantitative easing, and others, all represent monetary policy actions unrelated to the conventional target rate but that affect the term structure of interest rates. Understanding the transmission of these unconventional actions to long-term yields is the challenge that the next generation of models must meet.

Appendix

Discrete changes and the distribution of yields

Long-term yields evolve smoothly because the expectation operator is not restricted to the support of any random variable.[21] To see this, define the set of future dates where a meeting is scheduled, $\mathbb{S}_t$, and write the one-year yield, $y_t^{(i)}$, in terms of target rate expectations and a risk premium,

$$y_t^{(1)} = E_t \left[\frac{1}{365} \sum_{i=1}^{365} r_{t+i-1} \right] + rp_t^{(1)} = r_t + E_t \left[\sum_{i \in \mathbb{S}_t} c_i \Delta_{t+i} \right] + rp_t^{(1)},$$

where time is daily, $\Delta_{t+i} = r_{t+i} - r_{t+i-1}$, $c_i = \frac{365-i}{365}$ and $rp_t^{(1)}$ is an adjustment for risk. Then, on days with no policy rate changes (i.e., $r_t = r_{t+1}$), yield changes are given by

$$y_{t+1}^{(1)} - y_t^{(1)} = \sum_{i \in \mathbb{S}} (E_{t+1} - E_t) \left[c_i \Delta_{t+i} \right] + rp_{t+1}^{(1)} - rp_t^{(1)}, \tag{9.24}$$

which shows that yields can change smoothly as economic information arrives since expectations and, a fortiori, expectation changes are not restricted to the discrete support. Moreover, yields average the expected changes over a sequence of future meetings. Finally, risk premium variations can also evolve continuously.

But discrete target changes affect the distribution of yields changes. Note that the first term in Equation (9.24) is different on days where a policy meeting is held. On non-meeting days, this term is the change in the expectations of future target rate. On meeting days, it is the policy rate innovation, $n_{t+1} = E_t[r_{t+1} - r_t] - (r_{t+1} - r_t)$ (with a slight abuse of notation). Changes in expectations summarize the effect of a variety of "news" related to future policy and may be relatively close to a Gaussian distribution. In contrast, the innovations, n_{t+1}, can take only a few values

---

[21] But it is restricted to its range.

ex-post. In general, the expectation term, $E_t[r_{t+1}]$, does not lie close to a point on the support of r_{t+1} and the policy innovation n_{t+1} will "jump" to one of these points. Large yield changes should be more common on days with policy meetings.

To confirm this effect, I consider federal funds futures contracts with maturities between 1 and 6 months. I count occurrences of rate changes in bins with different change sizes on days with a scheduled policy meeting. The edges of the bins are -7.5, -2.5, 2.5 and 7.5 bps.[22] I consider each maturity separately. The sample runs from 1994 until 2011 and covers 144 schedule meetings. I repeat the analysis for other days when no meeting occurs. Table 9.9 reports for each bin the ratio of counts on meeting days to the average of counts across the preceding 20 non-meeting days. For each maturity, and for each bin, a ratio lower than one indicates that changes are less frequent on meeting days than on non-meeting days.[23]

As expected, small changes are less likely on meeting days. Overall, changes between -2.5 bps and 2.5 bps are between 15% and 25% less frequent on meeting days than on non-meeting days. In contrast, larger

Table 9.9 *Frequency ratio of changes in interest rates*

	Maturity					
$f_{t,n} - f_{t-1,n}$	1	2	3	4	5	6
$-\infty$ to -0.075	1.36	4.38	2.92	2.89	2.63	2.31
-0.075 to -0.025	5.74	1.41	1.66	1.43	1.41	1.28
-0.025 to 0.025	0.84	0.80	0.83	0.81	0.76	0.80
0.025 to 0.075	4.42	1.84	1.38	1.38	1.15	1.04
0.075 to ∞	1.54	5.00	2.43	2.05	2.75	2.05

Relative frequency of futures rate changes on days with and without policy meetings. Each column corresponds to a different contract maturity. I report the ratio of the number of times a futures rate changes on days with or without policy meeting, $P(x_i \le f_{t,n} - f_{t-1,n} \le x_{i+1} | I_t = 1)$ and $P(x_i \le f_{t,n} - f_{t-1,n} \le x_{i+1} | I_t = 0)$, respectively, where f_t is the rate on the n-month ahead contract, I_t is an indicator function equal to 1 when a meeting occurs, and x_i are the edges of the different bins used to compute the probabilities. P is the empirical distribution. Daily data from Jan. 3, 1994 to Dec. 30, 2011. Contract maturities between 1 and 6 months ahead.

[22] For comparison, the standard deviation of rate changes for the 6-month contract is 4.6 bps.

[23] See Section A for a description of Federal Funds futures contracts. Note that the results are robust to changes in the size of the bins and to changes in the number of days used to compute the average counts on non-meeting days.

rate changes are more frequent. Changes between 2.5 and 7.5 bps (in absolute value) are typically 50% more frequent on meeting days. The difference is much greater for the 1-month contract: there are very few changes of this magnitude on non-meeting days at this maturity. Finally, rate changes greater than 7.5 bps (in absolute value) are typically twice as likely on meeting days than on non-meeting days. Therefore, discrete changes in the target rate imply that yield changes have a more dispersed distribution following policy announcements.

References

Ahn, D.-H., Dittmar, R. and Gallant, A. R. (2002). Quadratic term structure models: theory and evidence. *Review of Financial Studies*, 15, 243–288.

Balduzzi, P., Bertola, G. and Foresi, S. (1997). A model of target changes and the term structure of interest rates. *Journal of Monetary Economics*, 39, 223–249.

Bech, M. L. and Klee, E. (2009). The mechanics of a graceful exit: interest on reserves and segmentation in the federal funds market. Working Paper 416, Federal Reserve Bank of New York.

Bhundia, A. J. and Chadha, J. S. (1998). The information content of 3-month sterling futures. *Economics Letters*, 61(2), 209–214.

Black, F. (1995). Interest rates as options. *Journal of Finance*, 50, 1371–1376.

Clarida, R., Galí, J. and Gertler, M. (2000). Monetary policy rules and macroeconomic stability: Evidence and some theory. *Quarterly Journal of Economics*, 115, 147–180.

Cochrane, J. and Piazzesi, M. (2002). The Fed and interest rates: a high-frequency identification. *American Economic Review*, 92, Papers and Proceedings, 90–95.

Cox, J., Ingersoll, J. and Ross, S. (1985). A theory of the term structure of interest rates. *Econometrica*, 53, 385–407.

Duffee, G. (1996). Idiosyncratic variation of Treasury bill yields. *Journal of Finance*, 51(2), 527–551.

Duffee, G. (2002). Term premia and interest rate forecasts in affine model. *Journal of Finance*, 57, 405–443.

Duffee, G. (2009). Sharpe ratios in term structure models. Working Paper, Johns Hopkins University.

Feldhütter, P. and Lando, D. (2008). Decomposing swap spreads. *Journal of Financial Economics*, 88(2), 375–405.

Ferrero, G. and Nobili, A. (2008). Futures contract rates as monetary policy forecasts. Technical Report 979, European Central Bank.

Feunou, B. and Fontaine, J. (2012). Discrete-choice term structure models: theory and applications. Banque du Canada, unpublished manuscript.

Fontaine, J.-S. (2011). Fed funds futures and the federal reserve. Working Paper, Bank of Canada.

Gürkaynak, R., Sack, B. and Swanson, E. (2007). Market based measures of monetary policy expectations. *Journal of Business and Economics Statistics*, 25, 201–212.

Hamilton, J. (1994). *Time Series Analysis*, Princeton: Princeton University Press.

Hamilton, J. (1996). The daily market for federal funds. *Journal of Political Economy*, **104**, 26–56.

Hamilton, J. (1997). Measuring the liquidity effect. *American Economic Review*, **87**(1), 80–97.

Hamilton, J. (2009). Daily changes in Fed funds futures prices. *Journal of Money, Credit and Banking*, **41**, 567–582.

Hamilton, J. and Jordà, O. (2002). A model of the federal funds rate target. *Journal of Political Economy*, **110**, 1136–1167.

Hamilton, J. and Okimoto, T. (2010). Sources of variations in holding returns for Fed funds futures contracts. *Journal of Futures Markets*, **31**, 205–229.

Kim, D. H. and Singleton, K. (2012). Term structure models and the zero bound: an empirical investigation of Japanese yields. *Journal of Economics*, **170**, 32–44.

Krueger, J. and Kuttner, K. (1996). The Fed funds futures rate as a predictor of Federal Reserve policy. *International Economic Review*, **16**, 865–879.

Leippold, M. and Wu, L. (2003). Design and estimation of multi-currency quadratic models. *European Finance Review*, 7, 47–73.

McFadden, D. L. (1984). Econometric analysis of qualitative response models. In *Handbook of Econometrics* (M. D. Intrilligator and Z. Griliches, eds.), Amsterdam: Elsevier.

Piazzesi, M. (2005a). Bond yields and the Federal Reserve. *Journal of Political Economy*, **113**, 311–344.

Piazzesi, M. (2005b). Affine term structure models. In *Handbook of Financial Econometrics* (Y. Ait-Sahalia and L. Hansen, eds.), Oxford: Elsevier.

Piazzesi, M. and Swanson, E. (2006). Futures prices as risk-adjusted forecasts of monetary policy. Technical Report 2006-23, Federal Reserve Bank of San Francisco.

Renne, J.-P. (2012). A model of the euro-area yield curve with discrete policy rates. Technical Report, Banque de France.

Rigobon, R. (2003). Identification through heteroskedasticity. *Review of Economics and Statistics*, **85**(4), 777–792.

Rudebusch, G. (1995). Federal reserve interest rate targeting, rational expectations, and the term structure. *Journal of Monetary Economics*, **35**(2), 245–274.

Sack, B. (2004). Extracting the expected path of monetary policy from futures rates. *International Economic Review*, **24**, 733–754.

Sentana, E. and Fiorentini, G. (2001). Identification, estimation and testing of conditionally heteroskedastic factor models. *Journal of Econometrics*, **102**(2), 143–164.

Sin, C. and White, H. (1996). Information criteria for selecting possibly misspecified parametric models. *Journal of Econometrics*, **71**(12), 207–225.

Skellam, J. (1946). The frequency distribution of the difference between two Poisson variates belonging to different populations. *Journal of the Royal Statistical Society*, **109**, 296.

Taylor, J. B. (1993). Discretion versus policy rules in practice. *Carnegie-Rochester Conference Series on Public Policy*, **39**, 195–214.

Thornton, D. L. (2006). The daily liquidity effect. Working Paper. Federal Reserve Bank of St. Louis.

Wright, J. (2012). What does monetary policy do to long-term interest rates at the zero lower bound? *Economic Journal*, **122**, F447–F466.

10 Developing a practical yield curve model: an odyssey

M. A. H. Dempster, Jack Evans and Elena Medova

10.1 Introduction and background

What happens if one wishes to implement an interest rate model based on current knowledge about the subject? Current knowledge means here state of the art or best practice, but not cutting edge. What would someone familiar with the recent literature and current practice be led to? The purpose of this chapter is to identify and describe the challenges presented by such an exercise.

The background of the exercise is the creation of a new global capital markets econometric model taking account of current developments, but in the spirit of earlier models developed for various financial services institutions; see, for example, Mulvey and Thorlacious (1998) (Towers Perrin), Dempster and Thorlacious (1998) (Swiss Re), Dempster and Arbeleche Grela (2003) (UniCredit) and the models currently in use by leading actuarial consultants. The emphasis in these 'economic scenario generators' is on their ability to be simulated forward over long horizons for pricing various financial products (Dempster et al., 2010), providing investment advice (Medova et al., 2008) and asset-liability management (Dempster et al., 2003). Since the pioneering system described in Mulvey and Thorlacious (1998), the keys to accurate scenario generation from these models are the yield curve models which forecast interest rates in each currency and upon which the determination of all other variables depend.

An immediate first question is what is *meant* by an interest rate model. Clearly the term covers many different creatures and so we will first describe some requirements for the exercise. However we also hope to illustrate the challenges involved in moving from naive desiderata,

We wish to acknowledge the major contributions made to this research by Miklós Reiter in both modelling and charting. We also thank the editors and two anonymous referees for suggestions which materially improved our chapter.

through practical specifications, to evaluation of some models described in the current literature. There are challenges at each stage.

Identifying what output is required from the model is probably the most straightforward aspect. After that there is a compromise to be made between hope and reality, and the two communicate only with a lot of work. Some of the issues are well known. For example, two major groups of model may be distinguished by whether they concentrate on matching a wide range of market prices for interest rate related products or instead aim to reflect realistic properties of the time series of rates and phenomena such as risk premia. This is not a logical distinction, but it is already a practical one in that a model builder cannot know what they need to address without considering the models actually available. Thus specification, even at this high level, is already dependent on what models are actually available, and the model builder, like the builders of the Channel Tunnel, must start from both ends and hope to meet in the middle. This is a common enough situation in life, but unfortunately in the present case there is no 'Which dynamic term structure model' publication containing a handy feature comparison table to save the model builder from having to read the literature on every model (although James and Webber (2000) is very helpful on the earlier literature).

The lack of such a current guide is not unexpected, but on the other hand there is no good reason why, to the best of our knowledge, such a survey article does not exist. Unfortunately, the situation is more challenging than simply having to read about each model individually, although there are certainly important features that can be inferred from reading the literature. For example, some models are intended for derivative pricing (e.g. de Jong et al., 2001) while others are intended for econometric study (e.g. Nelson and Siegel, 1987 and their descendants), although upon close examination this distinction becomes somewhat murky and has only recently begun to be explored in detail. Nevertheless, some important features we require are not addressed in the literature *at all*. The models therefore cannot be assessed on our requirements without first devoting significant effort to trial implementation.

The object of the exercise that led to this chapter was to understand how current best practice would look in the implementation of a dynamic term structure model of interest rates. A subsidiary question was whether or not an older model should be updated in the light of new developments. The model arrived at in this chapter is to be used to simulate *long-term* fixed income returns and to provide realistic scenarios for the future *prices* of interest rate linked liabilities. In the context of the model, *risk premia* should be realistically reflected and rates and returns in all *scenarios*, or paths, considered should be plausible when taken at face value. In addition, if at all possible the parameters of the model should be robustly determined by consideration of historical data. This is by no means a complete specification of such a model but, since we have already mentioned that there appears to be a distinction between econometric and derivative pricing models, we must accept that we are unlikely to be able to get every feature that we might want in a single model.

The remainder of this chapter is structured as follows. The next section contains a brief review of the current literature, followed by Section 10.3 which describes the process by which we arrived at our final model choice, requiring new research and described in Section 10.4. It is these two sections which we hope will provide the interested reader with some suggestions and *caveats*. Section 10.5 concludes, hinting at the issues involved in embedding yield curve models in a full capital market model for a currency area.

10.2   Literature review

As one might expect for such an important and complex subject, the literature on interest rate modelling is vast, and we cannot pretend to have read and processed it all. This chapter is about the search for an interest rate model suitable for our purposes and, as mentioned previously, we found the broadest range and most open-ended discussion in the book by James and Webber (2000). This book also has useful discussions on a wide range of implementation issues. The vast number of options available makes model selection a key issue; there is accordingly much discussion of it in the literature. Unfortunately, from our point of view most of this discussion is focused on areas that are not directly relevant to our situation. One recent paper that does address some of our concerns is Nawalkha and Rebonato (2011), which makes clear some of the limitations of derivative pricing models when they are applied for other purposes (but see also Longstaff et al., 2001). These issues led us to consider instead models oriented towards econometric estimation, and affine models in particular. What is involved in affine models was very clearly laid out by Dai and Singleton (2000), who put many affine models into a useful context. However, although their paper is very suggestive, estimation of these models is a much richer topic than a casual reading might lead one to expect. An overview of subsequent developments is supplied in Piazzesi (2010) and vital help with estimation comes from the trio of papers by Joslin, Singleton and Zhu (2011), Hamilton and Wu (2012) and Bauer, Rudebusch and Wu (2011). These three papers provide robust and efficient estimation methods which give a firm foundation to the conclusions derived from our explorations. Ultimately, we reject straightforward affine models for our purposes. Instead we pursue the idea of Fischer Black (1995) implemented previously in lower dimensional models by the Bank of Japan (see Ichiue and Ueno, 2005 and Ueno et al., 2006) and Kim and Singleton, 2011.

10.2.1 First challenge: lots of models

More than a decade ago, James and Webber (2000) were already able to describe tens of interest rate models. In the intervening years those that might *prima facie* be suitable for our purposes have not been whittled down to a more manageable number. The range of options is huge and this means that choices may need to be made before some avenues are fully explored.

The lack of a current catalogue of models is not merely an inconvenience, it is also indicative of the narrow application of many yield curve models, i.e. their understanding tends to require a narrow focus on the original application of the model. This means that someone seeking a model for a non-standard purpose will have to consider potential choices in some detail in order to determine their suitability. It also unfortunately means that there are limits to the extent that the required specification can be set down *in advance*; there is simply not enough information available about what is possible. Specification is a challenge to begin with, and the lack of comparison information in the current literature makes it difficult to understand what compromises will be required, or indeed available. This means that the task specification must necessarily be incomplete before the actual search begins.

On one hand, the specification must start incomplete and be improved upon as information about the relevant capabilities of models becomes available and their unexpected features are revealed. On the other hand, candidate models must be implemented far enough to assess their relevant properties. As investigations from the two sides make progress they can both be extended in the light of new information discovered and, with luck, be persuaded to meet in the middle.

10.2.2 What do we require?

The task here is to produce realistic stochastic forecasts of the long-term behaviour of various fixed income investments and interest rate linked liablities. That means that, among other things:

- rates must be realistic in each scenario, not only in aggregate;
- returns must be realistic given the economic environment;

- returns should reflect any market risk premium;
- the model should consistently address a wide range of fixed income products, e.g. bonds of different maturities;
- parameters should be objectively and empirically determined;
- simulations should accurately reflect initial conditions.

These requirements are pretty vague, but making them less so is as much a part of the modelling process as is achieving the result of our investigations. They will be made more precise and concrete when confronted with specific models. The above list is also likely far from complete, even if any particular issue could be put under one or more of the above umbrellas.

To give an example of what is meant by 'realistic', the popular Libor Market Model (see e.g. de Jong et al., 2001) can, under current actually occurring low interest rate conditions, require parameter estimates that make volatility so high that simulated cash returns are more volatile than actual equity returns with significant weight given to rates of more than 10,000%. Nevertheless, the model still works for its intended purpose because in a derivative pricing situation in banks it only needs to have the correct *aggregate* behaviour – which in our case is not adequate.

10.2.3 What's on offer?

It helps to attempt to categorise models first, however crudely. We have seen that for interest rate models the two most important areas are econometrics and derivative pricing. A case can be made that there is a third area, the descriptive models, such as the original Nelson–Siegel (1987) model. These provide functional forms which give economic descriptions of yield curves without direct consideration of the dynamic relationships they clearly imply. Similar requirements are heavily used in both of the other camps – for derivative pricing, to efficiently interpolate yield curves from real price data, and in econometrics, to provide convenient factor breakdowns of interest rates. However, as with the two main camps, our modelling case needs an explicit *dynamic* representation, so that a descriptive model can only be a *part* of our solution at best.

Derivatives pricing is a vigorous field which is intrinsically practical in its focus. That should be good news for us, but unfortunately the imperatives of derivative pricing are somewhat different from ours. In many applications a derivative pricing model must exactly match a wide range of market prices. To achieve this the models frequently incorporate two features that make them very difficult to use for our applications. The first is that they are mostly based on *risk neutral pricing* and pay no attention to the nature of any risk premia involved. Incorporating a risk premium therefore means extending the model in a typically uncharted way. To apply to our situation many of the implementations either will not work or have to be completely reworked. A more subtle issue is that models are frequently given multi-parameter term or cross-sectional structures which are determined outside their dynamics in order to achieve accurate pricing. This makes such models hard to reason about and estimate statistically. This issue is discussed extensively by Nawalkha and Rebonato (2011) from a slightly less specific point of view.

For the issue at hand the requirement for our model to be objectively and empirically determined translates into the following two more specific requirements:

- parsimony;
- time homogeneity.

As always we have limited data, so we first want the models to be parameterised by an appropriately *limited* number of parameters. Secondly, although time homogeneity can be seen as a particular aspect of parsimony, it also means that a model with this property makes it easier to understand what is going on inside the model, since it is more self-contained than the *double plus* models described by Nawalkha and Rebonato. The specification of their models removes a significant part of each model's ability to reflect market conditions. In practice, this is accommodated by appropriately adjusting a string of model parameters.

10.2.4 *Affine models*

Econometric interest rate modelling is dominated by *affine* models. This popularity reflects the attractive combination of tractability and a rich range of specifications. In certain forms they are closely linked to other econometric work horses such as *vector autoregression* (VAR) and an impressive amount of research has been done to apply these models to a wide range of situations. They owe their tractability to how simply, quickly and accurately *expectations*, and therefore implied bond prices and yields, can be calculated, making it easily feasible to build models of *changing* expectations. Such models specify *transition probabilities* between states in a (usually) finite-dimensional state space and allow *expected*, or mean, future states to be calculated explicitly analytically or in terms of easily solved ordinary differential or difference equations.

The affine property has been employed in many models, including the famous seminal works of Vasicek (1977) and Cox, Ingersol and Ross (1985). However, the links between the various specifications were not systematised until the work of Duffie and Kan (1996) and Dai and Singleton (2000), and their collaborators.

From the point of view of someone trying to narrow their modelling options, it is especially helpful that these authors provide a classification of affine models into a two-parameter family. One parameter represents the *dimension* of the model state space, while the second parameter is the *number* of those dimensions that are *bounded*. Roughly speaking, the evolution of the *unbounded* dimensions follow some sort of Ornstein Uhlenbeck process, while the *bounded* dimensions follow a Cox–Ingersoll–Ross, or Feller square root, process. The latter are *a priori* appropriate for modelling quantities that must remain positive, for example, volatilities or interest rates. Of course the details are more complex, but this is the picture that emerges from the literature.

More concretely, we represent the processes to be modelled in the notation of Dai and Singleton's paper. There they are presented as solutions Y to *stochastic differential equations* (SDEs) of the form:[1]

$$\mathrm{d}Y(t) = K(\Theta - Y(t))\mathrm{d}t + \Sigma\sqrt{s(t)}\mathrm{d}W(t), \qquad (10.1)$$

where Y is the n-dimensional *state* vector, W is an n-dimensional Brownian motion, Θ is a fixed point in the (Euclidean) Y space, K and Σ are $n \times n$ matrices and S is a diagonal matrix with each entry a constant affine function of Y. The *(instantaneous) short rate* r is then given by an affine function r of Y, with longer term *rates* being calculated as expectations of integrals of r.

In most cases we will work with two Y process measures, one describing the actual market evolution of the process and the other assumed for the purpose of pricing. The path measures, P and Q, underlying these two specifications are usually termed *real world (market)* and *risk neutral (pricing)* measures respectively, and are determined by instances of (10.1) which differ in their K and Θ terms.

Specifically, zero coupon *bond prices*, or *discount factors*, are given in terms of Y under the pricing measure Q as

$$r_t = \delta_0^Q + \delta_Y^Q{}' Y_t,$$
$$P_t(\tau) = E_t^Q\left[\exp\left(-\int_t^{t+\tau} r_s\,\mathrm{d}s\right)\right], \qquad (10.2)$$

where δ_0^Q and δ_y^Q are respectively a positive constant and a non-negative n-vector, prime denotes transpose, t is current time, τ denotes maturity and E_t^Q denotes conditional expectation under Q at time t. These expressions indicate the origin of the term (exponential) affine model.

---

[1] We indicate random entities, here conditionally random, using boldface.

Equivalent *yields to maturity* for all maturities τ, which we will term *rates* in this chapter, are given from bond prices by

$$y_t(\tau) := -\log P_t(\tau)/\tau. \tag{10.3}$$

The key feature of affine models is that for appropriate Y process descriptions the expectations in the bond prices of (10.2) are easily calculated, either in closed form or numerically. For some models, as noted above, bond prices or their corresponding rates may be evaluated analytically, see e.g. James and Webber (2000). For others, an n-vector R of rates in (10.2) may be calculated for each t in terms of the n state variables Y by numerically solving an n-dimensional vector *Ricatti* equation of the form

$$\partial R_t(\tau)/\partial\tau = (K' - \tau^{-1}I)R_t(\tau) + \frac{1}{2}(\sigma_{11}^2 R_{1t}(\tau)^2, \ldots, \sigma_{nn}^2 R_{nt}(\tau)^2)', \tag{10.4}$$

with initial condition $R_t(0) = 0$, to give $y_t(\tau) = r_t + R_t(\tau)'Y_t$. Here 0 denotes the n-zero vector and σ_{ii} denotes the ith diagonal entry of σ in (10.1). Expression (10.4) is an *ordinary differential equation* (ODE) with respect to rate maturity τ with other parameters determined by the specifications of (10.1) and (10.2).

The role of the affine function in determining the short rate highlights the fact that there will typically be multiple models that give indistinguishable rate evolution processes; in econometric terms these models are *not identified*. One of the main contributions of the Dai and Singleton paper is to specify a *normalised* form for identified affine models, at least for those models with maximum freedom.

There are similar formulae for state processes involving jumps, which is a subject for our future investigation. More useful from an estimation viewpoint is the existence of *discrete time* analogues for even complex versions of the state process evolution of these models. These analogues can sometimes considerably simplify the discretisation always necessary for estimation. In these cases, the ordinary differential equation (10.4) for numerically calculating expectations can be replaced with a difference equation which is much easier to solve. This approach is described in Dai, Le and Singleton (2010).

There are many *more* affine model specifications in the Dai and Singleton categories than those discussed in their paper, but these models should all be nested within at least one such category, so these authors' classification is a good place to start a model search. Ideally, we would examine *all* affine models systematically, but that is not possible – even in principle. Indeed, the practicalities are not so well worked out that there is an effective algorithm for selecting the best specification. Of course various statistical *information criteria* and other model selection tools can be applied, but doing so remains something of an art form, as is demonstrated by the recent literature.

Instead we start by taking a lead from the work of Litterman and Scheinkman (1991). They performed a principal components analysis of US yield curve (rates) data and concluded that at least three factors were necessary for a satisfactory representation of the dynamic behaviour of yield curves. Since we are determined to avoid complexity, we should also avoid using more than three factors if at all possible; so these models are our starting point.

10.3   Model evaluation

10.3.1   Basic considerations

The analysis presented here is based on data on gilt yields from the Bank of England web site. The data series extend from 1972 to the present and are freely downloadable. Among the series available are zero coupon yields (rates) for maturities at one month intervals at the short end and then at six monthly intervals out to up to 30 year maturity. This data is an excellent resource for development, but it is not ideal and may *not* be what we use in production. Its shortcomings include the fact that interpolation and coupon stripping is done using a model which is not necessarily consistent with the ones that we are evaluating, and which cannot distinguish 'on the run' effects and other similar microstructure considerations. There are also gaps in the data, although to be fair these mostly correspond to periods when certain maturities did not exist or were not liquid. Nevertheless, full zero coupon yield curve data at daily frequency extending as far back as the demise of Bretton Woods is extremely useful and is sufficient to address all the issues tackled here. We shall in fact use data at *monthly* frequency (at end of month) for the investigations reported in the sequel.

Model parameter estimation will be based on some version of *maximum likelihood estimation* (MLE) or its approximants. To this end we use numerical optimisation routines that combine an initial search method with an appropriate quasi-Newton method to refine the maximum achieved by the search algorithm. Since in practical use parameter estimates need to be frequently updated, we have a predilection for using market data at only a few data points on the yield curve and then interpolating or extrapolating other required maturities as necessary, e.g. for pricing. If the same number of observed points is used as the state space dimension, we can often considerably reduce the estimation computations by the direct inversion of square matrices.

This rules out, at least initially, most *filter-* or *method-of-moments-*based estimation of unobservable (latent) factors as too computationally expensive for our application. Moreover, although typically incorporating more observed rate data, all such complex methods require 'tender loving care' in each particular data instance, which is a difficult requirement in a production environment.

10.3.2 First candidate specification

The Dai and Singleton (2000) classification describes in detail four types of three-factor exponential affine model classified roughly according to how many of the factors are *bounded* (as noted above). Which to investigate?

It would be helpful to have a model that avoids negative rates. That can only happen completely in a model in which *all* factors are bounded, which means their models of $A_3(3)$ type. Such models can be thought of as three-factor extensions of the well known Cox, Ingersol and Ross (1985) square root (CIR) one factor model. They have been famously addressed in Chen and Scott (1993), so this should not be entirely unknown territory, and they *guarantee* non-negative rates.

The Dai and Singleton normal form for the stochastic differential equation (10.1) representation of this type is relatively simple:

$$Y(t) := \begin{pmatrix} y_1(t) \\ y_2(t) \\ y_3(t) \end{pmatrix},$$

$$K := \begin{pmatrix} \kappa_{11} & -\kappa_{12} & -\kappa_{13} \\ -\kappa_{21} & \kappa_{22} & -\kappa_{23} \\ -\kappa_{31} & -\kappa_{32} & \kappa_{33} \end{pmatrix},$$

$$\Theta := \begin{pmatrix} \theta_1 \\ \theta_2 \\ \theta_3 \end{pmatrix},$$

$$\Sigma := \begin{pmatrix} 1 & 0 & 0 \\ 0 & 1 & 0 \\ 0 & 0 & 1 \end{pmatrix},$$

$$S(t) := \begin{pmatrix} y_1(t) & 0 & 0 \\ 0 & y_2(t) & 0 \\ 0 & 0 & y_3(t) \end{pmatrix},$$

$$r(t) := \alpha + \beta y_1(t) + \gamma y_2(t) + \delta y_3(t). \tag{10.5}$$

The matrix K is non-negative on the diagonal and non-positive off the diagonal (i.e. $\kappa_{ij} \geq 0$) and the parameter vector Θ has positive elements, but otherwise they are allowed full freedom, while Σ is the identity matrix and S is a diagonal matrix with Y on the diagonal. As a result the instantaneous short rate can be given by an affine function of Y. We can calculate model-implied bond prices, and the corresponding rates using (10.3), in terms of the model-parameters by numerically solving the appropriate version of (10.4) to determine the corresponding likelihood function for maximum likelihood estimation with the observed rate data (see e.g. James and Webber, 2000).

For this model we have 28 coefficients to estimate – 12 for the market measure process, 12 for the pricing measure process and four for the affine form of the instantaneous rate. The risk premium is then the difference between the drift terms in the two process SDEs. Note, however, that although there are 28 degrees of freedom, 24 of them are bounded for technical reasons and the other four parameters, which correspond to the affine form of the instantaneous rate, must be restricted to be positive for economic reasons.

Unfortunately, using an $A_3(3)$ model in practice is not as smooth as we had hoped and problems arose even before estimating its maximum likelihood parameters. For a given parameter set such a model maps the positive orthant of a linear state space to the space of rates through a nonnegative affine map. This bounds each rate from below and means that simple stylised characteristics of yield curves, such as its *slope*, defined as the difference between short- and long-term rates, are also bounded. This limits the range of possible results, but unfortunately it is not the only restriction. There is a condition on Feller square root processes which must be satisfied if the process is to remain positive and there is also a link between the different rates through their derivation as expectations of integrals of the short rate under the Q pricing measure. Both these restrictions give the resulting model further stiffness.

The consequence is that the range of combinations of rates that can be achieved for a given parameter set is limited, and frequently will not span the set of observations. In particular, very low rates, negative yield curves and observations for which the middle rate was far from a linear interpolation between the long and short rates observed, all provided examples that were outside the span of apparently reasonable parameter sets. This problem is fairly intractable because the parameter sets are also bound by the need to match moments like the standard deviation of the short rate (which provides a lower bound for the mean of the process) and, through these requirements, tight restrictions on the range of parameters and spanned yield curves.

This is a problem on two fronts. On the one hand, for such a model the range of yield curves rendered to be not merely unlikely, but actually *impossible*, is uncomfortably large. On the other hand, many parameter sets could not provide likelihoods for all observations. This means that estimation first requires a search for valid specifications and it is not clear that there *are* any for the data set used in this chapter. Unless the other modelling possibilities prove to be even worse, these results imply a pretty direct failure of this model to provide realistic simulated yield curve scenarios.

The problems are, however, not only on the simulation side. If the model cannot fit even a minimal set of observations *exactly*, any estimation technique that uses observations directly or infers a *state* from direct inversion will fail too. Chen and Scott (2003) encountered this problem, as their comparisons between observed and fitted yield curves show. To get around the difficulty this poses for estimation, Chen and Scott resorted to a form of *Kalman filter* to *estimate* the expected state evolution path as an input into a maximum likelihood estimation for their state evolution parameters. This adds a whole extra layer of modelling, which from our viewpoint further undermines the $A_3(3)$ model type as a starting point for this investigation.

An indication of the problems with this model is given by the long-run mean reversion parameters of the instantaneous short rate implied by the estimate of K using our monthly data from January 1994 to December 2011. Although after a perturbation this gives a reasonable half life of 13.7 years in the market measure for the instantaneous short rate, this value is too fast under the pricing measure, which in this model is the same estimate under both measures.

Based on the investigation of one model alone – however disappointing the results – there is of course still the possibility that it is the best available. However, with the limitations in the performance of such a model in evidence right from the start – and the requirement for significant extra technical elaboration required even to begin to make progress – it seems reasonable to look elsewhere.

10.3.3 *Another candidate*

Having turned back from the square root process models, an obvious place to continue would be with one of the models examined in the Dai and Singleton (2000) paper. The concrete investigation in that paper concentrates on models of types $A_1(3)$ and $A_2(3)$. Since in general it appears that Gaussian models are easier to handle than CIR type models, an $A_1(3)$ type model might be preferred. Dai and Singleton present a restricted $A_1(3)$ model with a pleasing intuitive interpretation, originally given by Balduzzi, Das, Foresi and Sunderam (1996) and henceforth termed the *BDFS model*. This model proposes a short rate r with a stochastic mean ϑ and stochastic volatility v. Roughly speaking, the log short rate and the mean log short rate follow mean reverting Gaussian processes, while the volatility follows a CIR-type process, but the short rate is allowed sensitivity to innovations in the volatility.

More precisely, the (slightly extended) model process is given in the market measure P by

$$K := \begin{pmatrix} \kappa_{11} & 0 & 0 \\ 0 & \kappa_{22} & 0 \\ 0 & 0 & \kappa_{33} \end{pmatrix},$$

$$\Theta := \begin{pmatrix} \theta_1 \\ \theta_2 \\ \theta_3 \end{pmatrix},$$

$$\Sigma := \begin{pmatrix} 1 & 0 & 0 \\ \sigma_{21} & 1 & 0 \\ \sigma_{31} & \sigma_{32} & 1 \end{pmatrix},$$

$$S(t) := \begin{pmatrix} y_1(t) & 0 & 0 \\ 0 & \alpha & 0 \\ 0 & 0 & \beta y_1(t) \end{pmatrix},$$

$$r(t) := \delta + y_2(t) + y_3(t). \tag{10.6}$$

The risk neutral version under the Q measure will have the same form, but with different parameter values for K and Θ and so both models have a relatively parsimonious 12 parameters. A model equivalent to the original BDFS model is given by setting the parameters θ_1, θ_2, σ_{21}, and σ_{22} to zero, leaving only the innovations of r and y_3 correlated. For this affine model the short rate and the corresponding rates are once more available in analytical closed form under the pricing measure Q.

The model again has three factors, so we might once more hope to be able to estimate it successfully using either three points (rates) on the yield curve or three *principal components* from the data. A feature of affine models is that any point on the yield curve is modelled by an affine function of the state space and therefore so is any linear combination of them. Hence the linear combinations of rates that are the principal components of a finite data set are also modelled. As a result, a range of choices of estimation strategy are available – we can use a variety of combinations of three points on the yield curve, or even of *levels* of the first three principal components, as *observables*.

At first this approach appeared to go quite well. We were able to fit the observations for a variety of specifications, and distributions of the modelled yield curve points (rates) looked reasonable. For example,

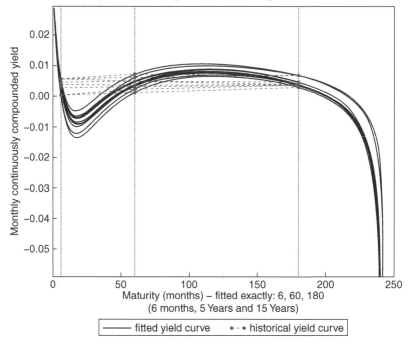

Modelled versus historical yield curves
BDFS model using MLE parameters
End of Month Bank of England Data from January 1994 to December 2011

Figure 10.1 BDFS model in-sample implied yield curves

in the chart presented in Figure 10.1 the $A_1(3)$ model was fitted to the 16-month, 5-year and 15-year rates. In general, the model had no trouble fitting the observations and the estimated moments appeared plausible.

So this approach appeared to be quite promising, until we plotted the out-of-sample rate evolutions implied by the model for various points on the yield curve together with those of the historical data (see Figure 10.1).

The dotted lines in Figure 10.1 are the in-sample paths of rates linearly interpolated between fitted yield curve points in the data over the 18 years (480 monthly observations) from 31 January 1994 to 31 December 2011, while the solid lines represent the corresponding paths of yield curve points implied from the model, both in-sample and out-of-sample, which latter are calculated by average values of simulated scenarios. The units of the vertical scale are in discount yield per month, so that the in-sample implied yield curves have rates from about –16% per annum (pa) at 18 months, can exceed 13% pa at 10 years and can each reach over -70% pa at 20 years. So not only would the implied yield curve not match observations, but its implications could be wildly implausible.

This chart was an unpleasant surprise, but it demonstrated some of the less obvious challenges involved in implementing an affine term structure model, including but not limited to:

- negative rates;
- explosive yield curves;
- the importance of rates beyond those directly fitted to data – both before and after the sample dates.

After seeing this we were struck by how rarely in the literature model implied yield curve plots are given over the in-sample data period, with the honourable exception of Chen and Scott's 1993 paper.

The implied yield curves shown above in Figure 10.1 clearly illustrated subtleties in the modelling that we had missed in our direct approach to estimating the model. Further investigation also revealed rather extreme values of the parameters. In particular, the yield curve blows up both before the sample begins and shortly after the longest observed term.

As a result, the estimated model again gave far too fast estimates of the mean reversion speed of the instantaneous short rate under the pricing measure, with a half life of 4.9 years under both the market and pricing measures.

If the original understanding of this model was that the square root state variable process was meant to capture the volatility of volatility, then the actual estimates are a significant disappointment. These estimation results could be interpreted as confirming the conclusion of Litterman and Scheinkman that three factors are necessary to capture the dynamic behaviour of the yield curve, but that stochastic volatility does *not* appear to be the natural third risk factor. This in turn suggests that a *mis-*specification of stochastic volatility is ill-suited to match the behaviour of a third yield curve point or principal component.

That being the case, we decided to start at the beginning and work with as simple a model as possible. Within the affine framework that means purely Gaussian, or extended Vasicek style, models.

10.3.4 Gaussian models

The basic *extended Vasicek model* – in the Dai–Singleton terminology, type $A_0(3)$ – is given in the market measure P by (10.1) with

$$
K := \begin{pmatrix} \kappa_{11} & 0 & 0 \\ \kappa_{21} & \kappa_{22} & 0 \\ \kappa_{31} & \kappa_{32} & \kappa_{33} \end{pmatrix},
$$

$$\Theta := \begin{pmatrix} \theta_1 \\ \theta_2 \\ \theta_3 \end{pmatrix},$$

$$\Sigma := \begin{pmatrix} \sigma_1 & 0 & 0 \\ 0 & \sigma_2 & 0 \\ 0 & 0 & \sigma_3 \end{pmatrix},$$

$$S := \begin{pmatrix} 1 & 0 & 0 \\ 0 & 1 & 0 \\ 0 & 0 & 1 \end{pmatrix},$$

$$r(t) := \delta_0 + \delta_1 y_1(t) + \delta_2 y_2(t) + \delta_3 y_3(t). \tag{10.7}$$

Estimating a complete specification means identifying 16 parameters.

This specification is not intended to restrict the process, but rather to represent a family that spans a range of specifications which are not equivalent. Since we wish to allow the broadest range of risk premia values, in order to fix the process in the pricing measure Q in the form above we must allow non-zero lower triangular values of K and zero the values of Θ. We assume a *fixed* risk premium so that market and pricing measure process SDEs differ only by the value of Θ, giving the risk neutral model 13 parameters.

Such a model and its variations are much easier to work with than other affine models. All these have closed form formulae for the distribution of the state over any time period and there is a big overlap with standard econometric techniques. It should therefore be easier to isolate and address the issues previously identified with the BDFS model.

With hindsight, this would have been the right place to start, but it was hard to identify *a priori* the challenges likely to be posed by attempts to implement superficially more attractive models. There are, of course, still many choices to be made with this model, and several other issues to address, but the behaviour of $A_0(3)$ models should be much more predictable.

10.3.5 Identification

One major change in going from the BDFS model to a pure Gaussian framework is that the default model is now *unrestricted*. That does not cause any immediate operational difficulties, but the initial results were not promising. Actually running the model does not cause problems and the behaviour of the directly calculated quantities looks reasonable, but plotting the implied yield curve paths (see Figure 10.2) once again reveals problems.

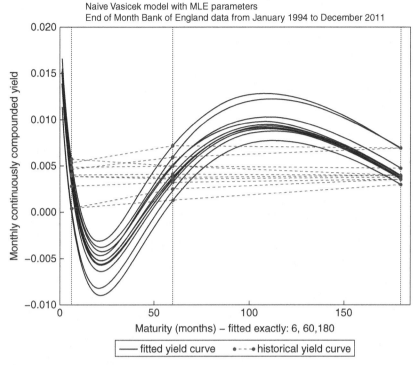

Figure 10.2 Vasicek model in-sample implied yield curves

The model implied yield curves in Figure 10.2 make even more violent swings than of the BDFS model, suggesting 2-year rates of over −20% pa and 10-year rates of over 60% *per annum*. Although at the time of writing there are some people talking as if these are in fact actually *possible* alternative scenarios, this seems unlikely to us.

So, what is the problem? One observation is that in the analysis applied we paid no attention at all to the behaviour of the rates *between* the modelled yield curve points, so we have only these three points to rely upon to deliver reasonable interpolations.

A more subtle issue lies within the estimation algorithm itself. The basic idea is that, given a parameter set, we can identify the state from each observation and determine a likelihood of each *transition* of the corresponding process which we can then use as a basis for likelihood optimisation. The problem is that we need to do this in terms of the *market* (physical) measure, while we can only determine the expectations needed to compute rates, or equivalently discount factors (zero-coupon bond prices), in terms of a *pricing* (risk neutral) *measure*. Working with the above assumption that the difference between the two is a *constant* (signed) factor market price of risk vector in the state process drift, as implied by (10.7), we can obtain its estimate.

However, the observations are not used to make a *direct* forecast of short-term rate changes and the model therefore has the freedom in the estimation to trade off between the risk premium and the mean factor change. This freedom leaves us with an *unidentified* model; but a lack of identification that is not transparently obvious. Until very recently this point was little discussed explicitly in the literature, presumably because much of the parameter estimation for these models often works with an over-identified *Generalised Method of Moments* (GMM) approach, which eradicates the problem.

In this instance unrealistic dynamics highlighted the inadequacy of our estimation procedure, and thus the lack of identification. Again this was manifest in the unrealistically fast short rate mean reversion in the pricing measure, with typical half-lives of 4.9 years in both P and Q measures. Although the surprisingly slow convergence of the likelihood optimisation calculations involved might also have provided a clue, this shortcoming was not immediately evident from the results.

The issue of identification and estimation is addressed in some detail in the recent papers of Joslin, Singleton and Zhu (2011) (JSZ) and Hamilton and Wu (2012) (HW). The basic estimation procedure used above is extended by requiring that in addition to the observations fitted *exactly* by the affine model, additional yield curve points are fitted *approximately,* using a *generalised least squares* criterion. This extra information is enough to tie down the interaction between the dynamics of the model and the risk premia, even when the specification of risk premia is expanded to allow the difference between the market and pricing measures to be an *affine function* of the state, rather than merely a *constant.* This broader specification of the risk premium allows statistical consideration of the fit of the model for points on the yield curve between perfectly fitted rates and also goes some way towards addressing the issue of return prediction raised in Cochrane and Piazzesi (2008).

Although the stochastic differential equation representation (10.1) of this model is familiar and suggestive, it does obscure a couple of its subtle points. Representations of multi-dimensional Gaussian processes in this framework demand the Cholesky square root of a matrix, which introduces extra degrees of freedom having no obvious meaning in the model. These can be dealt with by normalisation, e.g. by choosing a lower triangular form and positive diagonal entries in variable order, but the normalisation may obscure the symmetries of the model.

A second point is that the model is fundamentally a state space model with *observable* rates (yields) Y in a linear state space. If observables are affine functions of the state vector Y we can reparameterise the state space in terms of the given observables. The model can then be expressed in terms of the observables and it is again an affine model with parameters which differ from those of the original expression by application of a known affine transform. In affine models *expectations* of affine observables are again affine and as a result we can, without loss of generality, express an affine term structure model in terms of *rates*, or even the kind of linear combination of rates that results from a principal components analysis of yield curve observations. This brings term structure models much closer to traditional econometric methods and also means that different estimations can be expressed in terms of equivalent parameterisations for comparison purposes.

In our situation this means the state vector can be expressed in terms of specific observables (rates or principal components) and the discretisation of the $A_3(3)$ *JSZ/HW model* can be expressed in *vector auto-regressive* (VAR) model form in terms of *m*-vectors as

$$\Delta Y_t = k_0 + k_1 Y_t + \Sigma \varepsilon_t, \qquad (10.8)$$

where $m > n$ of (10.1) and Δ represents forward difference.

The parameter vector contains only the long-run means of the rates (or principal components) chosen to be fitted to the data *exactly*, their mean reversion rates and the rate covariance matrix Σ multiplying the independent uncorrelated standard normal Gaussian innovations vector ε. The *exactly fitted* rates are specified by appropriately specified zeroes in the full $m \times m$ Σ matrix. Here we will set $m := n + 1 = 4$.

10.3.6 Risk premia in affine models

Of vital interest in real world, or market measure, asset price models is the *risk premium*. From many points of view this premium (or premia) may be regarded as the whole point, but in models as complex as dynamic term structure models we need inevitably to be careful not to abuse, or to be misled by, a standard terminology designed to fit simpler models. Indeed, we must even be careful of the definite article above. To put these terms in an appropriate context for more general application to our situation, it is perhaps worth recapping their application in their native environment, the one factor *geometric Brownian motion* (GBM) model often used for reasoning about equity behaviour.

In such a model we first suppose that the asset price follows a GBM, possibly with a drift, so that the logarithm of price follows a Brownian motion. Next we suppose that the price represents the *expected* current value of the discounted asset price at any given time in the future. Usually two further assumptions, some variation of 'no free lunches' and constant coefficients, are also made. It turns out that the first of these conditions means that the current value of future state evolution follows a process with the same volatility as the actual price process, while considerations of the second type tend to restrict the process to a GBM with a possibly different, but also fixed, drift.

These specifications inherit the scale free quality of Brownian motion (or in discrete time, random walk) so that the distributions of current values of outcomes at future points differ only in their means and by amounts that depend on how far into the future we are looking. Therefore it makes sense to think of the fixed ratio between expected current value and expected future value as 'the' premium. This difference can also be realised through a utility function which displays a constant relative risk aversion, so the expected difference between expected utility and outcome can be seen as compensating for fear of negative outcomes and might therefore also be considered a risk premium.

All of these considerations apply to the fixed income models we study, but the intuitive identifications made above no longer go through straightforwardly. We must consider the following.

- We have multiple factors, so we might expect multiple premia.
- We are considering mean reverting Ornstein Uhlenbeck processes, not Brownian motions. The models are therefore not necessarily time homogeneous and so the finite time risk premia may depend upon the process state, although possibly not asymptotically. In our investigations so far we have treated the risk premia of the three factors (state variables) in our models as *constant*. More generally, depending on the circumstances, coefficients may only be fixed relative to the current value of a future fixed value, or similar benchmark, but that is mostly a distraction here.
- We are modelling fixed income investment returns via relatively simple rate distributions. Bond prices are non-linear in rates and their modelled returns are mostly path dependent. This complicates the link between the distribution of returns and the distributions of rates.
- Securities of different maturities have different dependencies on the same modelled variables. This means that the same risk premium-like phenomenon in the underlying process will have multiple manifestations at the asset return level.
- We have more complicated risk premium specifications. As described below, we can consider a wider range of risk premium specifications than are available in the equity sketch above.

- We have a more complicated justification. Formation of rate expectations that deviate from the implied market rates process is not quite as simple to rationalise in terms of a straightforward utility function as it is for a simple premium in equity models. In particular, the simple link between wealth preferences and expectations no longer holds.

For all these reasons the 'risk premium' in a Gaussian affine term structure model is complicated. Even more complicated models than we are considering share this property and add their own complexity. Nevertheless, the issue is too important to dismiss as complicated; there are intuitions to be gained and some analogies with the equity case to be determined by its examination.

Rates are prices, and as such they express the levels at which the market is willing to swap future cash flows. For example, the market regards as equivalent the prospects of rolling a deposit of cash and of buying a discount bond with maturity equal to the proposed cash roll. However this equivalence need not be based on naively calculated expectations, but rather on a range of conditional preferences.

We therefore assume that rates follow a stochastic process and that their term structure is determined by expectations, but *not simply* that the term structure corresponds to the expectations which full knowledge of the risk neutral state process and of the current state of the market would determine. There are various possible sources of discrepancy between these two expectations: non-linear preferences, systematic delusion, market composition,[2] etc., but under certain assumptions about the nature of the discrepancy it will only arise when there is uncertainty and may therefore be described as a 'risk premium'.

This view of the discrete time dynamics of the term structure is neatly captured in the Joslin, Singleton and Zhu (2011) and Hamilton and Wu (2012) approach to estimation of affine term structure models. Roughly speaking, they decompose the discretised process into the evolution of the risk neutral state and a *forecast error*. In affine models the state may be represented, as above, by a set of rates observed *exactly*. In simple cases, the parameters of that part of the model become a vector auto regression which can be estimated by well-understood techniques, including, for example, *ordinary least squares*.

Once the parameters of the exactly observed rates are determined, the forecasting parameters can be estimated by comparing the forecasts of additional observable rates implied by these rates with their data

---

[2] A related question is referred to as the *spanning* question, i.e. whether zero coupon bonds are sufficient instruments to specify the yield curve, or whether alternatively further instruments, such as bond options, or macroeconomic variables, such as inflation rate, are required to determine its parameter estimates and hence dynamics, see e.g. Guimarães (2012).

outcomes. Of course, the complexity and nature of this part of the estimation depends upon the specification of the model. Nevertheless, we can think of the overall model as a pair of models, one model describing historical market pricing behaviour and the other apparently in use for making forecasts, together with a link between them.

The simplest scenario is one in which the models are *identical* and this assumption, often going by the name of the *(rational)* *expectations hypothesis*, since then forecasts are *exact* in expectation (*see* Piazzesi, 2010), is quite common. Under this assumption there is no second step and the analysis is as straightforward as it can be. However, such a model cannot test the hypothesis it relies on and when the goal is an asset model the assumption is strong in a material way.

Next most simple would be to assume that the models differ by a *fixed* risk premium. This specification is deceptively natural in appearance in analogy with the equity case, but the considerations above demonstrate that its effects will not be the same. For example, if rates are given a *positive* risk premium, as might be expected in an equity model, that is to say that forward rates *understate* the mean of the distribution of future outcomes, a rolling cash deposit will show equity-like behaviour and give higher returns than the expectations hypothesis would imply. However, a rolling bond position would do the *opposite*.

This is not obviously implausible, but starting with an assumption of a positive risk premium for *bond* investments would seem just as plausible in isolation, though it would have the *opposite* consequences. Neither position is something one would want to accept without examination.

The initial attraction of affine models was that they allow a quick calculation of expectations and thus they allow models that compare expectations with outcomes to facilitate concrete and quantitative examination of one of the key features of term structure modelling. It is therefore desirable for expectations to be representable by an *affine* model. Moreover, Joslin, Singleton and Zhu (2011) are able to deploy the well developed machinery of vector auto regressions for estimation if the historical behaviour is represented by a model of that class. We are thus led by convenience and tractability to consider models where risk neutral expectations for pricing and historical market behaviour are *both* determined by affine models. If we further insist that the model be arbitrage free, a strong requirement, although high rewards for low risks are sadly hard to find and therefore should not be an accidental feature of a model, we are led by virtue of the Girsanov theorem to find that the Gaussian processes of the model under the two measures differ only in their *drift term*. Further, if we are to have any hope of using the model for statistical inference, we will want to make the model as parsimonious as possible, which leads to an assumption of *constant coefficients*. In explicit terms the model is as follows.

We begin by specifying the generalisation of (10.1) in continuous time under the market measure P as

$$d\mathbf{Y}(t) = K(\Theta - \mathbf{Y}(t) + \Pi)dt + \Sigma\sqrt{S(t)}d\mathbf{W}(t), \qquad (10.9)$$

where

$$\Pi = k_0^P + K_1^P\mathbf{Y}$$

is an *affine* state dependent vector *market price of risk (MPR)*. Although other possibilities for MPR specification, such as quadratic state dependence (see e.g. Leippold and Wu, 2003) are available, as noted above we shall see that the affine MPR specification leads to simple elegant estimation procedures in the discrete time equivalent of (10.9) given by (10.8).

The standard model for discrete time estimation of Gaussian affine interest rate models is a first order *vector autoregressive* (VAR) process $\mathbf{Y}$ written in the form of (10.8). In this model there are two processes operating on the same state space with the same value of Σ. We can write the equations for these two processes as

$$\Delta Y_t^Q = k_0^Q + K_1^Q Y_t^Q + \Sigma\varepsilon_t^Q,$$
$$\Delta Y_t^P = k_0^P + K_1^P Y_t^P + \Sigma\varepsilon_t^P. \qquad (10.10)$$

The first process in (10.9) is in the pricing measure Q, while the second process is in the market measure P. The *risk premium* process Π is specified by the difference between the drifts of the two processes to be an affine function of the state given by

$$\Pi_t = \left(k_0^P - k_0^Q\right) + \left(K_1^P - K_1^Q\right)Y_t^P. \qquad (10.11)$$

The (rational) *expectations* hypothesis corresponds to $k_0^P = k_0^Q$ and $K_1^P = K_1^Q$, while a *constant* risk premium corresponds to relaxing the restriction on the constant term in (10.11) to leave only $K_1^P = K_1^Q$.

Joslin, Singleton and Zhu (2011) developed a clever normalisation involving a rotation of the m-dimensional space of realisations of the full $\mathbf{Y}$ process to decompose its likelihood function into that of the n-dimensional risk neutral state process and that of the remaining $(m - n)$-dimensional observed processes conditional upon it. The log-likelihood of the transitions of the vector autoregression model (10.8) can therefore be expressed as a sum of squares and additional terms that depend upon the factor risk premia. The affine expression for the instantaneous short rate, r_t, is given by (10.2) in terms of the exactly measured state variables.

As a result the overall parameter estimation can be performed in two independent steps:

- the parameters of the n-dimensional state process under the risk neutral measure are first estimated via the simple, quick robust *ordinary least squares* regression procedure,
- then the risk premia are estimated by a slightly more complicated MLE calculation involving the $m - n$ extra observables and a helpful simplification based upon the Jordan form normalisation of the drift of the state process under the pricing measure, see Joslin, Singleton and Zhu (2011) for details.

This JSZ/HW specification nests the expectation and fixed risk premia hypotheses discussed above. The model satisfies the expectations hypothesis precisely when the discrepancy between the pricing and market processes vanishes and has a fixed risk premium if the discrepancy is constant. Estimating a model with this specification is therefore a way to examine the validity of these hypotheses.

If the discrepancy does not satisfy their restrictions, the risk premium will be stochastic or, more precisely, state dependent. That makes things significantly more complex than in the equity model described above, even before the obscuring complications described there. The impact of these complications may not be immediately obvious from the parameter values and the layers of indirection between the driving rate process and asset returns derived from it, so that the best understanding might be gained from consideration of finite time forecasts of the rates (or equivalently states of the model).

Both the pricing and market implied forecast distributions are Gaussian. This implies that their log densities are quadratic, as is their difference. What does this mean? For simplicity, consider the one factor case, where the effect of different risk premia is to move the pricing distribution within a two-dimensional space parameterised by the mean and dispersion of the forward distribution. The overall effect is to raise or diminish the emphasis on the extremes of the distribution versus its middle values and on its high versus the low values. The form of the difference in log densities shows that this is a complete characterisation. In higher dimensions, the situation is a little more complicated, because the emphases can be mixed and will not necessarily fall on the expected parameters, but the limited range of behaviours is similar. What must be remembered, however, is that the difference between expected means will not in general be *fixed*. Instead this difference will depend upon the starting state and in general, given a sufficiently extreme starting point, could be anything.

This is probably the clearest view of the model feature driving the risk premium. It can, of course, be traced back to the continuous time definition given in (10.9), but it does not provide an overall view of the implied distributions. Applying this definition to reason about asset returns is, as suggested above, considerably more difficult to characterise neatly. The correspondence between instrument duration and rate levels and the interaction with the state-dependent local risk premia introduces more complex functional forms whose non-linearity brings path dependency and so-called *convexity* effects. On top of all of these considerations, short- and long-term fixed income instruments can respond in opposite ways to the same change in rates.

The above specification is the most general where pricing and forecasting measures are both affine and equivalent, but further generalisations are possible, and some are described in the literature. Dai, Le and Singleton (2010) show how to use the Esscher transform to work with an affine forecasting measure and a more general pricing measure. The work of Joslin, Singleton and Zhu (2011) and Hamilton and Wu (2012) on the other hand opens the door to models where the pricing measure is affine but the forecast error might be more general. There are sensible arguments for the relevance of such specifications, but they can also produce a severe loss of tractability and inferential power.

10.3.7 *Care in likelihood optimisation*

However, both the above papers also highlight the issue of *local optima* in the type of augmented likelihood optimisation they employ. Indeed, Hamilton and Wu demonstrate that estimates obtained in Ang and Piazzesi's highly cited paper (Ang and Piazzesi, 2003) in fact correspond only to a *local* maximum, and that *global* maximum estimates not only correspond to a significantly higher likelihood, but also have *opposite* signs for key sensitivities.

Implementing all these considerations for the JSZ/HW model using four observed rates leads to a considerable improvement over the previously evaluated models using only three rates, but requires calculating tens or hundreds of optimisations from different starting points in order to have confidence in having attained the maximum augmented likelihood. This is an unwelcome burden.

Moreover, the results are not automatically a great deal more plausible. For example, the estimation of the model represented above sometimes gives the unpleasant behaviour shown in Figure 10.3.

This chart shows equivalent information to that of Figure 10.2 for a *locally optimal* parameter set obtained for the JSZ/HW model

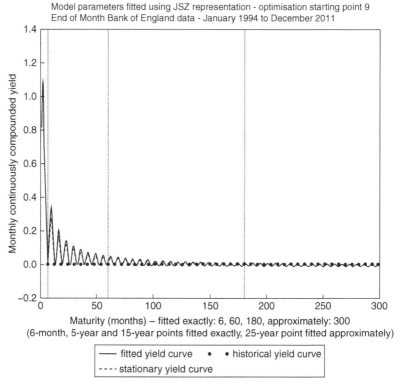

Maturity (months) – fitted exactly: 6, 60, 180, approximately: 300
(6-month, 5-year and 15-year points fitted exactly, 25-year point fitted approximately)

——— fitted yield curve   •   • historical yield curve
- - - - stationary yield curve

Figure 10.3 JSZ/HW model in-sample local optimum implied yield curves

incorporating the additions discussed above. The oscillation is caused by *complex* eigenvalues in the matrix drift component of the model. In a representative maximum likelihood estimation of the parameters of this model (under the pricing measure) which corresponds to a local optimum with maximal real eigenvalue 0.96076, the largest complex eigenvalue is 0.581612 ± 0.815219 i.

The steep gradient of the curve near the exact observation points (corresponding to the dotted vertical lines in Figure 10.3) means that only *very* small changes in the state variables are required to deliver the observed movements. Thus the resulting transition densities can have values of very large magnitude. There is, of course, no intrinsic reason that a solution of this type should not be the global augmented maximum, but its implications are of limited practical use to say the least.

High frequency oscillations like those illustrated above can be avoided by some combination of a judicious choice of yield curve points for approximate fitting, bounding the imaginary components of the eigenvalues of the drift matrix, and good fortune, so that the resulting estimates begin to look reasonably well behaved. The search for optimal solutions is carried out using several starting points and we have mostly been fortunate in finding that the best of these did *not* in fact have high frequency oscillations.

However, were we to be confronted with such a result, or if we needed to rely on an estimation technique not producing such an outcome, there are several approaches available to avoid it. The most direct method is to restrict the range of complex eigenvalues allowed. In the JSZ/HW method this is straightforward because it considers the Jordan normal form of the factor drift matrix and we can apply such limits to the drifts directly. It can also be useful in order to avoid the likelihood search path falling into a hole to apply a penalised buffer zone for the parameters which lies inside the region of those absolutely prohibited.

It is possible to extend this analysis to consideration of more rate data than four points on the yield curve, e.g. including more points *between* the exactly observed points, but the parameter estimation algorithm is made substantially more complex as a result.

10.3.8 Negative yield curves

High frequency oscillations can be reasonably straightforwardly suppressed using the techniques suggested above, but it is much harder to avoid estimated *negative* yield curves in this model. This is not simply the possibility of negative rates, but also the possibility of discount factors greater than 1 over long time periods. In some of the earlier models evaluated this was a problem, but, by this point having eliminated many of the explanations for such behaviour, the problem still arises with the JSZ/HW model.

Figure 10.4 shows more reasonably behaved yield curve evolution (data and model for various yield curve maturities) over the 20-year data period. Up to the observed data horizon (31 December 2011) the model fits the data well, but for the model yield curve forecast at 20 years forward the curve becomes *strongly negative*. The out-of-sample projected yield curves are derived by simulating (10.7) beyond the data span, using (10.8), and then averaging closed form model implied rates for each maturity across a large number (4000) of simulated *scenarios* to yield an accurate approximation of rates derived from the continuous time and space zero-coupon bond prices (10.2).

The root of the long-term negative yield curve problem is that the weightings of low rate scenarios are much heavier than those of high

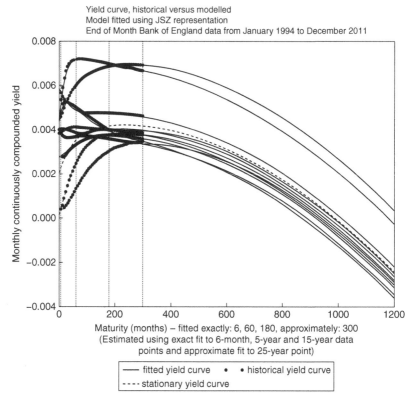

Figure 10.4 JSZ/HW model long-term implied yield curves in- and out-of-sample

rate scenarios in the scenario average rate calculations. Although it is not quite inevitable, this problem is obdurate and the restrictions on the combination of mean level, mean reversion and volatility necessary to prevent long-term negative rates can be unrealistic for realistic shorter term behaviour.

Explicit or computable formulae for expected rates are one of the key features of affine models, but these can be quite opaque and do not immediately give an intuition about what is going on, especially in higher dimensional versions.

The feature key to understanding is the distinction between the appropriate mean coordinates of the state process: the *current* expected rates, or yield to maturity of the appropriate zero-coupon bonds, and the corresponding *future* expected rates. The second are visible in the appropriate Ornstein Uhlenbeck equations and the first takes into account the monotonicity of discounting, so that low rates count for more than high rates. The expected rates, which actually determine the yield curve, also reflect the covariance of future rates with discount factors back to the current time point – the so-called *convexity adjustment*.

To illustrate this, consider the SDE of a simple *one-factor* short rate model under the pricing measure P given by

$$\mathrm{d}\boldsymbol{r}_t = \theta(\mu - r_t)\mathrm{d}t + \sigma\, d\boldsymbol{W}_t, \qquad (10.12)$$

with $\theta := 0.04$, $\kappa := 0.01$ and $\sigma := 0.04$. The short rate increment has a mean of 0.04, a future short rate that is asymptotically *zero* and rates derived from (10.2) and (10.3) that are *negative*. Even when the future short rate is asymptotically positive, rates can be negative. In fact, doubling the mean reversion rate θ gives negative rates despite the positive future short rate, and θ must be increased by a factor of 15 to make the implied yield curve positive in this example.

Our estimates for the JSZ/HW model typically suggest small values for mean reversion coefficients and therefore *slow* mean reversion which, given the positive probability of negative short rates, makes an ultimately negative yield curve very likely.

On the other hand, *fast* mean reversion implies *very* large risk premia and strong divergence from the expectations hypothesis which leads to unit roots under the market measure. Of course the recent regime of historically low interest rates does not help the situation, but the problem appears quite deep seated. Unit root model estimates will cause problems whatever the actual rates are.

10.3.9 Unit root solutions

Not only do unit root estimates bring negative yield curves, the range of returns given by a model with a unit or super unit root becomes extremely wide. In our opinion it is likely that many examples estimated in the literature to date have (super) unit roots. Moreover, we have found that implementations of the *small sample correction* suggested by Bauer, Rudebusch and Wu (2011) yield adjustments easily large enough to change a mean reverting estimate into one giving a random walk, or worse an *explosive* short rate process, by introducing a unit or super unit root. In a representative estimation of the JSZ/HW model this correction changed a maximal real eigenvalue 0.96138 into one of 1.03142. If we follow the authors' suggestions of applying a shrinkage factor or restricting the search range to mean reverting solutions, these heuristic techniques may have the desired result of expunging unit root estimates, but they delegate to other considerations the determination of whether or not the state process actually has a unit root.

Despite the significance of this issue it does not seem to be directly addressed in much of the literature. Clearly there is typically a problem with the amounts of data available, but the observation that this does not matter much for very short-term forecasts does not help determine parameters that have great significance for *long-term* behaviour. The literature frequently defers the decision on the long-term stability of the model to outside considerations and in general provides little help in the empirical determination of the estimated state process stability.

10.3.10 Negative rates

As it happens, our best estimates do *not* suggest unit roots and therefore we are not forced to consider wildly unprecedented risk characteristics. While it is regrettable that we cannot have both our first choice estimates and the ability to extrapolate indefinitely beyond the range of our observations, if we were only considering aggregate statistics over a short horizon we would probably be able to work with the models evaluated so far.

However, we need *every* simulated scenario to be plausible in its own right, not merely as part of an aggregate. At this point the issue of negative rates becomes a *genuine problem*.

Figure 10.5 shows the extent of this problem. It depicts quantiles of simulated 10-year interest rates from a recent starting point, 30 December 2011. Nearly 25% of scenarios are negative. If we merely assumed that those scenarios were zero instead of negative, the mean rate would be about 25 basis points higher – an amount too large to ignore. This is unacceptable even when other aspects of the model are well behaved.

10.3.11 Typical estimation only looks at conditional likelihood

Much recent interest rate data appears to have a strong downward trend, reflecting the fact that rates are currently very low. In the United Kingdom they were very *high* after the end of Bretton Woods and in the late 1980s. If we consider *only* the likelihood of the *transitions*, the trend will often be made plausible by strong mean reversion effects. Unfortunately, this can result in estimated models that make even recent history practically impossible. This is because analysis of *transitions* without considering the long-run relevance of *initial conditions* other than the first observation pays no attention to how the world got into this first state.

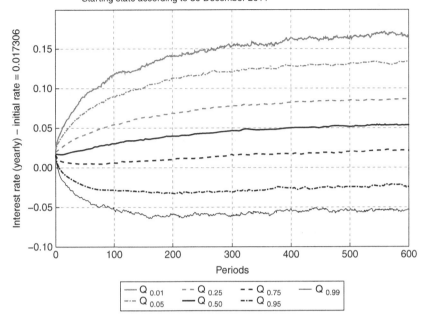

Figure 10.5 JSZ/HW 10-year rate distribution out-of-sample evolution quantiles from 30 December 2011

In terms of maximum likelihood estimation, considering only the transitions is considering only *conditional likelihood*. General descriptions of MLE and descriptions of univariate MLE usually concern a full or *unconditional* likelihood function involving a *specified* initial state, but for *multivariate* time series analysis this seems to be rarely considered. For instance, Hamilton's (1994) book opens discussions of maximum likelihood estimation with a full description of unconditional likelihood in the univariate case, but in the multivariate case it says that unconditional estimation is not attempted.

It is not difficult to derive the expression for the unconditional likelihood when the process is *stationary*, when the *long-run mean* estimate can be used as the initial state. However, using the unconditional likelihood makes estimation more difficult in a number of ways. Moreover, conditional likelihood estimation might be necessary to ensure that the stationarity assumption of rates is reasonable. The first order lags incorporated in the discretised versions of the models considered here make their full likelihood expressions much more complicated and standard least squares techniques no longer directly apply. Nevertheless, in our situation *unconditional* estimation appears to be the natural approach.

10.3.12 Gaussian models have constant volatility

The discussion so far has addressed relatively broad issues with the evaluated models – effectively the minimum requirements needed for viability. At the start of our attempts to implement an interest rate model there were other, subtler, issues on the agenda. One of these is an empirical link between the level of rates and the volatility of rates. The connection is well known and is illustrated in Rebonato's (2004) book. In stylised terms the behaviour referred to is *positive correlation* between volatility (measured in absolute terms) and the level of rates. In a purely Gaussian model there is no such link, so volatility will either be too high when rates are low or too low when they are high. This problem is quite subtle – models which have log-normal interest rates have a similar problem of inflexibility, but the sign of this behaviour is *reversed*. As a result, when historical rates are very low, very high levels of *parametric* volatility are required to match historical or option implied volatility levels.

10.3.13 Lessons learned

Before describing our implemented solution in the next section, we first discuss what we did for each model investigated so far and what we have learned from these exercises.

Draw a chart

Some of the problems we encountered were easily noticed by drawing a graph. Graphs of paths of yield curve points over the data period rarely feature in the literature (but see Dempster et al., 2010). The same comment applies to plotting quantiles of the evolving distribution of interest rates and returns. This is easier to do than most of the modelling, and provides an extremely useful context for model evaluation.

Take care of specifications

As a rule of thumb, when thinking about how big a model to build, it seems sensible to talk about the dimension of the state space of the model processes, but there is inflexibility in the CIR square root processes that means they do not map well to the three principal components identified in the Litterman and Scheinkman (1991) paper. From this point of view it is probably better to count the number of Gaussian variables in a model.

Use multiple likelihood optimisation starting points

The log-likelihood functions of models of this type have numerous local maxima. A single optimisation will most likely not give the global maximum. Unfortunately the parameter search space will typically be quite large and will require computationally intensive *multiple* optimisation starting point calculations, which luckily can be straightforwardly *parallelised.*

Consider using unconditional likelihood

Using unconditional likelihood makes some procedures more difficult or complex from specified initial states, but if the calculations are feasible there seems no reason why this should not be the default procedure. For Gaussian affine processes the computations are relatively simple. Taking unconditional likelihood into account in interest rate series where the rate levels at the beginning and end of the series are very different will tend to yield estimates with greater long-term variance. Unfortunate side effects of this are that the sample statistics of the time series are no longer the estimated model parameters and super-efficient least squares calculations can no longer be straightforwardly applied to calculate the parameter estimates. Even so, the required calculations are not terribly onerous.

10.4   Our solution

For our application negative yields are a *fatal* problem. However, in Gaussian models they are unavoidable and they cannot be sidestepped in forward solutions by simple measures such as setting any negative rate to zero, although other more complex procedures are available which alleviate, but do not eliminate, the difficulty.

Instead we applied an old idea of Fischer Black's. The idea asserts that interest rates generally come with a 'stuff it under the mattress' option in which investors just keep their money when faced with a negative interest rate. This means that we might model interest rates as *options* on some more fundamental, but possibly hard to observe, *shadow rates* in order to guarantee positive rates or set minimum rates.

The original idea is described, but not implemented, in Fischer Black's last (posthumously) published paper, see Black (1995). The corresponding yield curve model has been implemented a few times previously, often with Japanese interest rates in mind. Notable examples include papers by a group at the Bank of Japan (see Ueno et al., 2006 and Ichiue and Ueno, 2007) and by Kim and Singleton (2011), but with no more than *two* state variables. In our case, we need *three* state variables.

Specifically, the underlying process evolves in a three-dimensional state space like that of the JSZ/HW model, but now the forward yield observables are non-linear functions of the state space since they are represented in terms of expectations of integrals of an option payoff on short rate affine functions of the state space. As a result, unlike the JSZ/HW exponential affine model, coordinates are no longer uniform over the state space and translation between yields, which we can observe, and model states, about whose probabilities we can reason, is no longer a straightforward calculation.

In other words, we hypothesise an $A_0(3)$ model describing the evolution of a *shadow* instantaneous short rate of exactly the form described by (10.7) in the previous section, but additionally hypothesise that the *actual* short rate at time t is a zero strike call option on this rate, so that

$$r_{\text{actual},t} := \max\{0, r_{\text{shadow},t}\}. \qquad (10.13)$$

This is conceptually simple, and guarantees that expected rates for longer maturities are also non-negative but, as noted above, the non-linearity introduces considerable practical difficulty in moving from our rate (yield) observations to the corresponding state. Kim and Singleton (2011) equivalently perform this calculation for *discount factors* $P_t(\tau)$ by solving a quasilinear parabolic partial differential equation (PDE) of the form

$$\partial P_t/\partial \tau - \sum_{i,j=1}^{2} a_{ij}\partial^2 P_t/\partial y_i \partial y_j - \sum_{i=1}^{2} b_i \partial P_t/\partial y_i - cP_t = 0, \qquad (10.14)$$

with boundary values $P_t(0) = 1$ and sufficiently large state space bounds for the two rates y_1, y_2 of Y. However, the *alternating direction implicit* (ADI) finite difference scheme they use to solve (10.14) does not easily extend to accurate solution of the corresponding PDE in three dimensions and so far we have been unable to implement an effective alternative.

There are still avenues to explore in this direction, but for the time being we have adopted a technique which is a combination of closed form (numerical) rate calculations (see e.g. Kim and Singleton, 2011, appendix B) for short maturities and Monte Carlo simulation as in the previous section for longer ones. For longer maturities this takes account of the non-negligible convexity adjustment for the non-linear Black model which is accounted for *explicitly* for the linear Gaussian JSZ/HW model discussed above. The resulting procedure may be considered to be a refinement of solving the least squares fit of Monte Carlo simulated yields to each individual observation. This approach is very computationally intensive, but it does appear to provide very robust results.

10.4.1 Out-of-sample forecasts

We present here the quantiles of the simulated out-of-sample evolution over time of the distribution of the 10-year rate from for the new non-linear Black model. Figure 10.6 displays the out-of-sample diagram analogous to Figure 10.5 (from the same 30 December 2011 starting point) for this model.

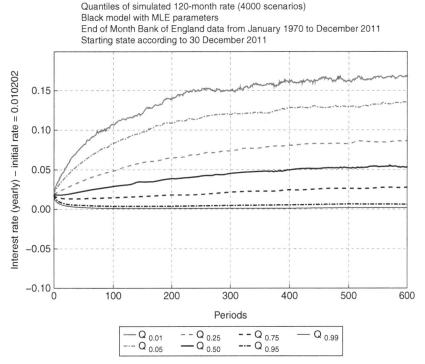

Figure 10.6 Black model non-negative 10-year rate distribution out-of-sample evolution quantiles from 30 December 2011

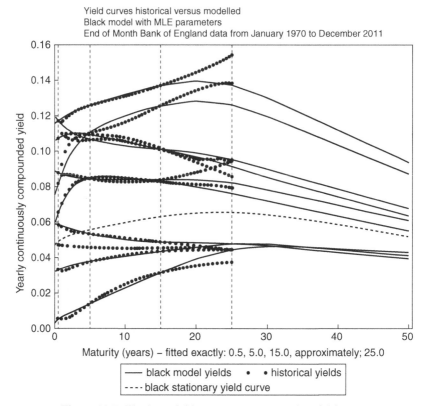

Figure 10.7 Black model long-term non-negative yield curves

Figure 10.7 shows the in- and out-of-sample long-term yield curve simulation forecasts for the new model analogous to that of Figure 10.4 and demonstrates the long-term scenario simulation performance of the Black model that our applications require.

Besides delivering positive rates and the direct connection between rates and expectations, the most notable difference between our earlier attempts and the Black model seems to be that it allows much *slower* short rate *mean reversion* estimates than alternatives, which is significant. For example, in the model that this research is meant to update (a development of the one described in Mulvey and Thorlacious, 1998) disequilibria have an estimated half life of approximately 4 years, while in this model the estimated half life is nearly 14 years in the market (physical) measure, and over 10,000 years in the pricing measure used for yield curve extrapolation. The difficulties such slow mean reversion would cause in a straightforward linear Gaussian model have been clearly illustrated above.

In concrete terms, this property of the new model means that we can reflect the possibility that interest rates in our main modelling targets – the UK, US and EU economies – remain extremely low, as Japan's have done for some time, while also entertaining the possibility that rates will blow up, like those of Italy and Spain currently. Indeed, the medium term distributions of short rates are bimodal. The underlying (shadow expectation) processes are still Ornstein Uhlenbeck processes, but the way states are non-linearly mapped to yield curves is different from the affine map of the earlier standard models.

10.5 Conclusion

In this chapter we have described a voyage of discovery that has resulted in a new tractable yield curve model which possesses the properties required by practitioners who intend to use long-term simulations from it for pricing, investment advice and asset liability management. Its estimation from sovereign interest rate data is computationally intensive, but straightforward and tractable, and is amenable to frequent updating, as is required by these applications.

Table 10.1 summarises the properties of the models evaluated in this chapter regarding well accepted stylised facts of yield curves and their models in the order in which both properties and models are discussed in the chapter. Our *non-linear* Black model possesses all

Table 10.1 *Properties of evaluated yield curve models with regard to stylised facts*

	Yield curve model					
Stylised fact properties	CIR	BDFS	Vasicek	JSZ/HW	JSZ/HW/ BRW	Black
	$A_3(3)$	$A_3(3)$	$A_3(3)$	$A_1(3)$	$A_0(3)$	$A_0(3)$
Mean reverting rates	Yes	Yes	Yes	Yes	No	Yes
Non-negative rates	Yes	No	No	No	No	Yes
Stochastic rate volatility	Yes	Yes	No	No	No	Yes*
Closed form bond prices	Yes	Yes	Yes	Yes	Yes	No
Replicates all observed curves	No	Yes	Yes	Yes	Yes	Yes
State dependent risk premia	No	No	No	Yes	Yes	Yes
Good for long-term simulations	No	No	No	No	No	Yes
Slow mean reversion under Q	No	No	No	No	No	Yes
+ve rate/volatility correlation	No	No	No	No	No	Yes
Effective in low rate regimes	No	No	No	No	No	Yes

* Rate volatilities are piecewise constant punctuated by random jumps to 0 at rate 0 boundary hitting points.

the desired properties except for closed form bond prices, but rapid effective simulation-based numerical techniques for bond pricing have been described in Section 10.4.

In ongoing work we are developing the interaction of this model with the other financial and economic variables in interacting capital market models of the four main currency areas. A first step explores the statistical interactions of our new yield curve model with macroeconomic variables such as inflation rate and GDP begun by Ang and Piazzesi (2003) in a macroeconomic context and extended in a manner more appropriate to capital market models by Dempster, Medova and Tang (2012). Specifically, we examine the relevance to the innovations of the state dynamics of the macroeconomic variables. We also expect to examine the spanning question using appropriate derivative price data and to investigate inflation influences on the yield curve using real bond data (see Guimarães, 2012 for the US case).

References

Ang, A. and Piazzesi, M. (2003). A no-arbitrage vector autoregression of term structure dynamics with macroeconomic and latent variables. *Journal of Monetary Economics*, **50**, 745–787.

Balduzzi, P. S., Das, R., Foresi, S. and Sunderam, R. (1996). A simple approach to three factor affine term structure models. *Journal of Fixed Income*, **6**, 43–53.

Bauer, M. D., Rudebusch, G. D. and Wu, J. C. (2011). Unbiased estimation of dynamic term structure models. Working Paper 2011–12, Federal Reserve Bank of San Francisco.

Black, F. (1995). Interest rates as options. *Journal of Finance*, **50**, 1371–1376.

Chen, R.-R. and Scott, L. (1993). Maximum likelihood estimation for a multifactor equilibrium model of the term structure. *Journal of Fixed Income*, **3**, 14–31.

Chen, R.-R. and Scott, L. (2003). Multi-factor Cox–Ingersoll–Ross models of the term structure: Estimates and tests from a Kalman filter model. *Journal of Real Estate Finance and Economics*, **27**, 143–172.

Cochrane, J. H. and Piazzesi, M. (2008). Decomposing the yield curve. Working Paper, Graduate School of Business, University of Chicago, 13 March 2008.

Cox, J. C., Ingersol, J. E. and Ross, S. A. (1985). A theory of the term structure of interest rates. *Econometrica*, **53**, 385–407.

Dai, Q. and Singleton, K. J. (2000). Specification analysis of affine term structure models. *Journal of Finance*, **50**, 1943–1978.

Dai, Q., Le, A. and Singleton, K. J. (2010). Discrete-time dynamic term structure models with generalized market prices of risk. *Review of Financial Studies*, **23**, 2184–2227.

de Jong, F., Driessen, J. and Pelsser, A. (2001). Libor market models versus swap market models for pricing interest rate derivatives: an empirical analysis. *European Finance Review*, **5**, 201–237.

Dempster, M. A. H. and Arbeleche Grela, S. (2003). Econometric modeling for asset liability management. Working Paper 13/03, Judge Institute of Management, University of Cambridge.

Dempster, M. A. H. and Thorlacious, A. E. (1998). Stochastic simulation of economic variables and asset returns: the Falcon asset model. *Proceedings of the 8th International AFIR Colloquium.* London: Institute of Actuaries, 29–45.

Dempster, M. A. H., Germano, M., Medova, E. A. and Villaverde, M. (2003). Global asset liability management. *British Actuarial Journal,* **9,** 137–216.

Dempster, M. A. H., Medova, E. A. and Tang, K. (2012). Presentation at Commodities Session, Global Derivatives, Trading and Risk Management Conference, Barcelona, 18th April 2012.

Dempster, M. A. H., Medova, E. A. and Villaverde, M. (2010). Long term interest rates and consol bond valuation. *Journal of Asset Management,* **11,** 113–135.

Duffie, D. and Kan, R. (1996). A yield-factor model of interest rates. *Mathematical Finance,* **6,** 379–406.

Guimarães, R. (2012). What's in a yield curve? Robust decompositions into risk and expectations. Bank of England, mimeo.

Hamilton, J. D. (1994). *Time Series Analysis.* Princeton: Princeton University Press.

Hamilton, J. D. and Wu, J. C. (2012). Identification and estimation of Gaussian affine term structure models. *Journal of Econometrics,* **168,** 315–331.

Ichiue, H. and Ueno, Y. (2007). Equilibrium interest rate and the yield curve in a low interest rate environment. Bank of Japan Working Paper Series, No. 07-E-18.

James, J. and Webber, N. (2000). *Interest Rate Modelling.* Chichester, UK: Wiley.

Joslin, S., Singleton, K. J. and Zhu, H. (2011). A new perspective on Gaussian dynamic term structure models. *Review of Financial Studies,* **24,** 926–970.

Kim, D. H. and Singleton, K. J. (2011). Term structure models and the zero bound: an empirical investigation of Japanese yields. Working Paper, Graduate School of Business, Stanford University.

Leippold, M. and Wu, L. (2003). Design and estimation of quadratic term structure models. *Review of Finance,* 47–73.

Litterman, R. and Scheinkman, J. A. (1991). Common factors affecting bond returns. *Journal of Fixed Income,* **1,** 54–61.

Longstaff, F. A., Santa-Clara, P. and Schwartz, E. S. (2001). The relative valuations of caps and swaptions: theory and empirical evidence. *Journal of Finance,* **56,** 2067–2109.

Medova, E. A., Murphy, J. K., Owen, A. P. and Rehman, K. (2008). Individual asset liability management. *Quantitative Finance,* **8,** 547–560.

Mulvey, J. M. and Thorlacious, A. E. (1998). The Towers Perrin global capital market scenario generation system. In: *Worldwide Asset and Liability Modeling* (W. T. Ziemba and J. M. Mulvey, eds.) Cambridge: Cambridge University Press, 286–312.

Nawalkha, S. K. and Rebonato, R. (2011). What interest rate model to use? Buy side versus sell side. ssrn.com/abstract=1723924.

Nelson, C. R. and Siegel, A. F. (1987). Parsimonious modeling of yield curves. *Journal of Business*, **60**, 473–489.

Piazzesi, M. (2010). Affine term structure models. In: *Handbook of Financial Econometrics*, Vol. 1 (Y. Aït-Sahalia and L. P. Hansen, eds.), Amsterdam: North-Holland, 691–766.

Rebonato, R. (2004). *Volatility and Correlation: the Perfect Hedger and the Fox.* Chichester, UK: Wiley.

Ueno, Y., Baba, N. and Sakurai, Y. (2006). The use of the Black model of interest rates as options for monitoring the JGB market expectations. Bank of Japan Working Paper Series, No. 06-E-15.

Vasicek, O. (1977). An equilibrium characterization of the term structure. Journal of Financial Economics, **5**, 177–188.

Part III

Policy

11 The repo and federal funds markets before, during, and emerging from the financial crisis

Morten Bech, Elizabeth Klee and Viktors Stebunovs

11.1 Introduction

This chapter examines the link between US overnight money markets, before, during, and emerging from the financial crisis that began in August 2007. In particular, the chapter focuses on the transmission of the monetary policy stance from the overnight federal funds market to the overnight US Treasury general collateral (GC) repurchase agreement (repo) market. In addition, the chapter estimates the liquidity effects in these two money markets over time, with an eye to gauging potential upward pressure on the two money market interest rates from hypothetical liquidity draining by the Federal Reserve.

To the best of our knowledge, there has been little recent work done using relatively modern econometric techniques which evaluates linkages between money markets. Much of the monetary policy transmission literature examines lower-frequency changes in interest rates, and then traces these changes through to real output and the rest of the economy. Often assumed to work seamlessly is the first step in this transmission – the transmission of the monetary policy stance from the federal funds market to other money markets. And as the recent financial crisis has demonstrated, seemingly resilient linkages between financial markets may suddenly weaken or disappear.

Given that these markets are the first markets in the monetary policy transmission chain, the focus on the money markets and their functioning during and emerging from the financial crisis is easily justifiable. For the policymakers, in particular, it is important to know whether the two money market interest rates co-move and what factors might set them

The views expressed are those of the authors and do not reflect those of the Bank for International Settlements, the Federal Reserve Board, or the Federal Reserve System.

apart and to what extent. In short, the major contribution of this chapter is a careful analysis of the interplay between the two money market interest rates from the monetary policy transmission and implementation point of view.

The federal funds and Treasury GC repo markets have been tightly linked, in part, because of the US monetary policy implementation framework. For many years, the Federal Open Market Committee (FOMC) has been setting a desired level for the interest rate at which depository institutions lend unsecured funds (reserves balances at the Federal Reserve) to other depository institutions overnight. This desired rate is called the target federal funds rate. To achieve the target federal funds rate, the Federal Reserve conducts open market operations – purchases and sales of US Treasury and federal agency securities using repos.

After the Federal Reserve initiates the monetary policy transmission process, the most immediate next step is for the federal funds rate to influence the behavior of other short-term interest rates. In order for monetary policy transmission to be effective, these other rates should move with the federal funds rate. As the participants in the federal funds market and other short-term markets frequently overlap, controlling for risk, collateral, and other frictions, all rate differences should be arbitraged quickly away. Consequently, short-term interest rates should move in tandem with the federal funds rate. In particular, it seems likely that repo rates and the federal funds rate would be very likely to move together, as both markets are involved in the earliest stages of the monetary policy transmission process.

But do they? While there are long periods when the Treasury GC repo rate and the federal funds rate move together, there are also notable times when they do not. For example, Figure 11.1 shows a spread between the federal funds rate and the Treasury GC repo rate. Although for much of the sample there appear to be only small differences between these two rates, there are spells when the spread widens considerably and the rate movements seem decoupled. One might question whether the monetary policy transmission mechanism is effective during these spells.

In order to provide perspective on the comovement of the two rates, this chapter characterizes the relationship between the federal funds rate and the Treasury GC repo rate during three periods: a period of relative calm in financial markets, from January 2002 to July 2007, the early stages of the financial crisis, from August 2007 to December 2008, and post-December 2008, after the FOMC set a target range for the federal funds rate of 0 to 25 basis points.

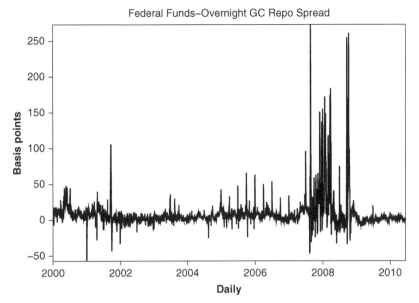

Figure 11.1 Spread between federal funds and Treasury GC repo

The sample breakdown is benchmarked to these two events: the suspension of redemptions by BNP Paribas on its investment funds in early August 2007 (the event that marked the beginning of the financial crisis in earnest) and the FOMC decision to establish a target range for the federal funds rate of 0 to 0.25 percent in mid-December 2008 (the event that marked the arrival of a zero lower bound for short-term interest rates and the effective cessation of temporary open market operations). Alternatively, the sample breakdown can be benchmarked to the Lehman Brothers bankruptcy in mid-September 2008. But given the brevity of the period between the Lehman Brothers bankruptcy and the arrival of the zero lower bound, the timing of the sample breakdown does not appear crucial for the results.[1]

The results suggest that pass-through from the federal funds rate to the repo deteriorated somewhat during the crisis and zero lower bound periods, likely due to limits to arbitrage and idiosyncratic market factors. In addition, during the early part of the crisis, the pricing of federal funds relative to repurchase agreements indicated a marked jump in perceived

[1] The Federal Reserve began to pay interest on depository institutions' required and excess balances in October 2008. Because of just a few changes in interest paid on reserves, which all occurred during the tumultuous times, the effects of this new policy tool on money market rates cannot be identified with confidence.

credit risk. Moreover, the liquidity effect in the federal funds market weakened with the increase in reserve balances over the crisis, implying a non-linear demand curve for federal funds. In contrast, the liquidity effects in the Treasury GC repo market, on balance, has remained unchanged. Consequently, emerging from the crisis, the two money market interest rates appear to co-move not as tightly as they did before the crisis. However, the presence of the liquidity effects in both the federal funds and repo markets implies that hypothetical liquidity draining by the Federal Reserve, for example via large-scale reverse repos, may boost somewhat the two money market rates in the absence of an increase in the policy rates, such as the target federal funds rate, the primary credit rate, or the rate paid on reserves. Our results shed some light on the weaker monetary policy transmission across interest rates for instruments of the same maturity (for the shortest of the maturities). As for the transmission of the monetary policy stance from the short-term rates to the longer-term rates along the yield curve, this traditional channel has clearly reached its limits in the zero lower bound environment with significant financial market segmentation. These limits, in fact, justify the Federal Reserve's non-conventional policy measures examined in Chapter 4 of this book.

The chapter proceeds as follows. Section 11.2 provides background on key overnight funding markets, both secured and unsecured. Section 11.3 describes the empirical framework for the results reported in Section 11.4. Section 11.5 concludes.

11.2   Background

This section reviews basic facts on the repo market and the federal funds market, as well as discussing monetary policy implementation.

The repo market

A repurchase agreement is a sale of a security coupled with an agreement to repurchase the security at a specified price at a later date.[2] It is economically similar to a collateralized loan, where the lender of cash receives securities as collateral. From the perspective of the borrower of cash, the transaction is called a "repo", and from the perspective of the lender of cash, it is a "reverse repo".[3]

---

[2] Frequently Asked Questions, Federal Reserve Bank of New York , 2010.

[3] There is a quirk in nomenclature when discussing the repo market and the Federal Reserve's balance sheet. For the Federal Reserve, repos are defined by the effect on the *counterparty*. Therefore, if the Federal Reserve lends securities and borrows funds, it is

Participation in the repo market is broad and includes depository institutions, the US government and its agencies, institutional investment funds, broker-dealers, money market mutual funds, and other entities.

There are two main methods of clearing and settling repos: direct (delivery versus payment) and tri-party. In a direct repo transaction, the securities holder initiates the transaction and the cash payment moves automatically as a result of the securities movement. Many of these transactions use the Fedwire Securities Settlement system for clearing and settlement, or they use the infrastructure provided by the Fixed Income Clearing Corporation (FICC). For a tri-party repo transaction, the transactions parties do not have to have their own infrastructure: both the borrower and the lender of securities must hold accounts at a clearing bank (either JPMorgan Chase or Bank of New York Mellon). The clearing banks offer services to customers that minimize transactions costs, including efficient collateral allocation and management, as well as extend a daylight overdraft to the borrower should the borrower of cash incur a daylight overdraft when the collateral is returned.[4]

Data on aggregate repo market activity over the sample period is not generally available.[5] However, there are a few sources of information on repo market volume which can help to characterize its size. One source is statistics compiled by the Federal Reserve Bank of New York (FRBNY) on repurchase agreements conducted by the primary dealers, which are the banks and broker-dealers that trade directly with the Open Market Desk (the "Desk") at FRBNY for the purposes of open market operations. As shown in Figure 11.2, the volume of repos in any collateral the primary dealers executed overnight nearly tripled between the early 2000s and late 2008, peaking at nearly $3 trillion before the Lehman Brothers bankruptcy. The volume of term repos expanded only modestly over the period. Similarly, trends in primary dealers' volume were less striking.

The repo market experienced significant strains during the financial crisis. For example, one of the reasons cited for the failure and takeover of Bear Stearns was its inability to access funding in the repo market.[6] As Figure 11.2 shows, outstanding amounts of repurchase agreements involving US government, federal agency, government

---

called a reverse repo, and if the Federal Reserve lends cash and borrows securities, it is called a repo.

[4] A daylight overdraft is a negative account balance normally resolved by the close of the business day.

[5] Some market observers attempt to estimate the size of the repo market; refer to Gorton (2010), for example.

[6] Refer to Fleming et al. (2010).

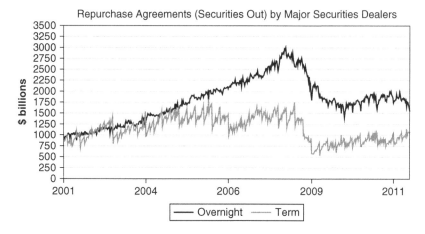

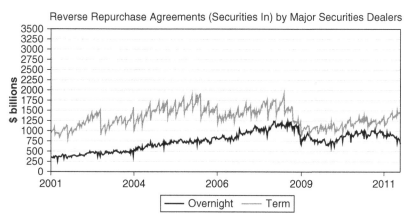

Figure 11.2 Primary dealers repurchase agreement volume

sponsored enterprise, mortgage-backed, corporate securities, equities, and other collateral by the primary US government securities dealers reporting to the Federal Reserve Bank of New York dropped significantly over the crisis and have not recovered since.

The broker-dealer volume reported above includes both direct trades and tri-party trades. The tri-party market grew substantially over the past decade, and according to data gathered by FRBNY in April 2010, there was about $474 billion in US Treasury tri-party repo volume.[7] Overall,

---

[7] Federal Reserve Bank of New York (2010).

then, the data from the primary dealers likely represents a significant fraction of total repo market activity.

The federal funds market

Federal funds are a liability of a depository institution that is issued or undertaken and held for the account of an office located in the US of another depository institution, foreign bank, Edge or Agreement Corporation, the US government or agency thereof, a Federal Home Loan Bank, or selected other institutions.[8] Anecdotal reports suggest that in the current environment, most funds are sold by Federal Home Loan Banks and other government-sponsored enterprises (GSEs), while most funds are bought by a limited number of banks. The rate at which these transactions occur is called the federal funds rate and the market in which these transactions occur is the federal funds market.

In some ways, the federal funds market is similar to the repo market, in that they are both short-term funding markets, but, there are important differences. Traditionally, the federal funds market was used by banks to buy funds in order to satisfy reserve requirements, to sell funds in excess of those requirements, and to fund payments settling in banks' accounts at the Federal Reserve. Previous research shows that funds rate behavior differed according to the day of the maintenance period.[9] Moreover, a short-term "liquidity effect", or a price response to changes in the level of reserve balances, has been identified in the federal funds market. In addition, participation in the federal funds market is restricted. This has the important implication that while many types of institution (both financial and non-financial) are theoretically able to participate in the repo market, the federal funds market is limited only to selected institution types (depository institutions and GSEs), which could hinder arbitrage across markets.

Although the federal funds market has been important for monetary policy implementation, the market is quite small and by many measures, its transaction volume is much lower than repo market volume. For example, Figure 11.3 plots federal funds transactions identified in the Fedwire data.[10] According to this series, federal funds market volume

---

[8] Refer to 12 CFR 204.2(a)(1)(vii)(A)(1) (Regulation D, Reserve Requirements of Depository Institutions).

[9] For example, refer to Hamilton (1996), Carpenter and Demiralp (2006), and Judson and Klee (2010).

[10] The data on federal funds volume are constructed using proprietary transaction-level data from the Fedwire Funds Service, using an algorithm pioneered by Furfine (1999)

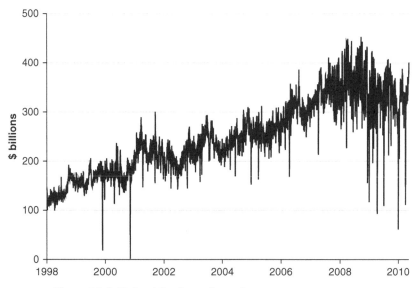

Figure 11.3 Federal funds market volume

ranges from around $100 billion in daily volume in 1998 to a peak above $400 billion in 2008, before falling closer to $300 billion in 2010. The decline in volume could be associated with the large volume of reserves outstanding emerging from the early part of the crisis, diminishing the possibility that institutions would be short on reserves. In addition, the interest on reserves might dampen the need for institutions to lend excess cash, as excess balances would earn interest.

Even though the volumes in these markets are quite different and there is imperfect overlap between the two markets, over much of the past decade or so, these rates have moved together quite closely. As is evident from the figure, rates in both markets were similar up until 2007. Because federal funds transactions are unsecured while repo transactions are secured, the repo rate is usually a bit below federal funds. Spreads

to match and form plausible overnight funding transactions, likely related to the federal funds market. The algorithm matches an outgoing Fedwire funds transfer sent from one account and received by another with a corresponding incoming transfer on the next business day sent by the previous day's receiver and received by the previous day's sender. This pair of transfers is considered a federal funds transaction if the amount of the incoming transfer is equal to the amount of the outgoing transfer plus interest at a rate consistent with the rates reported by major federal funds brokers. However, because we have no independent way to verify if these are actual federal funds transactions, our identified trades and characteristics of these trades are subject to error.

started to widen in the beginning of the financial crisis, from August 2007 onward, and then skyrocketed during the early crisis as investors flocked to the relative safety of secured overnight lending in repos.

11.2.1 Monetary policy implementation

There is a special connection between the federal funds market and the repo market for Federal Reserve monetary policy implementation. In the textbook version of monetary policy implementation, the Federal Reserve buys securities from dealers in the repo market, which gives the dealers cash which they deposit in their bank's accounts. In turn, the banks proceed to sell the funds in the federal funds market, hence increasing the supply of liquidity and reducing its price. By analogy, by selling securities in the repo market, the Federal Reserve increases the price of federal funds. By sizing this "open market operation" appropriately, the Federal Reserve could ensure that the effective federal funds rate is close to the target set by the FOMC. This operating procedure and target interest rate worked for many years. The Desk used repos almost daily to adjust the level of reserves so that federal funds would trade close to the target federal funds rate. Repo rates and federal funds rates traded in line with each other, and longer-term interest rates moved up and down with the federal funds rate.

Monetary policy implementation changed with the recent financial crisis, although not all at once. At the start of the crisis in August 2007, the Federal Reserve relied on larger-than-normal repo operations to inject liquidity into the federal funds market. Later, in the fall of 2008, the Federal Reserve conducted reverse repos in order to drain reserves from the system as well as to add some collateral back to the market. However, because reserve balances were elevated, the effective federal funds rate traded well below the target rate. In addition to the reverse repos, the Federal Reserve also conducted 28-day single-tranche repos, where the collateral pledged was agency MBS. The repos provided dealers with financing for agency MBS when the spread between one month agency MBS repo and one-month Treasury GC repo was particularly wide.[11] Although regular repo activity by the Desk ceased in the early part of 2009, in 2010 and 2011, the Desk conducted a series of small-value reverse repurchase agreements with a broad set of counterparties as part of its operational readiness program for tools to use in the future to drain reserve balances.

[11] For details, refer to Federal Reserve Bank of New York (2009).

In sum, although the repo market's role in monetary policy implementation has certainly changed in recent years, overall, it is likely to be a tool used for monetary policy implementation in the future.

11.3   Empirical preliminaries and framework

This section first performs some preliminary data analysis to provide justification for the statistical strategy used in this chapter. It then describes the primary estimating equation and reviews its ability to capture the three points deemed essential for judging the effectiveness of monetary policy transmission between the money markets.

11.3.1   Preliminary statistical analysis

The primary data used in this study are daily observations on the effective federal funds rate and the overnight Treasury GC repo rate from January 2, 2002 to June 16, 2010.[12] The daily effective federal funds rate is a volume-weighted average of rates on trades arranged by major brokers calculated and published by the Federal Reserve Bank of New York. The Treasury GC repo rate is a collateral-weighted average of a survey of all primary dealers conducted daily between 8:00 a.m. and 9:00 a.m.[13] Because a large fraction of federal funds market activity takes place in the late afternoon, the federal funds rate implicitly measures late-day funding activity, while the repo rate we use necessarily focuses on trading earlier in the day. Nevertheless, both measure activity when the respective markets are most active.[14]

The spread and correlations between federal funds and repo reviewed in Section 11.2 suggest that there could be a stable relationship between these two series over certain periods. These periods are benchmarked to the suspension of redemptions by BNP Paribas on its investment funds in August 2007 and the FOMC decision to establish a target range for the federal funds rate in December 2008. Reassuringly, Bai–Perron tests tend to indicate rather similar structural break dates, again around the discrete market events, and, in fact, the qualitative results are largely

---

[12]   In work not shown, we tested to see whether the introduction of a new discount window regime in 2003 affected our results; it did not.

[13]   Bartolini et al. (2011) also use this series in their work on the repo market.

[14]   The Desk obtains a federal funds indicative rate at 9:00 a.m. each morning. Although volumes associated with this rate are generally limited, we performed our analysis using this rate to see if using the end-of-day rate is different from this morning rate. Overall, we found the results to be quantitatively similar.

unaffected by the method of choice of sample periods. A series of augmented Dickey–Fuller tests performed over three subsamples – from January 2, 2002 to August 8, 2007, from August 9, 2007 to December 15, 2008, and from December 16, 2008 to June 2010 – suggest that the null of a unit root may be accepted for the first two periods, but may be rejected for the last period with the unchanged target federal funds rate and very high reserve balances.[15] In turn, Johansen co-integration tests show that the two rates are co-integrated in both the relatively stable period before the August 2007 start of the crisis, and in the window between the start of the crisis and the failure of Lehman Brothers.

Taken together, these results suggest the existence of distinct regimes for the relationship between the federal funds rate and the repo rate. As a result, portions of our analysis will divide the sample into these separate regimes and report statistics separately.

11.3.2 Empirical framework

The theoretical underpinning of our empirical framework is the arbitrage principle. In a frictionless environment with risk neutral agents, the Treasury GC repo and federal funds rate are bound by a strict arbitrage relationship as the participants in both the Treasury GC repo and federal funds market exhaust all opportunities to profit overnight from pricing anomalies in one market or the other. That is, the principle at work is simple arbitrage of lending overnight in one market at a higher rate than that of borrowing overnight in the other, subject to a risk premium: agents exploit pricing anomalies and trade until the differences between the two rates are driven to a minimum.[16] In other words, this arbitrage relationship – a no-arbitrage pricing condition – is equivalent to the existence of a linear pricing rule for the two types of overnight loan. And the no-arbitrage pricing condition does not rely on the validity of the expectations hypothesis. All that is required for the condition to hold is an environment free of arbitrage frictions, such as an agent not having access to one of the markets, for example, because of its high credit risk. Importantly, the existence of arbitrage is consistent with effective

---

[15] A constant has been included in the specification for all unit root tests. In addition, the optimal lag length used is based on the Schwarz information criterion (SIC).

[16] The existence of the risk premium in the frictionless environment reflects the fact that borrowing in the Treasury GC repo market is collateralized, while that in the federal funds market is not. Hence, a borrower will face a lower rate in the Treasury GC repo market than that in the federal funds market (because the cash flow to the lender, given the same probability of a borrower default on either type of a loan, is larger).

monetary policy transmission: the arbitrage is what ensures that the Treasury GC repo rate moves along with the effective federal funds rate.

Overnight money markets, at least before the financial crisis, are a natural candidate for testing the no-arbitrage pricing condition, as the market participants perceived arbitrage frictions to be quite low. Back then, the market participants with abundance of capital and liquidity were numerous; they viewed credit risk of money market transactions as inconsequential; and they could rely on unsophisticated traders at their funding desks to spot pricing anomalies and take advantage of them without hedging. It is likely that with the financial crisis things changed somewhat gradually, as the severity of the crisis was not immediately recognized.

Our empirical framework helps to shed some light on three points deemed essential for judging the effectiveness of monetary policy transmission from the federal funds to the repo markets: (1) the adjustment speed with which deviations from the long-term relationship between the two interest rates disappear; (2) the width of the federal funds rate spread over the repo rate; and (3) the sensitivity of the two money market interest rates to changes in liquidity supply.

These points have straightforward economic interpretation. The adjustment speed indicates how quickly arbitrage opportunities are exhausted. In turn, the width of the unsecured rate spread over the secured rate informs, in part, about the probability of counterparty default.[17] During times of stress, one may expect probability of default to jump, strengthening counterparty concerns and precluding arbitrage opportunities from being exhausted. At the same time, the transmission of the monetary policy stance will be rendered less effective, necessitating some intervention. The sensitivity of the interest rates to changes in liquidity supply – the liquidity effect – tells about the Federal Reserve's ability to push the rates closer to the target by adding or draining liquidity. A weak liquidity effect implies that liquidity additions or drainage should be substantial to achieve the desired outcome.

Our primary tool for evaluating these claims is a vector error correction model (VEC):

$$\Delta \mathbf{x_t} = \alpha \left(\beta' \mathbf{x_{t-1}} + \mathbf{c_0} \right) + \Phi(\mathbf{L}) \Delta \mathbf{x_t} + \Xi \mathbf{Z_t} + \mathbf{e_t} \qquad (11.1)$$

where $\mathbf{x_t}$ is the vector of federal funds and Treasury GC repo interest rates; β is the co-integrating vector for the error correction term that characterizes the long-run relationship between the repo and the federal

---

[17] The width of the spread also reflects the loan recovery rate, that depends on the intrinsic value of the collateral.

funds rate; c_0 is a constant in the error correction term; α is a vector of the adjustment speed coefficients. Because the α and β coefficients are not identified, we use the normalization proposed by Johansen (1995), which sets the first m components of the β vector to 1, where m is the number of co-integrating relationships.

The $\Phi(L)$ are auto-regressive coefficients to be estimated. We use three lags of all interest rates in the specification as suggested by the Schwarz Information Criterion (SIC) test.[18]

The other included variables are factors that likely shift the effective rate and the repo rate on a daily basis. These are captured in the Z_t vector, with coefficients to be estimated, Ξ. Z_t consists of four groups of variables which are used to evaluate the liquidity effect, proxy for financial market risk measures (a few are similar to those used in Collin-Dufresne et al. (2001)), plus some factors that are specific controls for the funds market and for the repo market, and a vector of calendar effects.

The first group of factors is used to identify the liquidity effect in each market, and in both markets simultaneously. The identification of the liquidity effect in the federal funds market in daily data was first suggested by Hamilton (1997). His innovation was to use a particular shock to supply of reserve balances (an unanticipated change in autonomous factors supplying reserve balances) to estimate the local slope of a demand curve for federal funds. This approach might suffer a couple of deficiencies in the crisis environment. First, Hamilton's exogenous shifter of supply of reserve balances is local in nature; it is quite small in magnitude and can help to identify the slope on rather steep segments on the demand curve.[19] Second, Hamilton's setup does not recognize the interplay between the federal funds and repo markets and allows for limited dynamic demand adjustments. More specifically, there are no cross effects between the federal funds and repo markets. Ideally, in a model with multiple money markets, a variety of instruments should be available. Some instruments should only affect the supply of reserve balances but not the availability of liquidity in the repo market and vice

---

[18] Although some tests occasionally reveal statistically significant autocorrelated lags further out, these are generally ten business days or more in the past. We balanced a more parsimonious specification versus controlling for all of these lags, and moreover, we believe that movements more than two weeks previously are likely irrelevant once other controls are included in the specification.

[19] When balances were low, the forecast miss allowed the researcher to trace out the demand curve and determine the liquidity effect without incurring problems of simultaneity. However, once reserve balances climbed to high levels, the level of the miss was minuscule relative to total balances, and in general, was not the most important factor adding unexpected reserve balances.

versa, whereas other instruments should affect liquidity in both markets. Choosing the "right" exogenous shocks to the supply curve takes some care. In turn, to address these issues, we use a number of different instruments.

One of the instruments we use is changes in the Treasury's General Account (TGA) at the Federal Reserve. As shown in the top panel of Figure 11.4, before the fall of 2008, the Treasury targeted an account balance at the Federal Reserve at a relatively constant level, typically $5 billion. Excess cash was invested in depository institution accounts through the Treasury Tax and Loan (TT&L) account system; the rate of return was typically the effective federal funds rate less 25 basis points. After the effective federal funds rate plummeted and reserve balances rose, the return that the Treasury received on TT&L investments was negligible, and the Desk ceased conducting open market operations on a daily basis to target a specific level of reserve balances. As a result of these policy changes, as shown in the bottom panel of Figure 11.4, the TGA level varied widely. Changes in the level of the TGA represent exogenous changes in the supply of reserve balances, and so are useful to trace out the demand curve in the federal funds market.

We use another instrument to show that the liquidity effect in the repo market is net Treasury securities issuance. These represent exogenous, known supply shocks, and the repo rate tends to increase after issuance dates, as the market absorbs the collateral. As a result, we can use this issuance to estimate the liquidity effect in the repo market.[20]

For the last subsample, we use changes in balances in another Treasury account at the Federal Reserve to identify the liquidity effect in the federal funds and repo markets. Starting in September 2008, at the request of the Federal Reserve, the Treasury announced a series of bill auctions separate from its primary borrowing program and deposited the proceeds of these auctions in an account at the Federal Reserve – the Supplementary Financing Account (SFA).[21] Just like the TGA, balances on this account drain reserves, and therefore changes in the level of this account can help to trace out the liquidity effect in the federal funds market. At the same time, issuance of SFA Treasury bills increases the amount of collateral financed in the repo market, helping to identify the liquidity in the repo market.

---

[20] It is true that Treasury securities issuance temporarily drains reserve balances. However, over the course of the issuance day, these balances, at least to some extent, end up on the accounts of depository institutions because of Treasury's outgoing payments.

[21] The SFA announcement did not appear to have an immediate impact on the money market rates. The settlements of SFA Treasury bills were not timed in response to gyrations in money markets.

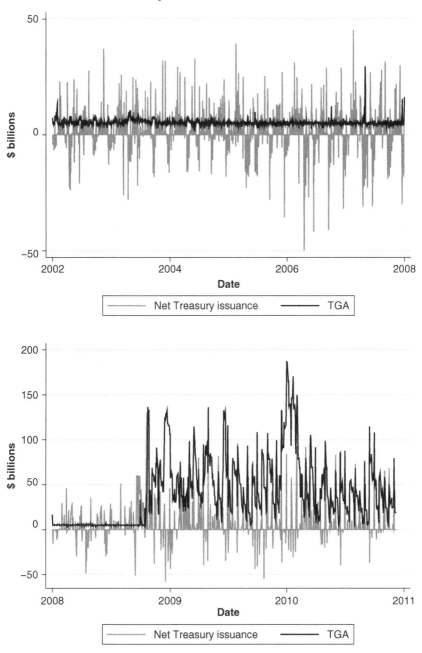

Figure 11.4 Net Treasury securities issuance and Treasury General Account balance

Our final instrument is related to Federal Reserve open market operations. Beginning in November 2008 and continuing through to March 2010, the Federal Reserve conducted a series of securities purchases with the intent of lowering longer-term interest rates. There were more than $1.7 trillion in "Large Scale Asset Purchases" (LSAPs) of Treasury securities, agency debt securities and agency mortgage-backed securities, which had the effect of adding a staggering amount of reserves to the Federal Reserve's balance sheet. The announcement of LSAPs had little immediate effect on money market rates; however, settlements of LSAPs resulted in an increase of reserve balances (and a decrease in collateral in the repo market) and exerted downward pressure on the money market rates. The LSAP amounts to be settled were known in advance; these amounts and the settlement dates were independent of the conditions in the federal funds and repo markets.[22] As a result, we can use the increment in the LSAPs each day as an instrumental variable in our estimation equations. The effects of the LSAPs, however, are less clear cut than some of our other instruments. LSAPs both add balances, thereby affecting the funds rate, and remove collateral, thereby affecting the repo rate. Consequently, this instrument likely affects both the funds and repo rates simultaneously, rather than one individually.

Beyond the rates and the liquidity effects, we also include other factors that likely affect the two money market interest rates. The next group controls for overall indications of financial risk. Over the estimation period, market sentiment changed dramatically with the advent of the financial crisis. As a result, indicators such as the Libor-OIS spread, the aggregate of US commercial bank capital ratios, and the monetary policy outlook – as proxied by the slope of the yield curve (the 10-year Treasury rate less the 2-year Treasury rate) – generally reflected more negative sentiment about the financial markets and the economy towards the second half of the sample.

The next group of controls includes factors specifically related to the repo market or the federal funds market. On the repo side, included is a measure of how heavily weighted primary dealers' books are toward trades with other dealers versus with non-dealers.[23] This gives some idea of market concentration in the Treasury market. To address market functioning, fails in Treasury securities are included as an independent

---

[22] Therefore, the LSAP settled amounts were not correlated with contemporaneous shocks affecting the money market interest rates.

[23] This variable is defined as transactions outside the dealer community as a share of total transactions, as reported in the weekly report of dealer positions, transactions, and Financing (FR 2004) available at: http://www.newyorkfed.org/banking/reportingforms/FR_2004A_B_C.html.

variable; these are reported by primary dealers to FRBNY on a weekly basis. In addition, actions on the Federal Reserve System Open Market Account (SOMA) Treasury portfolio are added as controls, including the level of Treasury securities lent through the SOMA securities lending programs. Again, securities lending tends to increase during times of market stress and particularly for any security that is trading on "special" in the market.[24]

On the federal funds side, we use a number of controls for the size of and participation in the federal funds market, including federal funds market volume, the number of sellers, and specifically, the quantity sold by the GSEs. In addition, we control for days when there is movement in the target federal funds rate; this variable equals the change in the target rate on days of FOMC announcements, but equals zero on all other days.

The final group of controls is *calendar*, a vector of maintenance period and other calendar effects. Previous work, including Hamilton (1996) and others, showed that these are significantly correlated with changes in the federal funds rate. Repo rates also move with calendar effects, as illustrated by Happ (1986) and Fleming et al. (2010). Reasons for these patterns include elevated payment flows on beginning- mid-, and end-month dates, as well as Treasury coupon securities issuance on these dates. Moreover, some research indicates that repo rates tend to exhibit maintenance period patterns as well, suggesting that there is some co-movement in the federal funds and repo rates that derives from the maintenance period construct (for example, Griffiths and Winters (1997)).

Preliminary estimation results, as well as some signs of volatility clustering in Figure 11.1, suggest that there exists heteroskedasticity of the residuals.[25] As a result, in conjunction with the mean equation described above, we also estimate variance and covariance processes with GARCH and TARCH components. This is a constant correlation form of generalized auto-regressive conditional heteroskedasticity formulated by Bollerslev (1990).

While our baseline methodology is a VEC model with GARCH/TARCH errors, in the last sample period, as discussed in Section 11.3.1, the rates do not have unit roots and are therefore are not co-integrated. As a result, we specify a VAR model similar to the VEC model and use a GARCH specification for the second moment equation and report results with Bollerslev–Wooldridge robust standard errors.

---

[24] For a discussion of specials markets in Treasury securities, refer to Duffie (1996), Fisher (2002), and others.

[25] We perform a White heteroskedasticity test which handily rejects the hypothesis of homoskedasticity in all three samples.

Operationally, we use a two-stage estimation procedure similar to Engle and Granger (1987). In the first stage, we test for co-integration of the repo rate and the federal funds rate. After establishing this, we construct the co-integrating term using ordinary least squares. This constructed term is included as an independent variable in our system GARCH estimation. Although it is possible that some efficiency is lost using this procedure, it allows us to use a GARCH specification relatively easily in the second stage estimation. Furthermore, significance of all coefficients is reported with respect to Bollerslev–Wooldridge robust standard errors.

11.4   Results

This section reviews the results over the three sample periods.

11.4.1   Normal times: 2002–2007

Table 11.1 provides results for the early part of the sample, a time of relative calm in financial markets. As shown by the constant term within the co-integrating relationship, the stationary series that is formed by the difference between the federal funds rate and the repo rate has a mean of about 2 basis points. This can be interpreted as the steady-state risk premium of federal funds over repo (assuming the recovery rate for a repo loan of about 1). In addition, over the early sample, the co-integrating equation coefficient (the β) suggest a relationship between federal funds and repo that is close to 1-to-1.

With the co-integrating term in hand, the remainder of Table 11.1 reports results from estimating the second stage VEC model with GARCH errors. The first set of columns report results for the repo equation; the second set report results for the federal funds equation. As indicated by the αs, the Treasury GC repo rate adjusts to deviations from the equilibrium relationship, as the α coefficient is statistically significant, but the federal funds rate does not. Moreover, we interpret statistically significant α terms as consistent with the existence of overnight arbitrage; that is, traders are willing to exploit pricing anomalies and trade until the differences between the two rates are minimized. Importantly, this arbitrage is consistent with effective monetary policy transmission.

There are three possible reasons why the federal funds rate does not appear to adjust to deviations from the co-integration relationship. First, over this sample period, the Desk was actively manipulating the federal

Table 11.1 *Normal times: January 2002–August 2007*

	Included observations: 1410							
Co-integrating vector:	Constant	–1.91			Slope	0.99		
	D(Repo rate)				D(Federal funds rate)			
Dependent variable	Coeff.	Std. Error	z-Stat.	Prob.	Coeff.	Std. Error	z-Stat.	Prob.
Speed of adjustment	–0.21	0.04	–5.30	0.00	–0.01	0.04	–0.19	0.85
D(Repo rate(–1))	–0.28	0.05	–5.52	0.00	–0.05	0.06	–0.83	0.41
D(Repo rate(–2))	–0.18	0.04	–4.63	0.00	–0.08	0.03	–2.76	0.01
D(Repo rate(–3))	–0.08	0.02	–3.37	0.00	–0.04	0.03	–1.62	0.10
D(Federal funds rate(–1))	0.03	0.05	0.53	0.59	–0.38	0.06	–6.13	0.00
D(Federal funds rate(–2))	0.06	0.05	1.34	0.18	–0.22	0.04	–5.87	0.00
D(Federal funds rate(–3))	0.04	0.03	1.34	0.18	–0.15	0.03	–5.38	0.00
Factor miss	0.05	0.10	0.51	0.61	–0.34	0.12	–2.72	0.01
Net Treasury sec. issuance	0.04	0.01	3.07	0.00	0.00	0.01	0.09	0.93
Net Treasury sec. issuance(–1)	0.02	0.01	1.81	0.07	0.00	0.01	–0.08	0.93
D(Libor-OIS spread)	0.11	0.09	1.13	0.26	–0.03	0.08	–0.36	0.72
D(Capital ratios)	19.55	10.15	1.93	0.05	21.42	19.36	1.11	0.27
D(Treasury yield curve slope)	0.06	0.04	1.47	0.14	–0.07	0.04	–1.88	0.06
D(Repo market composition)	0.03	0.17	0.18	0.86	0.06	0.17	0.34	0.73
D(Treasury sec. delivery fails)	–0.01	0.01	–0.80	0.43	0.00	0.01	–0.01	0.99
D(Securities lending)	0.00	0.05	–0.02	0.98	0.07	0.08	0.78	0.43
D(Federal funds volume)	0.05	0.01	4.64	0.00	0.11	0.01	8.27	0.00
D(Number of funds sellers)	0.00	0.00	1.97	0.05	–0.01	0.00	–2.70	0.01
D(Fed funds sold by GSEs)	–0.10	0.02	–5.96	0.00	–0.13	0.02	–7.39	0.00
D(Federal funds target rate)	0.16	0.12	1.29	0.20	0.15	0.10	1.51	0.13

Table 11.1 (cont.)

Included observations: 1410

Co-integrating vector:	Constant				Slope			
	-1.91				0.99			
	D(Repo rate)				D(Federal funds rate)			
Dependent variable	Coeff.	Std. Error	z-Stat.	Prob.	Coeff.	Std. Error	z-Stat.	Prob.
MP day 1	-1.81	1.44	-1.26	0.21	-2.05	1.03	-1.98	0.05
MP day 2	-4.53	1.42	-3.18	0.00	-5.17	1.00	-5.18	0.00
MP day 5	-1.76	1.43	-1.23	0.22	-2.05	1.03	-1.99	0.05
MP day 6	-2.92	1.46	-2.00	0.05	-3.93	1.06	-3.71	0.00
MP day 7	-2.84	1.42	-2.00	0.05	-3.86	1.00	-3.86	0.00
MP day 8	-1.90	1.42	-1.33	0.18	-2.08	1.03	-2.03	0.04
MP day 9	-3.16	1.42	-2.23	0.03	-4.29	1.02	-4.22	0.00
MP day 12	-1.54	1.42	-1.09	0.28	-2.46	1.00	-2.45	0.01
MP day 13	-2.84	1.47	-1.94	0.05	-5.35	1.05	-5.10	0.00
MP day 14	-3.32	1.43	-2.33	0.02	-3.66	1.07	-3.41	0.00
15th of the month	4.34	0.56	7.79	0.00	4.21	0.47	8.90	0.00
End of the month	2.45	0.52	4.68	0.00	3.66	0.51	7.13	0.00
25th of the month	0.51	0.40	1.27	0.20	3.64	0.43	8.44	0.00
End of the quarter	-7.69	3.08	-2.50	0.01	6.22	2.41	2.59	0.01
End of the year	-12.36	6.80	-1.82	0.07	-17.18	4.73	-3.63	0.00
Adjusted R^2	0.40				0.36			
Durbin–Watson statistic	1.94				1.74			

Note. Covariance specification: Constant Conditional Correlation with ARCH, TARCH, and GARCH components; end of the quarter calendar dummy. Bollerslev-Wooldridge robust standard errors.

funds market in order to achieve an effective rate near the target federal funds rate. As a result, the ability of the federal funds rate to adjust to movements in the repo rate may have been hindered. Second, the markets have different kinds of participants. For example, the Federal Financial Institutions Examination Council call report data indicate that both on the asset and liability sides of the balance sheet, repo holdings are concentrated in larger banks, while federal funds holdings tend to be more spread out. The data suggest that the top ten banks account for over 80 percent of commercial bank holdings of repo assets in some years, while the share of federal funds liabilities remains below 50 percent for nearly all of the sample, and medium-sized banks comprise a much larger share. If one assumes that larger, more sophisticated institutions are more likely to arbitrage differences, and that non-bank participants in the repo market also tend to be larger, more sophisticated institutions, then repo could potentially move back to equilibrium more readily than federal funds. And third, because repo transactions are secured, participants may be more willing to exploit pricing anomalies than they would if transactions were unsecured, as in the federal funds market.

The next six rows display the effects of past changes in rates on current ones. Own lags of the variables are statistically significant out to the third lag, consistent with some persistence in these series. The results for cross-market effects, when taken together, suggest limited causality from the repo market to the federal funds market, and no causality from the federal funds market to the repo market.[26] Although it appears from these short-run dynamics that the repo market may have been "ground zero" for monetary policy implementation, the fact that the two series are co-integrated in the long run suggest that these movements are transitory in nature and are not necessarily significant for long-run monetary policy transmission.

Turning to the liquidity variables, the next few lines in the table indicate that supply effects exist in both markets, and in general, a short-term liquidity effect existed. The coefficient on the unanticipated change in autonomous factors supplying reserves – the "factor miss" – for the federal funds equation suggests that for a $10 billion miss that adds balances, the effective federal funds rate declines by about 3 basis points. This liquidity effect is a little bit smaller than that estimated by Judson and Klee (2010), which could be a result of both the richer specification and different sample period. The effect of the miss is not significantly different from zero in the repo equation, as expected. By contrast, net

---

[26] Granger causality tests indicate that the repo market is more likely to drive the federal funds market than vice versa.

Treasury issuance tends to push up the repo rate, but has no discernible effect on the federal funds rate. The effect of net Treasury issuance on the repo rate tends to dissipate after the first day, implying that markets quickly return to their long-run relationship during this period. Still, according to the estimated coefficients, for a $10 billion increase in Treasury issuance, the change in the repo rate increases by about 0.4 of a basis point on the issuance day.

As for the risk variables, the estimated coefficients on the factors that control for overall indications of financial risk are broadly in line with intuition. During this period of relative calm, movements in the Libor-OIS spread were likely idiosyncratic, and therefore, did not have much connection to repo rates or to federal funds rates. Changes in the overall capital ratio of US commercial banks were positively associated with repo rates, but not associated with material movements in federal funds rates. By contrast to these other indicators, the change in the slope of the yield curve is associated with a more negative change in federal funds rates (at the 10 percent level); that is, as the yield curve slope steepens, changes in the federal funds rate become more negative. Interestingly, the repo rate is unaffected by changes in the slope of the yield curve.

Not surprisingly, there are different effects on the repo rate and on the funds rate of our various market-specific controls. Turning to those for the repo rate, as shown in the next line, the composition of dealers' books appears to have little impact on either the repo market or the federal funds market in this period. In addition, occasions with large amounts of fails in the Treasury market were also relatively sporadic over this period, and as such, changes in fails had little bearing on movements in the repo or federal funds rate. Consistently, securities lending by the Federal Reserve was also not correlated with changes in either rate.

For those variables included specifically to address conditions in the federal funds market, a positive change in federal funds market volume is associated with a movement up in both the federal funds and repo rates, reflecting demand for cash in both markets. The presence of more federal funds sellers pushes repo rates up and federal funds rates down, consistent with heightened cash supply. Supply of funds by GSEs works slightly differently, in that increases in GSE loan amounts tend to push both rates down; the point estimates suggest that this effect is a touch stronger for the repo rate than for the federal funds rate. This could be capturing a supply effect: if the GSEs have excess cash to invest, rates in both markets trade lower.

The final set of coefficients displays controls for calendar effects. Day-of-maintenance period factors are not significantly different from the first day of the maintenance period for repo on any day, while for federal funds, only the penultimate day of the maintenance period is significant. Day-of-month factors are also important. Both federal funds and repo tend to rise on mid-month and end-of-days, while repo also rises on the 25th of the month, when Fannie Mae makes principal and interest payments on their securities. Rates fall in the repo market on quarter-end but rise in the funds market, and both rates plummet on the last business day of the year.

The estimated ARCH and GARCH components, not shown, suggest that there the residuals are both auto-regressive and persistent.[27] The positive coefficients on the end of the quarter and the 15th of the month suggest systematic volatility on these days, consistent with large rate swings often seen on these days of the month.

11.4.2 *Early crisis: August 2007 to December 2008*

On August 9, 2007, BNP Paribas stopped redemptions on three investment funds and the financial crisis began in earnest. Over the next year-and-a-half, the Federal Reserve used a variety of unconventional policy measures to combat the financial crisis. During this period, the Federal Reserve cut the target federal funds rate by nearly 5 percentage points and provided the federal funds market with reserve balances in order to provide ample liquidity.

Despite these changes, the federal funds rate and the repo rate continued to co-move. Table 11.2 presents results for the crisis, from August 2007 through December 2008. Although December 2008 was likely not the end of the financial crisis, it marks the period before the funds rate fell to 25 basis points. As shown in the top panel, the mean of the stationary series that is formed by the difference between the federal funds rate and the repo rate jumped to 18 basis points, consistent with a perceived higher counterparty default probability. Moreover, repo market adjustment to arbitrage opportunities between the funds market and the repo market slowed considerably, and significant adjustment in federal funds continued to be absent.

There are a few reasons why the speed of adjustment may have changed. First, credit concerns in the unsecured federal funds market may have been greater than those in the secured repo market, creating conditions where investors were willing to leave arbitrage opportunities unexploited.[28] Second, some federal funds market investors may have

---

[27] The initial estimation results suggested no statistically significant TARCH effects.

[28] This phenomenon occurred in other markets as well; refer to Coffey et al. (2009) for evidence from the foreign exchange market.

Table 11.2 *Crisis: August 2007–December 2008*

	Included observations: 330							
Co-integrating vector:	Constant				Slope			
	−18.33				0.96			
	D(Repo rate)				D(Federal funds rate)			
Dependent variable	Coeff.	Std. Error	z-Stat.	Prob.	Coeff.	Std. Error	z-Stat.	Prob.
Speed of adjustment	−0.12	0.02	−5.59	0.00	0.01	0.01	0.34	0.73
D(Repo rate(−1))	−0.02	0.04	−0.53	0.60	−0.08	0.03	−2.62	0.01
D(Repo rate(−2))	−0.04	0.04	−1.17	0.24	0.03	0.01	1.79	0.07
D(Repo rate(−3))	−0.04	0.03	−1.32	0.19	0.01	0.01	0.58	0.56
D(Federal funds rate(−1))	0.22	0.05	4.65	0.00	−0.03	0.05	−0.76	0.45
D(Federal funds rate(−2))	0.18	0.07	2.67	0.01	−0.14	0.04	−3.33	0.00
D(Federal funds rate(−3))	0.06	0.04	1.34	0.18	−0.10	0.03	−3.58	0.00
Factor miss	−0.02	0.08	−0.22	0.82	0.05	0.05	1.01	0.31
Treasury General Acct. bal.	−0.09	0.02	−3.81	0.00	0.03	0.02	1.49	0.14
Net Treasury sec. issuance	0.17	0.04	4.87	0.00	0.04	0.04	1.20	0.23
Net Treasury sec. issuance(−1)	0.14	0.03	4.82	0.00	0.03	0.02	1.17	0.24
D(Supplement. Fin. Acct. bal.)	−0.08	0.12	−0.67	0.50	0.03	0.07	0.37	0.71
D(Libor-OIS spread)	−0.49	0.10	−5.08	0.00	0.12	0.06	1.89	0.06
D(Capital ratios)	221.78	89.88	2.47	0.01	−210.95	28.99	−7.28	0.00
D(Treasury yield curve slope)	−0.07	0.10	−0.71	0.47	−0.14	0.07	−2.01	0.04
D(Repo market composition)	5.62	1.55	3.63	0.00	0.33	0.58	0.57	0.57
D(Treasury sec. delivery fails)	0.00	0.02	−0.12	0.90	0.01	0.01	1.06	0.29
D(Securities lending)	0.23	0.16	1.46	0.14	0.36	0.13	2.69	0.01
D(Federal funds volume)	−0.01	0.04	−0.23	0.82	0.12	0.04	3.18	0.00
D(Number of funds sellers)	0.10	0.03	2.93	0.00	−0.06	0.03	−2.29	0.02
D(Fed funds sold by GSEs)	−0.01	0.06	−0.23	0.81	0.04	0.06	0.60	0.55
D(Federal funds target rate)	1.00	0.11	9.50	0.00	0.56	0.08	7.38	0.00

Table 11.2 (cont.)

Included observations: 330

Co-integrating vector:	Constant		-18.33		Slope		0.96	
	D(Repo rate)				D(Federal funds rate)			
Dependent variable	Coeff.	Std. Error	z-Stat.	Prob.	Coeff.	Std. Error	z-Stat.	Prob.
MP day 1	−140.49	87.08	−1.61	0.11	−108.69	40.85	−2.66	0.01
MP day 2	−143.03	87.06	−1.64	0.10	−116.99	40.84	−2.86	0.00
MP day 5	−142.25	87.03	−1.63	0.10	−111.92	40.92	−2.74	0.01
MP day 6	−144.76	87.07	−1.66	0.10	−112.80	40.87	−2.76	0.01
MP day 7	−145.06	87.07	−1.67	0.10	−110.84	40.86	−2.71	0.01
MP day 8	−140.57	87.07	−1.61	0.11	−110.32	40.85	−2.70	0.01
MP day 9	−146.22	87.10	−1.68	0.09	−116.51	40.84	−2.85	0.00
MP day 12	−139.91	87.09	−1.61	0.11	−111.14	40.81	−2.72	0.01
MP day 13	−146.60	87.06	−1.68	0.09	−114.72	40.79	−2.81	0.00
MP day 14	−146.48	87.05	−1.68	0.09	−110.56	40.82	−2.71	0.01
15th of the month	−1.59	2.17	−0.73	0.46	−1.55	1.93	−0.80	0.42
End of the month	−8.41	2.90	−2.90	0.00	1.23	2.57	0.48	0.63
25th of the month	−3.85	2.36	−1.63	0.10	7.79	1.97	3.95	0.00
End of the quarter	−47.10	7.55	−6.24	0.00	27.30	7.20	3.79	0.00
End of the year	−92.18	60.80	−1.52	0.13	−83.76	28.74	−2.91	0.00
Adjusted R^2	0.25				0.14			
Durbin–Watson statistic	1.87				2.02			

Note. Covariance specification: Constant Conditional Correlation with ARCH, TARCH, and GARCH components; end of the quarter calendar dummy. Bollerslev–Wooldridge robust standard errors.

experienced capital constraints, and were unwilling to expand their balance sheets in order to take advantage of arbitrage opportunities, similar to the phenomenon described by Brunnermeier and Pedersen (2009). Finally, the federal funds market was likely changing to some degree at this point in time, both in terms of participants and in the composition of reserve holdings. For example, some banks may have dropped out of the market as a result of the abundance of funds from the Term Auction Facility and other credit and liquidity programs.

The cross-correlation terms, shown in the next few lines of the table, provide further evidence of the co-movement of these rates. The funds market appears to lead changes in the repo market, and vice versa, although interestingly, own market correlations are a bit more muted than previously.[29]

The next few lines display the results associated with the liquidity effect. The level of the "factors miss" is not correlated with changes in either the repo rate or the funds rate over the period.[30] The coefficient on the factors miss is insignificant, as balances climbed towards the end of the sample, and similarly, the coefficient on the TGA is also insignificant, as it was allowed to float only towards the end of the sample. Increases in net Treasury issuance are associated with higher repo rates; the effect lingers for an extra day as the market absorbs the higher quantity of new collateral. The effect of net Treasury issuance on the funds market is limited during this period, however. The SFA balance does not significantly affect either rate.

Turning to the risk variables, positive changes in the Libor-OIS spread push the federal funds rate up and repo rates down, while positive changes in the slope of the yield curve are associated with decreases in the federal funds rate. Changes in risk-weighted capital ratios have significant effects on both the repo and the funds rate, although in opposite directions, as repos move up and funds move down.

The next few lines show the correlations of the market-specific factors with the repo and federal funds rates. Composition effects of dealers' books appear to have a strong influence on the repo rate during this period. As the share of transactions with entities other than dealers grew, the sensitivity of movements also became more pronounced. For a

---

[29] Granger causality tests indicate that the two money market interest rates cause each other.

[30] This result is likely influenced by the inclusion of the very high balances period from October to December 2008 in the sample; in results not reported, the factors miss is significant and negatively correlated with changes in the federal funds rate for a shorter sample period.

1 percentage point change in this ratio, the repo rate increases by about 6 basis points. Changes in the amount of securities lending by the Federal Reserve curiously affect changes in the funds rate; it may be the case that the federal funds market experiences strains as well when repo markets tighten up. Specific factors affecting the funds market have similar coefficients to the normal period, suggesting that the market still had some semblance of normal functioning. One key difference is that while movements in the repo rate were 1-to-1 with the target rate, movements in the funds rate were not.

Finally, maintenance-period frequency calendar effects are less relevant in the early crisis period, particularly those at the end of the maintenance period. By contrast, the month-end, quarter-end, and year-end effects are magnified, with changes in funds and repo rates exceeding 25 and 45 basis points, respectively. Window-dressing pressures for balance sheet reporting periods may have intensified during the early crisis period.

11.4.3 "Extended period": December 2008 to June 2010

On December 16, 2008, amid weak economic conditions, elevated reserve balances and a very low effective federal funds rate, the FOMC lowered its target rate to a range of 0 to 25 basis points.[31] Perhaps, in part, due to these factors and the absence of changes in the target rate over the period, augmented Dickey–Fuller tests show that during this period, the repo rate and the funds rate fail to exhibit unit roots, and as a result, the two rates are no longer co-integrated. Consequently, we use the model in VAR form.

Table 11.3 displays the results. Turning first to the lagged effects of the two rates, the results suggest that both own lags and cross-lags affect the repo rate, but only own lags of the federal funds rate significantly influence movements in that rate. This offers further evidence of some, but not complete, decoupling of the two rates. The fact that the coefficients are positive is consistent with some persistence in changes in rates that was less evident in earlier periods; that is, rates were more likely to revert to long-run averages during calmer markets.[32]

---

[31] At the same time, the interest rate paid on reserve balances was set to 25 basis points. To date, the target rate has remained at that level, and reserve balances are still quite elevated.

[32] Granger causality tests indicate that the federal funds market is more likely to drive the repo market than vice versa.

Table 11.3 *Extended period: December 2008–June 2010*

	Included observations: 385							
	Constant NA				Slope NA			
	Repo rate				Federal funds rate			
Dependent variable	Coeff. NA	Std. Error NA	z-Stat.	Prob.	Coeff. NA	Std. Error NA	z-Stat.	Prob.
D(Repo rate(−1))	0.67	0.05	12.53	0.00	0.04	0.03	1.70	0.09
D(Repo rate(−2))	0.02	0.06	0.40	0.69	−0.04	0.03	−1.11	0.27
D(Repo rate(−3))	0.12	0.05	2.32	0.02	0.01	0.02	0.24	0.81
D(Federal funds rate(−1))	0.42	0.07	5.68	0.00	0.85	0.06	15.15	0.00
D(Federal funds rate(−2))	0.06	0.10	0.63	0.53	0.06	0.07	0.92	0.36
D(Federal funds rate(−3))	−0.29	0.08	−3.68	0.00	0.01	0.05	0.26	0.79
Treasury General Acct. bal.	0.00	0.00	−1.37	0.17	0.00	0.00	−0.81	0.42
LSAP	0.00	0.01	−0.28	0.78	−0.01	0.00	−1.93	0.05
Net Treasury sec. issuance	0.04	0.00	10.27	0.00	0.01	0.00	4.59	0.00
Net Treasury sec. issuance(−1)	0.01	0.00	2.61	0.01	0.00	0.00	0.93	0.36
D(Supplement. Fin. Acct. bal.)	0.01	0.01	0.66	0.51	0.01	0.01	1.77	0.08
D(Libor-OIS spread)	−0.19	0.07	−2.61	0.01	0.00	0.04	0.11	0.91
D(Capital ratios)	31.70	3.59	8.83	0.00	11.09	4.07	2.72	0.01
D(Treasury yield curve slope)	0.01	0.02	0.46	0.64	0.00	0.01	0.30	0.76
D(Repo market composition)	0.00	0.19	−0.02	0.99	−0.09	0.10	−0.88	0.38
D(Treasury sec. delivery fails)	0.06	0.03	2.44	0.01	0.04	0.01	3.15	0.00
D(Securities lending)	0.02	0.07	0.26	0.79	0.00	0.03	0.00	1.00
D(Federal funds volume)	−0.05	0.02	−2.76	0.01	−0.01	0.01	−0.97	0.33
D(Number of funds sellers)	0.02	0.01	1.11	0.27	0.02	0.01	2.28	0.02
D(Fed funds sold by GSEs)	0.00	0.01	0.07	0.95	0.00	0.01	0.27	0.79

Table 11.3 (cont.)

Dependent variable	Constant				Slope			
	Included observations: 385							
	NA				NA			
	Repo rate				Federal funds rate			
	Coeff.	Std. Error	z-Stat.	Prob.	Coeff.	Std. Error	z-Stat.	Prob.
	NA				NA			
MP day 1	0.50	0.59	0.86	0.39	1.08	0.29	3.71	0.00
MP day 2	−0.68	0.40	−1.68	0.09	−0.47	0.21	−2.27	0.02
MP day 5	−0.30	0.40	−0.74	0.46	0.14	0.21	0.66	0.51
MP day 6	−1.86	0.37	−5.01	0.00	−0.27	0.21	−1.29	0.20
MP day 7	−1.53	0.41	−3.74	0.00	−0.37	0.20	−1.91	0.06
MP day 8	−0.16	0.45	−0.35	0.73	−0.21	0.19	−1.13	0.26
MP day 9	−0.54	0.40	−1.34	0.18	−0.34	0.20	−1.75	0.08
MP day 12	−0.75	0.37	−2.00	0.05	−0.27	0.21	−1.25	0.21
MP day 13	−1.85	0.37	−5.05	0.00	−0.34	0.21	−1.67	0.10
MP day 14	−1.42	0.40	−3.57	0.00	−0.25	0.22	−1.16	0.25
15th of the month	2.34	0.45	5.25	0.00	1.22	0.28	4.30	0.00
End of the month	−0.26	0.49	−0.52	0.60	0.20	0.25	0.81	0.42
25th of the month	0.09	0.45	0.20	0.84	−0.09	0.21	−0.45	0.65
End of the quarter	−9.01	3.29	−2.74	0.01	−2.84	2.21	−1.29	0.20
End of the year	−0.45	3.55	−0.13	0.90	−1.61	4.40	−0.37	0.71
Adjusted R^2	0.85				0.81			
Durbin–Watson statistic	2.13				1.78			

Note. Covariance specification: Constant Conditional Correlation with ARCH, TARCH, and GARCH components; end of the quarter calendar dummy. Bollerslev–Wooldridge robust standard errors.

The next four lines show that, despite high balances and ample Treasury securities issuance, there was still a liquidity effect in both markets. For the repo market, most of the liquidity effect was through net Treasury securities issuance; a $100 billion increase in net Treasury securities issuance pushed up the repo rate by about 4 basis points on the issuance day. Interestingly, this effect is similar to that before the crisis. For the federal funds market, the liquidity effect is evident primarily through LSAPs, net Treasury issuance, and the SFA balance. Note that each of these has a different effect on reserve balances. LSAPs add balances, which would cause the funds rate to fall. By contrast, net Treasury issuance increases the level of the TGA and therefore drains balances, supporting the federal funds rate. Finally, the SFA works similarly to the TGA and increases in this account drain balances, which also pushes up the federal funds rate. Our results suggest an extremely small liquidity effect of about 1 basis point per $100 billion in additional reserves, or 30 times smaller than that in the pre-crisis period, no matter the instrument used in identification. This finding implies a highly nonlinear demand for reserve balances with the essential flat slope in the neighborhood of high reserve balances.

Turning to the risk controls, although movements in the Libor-OIS spread had little effect on the funds market, they did have an effect on the repo market: for a 10 basis point change in this spread, the repo rate falls by about 2 basis points. Conversely, increases in capital ratios were associated with increases in the repo rate, but not correlated with the federal funds rate. Positive increases in capital ratios are associated with higher federal funds and repo rates. This is consistent with arbitrage in these markets, that is, amid higher capital ratios, banks are able to expand balance sheets and take advantage of the rate differential between federal funds and the interest on excess reserves rate. Unlike earlier periods, the slope of the yield curve exhibits little correlation with movements in either of these rates. Because policy was likely seen as being on hold for "an extended period", it is possible that other factors that might cause movements in this slope would not be associated with rate movements in very short-term funding markets.

For the specific market controls, repo collateral delivery fails were associated with larger changes in the federal funds and repo rates. During periods of high repo demand, fails increase and rates fall considerably, pushing these changes higher. Somewhat counterintuitively, as activity in the funds market increased, as indicated by the change in federal funds market volume, rates in both markets fell. However, the coefficients are fairly small and thus these changes were likely not economically meaningful during this period. Finally, increases in the number of funds sellers – an indicator of supply – is associated with higher federal funds rates, but changes in the quantity of funds sold by the GSEs was not significantly correlated with changes in these rates.

11.5   Conclusion

Our findings suggest that pass-through from the federal funds rate to the repo deteriorated somewhat since the financial crisis began, likely due to limits to arbitrage and idiosyncratic market factors. In particular, during the early part of the crisis, the pricing of federal funds relative to repurchase agreements indicated a marked jump in perceived credit risk. Moreover, the liquidity effect in the federal funds market weakened with the increase in reserve balances over the crisis, implying a highly non-linear demand curve for federal funds. In contrast, the liquidity effects in the Treasury GC repo market, on balance, has remained unchanged despite the extraordinarily large volume of Treasury securities issuance.

Consequently, emerging from the crisis, the two money market interest rates appear to co-move not as tightly as they did before the crisis, indicating that the effectiveness of the cross-sectional monetary policy transmission might be lower. However, the presence of the liquidity effects in both the federal funds and repo markets implies that hypothetical liquidity draining by the Federal Reserve, for example via large-scale reverse repos, may boost somewhat the two money market rates even in absence of an increase in the target federal funds rate or the rate paid on reserves. Because the demand curve for federal funds appears to be quite flat in the neighborhood of high reserve balances, upward pressure on the federal funds rate of initial liquidity draining is going to be very small, while the impact of subsequent liquidity draining should be more notable. In turn, as our evidence implies, both the increase of available collateral and the higher federal funds rate should boost the repo rate.

Policymakers and market participants alike care about the monetary policy transmission across both interest rates for instruments of the same maturity and that of different maturities. Our results shed some light on the former, for the shortest of the maturities. As for the latter, in the zero lower bound environment with significant financial market segmentation, the traditional approach to the monetary policy implementation – the reliance on the short-term interest rates to transmit the policy stance along the yield curve to the longer-term interest rates – has clearly reached its limits.[33] These limits, in fact, justify the Federal

---

[33] There is some evidence that the expectations hypothesis holds for the Treasury GC repo rates (for loans of maturities up to 90 days) but not for the federal funds rates in the post-crisis period. Hence, for the federal funds rate, the transmission even over the short tenors appears to be questionable. For details see Klee and Stebunovs (2012).

Reserve's unconventional policy measures examined in another chapter of this book.

References

Bartolini, L., Hilton S., Sundaresan S. and Tonetti, C. (2011). Collateral values by asset class: evidence from primary securities dealers, *Review of Financial Studies*, **24**(1), 248–278.

Bollerslev, T. (1990). Modeling the coherence in short-run nominal exchange rates: a multivariate generalized ARCH model, *Review of Economics and Statistics*, **72**(3), 498–505.

Brunnermeier, M. and Pedersen, L. (2009). Market liquidity and funding liquidity, *Review of Financial Studies*, **22**(6), 2201–2238.

Carpenter, S. and Demiralp, S. (2006). The liquidity, effect in the federal funds market: evidence from daily open market operations, *Journal of Money Credit, and Banking*, **38**(4), 900–920.

Coffey, N., Hrung, W. and Sarkar A. (2009). Capital constraints, counterparty risk, and deviation from covered interest rate parity, Federal Reserve Bank of New York Staff Report, No. 393, September.

Collin-Dufresne, P., Goldstein R. and Martin, J. S. (2001). The determinants of credit spread changes, *Journal of Finance*, **56**(6), 2177–2207.

Duffie, D. (1996). Special repo rates, *Journal of Finance*, **51**(2), 493–526.

Engle, R. and Granger, C. (1987). Cointegration and error-correction model: representation, estimation, and testing, *Econometrica*, **55**(2), 251–276.

Federal Reserve Bank of New York (2009). Domestic open market operations during 2008, January.

Federal Reserve Bank of New York (2010). Tri-party repo infrastructure reform, May 17.

Fisher, M. (2002). Special repo rates: an introduction, *Economic Review*, Federal Reserve Bank of Atlanta, Second Quarter.

Fleming, M., Hrung, W. and Keane, F. (2010). Repo market effects of the term securities lending facility, Federal Reserve Bank of New York Staff Report, No. 426.

Furfine, C. (1999). The microstructure of the federal funds market, *Financial Markets, Institutions, and Instruments*, **8**(5), 24–44.

Gorton, G. (2010). Questions and answers about the financial crisis, U.S. Financial Crisis Inquiry Commission, February 20.

Griffiths, M. and Winters, D. (1997). The effect of Federal Reserve accounting rules on the equilibrium level of overnight repo rates, *Journal of Business Finance and Accounting*, **24**(6), 815–832.

Hamilton, J. (1996). The daily market for federal funds, *Journal of Political Economy*, **104**(1), 26–56.

Hamilton, J. (1997). Measuring the liquidity effect, *American Economic Review*, **87**(1), 80–97.

Happ, S. (1986). The behavior of rates on federal funds and repurchase agreements, *The American Economist*, **30**(2), 22–32.

Judson, R. A. and Klee, E. (2010). Whither the liquidity effect? The impact of Federal Reserve open market operations in recent years, *Journal of Macroeconomics*, **32**(3), 713–731.

Johansen, S. (1995). Identifying restrictions of linear equations with applications to simultaneous equations and cointegration, *Journal of Econometrics*, **69**(1), 111–132.

Klee, E. and Stebunovs, V. (2012). Target practice: implementing the Federal Reserve's policy stance in a post-crisis environment, working paper, September.

12 Taylor rule uncertainty: believe it or not

Andrea Buraschi, Andrea Carnelli and Paul Whelan

"Not to be absolutely certain is, I think, one of the essential things in
rationality."

(Bertrand Russell in *Am I An Atheist Or An Agnostic?*)

12.1 Introduction

This chapter studies agents' perception of US monetary policy from
1986 to 2011 by fitting expected Taylor rules to a unique dataset
of macroeconomic forecasts. The use of subjective forecasts allows us
to investigate the extent to which agents believe the Fed are following a given policy function, and to quantify the uncertainty associated
with these beliefs. This is important since it allows us to study questions relating to the conduct of Central Bank policy. For example, in
recent years Chairman Bernanke has vigorously supported the idea that
announcements, if credible, can have the same effect as effective policy actions. This requires people to believe in the monetary rule that is
used to anchor expectations. By estimating subjective expected Taylor
rules, we provide a novel empirical identification scheme to address such
questions.

Since at least the tenure of Chairman Volcker, it has generally been
understood that US monetary policy is empirically well described by
a Taylor (1993) rule (see, among others, Levin, Wieland, and Williams
(2003)). Taylor rules are recipes that call for the adjustment of the policy
instrument (the federal funds rate in the case of the US) in response to
rising inflation and/or temporary deviations of output from its potential
level (see Clarida, Gali, and Gertler (1999)). The Fed's dual mandate of simultaneous price stability and output targeting is quite unique
with respect to other Central Banks. The European Central Bank, for
instance, has price stability as a primary objective, and full employment

The views expressed in this chapter are the authors' and do not necessarily represent the
views of The University of Chicago Booth School of Business or Imperial College London.

as a secondary objective. While a dual mandate may provide flexibility, it opens the door to additional policy uncertainty that may have important first-order effects on financial markets and economic activity (see, for instance, Bloom (2007), Pastor and Veronesi (2011), David and Veronesi (2011)). In general, uncertainty about the future path of policy can arise from three sources as agents may disagree on: (i) the expected path of arguments of the rule (the state variables); (ii) the parameters of the rule; or (iii) the functional form of the rule. We construct proxies for each source of disagreement by fitting constrained rules to the cross-section of agents' expectations, and unconstrained rules to the time-series of agents' expectations in order to quantify the relative importance of each source.

Cochrane (2011) shows that Taylor rule regressions suffer from an identification problem: when regressing federal funds rates on inflation, the econometrician recovers the autocorrelation coefficient of the monetary policy disturbance term, instead of the Central Bank's response coefficient to inflation. The intuition is that, in a rational expectations equilibrium, the dynamics of equilibrium inflation are the same as the monetary shocks. Since equilibrium interest rates depend on expected inflation, the same parameter that describes the dynamics of the monetary shocks also pins down how current interest rates depend on current inflation. More generally, *in*-equilibrium realized inflation should be equal to its target value, so that a time-series regression lacks the necessary variation of its right-hand-side variables. Thus, when agents have rational expectations, identifying Taylor rule loadings from time-series data presents a major econometric challenge. In this chapter, we remain agnostic about whether the representative agent expectations are rational and work directly with individual subjective probability measures. Whether aggregation and allocation of resources endows the representative agent with rational expectations is not of our direct concern. We use cross-sectional information from survey data to help identify the parameters of the expected policy rule under the assumption that agents may disagree on the future realization of the state variables but do not disagree on the policy parameters. This allows us to sidestep the identification issues implied by relying on the physical measure.

The dataset we exploit consists of monthly macroeconomic forecasts going out to five quarters from a set of professional economists from 1986 to 2011. First, we constrain the Taylor rule parameters to be constant both over time and across agents, and run time-series regressions on consensus forecasts. This specification allows us to identify the unconditional response coefficients perceived by the "consensus" agent without resorting to proxy expectations with model-dependent projections commonly deployed in the literature. Second, we relax the constraint that coefficients are constant over time and estimate time-varying responses by running dynamic cross-sectional regressions. The assumption behind these regressions is that agents must agree on the Taylor rule coefficients (the parameters of the model), but can disagree on its arguments. The cross-sectional regressions allow us to gauge the time-variation in the private sector's perception about the conduct of monetary policy, and to quantify the extent to which agents expect deviations from a Taylor rule with fixed parameters. Finally, we relax both constraints (time- and agent-invariance) and estimate time- and agent-specific Taylor rules by exploiting the multi-horizon dimension of the data. This latter specification is important for at least two reasons. First, by looking at the values of the individual estimates we can measure the degree of dispersion regarding the *parameters* of the model since the arguments (expectations on the state variables) for each individual are now observable. Second, these estimates allow us to conduct a non-parametric analysis of the state dependence of the point estimates. This allows us to study directly the extent to which the dual mandate introduces (or not) an element of uncertainty which varies across states of the world (i.e. low economic growth; high inflation).

Our empirical analysis highlights a number of novel results. First, when we compare the estimated coefficients obtained using survey consensus expectations to the estimates obtained from instrumental variable techniques (we follow the empirical approach by Clarida, Gali, and Gertler, 2000), we find substantial differences. This may be due either to the identification issue discussed by Cochrane (2011), or simply that agents expect the Central Bank to deviate from the announced policy rule. We think it is due to both. For instance, using survey data we find coefficients of 1.76 and 0.26 (for inflation and output gap, respectively), as opposed to 5.36 and −0.32, when we apply the IV-GMM technique used by Clarida, Gali, and Gertler (2000) to the 1986:1–2011:11 period using projections of empirical realizations of state variables. The last set of parameters implies that the policy rule is extremely sensitive to inflation and, indeed, we do not find the parameters robust to the use of different sets of instrumental variables. This hints at an identification problem.

Second, we investigate time dependence in the policy parameters by estimating dynamic cross-sectional regressions with time-varying loadings, and where dispersion in the residual is taken as a proxy for model uncertainty. We find considerable time-variation in the policy parameters implied by agents' expectations on future Fed fund rates, inflation, and the output gap. This is interesting since it suggests that agents have changed their expectations about the stance of the Central Bank considerably over time. However, we reject the hypothesis that agents expect the Fed to act more aggressively against inflation or output deviations during the latest Greenspan–Bernanke period than during the first part of the Greenspan tenure. Moreover, we find that the policy rule is nonlinear and state-dependent, suggesting that the Central Bank is expected to follow a relatively more aggressive contractionary policy when inflation shocks are excessively high (top quintile) and a relatively more accommodative policy when output gap is very low or negative (bottom quintile).

Third, we study the heterogeneity in agents' perception about the policy parameters by estimating time-series regressions at the individual level that quantify the degree of dispersion about the parameters of the Taylor rule. We find that the cross-sectional distribution is both large and time-varying. Moreover, estimating Taylor rules at the individual level allows us to proxy for the degree of uncertainty (ambiguity) about the parameters of the Taylor rule, which we find covaries strongly with the level of disagreement about these loadings. While these two concepts are theoretically different, the results suggest that disagreement can indeed be used as a reasonable empirical proxy for parameter uncertainty, at least in the specific context that we study.

Finally, taking both cross-sectional and time-series approaches together, we obtain three measures of policy uncertainty: (i) disagreement about the model; (ii) disagreement about the parameters of the model; and (iii) disagreement about the state variables of the model. All measures point toward a significant amount of time-variation in the extent to which agents believe that the Central Bank follows a Taylor rule. A revealing example is the period 2010–2011, when we find considerable disagreement about the stance on inflation. Similar periods also include 1989–1990, 1995–1996, and 2002–2004. Linking this decomposition to asset pricing, we show that both disagreement about the rule and disagreement about its arguments (inflation) are economically important drivers of Treasury variance risk with $\overline{R}^2$s of 29% and statistical significance at the 1% level.

12.1.1 Background and related literature

This chapter contributes to the vast literature on Taylor rules and monetary policy. A long-standing literature (see for instance Kydland and Prescott (1977), Barro and Gordon (1983)) argues that policies based on rules perform better than discretionary policies. Taylor (1993) studies monetary policy and concludes that a federal funds rule based on deviations of output and inflation from their targets captures reasonably well some stylized features of the data. Svensson (1997) argues that a Taylor rule can be interpreted as the optimal solution to the problem of a Central Bank whose loss function is quadratic in the deviations of output and inflation from their long-run targets. A more recent literature discusses the implications of Taylor rules in terms of the determinacy and stability of the implied equilibrium in the context of a New Keynesian economic framework (see Clarida, Gali, and Gertler (1999) for a thorough survey of the literature). King (2000) and Woodford (2003) discuss how the dynamic properties of equilibrium depend on the parameter values of the policy rule.

Since Taylor (1993), the literature has devoted considerable effort to estimating Taylor parameters and investigating their ability to describe the data. While some authors have focused on extending the Taylor rule by including lagged values of macro variables (see, for instance, Christiano, Eichenbaum, and Evans (1994, 1996), Clarida, Gali, and Gertler (1998)), others have proposed forward-looking Taylor rules based on forecasts of future output gap and inflation (see, for instance, Clarida and Gertler (1997) and Clarida, Gali, and Gertler (2000)). Forward-looking Taylor rules are appealing: they are consistent with a neo-classical forward-looking agent which induces the Central Bank to respond to the output and price level that are expected to prevail in the future. However, since expectations are not directly observable and, in addition, are endogenous to monetary shocks, the empirical implementation of forward-looking Taylor rules typically calls for the use of a set of instruments; for instance, the instrument set in Clarida, Gali, and Gertler (2000) includes: lagged federal funds rate, inflation, output gap, commodity price inflation, M2 growth, and term spread. The values of the estimated parameters have important implications with regards to the nature of the equilibria. It is often argued, for instance, that a necessary condition to obtain a locally unique equilibrium in New Keynesian models is that β, the Taylor sensitivity of the deviation of inflation to its target, is larger than 1. Woodford (2003) argues that this may be enough to allow expectations to coordinate upon that equilibrium rather than on one of the others. Studying expectations directly allows us to provide a set of estimates for these parameters which is potentially less model-sensitive.

Our work is also related to the literature on policy uncertainty. In terms of monetary policy, uncertainty can come in three forms: uncertainty about the state variables, uncertainty about the parameters of the policy rule, and uncertainty about whether a fixed rate-targeting rule can explain policy rule at all. Uncertainty has important policy implications: in the words of Greenspan (2004) "uncertainty is not just a pervasive feature of the monetary policy landscape; it is the defining characteristic of that landscape." Rudebusch (2001) shows that, when the Central Bank is uncertain about the values of the parameters of its reference macroeconomic model, the optimal policy rules call for a less vigorous response to innovations in the state variables. For a complete survey of this strand of literature, we refer the interested reader to Clarida, Gali, and Gertler (1999). More recently, some authors have studied the impact that policy uncertainty has on the real economy and financial markets: Baker, Bloom, and Davis (2011) construct an index of political uncertainty, while Pastor and Veronesi (2011, 2012) discuss the implications for asset prices. Our work differs from this strand of literature in one important respect: we address the issue of uncertainty from the perspective of the private sector. Unlike Clarida, Gali, and Gertler (1999), who analyze the issue of optimal policy when the Central Bank does not know with certainty the model/parameters of the macroeconomic model that drives the economy, we focus on the uncertainty faced by agents. The question we seek to address is: given that the private sector does not observe the rule followed by the Central Bank, what kind of rule do they expect the Central Bank to be following? Our unique dataset of forecasts allows us to address this question without making any assumption about the data generating process that the agents believe in.

12.2   Data

This section describes the dataset. All data span the period 1986:1– 2011:12 and are available at monthly frequency.

12.2.1 Survey data

We depart from the canonical literature on Taylor rules and propose new empirical measures of monetary policy uncertainty constructed directly from professional market participants' expectations regarding future Fed funds rates and macro-aggregates. The BlueChip Financial Forecasts Indicators (BCFF) is a monthly publication providing extensive panel data on expectations by agents who are working at institutions active in financial markets. Unfortunately, digital copies of BCFF are only currently available since 2001. We obtained, however, the complete BCFF paper archive (starting in 1986) directly from Wolters Kluwer and proceeded to enter the data manually. The digitization process required inputting around 750,000 entries of named forecasts plus quality control checking and was completed in a joint venture with the Federal Reserve Board. The resulting dataset represents an extensive and unique dataset to investigate the role of formation of expectations in monetary policy applications. Each month, BlueChip carry out surveys of professional economists from leading financial institutions and service companies regarding all maturities of the yield curve and economic fundamentals and are asked to give point forecasts at quarterly horizons out to five quarters ahead (six from January 1997). While exact timings of the surveys are not published, the survey is usually conducted between the 25th and 27th of the month and mailed to subscribers within the first five days of the subsequent month. The forecasts used here are real GDP (real GNP until February 1992), Consumer Price Inflation (CPI), and the federal funds rate (FF) at quarterly horizons out to $5Q$.[1]

12.2.2 Macro series

In what follows we compute implied consensus and subjective (at the individual level) measures of the output gap for which we use data on real GDP and the GDP price index from the Bureau of Economic Analysis (BEA). Additionally, we take consumer price index data from the Bureau of Labor Statistics (BLS).

12.3   Identification of Taylor rules with forecast data

We are interested to study agents' perceptions of how the Fed implements the Taylor rule. In this section, we review the theoretical framework and highlight the issue of identification. Let π_t denote the change in the price level from quarter $t-1$ to quarter t, annualized and in percentage points. Similarly, let x_t denote the output gap in quarter t, in percentage points. As standard in the literature, the output gap is defined as $x_t = \left(\frac{Y_t}{Y_t^*} - 1\right) \cdot 100$, where Y_t and Y_t^* denote actual and potential output at time t, respectively. Finally, let f_t denote the time t federal funds rate. According to the classic Taylor rule, current federal funds rates should be adjusted in reaction to changes in output gap and to deviations of the inflation rate from its target π^*:

$$f_t^* = f^* + \beta\left(\pi_t - \pi^*\right) + \gamma x_t. \tag{12.1}$$

---

[1] For instance, the $2Q$-ahead GDP forecast in April 2000 is the (annualized) expected GDP growth between end of June 2000 (the end of current quarter) and the end of September 2000 (the end of the next quarter).

This rule has a simple interpretation. In the absence of disturbances to the economy, the federal funds rate is constant and equal to f^*. If, on the other hand, either output deviates from its potential level, or inflation is not in line with its target, the Central Bank intervenes to stabilize the economy: the parameters β and γ capture the sensitivity to inflation and output stabilization, respectively. In practice, it has been observed that the Central Bank behaves less responsively to the state of the economy than implied by the benchmark Taylor rule; this is consistent with the Central Bank having preferences over the degree of variability of federal funds rates; also, the Central Bank might be interested to macro aggregates that are not realizing at time t. In order to accommodate "policy inertia" and backward-/forward-looking policies, the benchmark rule can be extended to include lagged federal funds and lags/leads in its arguments:

$$f_t = \rho(L)f_{t-1} + (1 - \rho)f_t^*$$
$$= \rho(L)f_{t-1} + (1 - \rho)\left(f^* + \beta\left(\pi_{t+j} - \pi^*\right) + \gamma x_{t+k}\right), \quad (12.2)$$

where $\rho(L) = \rho_1 + \rho_2 L + \cdots + \rho_n L^{n-1}$ and $\rho = \rho(1)$ capture the degree of interest rate smoothing.

This policy rule may, at first sight, appear simple to estimate. However, there is very little consensus in the literature about the magnitudes of the Taylor rule response coefficients. Levin, Wieland, and Williams (2003), for instance, observe that the literature proposes inflation loadings that range from 0.27 to 34.85, and output loadings that vary from 0 to 1. Different values of these coefficients have different equilibrium implications. Reference models in this literature require $\beta > 1$ and $\gamma \geq 0$ in order for a unique locally bounded equilibrium to exist. A more careful study of the Taylor equation suggests that these values are sensitive to a number of econometric issues. For instance, studies typically construct expectations using econometric methods based on realizations under the econometrician's measure. These procedures are sensitive to biases originating from model mis-specification, endogeneity, structural breaks, and omitted variables. Consensus forecasts, on the other hand, reflect the expectation prevailing on the market and thus allow us to dispense with the need of a VAR-based approach to modeling expectations. Unlike VAR-based approaches, the use of survey data does not require making assumptions about agents' information set and about the stability of the forecasting technology. For instance, Gavin and Mandal (2001) find that survey data represents a better source of Fed expectations so that replacing statistical with survey forecasts represents a solution to this particular problem.

At a deeper level, Cochrane (2011) highlights an important identification challenge that the econometrician faces in estimating the Taylor rule. To illustrate the argument consider, for the sake of simplicity, a Taylor rule that only responds to inflation, $f_t = f^* + \beta \pi_t + w_t$, where w_t is a monetary policy shock with correlation ρ_w. In equilibrium, the interest rate must also satisfy the representative agent's FOC, $f_t = f^* + E_t [\pi_{t+1}]$ (the Euler or, in this context, Fisher equation), yielding a process for equilibrium inflation expectations given by $E_t [\pi_{t+1}] = \beta \pi_t + w_t$. The solution to this process, provided that $|\beta| > 1$, is $\pi_t = -\frac{w_t}{\beta - \rho_w}$, i.e. equilibrium inflation is perfectly correlated with the monetary policy shock and thus it inherits its process, $E_t [\pi_{t+1}] = \rho_w \pi_t$. Plugging this latter identity into the Euler (Fisher) equation clearly shows that regressions of federal funds rates on inflation recover the autocorrelation of the monetary policy shock ρ_w rather than the Taylor response coefficient β. The point made by Cochrane (2011) is not specific to the simple macroeconomic model he adopts. In rational expectation models, the specification of the expectation process needs to be consistent with the postulated model itself and equilibrium attains in every point of time: since π_t never deviates from its equilibrium, one cannot estimate reactions of federal funds rates to deviations of inflation from target. This exposes a study of Taylor rules to a joint hypothesis problem and the estimated policy parameters are sensitive to the restrictions imposed to model the formation of expectations. This is a problem for empirical work and may explain the broad range of β and γ coefficients obtained by different studies.

Consensus forecasts allow us to dispense with the need to specify a model for the expectations. To see this point, consider a time-interval $[t, t + h]$ during which the response coefficients of the Taylor rule can be assumed to be fixed; by re-writing Equation (12.2) for time $t + h$, and taking expectations of both sides of the equation conditioning on the time t beliefs of agent i, we obtain

$$E_t^i [f_{t+h}] = \rho(L)E_t^i [f_{t+h-1}]$$

$$+ (1 - \rho)\left(f^* + \beta \left(E_t^i [\pi_{t+h+j}] - \pi^*\right) + \gamma E_t^i [x_{t+h+k}]\right). \quad (12.3)$$

Since we work directly with expectations obtained from survey data, both the left- and right-hand-side variables of the regression are observable. If one believes these expectations are formed conditional on a New-Keynesian model one still cannot say much about the conduct of actual monetary policy. We sidestep this issue since we ask to what extent do agents believe in the existence of a Taylor rule, and not how well a Taylor rule fits realizations of the data.

12.4 Time-invariant consensus Taylor rules

We proceed to ask our first question: for which policy parameters are agents' expectations consistent with a time- and state-invariant New-Keynesian Taylor rule? This question is important since different values have substantially different implications on the dynamic and economic properties of the equilibrium. In this exercise, we constrain the Taylor response coefficients to be constant over time and consider the expectations of the consensus agent. When expectations are directly observable using survey data, a simple estimation strategy for Equation (12.3) is to fix the horizons h, j, k, the number of lags for the lag polynomial $\rho(L)$, and estimate the parameters in a time-series regression of federal funds consensus forecasts on inflation and output gap consensus forecasts:

$$E_t^c\left[f_{t+h}\right] = a + r(L)E_t^c\left[f_{t+h-1}\right] + bE_t^c\left[\pi_{t+h} - \pi^*\right] + cE_t^c\left[x_{t+h}\right] + e_{t+h}^c,$$
(12.4)

where E^c denotes the expectation based on the consensus beliefs of the private sector. In this context, the interpretation of e_{t+h} is of a mean-zero observation error, not of a monetary shock. This is important since in order to identify the parameters the econometrician needs these shocks to be orthogonal to the right-hand-side variables. We can estimate the relationship with OLS. The structural parameters can be recovered from the reduced-form estimates as follows:

$$\beta = \frac{b}{1 - r(1)}, \quad \gamma = \frac{c}{1 - r(1)}.$$
(12.5)

Estimation of (12.4) requires empirical proxies for the forecasts. Our empirical measure for inflation expectations is the cross-sectional median of all time t forecasts for the inflation rate at horizon h; we fix the equilibrium rate of inflation π^* at 2%, as standard in the literature. Unfortunately, we only have forecasts about future GDP growth, but not on future output gaps. We construct output gaps as follows. We fit a Hodrick–Prescott filter (with a smoothing parameter of 14,400) to log output $y_t = \log(Y_t)$ and estimate the mean growth rate of the economy g^* as the average log difference of output. We construct potential output Y_t^* by taking the trend component of the filtered series, and construct conditional estimates of future potential output as $E_t[Y_{t+h}^*] = Y_t^* \exp\left(g_t^* \cdot h \cdot 3\right)$. Next, we obtain estimates of actual output using the

consensus growth rates, $E_t[Y_{t+h}] = Y_t \cdot \left(1 + \frac{E_t[g_{t+1}]}{400}\right) \cdot \left(1 + \frac{E_t[g_{t+2}]}{400}\right) \cdots$
$(1 + \frac{E_t[g_{t+h}]}{400})$. Finally, we construct the projected output gap for horizon
h as $E_t[x_{t+h}] = \left(\frac{E_t[Y_{t+h}]}{E_t[Y_{t+h}^*]} - 1\right) \cdot 100.$[2]

We begin by replicating the results in Clarida, Gali, and Gertler (2000) using their methodology applied to an updated sample up to December 2011 (Greenspan–Bernanke period). In this first regression both the left- and right-hand-side variables are the actual realizations of the economic variables of the Taylor rule.[3] Let $h_t = e_t \otimes Z_t$, with Z_t being a set of instruments available at time t, with

$$e_{a,t+h} = f_t - \left(a + r(L)f_t + b(E_t^s[\pi_{t+h}] - \pi^*) + cE_t^s[x_{t+h}]\right). \quad (12.6)$$

where expectations, E_t^s, are computed under the statistical measure available to the econometrician. The structural parameters are estimated by minimizing the standard GMM criterion function $\mathcal{J}_T = \frac{1}{T}h_t' W^{-1}h_t$. Since the explanatory variables are potentially endogenous, expectations of future inflation and output react to monetary shocks. In an attempt to solve this problem, Clarida, Gali, and Gertler (2000) consider a set of instrumental variables Z_t, defined as four lags of the federal funds rate, inflation, the output gap, a commodity price index, M2 money growth, and the 10 year – 3 month term spread. The results are summarized in Table 12.1, row (a). We assume the same lag structure as Clarida, Gali, and Gertler (2000), i.e., $\rho(L) = \rho_1 + \rho_2 L$, with $h = 1$ quarter. This specification mirrors the approach in Clarida, Gali, and Gertler (2000), which we use as a benchmark in all future specifications which follow. Estimates are reported in Table 12.1.

The results show that the slope coefficient on inflation is 5.36, while the slope for the output gap is negative and equal to -0.32. The results suggests that the Fed is extremely aggressive in responding to inflation shocks. If expected inflation increases by 100 basis points, the Fed reacts by increasing interest rates by 536 basis points. On the other hand, the parameters suggest that the Fed has an extremely accommodating stance on output. We find that extending the sample period leads to more extreme results than those reported by Clarida, Gali, and Gertler (2000).

---

[2] We examine the robustness of our results along two dimensions. First, we construct output gaps in real time, by fitting the Hodrick–Prescott filter and estimating mean growth rates recursively over a look-backwards rolling window. Second, we identify the trend component recursively by estimating a (rolling) quadratic function of time. The results are marginally affected.

[3] Expectations of inflation and the output gap, which enter as right-hand variables, are computed as linear projections of date t realized aggregates.

Table 12.1 *Consensus Taylor rule regressions*

	$\pi^\star$	β	γ	ρ	$\mathcal{J}_T(p)$
(a)	2.40	5.36	−0.32	0.96	14.06
	(0.32)	(0.14)	(0.02)	(0.11)	0.78
(b1)	2.01	1.68	1.49	0.89	14.62
	(0.21)	(0.08)	(0.06)	(0.14)	0.75
(b2)	1.81	1.36	1.59	0.90	14.46
	(0.17)	(0.05)	(0.05)	(0.15)	0.76
(c)	1.85	1.76	0.26	0.95	
	(0.07)	(0.10)	(0.09)	(0.13)	

Let $h_t = e_t \otimes Z_t$, with Z_t being a set of instruments available at time t. The structural
parameters are estimated by minimizing the GMM criterion function $\mathcal{J}_T = \frac{1}{T} h_t' W^{-1} h_t$.
Row (a) miminizes the moment conditions implied by

$$e_{a,t} = f_t - \left(a + r(L)f_t + b(E_t^{\mathrm{s}}[\pi_{t+h}] - \pi^*) + cE_t^{\mathrm{s}}[x_{t+h}] \right)$$

expectations, E_t^{s}, are computed from a 1st order VAR of inflation and the output gap, and
Z_t contain four lags of the federal funds rate, inflation, the output gap, a commodity price
index, M2 money growth, and the 10 year – 3 month term spread. Rows (b1) & (b2)
miminize the moment conditions implied by

$$e_{b,t} = f_t - \left(a + r(L)f_t + b(E_t^{\mathrm{c}}[\pi_{t+h}] - \pi^*) + cE_t^{\mathrm{c}}[x_{t+h}] \right),$$

with expectations of inflation forecast from survey data. Panel (b1) uses an instrument
vector Z_t containing four lags of the federal funds rate, inflation, the output gap, a
commodity price index, M2 money growth, and the 10 year – 3 month term spread.
Panel (b2) uses an instrument vector Z_t containing four lags of expectations (from
surveys) about the federal funds rate, inflation, and the output gap. Row (c) estimates

$$e_{c,t+4} = E_t^{\mathrm{c}}[f_{t+4}] - \left(a + r(L)E_t^{\mathrm{c}}[f_{t+4}] + b(E_t^{\mathrm{c}}[\pi_{t+5}] - \pi^*) + cE_t^{\mathrm{c}}[x_{t+5}] \right)$$

via OLS. Standard errors are reported in brackets. Hansen $\mathcal{J}_T$ tests and p-values are
reported in the final column. Structural parameters are recovered from their
reduced-form estimates, for example, $\beta = b/1 - r(1)$ and $\gamma = c/1 - r(1)$. All data spans:
1986:1–2011:12.

Using data spanning the Volcker–Greenspan period 1979:3–1996:4, the
authors report parameters equal to 2.15 and 0.93, respectively. Indeed,
while we follow their methodology, we find that the results are sensitive to
the set of instruments used. For instance, including two lags (12 moment
conditions) of Z_t instead of four (24 moment conditions) reduces the
p-value of the $\mathcal{J}_T$ test from 0.78 to 0.11.

Next, we consider a specification in which forecasts based on linear
projections of realized aggregates are replaced directly with consensus
expectations from surveys. This approach has the potential to partially
address the issue of sensitivity to different statistical specifications for

the VAR and choice of the instrumental variables. We repeat the same IV-GMM estimation and define

$$e_{b,t} = f_t - \left(a + r(L)f_t + b(E_t^c[\pi_{t+h}] - \pi^*) + cE_t^c[x_{t+h}] \right), \qquad (12.7)$$

again with $\rho(L) = \rho_1 + \rho_2 L$ and $h = 1$ quarter. In panels (b1) and (b2) expectations of inflation and the output gap are this time taken from survey data. Row (b1) estimates the parameters of the model using an instrument vector Z_t containing four lags of the federal funds rate, inflation, the output gap, a commodity price index, M2 money growth, and the 10 year − 3 month term spread. Row (b2) uses an instrument vector Z_t containing four lags of expectations (from survey data) about the federal funds rate, inflation, and the output gap. Both panels (b1) and (b2) miminize the moment conditions implied by (12.6).

The results, summarized in Table 12.1, show the slope coefficient on inflation is 1.68, while the slope for the output gap is now positive and equal to 1.49. The parameter values appear somewhat more realistic. The New-Keynesian literature requires that $\alpha \geq 0$ and $\beta > 1$ for the existence of a locally bounded equilibrium. These results are consistent with this restriction.

Last, we consider our preferred specification of choice, which include consensus expectation on both the left- and right-hand side of the regression:

$$e_{c,t+4} = E_t^c[f_{t+4}] - \left(a + r(L)E_t^c[f_{t+4}] + b(E_t^c[\pi_{t+5}] - \pi^*) + cE_t^c[x_{t+5}] \right).$$

In words, we consider a set of orthogonality conditions expressed in terms of $4Q$ ahead forecasts of the federal funds rate on $2Q$ and $3Q$ ahead forecasts of the federal funds rate, and $5Q$ ahead forecasts of the inflation rate and the output gap. This specification is not exposed to the Cochrane (2011) critique of lack of identification of the policy parameters and may offer some additional insights on the issue (albeit under the subjective probability measure). Row (d) summarizes the estimated structural parameters. Several important findings emerge. We find that the slope coefficient to inflation and output gap are 1.76 and 0.26, respectively. Both the loadings on inflation and the output gap are significant at any standard level. Importantly, the economic significance is in line with the "Taylor principle": the loading on the output gap is greater than zero, while the response to inflation is strictly greater than one. In general, we always find that the point estimate for $\rho = \rho_1 + \rho_2$ hints at a strong perception of policy inertia. Moreover, over the sample considered, the private sector has perceived monetary policy to be more focused on price, rather than output, stabilization.

A chi-square test of the restriction does not reject the null hypothesis that agents believe that a Taylor rule can describe monetary policy in the near future. However, this may be due to lack of power of the test. To examine this question, we now turn to relaxing the assumption that the parameters of the Taylor rule (under the subjective measure) are time and state independent. This will be the topic of the following sections.

12.5   Cross-sectional Taylor rules

Consensus regressions with time-invariant parameters allow us to identify the representative agent's unconditional perception of how the Federal Reserve conducted monetary policy between 1986 and 2011. It is, however, reasonable to assume that the stance of the Fed has changed greatly over time. For instance, anecdotal evidence points to the Fed being particularly concerned about a burst in inflation in the expansionary cycle up to the start of the 2008 crisis; these concerns were then sacrificed in favor of a stimulative regime aimed at stabilizing output after the collapse of Lehman Brothers. Many authors have tackled the issue of time-varying Taylor rule response coefficients (see, for instance, Clarida, Sarno, Taylor, and Valente (2006), Kim and Nelson (2006), and Sims and Zha (2006)). We estimate time-varying parameters by exploiting the panel structure of our dataset. In particular, we consider rolling windows of 6 months $\tau = t - 5, \ldots, t$ and run cross-sectional regressions:

$$E_\tau^i [f_{\tau+h}] = a_\tau + r_\tau(L) E_\tau^i [f_{\tau+h-1}] + b_\tau E_\tau^i \left[\pi_{\tau+h+j} - \pi^* \right]$$
$$+ c_\tau E_\tau^i [x_{\tau+h+k}] + e_{\tau+h}^i,$$

for all $i = 1, \ldots, N$, where the τ subscripts remind us that response coefficients are allowed to vary over time but are constrained to be equal across agents. We set $h = 4, L = 2, j = k = 1$. The implicit assumption here is that agents agree on the response parameters of the Taylor rule, but disagree on the macroeconomic forecasts. This assumption will be relaxed in the next section. We estimate the parameters by using panel regressions with common coefficients. Figures 12.1, 12.2, and 12.3 plot the time-series of the implied ρ, β, and γ (solid lines):[4]

The main message of the figures is that the perceived stance of the Central Bank is strongly time-varying. Importantly, the loading on inflation is not always strictly greater than one, as the estimates for the time-invariant rule would suggest. It is interesting to track the private sector's perception of the Central Bank's response to inflation. The

---

[4] Since ρ is often very to close or above one, we use its unconditional average when dividing by $(1 - \rho)$.

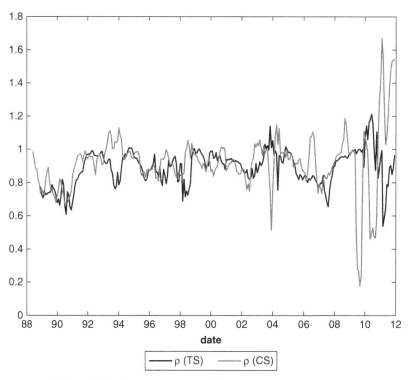

Figure 12.1 Interest rate smoothing
This figure shows the time-series of estimated smoothing parameters
from (i) the cross-section of expectations under the null hypothesis
that agents agree on the parameters of the Taylor rule (light grey); and
(ii) the time-series of agents' individual subjective rules allowing for
heterogeneity in the parameter of the Taylor rule (darker).

dynamics of the perceived inflation loadings are broadly consistent with
Greenspan's (2004) account of the evolution of the Fed's stance. In particular, β peaks between 1988 and 1989, and between 1994 and 1995,
periods in which the Fed engaged in actions of pre-emptive tightening
owing to the build-up of inflationary pressures (Greenspan, 2004). Interestingly, the perceived loading on inflation is low in 1999–2000, even
though the Fed was implementing a contractionary policy. Looking at
the 2008–2011 financial crisis, the dynamics of the perceived response to
inflation reveals that the Central Bank is perceived to be very concerned
with inflation at the end of 2007 (β hovers around 1), when the economy is still healthy. Following the faltering economy at the beginning
of 2008 and the Lehman collapse in September 2008, the loading of

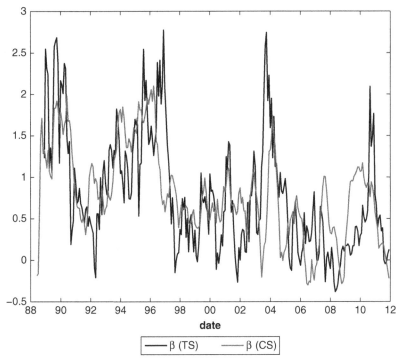

Figure 12.2 Inflation response
This figure shows the time-series of estimated loadings on inflation from (i) the cross-section of expectations under the null hypothesis that agents agree on the parameters of the Taylor rule (light grey); and (ii) the time-series of agents' individual subjective rules allowing for heterogeneity in the parameter of the Taylor rule (darker).

inflation drops dramatically, only to recover sharply in 2009 on concerns of the inflationary pressure exerted by the lax monetary policy. Figure 12.4 plots the time series of the regression $\overline{R}^2$; this can be interpreted as a gauge of the private sector's perception of how well the Taylor rule describes the actual policy implemented by the Fed. Interestingly, the $\overline{R}^2$ drops dramatically in 2009, suggesting that after Lehman the private sector had little confidence that the Central Bank would abide by a Taylor rule in implementing policy.

As a by-product of the cross-sectional regressions we also obtain a measure of the extent to which agents believe the Fed will deviate from the systematic component of the Taylor rule, i.e., deviations from an inflation target and the output gap. Figure 12.5 plots the cross-sectional

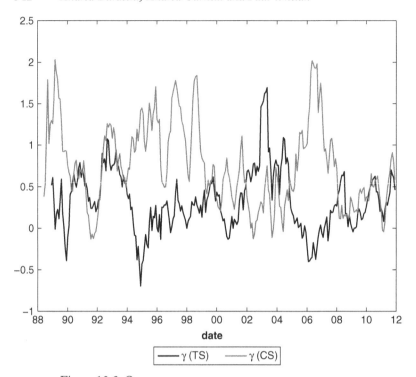

Figure 12.3 Output response
This figure shows the time-series of estimated loadings on the output
gap from (i) the cross-section of expectations under the null hypothesis
that agents agree on the parameters of the Taylor rule (light grey); and
(ii) the time-series of agents' individual subjective rules allowing for
heterogeneity in the parameters of the Taylor rule (darker).

mean-absolute deviation in the residuals from the above regressions. In
Section 12.7 we discuss this figure in the light of alternative sources of
uncertainty that may arise from expectations about future policy actions.

12.6   Individual Taylor rules

Finally, we estimate Taylor rules at the individual level over a 12-month
rolling window. For every individual i, we estimate:

$$E_\tau^i \left[f_{\tau+h}\right] = a_\tau^i + r_\tau^i (L) E_\tau^i \left[f_{\tau+h-1}\right] + b_\tau^i E_\tau^i \left[\pi_{\tau+h+j} - \pi *\right]$$
$$+ c_\tau^i E_\tau^i \left[x_{\tau+h+k}\right] + e_{\tau+h}^i,$$

$\tau = t, t-1, \ldots, t-11.$ We set $h = 3, 4, L = 2, j = k = 1.$

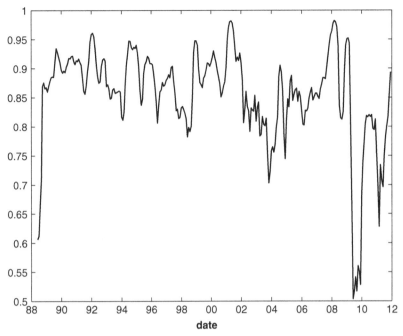

Figure 12.4 Cross-sectional $\bar{R}^2$
This figure shows the time-series of the $\bar{R}^2$ estimated from the cross-section of expectations under the null hypothesis that agents agree on the parameters of the Taylor rule.

12.6.1 Time series of point estimates

We compare the previous results with what would be obtained by using the median forecasts instead of panel regressions. The darker lines in Figures 12.1, 12.2, and 12.3 summarize the result. A comparison of the two dynamics allows us to test the hypothesis of homogeneous loadings across agents. Overall, the dynamics of the median estimates are not too different from those of the cross-sectional estimates. However, with a few exceptions, the level of the median agent's loading on inflation is lower than that uncovered by the cross-sectional regressions.

12.6.2 State dependence

It is revealing to study the properties of the perceived policy loadings by considering how they vary across different states of the world. We examine this issue by means of a non-parametric analysis. We consider

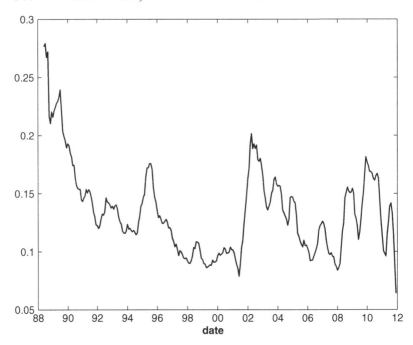

Figure 12.5 Disagreement about the Taylor rule
This figure shows a time-series of the median absolute deviation in the
residual estimated from the cross-section of expectations under the null
hypothesis that agents agree on the parameters of the Taylor rule.

two conditioning variables to proxy for different states of the world: the
inflation rate and the output gap expected to prevail at a 3-quarters
horizon;[5] given the dual mandate of the Fed, these are natural proxies
for the state of the economy. In particular, we sort Taylor rule coefficients into five quintiles based on the value of the conditioning variable.
Next, we examine whether there is any significant change in the median
response coefficient in each bucket. We construct confidence bands
around median M coefficients as $M \pm 2 \times MAD/\sqrt{N}$, where MAD is
the median absolute deviation of the coefficients in the relevant quintile,
and N is the respective number of observations.

Figure 12.6 summarizes the results. The bar charts on the left-hand
side are obtained by conditioning on future gap expectations, while the
bar charts on the right-hand side condition on future inflation expectations. The figures on the first row examine the median smoothing
parameter ρ. Policy inertia, while independent of the output gap state, is

[5] Changing the horizon of the forecast only marginally affects the results.

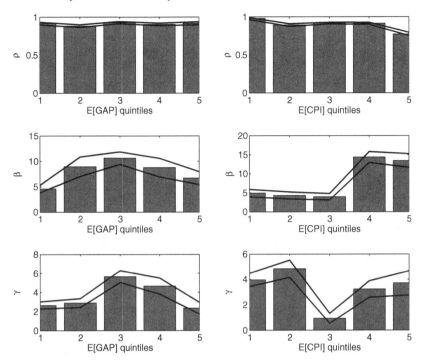

Figure 12.6 Non-parametric analysis
The figures feature median loading estimates (black bars) and confidence bands (grey lines) across different gap (left-hand side) and inflation (right-hand side) states. The first, second, and third rows feature median estimates of the ρ, β, and γ implied by the reduced-form estimates from individual regressions. Gap and inflation states are defined in terms of the level of 3Q-ahead forecasts prevailing at the time of the estimate. We sort Taylor rule coefficients into five quintiles based on the value of the conditioning variable. We construct confidence bands around median M coefficients as $M \pm 2 \times MAD/\sqrt{N}$, where MAD is the median absolute deviation of the coefficients in the relevant quintile, and N is the number of observations in the respective bucket.

decreasing in the inflation quintile: agents perceive lower policy persistence in high inflation states, probably because they expect the Central Bank to be willing to step in to control inflation bursts. The figures on the second row examine the state-dependence of the inflation response coefficients. The response to inflation increases on its forecasted level: the higher the expected increase in the level of prices, the more the Central Bank is expected to act decisively. A bit more surprising is the finding that the median inflation response parameter is above one only in states of high inflation expectations. The distribution of β across output gap states is tent-shaped: while this 'cross-dependence' is interesting on its own, it is hard to interpret it in the absence of a structural model relating real and nominal quantities. The dependence of γ on the output gap (third row) is strong: the response coefficient is around 0.2 when actual output is short of potential output, it rises to 0.5 and then falls back to 0.2 when the economy is strong. This is somewhat in contradiction of the notion of the 'Greenspan put': agents do not expect the Fed to lower the rates more aggressively than implied by a linear rule in periods of low GDP growth. Finally, inflation states seem to affect the gap response in a non-trivial way: the γ features an inverted tent-shape pattern. Overall, the figures point to strong state dependence in agents' perception of how the Central Bank responds to the economy. In light of these non-linearities, the results from Taylor rules estimated over the whole sample might overstate the implications for the existence of locally bounded equilibria.

12.7   Policy uncertainty

We now analyze the private sector's uncertainty about the policy response coefficients. We construct two measures of uncertainty. The first is aimed at capturing the disagreement among market participants: it is defined as the cross-sectional dispersion (median absolute deviation) of the point estimates of the policy response parameters; we denote the disagreement series for the inflation and output gap loadings by Ψ_t^β and Ψ_t^γ, respectively. The second measure, on the other hand, is engineered to capture the average ambiguity of agents about their estimates. It is defined as the median of the standard deviations of the point estimates of the policy response parameters. Intuitively, these standard errors capture how confident agents are, on average, about their guess of teh Federal Reserve's inertia and response to inflation and output gap. We denote this proxy for the inflation and output gap loadings by δ_t^β and δ_t^γ, respectively. These two proxies of uncertainty are potentially different: disagreement (across multiple agents) and ambiguity (multiple priors of a single agent) as they might carry independent information: the first variable uses cross-sectional information; the second one time-series information at the individual agent level.

Figures 12.7 and 12.8 plot the disagreement and ambiguity series for the loadings. It is interesting to consider the behavior of the series in

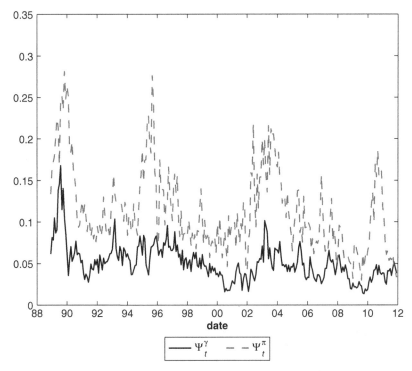

Figure 12.7 Disagreement about the parameters of the Taylor rule
This figure shows a time-series of the median absolute deviation (Ψ_t^γ, Ψ_t^π) in loadings estimated from individual Taylor rules allowing for parameter heterogeneity.

moments of macroeconomic and financial crisis. Our sample includes four important crises: the 1987–1988 stock market crash and the S&L crisis, the 1995 Mexican crisis, the 2001 Internet bubble burst, and the 2008–2009 credit crisis. Somewhat surprisingly, uncertainty about monetary policy is often high out of these windows. This has two important implications. First, measures of monetary policy uncertainty carry information over and above that contained in standard "fear" indices, such as the VIX. Second, since monetary policy uncertainty is not caused by exogenous macro shocks, it might be caused by the conduct of monetary policy itself. On the normative side, to the extent that the monetary authority intends to anchor the expectations of the private sector, these plots suggest that the Central Bank should be careful in engineering its communication policy.

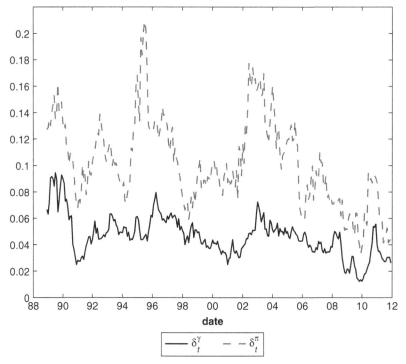

Figure 12.8 Ambiguity about the parameters of the Taylor rule
This figure shows a time-series of the ambiguity $(\delta_t^{\gamma}, \delta_t^{\pi})$ in load-ings estimated from individual Taylor rules allowing for parameter heterogeneity.

While disagreement carries potentially different theoretical informa-tion from ambiguity, it is interesting that the two measures are quite correlated in the data. Figure 12.9 and 12.10 are scatter plots of Ψ_t^{β} against δ_t^{β}, and Ψ_t^{γ} against δ_t^{γ}, respectively. Both plots suggest that the cross-sectional dispersion in beliefs about policy loadings is highly positively correlated to the average subjective uncertainty about policy loadings.

12.7.1 Understanding policy uncertainty

Our empirical results show that the private sector is faced with substan-tial uncertainty about how monetary policy is conducted. In this section we study the determinants of this uncertainty in order to address the following question: why does the private sector disagree on the expected

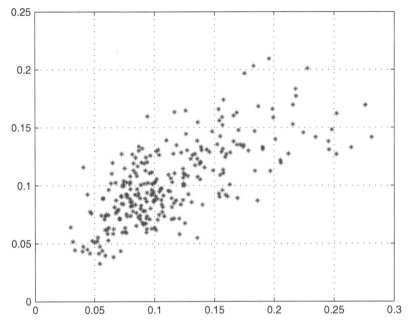

Figure 12.9 Disagreement vs ambiguity: inflation loading
This figure shows a scatter plot of the disagreement versus the ambiguity in inflation loadings for individual estimates allowed for parameter heterogeneity.

future path of monetary policy? If agents actually believe in a Taylor rule, does uncertainty stem from uncertainty about the stance of policy (i.e. Ψ_t^β and Ψ_t^γ), uncertainty in the path of state variables (i.e. Ψ_t^π and Ψ_t^x), or is it that agents simply don't believe in a Taylor rule (Ψ_t^T)? Answering these questions is important from the perspective of a Central Bank that attempts to anchor expectations.

All agents must agree on the price of date t tradable by no-arbitrage. However, in equilibrium, agents may disagree on future prices due to (i) heterogeneous priors, (ii) heterogeneous models, or (iii) asymmetric information. Since it is unlikely that agents hold private information about the conduct of monetary policy, we focus our attention on differences in opinions between agents who "agree to disagree" in the model or the parameters of the model. Figure 12.11 plots the time series of the 1- to 4-quarters ahead dispersion in analyst forecasts about the level of the federal funds rate. Some interesting observations emerge. Firstly, dispersion in forecasts increases with the forecast horizon, where private information is of little value, supporting the hypothesis that disagreement

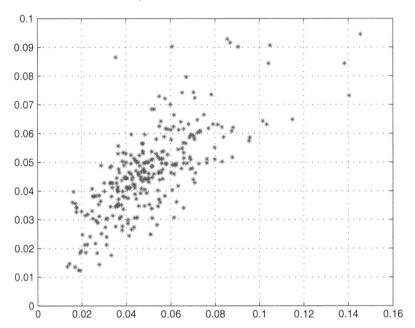

Figure 12.10 Disagreement vs ambiguity: output gap loading
This figure shows a scatter plot of the disagreement versus the ambiguity in output gap loadings for individual estimates allowed for parameter heterogeneity.

originates from heterogeneous priors or models.[6] Second, dispersion in beliefs does not converge, and is highly time-varying. Third, disagreement about monetary policy is largest in periods of active monetary policy. For example, consider the large upswing in policy uncertainty following 1994. A possible explanation for the increase in disagreement lies in the subjective policy model in the minds of agents at this time. In 1994 the Fed began a tightening cycle after leaving the target rate at 3% for nearly 15 months. Between 1994 and 1995 the target rate was raised six times, eventually peaking at 6%. How did such an aggressive sequence of rate decisions affect expectations about monetary policy? Recalling Figures 12.5, 12.7, and 12.8, we see a spike in the level of disagreement both in the extent to which the Fed were following a Taylor rule, and in the dispersion in parameters of the Taylor rule. Similar episodes are witnessed in the aftermath of the dot-com bubble and during the

[6] A similar observation is made by Patton and Timmermann (2010) using a different dataset. The authors study a learning model and conclude that heterogeneity in beliefs is unlikely to stem from heterogeneity in signals.

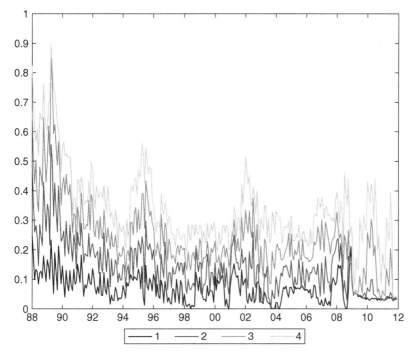

Figure 12.11 Monetary policy uncertainty
This figure plots the time series of 1- to 4-quarter ahead disagreement in federal funds rate forecasts. Disagreement, Ψ_t^{FF}, is computed as the cross-sectional mean absolute deviation in point estimates from the BlueChip financial forecasts dataset.

recent financial crisis. Furthermore, not only does the level of disagreement appear to vary with the conduct of policy, but so does the slope of the "term structure of disagreement". Figure 12.12 makes this point clear by plotting the time-series of the dispersion in 4-quarter ahead forecasts minus the dispersion in 1-quarter ahead forecasts. The slope of the uncertainty curve is large and persistent during the savings and loan crisis, the 1994–1995 rate hike period, the dot-com bubble, Lehman, and most recently during the euro crisis.

We test the determinants of Taylor rule uncertainty formally by projecting the 4-quarter ahead dispersion in federal funds forecasts on three sources of uncertainty: (i) disagreement about the arguments of the rule (Ψ_t^{π} and Ψ_t^{x}); (ii) disagreement about the parameters of the rule (Ψ_t^{β} and Ψ_t^{γ}); and (iii) uncertainty about the functional form of the rule (Ψ_t^{T}). We construct a proxy for the last type of uncertainty

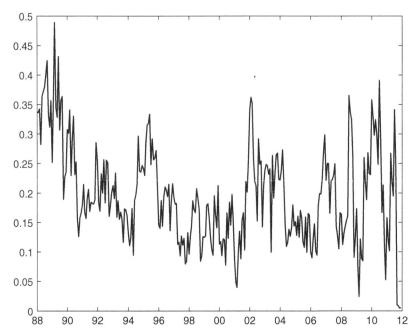

Figure 12.12 Term structure of uncertainty
This figure plots the time-series of 4-quarter ahead disagreement minus
1-quarter ahead disagreement in federal funds forecasts: $\Psi_t^{FF4} - \Psi_t^{FF1}$
where disagreement is computed as the cross-sectional mean abso-
lute deviation in point estimates from the BlueChip financial forecasts
dataset.

using the cross-sectional mean-absolute deviation in the *residuals* from
agents' dynamic cross-sectional regressions. This is intended to capture
the extent to which agents disagree on the outcome of the Taylor rule,
conditional on its arguments and policy parameters. Then, we run the
following regression:

$$\Psi_t^{FFA} = \text{const} + a_1 \Psi_t^{\beta} + a_2 \Psi_t^{\gamma} + a_3 \Psi_t^{T} + a_4 \Psi_t^{T} + a_5 \Psi_t^{x} + \varepsilon_t.$$

Table 12.2 reports the estimates of these regressions, for different choices
of the right-hand side variables. All variables are standardized, so that
regressors can be interpreted as the marginal change (in terms of standard deviations) in disagreement about future federal funds rates caused
by a one standard deviation move in monetary policy uncertainty. Specifications (i) and (ii) address the question whether disagreement about
federal funds rates is driven by disagreement about the monetary policy

Table 12.2 *Monetary policy uncertainty projections*

	(i)	(ii)	(iii)	(iv)	(v)	(vi)	(vii)
Ψ_t^{β}	0.22			0.11	0.34		0.20
	2.63			1.17	5.19		1.97
Ψ_t^{γ}		0.26		0.21	−0.17		0.14
		1.89		1.32	−1.94		1.15
Ψ_t^{T}			0.70		0.77	0.70	
			6.88		7.88	6.92	
Ψ_t^{π}						−0.12	0.24
						−1.38	2.22
Ψ_t^{x}						0.15	0.14
						1.70	0.91
$\overline{R}^2$	0.05	0.07	0.48	0.08	0.56	0.50	0.19

This table reports estimates of projections of disagreement in the 1-year (4-quarter) federal funds rate on (i) disagreement about the parameters of the Taylor rule (Ψ^{β}, Ψ^{γ}); (ii) disagreement about the functional form of the Taylor rule (Ψ^{T}); and (iii) disagreement about the expected arguments of the Taylor rule (Ψ^{π} and Ψ^{x}):

$$\Psi_t^{FF4} = const + a_1 \Psi_t^{\beta} + a_2 \Psi_t^{\gamma} + a_3 \Psi_t^{T} + a_4 \Psi_t^{\pi} + a_5 \Psi_t^{x} + \varepsilon_t.$$

t-stats in brackets are computed with 12 Newey–West lags. Both left- and right-hand variables are standardized. All data spans: 1986:1–2011:12

stance. When considered separately, disagreement about both inflation and output gap responses (Ψ_t^{β} and Ψ_t^{γ}) seem to be key drivers of disagreement about future rates: the statistical significance of the loadings is above standard thresholds (the *t*-statistics are 2.63 and 1.89, respectively), and the economic significance is important: a one standard deviation increase in the dispersion of inflation (gap) responses increases the dispersion in federal funds rates by 0.22 (0.26) standard deviations. When both Ψ_t^{β} and Ψ_t^{γ} appear among the regressors (specification (iv)), however, marginal significance disappears. Importantly, the coefficients of determination of all three regressions (5%, 7%, and 8%) point to a large portion of federal funds disagreement that cannot be traced back to uncertainty about the stance of monetary policy.

Next, we explore whether model uncertainty Ψ_t^{T} can explain cross-sectional dispersion in rates forecasts: specifications (iii) and (v) answer this question by running a univariate regression and controlling for Ψ_t^{β} and Ψ_t^{γ}, respectively. The empirical evidence from both specifications is clear. Both the statistical and economic significance of Ψ_t^{T} are large: changes in model uncertainty affect cross-sectional dispersion of forecasts almost one-for-one (0.70 and 0.77, respectively). Importantly, the R^2s (48% and 56%) suggest that half of the variation in forecasts can be traced back to model uncertainty.

12.7.2 Policy uncertainty and financial markets

Does monetary policy uncertainty impact financial markets? To address this question, we focus on two characteristics of bond markets: (a) the realized volatility of 30-year bond yields, calculated using intra-day bond yield data during the month between t and $t + 1$; (b) the volatility risk premium on Treasury bonds, namely the difference between the time-t implied volatility and the realized volatility between time t and time $t + h$.[7] We use the previous regressions to identify three separate forms of uncertainty. First, uncertainty about the future *state* of the economy, which is denoted by Ψ_t^{π} and Ψ_t^{x}.[8] Second, uncertainty about the *parameters* of the Taylor rule, which is denoted by Ψ_t^{β} and Ψ_t^{γ}.[9] Third, uncertainty about the *functional form* of the Taylor rule itself, which is denoted by Ψ_t^{T}.[10] Table 12.3 summarizes the results when we use these three proxies of uncertainty as explanatory variables for Treasury bond volatility. The t-statistics, reported in parentheses, are calculated using Hansen and Hodrick (1983) corrected standard errors.

Panel A reports the volatility regressions. We find that uncertainty about the functional form of the Taylor rule is very significant in explaining the dynamics of Treasury bond yield volatility, with a t-statistic equal to 5.27 and R^2 equal to 13%. In a multivariate regression, Taylor rule uncertainty is the most significant explanatory variable, subsuming the effect of the parameter uncertainty. This suggests not only that agents are uncertain about the real commitment of Fed in setting federal fund rates according to a linear rule, but that periods when this uncertainty is higher are also periods with higher interest rates volatility.

Panel B reports the results for volatility risk premium regressions. This second regression aims to capture whether uncertainty affects the premium that agents are willing to pay to insure against high volatility

---

[7] The Treasury volatility risk premium series was kindly provided by Andrea Vedolin, Philippe Mueller, and Yu-Min Yen. A detailed discussion of its construction is found in Mueller, Vedolin, and Yen (2012).

[8] These are measured by the cross-sectional difference in beliefs about future inflation and output.

[9] We proxy Ψ_t^{β} and Ψ_t^{γ} from the cross-sectional difference of individual model-implied parameters of the Taylor rule.

[10] This is defined on the basis of the residuals of the dynamic cross-sectional Taylor rule regressions. We compute the mean-absolute-deviation of these residuals as a proxy of uncertainty about the rule itself.

Table 12.3 *Treasury volatility risk premia*

Panel A	(i)	(ii)	(iii)	(iv)
ψ^π	0.37			0.26
	(3.25)			(2.44)
ψ^x	0.17			0.20
	(1.80)			(2.23)
ψ^T		0.36		0.24
		(5.27)		(3.72)
ψ^β			−0.19	−0.04
			(−2.24)	(−0.65)
ψ^γ			0.18	0.05
			(2.39)	(0.77)
$\overline{R}^2$	0.23	0.13	0.03	0.29
Panel B	**(i)**	**(ii)**	**(iii)**	**(iv)**
ψ^π	0.42			0.37
	(3.72)			(3.20)
ψ^x	−0.03			0.00
	(−0.32)			(−0.02)
ψ^T		0.18		0.05
		(2.70)		(0.79)
ψ^β			−0.22	−0.11
			(−3.14)	(−2.03)
ψ^γ			0.09	0.04
			(1.42)	(0.55)
$\overline{R}^2$	0.16	0.03	0.04	0.17

This table reports estimates from regressions of intra-month ($t \to t + 1$) annualized realized volatility and volatility risk premia on (i) disagreement about the parameters of the Taylor rule (ψ^β, ψ^γ); (ii) disagreement about the functional form of the Taylor rule (ψ^T); and (iii) disagreement about the expected arguments of the Taylor rule (ψ^π and ψ^x):

$$\text{Panel A: Vol}^{(30\text{yr})}_{t,t+1} = \text{const} + \sum_{i=1}^{5} \beta_i \psi_t(\star) + \varepsilon_{t+1},$$

$$\text{Panel B: VRP}^{(30\text{yr})}_{t,t+1} = \text{const} + \sum_{i=1}^{5} \beta_i \psi_t(\star) + \varepsilon_{t+1}.$$

Realised volatility is estimated from 5-minute returns on bond futures. t-statistics, reported in parentheses, are corrected for autocorrelation and heteroskedasticity using the Hansen and Hodrick (1983) GMM correction. $\overline{R}^2$ reports the adjusted R^2. Left- and right-hand variables are standardized for comparison reasons. A constant is included but not reported. Sample period: 1988:1–2011:12.

states. In univariate regressions, we find that uncertainty about the state of inflation Ψ_t^π is the most significant variable. While the residual uncertainty about the conduct of monetary policy and the functional form of the Taylor rule is very significant, it is subsumed by state uncertainty in multivariate regressions.

In general, these results highlight the importance of monetary policy uncertainty on asset prices. In addition to potentially affecting conditional expected excess returns, as already discussed in the extant ambiguity literature, policy uncertainty appears to have a significant effect on bond yield volatility.

12.8   Conclusion

The use of survey data allows us to measure expectations without making assumptions about agents' belief processes, or resorting to statistical projections using the econometrician's measure. We found substantial differences between the policy parameters estimated under the assumption of rational expectations and those obtained under subjective expectations. We uncovered substantial time- and state-dependence in the private sector's perception of how policy is conducted. We explored three different measures of policy uncertainty: uncertainty about the arguments, about the loadings, and about the functional form of the Taylor rule. Interestingly, we found that cross-sectional dispersion in the perceived policy parameters are highly correlated to the average individual uncertainty (ambiguity) about the parameters. Our approach offers a useful framework for analyzing the beliefs and learning process of the private sector about monetary policy, which may be of particular interest to policymakers when addressing questions related to expectation anchoring.

References

Baker, S. R., Bloom, N. and Davis, S. J. (2011). Measuring economic policy uncertainty. Working paper, Stanford University.

Barro, R. J. and Gordon D. B. (1983). Rules, discretion and reputation in a model of monetary policy. *Journal of Monetary Economics*, **12**, 101–121.

Bloom, N. (2007). The impact of uncertainty shocks. Discussion paper, National Bureau of Economic Research.

Christiano, L. J., Eichenbaum, M. and Evans, C. (1994). The effects of monetary policy shocks: some evidence from the flow of funds. Discussion paper, National Bureau of Economic Research.

Christiano, L. J., Eichenbaum, M. and Evans, C. L. (1996). Identification and the effects of monetary policy shocks, in *Financial Factors in*

Economic Stabilization and Growth (M. Blejer, Z. Eckstein, Z. Hercowitz and L. Leidenman, eds.), Cambridge: Cambridge University Press, pp. 36–74.

Clarida, R. H. and Gertler, M. (1997). How the Bundesbank conducts monetary policy, in *Reducing Inflation: Motivation and Strategy* (C. D. Romer and D. H. Romer, eds.), Chicago: University of Chicago Press.

Clarida, R., Gali, J. and Gertler, M. (1998). Monetary policy rules in practice: some international evidence. *European Economic Review*, **42**, 1033–1067.

Clarida, R., Gali, J. and Gertler, M. (1999). The science of monetary policy: a new Keynesian perspective. Discussion paper, National Bureau of Economic Research.

Clarida, R., Gali, J. and Gertler, M. (2000). Monetary policy rules and macroeconomic stability: evidence and some theory. *Quarterly Journal of Economics*, **115**, 147–180.

Clarida, R., Sarno, L. Taylor, M. and Valente, G. (2006). The role of asymmetries and regime shifts in the term structure of interest rates. CEPR discussion paper no. 4835.

Cochrane, J. H. (2011). Determinacy and identification with Taylor rules. *Journal of Political Economy*, **119**, 565–615.

David, A. and Veronesi, P. (2011). Investor and central bank uncertainty and fear measures embedded in index options. National Bureau of Economic Research working paper no. 16764.

Gavin, W. T. and Mandal, R. J. (2001). Forecasting inflation and growth: do private forecasts match those of policymakers? *Review – Federal Reserve Bank of St. Louis*, **83**, 11–20.

Greenspan, A. (2004), Risk and uncertainty in monetary policy, *American Economic Review*, **94**, 33–40.

Hansen, L. P. and Hodrick, R. J. (1983). Risk averse speculation in the forward foreign exchange market: an econometric analysis of linear models. *Exchange Rates and International Macroeconomics*, **3**, 113–142.

Kim, C. J. and Nelson, C. R. (2006). Estimation of a forward-looking monetary policy rule: a time-varying parameter model using ex post data. *Journal of Monetary Economics*, **53**, 1949–1966.

King, R. G. (2000). The new IS-LM model: language, logic, and limits. *Economic Quarterly-Federal Reserve Bank of Richmond*, **86**, 45–103.

Kydland, F. E. and Prescott, E. C. (1977). Rules rather than discretion: the inconsistency of optimal plans. *Journal of Political Economy*, 473–491.

Levin, A., Wieland, V. and Williams, J. C. (2003). The performance of forecast-based monetary policy rules under model uncertainty. *American Economic Review*, 622–645.

Mueller, P., Vedolin, A. and Yen, Y. (2012). Bond variance risk premia, ssrn.com/abstract=1787478 or dx.doi.org/10.2139/ssrn.1787478.

Pastor, L. and Veronesi, P. (2011). Political uncertainty and risk premia. Discussion paper, National Bureau of Economic Research.

Pastor, L. and Veronesi, P. (2012). Uncertainty about government policy and stock prices. *Journal of Finance*, **67**(4), 1214–1264.

Patton, A. J. and Timmermann, A. (2010). Why do forecasters disagree? Lessons from the term structure of cross-sectional dispersion. *Journal of Monetary Economics*, **57**, 803–820.

Rudebusch, G. D. (2001). Is the Fed too timid? Monetary policy in an uncertain world. *Review of Economics and Statistics*, **83**(2), 203–217.

Sims, C. A. and Zha, T. (2006). Were there regime switches in US monetary policy? *American Economic Review*, **96**, 54–81.

Svensson, L. E. O. (1997). Inflation forecast targeting: implementing and monitoring inflation targets. *European Economic Review*, **41**, 1111–1146.

Taylor, J. B. (1993). Discretion versus policy rules in practice. *Carnegie-Rochester Conference Series on Public Policy*, **39**, 195–214.

Woodford, M. (2003). *Interest and Prices: Foundations of a Theory of Monetary Policy.* Princeton: Princeton University Press.

Part IV

Estimating inflation risk

13 Inflation compensation and inflation risk premia in the euro area term structure of interest rates

Juan Angel García and Thomas Werner

13.1 Introduction

The term structure of interest rates is a fundamental source of information for monetary policymakers, especially for real yields, inflation expectations and risk premia. In particular, the yield spread between nominal and inflation-linked bonds, commonly referred to as the break-even inflation rate (BEIR), has become a key indicator of inflation expectations. Most major economies have issued inflation-linked debt in recent years, and detailed references to BEIRs in central bank publications and speeches (e.g. Bernanke, 2007; Trichet, 2005), research on the anchoring of inflation expectations (e.g. Gürkaynak, Levin and Swanson, 2010) and market commentary (e.g. *Wall Street Journal*, 2010) are increasingly common.

Monitoring developments in inflation expectations is crucial for a monetary policy oriented towards achieving price stability. Although BEIRs are available at different horizons and in real time, they are not a direct measure of inflation expectations. They reflect the overall inflation compensation that investors request to hold nominal bonds, comprising both the expected level of inflation and a premium to compensate

We thank Geert Bekaert, Francesco Giavazzi, Refet Gürkaynak, Peter Hördalh, Leonardo Iania, Philippe Mueller, Andrés Manzanares, Oreste Tristani and participants in the ECB workshop 'Measuring and interpreting the inflation risk premia for monetary policy', the Bank of Spain and the Central Bank of Cyprus for useful suggestions and comments. We are particularly indebted to participants in the CIMF-IESEG conference 'The yield curve and new developments in macrofinance: what have we learnt from the 2007–2010 financial crisis?' in Cambridge, UK, September 2011, our discussant James Steeley, the editor Mike Joyce and an anonymous referee for many useful comments and suggestions. Any remaining errors are our responsibility. The views expressed in this paper are those of the authors and do not necessarily reflect the views of the European Central Bank.

for inflation risks. Decomposing BEIRs into inflation expectations and inflation risk premia is therefore crucial for research and policy purposes.

This chapter focuses on the decomposition of BEIRs into their inflation expectations and inflation risk premium components in the euro area, and discusses the challenges posed by the financial crisis for the correct interpretation of the spread between the two types of yield in the euro area sovereign bond market. To estimate euro area BEIRs and inflation risk premia, we build a no-arbitrage term structure model along the lines of Ang, Bekaert and Wei (2008). To better identify the inflation risk premia, we also use inflation-linked bond yields to pin down real yields (e.g. D'Amico, Kim and Wei, 2010; Hördahl and Tristani, 2010), and survey inflation expectations to pin down the level of expected inflation (e.g. Dewachter and Lyrio, 2008; Chernov and Mueller, 2011).

The financial crisis that started in the summer of 2007 and intensified in the autumn of 2008 poses very serious challenges to extracting reliable information on BEIRs and inflation expectations to inform policymakers. Such difficulties were particularly strong in the euro area, where, in addition to the higher volatility of bond yields and the deterioration of market liquidity that took place all over the world, the presence of many sovereign issuers and the increasing discrimination by bond market investors tended to amplify those distortions and led to severe market segmentation at times. To account for liquidity distortions in the observed yields on conventional and inflation-linked bonds we allow for measurement errors along the term structure. We do not impose any restriction on the specification of these measurement errors, but we show that the fitting errors for both real and nominal yields are strongly related to several commonly used proxies for the liquidity premium. Our model estimates and a model-free series constructed using inflation-linked swap rates and survey inflation expectations follow quite similar dynamics.

Our main findings are as follows. The term structures of euro area BEIRs and inflation risk premia have been predominantly upward sloping but relatively flat. One-year forward BEIRs ending in five years averaged 2.25%, only 20 basis points higher than those ending in two years. However, since the start of the financial turbulence in mid-2007, and in particular following its intensification in the autumn of 2008, inflation compensation turned more volatile. The euro area BEIR curve was inverted for most of 2008 before steepening strongly in 2009, reflecting the volatility of realised inflation and revisions to short-term expected inflation during the crisis.

As regards the decomposition of BEIRs into inflation expectations and risk premia components, the term structure of inflation risk premia in the euro area also exhibits a predominantly upward slope but the spread across maturities is also quite compressed: on average the inflation risk premium was between 5 and 10 basis points within two years and about 25 basis points five years ahead. Moreover, long-term premia oscillated within a relatively narrow range of 0–50 basis points. Our estimates of inflation expectations embodied in bond yields, in line with the evidence from survey data, suggest a strong anchoring at medium-to-long maturities, while the long-term premium oscillated within a relatively narrow range of 0–50 basis points between 1999 and 2010. These results are in line with recent research on the euro area term structure (Hördahl and Tristani, 2010; Pericoli, 2011).

From a monetary policy point of view it is also important to understand the contribution of those two determinants to the volatility of BEIRs. We show that short horizon BEIRs are more volatile than longer term ones, with about two thirds of that volatility reflecting movements in short-term inflation expectations, and inflation risk premia playing a limited role. In contrast, the volatility of inflation compensation at longer horizons is almost wholly driven by inflation risk premia, while the limited contribution of long-term inflation expectations reflects a strong anchoring of euro area inflation expectations.

The chapter is organised as follows. Section 13.2 introduces our term structure model (full details are in Appendix A). Section 13.3 discusses our methodological approach to handle liquidity distortions and the relationship of our estimates of those distortions to standard indicators of the liquidity premium in bond markets. Section 13.4 reviews our main results for euro area BEIRs and provides some additional robustness checks. Section 13.5 concludes.

13.2   The term structure of inflation risk premia

The spread between the yield of a nominal bond (y_t^n) and the yield of a real bond (y_t^r) of maturity n reflects the inflation compensation requested by investors to hold nominal bonds. The requested compensation for inflation, or BEIR, however, comprises two very distinct components, namely the (average) level of inflation over the life of the bond $(E_t(\pi_{t,t+n}))$ and an additional risk premium (ϕ_t^n) required by bond holders as compensation for the risk of inflation turning out different from that expectation. Formally,

$$y_t^n - y_t^r = BEIR = E_t(\pi_{t,t+n}) + \phi_t^n. \qquad (13.1)$$

A serious challenge for interpreting developments in nominal yields and to estimate BEIRs is that not only the inflation risk premium but, to a large extent, also expected inflation are unobservable, and therefore need to be identified from the observed bond yields.

13.2.1   The model setup

To estimate the term structure of inflation risk premia, we employ a discrete-time affine term structure framework that links bond yields to the dynamics of short-term yields and inflation under no-arbitrage restrictions. Apart from modelling regime changes, the basic structure of our framework is similar to Ang, Bekaert and Wei (2008, ABW henceforth), so we here only stress the main features of the model and provide full model details in Appendix A.

No-arbitrage alone provides weak identifying restrictions for real yields and inflation risk premia. In line with recent literature, we therefore incorporate additional information to improve the decomposition of BEIRs. Specifically, to pin down real yields we incorporate inflation-linked bond yields in the estimation (see also D'Amico, Kim and Wei, 2010, DKW henceforth; Hördahl and Tristani, 2010; Pericoli, 2011). To help estimate inflation risk premia through Equation (13.1), we also incorporate survey data of inflation expectations at both short- and longer-term horizons (see Chernov and Mueller, 2011; Dewachter and Lyrio, 2008). This modelling approach has become relatively standard in recent years, and, for example, the Joyce et al. (2010) model for the UK term structure is also very similar to ours.[1]

The model has three state variables: two latent factors l_t^1, l_t^2, and actual inflation π_t as an observable factor. As is standard in the related literature, the state vector $X_t = (l_t^1\ l_t^2\ \pi_t)'$ follows a VAR(1) process $X_{t+1} = \mu + \Phi X_t + \Sigma \epsilon_{t+1}$. The matrices μ, Φ and Σ are specified as follows:

$$\mu = \begin{bmatrix} 0 \\ 0 \\ \mu_\pi \end{bmatrix}, \quad \Phi = \begin{bmatrix} \Phi_{11} & 0 & 0 \\ \Phi_{21} & \Phi_{22} & 0 \\ \Phi_{31} & \Phi_{32} & \Phi_{33} \end{bmatrix}, \quad \Sigma = \begin{bmatrix} 1 & 0 & 0 \\ 0 & 1 & 0 \\ 0 & 0 & \sigma_\pi \end{bmatrix}.$$

The real short rate $\hat{r}_t$ is an affine function of the state vector $\hat{r}_t = \delta_0 + \delta_1' X_t$. To make the real rate dependent on the latent factors but not on inflation,[2] we restrict the δ_1 vector to $(\delta_{1,1}\ \delta_{1,2}\ 0)$. To model the

---

[1] For our purpose in this paper we chose the most parsimonious structure needed to fit the data. Joyce et al. (2010) employ an additional latent factor in their model, but, in the euro area, the first two principal components already explain more than 99% of the variation in the real term structure.

[2] Theoretically, by imposing this restriction we exclude the Mundell–Tobin effect that gives a direct effect of inflation on the real interest rate.

term structure of real yields, we specify the real pricing kernel[3] as an exponential function of the market price of risk λ_t:

$$\hat{M}_t = \exp\left(-\hat{r}_t - \frac{1}{2}\lambda_t'\lambda_t - \lambda_t'\epsilon_{t+1}\right).$$

The market price of risk, in turn, is a linear function of the state variables $\lambda_t = \lambda_0 + \lambda_1 X_t$, with

$$\lambda_0 = \begin{bmatrix} \lambda_{0,1} \\ \lambda_{0,2} \\ \lambda_{0,3}^* \end{bmatrix}, \quad \lambda_1 = \begin{bmatrix} \lambda_{1,11} & \lambda_{1,12} & \lambda_{1,13}^* \\ \lambda_{1,21} & \lambda_{1,22} & \lambda_{1,23}^* \\ \lambda_{1,31}^* & \lambda_{1,32}^* & \lambda_{1,33}^* \end{bmatrix}.$$

We consider two specifications of the market prices of risk. In our baseline specification inflation does not affect the term structure of real interest rates (all λ^* elements of λ_1 are restricted to zero), so the real pricing kernel is not a function of current inflation. As discussed in detail in Chernov and Mueller (2011), most of the currently discussed general equilibrium models are in line with this assumption. The finance literature focuses on endowment economies where the real pricing kernel, and in turn risk premia, are functions of consumption growth and other real state variables. But even models that endogenise inflation via a Taylor rule do not feature a direct influence of inflation onto the real pricing kernel.[4] We, however, also test for the role of inflation in the real pricing kernel by estimating a model version with all λ^* elements of λ_1 unrestricted. As both model specifications provide very similar estimates of BEIRs and inflation risk premia, we focus below on the baseline specification.

Using the affine term structure framework we can derive closed-form solutions for real and nominal bond prices. For a given maturity n, bond prices are exponentially affine functions of the state vector. For example, in the case of real bond prices, the solutions have the form (solutions for nominal bonds can be found in Appendix A):

$$\hat{P}_t^n = \exp\left(\hat{A}_n + \hat{B}_n' X_t\right).$$

---

[3] The no-arbitrage condition implies the existence of a stochastic discount factor (or pricing kernel) that allows for consistent pricing of all assets. Following most of the literature, we start modelling the real pricing kernel, relevant for pricing assets in real terms, and derive a consistent nominal pricing kernel introducing inflation.

[4] The effect of inflation on the real pricing kernel should not be confused with the recent debate on *unspanned* inflation. In this literature, there is some evidence put forward that factors derived from the nominal yield curve, like principal components, are sufficient to explain all variations in the cross-section of the term-structure. Inflation, in this sense, does not add any information to modelling the cross-section of nominal yields and is therefore *unspanned* (see, e.g. Wright, 2011).

The constants $\hat{A}_n$ and the factor loadings $\hat{B}'_n$ can be recursively computed using the system of Riccati equations (with $\hat{A}_1 = -\delta_0$ and $\hat{B}'_1 = -\delta_1$ as initial conditions):

$$\hat{A}_{n+1} = -\delta_0 + \hat{A}_n + \hat{B}'_n(\mu - \Sigma\lambda_0) + \frac{1}{2}\hat{B}_n \Sigma\Sigma\hat{B}'_n,$$

$$\hat{B}'_{n+1} = -\delta'_1 + \hat{B}'_n(\Phi - \Sigma\lambda_1).$$

13.2.2 Data and estimation method

Data

Our estimation is based on monthly data from January 1995 to September 2010. The nominal zero-coupon yields (3-month, and 1-, 2-, 3- and 5-year) are from Bloomberg.[5] Real zero-coupon yields (2-, 3-, and 5-year) since February 2004 are estimated from inflation-linked bond yields following Ejsing et al. (2007). The euro area comprises a large number of sovereign issuers, and in some cases the rating of the bonds of those issuers changed significantly over our sample, but our bond yields are exclusively based on high-rated bonds (issued by France and Germany and AAA-rated throughtout our sample). As our inflation measure, we use year-on-year rates of change in the euro area HICP figures as reported by Eurostat, since they match the ECB inflation objective and the survey-based measures of inflation expectations from the ECB's SPF (to be described in detail below).

Table 13.1 reports some basic statistics of the euro area yield curve data over the sample 1999M1–2010M9. In addition to full sample statistics, the table also reports statistics for a pre-financial crisis subsample 1999M1–2007M6 that we use as reference period to shelter our analysis from the yield data distortions stemming from the financial turbulence since the summer of 2007. In particular, the time-varying nature of the liquidity premium embodied in nominal and real bond yields worldwide since mid-2007 is difficult to correct for (see discussions in Campbell et al., 2009; DKW, 2010) and can potentially cloud the relationship we aim at unveiling here. Details of our modelling approach are described in detail below, but, for completeness, we also briefly discuss here the main characteristics of the BEIRs.

The euro area nominal, real and BEIR curves have been on average upward sloping but relatively flat during the ECB era. These curves display significantly higher volatility at the short-end than over longer

---

[5] Nominal yields before 1999 are yields derived from German government bonds.

Table 13.1 *Summary statistics of euro area yield curve data*

	Central moments (Full-sample: 1999M1–2010M9)				Central moments (Pre-crisis: 1999M1–2007M6)				Autocorrelation (Full-sample)		
	Mean	STDev.	Skew	Kurtosis	Mean	STDev.	Skew	Kurtosis	Lag 1	Lag 2	Lag 3
Nominal yields											
1-year yield	2.98	1.18	−0.37	−0.61	3.15	0.93	0.58	−0.69	0.97	0.94	0.89
2-year yield	3.17	1.07	−0.31	−0.66	3.35	0.87	0.42	−0.96	0.97	0.93	0.88
5-year yield	3.74	0.85	−0.13	−0.73	3.88	0.75	0.24	−1.14	0.97	0.93	0.90
Real yields											
2-year yield	1.10	0.75	0.00	−0.87	0.77	0.51	0.42	−1.07	0.95	0.90	0.85
5-year yield	1.36	0.56	0.12	−0.67	1.23	0.34	−0.34	−1.02	0.93	0.86	0.81
Forward BEIRs											
1-year BEIR	1.98	0.46	−0.56	1.33	2.04	0.23	−0.39	0.90	0.95	0.88	0.78
1-year forward BEIR ending in two years	2.03	0.24	−0.49	−0.38	2.07	0.16	0.44	−0.87	0.96	0.90	0.82
1-year forward BEIR ending in five years	2.23	0.14	0.23	−0.34	2.25	0.14	0.33	−0.59	0.92	0.81	0.73

Table statistics refer to the monthly data over the period 1999M1–2010M9 used in the estimation of our term structure model. Nominal yields are (AAA) zero-coupons as reported in Bloomberg; real yields are zero-coupon adjusted for inflation seasonality estimated following Ejsing et al. (2007), and their statistics refer to the period 2004Q1–2010Q3 due to the limited number of inflation-linked bonds available for their estimation before 2004; forward breakeven inflation rates (or inflation compensation) are based on our benchmark term structure model as described in Section 13.2.

horizons, which in the case of the nominal and the BEIR curves reflects the strong anchoring of inflation expectations in the euro area. Yields nonetheless exhibit significant persistence at all horizons.

Looking at the pre-crisis subsample allows us to ascertain some effects of the financial crisis on euro area yield curves. The financial crisis period is characterised by, on average, lower but more volatile yields. In addition to higher volatility, observed real yields exhibited higher average values, most likely reflecting severe liquidity premia that cautions against the direct calculation of BEIRs as spreads between nominal and real yields. In contrast, the mean and volatility of our model-based BEIRs, on average, remained relatively stable over the whole sample, particularly at longer horizons, which is more reassuring for our analysis in this chapter.

Finally, although all the series exhibit some mild non-Gaussian features like skewness and excess kurtosis over the sample, the Gaussian assumption does not seem to be unreasonable as a first approximation for gauging reliable estimates of the euro area term structure of inflation risk premia and its dynamics and to compare them to the dynamics of perceived inflation risks.

State and observation equations

The measurement and transition equations from the state-space representation of the model can be expressed as $w_t = d + ZX_t + \eta_t$ and $X_t = \Phi X_{t-1} + \Sigma \epsilon_t$. The observed data vector w_t contains real and nominal bond yields, inflation and survey inflation expectations. The vector d and the matrix Z reflect the bond price equations that link the state variables (latent factors) and the observed data (see Appendix A for details).

Kalman filtering and optimisation

We use Kalman filtering techniques in the estimation because they offer two main advantages in our setting. First, we incorporate additional data in the estimation as they become available. For example, we incorporate yields from inflation-linked bonds only from 2004 onwards, given the limited number of bonds available to estimate the real term structure before that date (see Ejsing et al., 2007).

Second, we allow for measurement errors in the fitting of most observed variables to account for the characteristics of our data. For example, we fit real and nominal bond yields at all maturities up to a measurement error. Moreover, to capture the fact that the inflation-linked bond yields are likely to be somewhat less liquid than nominal bonds, we allow for a higher measurement error in real bond yields.

Table 13.2 *Volatility of survey and model inflation expectations*

Horizon	Survey inflation expectations	Model without surveys	Model including surveys
in one year	20	25	18
in two years	11	17	8
in five years	5	8	3

The table entries are the standard deviations of survey inflation expectations and the corresponding estimates from our benchmark term structure model specification for each horizon, in basis points. Our survey data are from the ECB's Survey of Professional Forecasters. Results from two versions of the term structure model, including and not including survey data in the estimation, are reported. The higher volatility of the model inflation expectations without survey data translates into too low a volatility of inflation risk premia estimates.

Survey inflation expectations from the ECB's Survey of Professional Forecasters (ECB's SPF) are a key element in our setting,[6] but they are only available since 1999, and at a quarterly frequency.[7] The state-space formulation also fits well with those features of the survey data. By fitting survey inflation expectations up to a measurement error we do not impose that model inflation expectations are exactly those from surveys, and this helps capture the strong anchoring of inflation expectations at long horizons (see Table 13.2). Importantly, better estimation of the term structure of inflation expectations using survey expectations does not come at the cost of fitting financial data. Table 13.3 shows that the fitting of nominal yields in the model including survey data is as good as, and often somewhat better than, that of the model without including survey information. These results for euro area data corroborate the findings of Kim (2009) and Chernov and Mueller (2011) for the US economy.[8] As inflation is included as an observable variable in the state vector, model-based measures of expected inflation are, for all forecast horizons, a function of the states in time t. For example, the

---

[6] See García (2003) for an introduction to the ECB's SPF.

[7] We use mean inflation expectations estimated from the probability forecasts (in the form of histograms) at the 1-, 2- and 5- year horizons. Those means are estimated by fitting a continous density to the SPF histograms following García and Manzanares (2007).

[8] Since pinning down inflation expectations is crucial for estimating inflation risk premia, the use of survey inflation expectations in the estimation of term structure models has become a standard practice (e.g. DKW, 2010; Hördahl and Tristani, 2010; Joyce et al., 2010).

Table 13.3 *The fitting of nominal bond yields under different model specifications*

Horizon	Model without surveys	Model including surveys
One year ahead	12	13
Two years ahead	6	7
Five years ahead	10	7

The table entries report the root-mean-square fitting errors for the nominal yields in models including and not including survey inflation expectations. Using survey data does not increase fitting errors significantly.

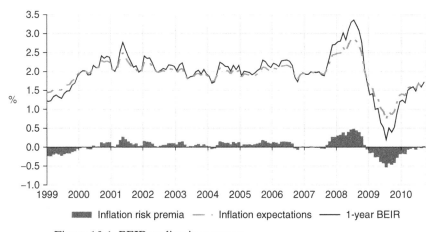

Figure 13.1 BEIR ending in one year

model-based inflation expectation for inflation five years (60 months) ahead can be computed as follows:[9]

$$E_t^{\text{model}}[\pi_{t+60}] = e_3(I - \Phi^{60})(I - \Phi)^{-1}\mu + e_3\Phi^{60}X_t.$$

Figures 13.1 to 13.3 show the model estimates for inflation compensation, inflation expectations and inflation risk premia one, two and five years ahead, and Figure 13.4 displays the model's ability to fit nominal, real yields and survey inflation expectations at different horizons. A vertical line differentiates the pre-crisis period 1999Q1–2007Q2 and the full sample, and we will discuss specific modelling challenges for the second period below. Table 13.4 lists parameter estimates and confidence bounds computed using MCMC, following Chernozhukov and Hong (2003).

---

[9] e_3 is a vector of zeros apart from its third element, a one, which selects inflation from the state vector.

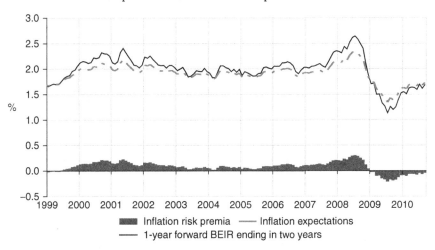

Figure 13.2 One-year forward BEIR ending in two years

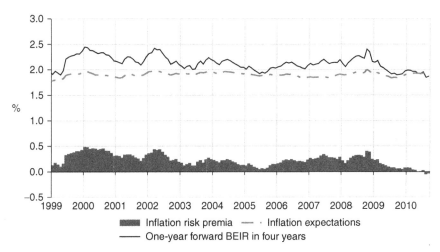

Figure 13.3 One-year forward BEIR ending in five years
Note: The charts depict the decomposition of break-even inflation rates (BEIRs, or inflation compensation) into the expected level of inflation and the inflation risk premium associated with it using the benchmark specification of the term structure model described in Section 13.2. Data are in percentage points.

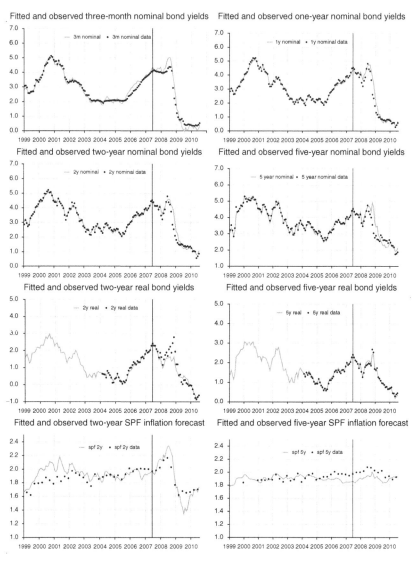

Figure 13.4 Term structure model measurement equations: fitted and observed values

Note: The charts depict the fitted and observed values for nominal and real bond yields and inflation expectations under the benchmark term structure model specification discussed in Section 13.2. Data are in percentage points. The vertical line, at June 2007, distinguishes the pre-crisis from the full sample periods.

Table 13.4 *Parameter estimation (benchmark model specification)*

	Estimated parameters	99% Confidence bounds	
		lower bound	upper bound
$\mu_\pi * 1200$	0.1570	0.0362	0.2088
Φ_{11}	0.9591	0.8651	0.9993
Φ_{22}	0.9592	0.9288	0.9999
Φ_{33}	0.9206	0.8888	0.9849
Φ_{21}	0.0896	0.0295	0.1903
$\Phi_{31} * 1200$	0.0022	0.0004	0.0138
$\Phi_{32} * 1200$	-0.0023	-0.0030	-0.0001
$\sigma_\pi * 12 * 10^5$	0.0292	0.0055	0.0895
$\lambda_{0,1}$	-0.3039	-0.7257	-0.0055
$\lambda_{0,2}$	0.4344	0.0690	0.7599
$\lambda_{1,11}$	-0.0047	-0.0102	-0.0014
$\lambda_{1,12}$	0.0170	0.0078	0.0358
$\lambda_{1,21}$	0.0429	0.0037	0.0564
$\lambda_{1,22}$	-0.0513	-0.0639	-0.0031
$\delta_0 * 1200$	1.2243	1.2243	1.2243
$\delta_{1,1} * 100$	0.0123	0.0004	0.0110
$\delta_{1,2} * 100$	-0.0112	-0.0239	-0.0035
$\tilde{\sigma}_\epsilon^2(1) * 12 * 10^5$	0.0129	0.0026	0.0162
$\tilde{\sigma}_\epsilon^2(2) * 12 * 10^5$	0.0090	0.0038	0.0504
$\tilde{\sigma}_\epsilon^2(3) * 12 * 10^5$	0.0149	0.0091	0.1011

The table entries show the estimates for the key parameters of the model. Confidence bounds are constructed by an MCMC approach as advocated by Chernozhukov and Hong (2003).

13.3 Measurement errors and the liquidity premium in euro area bond yields

Modelling the term structure of interest rates during the financial crisis poses some additional difficulties, but the estimation of the inflation risk premium is especially challenging. Strong and time-varying liquidity distortions are likely to affect nominal and inflation-linked bonds asymmetrically since the intensification of the financial crisis in the autumn of 2008 (see e.g. Campbell et al., 2009). Without controlling for them, the analysis of inflation compensation and inflation risk premia would be misleading. As explained above, our estimation approach allows for nominal and inflation-linked bond yields to be fitted with different measurement errors.

One possible approach to capture the liquidity gap between inflation-linked and nominal bonds is to introduce an additional factor as in

D'Amico et al. (2010); our experience suggests that while such an approach can account for the liquidity premium in the early years of the inflation-linked bond markets (as D'Amico et al., 2010, for TIPS and Fontaine and García, 2012, for nominal Treasuries) it may trigger identification problems in periods of intense market turbulence, as is the case at the end of our sample, and therefore increase the risk of model mis-specification. In the euro area this is particularly problematic because it is the only inflation-linked bond market with four different sovereign issuers (France, Germany, Italy and Greece), thereby combining different and time varying ratings. We restrict our term structure analysis to AAA-rated nominal and inflation-linked bonds (i.e. those issued by France and Germany), but find that obtaining liquidity proxies to identify liquidity factors in the euro area term structure is problematic, and conditioning the model estimation on a liquidity factor loosely identified risks serious model mis-specification.

Our practical approach is as follows. First we estimate the model for the pre-crisis period 1995M1–2007M6. This allows us to shelter the parameter estimation from the distortions and potential bond market mispricing during the financial crisis, when arbitrage opportunities across the nominal and inflation-linked markets were likely to persist (see Fleckenstein et al., 2011). We conjecture that a substantial part of the measurement errors during the financial crisis period are related to liquidity premia. This section shows some empirical evidence supporting that conjecture.

The measurement errors in our model indeed show substantial increases not only in the autumn of 2008, when portfolio reallocation from inflation-linked into nominal bonds and strong flight-to-safety flows into nominal bonds led to strong declines in observed breakeven inflation rates, but also in the first half of 2009 at short horizons as well as in the spring of 2010 with the intensification of the sovereign debt concerns in some euro area countries. Specifically, Figure 13.5 provides evidence supporting the presence of a sizable negative distortion in nominal bond yields and a strong positive one in real yields due to varying market liquidity, whose evolution over the crisis explains a large part of the volatility of observed BEIRs calculated from them, as argued in our discussion of Table 13.1.

To gauge the relative importance of measurement errors and the inflation risk premia over time resulting from our modelling approach, Table 13.5 provides a decomposition of the average values of spot BEIRs at one-, two- and five-year horizons into expected inflation, the inflation risk premium and measurement errors over several years. Note that Table 13.5 provides a mechanical decomposition of spot BEIRs,

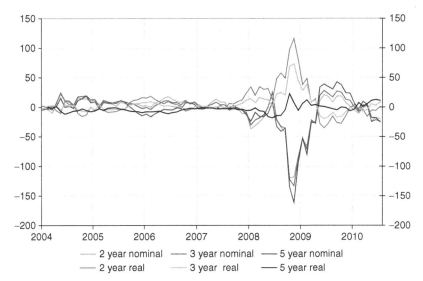

Figure 13.5 Measurement errors for nominal and real yields: observed over fitted values
Note: The chart shows the difference between observed and fitted nominal and real yields for different horizons, in basis points. In contrast to the relatively minor measurement errors between 2004 and 2007, the sharp deterioration in liquidity conditions following the collapse of Lehman Brothers and the intensification of the financial crisis in late 2008 triggered a substantial rise in real yields (as reflected in positive measurement errors) and a fall in nominal yields (as reflected in negative measurement errors), which led to sharp declines in observed breakeven inflation rates. Although somewhat attenuated thereafter, distortions remained relatively high for the rest of our sample period.

which reflect expected averages over their whole horizon rather than the one-year forward BEIRs used in Table 13.1 and Figures 13.1–13.3. This, for example, explains the presence of a negative inflation risk premium even at the five-year horizon (i.e. on average over the next five years) in the later part of our sample, while in Figure 13.3 (see also Figure 13.6) a significantly lower but nonetheless positive inflation risk premium component is observed in the one-year forward BEIR ending in five years.

Turning to the importance of measurement errors, we can differentiate between three periods. In 2004 and 2005, the inflation risk premium was quite low (about 10 basis points) and merely above the magnitude of the measurement errors. Over 2006 and 2007, in contrast,

Table 13.5 *Model decomposition of spot breakeven inflation rates*

	2004	2005	2006	2007	2008	2009	2010
Two-year horizon							
Observed breakeven inflation rate	2.12	2.04	2.11	2.08	1.69	1.11	1.47
of which							
expected inflation	1.93	1.92	1.99	2.03	2.35	1.33	1.62
inflation risk premium	0.07	0.07	0.09	0.09	0.26	−0.23	−0.06
measurement errors	0.11	0.05	0.03	−0.04	−0.93	0.00	−0.09
Three-year horizon							
Observed breakeven inflation rate	2.12	2.04	2.10	2.10	1.82	1.31	1.48
of which							
expected inflation	1.92	1.90	1.96	1.99	2.24	1.46	1.67
inflation risk premium	0.08	0.07	0.11	0.13	0.25	−0.15	−0.06
measurement errors	0.12	0.07	0.03	−0.02	−0.67	0.00	−0.13
Five-year horizon							
Observed breakeven inflation rate	2.15	2.04	2.10	2.13	1.96	1.61	1.58
of which							
expected inflation	1.92	1.89	1.93	1.94	2.12	1.62	1.76
inflation risk premium	0.11	0.08	0.14	0.18	0.26	−0.06	−0.03
measurement errors	0.11	0.07	0.03	0.00	−0.42	0.06	−0.15

The table shows a decomposition of the average values of spot BEIRs at one-, two- and five-year horizons into expected inflation, inflation risk premia and measurement errors between 2004 and 2010 over several years according to the term structure model discussed in the chapter.

inflation risk premia rose (almost doubled to around 20 basis points at the five-year horizon) and remained well above the corresponding measurement errors. During the financial crisis period, however, and in particular around the intensification of the financial market turbulence following the bankruptcy of Lehman, measurement errors increased considerably, well above the levels of inflation risk premia.

Regressing the model-implied measurement errors on several proxies for liquidity premia suggests that they captured a large part of the liquidity distortions in bond markets following Lehman's bankruptcy (see Table 13.6). Specifically, we regress the two- and five-year measurement errors for both nominal (columns 1 to 4) and real yields (columns 5 to 8) on different liquidity proxies.

For nominal bond yield errors we use LIBOR-OIS spreads, agency spreads from the German governmental agency KfW (Kreditanstalt fur Wiederaufbau) bond yields over German Treasury bonds, and asset swap spreads for nominal bonds. The LIBOR-OIS spread has been a closely watched barometer of distress in money markets in developed economies on both sides of the Atlantic since 2007. The higher the OIS spread the higher the gap between observed and liquidity-free yields, so a positive coefficient should be expected (as in columns 1 and 3). KfW bonds are fully guaranteed by the German government, so any difference between their yields and Bund yields cannot be attributed to default risk and must reflect different liquidity. Longstaff (2004) shows that bond spreads for similar US agencies capture flight-to-safety episodes well, and indeed KfW spreads have been used as proxies for liquidity in euro area bond markets in Schwarz (2010) for example. Since the bonds used in our analysis are AAA-rated, it is logical to assume that flight-to-safety flows on nominal bonds during the financial crisis should depress bond yields and therefore lead to a negative (and significant) coefficient in the measurement-error regression (as indeed in columns 1 to 4 in Table 13.6). In turn, asset-swap spreads should capture the evolution of the cost of financing a long position in the bonds market. Since a deterioration of the liquidity of the bond should be associated with a wider asset swap spread over LIBOR in the swap deal, a positive coefficient should be expected, which is in line with what we find.

To assess the information content of the model-based errors in real yields, we perform two different regressions for each maturity. The first regression uses two specific measures of liquidity for inflation-linked bonds, namely the relative trading volume in inflation-linked bonds versus that in the market as whole for all bonds and the Roll (1984) effective bid–ask spread. The relative trading variable should capture additional search costs in the smaller inflation-linked bond market, and therefore a negative coefficient should be expected. Roll's effective bid–ask spread for individual bonds is a widely used illiquidity indicator in the market microstructure literature, and we should therefore expect a positive coefficient on our model measurement errors. The indicator is based on the serial dependence of individual bond prices, and to capture overall market conditions we here employ the cross-sectional median (see García and Moreno, (2013), for additional details).[10] The second regression follows Pflueger and Viceira (2011) and uses the KfW agency spreads, relative trading volume and the (median) asset swap spread for inflation-linked bonds.

[10] Specifically, García and Moreno (2013) consider several indicators of illiquidity for IL bonds (Roll, Amihud, zero-return, as well as bond characteristics and trading patterns). The Roll indicator uses the serial dependence of price changes observed in market transactions to construct a simple yet empirically robust measure of the impact of trading frictions in the euro area inflation-linked bond market, as originally proposed by Roll (1984) and recently advocated by Bao et al. (2011) for the US corporate bond market.

Table 13.6 *Bond liquidity measures and model-based distortions in observed bond yields*

	Nominal yields				Real yields			
	Two year		Five year		Two year		Five year	
Agency spread (KfW-Bund)	-1.25 [-11.39]	-1.10 [-13.11]	-1.60 [-8.8]	-0.98 [-6.3]	1.55 [5.20]		0.08 [0.85]	
OIS Spread	0.40 [2.23]		1.32 [5.81]					
Asset swap spread		0.52 [3.09]		1.12 [3.51]		-0.71 [-3.74]		0.11 [1.90]
IL bonds relative trading volume					7.17 [0.11]	-32.31 [-0.45]	-60.71 [-1.24]	-52.17 [-1.79]
IL bonds effective bid-ask spread					1.16 [2.44]		0.29 [3.37]	
Adjusted R^2	**0.76**	**0.78**	**0.60**	**0.47**	**0.24**	**0.65**	**0.18**	**0.41**
Joint significance test (p-value)	0.00	0.00	0.00	0.00	0.00	0.00	0.00	0.00

Each column reports a regression of the model measurement errors on different proxies for liquidity in euro area bond markets. Agency spreads are from the German governmental agency KfW (Kreditanstalt fur Wiederaufbau) bonds over German Treasury bonds, and should capture flight-to-safety flows following Longstaff (2004) for US agency bonds. Effective bid–ask spreads for inflation-linked bonds are from Garcia and Moreno (2013) and are calculated using the serial correlation in bond transaction prices following Roll (1984). Asset-swap spreads reflect the median spreads over LIBOR among inflation-linked and conventional bonds in par-par asset swaps, and are from Barclays Capital. The relative transaction volume should reflect search costs in the smaller inflation-linked bond market and is calculated from bond transactions in the MTS electronic platform system. Sample is 2006M1–2010M7, and regressions include a constant that is not tabulated. T-statistics based on robust (Newey–West) standard errors are in square brackets.

Most of the liquidity proxies have the expected signs and turn out to be strongly significant, being able to explain between 50 and 75% of the variation of measurement errors for nominal bonds, and a somewhat lower 20–65% of the real yield distortions. Overall we interpret these results, where several different indicators appear to be needed to capture the liquidity distortions in both nominal and real yields and across maturities during the financial crisis, as reflecting the difficulties of measuring liquidity premia in euro area bond markets at different horizons and supporting our approach not to impose any particular variable to identify them in the estimation of our model.

13.4 Inflation compensation and inflation risk premia

This section describes the key features of inflation compensation in the euro area between 1999M1 and 2010M9, and, in particular, the role of inflation expectations and inflation risk premia at different horizons. We focus on one-year forward rates of inflation compensation ending in one, two and five years, because we collect survey inflation forecasts at those horizons, and they are a key element in our model.[11]

Table 13.7 reports the main characteristics of inflation compensation (BEIRs), expected inflation and the inflation risk premium (see also Figures 13.1 to 13.3). The term structure of euro area inflation compensation is upward sloping but relatively flat, and, with the intensification of the crisis in the autumn of 2008, inflation compensation turned more volatile. The term structure of inflation risk premia is also upward sloping and compressed, with long-term premia oscillating within a relatively narrow range of 0–50 basis points. Inflation expectations are strongly anchored at medium-to-long maturities.

These results are broadly in line with some recent research on the euro area term structure (Hördahl and Tristani, 2010; Pericoli, 2011). The size of the inflation risk premia may look small but it has to be borne in mind that our sample includes about three years of the financial crisis, and the economic downturn associated with it diminished *upside* inflation risks substantially, while keeping inflation expectations strongly anchored at levels below but close to 2%. From a more technical point of view, the term premium in the term structure of interest rates comprises not only the inflation risk premium but also an additional Jensen's inequality term that may depend on inflation uncertainty and arises from the relative convexity of nominal and inflation-linked bonds.

---

[11] Note that Equation (13.1) also establishes the link between forward inflation compensation, inflation expectations and forward inflation risk premia.

Table 13.7 *Decomposition of inflation compensation (BEIRs)*

Panel A: average levels of inflation expectations and risk premia

One-year forward	Expected inflation	Inflation risk premium
in one year	1.94	0.03
in two years	1.91	0.08
in five years	1.90	0.23

Panel B: in-sample variance decomposition of inflation compensation

One-year forward	Expected inflation	Inflation risk premium
in one year	0.70	0.30
in two years	0.65	0.35
in five years	0.15	0.85

Figures are averages of the monthly estimates of inflation compensation (BEIRs), expected inflation and inflation risk premia from our term structure model over the sample 1999M1–2010M9. The relative contributions of each component to the variance of inflation compensation are calculated according to

$$\frac{\text{Cov}(\text{BEIR}_t^n, E_t(\pi_t^n))}{\text{Var}(\text{BEIR}_t^n)} + \frac{\text{Cov}(\text{BEIR}_t^n, \phi_t^n)}{\text{Var}(\text{BEIR}_t^n)} = 1.$$

A calibration of that term using the standard deviations of nominal and inflation-linked bonds reported in Table 13.1 and the model parameters in Table 13.4 suggests that at the five-year horizon we consider in this chapter it may be around 6 basis points, and therefore does not alter the main conclusions of our analysis.[12]

To help interpret euro area BEIRs, Table 13.5 reports the relative contributions of inflation expectations and inflation risk premia to the volatility of overall inflation compensation. As reported in Table 13.1, short horizon BEIRs are more volatile than longer-term ones, and about two-thirds of that volatility reflects movements in short-term inflation expectations, with inflation risk premia playing a limited role. In contrast, the volatility of inflation compensation at longer horizons is almost fully driven by inflation risk premia, while the limited contribution of long-term inflation expectations reflects a strong anchoring of euro area inflation expectations. This result highlights the importance of accounting for this feature of inflation expectations when modelling long-term inflation risk premia. In this regard, our model-based inflation expectations, which combine information from both survey and financial data,

---

[12] We are very grateful to our discussant James Steeley for pointing this out to us (see Steeley, 1997, for additional details).

suggest that long-term inflation expectations among market participants may be even more firmly anchored than survey data suggest: with a standard deviation of 0.04, our model-based inflation expectations fluctuate less than the survey long-term inflation expectations.

13.4.1 Robustness check: model-free inflation risk premium

Inflation-linked swap rates (ILS henceforth) provide an alternative measure of inflation compensation. As standard swaps, in a zero-coupon ILS one party agrees to pay the realised inflation rate over the swap horizon, the floating leg, in exchange for a given inflation rate, the fixed leg of the swap. The euro area ILS market has developed very rapidly since 2003, partly as a financial innovation to cope with the limitations of the euro area inflation-linked bond market in its early years.[13] Indeed, IL swaps are actively traded at a wide range of maturities and can be used to gauge inflation compensation over the horizons of our survey risk measures. In contrast to inflation compensation measures from term structure models, ILS-based measures: (i) do not require the estimation of nominal and real term structures; (ii) are less prone to liquidity distortions than BEIRs calculated as the yield spread between conventional and inflation-linked bonds due to the recent turbulence in financial markets. Haubrich et al. (2011), for example, use them to estimate US inflation expectations and related premia during the financial crisis period.

Contrasting measures of inflation compensation and inflation risk premia from term structure models and from the ILS swap market may offer some interesting insights that may be particularly useful in periods of intense market turbulence. A shortcoming of ILS for monetary policy purposes during the financial crisis is, however, that a liquid ILS market only started in late 2004–2005, so their sample is more limited than what can be estimated using term structure techniques. On the other hand, although not completely isolated from liquidity distortions in the bond market, as bond and ILS measures are linked by arbitrage via asset-swap activity, the impact of liquidity distortions in ILS rates is likely to be more limited than in the bond market.[14]

As for our model-based long-term inflation compensation measures, we calculate one-year forward ILS rates ending in five years.[15] We then

---

[13] For an overview of the development of the euro area ILS market and some international comparisons see García and Van Rixtel (2007) and references therein.

[14] Some supporting evidence can be found in García and Moreno (2013).

[15] Traded inflation-linked swaps, as inflation-linked bonds, incorporate a three-month indexation lag. Although at the horizons we use them here the effect on the relevant expectations is minimal, we do take it into account when matching the survey expectations in our calculations.

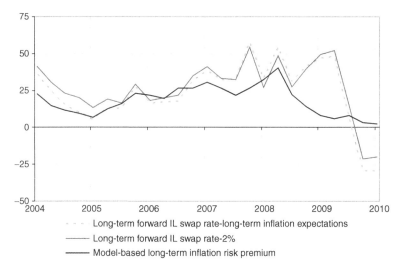

Figure 13.6 Estimated and model-free measures of long-term inflation risk premium (in basis points)
Note: The one-year forward inflation risk premium four years ahead is based on our term structure model and inflation-linked swap rates. Model-free estimates of the long-term inflation risk premium are constructed using forward inflation-linked swap rates and survey (mean) inflation expectations from the ECB's Survey of Professional Forecasters (ECB's SPF) to match the month in which the survey was conducted, in basis points. Sample 2004Q1–2010Q3.

obtain two alternative estimates of inflation risk premium out of those inflation compensation measures. The first one, our survey-based premium, is calculated by subtracting the five-year-ahead (mean) inflation expectation from the ECB's SPF from the ILS forward rate. The second, a *crude* swap-based premium measure, is constructed by subtracting a fixed inflation rate of 2% from that ILS forward rate.

Figure 13.6, which displays our model-based long-term inflation risk premium together with those two model-free proxies based on the ILS, illustrates the main points discussed above. Our model-adjusted estimates and the model-free series follow similar dynamics over the last ten years. This being said, the challenges imposed by the financial crisis are also clearly visible in the figure, with a mild deterioration in the co-movement of the series from mid-2007 with the beginning of the tensions in the money markets and particularly the intensification of the market turbulence in the autumn of 2008. Indeed, the correlation between the series decreased from 0.84 between 2004 and mid-2007 to less than 0.6 in the second part of the sample. Furthermore, the financial crisis led to more volatile model-free series, exacerbating both the level of the inflation risk premia between 2007 and most of 2008 due to the surge in oil prices, but also the downward correction as the depth and length of the expected economic downturn was gradually gaining momentum over 2009.

13.5   Concluding remarks

The goal of this chapter was to investigate the challenges posed by the financial crisis for the interpretation of movements in the term structure of interest rates in the euro area. In particular we focused on the impact of liquidity distortions on inflation-linked and conventional bond yields.

We estimated a no arbitrage model of the term structure and incorporated information on inflation-linked yields and survey measures of inflation expectations in its estimation. To minimise potential risks of mis-specification, our approach was to estimate the term structure model using the pre-crisis period and assess potential distortions to nominal and inflation-linked bond yields indirectly by analysing the residuals during the crisis period. Beyond reporting some stylised facts about the term structures of inflation compensation, inflation expectations and inflation risk premia, we also showed that liquidity distortions in the euro area market for inflation-linked and conventional bonds were substantial during the financial crisis.

Our approach is admittedly indirect, but sheds some light on the nature of the distortions affecting BEIRs during the financial crisis period. A more direct approach could focus on how best to integrate crisis-related distortions in bond yields as part of the estimation procedure. It is, however, not clear whether a direct modelling of liquidity premia by a single additional factor, as proposed, e.g., by D'Amico et al. (2010) is an optimal approach. Our results suggest that the liquidity distortions display significant variation over time, vary across maturities and are quite different for nominal and inflation-linked bonds. Moreover, our model errors are related to a large number of financial and liquidity indicators, and it is not clear how such complex effects can be integrated into the affine term structure framework. An alternative approach would be to model measurement errors as a potentially persistent process, as proposed by Ireland (2004) in a DSGE context, and analyse distortions in bond yields in a second step, as proposed in this chapter. We leave that investigation for further research.

Appendix A

Term structure model specification

A.1   Bond prices

A.1.1   Real bond prices

The price of a one-period real bond $\hat{P}_t^1$ in time t is the expected value of the pricing kernel in time $t + 1$:

$$\hat{P}_t^1 = E_t(\hat{M}_{t+1}).$$

Substituting the pricing kernel (stochastic discount factor) with $-r_t - \frac{1}{2}\lambda_t'\lambda_t - \lambda_t'\epsilon_{t+1}$ and applying the basic properties of the normal distribution,[16] we get

$$\hat{P}_t^1 = E_t(\exp(-r_t - \frac{1}{2}\lambda_t'\lambda_t - \lambda_t'\epsilon_{t+1})) = \exp(-r_t) = \exp(-\delta_0 - \delta_1' X_t).$$

Comparing this equation with the exponentially affine pricing equation $\hat{P}_t^1 = \exp(\hat{A}_1 + \hat{B}_1' X_t)$ gives the starting values for the recursive computation of the factor loadings $\hat{A}_1 = -\delta_0$ and $\hat{B}_1' = -\delta_1$.

In general, the price of an $n + 1$ maturity bond in time t is the expected value of the (stochastically) discounted price of the same bond at time $t + 1$ value of a maturity n bond

$$\hat{P}_t^{n+1} = E_t(\hat{M}_{t+1}\hat{P}_{t+1}^n).$$

Substituting the definition of the pricing kernel and applying the exponentially affine pricing rule gives

$$\hat{P}_t^{n+1} = E_t\left[\exp\left(-r_t - \frac{1}{2}\lambda_t'\lambda_t - \lambda_t'\epsilon_{t+1}\right)\exp\left(\hat{A}_n + \hat{B}_n' X_{t+1}\right)\right].$$

Substituting further for X_{t+1} and rearranging gives

$$\hat{P}_t^{n+1} = E_t\left[\exp\left(-r_t - \frac{1}{2}\lambda_t'\lambda_t - \lambda_t'\epsilon_{t+1} + \hat{A}_n + \hat{B}_n'(\mu + \Phi X_t + \Sigma\epsilon_{t+1})\right)\right]$$

$$= \exp\left(-r_t - \frac{1}{2}\lambda_t'\lambda_t + \hat{A}_n + \hat{B}_n'(\mu + \Phi X_t)\right)E_t\left[\exp\left((\hat{B}_n'\Sigma - \lambda_t')\epsilon_{t+1}\right)\right].$$

---

[16] If X is a normal distributed random variable, $Y = e^x$ is log-normal distributed with $E(Y) = e^{E(x) + \frac{1}{2}\mathrm{Var}(x)}$.

Using properties of the normal distribution gives[17]

$$\hat{P}_t^{n+1} = \exp\left(-r_t - \frac{1}{2}\lambda_t'\lambda_t + \hat{A}_n + \hat{B}_n'(\mu + \Phi X_t)\right.$$
$$\left. + \frac{1}{2}(\hat{B}_n'\Sigma - \lambda_t')(\hat{B}_n'\Sigma - \lambda_t')'\right).$$

Using the affine pricing rule $\hat{P}_t^{n+1} = \exp\left(\hat{A}_{n+1} + \hat{B}_{n+1}'X_t\right)$ on the right side of this equation and substituting for the market price of risk $\lambda_t = \lambda_0 + \lambda_1 X_t$ and the short rate $r_t = -\delta_o - \delta_1'X_t$ gives

$$\exp\left(\hat{A}_{n+1} + \hat{B}_{n+1}'X_t\right) = \exp\left(-\delta_0 + \hat{A}_n + \hat{B}_n'(\mu - \Sigma\lambda_0) + \frac{1}{2}\hat{B}_n\Sigma\Sigma\hat{B}_n'\right.$$
$$\left. + (\hat{B}_n'(\Phi - \Sigma\lambda_1) - \delta_1')X_t\right).$$

Equating the constant terms and the terms multiplied by X_t on both sides of this equation gives

$$\hat{A}_{n+1} = -\delta_0 + \hat{A}_n + \hat{B}_n'(\mu - \Sigma\lambda_0) + \frac{1}{2}\hat{B}_n\Sigma\Sigma\hat{B}_n',$$
$$\hat{B}_{n+1}' = -\delta_1' + \hat{B}_n'(\Phi - \Sigma\lambda_1).$$

A.1.2   Nominal bond prices

Nominal bonds are priced by using the nominal pricing kernel M_{t+1} instead of the real pricing kernel. Both pricing kernels are linked by inflation, $M_{t+1} = \hat{M}_{t+1}/\Pi_{t+1}$. This implies for the log pricing kernel[18] $m_{t+1} = \log(M_{t+1}) = \hat{m}_{t+1} - \pi_{t+1}$.

Using the definition of the real pricing kernel and the fact that inflation π_t is included in the state vector,[19] the log nominal pricing kernel can be written as

$$m_{t+1} = -r_t - \frac{1}{2}\lambda_t'\lambda_t - \lambda_t'\epsilon_{t+1} - e_N'X_{t+1}.$$

In the next step, the price of a one-period nominal bond can be computed by

$$P_t^1 = \exp(A_1 + B_1 X_t) = E_t\left[\exp\left(-r_t - \frac{1}{2}\lambda_t'\lambda_t - \lambda_t'\epsilon_{t+1} - e_N'X_{t+1}\right)\right].$$

---

[17] Note that Σ is symmetric, that is $\Sigma' = \Sigma$.
[18] Using $\pi_{t+1} = \log(\Pi_{t+1})$ and $\hat{m}_{t+1} = \log(\hat{M}_{t+1})$
[19] As inflation π_t is the last variable in the state vector X_t which is of dimension N, the vector e_N (which contains only zeros with the exception of the element N which is one) can be used to extract π from the state vector.

Substituting for r_t and X_{t+1} and rearranging terms gives

$$\exp(A_1 + B_1 X_t)$$

$$= E_t \left[\exp\left(-\delta_0 - (\delta_1' + e_N'\Phi)X_t - \frac{1}{2}\lambda_t'\lambda_t - e_N'\mu - (\lambda_t' + e_N'\Sigma)\epsilon_{t+1} \right) \right]$$

$$= \exp\left(-\delta_0 - (\delta_1' + e_N'\Phi)X_t - \frac{1}{2}\lambda_t'\lambda_t - e_N'\mu \right) E_t \left[\exp\left(-(\lambda_t' + e_N'\Sigma)\epsilon_{t+1} \right) \right].$$

Solving the expectations term and substituting for λ_t we get[20]

$$\exp(A_1 + B_1 X_t)$$

$$= \exp\left(-\delta_0 - (\delta_1' + e_N'\Phi)X_t - e_N'\mu + \frac{1}{2}e_N'\Sigma\Sigma e_N + e_N'\Sigma\lambda_0 + e_N'\Sigma\lambda_1 X_t \right).$$

Equating constant terms and terms multiplied by X_t on both sides gives

$$A_1 = -\delta_0 - e_N'\mu + \frac{1}{2}e_N'\Sigma\Sigma e_N + e_N'\Sigma\lambda_0),$$

$$B_1' = e_N'\Sigma\lambda_1 - (\delta_1' + e_N'\Phi).$$

In general, similar to the case of real bond prices, we have

$$P_t^{n+1} = \exp\left(A_{n+1} + B_{n+1}' X_t \right)$$

$$= E_t[\exp(-\delta_0 + \delta_1' X_t - \frac{1}{2}\lambda_t'\lambda_t - \lambda_t'\epsilon_{t+1} - e_N'X_{t+1} + A_n + B_n'X_{t+1})].$$

After substituting for X_{t+1} we get

$$\exp\left(A_{n+1} + B_{n+1}' X_t \right) = E_t[\exp(-\delta_0 + \delta_1' X_t - \frac{1}{2}\lambda_t'\lambda_t$$

$$+ ((B_n' - e_N')\Sigma - \lambda_t')\epsilon_{t+1} + A_n + (B_n' - e_N')\mu + (B_n' - e_N')\Phi X_t)].$$

Solving for the expectation term[21] and substituting for λ_t gives, after rearrangements,

$$\exp\left(A_{n+1} + B_{n+1}' X_t \right) = \exp\left[-\delta_0 + A_n + (B_n - e'N)(\mu - \Sigma\lambda_0) \right.$$

$$\left. + \frac{1}{2}(B_n - e'N)\Sigma\Sigma(B_n - e'N) + ((B_n - e'N)\Phi - \delta_1' - (B_n - e'N)\Sigma\lambda_1)X_t \right].$$

Again, after equating constant terms and terms multiplied by X_t on both sides of the equation we get

---

[20] We use the relationship $(\lambda_t' + e_N'\Sigma)(\lambda_t' + e_N'\Sigma)' = (\lambda_t' + e_N'\Sigma)(\Sigma'e_N + \lambda_t) = e_N'\Sigma\Sigma e_N + \lambda_t'\lambda_t + 2e_N'\Sigma\lambda_t$.

[21] We use the relationship $((B_n' - e_N')\Sigma - \lambda_t')((B_n' - e_N')\Sigma - \lambda_t')' = ((B_n' - e_N')\Sigma - \lambda_t')(-\lambda_t + \Sigma(B_n' - e_N')') = \lambda_t'\lambda_t + (B_n' - e_N')\Sigma\Sigma(B_n' - e_N')' - 2(B_n' - e_N')\Sigma\lambda_t$.

$$A_{n+1} = -\delta_0 + A_n + (B'_n - e'_N)(\mu - \Sigma\lambda_0) - \frac{1}{2}(B'_n - e'_N)\Sigma\Sigma(B'_n - e'_N)',$$

$$B'_{n+1} = (B'_n - e'_N)(\Phi - \Sigma\lambda_1) - \delta'_1.$$

A.2 State-space representation

In order to use Kalman filter estimation techniques, we first express the affine term structure model in a state-space form:

$$w_t = d + ZX_t + \eta_t \quad \text{(measurement equation)},$$
$$X_t = \Phi X_{t-1} + \Sigma\epsilon_t \quad \text{(state equation)}.$$

The vector d and the matrix Z, which link the state variables (latent factors) with the observed data, are constructed by using the coefficients $\hat{A}_n$, $\hat{B}_n$, A_n, and B'_n described in Section A.1. The transformations of the bond prices into bond yields are done by using the relation $P_t^n = \exp(-y_t^n n)$ or $y_t^n = -\log(P_t^n)/n$.

The vector of observed data w_t contains the bond yields and, if the model includes them, the SPF inflation expectations:

$$
\mathbf{w}_t = \begin{bmatrix} y_t^3 \\ y_t^{12} \\ y_t^{24} \\ y_t^{36} \\ y_t^{60} \\ \pi_t \\ \hat{y}_t^{24} \\ \hat{y}_t^{36} \\ \hat{y}_t^{60} \\ E_t^{\text{SPF}}[\pi_{t+12}] \\ E_t^{\text{SPF}}[\pi_{t+24}] \\ E_t^{\text{SPF}}[\pi_{t+60}] \end{bmatrix},
\mathbf{d} = \begin{bmatrix} -A_3/3 \\ -A_{12}/12 \\ -A_{24}/24 \\ -A_{36}/36 \\ -A_{60}/60 \\ 0 \\ -\hat{A}_{24}/24 \\ -\hat{A}_{36}/36 \\ -\hat{A}_{60}/60 \\ e_3(I - \Phi^{12})(I - \Phi)^{-1}\mu \\ e_3(I - \Phi^{24})(I - \Phi)^{-1}\mu \\ e_3(I - \Phi^{60})(I - \Phi)^{-1}\mu \end{bmatrix},
\mathbf{Z} = \begin{bmatrix} -B_3/3 \\ -B_{12}/12 \\ -B_{24}/24 \\ -B_{36}/36 \\ -B_{60}/60 \\ (0,0,1) \\ -\hat{B}_{24}/24 \\ -\hat{B}_{36}/36 \\ -\hat{B}_{60}/60 \\ e_3\Phi^{12} \\ e_3\Phi^{24} \\ e_3\Phi^{60} \end{bmatrix}.
$$

The structure of the variance–covariance matrix of the measurement errors is as follows:

$$
\begin{bmatrix} \sigma_\epsilon^2(1) & 0 & \cdots & 0 \\ 0 & \sigma_\epsilon^2(2) & \cdots & 0 \\ \vdots & \vdots & \ddots & \vdots \\ 0 & 0 & \cdots & \sigma_\epsilon^2(12) \end{bmatrix}.
$$

We impose the following restrictions in its main diagonal elements:

$$\sigma_\epsilon^2(1), \ldots, \sigma_\epsilon^2(5) = \tilde{\sigma}_\epsilon^2(1),$$
$$\sigma_\epsilon^2(6) = 0,$$
$$\sigma_\epsilon^2(7), \ldots, \sigma_\epsilon^2(9) = \tilde{\sigma}_\epsilon^2(2),$$
$$\sigma_\epsilon^2(10), \ldots, \sigma_\epsilon^2(12) = \tilde{\sigma}_\epsilon^2(3),$$

which implies that (i) inflation π_t is measured without error; (ii) data freely determines the variances of the measurement errors for nominal yields, real yields and survey inflation expectations. The transition equation of the state-space is identical to the transition equation described in the main text.

References

Ang, A., Bekaert, G. and Wei, M. (2008). The term structure of real rates and inflation expectations, *Journal of Finance*, **63**, 797–849.

Bao, J., Pan, J. and Wang, J. (2011). The illiquidity of corporate bonds, *Journal of Finance*, **66**(3), 911–946.

Bernanke, B. (2007). Inflation expectations and inflation forecasting, Monetary Workshop of the NBER Summer Institute, Cambridge, MA.

Campbell, J., Schiller, R. and Viceira, L. (2009). Understanding inflation-indexed bond markets, *Brookings Papers on Economic Activity*, 7, 79–120, Spring.

Chernov, M. and Mueller, P. (2011). The term structure of inflation expectations, *Journal of Financial Economics*, **106**(2), 367–394.

Chernozhukov, V. and Hong, H. (2003). An MCMC approach to classical estimation, *Journal of Econometrics*, **115**, 293–346.

D'Amico, S., Kim, D. and Wei, M. (2010). Tips from TIPS: the informational content of Treasury inflation-protected security prices, Finance and Economics Discussion Series 2010-19. Board of Governors of the Federal Reserve System (U.S.).

Dewachter, H. and Lyrio, M. (2008). Learning, macroeconomic dynamics and the term structure of interest rates. In *Asset Pricing and Monetary Policy* (J. Campbell, ed.), Chicago: University of Chicago Press.

Ejsing, J., García, J. A. and Werner, T. (2007). The term structure of euro area break-even inflation rates: the impact of seasonality, ECB Working Paper Series No. 830, November.

Fontaine, J.-S. and García R. (2012). Bond liquidity premia, *Review of Financial Studies*, **25**(4), 1207–1254.

Fleckenstein, M., Longstaff, F. A. and Lustig, H. (2011). Why does the Treasury issue TIPS? The TIPS-Treasury bond puzzle, NBER Working Paper No. 16358.

García, J. A. (2003). An introduction to the ECB's survey of professional forecasters, ECB Occasional Paper, no. 8.

García, J. A. and Manzanares, A. (2007). What can probabilistic forecasts tell us about inflation risks? ECB Working Paper series, no. 825.

García, J. A. and Moreno, A. (2013). The illiquidity of inflation-linked bonds in the euro area, ECB Working Paper series, forthcoming.

García, J. A. and van Rixtel, A. (2007). Inflation-linked bonds from a central bank's perspective, ECB Occasional Paper, no. 62, June.

Gürkaynak, R., Levin, A. and Swanson, E. (2010). Does inflation targeting anchor long-run inflation expectations? Evidence from long-term bond yields in the U.S., U.K., and Sweden, *Journal of the European Economic Association*, **8**(6), 1208–1242.

Haubrich, J., Pennacchi, G. and Ritchken, P. (2011). Inflation expectations, real rates and risk premia: evidence from inflation swaps, Federal Reserve Bank of Cleveland Working Paper 11-07.

Hördahl, P. and Tristani, O. (2010). Inflation risk premia in the US and the euro area, BIS Working Paper, no. 325, November.

Ireland, P. N. (2004). A method for taking models to the data, *Journal of Economic Dynamics and Control*, **28**, 1205–1226.

Joyce, M., Lildholdt, P. and Sorensen, S. (2010). Extracting inflation expectations and inflation risk premia from the term structure: a joint model of the UK nominal and real yield curves, *Journal of Banking & Finance*, **34**(2), 281–294.

Kim, D. (2009). Challenges in macro-finance modelling, *Federal Reserve Bank of Saint Louis Review*, September/October.

Longstaff, F. (2004). The flight to liquidity premium in U.S. Treasury bond prices. *Journal of Business*, **77**, 511–526.

Pericoli, M. (2011). Expected inflation and inflation risk premium in the euro area and in the United States, CIMF-IESEG conference *The yield curve and new developments in macrofinance: what have we learnt from the 2007–2010 financial crisis*. Cambridge, UK, September 2011.

Pflueger, C. E. and Viceira, L. (2011). An empirical decomposition of risk and liquidity in nominal and inflation-indexed government bonds, NBER Working Paper, no. 16892.

Roll, R. (1984). A simple implicit measure of the effective bid–ask spread in an efficient market, *Journal of Finance*, **39**, 1127–1139.

Schwarz, K. (2010). Mind the gap: disentangling credit and liquidity in risk spreads, Mimeo, University of Pennsylvania, October.

Steeley, J. M. (1997). A two factor model of the UK yield curve, *Manchester School*, **65**, 32–58.

Wall Street Journal (2010). Look to TIPS, Not Fed, for inflation Tips, January 27.

Wright, J. H. (2011). Term premia and inflation uncertainty: empirical evidence from an international panel dataset, *American Economic Review*, **101**, 1514–1534.

14 The predictive content of the yield curve for inflation

Hans Dewachter, Leonardo Iania and Marco Lyrio

14.1 Introduction

It is hard to overestimate the importance of inflation forecasting. Since most prices are sticky and a number of contracts imply long-term commitments in nominal terms, forward-looking economic agents tend to have implicitly in their decision-making process some form of forecasting of the general price level in the economy. For example, the prediction of inflation guides firms and employees during the negotiation of labour contracts, and influences investors in the evaluation of asset prices. This central role of inflation expectations in the economy also creates a mandate for central banks to achieve predictable (and low) inflation rates. Therefore, inflation forecasting is also important from a central banking perspective; inflation projections typically serve as an important element in the monetary policy decision process.

Notwithstanding the importance of inflation forecasting, it has been difficult to develop satisfactory forecasting models that generate both accurate and timely inflation forecasts. The significant publication lags of crucial information variables limit the use of various model-based or survey-based approaches and have introduced market-based alternatives. The latter circumvent the issue of publication lags by limiting the information set to observable financial variables and hence have the potential to provide timely inflation forecasts. Examples of this approach include the well-known breakeven inflation rate or, more recently, the use of inflation swaps. However, the success of the latter approach crucially hinges on the dominance of the expectations component in the time variation of the derived measures. While such an assumption may be reasonable in tranquil periods, it is clearly not the case during more

The views expressed are solely our own and do not necessarily reflect those of the National Bank of Belgium.

turbulent periods, where marked increases in risk and liquidity premia may blur the information content of market-based measures.

In recent work, Faust and Wright (2011) analyse seventeen methods to forecast inflation, including survey-based, model-based, and financial market-based measures. They compare models from a statistical perspective only, thus ignoring timeliness. Interestingly, they find that subjective forecasts (e.g. surveys) of inflation outperform most model-based forecasts in terms of out-of-sample root-mean-square error (RMSE), and that the random walk-based model of Atkeson and Ohanian (2001) does remarkably well in forecasting inflation. They also find that market-based measures of inflation expectations are simply too volatile to represent rational forecasts of long-run levels of inflation. These measures most likely incorporate not only inflation expectations but also inflation risk premia and liquidity premia.

Two recent papers corroborate the finding that inflation and liquidity risk premia blur the information content of market-based measures, i.e. Joyce et al. (2010) and D'Amico et al. (2010). Joyce et al. (2010) use a term structure model for nominal and real bond yields to decompose the UK yield curve into expected real short rates, expected inflation, real term premia, and inflation risk premia. The authors report the importance of inflation risk premia in the variation of long-term bond yields. D'Amico et al. (2010) study the US bond market. They use data on nominal bond yields and Treasury Inflation-Protected Securities (TIPS), supplemented by survey forecasts of interest rates. Their results indicate the existence of a substantial but declining liquidity premium in the TIPS market from 1999 until around 2004, which remained at a relatively low level until 2007.

In Dewachter et al. (2012), we revisit the potential of market-based measures for inflation forecasting once these measures are handled by a macro-finance model. We focus on information contained in the yield curve and address the issue of the excess volatility ('nuisance') due to time-varying liquidity and risk premia. In particular, we concentrate on the most popular yield curve variable used to forecast macroeconomic aggregates such as real activity and inflation, i.e. the yield spread.[1] Although the predictive power of this variable for real activity seems well established, its forecasting ability for inflation is weaker (see Kozicki, 1997).

---

[1] The yield spread is the difference between yields on long- and short-term government bonds. Examples of publications investigating the forecasting power of the term spread for economic activity are, among others, Estrella and Hardouvelis (1991), Estrella and Mishkin (1998), Plosser and Rouwenhorst (1994) and Stock and Watson (1989). For inflation, see, for example, Fama (1990), Mishkin (1990), Estrella and Mishkin (1997) and Jorion and Mishkin (1991).

More specifically, in Dewachter et al. (2012) we investigate whether a decomposition of yield spreads into an expectations and a term premium component increases the predictive power to forecast inflation.[2] By decomposing the yield spread, we explicitly allow for a potentially different impact, in terms of size and sign, of the expectations and term premium components on inflation forecasts. This is relevant since macroeconomic and financial shocks have different contributions to the dynamics of each of the yield spread components. We find that the yield spread decomposition is crucial to forecast inflation for most forecasting horizons.

In this chapter, we investigate the robustness of our earlier findings by focusing on a different measure of inflation over an extended sample period. As in Dewachter et al. (2012), the decomposition of the yield spread into an expectations and a term premium component is based on the extended macro-finance model (EMF) of Dewachter and Iania (2011). The EMF model augments standard macro-finance models of the term structure of interest rates with the inclusion of three financial factors and two stochastic trends. The first two financial factors in the EMF model reflect financial strains in the money market, while the third financial factor captures time variation in bond risk premia. The two stochastic trends allow for highly persistent processes capturing the time variation in long-run inflation expectations and in the equilibrium real rate, two key components of long-run interest rate expectations. The model is applied to the US economy and estimated with Bayesian techniques.

Our main findings are twofold. First, we identify the importance of financial shocks in the dynamics of bond yields. We show that macroeconomic factors alone are not able to capture much of the variation in yield spreads and attribute an important role to financial factors. We illustrate the importance of financial shocks, in particular liquidity and risk premium shocks, in the evolution of yield spreads during the period 2004–2012. This includes the period in which the behaviour of world bond markets was described by the former Federal Reserve Chairman Alan Greenspan as a 'conundrum', and the current financial crisis. Second, in an in-sample exercise, we show that the yield spread decomposition increases significantly the predictive power of yield spreads to forecast inflation. This is the case since the dynamics of long-term yields are heavily influenced by term premium movements which occur

---

[2] Other studies decomposing the yield spreads into an expectation and a term premium component to forecast GDP growth are Hamilton and Kim (2002), Ang et al. (2006) and Favero et al. (2005), among others. We are not aware of any study that uses such a decomposition to forecast inflation.

mainly due to financial shocks. We investigate whether such a decomposition adds forecasting power beyond that achieved with the random walk-based model proposed by Atkeson and Ohanian (2001), and the inclusion of control variables.

The remainder of the chapter is organised as follows. Section 14.2 explains briefly the EMF model and discusses the implied decomposition of the yield curve into expectations and term premium components. Section 14.3 describes the data and the Bayesian model specification used to estimate the EMF model. Section 14.4 analyses the model-implied term premia and focuses on the yield spread decomposition, and its impact in the forecasting of inflation. The main findings are summarised in the conclusion.

14.2   A macro-finance model with financial factors

As is well known, one can decompose the yield on a n-period zero-coupon bond at time t, $y_t^{(n)}$, into an expectations and a term premium component:

$$y_t^{(n)} = \underbrace{\frac{1}{n}\sum_{\tau=0}^{n-1} E_t\left[y_{t+\tau}^{(1)}\right]}_{\text{expectations component}} + \underbrace{\chi_t^{(n)}}_{\text{term premium component}}. \tag{14.1}$$

The expectations component is the average expected one-period interest rate over the remaining maturity of the bond, and the term premium component is the additional compensation required to lock in the money over n periods instead of rolling over $n-1$ times an investment in a one-period bond. This section introduces the macro-finance model used in this chapter and derives the model-implied components of Equation (14.1).

14.2.1   Macro-finance framework

A general macro-finance model can be described by four main assumptions. First, the pricing kernel, m_t, which represents an investor's intertemporal marginal rate of substitution, is assumed to be log-normally distributed and is defined as an exponentially affine function of the risk-free rate, i_t, and a set of Gaussian structural shocks, ε_{t+1}:

$$m_{t+1} = \exp\left(-i_t - \frac{1}{2}\Lambda_t'\Lambda_t - \Lambda_t'\varepsilon_{t+1}\right), \qquad \varepsilon_{t+1} \sim N(0, I), \tag{14.2}$$

where Λ_t are the market prices of risk for the structural shocks. Second, following Duffee (2002), the risk-free interest rate and the prices of risk are restricted to be affine functions of the factors, X_t:

$$i_t = \delta_0 + \delta_1' X_t,$$
$$\Lambda_t = \Lambda_0 + \Lambda_1 X_t. \tag{14.3}$$

Third, the law of motion of the state vector under the historical probability measure follows a first-order vector error correction model (VECM) transition equation:

$$X_{t+1} = C + \Phi X_t + \Sigma \varepsilon_{t+1}. \tag{14.4}$$

Finally, invoking the no-arbitrage assumption, we can compute the price of an n-period bond at time t by solving the following relation recursively:

$$P_t^{(n)} = E_t \left[m_{t+1} P_{t+1}^{(n-1)} \right], \tag{14.5}$$

with the initial condition $P_t^{(0)} = 1$. The resulting yields are linear functions of the state vector:

$$y_t^{(n)} \equiv -\frac{\ln P_t^{(n)}}{n} = A_{y,n} + B_{y,n} X_t, \tag{14.6}$$

where $A_{y,n} = -a_{y,n}/n$ and $B_{y,n} = -b_{y,n}/n$, with $a_{y,n}$ and $b_{y,n}$ satisfying the standard no-arbitrage difference equations (see Ang and Piazzesi, 2003 and Duffee, 2002).

The model summarised by Equations (14.4) and (14.6) implies affine representations for the expectations and term premium components, as defined in Equation (14.1). More specifically, the expectations component can be written as:

$$\frac{1}{n}\sum_{\tau=0}^{n-1} E_t \left[y_{t+\tau}^{(1)} \right] = \frac{1}{n}\sum_{\tau=0}^{n-1} \left[A_{y,1} + B_{y,1} E_t X_{t+\tau} \right] = A_{e,n} + B_{e,n} X_t, \tag{14.7}$$

where $A_{e,n} = -a_{e,n}/n$ and $B_{e,n} = -b_{e,n}/n$, with $a_{e,n}$ and $b_{e,n}$ determined by the following difference equations:

$$a_{e,n} = a_{e,n-1} + b_{e,n-1} C + \frac{1}{2} b_{e,n-1} \Sigma \Sigma' b_{e,n-1}' - \delta_0,$$
$$b_{e,n} = b_{e,n-1} \Phi - \delta_1', \tag{14.8}$$

given the initial conditions $a_{e,0} = 0$ and $b_{e,0} = [0, ..., 0]$.

The term premium implied by the above framework can be obtained directly from the affine representation for the yield curve and the expectations component:

$$\chi_t^{(n)} = A_{y,n} - A_{e,n} + \left(B_{y,n} - B_{e,n} \right) X_t. \tag{14.9}$$

In order to close the model, we just need to specify the set of factors used in it. In the next section, we use the EMF model for this purpose.

14.2.2 The extended macro-finance model

The EMF model contains eight state variables which can be sorted in three groups: (i) three observable macroeconomic factors (inflation, π_t, the output gap, y_t, and the central bank policy rate, i_t^{cb}); (ii) three latent financial factors, two related to the overall liquidity and counterparty risk in the money market ($l_{1,t}$ and $l_{2,t}$, respectively) and one driving the one-period bond risk premia ($l_{3,t}$); (iii) two stochastic trends modelling the long-run equilibrium of inflation, π_t^*, and the equilibrium real rate, ρ_t. The state vector X_t introduced in Equation (14.4) is, therefore, given by

$$X_t = [\pi_t, y_t, i_t^{cb}, l_{1,t}, l_{2,t}, l_{3,t}, \pi_t^*, \rho_t]'. \qquad (14.10)$$

The inclusion of the three observable macroeconomic variables is standard in macro-finance models while the introduction of liquidity factors is motivated by the recent works of Christensen et al. (2009), Feldhütter and Lando (2008) and Liu et al. (2006). In our model, the liquidity factors are related to tensions in the money market. We focus our attention on a standard measure of funding liquidity in the money market, the TED spread (i.e. the difference between the unsecured money market rate, i_t^{mm}, and the Treasury bill (T-bill) rate, $y_t^{(1)}$). We decompose this spread into two components, see Equation (14.11) below. The first component is the spread factor $l_{1,t}$, which represents a proxy for the convenience yield from holding Treasury bills and can be seen as a flight-to-quality component. The second component is the spread factor $l_{2,t}$, which reflects a credit component and measures counterparty risk as it is given by the difference between the unsecured and the secured or collateralised money market rate, i_t^{repo}. Formally:

$$\text{TED}_t = i_t^{mm} - y_t^{(1)} = l_{1,t} + l_{2,t},$$
$$l_{1,t} = i_t^{repo} - y_t^{(1)}, \quad \text{and} \quad l_{2,t} = i_t^{mm} - i_t^{repo}. \qquad (14.11)$$

The third financial factor ($l_{3,t}$) captures the time variation in the one-period bond premium and therefore measures the risk attitude in the market. The motivations for the inclusion of this factor are twofold. First, Dewachter et al. (2012) show, for a dataset similar to ours, that realised excess returns display strong collinearity across maturities, indicating the presence of a dominant factor in bond risk premia. Second, Cochrane and Piazzesi (2005), Cochrane and Piazzesi (2009) and Joslin et al. (2009) give evidence that a substantial fraction of the variation in bond risk premia cannot be explained by macroeconomic factors but should be modelled with an additional return-forecasting factor. In the EMF framework, this factor is identified by restrictions on the prices of risk (Λ_1) such that it accounts for all the variation in the one-period bond premium.[3]

We now turn to the two stochastic trends. A number of recent papers have suggested modelling the yield curve dynamics as a cointegrated or near-cointegrated system. The EMF model introduces two stochastic trends, π_t^* and ρ_t, representing the long-run equilibrium inflation rate and the equilibrium real rate, respectively. We ensure this macroeconomic interpretation by imposing the following cointegrating restrictions in the transition equation (14.4):

$$\lim_{s \to \infty} E_t\left[\pi_{t+s}\right] = \pi_t^*, \quad \text{and} \quad \lim_{s \to \infty} E_t\left[i_{t+s}^{cb}\right] = \rho_t + \pi_t^*. \tag{14.12}$$

As shown in, for example, Dewachter and Lyrio (2006), Cochrane and Piazzesi (2009) and Dewachter and Iania (2011), the introduction of stochastic trends in macro-finance models alters the model dynamics significantly. Specifically, unlike standard macro-finance models with fixed equilibrium levels for inflation and interest rates, the EMF model allows for time variation in the long-run expectations of these variables. From the perspective of the current chapter, allowing for stochastic trends in the factor dynamics is important as it affects significantly the model-implied expectations and term premium components, especially at the long end of the maturity spectrum.

14.3   Estimation

14.3.1   *Data*

We estimate the EMF model on US quarterly data over the period 1960:Q1–2012:Q1 (209 observations). The variables included in the sample can be divided in four groups. (*i*) *Standard macroeconomic series.* This group consists of the core PCE inflation (which excludes food and energy prices), the output gap constructed from data provided by the Congressional Budget Office (CBO), and the central bank policy rate represented by the effective federal funds rate. The data are obtained from the Federal Reserve Bank of St. Louis FRED database. (*ii*) *Yield curve data.* We use per annum zero-coupon yield data for maturities of 1, 4, 8, 12, 16, 20 and 40 quarters from the Fama-Bliss Center

---

[3] These restrictions are $\Lambda_1(i,j) = 0$, $\forall j \neq 6$ and $\forall i$.

for Research in Security Prices (CRSP) bond files with the exception of 40-quarter yields obtained from Gürkaynak et al. (2007). (*iii*) *Money market spreads*. This group consists of money market rates used to identify the decomposition of the TED spread into a convenience yield ($l_{1,t}$) and a credit-crunch or counterparty risk factor ($l_{2,t}$). We use the 1-quarter eurodollar (Ed) rate and the 1-quarter London Interbank offered rate – LIBOR (Lb) – from Datastream to identify the credit-crunch factor. We supplement the LIBOR data with data on the eurodollar given that the latter series dates back further in time.[4] We also use the 1-quarter T-bill rate to identify the convenience yield. All spreads are computed relative to the secured money market rate represented by the government-backed collateral repo rate (GC-repo) from Bloomberg (ticker RPGT03M). (*iv*) *Additional series used to identify the two stochastic trends in the model.* We use survey data on the average 4- and 40-quarter inflation forecasts to identify long-run inflation expectations (π_t^*). The data are from the Survey of Professional Forecasters (Federal Reserve Bank of Philadelphia). We also use data on the potential output growth, measured as the quarterly growth of CBO potential output, to identify the equilibrium real rate (ρ_t).

14.3.2 Econometric setting

The EMF model contains a total of 92 parameters represented by the vector θ. We estimate the model using standard Bayesian MCMC techniques based on informative priors. We rewrite the state space dynamics in Equation (14.4) making explicit the dependence on the parameter vector θ:

$$X_{t+1} = C(\theta) + \Phi(\theta)X_t + \Sigma(\theta)\varepsilon_{t+1}, \quad \varepsilon_{t+1} \sim N(0, I). \quad (14.13)$$

The measurement equation relates the observed data Z_t to the state vector X_t:

$$Z_t = A(\theta) + B(\theta)X_t + S(\theta)\eta_t, \quad \eta_t \sim N(0, I). \quad (14.14)$$

As mentioned before, we use four groups of information variables in the measurement equation. The observed series in Z_t consist of (*i*) macroeconomic variables ($Z_{\text{mac},t}$), (*ii*) yield curve data ($Z_{\text{y},t}$), (*iii*) money market spreads ($Z_{\text{mm},t}$), and (*iv*) data used to identify the two long-run trends in the model ($Z_{\text{LR},t}$).

---

[4] Given that the eurodollar and the LIBOR rates are closely related, we use the former as an additional proxy for the credit-crunch factor.

The vector of constants $A(\theta)$, the matrix of factor loadings $B(\theta)$, and the matrix $S(\theta)$ are partitioned into four blocks:

$$A(\theta) = [A'_{\text{mac}}, A'_{\text{y}}, A'_{\text{mm}}, A'_{\text{LR}}]', \tag{14.15}$$

$$B(\theta) = [B'_{\text{mac}}, B'_{\text{y}}, B'_{\text{mm}}, B'_{\text{LR}}]', \tag{14.16}$$

$$S(\theta) = \text{diag}(S'_{\text{mac}}, S'_{\text{y}}, S'_{\text{mm}}, S'_{\text{LR}}). \tag{14.17}$$

A number of observations can be made. First, we assume that the three macroeconomic variables $(\pi_t, y_t, i_t^{\text{cb}})$ are observed without errors, implying that $A_{\text{mac}} = 0_{3 \times 1}$, $B_{\text{mac}} = [I_{3 \times 3}, 0_{3 \times 5}]$, and $S_{\text{mac}} = 0_{3 \times 1}$. Second, all yields are measured with an error and are related to the state variables through the no-arbitrage equation (14.6). Third, we use three money market spreads to identify the convenience yield and credit-crunch factors ($l_{1,t}$ and $l_{2,t}$, respectively). We use two measures for the TED spread since LIBOR rates are only available from 1986:Q2 onwards. For the period 1971:Q2–1986:Q1, we use the TED spread based on the eurodollar rate $(i_t^{\text{Ed}} - y_t^{(1)})$. After that, the TED spread is based on the LIBOR rate $(i_t^{\text{Lb}} - y_t^{(1)})$. Both are used to identify the credit-crunch factor ($l_{2,t}$). We assume there is a spread between the eurodollar and LIBOR rates equal to a constant, c_{Ed}, plus an idiosyncratic shock, $\eta_{\text{Ed},t}$.

$$i_t^{\text{Ed}} = y_t^{(1)} + c_{\text{Ed}} + l_{1,t} + l_{2,t} + s_{\text{Ed}} \eta_{\text{Ed},t}. \tag{14.18}$$

The third spread is based on the GC-repo rate $(i_t^{\text{GC}} - y_t^{(1)})$ and identifies the convenience yield ($l_{1,t}$) perfectly.

Finally, survey data on 4- and 40-quarter average inflation forecasts $F_{\pi,t}^{(4)}$ and $F_{\pi,t}^{(40)}$ are used to identify the stochastic trend for inflation. The loadings for these survey expectations are implied by the transition equation (14.4). The stochastic trend for the real rate is identified by the growth rate of potential output:

$$\Delta y_t^{\text{pot}} = \alpha + \beta_\rho \rho_t + s_{\Delta y^{\text{pot}}} \eta_{\Delta y^{\text{pot}},t}, \tag{14.19}$$

where y_t^{pot} denotes log potential output. We allow for measurement errors in each of the series: $S_{\text{LR}} = [s_{F_{\pi,t}^{(4)}}, s_{F_{\pi,t}^{(40)}}, s_{\Delta y^{\text{pot}}}]'$.

The log-likelihood function is obtained from the prediction error decomposition implied by the measurement Equation (14.14), by exploiting the linearity and normality of the system composed by equations (14.13) and (14.14), and making use of Kalman filter recursions (see Harvey, 1991).

The type of distribution, mean, and standard deviation for the prior of the parameter vector θ are the same as the ones in Dewachter et al.

(2012). Overall, we use relatively loose priors characterised by large standard deviations of the prior distributions. Most of the priors reflect standard beliefs regarding macroeconomic dynamics. The priors incorporate significant inertia in the dynamics of macroeconomic variables and impose a delayed deflationary impact of changes in the policy rate. Also, the priors for the dynamics of the policy rate reflect a Taylor-rule type of monetary policy. The prior distributions on the impact matrix Σ identify a supply, a demand, and a policy rate shock, while modelling the financial shocks as demand shocks affecting inflation and the output gap negatively. Finally, the priors for the prices of risk are constructed such that the EMF model implies an upward-sloping yield curve (see also Chib and Ergashev, 2009).

14.4   Empirical results

The EMF model presented in Section 14.2 is estimated using core PCE as a measure of inflation.[5] Dewachter and Iania (2011) provide a careful evaluation of the model's performance in fitting the yield curve using a comparable dataset. As one of the motivations to use the EMF model is to distinguish between expectations and risk premium components, Section 14.4.1 illustrates the relevance of this type of yield curve decomposition. Having used the EMF model to decompose yield spreads into an expectations and a term premium component, in Section 14.4.2 we assess the importance of such decomposition to forecast inflation.

14.4.1 Yield spread decomposition

Figure 14.1 shows the decomposition of the 10-year yield spread into an expectations and a term premium component. The top panel of Figure 14.1 shows the 10-year yield spread implied by the EMF model, while the middle and bottom panels display its expectations and term premium components, respectively. This figure shows that a significant part of the yield spread movement is due to the time variation in the term premium. This fact confirms the well-known rejection of the expectations hypothesis[6] and has significant economic implications. In

---

[5] For brevity, we do not report the parameter estimates here. The use of alternative measures of inflation deliver similar results. All additional results are available upon request.

[6] See Fama (1984), Jones and Roley (1983), Mankiw and Summers (1984) and Shiller et al. (1983). For more recent studies, see Cochrane and Piazzesi (2005, 2009), Duffee (2011) and Joslin et al. (2009). These papers report statistically and economically significant time-varying risk premia.

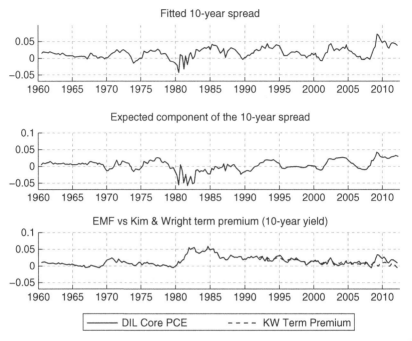

Figure 14.1 10-year yield spread: fitted value and expectations and term premium components
Note: The top panel plots the fitted spread of the 10-year yield less the 1-quarter yield of the EMF model. The middle panel depicts the EMF model-implied expected average 1-quarter yield over a period of 10 years minus the 1-quarter yield of the EMF model. The bottom panel plots the EMF model-implied term premium for the 10-year bond and the term premium of Kim and Wright (2005) (dashed line).

particular, it implies that the one-to-one relation between yield spreads and expected short rates breaks down, making the informational content of yield spreads with respect to future macroeconomic variables less clear.[7] A decomposition of the yield curve, therefore, may help identify the macroeconomic information contained in the yield curve.

Given the empirical relevance of the time variation in the term premia, the next step is to identify the economic and financial forces behind movements of the yield spread, and its expectations and term premium

---

[7] Our term premium component is also similar to the Kim and Wright (2005) measure, selected by Rudebusch et al. (2007) as the most representative among a number of measures analysed. The Federal Reserve Board provides data to generate the term premium from the Kim and Wright (2005) model, which is a standard latent factor model augmented with survey data.

Table 14.1 *Variance decomposition of yield spreads*

	(a) Yield spread				(b) Expectations comp.				(c) Term prem. comp.			
	σ^M	σ^{MP}	σ^L	σ^{RP}	σ^M	σ^{MP}	σ^L	σ^{RP}	σ^M	σ^{MP}	σ^L	σ^{RP}
Horizon	4-qtr yield spread				4-qtr yield spread				4-qtr yield spread			
4 qtr	0.03	0.26	0.18	0.54	0.06	0.86	0.09	0.00	0.00	0.01	0.22	0.76
40 qtr	0.04	0.21	0.21	0.53	0.07	0.83	0.10	0.00	0.01	0.08	0.22	0.69
Horizon	40-qtr yield spread				40-qtr yield spread				40-qtr yield spread			
4 qtr	0.10	0.48	0.08	0.34	0.07	0.84	0.09	0.00	0.01	0.12	0.06	0.81
40 qtr	0.12	0.32	0.32	0.25	0.09	0.76	0.15	0.00	0.01	0.18	0.22	0.59

σ^M = macro; σ^{MP} = monetary policy; σ^L = liquidity; σ^{RP} = risk premium.

components. To analyse the information content of each of these variables, we perform a variance decomposition, which allows us to identify the dominant shocks driving each of the components.[8]

Table 14.1 summarises the results for yield spreads of maturities 4 and 40 quarters, and also for forecasting horizons of 4 and 40 quarters. To simplify interpretation, we present the effect of four groups of shocks: *macro shocks*, which include supply, demand, long-run inflation, and equilibrium real rate shocks; *monetary policy shocks*; *liquidity shocks*, which include flight-to-quality and credit-crunch shocks; and *risk premium shocks*, which represent the shocks to the return-forecasting factor.

Yield spreads are marginally influenced by macro shocks. Panel (a) shows that short-term yield spreads are dominated by risk premium shocks, with monetary policy and liquidity shocks becoming more important for long-term yield spreads. From Panel (b), we observe that the expectations component of yield spreads are dominated by monetary policy shocks. In contrast, the term premium component of the yield spreads shown in Panel (c) is dominated by risk premium shocks at all maturities and forecasting horizons. Liquidity shocks play a significant role for longer forecasting horizons while monetary policy shocks gain in importance for bonds with longer maturities.

The results of the variance decomposition indicate that the expectations component of the spread is dominated by macro- and monetary-policy shocks, while the term premium component mainly reflects

[8] Shocks are obtained using a Cholesky decomposition on the conditional variance–covariance matrix. The ordering of the variables is the same as the one in the state vector (Equation (14.10)).

financial shocks. Such differences in compositions could entail differences in the information content of the respective components with respect to inflation forecasting, an issue taken up in Section 14.2.

The estimation of the EMF model also gives us the possibility of analysing the historical contribution over time of the realised shocks to each of the factors in the model. In particular, we are interested in the relevance of the financial shocks that hit the economy during two recent periods, the so-called bond market conundrum between 2004 and 2006, and the financial crisis that started in mid-2007. Figures 14.2 and 14.3 display the historical decomposition of the 1-quarter yield, the 10-year yield, and the 10-year yield spread in terms of the eight shocks in the EMF model over these two periods.

The conundrum period was characterised by a directional divergence between short- and long-term yields. From mid-2004 to mid-2006, there

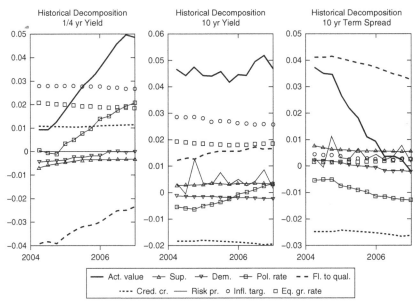

Figure 14.2 Historical decomposition: conundrum period
Note: The contribution of the shocks is evaluated at the mode of the posterior distribution of the parameters. 'Act. value' is the historical (actual) data, 'Sup.' stands for supply shocks, 'Dem.' for demand shocks, 'Pol. rate' for policy rate shocks, 'Fl. to qual.' for flight-to-quality shocks, 'Cred. cr.' for credit-crunch shocks, 'Risk pr.' for risk premium shocks, 'Infl. targ.' for long-run inflation shocks, and 'Eq. gr. rate' for equilibrium growth rate shocks.

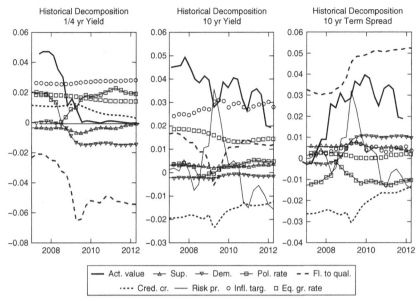

Figure 14.3 Historical decomposition: current financial crisis
Note: The contribution of the shocks is evaluated at the mode of the posterior distribution of the parameters. 'Act. value' is the historical (actual) data, 'Sup.' stands for supply shocks, 'Dem.' for demand shocks, 'Pol. rate' for policy rate shocks, 'Fl. to qual.' for flight-to-quality shocks, 'Cred. cr.' for credit-crunch shocks, 'Risk pr.' for risk premium shocks, 'Infl. targ.' for long-run inflation shocks, and 'Eq. gr. rate' for equilibrium growth rate shocks.

was a trend-wise increase in short-term rates from 1 per cent to almost 5 per cent (left panel of Figure 14.2). Despite this increase, long-term rates remained around 4.5 percent during most of this period with a slight increase by mid-2006 (middle panel of Figure 14.2). This break in the co-movement between short and long rates has been hard to interpret and has been labelled by the former Fed Chairman Alan Greenspan as a conundrum. It translated into a sharp decrease in the long-term yield spread, shown in the right panel of Figure 14.2. According to Rudebusch et al. (2006), benchmark macro-finance models (only containing macro-factors and shocks) cannot account for this disconnection in the dynamics of short- and long-term rates. The EMF model relates this directional divergence between short and long yields to the occurrence of significant financial and monetary policy shocks. The decomposition shown in the right panel of Figure 14.2 reveals that a significant part of the decrease in the long-term yield spread during this period is explained by a decrease in the contribution of risk premium shocks, liquidity shocks (flight-to-quality) and monetary policy shocks.

The current financial crisis was characterised by unprecedented cuts in the federal funds rate, dropping by 5pp from 2007:Q4 to 2009:Q4, and a sharp increase in the slope of the yield curve, which increased by 3pp over the same period of time (Figure 14.3). Our model explains this decoupling between the long- and short-end of the yield curve by means of financial, demand and policy rates shocks. The initial increase of the term spread was due to monetary policy shocks followed by flight-to-quality, demand and risk premium shocks. Interestingly, our model assigns an important role to the latter shocks in the increase of the spread. According to our model, investors became increasingly more risk averse during the crisis, a trend that was reversed by the beginning of 2009 after the approval of the rescue plan by the US authorities at the end of 2008.

The main message from this analysis is that the occurrence of financial shocks seems to have been important during the two periods analysed and therefore distorted the conventional information conveyed by movements in the yield curve. In the next section, we assess the predictive content of yield spreads and their decomposition into expectations and a term premium component for inflation predictions.

14.4.2 Inflation forecasting

The results from the previous section provide evidence of a time-varying term premium in long-term bonds which might affect the information content of yield spread changes. In addition, variance decompositions and historical decompositions show clearly the importance of financial shocks in the variation of the term premium component of bond yields whereas the expectation component is driven mainly by macro-shocks. Therefore, to the extent that macro- and financial shocks carry different information for future inflation, one might expect that yield spread decompositions could improve the forecasting performance relative to models only including the yield spread.

In this section, we assess whether by decomposing yield spreads ($\mathrm{Spr}_t^{(n)}$) into an expectations ($\mathrm{Spr}_t^{e,(n)}$) and a term premium ($\chi_t^{(n)}$) component we are able to improve the forecasting power for inflation, where:

$$\mathrm{Spr}_t^{(n)} = y_t^{(n)} - y_t^{(1)} = \mathrm{Spr}_t^{e,(n)} + \chi_t^{(n)}. \qquad (14.20)$$

Ours is an in-sample forecasting exercise and takes into consideration the findings of Faust and Wright (2011), which suggest that the random walk-based model proposed by Atkeson and Ohanian (2001) (RW-AO) works remarkably well in forecasting inflation. We therefore investigate the forecasting power of decomposed yield spreads beyond the one obtained with a random walk-based model and the inclusion of control variables.[9]

The RW-AO model predicts that inflation k periods ahead is equal to the average of quarterly inflation over the past four quarters, $\bar{\pi}_{t-3,t} = \frac{1}{4}\sum_{j=0}^{3}\pi_{t-j}$. Hence, we evaluate the predictive power of yield spreads – and their decomposition in expectations and term premium components – to predict the deviation of future inflation k periods ahead from the forecast based on the RW-AO model at time t, $\bar{\pi}_{t-3,t}$. The four models we estimate can be represented by the general regression as follows:

$$\pi_{t+k} - \bar{\pi}_{t-3,t} = \alpha + \beta^{\text{EC+TP}}(\text{Spr}_t^{\text{e},(n)} + \chi_t^{(n)}) + \beta^{\text{TP}}\chi_t^{(n)}$$
$$+ \gamma(\pi_t - \bar{\pi}_{t-4,t-1}) + \delta y_t^{(1)} + \varepsilon_{t+k}, \qquad (14.21)$$

where π_{t+k} is the level of inflation between quarters $t + k - 1$ and $t + k$, expressed in annual terms. We allow for a set of control variables, that is the deviation of current inflation from the average of quarterly inflation over the periods $t - 4$ and $t - 1$, $\pi_t - \bar{\pi}_{t-4,t-1}$, and the short-term interest rate, $y_t^{(1)}$. The RW-AO model can therefore be recovered by making $\beta^{\text{EC+TP}} = \beta^{\text{TP}} = \gamma = \delta = 0$. We predict inflation 1, 4 and 8 quarters ahead (k) using 4-, 20- and 40-quarter (n) yield spreads.

We provide our results in Table 14.2. The results for Model 1 show that yield spreads alone are not statistically significant for any of the horizons considered, leading to very low adjusted R^2s. In other words, yield spreads alone do not add forecasting power beyond the RW-AO model. Using decomposed yield spreads (Model 2), however, we observe a significant increase in the adjusted R^2 for all forecasting horizons and spread maturities. Moreover, the t-statistics for the β^{TP}s clearly reject the null hypothesis $H_0 : \beta^{\text{TP}} = 0$, showing the statistical significance of the yield spread decomposition. If we allow for control variables instead of decomposing the yield spread (Model 3 versus Model 1), we also observe a significant increase in the adjusted R^2. However, a comparison between Models 1 and 2 and Models 1 and 3 shows that for horizons above one year the yield spread decomposition has a larger effect (increase) on the adjusted R^2 than the inclusion of control variables. The results

---

[9] As mentioned before, Faust and Wright (2011) also show that subjective forecasts of inflation outperform most model-based forecasts. We do not include those in our forecasting exercise since we choose to restrict the analysis to financial market information which is readily available.

Table 14.2 *Forecasting core PCE inflation*

Mod. 1

$$\pi_{t+k} - \bar{\pi}_{t-3,t} = \alpha + \beta \mathrm{Spr}_t^{(n)} + \varepsilon_{t+k}$$

hor. (k)	1 qtr			4 qtr			8 qtr		
mat. (n)	4 qtr	20 qtr	40 qtr	4 qtr	20 qtr	40 qtr	4 qtr	20 qtr	40 qtr
α	0.001	0.002	0.002	0.000	0.002	0.002	-0.003	-0.002	-0.002
	(0.001)	(0.002)	(0.002)	(0.002)	(0.003)	(0.003)	(0.002)	(0.002)	(0.002)
β	-0.098	-0.168*	-0.110	0.048	-0.190	-0.124	0.764*	0.183	0.147
	(0.210)	(0.093)	(0.069)	(0.323)	(0.147)	(0.109)	(0.449)	(0.146)	(0.107)
Adj. R^2	-0.003	0.031	0.022	-0.005	0.017	0.011	0.036	0.008	0.009

Mod. 2

$$\pi_{t+k} - \bar{\pi}_{t-3,t} = \alpha + \beta^{\mathrm{EC+TP}}(\mathrm{Spr}_t^{e,(n)} + \chi_t^{(n)}) + \beta^{\mathrm{TP}}\chi_t^{(n)} + \varepsilon_{t+k}$$

hor. (k)	1 qtr			4 qtr			8 qtr		
mat. (n)	4 qtr	20 qtr	40 qtr	4 qtr	20 qtr	40 qtr	4 qtr	20 qtr	40 qtr
α	0.003***	0.003***	0.004**	0.004***	0.005**	0.007***	0.002	0.004**	0.006***
	(0.001)	(0.001)	(0.002)	(0.002)	(0.002)	(0.003)	(0.002)	(0.002)	(0.002)
$\beta^{\mathrm{EC+TP}}$	-0.048	-0.060	-0.067	0.450	0.024	-0.041	2.290***	0.528***	0.300***
	(0.297)	(0.083)	(0.060)	(0.403)	(0.124)	(0.093)	(0.514)	(0.120)	(0.089)
β^{TP}	-0.516**	-0.203***	-0.201***	-1.300***	-0.465***	-0.435***	-2.545***	-0.784***	-0.662***
	(0.203)	(0.059)	(0.053)	(0.291)	(0.081)	(0.074)	(0.423)	(0.112)	(0.099)
Adj. R^2	0.083	0.087	0.090	0.147	0.159	0.164	0.247	0.242	0.219

Mod. 3

$$\pi_{t+k} - \bar{\pi}_{t-3,t} = \alpha + \beta \mathrm{Spr}_t^{(n)} + \gamma(\pi_t - \bar{\pi}_{t-4,t-1}) + \delta y_t^{(1)} + \varepsilon_{t+k}$$

hor. (k)	1 qtr			4 qtr			8 qtr		
mat. (n)	4 qtr	20 qtr	40 qtr	4 qtr	20 qtr	40 qtr	4 qtr	20 qtr	40 qtr
α	0.001	0.004***	0.005**	0.004**	0.010***	0.012***	0.010***	0.014***	0.017***
	(0.001)	(0.001)	(0.002)	(0.002)	(0.002)	(0.003)	(0.003)	(0.003)	(0.004)

β	−0.059	−0.130**	−0.116**	0.035	−0.264**	−0.257***	0.607*	−0.061	−0.147
	(0.149)	(0.059)	(0.047)	(0.265)	(0.109)	(0.082)	(0.363)	(0.114)	(0.090)
γ	0.485***	0.453***	0.451***	0.451**	0.380*	0.368*	0.192	0.160	0.129
	(0.102)	(0.102)	(0.102)	(0.214)	(0.208)	(0.207)	(0.156)	(0.153)	(0.152)
δ	−0.020	−0.040**	−0.051**	−0.083**	−0.126***	−0.153***	−0.219***	−0.241***	−0.271***
	(0.020)	(0.019)	(0.020)	(0.037)	(0.036)	(0.037)	(0.040)	(0.046)	(0.050)
Adj. R^2	0.236	0.252	0.253	0.119	0.151	0.162	0.180	0.155	0.164

$$\pi_{t+k} - \bar{\pi}_{t-3,t} = \alpha + \beta^{EC+TP}\left(Spr_t^{e,(n)} + \chi_t^{(n)}\right) + \beta^{TP}\chi_t^{(n)} + \gamma\left(\pi_t - \bar{\pi}_{t-4,t-1}\right) + \delta y_t^{(1)} + \varepsilon_{t+k}$$

Mod. 4 hor. (k)	1 qtr			4 qtr			8 qtr		
mat. (n)	4 qtr	20 qtr	40 qtr	4 qtr	20 qtr	40 qtr	4 qtr	20 qtr	40 qtr
α	0.001	0.001	0.002	0.003	0.003	0.007*	0.002	0.001	0.008
	(0.002)	(0.002)	(0.002)	(0.003)	(0.003)	(0.004)	(0.004)	(0.005)	(0.005)
β^{EC+TP}	0.015	−0.002	−0.019	0.576	0.111	−0.038	2.240**	0.634***	0.238
	(0.369)	(0.085)	(0.061)	(0.646)	(0.155)	(0.111)	(0.890)	(0.219)	(0.154)
β^{TP}	−0.341	−0.144	−0.131	−1.242*	−0.462***	−0.349**	−2.464***	−0.868***	−0.575***
	(0.374)	(0.103)	(0.089)	(0.637)	(0.175)	(0.149)	(0.835)	(0.241)	(0.201)
γ	0.438***	0.437***	0.436***	0.327	0.321	0.316	0.059	0.064	0.067
	(0.105)	(0.105)	(0.105)	(0.214)	(0.213)	(0.209)	(0.178)	(0.169)	(0.165)
δ	0.004	0.008	0.003	0.013	0.024	−0.019	−0.008	0.046	−0.044
	(0.041)	(0.040)	(0.042)	(0.080)	(0.078)	(0.080)	(0.092)	(0.101)	(0.106)
Adj. R^2	0.257	0.258	0.259	0.188	0.198	0.200	0.241	0.237	0.213

The standard errors of the coefficients are in parentheses. ***, **, and * indicate that the value is statistically significant at the 1%, 5%, and 10% level, respectively. We estimate the model over the period 1960:Q1–2008:Q4.

of Model 4, moreover, show that even allowing for control variables the yield spread decomposition is in most cases still statistically significant. Furthermore, the increase in the adjusted R^2 is higher for longer forecasting horizons. Comparing the coefficients for the yield spread (β) and its components (β^{EC+TP} and β^{TP}) in Models 3 and 4, respectively, we observe that allowing for separate effects from the yield spread components increases the information content of the yield spread, i.e. the separate coefficients increase in magnitude due to their opposite signs.

In all cases where the expectations component is statistically significant it has a positive association with future inflation, indicating that markets expect short-term rates to increase with increasing inflation. On the contrary, the total impact of the term premium ($\beta^{EC+TP} + \beta^{TP}$) is always negative. These differences in sign cannot be captured by regressions involving only the spread itself. Despite the robustness of the negative impact of the term premium on future inflation, further research on the determinants of the link between perceived risk aversion and subsequent inflation dynamics is required. We conclude that the yield spread decomposition is crucial for forecasting inflation and becomes more important as the forecasting horizon increases.

14.5   Conclusion

We used the EMF model of Dewachter and Iania (2011) to decompose yield spreads into an expectations and a term premium component and assessed whether this decomposition increases the forecasting power of yield spreads for inflation. Our formal tests investigated whether this decomposition adds predictive power beyond the one obtained by the random walk-based model proposed by Atkeson and Ohanian (2001). We also tested the robustness of the results to the inclusion of control variables. The EMF model was chosen for this task due to its ability to identify the macroeconomic and financial driving forces behind movements in the yield curve. The set of financial factors, incorporated in the EMF macro-finance model, includes liquidity (flight-to-quality and credit-crunch) and risk premium factors.

The estimates from the EMF model show a significant time-varying risk premium, confirming the results in the literature which reject the expectations hypothesis. We illustrated the time variation in the term premium component of long-term bonds which might affect the information content of yield spread changes. We also showed the importance of financial shocks in the variation of the term premium component of bond yields with the use of a variance decomposition. This finding is in line with the recent literature indicating that macroeconomic factors cannot account for the time variation in term premia. The importance of financial shocks is also evident from the historical decomposition of long-term yield spreads during the period 2004–2012. Finally, we showed that the yield spread decomposition increases significantly the forecasting power of yield spreads for inflation for most forecasting horizons. Also, in general, the inclusion of control variables such as the short-term interest rate and the lagged dependent variable does not drive out the predictive power of the yield spread decomposition.

Faust and Wright (2011) caution against the use of market-based measures of inflation expectations (e.g. breakeven inflation). Our results indicate that the potential danger mentioned by Faust and Wright (2011) of using these measures might be associated with the presence of term premium components, which can only be filtered with the use of a proper macro-finance model. We show that the EMF model is one possible way to differentiate between expectations and term premium components. And, by using the model-implied decomposition, high-frequency financial market data can be used to infer market inflation expectations.

References

Ang, A. and Piazzesi, M. (2003). A no-arbitrage vector autoregression of term structure dynamics with macroeconomic and latent variables. *Journal of Monetary Economics*, **50**(4), 745–787.

Ang, A., Piazzesi, M. and Wei, M. (2006). What does the yield curve tell us about GDP growth? *Journal of Econometrics*, **131**(1–2), 359–403.

Atkeson, A. and Ohanian, L. E. (2001). Are Phillips curves useful for forecasting inflation? *Federal Reserve Bank of Minneapolis Quarterly Review*, **25**(1), 2–11.

Chib, S. and Ergashev, B. (2009). Analysis of multifactor affine yield curve models. *Journal of the American Statistical Association*, **104**(488), 1324–1337.

Christensen, J. H. E., Lopez, J. A. and Rudebusch, G. D. (2009). Do central bank liquidity facilities affect interbank lending rates? Working Paper Series 2009-13, Federal Reserve Bank of San Francisco.

Cochrane, J. H. and Piazzesi, M. (2005). Bond risk premia. *American Economic Review*, **95**(1), 138–160.

Cochrane, J. H. and Piazzesi, M. (2009). Decomposing the yield curve. *AFA 2010 Atlanta Meetings Paper*.

D'Amico, S., Kim, D. H. and Wei, M. (2010). Tips from TIPS: the informational content of Treasury Inflation-Protected Security prices. Finance and Economics Discussion Series 2010-19, Board of Governors of the Federal Reserve System (US).

Dewachter, H. and Iania, L. (2011). An extended macro-finance model with financial factors. *Journal of Financial and Quantitative Analysis*, **46**, 1893–1916.

Dewachter, H. and Lyrio, M. (2006). Macro factors and the term structure of interest rates. *Journal of Money, Credit and Banking*, **38**(1), 119–140.

Dewachter, H., Iania, L. and Lyrio, M. (2012). Information in the yield curve: a macro-finance approach. *Journal of Applied Econometrics*, forthcoming.

Duffee, G. R. (2002). Term premia and interest rate forecasts in affine models. *Journal of Finance*, **57**(1), 405–443.

Duffee, G. R. (2011). Information in (and not in) the term structure. *Review of Financial Studies*, **24**, 2895–2934.

Estrella, A. and Hardouvelis, G. A. (1991). The term structure as a predictor of real economic activity. *Journal of Finance*, **46**(2), 555–76.

Estrella, A. and Mishkin, F. S. (1997). The predictive power of the term structure of interest rates in Europe and the United States: implications for the European Central Bank. *European Economic Review*, **41**(7), 1375–1401.

Estrella, A. and Mishkin, F. S. (1998). Predicting U.S. recessions: financial variables as leading indicators. *Review of Economics and Statistics*, **80**(1), 45–61.

Fama, E. F. (1984). The information in the term structure. *Journal of Financial Economics*, **13**, 509–528.

Fama, E. F. (1990). Term-structure forecasts of interest rates, inflation and real returns. *Journal of Monetary Economics*, **25**(1), 59–76.

Faust, J. and Wright, J. H. (2011). Forecasting inflation. Unpublished manuscript, Johns Hopkins University.

Favero, C., Kaminska, I. and Söderström, U. (2005). The predictive power of the yield spread: further evidence and a structural interpretation. CEPR Discussion Papers 4910.

Feldhütter, P. and Lando D. (2008). Decomposing swap spreads. *Journal of Financial Economics*, **88**(2), 375–405.

Gürkaynak, R. S., Sack, B. and Wright, J. H. (2007). The U.S. treasury yield curve: 1961 to the present. *Journal of Monetary Economics*, **54**(8), 2291–2304.

Hamilton, J. D. and Kim, D. H. (2002). A reexamination of the predictability of economic activity using the yield spread. *Journal of Money, Credit and Banking*, **34**(2), 340–60.

Harvey, A. C. (1991). *Forecasting, Structural Time Series Models and the Kalman Filter*. Cambridge: Cambridge University Press.

Jones, D. S. and Roley, V. V. (1983). Rational expectations and the expectations model of the term structure: a test using weekly data. *Journal of Monetary Economics*, **12**, 453–465.

Jorion, P. and Mishkin, F. S. (1991). A multicountry comparison of term-structure forecasts at long horizons. *Journal of Financial Economics*, **29**(1), 59–80.

Joslin, S., Priebsch, M. and Singleton, K. J. (2009). Risk premium accounting in macro-dynamic term structure models. Unpublished manuscript.

Joyce, M. A., Lildholdt, P. and Sorensen, S. (2010). Extracting inflation expectations and inflation risk premia from the term structure: a joint model of the UK nominal and real yield curves. *Journal of Banking and Finance*, **34**(2), 281–294.

Kim, D. H. and Wright, J. H. (2005). An arbitrage-free three-factor term structure model and the recent behavior of long-term yields and distant-horizon forward rates. Finance and Economics Discussion Series 2005-33, Board of Governors of the Federal Reserve System (US).

Kozicki, S. (1997). Predicting real growth and inflation with the yield spread. *Economic Review*, Q IV, 39–57.

Liu, J., Longstaff, F. A. and Mandell, R. E. (2006). The market price of credit risk: an empirical analysis of interest rate swap spreads. *Journal of Business*, **79**(5), 2337–2359.

Mankiw, N. G. and Summers, L. H. (1984). Do long-term interest rates overreact to short-term interest rates? *Brookings Papers on Economic Activity*, **1**, 223–242.

Mishkin, F. S. (1990). The information in the longer maturity term structure about future inflation. *Quarterly Journal of Economics*, **105**(3), 815–828.

Plosser, C. I. and Rouwenhorst, G. K. (1994). International term structures and real economic growth. *Journal of Monetary Economics*, **33**(1), 133–155.

Rudebusch, G. D., Sack, B. P. and Swanson, E. T. (2007). Macroeconomic implications of changes in the term premium. *Federal Reserve Bank of St. Louis Review*, **84**(4), 241–269.

Rudebusch, G. D., Swanson, E. T. and Wu, T. (2006). The bond yield 'conundrum' from a macro-finance perspective. *Monetary and Economic Studies*, **24**(S-1), 83–109.

Shiller, R. J., Campbell, J. Y. and Schoenholtz, K. L. (1983). Forward rates and future policy: interpreting the term structure of interest rates. *Brookings Papers on Economic Activity*, **1**, 173–217.

Stock, J. H. and Watson, M. W. (1989). New indexes of coincident and leading economic indicators. *NBER Macroeconomics Annual 1989*, **4**, 351–409.

15 Inflation risk premium and the term structure of macroeconomic announcements in the euro area and the United States

Marcello Pericoli

15.1 Introduction

Over the past decade government-issued inflation-indexed, or index-linked, bonds have become available in a number of euro-area countries and have provided a fundamentally new instrument popular among institutional investors and households, especially for retirement saving. From a policy perspective, inflation-indexed bonds can be used to extrapolate inflation expectations at different maturities. In fact, bonds linked to an inflation index differ from the corresponding standard bonds in respect of expected inflation and inflation risk premia as well as of maturities, coupon rates and cash-flow structures. In addition, as index-linked bonds have different maturities, an entire spectrum of inflation expectations and inflation risk premia can be derived from the comparison with standard nominal bonds. Hence, stemming from the no-arbitrage affine Gaussian term structure literature developed for standard bonds, some recent papers have investigated a theoretical and empirical framework to jointly price standard and index-linked bonds based on a small number of common factors. The novelty of this stream of literature, to which this chapter belongs, is to have consistent, i.e. arbitrage-free, estimates of the real and nominal interest rates as well as expected inflation rates and inflation risk premia.

This chapter estimates a no-arbitrage affine Gaussian term structure model for nominal and real zero-coupon interest rates implied

I would like to thank Michael Ehrmann, Paul Mizen, Lucio Sarno, Alessandro Secchi, Christian Speck and participants at the conference 'The Yield Curve and New Developments in Macro-finance. What have we learnt from the 2007–2010 financial crises?' organised by IESEG and the University of Cambridge, the 2012 Eastern Finance Association meeting, the ICEF seminar of the University of Venice 'Ca' Foscari' for comments. Responsibility for any errors is, of course, entirely my own.

in government bonds with macroeconomic surprises in the euro area and the United States. This class of model enables a model-implied constant-maturity inflation compensation (or model-implied breakeven inflation rate), obtained as the difference between the estimated nominal and real zero-coupon rates, to be split into the expected component (i.e. the expected inflation) and the premium requested by investors to hedge against unexpected changes in inflation, namely the inflation risk premium. This chapter aims to build a bridge between models with nominal and index-linked bonds, on the one hand, and multifactor models of the term structure with observable variables à la Ang and Piazzesi (2003) and interest-rate models with macroeconomic surprises, on the other hand, by introducing the surprises inside the no-arbitrage affine Gaussian term structure framework. However, this chapter does not consider macro-factors such as inflation and industrial production as it uses weekly data and, therefore, focuses on information available in real time. The impact of macroeconomic surprises on the nominal and real term structure is measured by the factor loadings associated with each piece of news and their impulse response function. When the surprises of macroeconomic announcements are plugged into the term structure model, it is possible to estimate the impact of surprises on the entire term structure, both nominal and real, which is consistent with the absence of arbitrage in the bond markets.

A model which jointly estimates the expected inflation, the inflation risk premium and the impact of macroeconomic surprises presents three advantages with respect to the use of the regression of real and nominal interest rates on surprises. First, over longer time horizons, the breakeven inflation rate can substantially differ from the expected inflation as the compensation requested by investors for uncertainty about future inflation rates – i.e. the inflation premium – can be considerable. Second, real and nominal interest rates are estimated on the basis of a common set of factors which drive the entire nominal and real term structure; so this class of model is capable of giving an economic intuition of the drivers of the nominal and real term structures. Third, this class of model gives fresh and readily available updates of market responses to surprises in inflation expectations and interest rates, key ingredients in monetary policy decisions.

This chapter differs with respect to the previous macro-finance literature. First, it uses weekly data for the euro area; previous works with weekly data include those by Risa (2001) for the United Kingdom and Adrian and Wu (2010) for the United States. Second, the three latent factors are interpreted as a transformation of observable financial variables and this helps assign an economic interpretation to these factors, which drive the shape of the nominal and real term structures. Third, the same methodology is applied to the euro area and the United States, allowing a consistent comparison between the two markets. The use of weekly data is essential when this class of model is used by monetary policymakers to evaluate inflation expectations and inflation risk premia.

This chapter draws on an extensive literature which establishes the significance to the bond market of various scheduled macroeconomic and monetary policy announcements. Usually bond markets are forward-looking and incorporate both expected macroeconomic data and expected monetary policy interest rates; thus, only unexpected changes, e.g. surprises, can generate variations in bond market prices.

Obviously, macroeconomic and monetary policy announcements are strongly interconnected. On the one hand, changes in the interest rates across the maturity spectrum due to macroeconomic surprises can reveal information about markets' beliefs regarding the monetary policy reaction function. Usually markets expect central banks to react to surprises in the medium term and not in the short term since, as more new information accumulates, the central bank is likely to react. On the other hand, changes in the interest rates across the maturity spectrum due to monetary surprises can give a rough signal of the market's assessment of monetary policy credibility. In a credible inflation targeting regime, an increase in the policy rate is compatible with a reduction in long-term rates and a decrease in far-ahead forward inflation rates. Similarly, if far-ahead forward inflation is relatively stable and insensitive to macroeconomic surprises, then the monetary policy stance has been reasonably successful in anchoring long-term inflation expectations.

All in all, in spite of the announcements' importance, few studies examine their impact on the term structure as a whole. Most studies have looked at a single interest rate, a few rates from one part of the maturity spectrum, or a short-term rate and a long-term rate. Even when they do consider more than a single rate, there is typically no attempt to relate surprises across maturities. The aim of this chapter is to help fill this gap by analysing the reaction of nominal and real interest rates, as well as forward inflation rates, to macroeconomic and monetary policy surprises in the United States and the euro area. Moreover, the no-arbitrage affine term structure model allows for consistent comparison across the entire maturity spectrum. Lastly, the outbreak of the financial crisis in August 2007 is an event study that allows a comparison of the bond market in tranquil and turbulent times. The framework of this chapter enables a comparison of both the credibility of the monetary policy stance in the two areas and the changing aspects of macroeconomic surprises.

The results show that nominal rates are impacted by macroeconomic surprises in growth, the labour market and economic outlook in the United States and by surprises in inflation in the euro area. These results may be due to differences in the mandates of the monetary authorities, which is dual in the United States and hierarchical in the euro area. Moreover, monetary policy shocks make short-term breakeven inflation rates increase in the United States, while they do not change breakeven inflation rates across the maturity spectrum in the euro area. These different responses to monetary shocks highlight dissimilarities between the markets' perception of monetary policy targets.

The chapter is organised as follows. Section 15.2 reviews the literature on models for joint nominal and real term structures. Section 15.3 describes the data for the nominal and real rates and the methodology for computing the surprises. Section 15.4 presents the effects of surprises on interest rates. The affine Gaussian term structure model is presented in Section 15.5 while Section 15.6 presents the results. Section 15.7 concludes.

15.2   The literature

15.2.1   Nominal and real affine term structure models

Recent papers on the term structure of inflation can be divided into two broad groups. The first uses the standard setup of the no-arbitrage Gaussian affine term structure models of nominal and real interest rates with some identification assumptions meant to increase the power of the estimates; along this line of research there are Evans (1998), Risa (2001), Joyce et al. (2010), Ang et al. (2008), D'Amico et al. (2008), Christensen et al. (2010), García and Werner (2010), Adrian and Wu (2010) and Haubrich et al. (2011, 2012). Alternatively, a second stream of work uses standard new Keynesian macro-finance models which encompass financial and macro variables; the works by Chernov and Mueller (2012) and Hördahl and Tristani (2010) belong to this line of research. This chapter belongs to the first category of papers.

Evans (1998) and Risa (2001) use a no-arbitrage Gaussian affine term structure model and study the term structure of real and nominal rates, expected inflation, and inflation risk premia derived from the prices of index-linked and nominal debt in the United Kingdom. Both authors find strong evidence of variable inflation risk premia throughout the term structure and, furthermore, reject both the Fisher hypothesis and versions of the expectations hypothesis for real rates. In these papers the variability of the nominal to real yield spread is mostly due to inflation at the short end and to its premium at the long end.

Ang et al. (2008) develop a term structure model with regime switches, time-varying prices of risk and inflation to identify these components of the nominal yield curve. They find that the unconditional real rate curve in the United States is fairly flat at around 1.3%. In one real rate regime, the real term structure is steeply downward sloping. An inflation risk premium that increases with maturity fully accounts for the generally upward sloping nominal term structure.

Christensen et al. (2010) show that the affine arbitrage-free Nelson–Siegel model can be estimated for a joint representation of nominal and real yield curves in the United States. The results suggest that long-term inflation expectations have been well anchored over the past few years in the United States and that the inflation risk premia, while volatile, have been close to zero on average. Haubrich et al. (2011, 2012) estimate the term structure of inflation expectations and inflation risk premia by means of data on inflation swap rates, nominal Treasury yields and survey forecasts of inflation. The use of inflation swap rates rules out the problems connected with the illiquidity of the index-linked Treasuries. They find that the short-term real interest rate is typically the most volatile component of the yield curve, that expected inflation over short horizons is also volatile, that investors' expectations of longer-term inflation have declined substantially over the last twenty years, and that the 10-year inflation risk premium has varied between 23 and 55 basis points. Joyce et al. (2010) and D'Amico et al. (2008) document the importance of using index-linked bonds for accurate predictions of inflation for the United Kingdom and for the United States, respectively.

García and Werner (2010) document that no-arbitrage Gaussian affine term structure models fit data well in the euro area, but lack economic interpretation; so the authors introduce survey inflation risks and show that perceived asymmetries in inflation risks help interpret the dynamics of long-term inflation risk premia, even after controlling for a large number of macro and financial factors. Similarly Adrian and Wu (2010) present estimates of the term structure of inflation expectations, derived from an affine model of real and nominal yield curves for the United States. The model features stochastic covariation of inflation with the real pricing kernel. The authors fit the model not only to yields, but also to the yields' variance–covariance matrix, thus increasing the identification power, and find that model-implied inflation expectations can differ substantially from breakeven inflation rates when market volatility is high.

Within the second set of works, Chernov and Mueller (2012) use evidence from the term structure of inflation expectations to address the question of whether or not monetary policy is effective. They show that the inflation premia and out-of-sample estimates of long-term inflation suggest that US monetary policy became effective over time. As an implication, their model outperforms standard macro-finance models in inflation and yield forecasting. Hördahl and Tristani (2010) extend a traditional New-Keynesian macro-finance model by encompassing the nominal and the real term structure and introduce survey data on inflation and interest rate expectations at various future horizons. They show that in the euro area and in the United States, inflation risk premia are relatively small, positive, and increasing in maturity. The cyclical dynamics of long-term inflation risk premia are mostly associated with changes in output gaps, while their high-frequency fluctuations appear to be aligned with variations in inflation. However, inflation premia are countercyclical in the euro area, while they are procyclical in the United States.

15.2.2   Surprises and term structure models

While in the 1980s the literature focused on money supply announcements (Grossman, 1981; Urich and Wachtel, 1981; Roley and Walsh, 1985; and Cook and Hahn, 1987), work in the 1990s documented the importance of employment, the producer price index, consumer price index, and other announcements on interest rates (Hardouvelis, 1988, and Edison, 1996). Most announcement studies, based on daily and high frequency data, document that the price response to scheduled macroeconomic announcements is typically completed within one or two minutes (Ederington and Lee, 1993, and Fleming and Remolona, 1999a, b); in the US bond market, the largest five-minute price changes occur immediately after the release of scheduled macroeconomic announcements (Fleming and Remolona, 1997). Piazzesi (2001) estimates the effects of macroeconomic forecasts and monetary surprises on the US fixed income market with daily data by means of an affine term structure model augmented with jumps. Ehrmann and Fratzscher (2005) investigate whether the degree of interdependence between the United States and the euro area has changed with EMU by analysing the effects of surprises on daily short-term interest rates in the two economies. They find a strongly increased interdependence of money markets around EMU. Spillover effects from the United States to the euro area remain stronger than in the opposite direction, even if US markets have recently started reacting to euro area developments.

In the same vein, few studies evaluate the effect of inflation targeting on long-term inflation expectations by comparing the behaviour of bond yield data. Gürkaynak, Levin, and Swanson (2010) present an analysis on how forward interest rates and far-ahead forward inflation rates respond to unexpected monetary announcements in the United States, the United Kingdom and Sweden. If the steady-state inflation rate is constant over time and known by all agents – that is, if inflation expectations are well anchored – then standard macroeconomic models predict that inflation should return to its steady state well within ten years after a shock (Gürkaynak et al. 2005). To test whether this prediction is satisfied in the data, the analysis must look beyond the effects of economic announcements on the first few years of the term structure and focus instead on the response of far-ahead forward interest rates and inflation compensation to the announcement. Despite the novelty of these papers, the literature still lacks an analysis of announcement effects on the entire term structure.

15.3   The data

15.3.1   *Nominal and real zero-coupon rates*

Nominal and real zero-coupon interest rates for the euro area are estimated from end-of-week quotes of French government bonds by means of the smoothing B-spline methodology first introduced by Fisher et al. (1995) and presented in Pericoli (2013). Data range from January 2002 to April 2012. The use of French government bonds is motivated by the large number of French index-linked issues with the highest class of rating among euro-area countries; Italian index-linked government bonds have a lower rating while the few issues of German index-linked bonds are characterised by a much shorter history.

The nominal term structure is estimated by using the quotes of the euro repo rates with maturity at 1 week, 2 weeks, 3 weeks, 1 month, 2 months, 3 months, 6 months, 9 months, 12 months for the short term, of the BTANs (Bon à Taux Annuel Normalisé) with maturity greater than 1 year and below 5 years, and of standard OAT (Obligations Assimilables au Trésor) with maturity greater than 1 year. The real term structure for the euro area is estimated using OAT€i, i.e. OAT indexed to the euro-area harmonised index of consumer prices (HICP) ex-tobacco, the reference price index of the euro area. This work considers French index-linked bonds. End-of-week mid-quotes are obtained from Bloomberg and Thomson Financial Reuters.

The nominal and real term structures for the United States are taken from the weekly data estimated by Gürkaynak et al. (2007 and 2010).[1]

15.3.2 Macroeconomic and monetary surprises

Surprises are defined as unexpected releases with respect to the median forecasts released by Bloomberg. They are built in such a way that good surprises, for instance a decrease in the unemployment rate, trigger an increase in long-term yields, while negative surprises provoke a decrease. This chapter uses the original estimates of the macroeconomic surprises even if most of the figures released in the euro area and in the United States are initially preliminary estimates, and are subject to review in follow-up announcements. Most of the macroeconomic datasets in empirical papers use the revised estimates for every macroeconomic figure.[2]

Let $S_{t,i}$ denote the surprise at time t in the figures indexed by i as follows:

$$S_{t,i} = \frac{R_{t,i} - F_{t,i}}{\sigma_{S_i}}, \tag{15.1}$$

where $F_{t,i}$ is the market median consensus about the upcoming figures i for t, the date of release; $R_{t,i}$ is the announcement (the first estimate) at time t of the same figure i. To make surprises comparable, they are scaled using their historical standard deviation, σ_{S_i}. This way of proceeding is very common in the literature, see for example Fleming and Remolona (1999a,b) and Gürkaynak et al. (2005). The Bloomberg median survey forecasts as a measure of the market consensus for a given figure at a given date; thus, $F_{t,i}$ will be approximated by the last forecast in the Bloomberg database for each announcement.

Table 15.1 reports the macroeconomic surprises used in the estimates for the United States and the euro area. For both areas, surprises can

---

[1] Weekly updates are available at www.federalreserve.gov/econresdata/researchdata.htm.

[2] The Bloomberg calendar contains the Bloomberg forecasts for each of these figures, which are formed using the fiftieth empirical percentile of the distribution of a survey made of the forecasts of several bank economists, regarding a precise figure. The use of the median as a measure of the expectations makes the forecast robust to the influence of ill-intentioned economists who might want to shift the forecast in order to make the most of it. This forecast is extensively used by market participants. For each figure that is predicted by Bloomberg's collection of economists' forecasts, the median is regularly updated until every economist answers the survey, which can take up to two weeks. We retained the last median computed by the Bloomberg services, so as to match both the practitioners' and academic approach.

Table 15.1 *Economic variable surprises*

Bloomberg code	description	freq.	mean × 10²	std. dev	min	max	field
United States							
GDP CQOQ	GDP Chained 2005 Dollars	Q	−3.45	0.28	−4.17	2.08	growth
IP CHNG	Industrial Production	M	−10.59	0.36	−5.49	3.02	growth
USTBTOT	Trade Balance Bal. of Payments	M	−1.48	2.96	−2.96	3.57	growth
RSTAMOM	Adj, Retail - Food Serv. Sales	M	2.1	0.7	−2.25	6.49	growth
DGNOCHNG	Durable Goods New Orders Ind.	M	−2.66	2.7	−3.03	3.99	growth
INJCJC	Initial Jobless Claims	W	26.82	21.24	−3.9	33.76	labour market
USURTOT	Unemployment Rate	M	−13.32	0.14	−3.35	2.68	labour market
NFP TCH	Employees on Nonfarm Payrolls	M	−24.73	89.61	−3.54	2.09	labour market
PPI CHNG	PPI by Proc. Stage Finish. Goods	M	6.64	0.48	−2.46	3.49	inflation
CPI CHNG	CPI Urban Consumers	M	−3.26	0.13	−2.99	2.99	inflation
NAPMPMI	ISM Manufacturing PMI SA	M	5.96	1.99	−3	3.7	future ec. act.
CONCCONF	Conference Board Cons. Conf.	M	−0.85	4.94	−2.82	2.49	future ec. act.
Euro area							
EUGNEMUQ	Eurostat GDP Constant Prices	Q	−20.25	0.05	−5.02	1.67	growth
EUITEMUM	Eurostat Ind. Prod. Ex Constr.	M	−8.86	0.53	−3.35	1.86	growth
EUNOEZM	Eurostat New Orders	M	6.75	2.04	−2.78	3.32	growth
RSSAEMUM	Eurostat Retail Sales Volume	M	−24.9	0.63	−2.69	4.9	growth
XTTBEZ	Eurostat Trade Eurozone	M	2.22	5.40	−14.80	12.60	growth
EUCATLBA	Eurozone BOP CA	M	−1.45	6.71	−21.4	12.4	growth
UMRTEMU	Eurostat Unemployment Rate	M	8.54	0.91	6.90	10.1	labour market

ECCPEMUM	CPI All Items	M	2.15	0.07	−4	2.66	inflation
EUPPEMUM	PPI Industry Ex Constr.	M	−10.26	0.14	−6.02	2.67	inflation
GRZEEUEX	ZEW Expectation of Ec. Growth	M	1.39	7.74	−2.6	2.42	future ec. act.
PMITSEZ	Services PMI Markit Survey	M	3.73	0.56	−3.91	3.02	future ec. act.
PMITMEZ	Manufact. PMI Markit Survey	M	5.08	0.3	−2.32	3.65	future ec. act.
EUBCI	EC Business Climate	M	9.61	0.19	−2.8	2.5	future ec. act.
EUCCEMU	EC Consumer Confidence	M	−8.62	1.28	−3.12	3.9	future ec. act.
EUESEMU	EC Economic Sentiment	M	4.02	1.5	−3.72	2.46	future ec. act.
ECPMICOU	EC Composite PMI Output	M	9.89	0.37	−2.66	3.19	future ec. act.
ECMA3MTH	ECB M3 Money Supply	M	0.02	0.46	−2.76	2.76	money

Source: Bloomberg. For each economic variable the surprise is computed as the difference between the actual release (Bloomberg datatype is ACTUAL_RELEASE) and the median of the survey (Bloomberg data type is BN_MEDIAN_SURVEY) and is standardised by its standard deviation. EC stands for European Commission. Q/M/W indicates that data are released at a quarterly, monthly and weekly frequency. The mean is the arithmetic average of the standardised surprise as in Equation (15.1), std. dev. is the standard deviation of the surprise, e.g. the denominator in Equation (15.1), min and max are the minimum and the maximum of the standardised surprise given by Equation (15.1). For the euro area, the first (advanced) release of GDP growth is used. For the United States the first (advanced) release of GDP growth is used. For the euro area, the first (advanced) releases of the euro area GDP growth and the Composite PMI are used.

be divided into four major groups; the first set of surprises encompasses data related to economic growth, the second to labour market conditions, the third to inflation and the fourth to the tone of future economic activity.

For the United States, macroeconomic data are released monthly with the exception of the initial jobless claims, which has a weekly frequency, and the GDP rate of growth, which is quarterly. Economic growth surprises are related to the GDP rate, industrial production, the trade balance, retail sales and durable orders. Labour market indicators are non-farm payrolls, initial jobless claims and the unemployment rate. Inflation pressure indicators are the consumer price index (CPI) and the producer price index (PPI). Finally, the two indicators of future economic activity are the ISM Manufacturing Purchasing Managers Index (the former NAPM index) and the Conference Board Consumer Confidence Index.

In the euro area all surprises have a monthly frequency except for GDP. Economic growth surprises are given by the GDP rate of growth, industrial production, new orders, retail sales, external trade of the euro area and the current account. Signals on labour market conditions are given by the unemployment rate. Inflation indications are expressed by means of the CPI and PPI. Future economic activity by the Composite Purchasing Managers Index (PMI), the advanced release of the Manufacturing PMI, the Services PMI, the ZEW Survey on expectations of economic growth, and the Business Climate.

As with macroeconomic data releases, the surprise component of monetary policy announcements in each monetary area measures the effects of these announcements on interest rates. Rather than using the median of professional forecasts to measure expectations, however, this chapter uses the one-week change in a short-term interest rate, such as the 30-day futures on federal funds for the United States and the 1-month Eonia swap index rate (the 1-month Overnight Index Swap from January 2002 until July 2005) for the euro area, around each monetary policy announcement to measure the surprise component of the announcement. The advantage of using market-based measures of monetary policy surprises is that they are of higher quality and are available essentially continuously (see, for example, Krueger and Kuttner, 1996; Rudebusch and Wu, 2008; Gürkaynak, Sack, and Wright, 2007, 2010).

Obviously, there can be an interaction between monetary policy surprises and macroeconomic surprises. For example, a bad surprise about labour market conditions can influence the decision of the central bank on the stance of monetary policy.

The role of monetary aggregates

Among economic releases a different role is played by monetary aggregates in the United States and in the euro area. There is no question that central banks should monitor monetary developments and assess their implications for price stability, thus affecting nominal and real interest rates. However, monetary aggregates have partially lost their pivotal role in both areas.

During the Volcker years once a week the financial press anticipated, tried to forecast, and then commented on the weekly releases of M2. Markets also reacted to and attempted to anticipate monetary data in the United States. Today M2 and M3 aggregates are almost completely ignored by markets. On 23 March 2006, the Federal Reserve ceased publication of the M3 monetary aggregate, along with that of large-denomination time deposits, repurchase agreements, and eurodollars, while continuing to publish institutional money market mutual funds. According to the Federal Reserve, M3 does not appear to convey any additional information about economic activity that is not already embodied in M2 and has not played a role in the monetary policy process for many years. Consequently, the Federal Reserve judged that the costs of collecting the underlying data and publishing M3 outweigh the benefits. Nonetheless, the M2 aggregate is a large component of the Conference Board's US Leading Index, making up more than 30% of the index, which contains ten indicators. In order to compare the role of monetary aggregates in the United States with that in the euro area, the surprise on US M2 is computed as the weekly deviations of M2 from its exponential trend.

In contrast with the United States, the release of monetary aggregates in the euro area is highly considered as its growth rate is one of the two pillars of the area's monetary policy strategy. The monetary and economic analyses are intended to complement each other and aim to develop a deeper insight into the risks to price stability at various horizons in order to ensure that the most appropriate policy decisions are made. The European Central Bank's (ECB) two-pillar strategy is one response to the difficulty of finding a single model or analytical framework which encompasses both the economic and monetary analyses in a meaningful way. Its approach is motivated by the historical evidence that money growth and inflation are closely related in the medium to long run and is intended to ensure policy retains a medium-term focus by reducing the chances of over-reacting to the transient impacts of shocks. One element of the ECB's monetary pillar is the reference value for M3 growth. A growth rate of M3 in excess of the reference value of 4.5% per annum is, in principle, regarded as signalling a risk to inflation over the medium term, although it does not imply a mechanical policy reaction. The ECB looks also at whether special factors such as portfolio shifts or financial innovation may be distorting the relationship.

15.4   The effects of surprises on interest rates

As a first step the change in nominal and real interest rates is regressed separately on macroeconomic and monetary surprises, namely

$$\Delta Y_t = \alpha + \beta \cdot S_t + v_t, \tag{15.2}$$

where Y_t is the vector of nominal and real interest rates and S is defined by (15.1). The results are shown in Table 15.2. The impact of macroeconomic surprises on the nominal term structure of the euro area is significant only for the CPI and the PMIs, the most followed indicators of future economic activity, and for monetary policy surprises. No significant impact is found for surprises in economic growth and labour market conditions. As for the United States, the impact of CPI and ISM surprises is increasing at the short end of the nominal term structure and decreasing afterwards, with the largest impact at around 4-year maturity. Conversely, the impact of a monetary surprise is decreasing along the maturity spectrum but always significant.

As regards the impact of macroeconomic surprises on the real term structure of the euro area, the results differ slightly. Macroeconomic surprises are positive and significant both for the CPI, for the short and medium term, and for the PPI, for the long term only. Business climate surprises have a negative impact on the medium-term segment of the real term structure. Finally, monetary policy surprises have a positive and significant impact on real rates, which clearly resembles that obtained for nominal rates.

The impact of macroeconomic surprises on the nominal term structure of the United States is particularly strong for retail sales, for the three labour market indicators (i.e. jobless claims, unemployment rate and non-farm payrolls) and for the ISM index, the main future economic activity indicator. Among the inflation indicators, only the CPI affects nominal interest rates at the long end while the PPI has no effect. Monetary policy surprises impact short-term interest rates up to 4-year maturity. More interestingly, the impact of these surprises is first increasing and then decreasing, showing the shape also found by Fleming and Remolona (1999a,b) with higher frequency data. In particular, the impact of macroeconomic surprises appears greater for interest rates between 3 and 5 years of maturity. Only CPI surprises show a clear

Table 15.2a *USA: impact of surprises*

| | nominal interest rates | | | | | | | | | |
	1y	2y	3y	4y	5y	6y	7y	8y	9y	10y
Adv. GDP	0.37	1.37	1.08	0.98	0.91	0.59	0.39	0.28	0.34	0.09
Ind. prod.	0.07	0.97	0.92	0.56	0.33	0.09	−0.43	−0.67	−0.72	−1.02
BOP	−0.36	0.03	0.68	1.05	1.21	1.43	1.47	1.61	1.73	*1.77*
Retail	**3.77**	**5.11**	**5.30**	**5.35**	**5.49**	**5.48**	**5.25**	**5.11**	**4.97**	**4.67**
Dur. goods	0.45	1.05	1.11	1.17	1.20	1.16	1.13	1.08	1.04	0.95
Job. claims	**−2.27**	**−2.40**	**−2.66**	**−2.63**	**−2.26**	**−2.27**	**−2.29**	**−2.21**	**−2.22**	**−2.33**
Unemp.	*−1.35*	**−2.15**	**−2.51**	**−2.56**	**−2.48**	**−2.45**	**−2.49**	**−2.41**	**−2.54**	**−2.67**
NF payroll.	**4.07**	**5.63**	**5.63**	**5.61**	**5.68**	**5.40**	**5.10**	**4.55**	**4.24**	**4.21**
CPI	0.67	0.94	1.18	1.42	1.62	*1.82*	*1.98*	**2.21**	**2.52**	**2.58**
PPI	1.45	1.45	1.61	1.62	1.63	1.73	*1.77*	*1.91*	**2.13**	**2.27**
ISM	**3.29**	**4.46**	**4.68**	**4.70**	**4.82**	**4.71**	**4.47**	**4.35**	**4.20**	**3.83**
Cons. conf.	0.46	0.31	0.44	0.34	0.21	0.17	−0.04	−0.09	0.10	0.40
M2	0.27	0.42	*0.48*	0.52	0.50	0.44	0.36	0.31	0.26	0.20
Mon. pol.	**0.70**	**0.51**	**0.47**	**0.42**	**0.34**	*0.27*	0.21	0.19	0.19	0.16

| | real interest rates | | | | | | | | | |
	1y	2y	3y	4y	5y	6y	7y	8y	9y	10y
	1	2	3	4	5	6	7	8	9	10
Adv. GDP	−14.95	−6.20	−2.48	−1.03	−0.54	−0.46	−0.56	−0.71	−0.87	−1.02
Ind. prod.	*−7.07*	−4.72	−1.49	0.11	0.67	0.81	0.83	0.81	0.80	0.79
BOP	0.34	0.12	0.29	0.54	0.73	0.95	1.12	1.27	*1.39*	*1.49*
Retail	−2.40	0.85	2.23	**2.77**	**2.81**	**2.81**	**2.74**	**2.66**	**2.58**	**2.52**
Dur. goods	−3.46	−1.48	−0.07	0.70	1.10	1.28	1.32	1.28	1.20	1.09
Job. claims	0.70	−1.86	**−2.05**	**−1.92**	**−1.73**	**−1.59**	*−1.47*	*−1.36*	*−1.26*	*−1.17*
Unemp.	*−7.13*	−2.69	−1.12	−0.69	−0.60	−0.68	−0.77	−0.83	−0.87	−0.88
NF payroll	−1.93	1.83	**3.59**	**4.22**	**4.27**	**4.15**	**3.96**	**3.77**	**3.60**	**3.46**
CPI	−0.51	−0.81	−0.56	−0.34	−0.10	0.13	0.34	0.50	0.62	0.70
PPI	−1.93	−2.09	−1.88	−1.56	−0.98	−0.73	−0.53	−0.39	−0.30	−0.23
ISM	0.16	2.17	**2.59**	**2.53**	**2.38**	**2.26**	**2.20**	**2.17**	**2.17**	**2.17**
Cons. conf.	**9.69**	**4.83**	*2.20*	0.71	−0.11	−0.54	−0.76	−0.87	−0.91	−0.93
M2	−1.28	−0.64	−0.36	−0.24	−0.19	−0.17	−0.16	−0.15	−0.14	−0.12
Mon. pol.	0.17	0.19	0.12	0.03	−0.03	−0.05	−0.05	−0.05	−0.05	−0.05

The table shows the estimates of the βs in the multivariate regression (15.2); in bold (italics) the coeffcients significant at the 95 (90) per cent significance level. Standard errors are computed using five Newey–West lags for correcting autocorrelation and heteroskedasticity. Surprises for M2 are computed as deviations of the weekly monetary aggregate M2 from its exponential trend.

Table 15.2b *Euro area: impact of surprises*

	1y	2y	3y	4y	5y	6y	7y	8y	9y	10y
					Nominal interest rates					
Adv. GDP	1.20	0.91	0.61	0.29	−0.05	−0.37	−0.65	−0.88	−1.05	−1.18
Ind. prod.	**2.47**	**2.41**	**2.35**	**2.33**	**2.35**	**2.35**	**2.28**	**2.15**	**1.96**	**1.74**
New. orders	−0.44	−0.58	−0.67	−0.72	−0.75	−0.75	−0.69	−0.59	−0.45	−0.27
Ret. sales	1.12	0.88	0.67	0.48	0.30	0.15	0.04	-0.02	-0.04	-0.04
Trade	−1.18	−1.29	−1.33	−1.33	−1.32	−1.30	−1.25	−1.18	−1.11	−1.04
BOP	0.90	0.76	0.62	0.47	0.33	0.22	0.14	0.10	0.08	0.07
Unemp.	**−40.39**	**−37.60**	**−34.87**	**−33.31**	**−32.95**	**−32.67**	**−31.65**	**−29.73**	**−27.12**	*−24.19*
CPI	*3.17*	**3.15**	**3.14**	**3.03**	**2.80**	*2.53*	**2.27**	*2.06*	1.89	1.76
PPI	**3.04**	**2.41**	*1.83*	1.39	1.11	0.92	0.78	0.67	0.58	0.49
ZEW	*2.77*	*2.44*	2.05	1.71	1.48	1.34	1.26	1.23	1.22	1.24
Adv. Man. PMI	**3.55**	**3.73**	**3.89**	**3.93**	**3.83**	**3.65**	**3.44**	**3.23**	**3.04**	**2.91**
Serv. PMI	0.60	1.21	1.73	2.15	*2.49*	**2.73**	**2.88**	**2.95**	**2.96**	**2.93**
Comp. PMI	3.63	**4.12**	**4.57**	**4.93**	**5.18**	**5.31**	**5.31**	**5.22**	**5.07**	**4.91**
Bus. clim.	*2.34*	*2.18*	*1.98*	1.69	1.32	0.97	0.67	0.47	0.34	0.28
Cons. conf.	*2.26*	*1.96*	1.65	1.32	0.97	0.64	0.33	0.05	−0.20	−0.43
Ec. sent.	*2.42*	*1.93*	1.44	0.99	0.59	0.25	−0.02	−0.25	−0.43	−0.60
M3	*0.02*	**0.03**	**0.03**	**0.03**	**0.02**	0.02	0.02	0.02	0.01	0.01
Mon. pol.	0.02	0.04	0.07	0.09	*0.11*	**0.13**	**0.14**	**0.14**	**0.14**	**0.14**
					Real interest rates					
Adv. GDP	0.51	0.34	0.20	0.12	0.08	0.06	0.05	0.02	−0.03	−0.08
Ind. prod.	2.58	2.56	*2.53*	**2.48**	**2.40**	**2.26**	**2.04**	*1.76*	1.45	1.15
New orders	−2.30	−2.02	−1.78	−1.64	−1.57	−1.46	−1.23	−0.87	−0.43	0.04
Ret. sales	1.82	1.59	1.36	1.11	0.87	0.66	0.50	0.41	0.36	0.34
Trade	−0.68	−0.79	−0.89	−0.97	−1.01	−1.01	−0.97	−0.90	−0.81	−0.72
BOP	0.96	0.92	0.91	0.94	1.01	1.04	1.01	0.89	0.71	0.47
Unemp.	*−56.64*	*−47.17*	*−38.43*	*−31.25*	−25.84	−21.77	−18.63	−16.20	−14.38	−13.12
CPI	**6.23**	**5.72**	**5.17**	**4.58**	**3.95**	**3.36**	**2.86**	**2.46**	*2.14*	1.91
PPI	**2.71**	*2.68*	*2.64*	**2.60**	**2.56**	**2.50**	**2.43**	**2.33**	**2.22**	**2.11**
ZEW	−0.13	0.04	0.19	0.32	0.43	0.53	0.60	0.66	0.70	0.73
Adv. Man. PMI	2.12	2.61	2.99	*3.22*	**3.31**	**3.30**	**3.23**	**3.12**	**2.98**	**2.84**
Serv. PMI	1.15	1.23	1.31	1.37	1.42	1.47	1.51	1.56	1.61	1.66
Comp. PMI	0.84	0.88	0.90	0.88	0.83	0.73	0.61	0.47	0.33	0.21
Bus. clim.	−1.98	−2.05	−2.08	−2.02	−1.86	−1.68	−1.52	−1.40	−1.32	−1.28
Cons. conf.	1.78	1.22	0.76	0.46	0.33	0.23	0.08	-0.13	−0.40	−0.69
Ec. sent.	−0.44	−0.74	−0.98	−1.10	−1.13	−1.15	−1.23	−1.37	*−1.57*	**−1.80**
M3	**0.05**	**0.04**	**0.03**	**0.03**	*0.02*	0.01	0.01	0.01	0.01	0.01
Mon. pol.	16.90	*17.57*	**18.20**	**18.72**	**19.13**	**19.47**	**19.77**	**20.03**	**20.22**	**20.31**

The table shows the estimates of the βs in the multivariate regression (15.2); in bold (italics) the coefficients significant at the 95 (90) per cent significance level. Standard errors are computed using five Newey–West lags for correcting autocorrelation and heteroskedasticity. The first releases (advanced) of GDP growth and Manufacturing PMI are used.

increasing trend which reaches its maximum for the 9/10-year rates. As expected, monetary policy shock impacts fade as maturities increase.

Real interest rates in the United States are much less affected by surprises than their corresponding nominal rates. Moreover, the impact seems somewhat controversial as both industrial production and the ISM surprises show a negative impact on medium-term and long-term real rates. Consumer confidence, another much followed indicator of future economic activity, also has a positive impact on long-term real rates. Finally, monetary policy surprises show a negative impact on real rates from 1- to 5-year maturity; these results, combined with those seen above for nominal rates, signal that markets change their perception on breakeven inflation rates at the shortest maturities.

All in all, the comparison between the impact of macroeconomics and monetary surprises on nominal and real rates shows that: (1) in the United States nominal rates are more affected than the corresponding euro area rates; (2) in the United States growth, labour market and future economic activity indicators have a clear and significant impact on nominal rates while in the euro area only inflation indicators and future economic activity indicators have a significant impact; (3) the factor loadings of macroeconomic surprises are hump-shaped, i.e. they increase at short maturities and decrease after the 5-year maturity; (4) monetary policy surprises have an impact on nominal rates, which is decreasing along the maturity spectrum; (5) monetary policy surprises have a negative impact on real rates in the United States and a positive impact on real rates in the euro area.

From points (2) and (5) it emerges that nominal rates are impacted by macroeconomic surprises in growth, the labour market and economic outlook in the United States and by surprises in inflation in the euro area. These results can be due to differences in the mandates of the monetary authorities, which is dual in the United States and hierarchical in the euro area. Moreover, monetary policy shocks make short-term breakeven inflation rates increase in the United States, while they do not change breakeven inflation rates across the maturity spectrum in the euro area. These differences in responses to monetary shocks also highlight the dissimilarities between the markets' perception of monetary policy targets.

15.5   The model

15.5.1   The plain-vanilla estimation problem

This chapter uses a no-arbitrage standard Gaussian affine term structure model, set in discrete time, as in the majority of the recent literature about macro term structure models. The term structures for nominal and real interest rates are linked through the pricing kernel corrected by the inflation rate (see Appendices). This model follows the original setup by Evans (1998), successively enriched by Risa (2001), García and Werner (2010) and Adrian and Wu (2010). The term structure model is expressed in the state-space form

$$Y_t = A + HX_t + R\eta_t \quad \text{(observation equation)},$$
$$X_t = \mu + \rho X_{t-1} + \Sigma\varepsilon_t \quad \text{(state equation)},$$
$$R \perp \Sigma, \tag{15.3}$$

where $A = [\widehat{A}_1, \ldots, \widehat{A}_N, A_1, \ldots, A_R]$ is an $(N+R) \times 1$ vector, $H = [\widehat{B}, B]^\top$ is an $(N+R) \times k$ matrix, N and R are the number of nominal and index-linked bonds used in the estimation, $\varepsilon_t \sim N(0, I_k)$ and $\eta_t \sim N(0, I_{N+R})$. The matrix Y_t contains the N nominal zero-coupon rates with annual maturity from 3 to 10 years and the R real zero-coupon rates with annual maturity from 3 to 10 years. k defines the number of latent factors in matrix X_t, namely $[l_t^1, l_t^2, \pi_t]$, which can be interpreted as two interest-rate factors and an inflation factor. For a complete formal definition see the Appendices.

The expected inflation for different horizons can be obtained from Equation (15.3). Let $e_K = (0, 0, 1)^\top$ so that $e_K^\top X$ picks the latent factor related to inflation; thus the conditional expectation of inflation for τ periods ahead is given by

$$E_t(\pi_{t+\tau}) = E_t(e_K^\top X_{t+\tau}) = \tau \cdot [0 \ 0 \ 1] \cdot \left[(I - \rho)^{-1} (I - \rho^\tau) \mu + \rho^\tau \cdot X_t \right]. \tag{15.4}$$

The comparison between the nominal and real term structure gives the inflation compensation requested by investors to hold standard nominal bonds. This compensation, known as the breakeven inflation rate (BEIR), is equal to the difference between the nominal and real interest rates, namely $\text{BEIR}_t^n = y_t^n - r_t^n$, where y_t^n is the nominal interest rate at time t for maturity n, and r_t^n is the corresponding real interest rate. However, the BEIR is not a pure expectation of the inflation rate since, as shown by Evans (1998), it can be thought of as the sum of the expected inflation rate at time t during the n periods to maturity and the inflation risk premium at period t, γ_t^n,[3] which, using Equation (15.4), can be written as

---

[3] It can be shown that if variables are jointly log-normal, this risk premium is given by $\gamma_t^n = \text{Cov}(m_t^n, \pi_t^{e,n}) - \frac{1}{2}\text{Var}(\pi_t^{e,n})$, where m_t^n is the stochastic discount factor between period t and $t + n$ and $\pi_t^{e,n}$ the expected inflation rate over the same period; in other words, the premium requested by investors to hold indexed-linked bonds and to hedge against unexpected changes in inflation depends on the covariance between the marginal

$$\gamma_t^n = \text{BEIR}_t^n - E_t(\pi_{t+\tau})$$

$$= y_t^n - r_t^n - \frac{1}{\tau}E_t(e_K^\top X_{t+\tau}). \tag{15.5}$$

This premium, in a standard representative-agent power-utility model, is positive when the covariance between the stochastic discount factor and inflation is negative, in other words when expected consumption growth is low and inflation is high.

15.5.2 The surprises-augmented model

Model (15.3) can be augmented by introducing the surprises contained in the macroeconomic data releases. Thus the model becomes a state-space system with unobservable and observable variables and can be treated according to the specification of Pericoli and Taboga (2008). The augmented model is obtained by adding a new set of variables in the state equation of (15.3), namely

$$
\begin{aligned}
Y_t &= \overline{A} + \overline{H}X_t + R\eta_t \quad \text{(observation equation)},\\
\overline{X}_t &= \overline{\mu} + \overline{\rho}\overline{X}_{t-1} + \overline{\Sigma}\overline{\varepsilon}_t \quad \text{(state equation)},\\
R &\perp \Sigma,
\end{aligned}
\tag{15.6}
$$

with

$$
\overline{A} = \begin{bmatrix} \widehat{A}+\widehat{E} \\ A+E \end{bmatrix}, \overline{H} = \begin{bmatrix} \widehat{B} & \widehat{G} \\ B & G \end{bmatrix}, \overline{\rho} = \begin{bmatrix} \rho & \phi \\ {}_{k\times k} & {}_{k\times M} \\ 0 & \rho_{\text{uo}} \\ {}_{M\times k} & {}_{M\times M} \end{bmatrix},
$$

$$
\overline{\mu} = [\mu, \mu_S]^\top, \overline{X}_t = [X_t, S_t]^\top, \overline{\Sigma} = \begin{bmatrix} \Sigma & 0 \\ 0 & \Sigma_S \end{bmatrix}, \overline{\varepsilon}_t = [\varepsilon_t, v_t \cdot \mathfrak{I}_t],
$$

where S_t is the row vector of matrix

$$
\underset{T\times M}{S} = \begin{bmatrix}
S_{1,1} & 0 & \cdots & 0 \\
\vdots & \vdots & \ddots & \vdots \\
0 & S_{2,t-1} & \cdots & 0 \\
S_{1,t} & 0 & \cdots & 0 \\
0 & 0 & \cdots & S_{M,t+1} \\
\vdots & \vdots & \ddots & \vdots \\
0 & S_{2,T} & \cdots & 0
\end{bmatrix},
$$

rate of substitution (the stochastic discount factor) and the inflation rate; the second term is a convexity adjustment, inferred from a Jensen inequality. Sometimes, the first term of the inflation risk premium, $\text{Cov}(m_t^n, \pi_t^{e,n})$, is referred to as the 'pure inflation risk premium'.

X is the usual set of K latent factors, S is the set of M known surprises (an M-dimensional vector, $M \in \mathbb{N}$) equal to the surprise at the time of the announcement and nil otherwise, ϕ is an $M \times M$ matrix which links unobserved factors X with surprises S, Σ_S is an $M \times M$ diagonal matrix, μ_S is an $M \times 1$ vector of drifts, $\widehat{E}$ and E are the $(N + R) \times 1$ vector of drifts for the nominal and real rates in the observation equation associated with surprises S and $\widehat{G}$ and G are $(N \times M)$ and $(R \times M)$ matrices, respectively, of loadings for nominal and real rates in the observation equation associated with surprises S, $\eta_t \sim N(0, I_{N+R})$, $\varepsilon_t \sim N(0, I_K)$. $v_t \sim N(0, I_M)$ is a vector of white noise for the M announcements and $\mathfrak{I}_t$ is an indicator variable which takes the value 1 when the variable S_t is different from 0 and nil otherwise. ρ_{uo} is an $(M \times M)$ diagonal matrix which describes the dynamics of the surprises S.

For ease of computation, model (15.6) is estimated with the monetary surprise and four macroeconomic surprises regarding growth (retail sales in the United States and in the euro area), inflation (CPI in the United States and in the euro area), the labour market (jobless claims in the United States and the unemployment rate in the euro area), and future economic activity (ISM in the United States and advanced manufacturing PMI in the euro area); thus S becomes a $T \times 5$ matrix. The novelty of the estimates of the factor loadings $\widehat{G}$ and G is given by the fact that they are obtained through a pricing model which is arbitrage-free and thus capable of giving consistent loadings across the maturity spectrum; see the Appendices for a formal definition.

Based on the state space representation in (15.6), the factors are filtered according to the Kalman filter. Given estimates of the latent factors $\widehat{X}_t$, the parameters can be estimated by maximum likelihood, based on the conditional distribution of $Y_t | Y_{t-1}$ for each observation.

15.6   Results

The results show that model (15.6) is capable of jointly estimating the nominal and real term structures for the euro area and for the United States (Table 15.3). Parameter estimates are presented in Table 15.4. Root mean squared errors are in line with those obtained by Ang and Piazzesi (2003) for the United States while they are smaller in the euro area.

An important step towards a better understanding of the mechanics of a reduced-form no-arbitrage model like (15.6) consists of assigning an economic interpretation to the latent factors since it helps to provide a deeper insight into the economic forces driving bond prices. Pericoli (2012b) documents that latent factors can be interpreted as

Table 15.3a *United States: yield pricing errors in basis points*

	nominal			real		
	mean	RMSE	std.dev.	mean	RMSE	std.dev.
3-yr	10.48	26.76	24.64	0.24	15.37	15.38
4-yr	−0.12	21.49	21.50	0.63	14.86	14.86
5-yr	−3.82	20.62	20.28	1.46	15.34	15.28
6-yr	−4.02	20.01	19.62	2.00	15.28	15.16
7-yr	−2.49	19.84	19.70	2.10	15.08	14.94
8-yr	−0.28	20.36	20.37	1.78	15.00	14.90
9-yr	2.02	21.46	21.38	1.10	15.17	15.14
10-yr	4.02	22.85	22.51	0.13	15.65	15.66

Statistics of weekly data from January 2002 to April 2012. Pricing error is defined as the percentage point difference ×100 between the current and the estimated yield. RMSE is the root mean squared error of the error in basis points; std.dev. is the standard deviation of the error in basis points.

Table 15.3b *Euro area: yield pricing errors in basis points*

	nominal			real		
	mean	RMSE	std.dev.	mean	RMSE	std.dev.
3-yr	1.38	14.65	14.60	−0.12	18.30	18.31
4-yr	1.04	15.34	15.32	−0.85	16.05	16.05
5-yr	1.36	16.37	16.33	−0.54	14.82	14.82
6-yr	1.81	17.27	17.19	0.14	14.29	14.30
7-yr	2.11	17.96	17.85	0.75	14.17	14.17
8-yr	2.17	18.44	18.33	1.12	14.26	14.23
9-yr	1.99	18.85	18.76	1.22	14.54	14.50
10-yr	1.65	19.32	19.27	1.09	15.09	15.06

Statistics of weekly data from January 2002 to April 2012. Pricing error is defined as the percentage point difference ×100 between the current and the estimated yield. RMSE is the root mean squared error of the error in basis points; std.dev. is the standard deviation of the error in basis points.

the cross-sectional average of the real term structure (first factor), the slope of the real term structure computed as the difference between the 10-year and 3-year real zero-coupon rate (second factor) and the 10-year breakeven inflation rate (third factor). This last factor is a wedge between the nominal and the real interest rate. Standard three-factor models introduced by the seminal work of Litterman and Scheinkman (1991) identify the nominal term structure average, the slope of the nominal term structure and the curvature of the nominal term structure

Table 15.4 *Parameter estimates*

US	coefficient	std.err.	euro area	coefficient	std.err.
ρ_{11}	0.998	0.304	ρ_{11}	0.989	0.134
ρ_{21}	−0.004	0.151	ρ_{21}	−0.001	0.340
ρ_{22}	0.999	0.027	ρ_{22}	0.996	1.064
ρ_{31}	−0.000	0.086	ρ_{31}	0.008	0.028
ρ_{32}	−0.000	0.013	ρ_{32}	−0.007	0.061
ρ_{33}	0.993	0.008	ρ_{33}	0.989	0.005
μ_π	0.030	48.341	μ_π	0.060	39.359
σ_π	−0.268	0.494	σ_π	−0.114	0.086
δ_0	−40.895	5.439	δ_0	−72.063	48.945
$\delta_{1,1}$	0.246	216.415	$\delta_{1,1}$	0.133	0.744
$\delta_{1,2}$	−66.370	56.304	$\delta_{1,2}$	−122.733	312.417
$\delta_{1,3}$	12.352	0.000	$\delta_{1,3}$	−18.485	0.000
$\lambda_{0,1}$	0.016	4.205	$\lambda_{0,1}$	−0.025	3.918
$\lambda_{0,2}$	1.372	1.181	$\lambda_{0,2}$	1.173	1.320
$\lambda_{0,3}$	0.023	13.151	$\lambda_{0,3}$	0.008	40.025
$\lambda_{1,11}$	0.006	0.307	$\lambda_{1,11}$	−0.008	0.134
$\lambda_{1,12}$	1.996	0.026	$\lambda_{1,22}$	1.940	2.374
$\lambda_{1,13}$	6.930	0.000	$\lambda_{1,33}$	172.666	0.000
$\lambda_{1,21}$	0.284	0.298	$\lambda_{1,12}$	−0.005	0.005
$\lambda_{1,22}$	−0.000	3.890	$\lambda_{1,21}$	−0.161	6.228
$\lambda_{1,23}$	−0.002	16.362	$\lambda_{1,13}$	−0.000	0.002
$\lambda_{1,31}$	0.091	0.025	$\lambda_{1,23}$	0.042	0.680
$\lambda_{1,32}$	0.003	6.492	$\lambda_{1,31}$	−1.424	6.602
c_N	0.001	0.075	c_N	0.089	0.151
d_N	0.023	1.124	c_R	−0.010	0.645
c_R	−0.015	1.192	d_N	−0.046	0.118
d_R	−0.005	1.035	d_R	0.049	0.053

The table reports the estimates of model (15.3) for the euro area and for the United States. Parameters for the surprises are not reported. Standard errors are computed with the outer product.

as the main driving forces of the nominal term structure. By contrast, model (15.6) considers two real factors (the average of the real rates and the slope of the real term structure) and an inflation factor (which summarises the information embedded in the slope of the nominal term structure and in its curvature). Table 15.5 documents that the correlation between the first latent factor and the average of the real rates is large in both areas even if it decreases from September 2008 to April 2012. Moreover, the correlation between the second latent factor and the slope of the real term structure is large, but becomes negative in the euro area during the crisis. Finally, the correlation between the third

Table 15.5 *Correlation of latent factors with observable variables*

United States	Jan '98–Apr '12	Jan '98–Sep '08	Sep '98–Apr '12
1st factor – average real rates	0.78	0.68	0.67
2nd factor – slope of real rates	0.47	0.64	0.40
3rd factor – BEIR	0.93	0.92	0.98

Euro area	Jan '02–Apr '12	Jan '02–Sep '08	Sep '98–Apr '12
1st factor – average real rates	0.95	0.94	0.84
2nd factor – slope of real rates	0.53	0.49	−0.16
3rd factor – BEIR	0.72	0.73	0.77

The table reports the absolute value of the correlation between the three latent factors, defined in the column as 1st, 2nd and 3rd, and the observable variables, defined as the average of real rates, the slope of real rates – the difference between the 10-year and the 3-year real rate – and the 10-year BEIR.

latent factor and the breakeven inflation rate is large and increases from September 2008.

Estimates of long-term inflation expectations given by Equation (15.4) are plotted in the top panels of Figures 15.1 and 15.2 for the United States and the euro area. In the United States the 10-year expected inflation rate records some swings at around 2 per cent from 1998 until the middle of 2004, when it starts showing steady values with much smaller variations; from the end of 2004 until the middle of 2008 the average of the 10-year expected inflation is equal to 2.2 per cent. The 10-year expected inflation rate drops in the second half of 2008 to almost nil and steadily increases in the course of 2009 up to 2 per cent. The 10-year breakeven inflation rate tracks the corresponding expected inflation quite closely until mid-2001 but records higher values afterwards. This explains why the US 10-year inflation risk premium, given by the difference between the breakeven inflation and expected inflation rates, is almost nil until mid-2001 while in the following years it surges to an average of 0.40 percentage points. An alternative indication of inflation expectations comes from the expected forward inflation rate (bottom panels of Figures 15.1 and 15.2). The expected forward inflation rates, i.e. the 5-year expected inflation rate 5 years ahead, is very stable at an average of around 2.1 per cent; only in the last quarter of 2008 it declines to below 2 per cent but rapidly comes back to its long-term average. Correspondingly, the forward inflation risk premium, given by the difference between the 5–10 year breakeven forward and expected forward inflation rate, is nil on average from 1998 to mid-2001 and around 0.4 percentage points from early 2001 to mid-2005. It then drops to 0.2 percentage

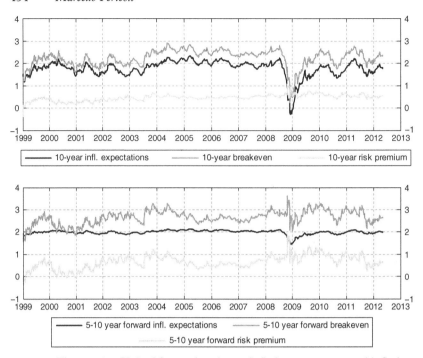

Figure 15.1 United States: breakeven inflation rates, expected inflation rates and risk premia. The 10-year expected inflation rate is given by Equation (15.4), namely

$$\tfrac{1}{520}E_t(e_K^\top \widehat{X}_{t+520}) = [0\ 0\ 1] \cdot \left[(I - \widehat{\rho})^{-1}\left(I - \widehat{\rho}^{520}\right), \widehat{\mu} + \widehat{\rho}^{520} \cdot \widehat{X}_t\right],$$

where 520 is the 10-year forecasting period in weeks and $\widehat{\ }$ above a parameter stands for its estimate. The 5–10 year expected forward inflation rate is given by

$$2 \times \tfrac{1}{520}E_t(e_K^\top \widehat{X}_{t+520}) - \tfrac{1}{260}E_t(e_K^\top \widehat{X}_{t+260}),$$

where 260 is the 5-year forecasting period in weeks. The 10-year inflation risk premium is the difference between the 10-year breakeven inflation rate and (15.4); the 5–10 year forward risk premium is the difference between the 5–10 year breakeven forward inflation rate and the 5–10 year forward expected inflation rate.

points, until the start of the subprime crisis in August 2007. In 2008, against the backdrop of an extremely expansive monetary stance, it increases to over 0.5 percentage points and remains above this level.

In the euro area the picture differs slightly. The 10-year expected inflation rate is steadily below the 2% monetary policy target from 2002 until

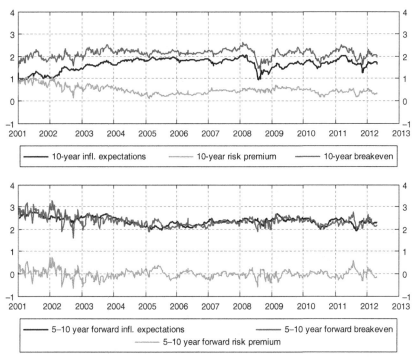

Figure 15.2 Euro area: breakeven inflation rates, expected inflation rates and risk premia. The 10-year expected inflation rate is given by Equation (15.4), namely

$$\tfrac{1}{520}E_t(e_K^\top \widehat{X}_{t+520}) = [0\ 0\ 1] \cdot \left[(I - \widehat{\rho})^{-1}\left(I - \widehat{\rho}^{520}\right)\widehat{\mu} + \widehat{\rho}^{520} \cdot \widehat{X}_t\right],$$

where 520 is the 10-year forecasting period in weeks and $\widehat{}$ above a parameter stands for its estimate. The 5–10 year expected forward inflation rate is given by

$$2 \times \tfrac{1}{520}E_t(e_K^\top \widehat{X}_{t+520}) - \tfrac{1}{260}E_t(e_K^\top \widehat{X}_{t+260}),$$

where 260 is the 5-year forecasting period in weeks. The 10-year inflation risk premium is the difference between the 10-year breakeven inflation rate and (15.4); the 5–10 year forward risk premium is the difference between the 5–10 year breakeven forward inflation rate and the 5–10 year forward expected inflation rate.

2004. It averages above 1.8 per cent from 2004 until 2008, when it drops to 1.4 per cent. From mid-2009 to the end of 2010 it is close to 1.8 per cent. By contrast to the United States, in the euro area there is a strong correspondence between the 10-year expected inflation and the 10-year breakeven rates from 2005 until 2008. Accordingly, the 10-year inflation risk premium average is very tiny in this period. The indication stemming from the expected forward rates are similar; the expected forward inflation rates, i.e. the 5-year expected inflation rate 5 years ahead, is stable at around an average of 1.8 per cent with a minor drop in the last quarter of 2008. The forward inflation risk premium, given by the difference between the 5–10 year breakeven forward and expected forward inflation rates, records wide oscillations given by the large variability of the 5–10 year breakeven forward inflation rate. However, it is on average around 0.5 percentage points from 2005. A caveat is warranted. In actual fact, the results for the euro area for the 2002–2004 period can be biased by the small number of index-linked bonds as well as by their extremely low liquidity.

15.6.1 *Expected inflation and inflation risk premia during the crisis*

The comparison between expected forward inflation rates and forward risk premia in the euro area and in the United States highlights some differences between the two areas. In the euro area, against the background of an expected forward inflation rate well anchored below 2 per cent, the forward inflation risk premium has recorded constant figures of around 0.5 percentage points. The two variables have barely changed since the adoption of unconventional monetary policy measures in the aftermath of the financial crisis. A first bold wave of unconventional monetary policy measures put forward by the ECB started at the beginning of October 2008. A second wave, coinciding with the deterioration of the euro-area government debt markets, started on May 2010.[4] The spot 10-year inflation risk premium did not significantly change either in October

---

[4] In the euro area the main measures are: in October 2008, the adoption of the Fixed-Rate Full-Allotment procedure (FRFA) on money market rates and the expansion of the collateral eligible for Eurosystem credit operations; in May 2009, the outright purchases in the primary and secondary market of covered bonds (Covered Bonds Purchasing Programme, CBPP) and the lengthening of the refinancing operations through the long-term 12-month operations; in May 2010 the outright purchases of euro-area government bonds in the secondary market (Securities Markets Programme, SMP; the SMP was enlarged in August 2011 when the debt crisis propagated to the entire euro area). In December 2011 and in February 2012 the ECB introduced two 3-year Longer-Term Refinancing Operations. See Cecioni et al. (2011) for a survey of the unconventional measures.

2008 or in the second half of 2010; similarly the 5–10 year forward risk premium temporarily decreased in the second half of 2010. All in all, there is no clear effect on risk premia stemming from the unconventional measures.

Conversely, in the United States the sequence of unconventional monetary policy measures, intended to provide quantitative easing, changed the perception of expected forward inflation rates by market participants and determined a substantial and non-negligible inflation risk premium. In particular, the forward inflation risk premium showed a sudden surge first in late 2008, when speculation about the first wave of unconventional measures (the so-called Quantitative Easing 1, QE1, operative from March 2009 until February 2010) emerged, and again in early August 2010, when speculation about the second wave of measures (the so-called Quantitative Easing 2, QE2, in place since November 2010) started to intensify. In September 2011, the Federal Reserve announced the implementation of a plan to purchase bonds with maturities of six to thirty years and to sell bonds with maturities of less than three years (Operation Twist). The aim of this plan was to do what QE has tried to do, without printing more money and without expanding the Federal Reserve's balance sheet, therefore hopefully avoiding the inflationary pressure associated with QE.

15.7   The effects of surprises on the term structure

From (15.6) it is possible to extract the factor loadings of surprises, e.g. the change in nominal and interest rates which follows a macroeconomic or monetary policy surprise. A simple back-of-the-envelope calculation shows that changes in interest rates are obtained by subtracting Y_t from Y_{t-1}, which yields

$$
\begin{aligned}
Y_t - Y_{t-1} &= \overline{H}\left(\overline{X}_t - \overline{X}_{t-1}\right) + R\eta_t - R\eta_{t-1} \\
&= \overline{H}\left(\overline{\rho}\overline{X}_{t-1} + \overline{\Sigma\varepsilon}_t - \overline{X}_{t-1}\right) + R\eta_t - R\eta_{t-1} \\
&= \overline{H}(\overline{\rho} - I)\overline{X}_{t-1} + u_t,
\end{aligned}
\tag{15.7}
$$

where $u_t = \overline{H\Sigma\varepsilon}_t + R\eta_t - R\eta_{t-1}$ and $\overline{H}(\overline{\rho} - I)$ are the factor loadings for the factor $\overline{X}$. The factor loading on interest rate differentials for the five surprises are given by $[0, 0, 0, 1, 1, 1, 1, 1]^{\top}\overline{H}(\overline{\rho} - I)$. These factor loadings obtained from model (15.6) correspond to those obtained from the simple unconstrained regression (15.2).

15.7.1 *Monetary policy surprises*

Factor loadings of monetary policy surprises are plotted in Figure 15.3. This model is capable of obtaining a sequence of factor loadings for nominal rates different from real rates; for the United States shocks the loadings for nominal rates are positive and decreasing while those for real rates are negative and increasing. For the euro area both sequences of factor loadings are positive but decreasing. The model is not capable of estimating the intersection of the nominal and real sequences of loadings at around 7-year maturity. Differences between constrained and unconstrained factor loadings are small for nominal rates in both areas and slightly larger for real rates, especially in the euro area.

A comparison of factor loadings before and after the collapse of Lehman Brothers, in September 2008, reveals interesting features (Table 15.6). In normal times, i.e. before the Lehman collapse, in the United States nominal rates reacted to monetary surprises especially at the short end of the term structure while the impact was nil on euro area nominal rates. Since the Lehman collapse nominal rates react much less in the United States and the impact is negligible on shorter-term euro-area nominal rates. Unexpectedly, monetary surprises have a positive impact on longer-term euro-area real rates. These results suggest that monetary authorities may surprise markets in normal times in the United States while the communication of the monetary policy stance is much clearer in the euro area, as bond markets are rarely surprised by the ECB.

The model can also be used to extract the impulse response function from monetary surprises. Figure 15.4 reports the impulse of forward

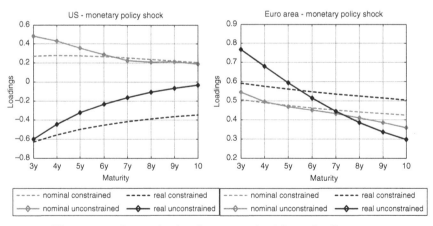

Figure 15.3 Constrained and unconstrained factor loadings

Table 15.6 *Monetary surprises on nominal and real rates before and after the Lehman collapse*

United States	1 yr	2 yr	3 yr	4 yr	5 yr	6 yr	7 yr	8 yr	9 yr	10 yr
nominal rates										
full sample	**0.70**	**0.51**	**0.47**	**0.42**	**0.34**	0.27	0.21	0.19	0.19	0.16
pre-Lehman	**0.67**	**0.45**	**0.41**	**0.38**	**0.32**	**0.31**	**0.32**	**0.30**	0.26	0.24
post-Lehman	**0.77**	**0.71**	**0.66**	**0.55**	0.39	0.11	−0.20	−0.21	−0.06	−0.09
real rates										
full sample	0.17	0.19	0.12	0.03	−0.03	−0.05	−0.05	−0.05	−0.05	−0.05
pre-Lehman	−0.03	0.24	0.27	**0.25**	0.23	0.20	0.19	0.17	0.16	0.15
post-Lehman	0.82	0.00	−0.40	−0.75	−0.90	−0.92	−0.89	−0.84	−0.79	−0.75

Euro area	1 yr	2 yr	3 yr	4 yr	5 yr	6 yr	7 yr	8 yr	9 yr	10 yr
nominal rates										
full sample	0.02	0.04	0.07	0.09	0.11	0.13	**0.14**	**0.14**	**0.14**	**0.14**
pre-Lehman	0.16	0.17	0.18	0.18	0.17	0.16	0.16	0.16	0.17	**0.18**
post-Lehman	−0.03	0.00	0.04	0.07	0.10	0.12	0.13	0.14	0.13	0.13
real rates										
full sample	0.17	0.18	**0.18**	**0.19**	**0.19**	**0.19**	**0.20**	**0.20**	**0.20**	**0.20**
pre-Lehman	0.37	0.33	0.28	0.24	0.20	0.17	0.14	0.12	0.11	0.11
post-Lehman	0.10	0.13	0.15	0.17	**0.19**	**0.21**	**0.22**	**0.23**	**0.24**	**0.24**

For the United States the full sample runs from January 1998 until April 2012, the pre-Lehman from January 1998 until August 2008, and the post-Lehman from September 2008 until April 2012. For the euro area the full sample runs from January 2002 to April 2012, the pre-Lehman from January 2002 until August 2008, and the post-Lehman from September 2008 until April 2012. Coefficients of monetary surprises estimated with model (15.6); in bold the coefficients are significant at the 95% level; standard errors are computed with the outer product.

inflation rates between 5 and 10 years and between 9 and 10 years in the two areas. As expected, in the United States a positive monetary shock makes the forward inflation rates increase, and has the opposite effect on nominal and real rates. Conversely, in the euro area a monetary shock makes the forward inflation rates decrease. In both areas the effects of monetary surprises fade after five weeks.

15.7.2 *Macroeconomic surprises*

As a second step, model (15.6) is estimated by combining five surprises (four macroeconomic and one monetary) in both areas. The results are consistent with those obtained in the unconstrained model (15.2). Figure 15.5 shows the cross-correlogram between macroeconomic and

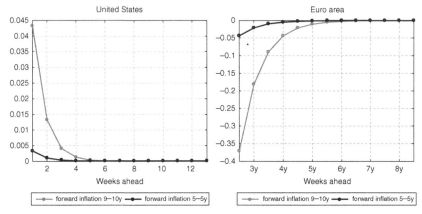

Figure 15.4 Impulse response function of forward inflation rates
Note: The figure plots the factor loadings of the unconstrained model (15.2) and those of the constrained model (15.6) given by Equation (15.7) for nominal and real rates. Impulse response functions are obtained by (15.7) by one standard deviation shock of the monetary surprise.

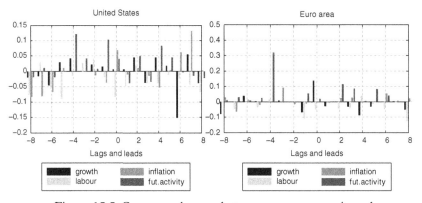

Figure 15.5 Cross-correlogram between macroeconomic and monetary news
Note: The figure plots the cross-correlogram between the news on growth, the labour market, inflation and future economic activity on one side, and monetary policy surprises on the other.

monetary surprises, i.e. the leads and lags between data surprises and unexpected monetary policy decisions. As expected, monetary surprises show some dependence on macroeconomic surprises; in fact, a surprise in the labour market can affect the next monetary policy move. Then a certain degree of interlinking among surprises is important in evaluating their impact on the nominal and real term structures. The cross-correlogram in both areas show that labour market surprises are followed by a surprise with the opposite sign in both areas; similarly, surprises in growth and in future economic activity are followed by a monetary surprise of the same sign. There is no clear dependence between inflation surprises and monetary policy surprises.

Like monetary surprises, the comparison between factor loadings before and after the collapse of Lehman Brothers reveals important differences between the two bond markets (Table 15.7). In normal times, i.e. before the Lehman collapse, in the United States nominal rates reacted to surprises in economic growth (retail sales), the economic outlook (ISM) and the labour market (jobless claims; in this case only for the shortest maturities). During the crisis the economic growth impact disappears, the labour market effect shows up with very large factor loadings, and the economic outlook effect almost doubles. In the euro area, the only relevant effect in normal times is that of inflation (CPI), which is substituted by the economic outlook impact (Manufacturing PMI) during the crisis period. The results suggest that nominal rates in the United States are driven by surprises in the real economy, both in normal and in crisis periods, but during the crisis supply-side (labour market) conditions have taken over the role played by the demand-side (retail sales) conditions; moreover, inflation never surprises nominal rates. On the contrary, in the euro area only inflation surprises impact nominal rates in normal times.

The impact on real rates is sometimes difficult to interpret. In the United States, before the Lehman collapse economic-growth and economic-outlook surprises impact real rates across the maturity spectrum; no surprise is relevant during the crisis period. In the euro area, only labour market surprises impact longer-term real rates before the Lehman collapse, while inflation scares produce a large increase in real rates after September 2008.

The impulse response function of shocks in the macroeconomic surprises shows that nominal rates react more than the corresponding real rates (Figure 15.6). Growth and labour market surprises have a short decay and their effects vanish after approximately six weeks. Conversely, surprises in inflation and future economic activity are much more persistent in both areas. This difference in the shocks' duration can reflect the forward nature of inflation and future economic-activity indicators with respect to growth and labour market announcements; this finding is confirmed by the dependence of monetary policy shocks and future surprises on inflation and future economic activity, as demonstrated by the positive cross-correlogram of leads.

Table 15.7 *Macroeconomic surprises on nominal and real rates before and after the Lehman collapse*

US	nom. rate	1 yr	2 yr	3 yr	4 yr	5 yr	6 yr	7 yr	8 yr	9 yr	10 yr
pre-Lehman	retail	4.64	6.18	6.33	6.18	6.16	6.05	5.91	5.83	5.59	5.25
post-Lehman	retail	1.31	2.06	2.34	2.95	3.55	3.81	3.34	3.05	3.17	2.96
pre-Lehman	job.claims	-2.55	-2.40	-2.29	-2.10	-1.72	-1.63	-1.53	-1.46	-1.49	-1.51
post-Lehman	job.claims	-1.39	-2.54	-4.13	-4.68	-4.38	-4.76	-5.19	-5.11	-5.00	-5.48
pre-Lehman	CPI	0.53	1.05	1.27	1.45	1.65	1.75	1.71	1.64	1.62	1.64
post-Lehman	CPI	1.04	0.50	0.81	1.23	1.45	1.96	2.75	3.96	5.32	5.52
pre-Lehman	ISM	2.94	4.02	4.20	4.16	4.13	4.04	4.00	3.89	3.58	3.18
post-Lehman	ISM	4.17	5.59	5.90	6.06	6.55	6.38	5.69	5.55	5.78	5.49

US	real rate	1 yr	2 yr	3 yr	4 yr	5 yr	6 yr	7 yr	8 yr	9 yr	10 yr
pre-Lehman	retail	-0.50	2.00	3.28	3.84	4.04	4.04	3.95	3.83	3.69	3.56
post-Lehman	retail	-7.75	-2.42	-0.75	-0.31	-0.68	-0.70	-0.71	-0.66	-0.58	-0.45
pre-Lehman	job.claims	-0.49	-1.82	-1.96	-1.85	-1.66	-1.50	-1.37	-1.25	-1.15	-1.08
post-Lehman	job.claims	4.97	-2.14	-2.52	-2.34	-2.14	-2.06	-1.97	-1.88	-1.77	-1.65
pre-Lehman	CPI	-1.13	0.47	0.19	0.02	-0.01	0.05	0.14	0.24	0.33	0.41
post-Lehman	CPI	1.47	-5.05	-3.06	-1.61	-0.51	0.31	0.90	1.27	1.48	1.56
pre-Lehman	ISM	2.16	3.73	3.75	3.45	3.22	2.99	2.84	2.74	2.66	2.60
post-Lehman	ISM	-4.63	-1.52	-0.13	0.37	0.45	0.58	0.72	0.88	1.05	1.22

Euro area	nom. rate	1 yr	2 yr	3 yr	4 yr	5 yr	6 yr	7 yr	8 yr	9 yr	10 yr
pre-Lehman	retail	0.99	1.10	1.20	1.21	1.14	1.04	0.96	0.91	0.89	0.91
post-Lehman	retail	1.01	−0.24	−1.31	−2.08	−2.54	−2.79	−2.93	−3.01	−3.04	−3.05
pre-Lehman	Unenmp.	−14.21	−19.96	−24.83	−29.14	−32.70	−34.81	−35.07	−33.64	−30.93	−27.53
post-Lehman	Unenmp.	**−64.81**	−52.95	−42.18	−34.59	−30.40	−27.98	−25.95	−23.82	−21.55	−19.34
pre-Lehman	CPI	3.35	**3.35**	**3.42**	**3.40**	**3.24**	**3.02**	**2.80**	**2.61**	**2.44**	**2.30**
post-Lehman	CPI	2.85	2.72	2.44	2.02	1.54	1.08	0.70	0.42	0.23	0.11
pre-Lehman	Man.PMI	−4.37	−3.64	−2.50	−1.85	−1.94	−2.34	−2.61	−2.64	−2.43	−2.05
post-Lehman	Man.PMI	**4.34**	**4.46**	**4.52**	**4.50**	**4.40**	**4.24**	**4.03**	**3.80**	**3.58**	**3.40**

Euro area	real rate	1 yr	2 yr	3 yr	4 yr	5 yr	6 yr	7 yr	8 yr	9 yr	10 yr
pre-Lehman	Retail	2.96	2.52	2.09	1.66	1.24	0.89	0.62	0.44	0.33	0.27
post-Lehman	Retail	−2.02	−1.56	−1.12	−0.74	−0.43	−0.17	0.06	0.25	0.40	0.50
pre-Lehman	Unenmp.	−56.78	−50.39	−44.77	−41.19	−39.52	**−38.21**	**−36.12**	**−32.98**	**−29.01**	−24.65
post-Lehman	Unenmp.	−52.27	−39.88	−28.14	−17.33	−8.03	−1.12	2.94	4.30	3.43	0.93
pre-Lehman	CPI	5.37	4.65	3.93	3.24	2.59	2.00	1.48	1.04	0.67	0.36
post-Lehman	CPI	**9.13**	**9.22**	**9.19**	**8.88**	**8.30**	**7.70**	**7.23**	**6.93**	**6.80**	**6.78**
pre-Lehman	Man.PMI	7.78	7.25	6.80	6.53	6.35	6.03	5.40	4.46	3.28	1.98
post-Lehman	Man.PMI	1.57	2.16	2.62	2.91	3.02	3.04	3.02	2.99	2.96	2.93

For the United States the pre-Lehman period runs from January 1998 to August 2008, and the post-Lehman from September 2008 to April 2012. For the euro area, the pre-Lehman period runs, from January 2002 until August 2008, and the post-Lehman from September 2008 until April 2012. The coefficients of macroeconomic surprises are estimated with model (15.6); the coefficients in bold are significant at the 95% level; standard errors are computed with the outer product.

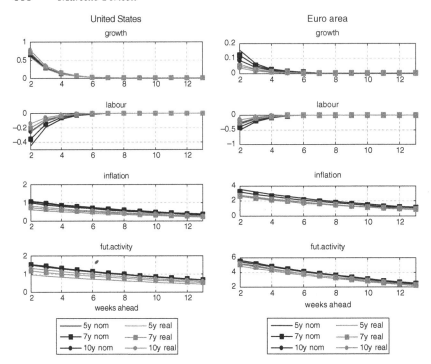

Figure 15.6 Impulse response functions

Note: The figure plots the impulse response function of the constrained model (15.6) given by Equation (15.7) for nominal and real rates. Impulse response functions are obtained by (15.7) by one standard deviation shock of the monetary surprise. Growth refers to news on retail sales in the United States and in the euro area, inflation to news on CPI in the United States and in the euro area, the labour market to news on jobless claims in the United States and the unemployment rate in the euro area, future economic activity to ISM in the United States and PMI in the euro area.

15.8   Number of factors and robustness checks

In order to test the performance of the three-factor model, the same model with two and four factors has been tested. The problem of selecting the number of factors is cumbersome; likelihood ratio tests cannot be used to test for the number of statistically relevant factors, as some of the parameters become unidentified under the null. Previous works use three factors (D'Amico et al., 2008; Christensen et al., 2010; and García and Werner, 2010), four factors (Risa, 2001) and five factors (Adrian and Wu, 2010). The criterion for using three factors in this chapter is based on the cumulative explained variance of nominal and real interest rates obtained by a principal component analysis. For the euro area bond market, variances explained by the first, second, third and fourth principal factors are 88.5%, 8.4%, 2.8% and 0.2%, respectively; those for the United States market are 91.3%, 7.1%, 1.4% and 0.2%. Then, in both markets the first three factors explain more than 99.5% of the total variance and this is deemed sufficient for choosing three factors. A more thorough analysis can be made either by comparing out-of-sample errors of the pricing equations, as in Risa (2001), or by cross-validation. It appears that, in the case of two factors, the fit is not able to capture the dynamics of the term structure; in fact the unique real latent factor, which proxies the cross-sectional average of real rates, is not capable of capturing the cross-sectional dispersion among interest rates. With four factors, the model tends to overfit the term structures both for real and nominal interest rates.

The validity of estimates have also been tested by means of a number of robustness checks. First, model (15.6) has been enriched by introducing surveys of inflation expectations. Second, a proxy of economic growth has been introduced. This section briefly reviews the main findings of the robustness checks.

Surveys of inflation expectation are introduced in the model in order to improve its identification power, as in Chernov and Mueller (2012), D'Amico et al. (2008), García and Werner (2010) and Hördahl and Tristani (2010). Alternatively, Adrian and Wu (2010) use time-varying conditional covariation between real and inflation factors to increase the identification power of the model. Haubrich et al. (2011, 2012) combine the use of surveys of inflation expectation with four volatility state variables which completely determine the risk premia. A natural way to increase the identification power of the model is to use the short-term interest rate in the estimates. Model (15.6) is then estimated by inserting the 3-month repo interest rate in the Y matrix. The repo rate is preferred to the inter-bank rate and to the eurocurrency rate as it does not contain premiums for counterparty risks. The results are very similar to those presented above.

Model (15.6) has been estimated with each of the macroeconomic surprises available from Bloomberg for the United States, the euro area, and the three largest euro-area countries – namely Germany, France and Italy. The results show that no other macroeconomic surprises in the United States and in the euro area impact nominal and real interest rates at a weekly frequency. Only the consumer price indices of the three largest euro-area countries have an effect on the short-term segment of the nominal term structure; this effect can be explained by the relative weight of the inflation rate of each of these countries on the aggregate euro-area inflation rate. Monetary surprises in the United States have also been calculated as surprises in the expected federal funds target rate.

Finally, in the euro area surprises for the advanced GDP, the preliminary GDP, the final manufacturing PMI, the advanced services PMI, the advanced composite PMI, and the advanced consumer confidence have been computed and used individually in model (15.6). In the United States the surprise for the preliminary and the final GDP have been computed and used individually in model (15.6). The results are substantially similar to those presented in the chapter.

15.9   Conclusion

The chapter documents the impact of surprises on the real and nominal term structure, in the euro area and the United States, in the last twelve years. The interaction between an affine Gaussian term structure model augmented with macroeconomic surprises is capable of describing, at the same time, the evolution of nominal and of real interest rates by means of a small number of latent factors and the response of real and nominal rates to surprises in economic data releases as well as to monetary surprises. The model is also capable of providing the spot long-term inflation expectation and the forward long-term inflation expectation implied in the nominal and real term structure together with the corresponding inflation risk premia. Inflation risk premia show large values and ample variability in the United States while they are smaller and more stable in the euro area.

Long-term expected forward inflation rates, a common indicator of inflation expectations, are on average below breakeven forward inflation rates in the United States, at around 2.1 per cent from 2002 until 2010; this implies that the forward inflation risk premium is on average positive in a range of 0.2 to 0.4 percentage points in the United States. The forward inflation risk premia became sizable around the start of the late-2000s financial crisis and considerably increased in the United States just before the adoption of the first unconventional measures of monetary policy, known as QE1, in March 2009. In contrast, in the euro area expected forward inflation rates remained well anchored at around 1.8 per cent and the forward inflation risk premium was unchanged even after the adoption of the unconventional monetary policy measures following the peaks of the financial crisis, in October 2008 and in May 2010.

As far as macroeconomic surprises are concerned, this work contributes to this field of literature by consistently analysing the impact of surprises on nominal and real rates. Most studies look at a single bill yield, a few yields from one part of the maturity spectrum, or a short-term yield and a long-term yield. Even when they do consider more than a single yield, there is typically no attempt to relate announcement effects across maturities. This chapter innovates this strand of the literature, which still lacks an analysis for the entire yield curve.

The results show that nominal rates are impacted by macroeconomic surprises in growth, the labour market and economic outlook in the United States and by surprises in inflation in the euro area. These preliminary results can be due to the difference in the mandate of the monetary authorities, which is dual in the United States and hierarchical in the euro area. Moreover, monetary policy shocks make short-term breakeven inflation rates increase in the United States, while they do not change breakeven inflation rates across the maturity spectrum in the euro area. These different responses to monetary shocks highlight dissimilarities between the markets' perception of monetary policy targets.

Appendix A

The real term structure

The model consists of three equations. The first equation describes the dynamics of the vector of state variables X_t (a k-dimensional vector, $k \in \mathbb{N}$):

$$X_t = \mu + \rho X_{t-1} + \Sigma \varepsilon_t, \tag{15.8}$$

where $\varepsilon_t \sim N(0, I_k)$, μ is a $k \times 1$ vector and ρ and Σ are $k \times k$ matrices. Without loss of generality, it can be assumed that Σ is lower triangular. Furthermore, to ensure stationarity of the process, we assume that all the eigenvalues of ρ strictly lie inside the unit circle. The probability measure associated with the above specification of X_t will be denoted by P. X_t is a matrix containing k latent factors, which can be thought of as $k-1$ real factors and one inflation factor.

The second equation relates the one-period interest rate $r_t^1 = r_t$ to the state variables (positing that it is an affine function of the state variables):

$$r_t = -\delta_0 - \delta_1 X_t, \tag{15.9}$$

where δ_0 is a scalar and δ_1 is a $k \times 1$ vector with the last element equal to zero as the real rate is not affected by the inflation rate.

The third equation is related to bond pricing in an arbitrage-free market. A sufficient condition for the absence of arbitrage on the bond market is that there exists a risk-neutral measure Q, equivalent to P, under which the process X_t follows the dynamics

$$X_t = \overline{\mu} + \overline{\rho} X_{t-1} + \Sigma \eta_t, \tag{15.10}$$

where $\eta_t \sim N(0, I_k)$ under Q and such that the price at time t of a bond paying a unitary amount of cash at time $t + n$ (denoted by p_t^n) equals

$$p_t^n = \mathrm{E}_t^Q \left[\exp(-r_t) p_{t+1}^{n-1} \right], \tag{15.11}$$

where E_t^Q denotes expectation under the probability measure Q, conditional upon the information available at time t.

The vector $\overline{\mu}$ and the matrix $\overline{\rho}$ are in general different from μ and ρ, while equivalence of P and Q guarantees that Σ is left unchanged. The link between the risk-neutral distribution Q and the physical distribution P is given by the (time-varying) price of risk which is affine in the state variables:

$$\lambda_t = \lambda_0 + \lambda_1 X_t,$$

where $\lambda_0 = \Sigma^{-1}(\mu - \overline{\mu})$ and $\lambda_1 = \Sigma^{-1}(\rho - \overline{\rho})$. According to Cameron, Martin and Girsanov's theorem (see, e.g. Kallenberg, 1997)

$$\mathrm{E}_t^P \left[\frac{dQ}{dP} \right] = \prod_{j=1}^{\infty} \exp \left[-\frac{1}{2} \lambda_{t+j-1}^\top \lambda_{t+j-1} - \lambda_{t+j-1}^\top \varepsilon_{t+j} \right],$$

so that the real pricing kernel

$$m_{t+1} = \exp \left(-r_t - \frac{1}{2} \lambda_t^\top \lambda_t - \lambda_t^\top \varepsilon_{t+1} \right) \tag{15.12}$$

can be used to recursively price bonds:

$$p_t^n = \mathrm{E}_t^P \left[m_{t+1} p_{t+1}^{n-1} \right]. \tag{15.13}$$

Note that within this Gaussian framework, bond yields are affine functions of the state variables:

$$r_t^n = -\frac{1}{n} \ln(p_t^n) = A_n + B_n X_t,$$

where r_t^n is the yield at time t of a bond maturing in n periods and A_n and B_n are coefficients obeying the following simple system of Riccati equations, derived from (15.11):[5]

---

[5] A proof by induction for a more general case can be found in, for example, Dai and Singleton (2000).

$$A_1 = -\delta_0,$$
$$B_1 = -\delta_1,$$
$$A_{n+1} = -\delta_0 + A_n + B_n(\mu - \Sigma\lambda_0) - \frac{1}{2}B_n\Sigma\Sigma B_n,$$
$$B_{n+1} = -\delta_1 + B_n(\rho - \Sigma\lambda_1). \tag{15.14}$$

Define $A = [A_1, \ldots, A_{n+1}]$, an $(n+1) \times 1$ vector and $B = [B_1, \ldots, B_{n+1}]$, an $(n+1) \times k$ matrix which enter models (15.3) and (15.6).

The yields $\tilde{r}_t^n$ and the bond prices $\tilde{p}_t^n$ that would obtain in an arbitrage-free market populated by risk-neutral investors are instead obtained setting the prices of risk to zero ($\lambda_t = 0$) in (15.12) and (15.13):

$$\tilde{p}_t^n = E_t^P\left[\exp\left(-r_t\right)\tilde{p}_{t+1}^{n-1}\right].$$

They obey the same system of recursive equations (15.14), where $\overline{\mu}$ and $\overline{\rho}$ are substituted by μ and ρ. Subtracting the risk-neutral yields $\tilde{r}_t^n$ thus calculated from the actual yields r_t^n, one obtains the term risk premia ϕ_t^n:

$$\phi_t^n = r_t^n - \tilde{r}_t^n,$$

which is the additional interest per unit of time required by investors for bearing the risk associated with the fluctuations of the price of a bond expiring in n periods. Such premia are in general time varying, and they are constant only when $\lambda_1 = 0$, i.e. for $\rho = \overline{\rho}$.

Appendix B

The nominal term structure

Nominal bond prices are determined by the nominal pricing kernel $\widehat{M}$ which is linked to the real pricing kernel through the inflation rate, Π, i.e. the change in the consumer price index. Given the relation $\widehat{M}_{t+1} = M_{t+1}/\Pi_{t+1}$, the log nominal pricing kernel is given by

$$\begin{aligned}
\log\widehat{M}_{t+1} = \widehat{m}_{t+1} &= m_{t+1} - \pi_{t+1} \\
&= m_{t+1} - \exp(e_K^\top X_{t+1}) \\
&= \exp\left(-r_t - \frac{1}{2}\lambda_t^\top\lambda_t - \lambda_t^\top\varepsilon_{t+1} - e_K^\top X_{t+1}\right),
\end{aligned}$$

where $e_K = (0, \ldots, 0, 1)^\top$ and thus $e_K^\top X_{t+1}$ picks the inflation rate. Using the affine pricing rule, the price of a nominal bond is given by

$$
\exp\left(\widehat{A}_{n+1} + \widehat{B}_{n+1}^\mathrm{T} X\right) = \exp\left[-\delta_0 + \widehat{A}_n + \left(\widehat{B}_n - e_K^\top\right)(\mu - \Sigma\lambda_0)\right.
$$
$$
-\frac{1}{2}\left(\widehat{B}_n - e_K^\top\right)\Sigma\Sigma\left(\widehat{B}_n - e_K^\top\right)^\mathrm{T}
$$
$$
\left. +\left(-\delta_1 + \left(\widehat{B}_n - e_K^\top\right)(\rho - \Sigma\lambda_1)\right)X_t\right],
$$

where

$$
\widehat{A}_1 = -\delta_0 - e_K^\top\mu + \frac{1}{2}e_K^\top\Sigma\Sigma e_K + e_K^\top\Sigma\lambda_0,
$$
$$
\widehat{B}_1 = -\left(\delta_1 + e_K^\top\rho\right) + e_K^\top\Sigma\lambda_1,
$$
$$
\ldots
$$
$$
\widehat{A}_{n+1} = -\delta_0 + \widehat{A}_n + \left(\widehat{B}_n - e_K^\top\right)(\mu - \Sigma\lambda_0),
$$
$$
-\frac{1}{2}\left(\widehat{B}_n - e_K^\top\right)\Sigma\Sigma\left(\widehat{B}_n - e_K^\top\right)^\mathrm{T},
$$
$$
\widehat{B}_{n+1} = -\delta_1 + \left(\widehat{B}_n - e_K^\top\right)(\rho - \Sigma\lambda_1). \tag{15.15}
$$

Define $\widehat{A} = [\widehat{A}_1, \ldots, \widehat{A}_{n+1}]$, an $(n+1) \times 1$ vector and $\widehat{B} = [\widehat{B}_1, \ldots, \widehat{B}_{n+1}]$, an $(n + 1) \times k$ matrix which enter models (15.3) and (15.6).

Appendix C

The model with macroeconomic and monetary surprises

The drifts, E, and the loadings, G, for real rates associated with surprises S are defined by the usual system of Riccati equations:

$$
E_1 = -\gamma_0,
$$
$$
G_1 = -\gamma_1,
$$
$$
E_{n+1} = -\gamma_0 + E_n + G_n(\mu_S - \Sigma_S\theta_0) - \frac{1}{2}G_n\Sigma_S\Sigma_S G_n,
$$
$$
G_{n+1} = -\gamma_1 + G_n(\phi - \Sigma_S\theta_1). \tag{15.16}
$$

Define $E = [E_1, \ldots, E_{n+1}]$, an $(n+1) \times 1$ vector and $G = [G_1, \ldots, G_{n+1}]$, an $(n+1) \times M$ matrix which enter model (15.6). The equivalent equations for nominal rates have the same recursive structure, namely

$$\widehat{E}_1 = -\widehat{\gamma}_0 - \iota_M^\top \mu_S + \frac{1}{2}\iota_M^\top \Sigma_S \Sigma_S \iota_M + \iota_M^\top \Sigma \theta_0,$$

$$\widehat{G}_1 = -\left(\widehat{\gamma}_1 + \iota_M^\top \phi\right) + \iota_M^\top \Sigma_S \theta_1,$$

$$\widehat{E}_{n+1} = -\widehat{\gamma}_0 + \widehat{E}_n + \left(\widehat{G}_n - \iota_M^\top\right)(\mu_S - \Sigma_S \theta_0)$$
$$- \frac{1}{2}\left(\widehat{G}_n - \iota_M^\top\right)\Sigma_S \Sigma_S \left(\widehat{G}_n - \iota_M^\top\right),$$

$$\widehat{G}_{n+1} = -\widehat{\gamma}_1 + \left(\widehat{G}_n - \iota_M^\top\right)(\phi - \Sigma_S \theta_1), \tag{15.17}$$

where ι_M is an $(M \times 1)$ vector of parameters. Define $\widehat{E} = [\widehat{E}_1, \ldots, \widehat{E}_{n+1}]$, an $(n+1) \times 1$ vector and $\widehat{G} = [\widehat{G}_1, \ldots, \widehat{G}_{n+1}]$, an $(n+1) \times M$ matrix which enter model (15.6). Note that the equation of the real pricing kernel becomes

$$m_{t+1} = \exp\left(-r_t - \frac{1}{2}\overline{\lambda}_t^\top \overline{\lambda}_t - \overline{\lambda}_t^\top \varepsilon_{t+1}\right), \tag{15.18}$$

where

$$\overline{\lambda}_t = [\lambda_0, \theta_0] + \begin{bmatrix} \lambda_1 & 0 \\ 0 & \theta_1 \end{bmatrix}\begin{bmatrix} X_t \\ S_t \end{bmatrix}.$$

Appendix D

The specification of the model

The complete model (15.6) is defined by the following parameters

$$\rho = \begin{bmatrix} \rho_{11} & 0 & 0 \\ \rho_{21} & \rho_{22} & 0 \\ \rho_{31} & \rho_{32} & \rho_{33} \end{bmatrix}, \phi = \begin{bmatrix} \phi_{11} & \cdots & \phi_{15} \\ \vdots & \ddots & \vdots \\ \phi_{31} & \cdots & \phi_{35} \end{bmatrix},$$

$$\rho_{uo} = \begin{bmatrix} \rho_{uo,11} & 0 & 0 & 0 & 0 \\ 0 & \rho_{uo,22} & 0 & 0 & 0 \\ 0 & 0 & \rho_{uo,33} & 0 & 0 \\ 0 & 0 & 0 & \rho_{uo,44} & 0 \\ 0 & 0 & 0 & 0 & \rho_{uo,55} \end{bmatrix},$$

$$\mu = (0, 0, \mu_\pi), \mu_S = (\mu_S^1, \mu_S^2, \mu_S^3, \mu_S^4, \mu_S^5),$$
$$\delta_0 = 0, \delta_1 = (\delta_1^1, \delta_1^2, 0), \gamma_0 = 0, \gamma_1 = (\gamma_1^1, \gamma_1^2, \gamma_1^3, \gamma_1^4, \gamma_1^5),$$

$$\Sigma = \begin{bmatrix} 1 & 0 & 0 \\ 0 & 1 & 0 \\ 0 & 0 & \sigma_\pi \end{bmatrix}, \; \Sigma_S = \begin{bmatrix} \sigma_{S,11} & 0 & 0 & 0 & 0 \\ 0 & \sigma_{S,22} & 0 & 0 & 0 \\ 0 & 0 & \sigma_{S,33} & 0 & 0 \\ 0 & 0 & 0 & \sigma_{S,44} & 0 \\ 0 & 0 & 0 & 0 & \sigma_{S,55} \end{bmatrix},$$

$$\lambda_0 = (\lambda_0^1, \lambda_0^2, \lambda_0^3)^\top, \; \theta_0 = (\theta_0^1, \theta_0^2, \theta_0^3, \theta_0^4, \theta_0^5)^\top = 0,$$

$$\lambda_1 = \begin{bmatrix} \lambda_{1,11} & \lambda_{1,12} & \lambda_{1,13} \\ \lambda_{1,21} & \lambda_{1,22} & \lambda_{1,23} \\ \lambda_{1,31} & \lambda_{1,32} & 0 \end{bmatrix}, \; \theta_1 = \begin{bmatrix} \theta_{1,11} & 0 & 0 & 0 & 0 \\ 0 & \theta_{1,22} & 0 & 0 & 0 \\ 0 & 0 & \theta_{1,33} & 0 & 0 \\ 0 & 0 & 0 & \theta_{1,44} & 0 \\ 0 & 0 & 0 & 0 & \theta_{1,55} \end{bmatrix},$$

$$\sigma_N(\tau) = c_N + d_N/\sqrt{\tau}, \text{ for } \tau = 3, \ldots, 10,$$

$$\sigma_R(\tau) = c_R + d_R/\sqrt{\tau}, \text{ for } \tau = 3, \ldots, 10.$$

Pericoli and Taboga (2008) show that, without loss of generality, it is possible to assume that ρ is lower triangular and that the matrix Σ is diagonal with all diagonal elements equal to one but the last. The matrix R is a 16×16 diagonal matrix whose main diagonal is given by $R = \text{diag} [\sigma_N(3), \ldots, \sigma_N(10), \sigma_R(3), \ldots, \sigma_R(10)]$, where $\sigma_N(\tau)$ and $\sigma_R(\tau)$ are the standard deviations of the nominal and real bond with maturity τ. Furthermore, let's assume that the standard deviation of the observation errors is non-increasing in the term to maturity τ, i.e. the volatility is lower for bonds with longer maturities; this notation can reflect several possible definitions of the observation error; when d_N and d_R are equal to zero the price errors are constant across maturities (Risa, 2001).

References

Adrian, T. and Wu, H. (2010). The term structure of inflation expectations, Federal Reserve Bank of New York Staff Reports, No. 362, August.

Ang, A. and Piazzesi, M. (2003). A no-arbitrage vector autoregression of term structure dynamics with macroeconomic and latent variables, *Journal of Monetary Economics*, 50, 745–787.

Ang, A., Bekaert, G. and Wei, M. (2008). The term structure of real rates and inflation expectations, *The Journal of Finance*, 63, 797–849.

Cecioni, M., Ferrero, G. and Secchi, A. (2011). Unconventional monetary policy in theory and in practice, Questioni di Economia e Finanza, Banca d'Italia, No. 102, September.

Chernov, M. and Mueller, P. (2012). The term structure of inflation expectations, *Journal of Financial Economics*, 106(2), 367–394.

Christensen, J. H. E., Lopez, J. A. and Rudebusch, G. D. (2010). Inflation expectations and risk premiums in an arbitrage-free model of nominal and real bond yields, *Journal of Money, Credit and Banking*, 42(6), 143–178.

Cook, T. and Hahn, T. (1987). The reaction of interest rates to unanticipated Federal Reserve actions and statements: implications for the money announcement controversy, *Economic Inquiry*, 25, 511–534.

Dai, Q. and Singleton, K. J. (2000). Specification analysis of affine term structure models, *The Journal of Finance*, 55, 1943–1978.

D'Amico, S., Kim, D. H. and Wei, M. (2008). Tips from TIPS: the informational content of Treasury Inflation-Protected Security prices, Finance and Economics Discussion Series, Federal Reserve Board, No. 30.

Ederington, L. H. and Lee, J. H. (1993). How markets process information: news releases and volatility, *The Journal of Finance*, 48(4), 1161–1191.

Edison, H. J. (1996). The reaction of exchange rates and interest rates to news releases. International Finance Discussion Paper, Federal Reserve Board, No. 570, October.

Ehrmann, M. and Fratzscher, M. (2005). Equal size, equal role? Interest rates interdependence between the euro area and the United States, *The Economic Journal*, 115 (October), 928–948.

Evans, M. (1998). Real rates, expected inflation, and inflation risk premia, *The Journal of Finance*, 53, 187–218.

Fisher, M., Nychka, D. and Zervos, D. (1995). Fitting the term structure of interest rates with smoothing splines, Finance and Economics Discussion Series, Federal Reserve Board, No. 95–1.

Fleming, M. J. and Remolona, E. M. (1997). What moves the bond market?, *Federal Reserve Bank of New York Economic Policy Review*, December, 31–50.

Fleming, M. J. and Remolona, E. M. (1999a). Price formation and liquidity in the U.S. Treasury market: the response to public information, *The Journal of Finance*, 54(5), 1901–1915.

Fleming, M. J. and Remolona, E. M. (1999b). The term structure of announcement effects, BIS Working Paper, No. 71, June.

García, J. A. and Werner, T. (2010). Inflation risk and inflation risk premia, ECB Working Paper, No. 1162, March.

Grossman, J. (1981). The 'rationality' of money supply expectations and the short-run response of interest rates to monetary surprises, *Journal of Money, Credit and Banking*, 13, 409–424.

Gürkaynak, R. S., Sack, B. and Swanson, E. (2005). The sensitivity of long-term interest rates to economic news: evidence and implications for macroeconomic models, *American Economic Review*, 95(1), 425–436.

Gürkaynak, R. S., Sack, B. and Wright, J. H. (2007). The U.S. Treasury yield curve: 1961 to the present, *Journal of Monetary Economics*, 54(8), 2291–2304.

Gürkaynak, R. S., Sack, B. and Wright, J. H. (2010). The TIPS yield curve and inflation compensation, *American Economic Journal: Macroeconomics*, 2(1): 70–92.

Gürkaynak, R. S., Levin, A. and Swanson, E. (2010). Does inflation targeting anchor long-run inflation expectations? Evidence from the U.S., UK, and Sweden, *Journal of the European Economic Association*, 8(6), 1208–1242.

Hardouvelis, G. A. (1988). Economic news, exchange rates and interest rates, *Journal of International Money and Finance*, 7, 23–35.

Haubrich, J., Pennacchi, G. and Ritchken, P. (2011). Estimating real and nominal term structures using Treasury yields, inflation, inflation forecasts, and inflation swap rates, Federal Reserve Bank of Cleveland, Working Paper, March 11/07.

Haubrich, J., Pennacchi, G. and Ritchken, P. (2012). Inflation expectations, real rates, and risk premia: evidence from inflation swaps, *Review of Financial Studies*, 5(5), 1588–1629.

Hördahl, P. and Tristani, O. (2010). Inflation risk premia in the US and the euro area, ECB Working Paper, No. 1270, December.

Joyce, M., Lildholdt, P. and Sorensen, S. (2010). Extracting inflation expectations and inflation risk premia from the term structure: a joint model of the UK nominal and real yield curves, *Journal of Banking and Finance*, 34, 281–294.

Kallenberg, O. (1997). *Foundations of Modern Probability*, New York: Springer.

Krueger, J. T. and Kuttner, K. N. (1996). The Fed funds futures rate as a predictor of federal reserve policy, *Journal of Futures Markets*, 16, 865–879.

Litterman, R. and Scheinkman, J. A. (1991). Common factors affecting bond returns, *Journal of Fixed Income*, 1, 54–61.

Pericoli, M. (2012). Expected inflation and inflation risk premium in the euro area and in the United States, Temi di discussione, Banca d'Italia, No. 842.

Pericoli, M. (2013). Real term structure and inflation compensation in the euro area, *International Journal of Central Banking*, forthcoming.

Pericoli, M. and Taboga, M. (2008). Canonical term-structure models with observable factors and the dynamics of bond risk premia, *Journal of Money, Credit and Banking*, 40(7), 1471–1488.

Piazzesi, M. (2001). An econometric model of the yield curve with macroeconomic jump effects, NBER Working Paper, No. 8246, April.

Risa, S. (2001). Nominal and inflation indexed yields: separating expected inflation and inflation risk premia, Columbia University, Mimeo.

Roley, V. V. and Walsh, C. E. (1985). Monetary policy regimes, expected inflation and the response of interest rates to money announcements. *Quarterly Journal of Economics*, 100, Supplement, 1011–1039.

Rudebusch, G. D. and Wu, T. (2008). A macro-finance model of the term structure, monetary policy and the economy, *Economic Journal*, 118, 906–926.

Urich, T. and Wachtel, P. (1981). Market response to the weekly money supply announcements in the 1970s, *The Journal of Finance*, 36, 1063–1072.

Part V

Default risk

16 A term structure model for defaultable European sovereign bonds

Priscilla Burity, Marcelo Medeiros and Luciano Vereda

16.1 Introduction

The recent economic crisis, triggered by problems in the subprime mortgage market in the USA, has hit economies around the world. Systemic banking fragility associated with the deterioration of the economic outlook and fiscal stimulus packages left behind quite fragile fiscal positions. The banking crisis has turned into a sovereign debt crisis. The details regarding the origins of the euro zone crisis are discussed in Chapter 3 by Durré and Smets. Here, we explore the fact that increases in countries' fiscal deficit and debt levels can bring an increased perception of sovereign risk. In the sovereign bond markets, this movement can cause higher yields on bonds of these countries to finance their debt.

Following Ang and Piazzesi (2003), we use an arbitrage-free affine term structure model to assess how European sovereign yield spreads (measured as the difference between the relevant countries' bond yield and Germany's bond yield) are affected by fiscal variables. The countries we study are Italy, Greece and Spain. We use monthly data from January 1999 to March 2010 for Italy and Spain, and from January 2001 to March 2010 for Greece. We also check how some of the results change when the sample is extended further, with the deepening of the debt crisis.

In the literature on the European sovereign bond market, the papers tackling the role of fiscal variables on bond yield spreads are not conclusive. Focusing on the European bond market, Bernoth, von Hagen and Schuknecht (2004) and Schuknecht, von Hagen and Wolswijk (2008) studied the relationship between fiscal variables and spreads for some

The authors are grateful for extremely helpful comments from Michael Dempster, Mike Joyce and an anonymous referee.

selected maturities.[1] The basic equation of the two articles has spreads as dependent variables and fiscal variables and the maturity of bonds (among other things) as explanatory factors, with no restriction of no-arbitrage. The authors find a positive effect from deficit and debt levels. In a more general approach, using a sample of 26 countries, Longstaff et al. (2011) found that the excess returns from investing in sovereign credit are largely compensation for bearing global risk, and that there is little or no country-specific credit risk premium. Using data from USA, Germany and Italy, Marattin, Paesani and Salotti (see Chapter 17) show that fiscal fundamentals significantly affect long-term interest rates. Our goal is to use the tools developed by the literature on term structure models summarised above to answer the questions traditionally raised by the literature on the European sovereign bond market.

The no-arbitrage modelling approach we use has advantages in comparison to an unrestricted vector autoregression (VAR) or single equation approach, like Bernoth, von Hagen and Schuknecht (2004), Schuknecht, von Hagen and Wolswijk (2008) and Georgoutsos and Migiakis (2010). First, it allows us to assess the impact of fiscal shocks on the whole yield curve, not only on observed yields. VAR models have little to say about how yields to maturities not included in the model move. Second, in VAR models the implied movements of yields in relation to each other may not rule out arbitrage opportunities. Third, the no-arbitrage approach allows us to model the relationship between macroeconomic variables and yield spreads. We know of no other work that addresses the relationship between fiscal variables and the term structure of bond yields for countries in the euro zone in an arbitrage-free term structure model environment.

We believe that the three euro-area countries in this analysis – Spain, Greece and Italy – are representative of the group of European countries that has faced debt financing problems more recently. In summary, our main question is: to what extent can their yield spreads can be attributed to economic fundamentals? In particular, we are interested in the con-tribution of deficit and debt in the expansion of sovereign spreads in the years after the onset of the economic crisis in 2007. Our idea is to distinguish the effects of fiscal shocks from the effects of shocks to other macroeconomic variables and potentially relevant indicators of risk aversion.

The remainder of this chapter is organised as follows. In Section 16.2 we present the model. The data are discussed in Section 16.3. The

---

[1] It is standard in this literature to evaluate, instead of the bond yields themselves, the spreads in relation to the yields on German securities. Schuknecht, von Hagen and Wolswijk (2008) also studied the Canadian government bond market.

estimation strategy is presented in Section 16.4. The results are shown in Section 16.5. In Section 16.6 we check how some of the results change when the sample is extended to December 2011, with the deepening of the debt crisis. In Section 16.7, we discuss robustness and finally, Section 16.8 concludes.

16.2 Model

Our strategy consists of estimating a term structure model for Germany and then estimating the spreads between the yields to maturity of bonds from Italy, Greece and Spain (the group we will call IGS) and bonds from Germany. These two steps require the previous estimation of the process for the short rate and the dynamics of factors. In this section, we present the term structure models for Germany (Subsection 16.2.1) and the IGS countries (Subsection 16.2.2). The short rate and factors equations are also discussed.

16.2.1 Term structure model for non-defaultable bonds

The pricing model of securities issued by the German government which, according to our assumptions, are non-defaultable securities, follows from Ang and Piazzesi (2003). The short rate r_t follows an affine function of all state variables, grouped in the vector X_t of dimension K; see Duffie and Kan (1996):

$$r_t = \delta_0 + \delta_1' X_t. \tag{16.1}$$

The composition of X_t will be discussed below and includes important fiscal variables. We assume that the standardised (zero mean and unit variance) X_t follows a first-order Gaussian VAR.[2]

$$X_t = \phi X_{t-1} + \Sigma u_t, \tag{16.2}$$

where u_t is a Gaussian vector of uncorrelated shocks of variance one.
The price at t of an $(N+1)$-period bond can be written as

$$V_t^{(N+1)\text{Ge}} = \exp\left(\overline{A}_{N+1} + \overline{B}'_{N+1} X_t^{\text{Ge}}\right), \tag{16.3}$$

where $\overline{A}_{N+1}$ and $\overline{B}'_{N+1}$ satisfy well-known Riccati difference equations (see Appendix A for a summary).

---

[2] The VAR order was chosen by the Schwarz information criterion in a range between 0 and 6.

16.2.2   Term structure model for defaultable bonds

In this subsection we consider the model for pricing securities issued by the IGS countries which, according to our assumptions, are defaultable securities. Consider a defaultable bond that at t promises to pay V_{t+N} at maturity date $t + N$ and nothing before that. For any period $s \geq t$, let: $h_s \in [0, 1]$ be the conditional probability at s of default between s and $s + 1$; φ_s be the recovery value, in units of account, in the case of default; M_s be the stochastic discount factor (or pricing kernel) in S of the representative buyer. Therefore, the present value of this bond at t, V_t, is given by (see Duffie and Singleton, 1999)

$$V_t = h_t \mathrm{E}_t \left(M_{t+1} \varphi_{t+1} \right) + (1 - h_t) \, \mathrm{E}_t \left(M_{t+1} V_{t+1} \right). \tag{16.4}$$

We make the following assumptions.

Assumption 16.1 *In case of default, the recovery value is proportional to the face value of the bond:*

$$\varphi_s = (1 - L_s) \, V_s, \tag{16.5}$$

where L_s denotes the proportional loss at s.

Assumption 16.1 follows Pan and Singleton (2008) and must be thought of as case-specific. Substituting (16.5) into (16.4), we have (Bonomo and Lowenkron, 2008)

$$
\begin{aligned}
V_t &= h_t \, \mathrm{E}_t \left[M_{t+1} \left(1 - L_{t+1} \right) V_{t+1} \right] + (1 - h_t) \, \mathrm{E}_t \left[M_{t+1} V_{t+1} \right] \\
&= \mathrm{E}_t \left[M_{t+1} \left(1 - h_t L_{t+1} \right) V_{t+1} \right].
\end{aligned}
$$

It is common in this literature to allow liquidity to affect pricing.[3] We make the simplifying assumption that illiquidity of the security translates into a fractional cost of rate l. Hence, the total discount rate of the security due to default and illiquidity risks is

$$V_t = \mathrm{E}_t \left[M_{t+1} \Theta_{t+1} V_{t+1} \right], \tag{16.6}$$

where $\Theta_{t+1} \equiv 1 - h_t L_{t+1} - l_{t+1}$ is a measure of default and liquidity risk. We assume that $\ln \Theta_{t+1}$ is linear in the factors X_t, i.e., $\ln \Theta_t = \theta_t = \theta_0 + \theta_1' X_t = \theta_0 + \theta_1' \Phi X_{t-1} + \theta_1' \Sigma \varepsilon_t$. We also need to impose an additional assumption

Assumption 16.2 *For every s, $\Theta_s > 0$.*

Assumption 16.2 states that the discount applied on defaultable bonds cannot be larger than 100%. In the absence of liquidity effects, it means

---

[3] See Duffie and Singleton (1999) and Duffie, Pedersen and Singleton (2003).

that the case where the probability assigned to default is 100% and, in case of default, the loss rate is 100%, never occurs.

Note that the stochastic discount factor used in the pricing model of a defaultable bond is $M_{t+1}\Theta_{t+1}$, which is the stochastic discount factor M_{t+1} of the representative buyer of the non-defaultable bond (bonds issued by the German government) adjusted for the default and liquidity risk Θ_{t+1}. Once Θ_{t+1} carries information on the recovery rate in case of default, probability of default and liquidity effects on the price of the bond, we should think of Θ_{t+1} as maturity-specific. Therefore, we should rewrite Equation (16.6) as

$$V_t^{N+1} = E_t\left[M_{t+1}\Theta_{t+1}^N V_{t+1}^N\right]. \tag{16.7}$$

We assume the following simplifying assumption about $\ln\Theta_t^N$

Assumption 16.3 $\ln\Theta_t^N$ *has three additive components: a constant, a component linear in the maturity and a component linear in the state variables:*

$$\ln\Theta_t^N = \theta_t^N = \theta_0^N + \theta_1'X_t = \theta_{00} + N\theta_{01} + \theta_1'X_t. \tag{16.8}$$

A crucial implication of Assumption 16.3 is that $\ln\Theta_t^N$ varies (linearly) with the maturity, but the effect of the state variables on $\ln\Theta_t^N$ does not depend on the maturity. Given the model described above, the following proposition determines the prices of defaultable bonds. Thereafter, prices and other variables related to a specific country in the group of the IGS will be indexed by i.

Proposition 16.1 *If $M_{t+1}\Theta_{t-1}^{(N)i}V_{t-1}^{(N)i}$ follows a log-normal distribution and under Assumptions 16.1 to 16.3, the restriction of no arbitrage implies that the price at t of a defaultable $(N+1)$-maturity bond (in the case we are evaluating, a bond issued by one of the IGS governments) can be written as $v_t^{(N+1)} = v_t^{(N+1)Ge} + \overline{D}_{(N+1)}^i + \overline{E}_{(N+1)}^i X_t^i$, where lowercase letters denote variables in log, X_t^i represents the matrix of factors for all countries and*

$$\overline{D}_{N+1}^i = \theta_0^{(N)i} + \overline{D}_N^i + \left(\theta_1^i + \overline{E}_N^i\right)' \Sigma^i \left[J'\left(\Sigma^{Ge'}\overline{B}_N - \lambda_0\right)\right.$$

$$\left. + \frac{1}{2}\Sigma^i\left(\theta_1^i + \overline{E}_N^i\right)\right], \tag{16.9}$$

$$\overline{E}_{N+1}^i = \left(\theta_1^i + \overline{E}_N^i\right)'\left(\Phi^i - \Sigma^i J'\lambda_1'J\right). \tag{16.10}$$

Here, J is a selection matrix such that $X_t^{Ge} = JX_t^i$ and $y_t^{(N)i}$ is given by $y_t^{(N)i} = -\frac{v_t^{(N+1)i}}{N} = y_t^{(N)Ge} + D_N + \overline{E}_N^i X_t^i$. The spreads $s_t^{(N)i} \equiv y_t^{(N)i} - y_t^{(N)Ge}$ can be written as

$$s_t^{(N)i} = D_N + \overline{\mathrm{E}}_N^{i'} \mathrm{X}_t^i, \tag{16.11}$$

where $D_N = -\frac{\overline{D}_N}{N}$ *and* $\mathrm{E}_N = -\frac{\overline{\mathrm{E}}_N}{N}$.

Proof   See Appendix B.   □

Spreads are affine functions of factors. Once we have yields on bonds of different maturities, we estimate the parameters by imposing no-arbitrage restrictions on cross-section estimates given by Equations (16.9) and (16.10). For the defaultable bonds model, we need to estimate the parameters $\psi^i = \left(\phi^i, \sum^i, \theta_{00}^i, \theta_{01}^i, \theta_1^i\right)$, for $i =$ Italy (It), Spain (Sp) and Greece (Gr). Note that θ_{00}^i and θ_{01}^i are scalars, θ_1^i is a K^i-dimensional vector, and ϕ^i and $\sum^i$ are $K^i \times K^i$ matrices. Hence, with no restrictions imposed, ψ^i can be written as a $(2+K^i+2K^{i2})$-dimensional vector of parameters.[4]

16.3   Data

The countries we study are Germany, Italy, Greece and Spain. We use monthly data from January 1999 to March 2010 for Italy and Spain, . and from January 2001 to March 2010 for Greece.[5] We use prices of zero-coupon bonds with maturities of 3, 6, 12, 24, 36, 48, 60, 84 and 120 months, extracted from Bloomberg. Factors are divided into macroeconomic variables, a risk indicator and yields-related variables. The macroeconomic variables are: industrial production (IP), inflation (I), deficit (excluding interest payments) as a ratio of GDP (Def), and debt as a ratio of GDP (Deb).[6] The high-yield risk indicator is Moody's Baa Corporate Bond Yield (HY).[7] Industrial production and inflation are measured as the annual changes of the respective indices.

The yields-related variables are the three first principal components of yields (for Germany) or spreads (for the IGS countries) estimated from an eigenvalue decomposition of the observed yields (spreads) covariance

---

[4] Note that, if some variables that are included in the German model are also included in the defaultable bonds model, ψ^i and ψ^{Ge} share some of the VAR parameters of the country i (ϕ^i and $\sum^i$). Parameters in ψ^{Ge} are presented in Appendix B.

[5] Greece joined the European Monetary Union in 2001.

[6] The ideal fiscal variables would be the expected path of deficit and debt within a period ahead (say, twelve months), because fiscal positions usually are partially anticipated. In the absence of this ideal variable, we use the variables themselves, which is certainly a caveat.

[7] We use the Baa yield instead of the spread AAA-Baa as the former has more variability (and more information) than the spread.

Table 16.1 *Autocorrelation of yields, spreads and the three first principal components (PC1, PC2 and PC3) of yields (or spreads, for the IGS countries) orthogonalised with respect to the macroeconomic and risk factors*

Lags	Yields (Germany) and spreads (Spain, Italy and Greece) maturities									PC1	PC2	PC3
	3	6	12	24	36	48	60	84	120			
Germany												
0	1.00	1.00	1.00	1.00	1.00	1.00	1.00	1.00	1.00	1.00	1.00	1.00
1	0.97	0.97	0.97	0.96	0.95	0.95	0.95	0.95	0.95	0.74	0.61	0.73
2	0.93	0.92	0.92	0.90	0.89	0.83	0.88	0.89	0.89	0.49	0.46	0.58
3	0.87	0.87	0.86	0.83	0.83	0.82	0.82	0.84	0.84	0.28	0.39	0.49
Spain												
0	1.00	1.00	1.00	1.00	1.00	1.00	1.00	1.00	1.00	1.00	1.00	1.00
1	0.77	0.78	0.87	0.91	0.94	0.95	0.95	0.94	0.96	0.54	0.45	0.07
2	0.58	0.62	0.73	0.82	0.87	0.89	0.90	0.89	0.92	0.29	0.09	0.05
3	0.47	0.56	0.61	0.70	0.78	0.81	0.84	0.81	0.86	0.21	−0.09	0.07
Italy												
0	1.00	1.00	1.00	1.00	1.00	1.00	1.00	1.00	1.00	1.00	1.00	1.00
1	0.66	0.61	0.77	0.86	0.91	0.92	0.94	0.93	0.95	0.40	0.47	0.50
2	0.57	0.53	0.57	0.69	0.78	0.79	0.84	0.84	0.90	0.11	0.19	0.21
3	0.52	0.47	0.41	0.51	0.62	0.65	0.72	0.74	0.83	−0.05	0.05	0.12
Greece												
0	1.00	1.00	1.00	1.00	1.00	1.00	1.00	1.00	1.00	1.00	1.00	1.00
1	0.81	0.82	0.83	0.34	0.87	0.88	0.89	0.89	0.90	0.65	0.57	0.35
2	0.55	0.55	0.57	0.61	0.68	0.70	0.73	0.73	0.77	0.27	0.27	−0.02
3	0.30	0.29	0.33	0.37	0.46	0.49	0.54	0.54	0.62	0.01	−0.09	0.11

matrix, orthogonalised with respect to the macroeconomic and risk factors; see Cochrane and Piazzesi (2008). These yields and spread factors represent variables other than the factors considered above. It was shown by Litterman and Scheinkman (1991) and Ang and Piazzesi (2003) that three latent factors are appropriate to capture most salient features of the yield curve.[8]

As a practical matter, these remaining factors have the role of capturing most of the persistence of yields (and spreads, for the IGS countries). As we see in Table 16.1, a large portion of the autocorrelation of yields

---

[8] A number of recent papers (Joslin, Priebsch and Singleton, 2011; Joslin, Le and Singleton, 2011; Duffee, 2011) have criticised the assumptions underlying the approach of Ang and Piazzesi (2003) and similar term structure models such as this model, which imply that macroeconomic factors are fully explained by the term structure – a fact that is not empirically supported. This chapter does not address these particular issues, which might have a bearing on the results.

Table 16.2 *Debt to GDP ratio from 2000Q1 to 2010Q3 – Granger causality tests*

Null hypothesis	Lag = 1		Lag = 2		Lag = 3		Lag = 4	
	Obs	Probability[a]	Obs	Probability[a]	Obs	Probability[a]	Obs	Probability[a]
Greece's debt does not Granger cause Germany's debt	37	0.24	36	0.01***	35	0.02**	34	0.08*
Germany's debt does not Granger cause Greece's debt		0.22		0.16		0.11		0.29
Italy's debt does not Granger cause Germany's debt	40	0.72	39	0.43	38	0.25	37	0.70
Germany's debt does not Granger cause Italy's debt		0.15		0.09*		0.06*		0.01***
Spain's debt does not Granger cause Germany's debt	40	0.82	39	0.03***	38	0.03**	37	0.11
Germany's debt does not Granger cause Spain's debt		0.00***		0.54		0.13		0.07*
Italy's debt does not Granger cause Greece's debt	37	0.35	36	0.46	35	0.72	34	0.19
Greece's debt does not Granger cause Italy's debt		0.00***		0.00***		0.01***		0.0***
Spain's debt does not Granger cause Greece's debt	37	0.27	36	0.00***	35	0.01***	34	0.04**
Greece's debt does not Granger cause Spain's debt		0.00***		0.75		0.90		0.95
Spain's debt does not Granger cause Italy's debt	40	0.98	39	0.00***	38	0.00***	37	0.00***
Italy's debt does not Granger cause Spain's debt		0.00***		0.58		0.53		0.09

(a) F-distribution

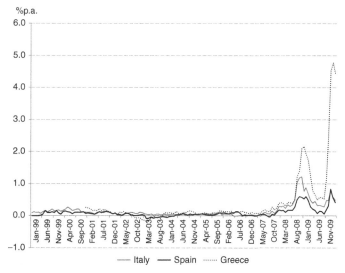

Figure 16.1 1-year sovereign bond yield spread (% pa) – selected countries
Source: Eurostat.

and spreads is captured by the three first principal components of yields orthogonalised with respect to the macroeconomic and risk factors.

Sources for the macroeconomic variables are Eurostat (all variables except HY) and the Board of Governors of the Federal Reserve System (HY). Fiscal balance, debt and GDP monthly data are not available. Monthly data for these variables were constructed from their quarterly observations and from monthly data of some coincident indicators, such as energy consumption, unemployment rate, imports and exports. For details, see Appendix C.

16.3.1 A first look at the data

In the European case, specifically in the cases of Italy, Greece and Spain, Figures 16.1 to 16.3 suggest that there is a relationship between deficit and sovereign yield spreads. Note in Figure 16.1 that from 1999 to early 2008, the 1-year yield spread between each of the IGS and Germany sovereign bonds was very low, in accordance with the interest-rate parity theory. From the mid 2008 onwards, this spread began to widen. See in Figure 16.2 that the budget deficit of these selected countries has also increased significantly since 2008. Figure 16.3 shows the 4-quarter moving average of deficit and 1-year bond yield spreads of IGS (the last graph

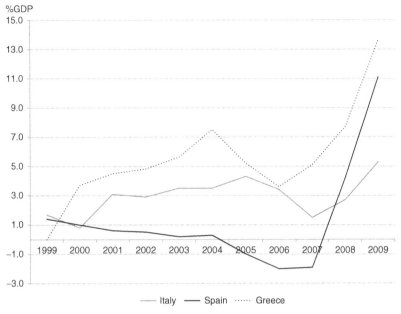

Figure 16.2 Central government budget deficit
Source: Eurostat.

shows the mean of these variables among the countries). The figure suggests that deficits are closely related to spreads. Spreads, as well as deficit
rates, assumed different dynamics from 2008 on, but, very importantly,
there is no evident reason to believe that the relationship between deficit
and spreads has ever changed.

16.4   Estimation strategy

We use the following multi-step estimation procedure[9]

1. Non-defaultable bonds estimation

   (a) We estimate the short rate Equation (16.1) and the macro
   dynamics (16.2) by ordinary least squares (OLS), obtain-
   ing $\hat{\delta}_0^{Ge}, \hat{\delta}_1^{Ge}, \hat{\Phi}^{Ge}$ and $\hat{\sum}^{Ge}$.

   (b) We estimate the yield equation (A.5; see Appendix A) also by
   OLS imposing restrictions (A.3) and (A.4). In this step, we obtain

---

[9] Our estimation strategy involves a sequence of ordinary least squares estimates which,
although consistent, might be inefficient compared to system estimation by maximum
likelihood. However, we decided to keep the OLS estimates due to its simplicity of
implementation. A similar strategy has been used in Ang and Piazzesi (2003).

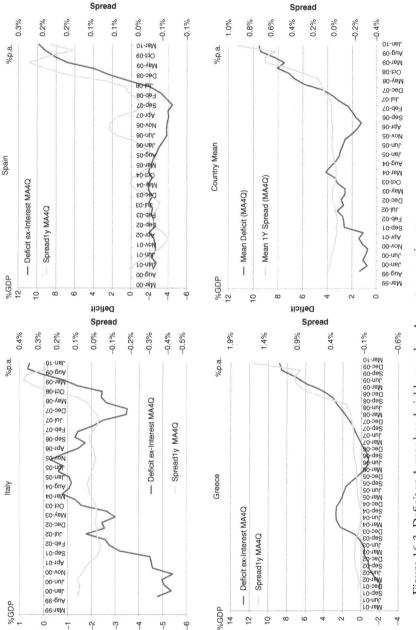

Figure 16.3 Deficit vs 1-year bond yield spreads – 4 quarters moving average

$\hat{\lambda}_0$ and $\hat{\lambda}_1$. We make the simplifying assumption that the matrix λ_1 in Equation (A.2) is diagonal.[10]

2. Defaultable bonds

   (a) We estimate the short rate spread Equation (16.1) and the analogous macro dynamics (16.2) for country i by OLS, obtaining $\hat{\delta}_0^i, \hat{\delta}_1^i, \hat{\phi}^i$ and $\hat{\sum}^i$.

   (b) We estimate the yield Equation (16.11) also by OLS using previously estimated parameters $\hat{\psi}^{\text{Ge}}$ and imposing restrictions (16.9) and (16.10). In this step, we obtain $\hat{\theta}_{00}^i, \hat{\theta}_{01}^i$ and $\hat{\theta}_1^i$.

In the non-defaultable bonds model, the state variables X_t^{Ge} are HY_t and all macroeconomic and yields-related variables from Germany, in the order HY_t, IP_t, CPI_t, Def_t, Deb_t, $PC1_t$, $PC2_t$, $PC3_t$. In the defaultable bonds model, state variables X_t^i are HY_t and all macroeconomic and yields-related variables from Germany and the country i. X_t^i includes the first three principal components of spreads for country i. In this model, the variables are ordered the same way. First HY_t, then the German ones, and then the specific country variables (i.e., $K = 8$ and $K^i = 15$). As some variables included in the Germany non-defaultable model are also included in the defaultable bonds model, $\left(\phi^i, \sum^i\right)$ and $\left(\phi^{\text{Ge}}, \sum^{\text{Ge}}\right)$ share some parameters. The way ϕ^i and $\sum^i$ are constructed (and the assumptions on them) can be seen in Equations (16.12) to (16.13). The estimation of $\hat{\sum}^{\text{Ge}}$ and $\hat{\sum}^i$ requires the estimation of a structural VAR. It is assumed that $\sum$ is a lower triangular Cholesky matrix such that $\text{Cov}\left(\sum u_t \sum'\right) = \sum \sum'$. See details in Appendix D.

$$\phi_{15 \times 15}^i = \begin{pmatrix} \phi_{8 \times 8}^{\text{Ge}} & \mathbf{0}_{8 \times 7} \\ \phi_{7 \times 15}^{ii} & \end{pmatrix}, \tag{16.12}$$

$$\Sigma_{15 \times 15}^i = \begin{pmatrix} \Sigma_{8 \times 8}^{\text{Ge}} & \mathbf{0}_{8 \times 7} \\ \Sigma_{7 \times 15}^{ii} & \end{pmatrix}. \tag{16.13}$$

A possible drawback of this approach is the lack of feedback effects from IGS to Germany. We expect that it is partially solved by the inclusion of the Moody's risk indicator in the model for Germany. See the scatter-plots in Figure 16.4. The correlation between Moody's high yield and yields on bonds of longer maturities is large: for 10-year bond yields, it is 0.83 for Italy, 0.79 for Spain and 0.61 for Greece. The Cholesky

---

[10] Results are not very sensitive to this restriction on λ_1. As an exercise, we estimate the model imposing that λ_1 is block-diagonal as in Ang and Piazzesi (2003) and the results are very similar. Technical reasons made Duffee (2011) also impose restrictions on λ_1. See Duffee (2011) for a discussion.

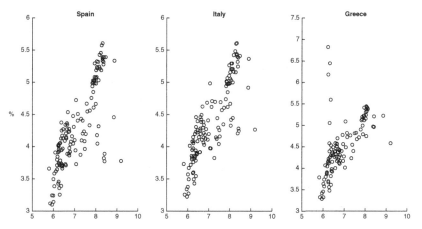

Figure 16.4 Moody's high yield (x-axis) and 10-year bond yields (y-axis), scatter-plots

identification also precludes simultaneous effects. However, as we are considering monthly data we believe this is a minor problem.

16.5   Results

16.5.1   Parameter estimates

Tables 16.3 to 16.6 in Appendix F show parameter estimates for the non-defaultable (Table 16.3) and defaultable bonds models (Tables 16.4 for Italy, 16.5 for Spain and 16.6 for Greece). In both models, standard errors are calculated through a non-parametric bootstrap procedure (using 400 repetitions).[11] The reported standard errors for the non-defaultable bonds model parameters ψ^{Ge} take into account all the steps of estimation (steps 1(a) and 1(b) in Section 16.4). The reported standard errors for the defaultable bonds model parameters ψ^i take into account the steps of estimation of the parameters of the model (steps 2(a) and 2(b) in Section 16.4), taking $\hat{\psi}^{Ge}$ as constant.[12]

Note that in Tables 16.4 to 16.6 the estimated parameters $\hat{\theta}^i_{00}$, $\hat{\theta}^i_{01}$ and $\hat{\theta}^i_1$, related to the measure of default and liquidity risk, seem to have no statistical significance. In this chapter, we are going to focus

---

[11] See Horowitz (2001) and Davison and Hinkley (1997). Details in Appendix E.

[12] Note that step 2(b) depends on previously estimated $\hat{\psi}^{Ge}$. The bootstrap procedure used to estimate the reported standard errors for the defaultable bonds model parameters $\hat{\psi}^i$ takes $\hat{\psi}^{Ge}$ as constant.

our analysis on the impulse response functions and the estimated factor loadings across maturities. We believe this result does not rule out the existence of default and liquidity premia because the recent regime (in which investors distinguish between German and IGS debts) comprises only around 20% of the total number of observations in the sample, hampering the task of estimating parameters with precision.

16.5.2   *What has been driving the spreads?*

From Equation (16.11), we know that the effect of each factor on the yield curve is determined by the weights E^N that the term structure model assigns to each spread for bonds of maturity N. Figure 16.5 plots the one year bond yield spread estimated composition, i.e., the weights of factors in the 1-year bond yield spread (i.e., for $N = 12$) multiplied by the current values of the corresponding factor over time. Factors Ge are Germany related variables, and Fiscal are deficit and debt. The factors Others are industrial production, inflation and the principal components of the spreads.[13]

In the case of Italy, note that the recent rise in spreads has been driven mainly by Italy's debt and variables related to Germany. Market stress (HY) has also played an important role. The Germany related variables have been even more important for the widening of Spain's spreads, with smaller influence of the Others, Debt, Deficit and HY. Figure 16.6 plots the weights only of Germany-related factors E^N in the 1-year bond yield spread multiplied by the current values of the corresponding factor over time. It shows that, for both Italy and Spain, among the Germany related variables, the most important ones for the widening of spreads are Germany's fiscal variables. The results are intuitive: markets see Germany as a lender of last resort for the largest economies in the EMU.

For Greece, the rise in spreads has been driven mainly by Greece's own debt (Figure 16.5), with smaller influence of variables other than the factors considered (represented by the principal components of spreads), the Greek deficit and the Germany-related factors.

16.5.3   *Factor loadings along the spread curve*

As mentioned, the effect of each factor on the yield curve is determined by the weights E^N that the term structure model assigns on each spread of maturity N. Figure 16.7 plots the weights of HY, Germany's debt,

---

[13] We will focus the analysis on the role of HY and fiscal variables.

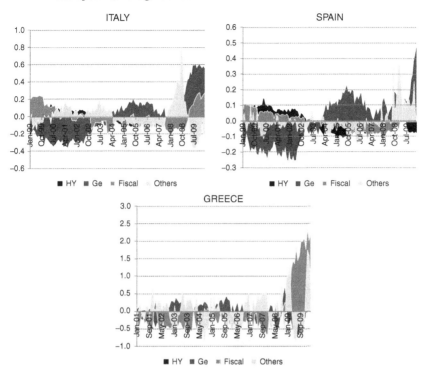

Figure 16.5 1-year bond yield spread estimated composition
Note: Composition based on E^N factor weights in the 1-year bond yield spread (i.e., for $N = 12$) multiplied by the current values of the corresponding factor over time. The factors Others are IP, Inf and the principal components of the spreads (summed up in PC). Factors Ge are Germany related variables. Factors Fiscal are Def and Deb. Y-axis scales are different among countries for a better visualisation.

industrial production, inflation debt and deficit as a function of yield maturity for the three countries.

A common interesting feature is that the weight of the own country's debt is larger around the maturity of 12 months. For Italy and Spain, Germany's debt plays the most important role until the maturity of 112 and 69 months, respectively. In the case of Greece, the own country's debt is the most relevant variable in the determination of spreads. For all countries, market stress (HY) is the variable that has the largest weight over longer maturities (from 113 months on for Italy, 70 months on for Spain and 85 months for Greece). The weight on activity is always negative, which is quite intuitive: economic growth is perceived as reducing sovereign risk.

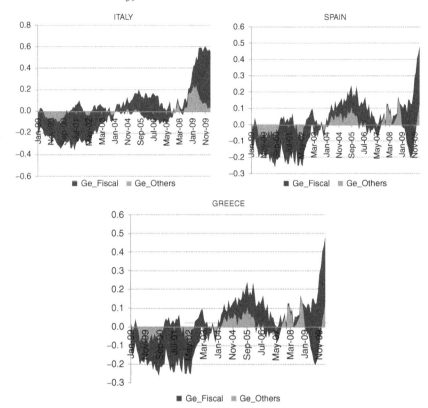

Figure 16.6 1-year bond yield spread estimated composition – only Germany-related factors

Note: Composition based on Germany related factors. Composition based on the E^N factor weights in the 1-year bond yield spread (i.e., for $N = 12$) multiplied by the current values of the corresponding factor over time. Factors Other are Ge_IP, Ge_Inf, and the principal components of the Germany's yields (Ge_1PC to Ge_3PC). Factors Ge_Fiscal are Ge_Def, Ge_Deb.

16.5.4 *Impulse responses*

Our term structure model allows us to obtain the response of yields to shocks at all horizons, including maturities omitted in estimation. The impulse responses (IRs) for all maturities are known analytical functions of the parameters. Figures 16.8 to 16.10 show the IRs of 12, 60 and 120 months for the three countries. These figures show the movements of the yield curve at different maturities (in rows) in response

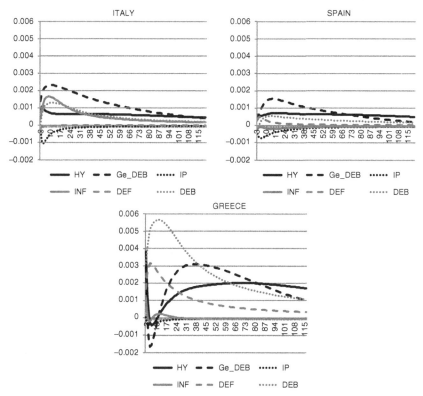

Figure 16.7 E^N factor loadings of HY, Ge$_{Deb}$, IP, Infl, Def and Deb for the three countries as a function of maturity N

to one-standard-deviation shocks in HY, Germany's debt, the country's own debt and deficit (in columns).[14]

For Italy (see Figure 16.8), the variable that causes the largest impact is market stress (HY), followed by Germany's debt and the country's own debt (Deb). A shock of one standard deviation to HY, for example, causes an initial response of the 1-year yield spread of 35% of its standard deviation (0.023×10^{-2} of 0.066×10^{-2}).[15] A shock of one

---

[14] As for the reported parameter estimates, reported standard errors for the impulse responses (defaultable bonds model) takes into account the steps of estimation of the parameters of the model (steps 2(a) and 2(b) in Section 16.4.1), taking $\hat{\varphi}^{Ge}$ as constant.

[15] Such small numbers are expected: Recall that $s_t^{(N)i} \equiv y_t^{(N)i} - y_t^{(N)Ge}$, where $y_t^{(N)i} = \ln\left(1 + Y_t^{(N)i}/100\right)$. If Italy's 1-year bond yield is, say, 3% per year, $Y_t^{(12)It} = 3$. If Germany's 1-year bond yield is, say, 2.7% per year, $Y_t^{(12)Ge} = 2.7$ and $S_t^{(12)It} \equiv y_t^{(12)It} - y_t^{(12)Ge} = \ln(1.030) - \ln(1.027) \cong 0.003$.

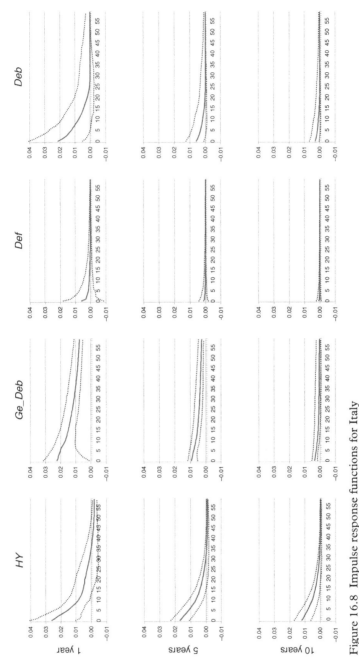

Figure 16.8 Impulse response functions for Italy

Note: All impulse responses (IR's) are from one standard-deviation shocks in HY, Ge_Deb, Def and Deb. IRs for 12-month (top row), 60-month (middle row) and 120-month (bottom row) yield spreads. Confidence intervals of 95%. X-axis scales are different among countries for better visualisation. Responses are multiplied by 100.

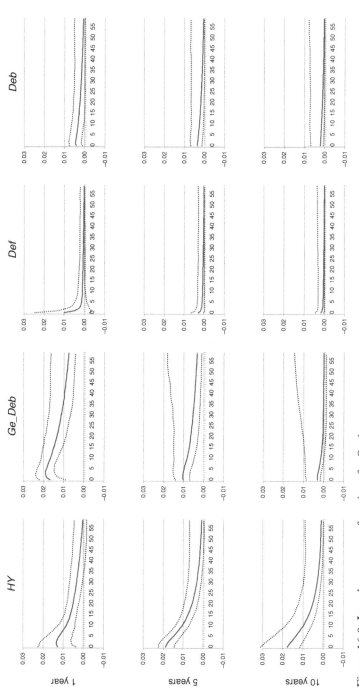

Figure 16.9 Impulse response functions for Spain

Note: All impulse responses (IR's) are from one-standard-deviation shocks in HY, Ge_De, Def and Deb. IRs for 12-month (top row), 60-month (middle row) and 120-month (bottom row) yield spreads. Confidence intervals of 95%. X-axis scales are different among countries for better visualisation. Responses are multiplied by 100.

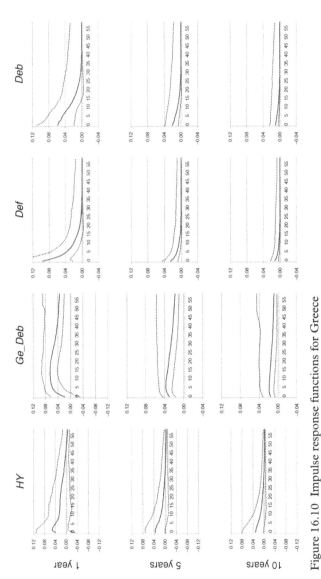

Figure 16.10 Impulse response functions for Greece

Note: All impulse responses (IR's) are from one-standard-deviation shocks in HY, Ge_Deb Def and Deb. IRs for 12-month (top row), 60-month (middle row) and 120-month (bottom row) yield spreads. Confidence intervals of 95%. X-axis scales are different among countries for better visualisation. Responses are multiplied by 100.

standard deviation to Ge$_{Deb}$ causes an initial response of the 1-year yield spread of 34% of its standard deviation (0.022 × 10^{-2}) and, from the country's debt, 27% (0.018 × 10^{-2}).[16] The responses to shocks to HY, Germany's debt and the country's own debt get weaker as the maturity increases.

For Spain, Figure 16.9 shows that Germany's debt is the variable that causes the largest impact, followed by market stress (HY) and the country's own debt. A shock of one standard deviation to Germany's debt causes an initial response of the 1-year yield spread of 55% of its standard deviation (0.018 × 10^{-2} of 0.032 × 10^{-2}), from HY, 40% (0.013 × 10^{-2}) and, from the country's own debt, 14% (0.004 × 10^{-2}). Finally, yield spreads of Greece (Figure 16.10) respond more strongly to shocks to debt and deficit levels. A shock of one standard deviation to Def causes an initial response of the 1-year yield spread of 30% of its standard deviation (0.08 × 10^{-2} of 0.28 × 10^{-2}) and from Deb, 20% (0.06 × 10^{-2}).

For all countries, the responses of spreads of different maturities to shocks to inflation are not statistically significant at the 5% level. This result can be explained by the fact that these countries are in a monetary union, and the country-specific interest rate is not a monetary policy instrument. Only for Greece do the responses of spreads to activity shocks have statistical significance, again suggesting that economic growth (measured here by industrial production growth) is perceived as reducing sovereign risk.

16.5.5 The path of Θ_t

From Equation (16.6), we know that Θ_t is a measure of default risk. Keeping l_t constant, the smaller Θ_t, the larger is $h_t L_t$, i.e., the larger the probability of default and/or the proportional loss in case of default. We allowed Θ_t to change over time and across maturities. The path of $\hat{\Theta}_t$ for maturities of 1, 5 and 10 years for Italy, Spain and Greece are shown in Figure 16.11.

Over the whole period of analysis (and with absolutely no restrictions on the estimated parameters), $\hat{\Theta}_t$ is around 1 for all maturities for the three countries, indicating that the discount on bond prices because of default and liquidity risks was always of small magnitude. Markets probably expected that the ECB would become a lender of last resort in such an extreme scenario (i.e. if one of its members experienced a

---

[16] The analysis based on standard deviations must be taken with caution because Figure 16.1 indicates that the spreads' standard deviation changes greatly over time.

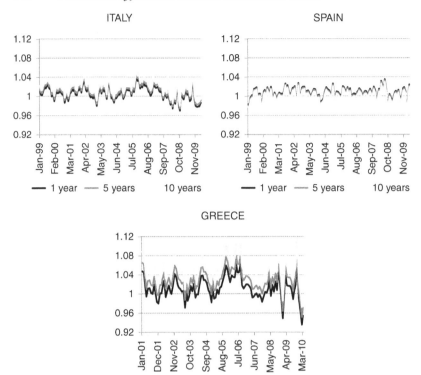

Figure 16.11 Path of Θ_t for maturities of 1, 5 and 10 years for Italy, Spain and Greece

Note: $\ln \Theta_t^N$ follows the process $\ln \Theta_t^{iN} \equiv \Theta_t^{iN} = \Theta_{00}^i + N\Theta_{01}^i + \theta_1^{i'}X_t^i$, where N is the maturity and X_t^i is Germany's and country i's factors.

severe liquidity constriction), in spite of the no-bailout clause in the EU treaty (Article 104b). Although a clear tendency in Θ_t cannot be seen, the historical lowest levels of Θ_t were reached after 2008 (April and October 2008 for Italy, September 2008 and January 2010 for Spain, and February 2010 and January 2009 for Greece).

An interesting common feature in the path of Θ_t for Italy and Greece is that, the shorter the maturity, the smaller is Θ_t. In the case of Spain, although the difference of Θ_t across maturities is much smaller, the opposite happens: the longer the maturity, the smaller is Θ_t. This difference may be attributed to the different roles played by liquidity and default risk across maturities and across countries.

16.6   Extending the sample

Our sample ends in March 2010, and from then, the successive plans to restore confidence in the euro area have failed. The market cost of borrowing reached unsustainable levels for many banks and a significant number of governments that share the euro. Figure 16.12 plots one-year sovereign bond yield spreads for Italy, Spain and Greece. The figure is analogous to Figure 16.1, with data extended to December 2011. The vertical dashed line indicates March 2010, the last month included in our original data. Right after March 2010, the spreads on Greece's sovereign bonds took an almost vertical path – the maximum value, reached in December 2011, was of 123.9% p a. Figure 16.13 plots one-year sovereign bond yield spreads only for Italy and Spain, for a better visualisation of the data on these countries. Sovereign bond yield spreads of these countries also increased dramatically, reaching a maximum of 5.2% pa for Spain and 6.4% pa for Italy in November 2011. Especially in Greece's case, we do not expect that the model in this chapter will explain this phenomenon, as it was driven by a series of political factors, especially the reduced executive decision-making capability in the

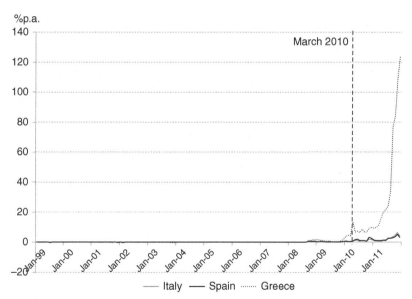

Figure 16.12 1-year sovereign bond yield spread (% pa) – Italy, Spain and Greece
Source: Bloomberg.

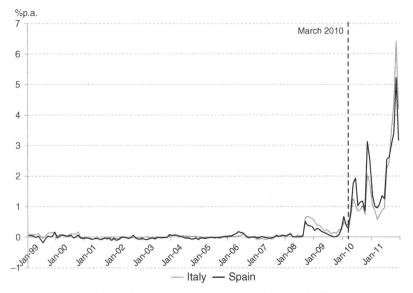

Figure 16.13 1-year sovereign bond yield spread (% pa) – Italy and Spain. Sample: January 1999 to December 2011
Source: Bloomberg

European Union and euro area institutional framework, which helps to explain the insufficient policy response.

As an exercise, we ran our model for Italy and Spain using the data from January 1999 to December 2011. As we will see, the main results did not change. We present two sets of results: factor loadings in Figure 16.14 and impulse response functions in Figures 16.15 and 16.16.[17]

Figure 16.14 is analogous to Figure 16.7. For both Italy and Spain, Germany's debt plays the most important role at the short end of the yield curve. For Italy, Germany's debt has the larger weight on bonds of maturities up to one year and over 69 months. For Spain, Germany's debt has a larger weight on bonds of maturities up to six months. The own country's debt is the most relevant variable in the determination of yield spreads on bonds in the middle part of the curve for Italy and also at the long end for Spain. The negative weights on HY and deficit are an odd result. The negative weight on the deficit of both countries is probably due to the fact that plans to restore confidence in the euro promoted some reduction in deficit levels at a moment of

---

[17] Other results are available upon request.

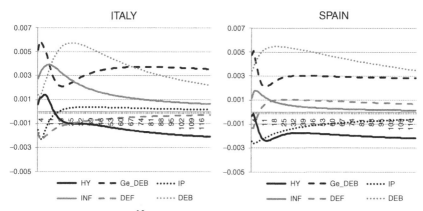

Figure 16.14 E^N factor loadings of HY, Ge$_{Deb}$, IP, Infl, Def and Deb for Italy and Spain as a function of maturity N. Sample: January 1999 to December 2011

high uncertainty. Figure 16.17 shows the path of deficits in the three countries.

The bottom line from the comparison of Figures 16.7 and 16.14 is that the countries' debt seems to have gained a larger weight in the determination of spreads. For all countries, market stress (HY) is the variable that has the largest weight at longer maturities (from 113 months for Italy, 69 months for Spain and 73 months for Greece). The weight on activity (measured by industrial production) is always negative, which is quite intuitive: economic growth is perceived as reducing sovereign risk.

Looking at Figures 16.15 and 16.16, we note at least three differences in comparison with the impulse responses in Figures 16.8 and 16.9. The first is the short-term responses of yield spreads to shock to HY, which now is negative. The second is the magnitude of the impact, which is larger now. This second fact is probably due to the higher levels of spreads observed at the end of the sample. Finally, it seems that the nature of the responses is almost the same – for Italy the variables that cause the largest impact are Germany's debt and the country's own debt (Deb), and for Spain Germany's debt is the variable that causes the largest impact, followed by market stress (HY) and the country's own fiscal variables. Therefore, for Italy and Spain, it seems that the dynamics of the variables' interaction is pretty much the same when the sample is extended. But, given the vertical path of the yield spread on Greece's sovereign bonds in the last months, we do not expect that the same is true for this country.

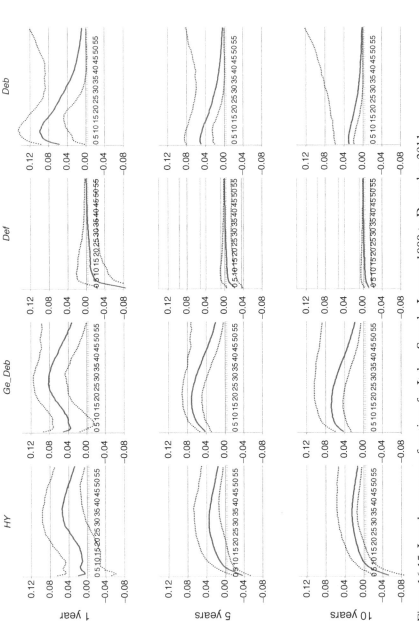

Figure 16.15 Impulse response functions for Italy – Sample: January 1999 to December 2011

Note: All impulse responses (IR's) are from one-standard-deviation shocks to HY, Ge_De, Def and Deb. IR's for 12-month (top row), 60-month (middle row) and 120-month (bottom row) yield spreads. Confidence intervals of 95%. Responses are multiplied by 100.

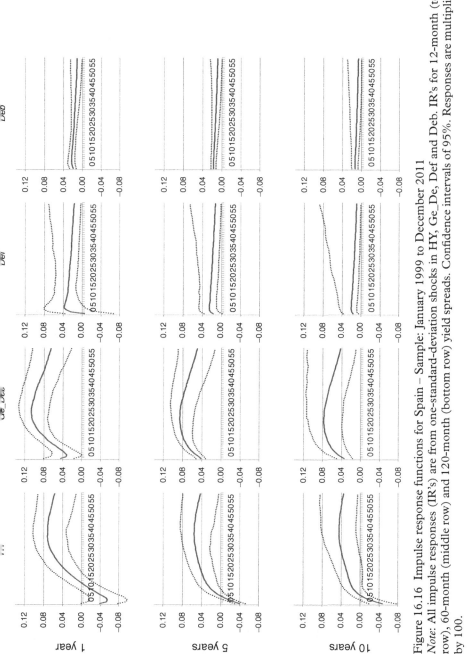

Figure 16.16 Impulse response functions for Spain – Sample: January 1999 to December 2011

Note: All impulse responses (IR's) are from one-standard-deviation shocks in HY, Ge_De, Def and Deb. IR's for 12-month (top row), 60-month (middle row) and 120-month (bottom row) yield spreads. Confidence intervals of 95%. Responses are multiplied by 100.

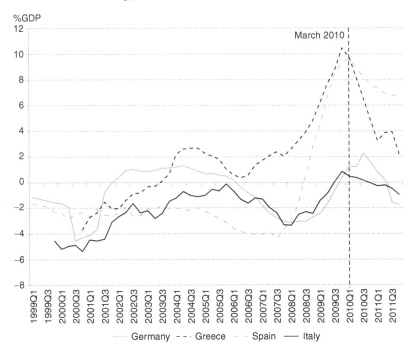

%GDP

Germany   - - · Greece   — Spain   —— Italy

Figure 16.17 Deficit (ex-interest rate payments) as a percentage of GDP

16.7   Robustness

The importance of Germany's debt in the determination of the bond yield spreads of Spain and Italy found so far raises valid concerns about the role of regional contagion. Indeed, in our model, fiscal variables from a certain IGS country enter only in the equations of its own spreads and one may be concerned that the trend in German debt levels is picking up something not in the model. A consequence of that would be that shocks to other variables – say, Greece's debt – could be the real important source of developments in Italy's or Spain's sovereign spreads and a possible correlation between Greece's and Germany's variables would produce the wrong result that Germany's fiscal variables are the ones that are important in the determination of the bond yield spreads of Spain and Italy.

In order to address this point, we performed Granger causality tests, presented in Table 16.2.[18] We can see that we do not reject the null

---

[18] These tests were performed with the original quarterly debt data, available only from the first quarter of 2000.

hypothesis that other countries' debts Granger-cause Germany's debt until a lag of two quarters. This indicates that shocks from other countries' debt eventually impact Germany's debt but it takes a while.

16.8   Conclusion

Following Ang and Piazzesi (2003), we use an arbitrage-free affine term structure model in which sovereign bond yield spreads are used as dependent variables in an equation that includes, among others, fiscal variables. Our main question is to what extent can these yield spreads be attributed to economic fundamentals? In particular, we are interested in the contribution of deficit and debt levels in pushing up sovereign spreads throughout the years after the onset of the economic crisis of 2007. Our idea is to distinguish the effects of fiscal shocks from the effects of shocks to other macroeconomic variables and potentially relevant indicators of risk aversion. We chose three euro-area countries for this analysis: Spain, Greece and Italy.

It is important to stress that the aim of this chapter is to understand what drives European yield spreads rather than to promote a particular modelling innovation. Factors in the model follow a first-order VAR in levels and identification of shocks is made via a Cholesky decomposition.[19] We searched for some support in the literature to order the factors, but we are obviously subject to criticism about both the ordering of variables and the use of Cholesky decomposition itself. Another possible drawback is the lack of feedback effects from IGS to Germany. We expect that it is partially solved by the inclusion of the Moody's risk indicator in the model for Germany, which seems to be highly correlated to yields on bonds especially of longer maturities.

As for Marattin, Paesani and Salotti (see Chapter 17), fundamentals matter. Our results show that the country's own debt has been playing an important role in the recent widening of spreads, especially for Greece and Italy. For Italy, the variable that causes the largest impact is the market stress, followed by Germany's debt and the country's own debt. A shock of one standard deviation to HY causes an initial response of the 1-year yield spread of 35% of its standard deviation. A shock of one standard deviation to Ge_{Deb} causes an initial response of the 1-year yield spread of 34% of its standard deviation and, from the country's debt, 27%. The responses to shocks to HY, Germany's debt and the country's

---

[19] We estimate an unrestricted VAR in levels assuming that the variables are either cointegrated or stationary. This assumption is supported by the shape of the estimated impulse response functions. If the variables in the VAR were non-stationary and not cointegrated, we would have seen non-convergent impulse responses.

own debt get weaker as the maturity increases. Yield spreads of Greece respond more strongly to shocks to debt and deficit. A shock of one standard deviation to Def causes an initial response of the 1-year yield spreads of 30% of its standard deviation, and from Deb, 20%.

For Spain, the recent rise in spreads is being driven mainly by variables related to Germany (amongst which German debt is the most important one), and market stress (represented by the high yield index). A shock of one standard deviation to Germany's debt causes an initial response of the 1-year yield spread of 55% of its standard deviation, from HY, 40% and, from the country's own debt, 14%.

For all countries, the responses of spreads of different maturities to shocks to inflation are not statistically significant at the 5% level. This result can be explained by the fact that these countries are in a monetary union, and country-specific interest rates are not a monetary policy instrument. Only for Greece do the responses of spreads to activity shocks have statistical significance, again suggesting that economic growth (measured here by industrial production growth) is perceived as reducing sovereign risk.

Appendix A   Riccati difference equations

The stochastic discount rate M_{t+1} can be written as

$$M_{t+1} = \exp\left\{-\tfrac{1}{2}\lambda_t'\lambda_t - \delta_0 - \delta_1'X_t - \lambda_t'\varepsilon_{t+1}\right\}, \tag{A.1}$$

where λ_t is the market price of risk (time variant) associated with the sources of uncertainty ε_t. λ_t is parameterised as an affine function of the state variables:

$$\lambda_t = \lambda_0 + \lambda_1'X_t, \tag{A.2}$$

for a $K \times 1$ vector λ_0 and a $K \times K$ matrix λ_1. From Ang and Piazzesi (2003), we know:

Result 16.1 *If $M_{t+1}V_{t+1}^{(N)}$ follows a log-normal distribution, the restriction of no arbitrage implies that*

$$\overline{A}_{N+1} = \overline{A}_N + \overline{B}_N'\left(-\Sigma^{\mathrm{Ge}}\lambda_0\right) + \frac{1}{2}\overline{B}_N'\Sigma^{\mathrm{Ge}}\Sigma_{N'}^{\mathrm{Ge}}\overline{B}'\delta_0^{\mathrm{Ge}}, \tag{A.3}$$

$$\overline{B}_{N+1}' = \overline{B}_N'\left(\Phi^{\mathrm{Ge}} - \Sigma^{\mathrm{Ge}}\lambda_1'\right) - \delta_1^{\mathrm{Ge}'} \tag{A.4}$$

with $\overline{A}_1 = -\delta_0^{\text{Ge}}$ and $\overline{B}_1' = -\delta_1^{\text{Ge}'}$. The yield $y_t^{(N)}$ at t of a bond with maturity N is given by

$$y_t^{(N)\text{Ge}} = -\frac{\log\left(V_t^{(N)\text{Ge}}\right)}{N} = A_N + B_N' X_t^{\text{Ge}}, \qquad (A.5)$$

where $A_N = -\overline{A}_N/N$ and $B_N = -\overline{B}_N/N$. In short, we need to esti-mate the parameters $\psi^{\text{Ge}} = \left(\delta_0^{\text{Ge}}, \delta_1^{\text{Ge}}, \phi^{\text{Ge}}, \sum^{\text{Ge}}, \lambda_0, \lambda_1\right)$. Recall that δ_0^{Ge} is a scalar; δ_1^{Ge} and λ_0 are K-dimensional vectors; $\phi^{\text{Ge}}, \sum^{\text{Ge}}$ and λ_1 are $K \times K$ matrices. Before restrictions are imposed, ψ^{Ge} can be written as a $(1+2K+3K^2)$-dimensional vector of parameters.

Appendix B   Proof of Proposition 16.1

The proof of Proposition 16.1 has two steps: in the first one, we prove that, given our assumptions, the short rate spread $s_t^1 \equiv y_t^1 - y_t^{1\text{Ge}}$ is linear in X_t; in the second step, we show that, given that the short rate spread is linear in X_t and the dynamics of Germany's yield curve are given by Result 1, spreads of other maturities are given by Equations (16.9) to (16.11).

The short rate spread $s_t^1 \equiv y_t^1 - y_t^{1\text{Ge}}$ is linear in X_t. Consider V_t^N, the price at t of a bond that pays no coupon and makes a payment of \$1 at time $t + N$. For $N = 0$, $V_t^N = 1$. Hence, Equation (16.7) can be written as

$$V_t^1 = E_t[M_{t+1}\Theta_{t+1}^0]. \qquad (B.1)$$

If $M_{t+1}\Theta_{t+1}^N V_{t+1}^N$ follows a log-normal distribution, Equation (B.1) gives $v_t^1 = E_t[m_{t+1}+\theta_{t+1}^0]+\frac{1}{2}\text{Var}_t[m_{t+1}+\theta_{t+1}^0]$, where lowercase letters denote variables in log. Substituting Equations (16.8) and (A.1), we have

$$= E_t\left[-\frac{1}{2}\lambda_t'\lambda_t - \delta_0^{\text{Ge}} - \delta_1^{\text{Ge}'}X_t^{\text{Ge}} + \theta_{00} + \theta_1'\Phi X_t\right]$$
$$+ \frac{1}{2}\text{Var}_t[1\lambda_t'\varepsilon_{t+1}^{\text{Ge}} + \theta_1'\Sigma\varepsilon_{t+1}]$$
$$= -\frac{1}{2}\lambda_t'\lambda_t - \delta_0^{\text{Ge}} - \delta_1^{\text{Ge}'}X_t^{\text{Ge}} + \theta_{00} + \theta_1'\Phi X_t$$
$$+ \frac{1}{2}\text{Var}_t\left[\left(-\lambda_t'J + \theta_1'\Sigma\right)\varepsilon_{t+1}\right],$$

where J is a selection ($K^{\text{Ge}} \times K$)-dimensional matrix such that $\varepsilon_t^{\text{Ge}} = J\varepsilon_t$. Note that $JJ' = I_{K^{\text{Ge}}}$. So, $v_t^1 = -\delta_0^{\text{Ge}}-\delta_1^{\text{Ge}'}X_t^{\text{Ge}}+\theta_{00}+\theta_1'\Phi X_t-\theta_1'\sum J'\lambda_t+\frac{1}{2}\theta_1'\sum\sum'\theta_1$. Substituting Equation (A.2), $v_t^1 = -\delta_0^{\text{Ge}}-\delta_1^{\text{Ge}'}X_t^{\text{Ge}}+\theta_{00}+$

$\theta_1' \Phi X_t - \theta_1' \sum J' \left(\lambda_0 + \lambda_1' X_t^{Ge} \right) + \frac{1}{2} \theta_1' \sum \sum' \theta_1$. We know from Equation (16.1) that

$$v_t^{1Ge} = -r_t^{Ge} = -\delta_0^{Ge} - \delta_0^{Ge'} X_t^{Ge}.$$

So,

$$v_t^1 = v_t^{1Ge} + \left[\theta_{00} - \theta_1' \sum J' \lambda_0 + \frac{1}{2} \theta_1' \sum \sum{}' \theta_1 \right] + [\theta_1' (\Phi - \sum J' \lambda_1' J)] X_t.$$

It means that

$$v_t^1 = v_t^{1Ge} + \overline{D}_1 + \overline{E}_1' X_t, \tag{B.2}$$

where $\overline{D}_1 = \left[\theta_{00} - \theta_1' \Sigma J' \lambda_0 + \frac{1}{2} \theta_1' \Sigma \Sigma' \theta_1 \right]$, and $\overline{E}_1' = \left[\theta_1' (\Phi - \Sigma J' \lambda_1' J) \right]$. Equation (B.2) can be written the following way: $s_t^1 \equiv y_t^1 - y_t^{1Ge} = -v_t^1 + v_t^{Ge} = D_1 + E_1' X_t$, where $D_1 = -\overline{D}_1$ and $E_1 = -\overline{E}_1$.

Second step: given that the short rate spread is linear in X_t and the dynamics of the Germany yield curve is given by Result 1, spreads of other maturities are given by Equations (16.9) to (16.11). From Equation (16.7), and assuming that $M_{t+1} \Theta_{t+1}^N V_{t+1}^N$ follows a log-normal distribution, we have

$$v_t^{N+1} = E_t \left[m_{t+1} + \theta_{t+1}^N + v_{t+1}^N \right] + \frac{1}{2} \text{Var}_t \left[m_{t+1} + \theta_{t+1}^N + v_{t+1}^N \right].$$

Take $N = 1$. Substituting Equations (A.1), (A.2), (16.2), (B.2) and (16.8) into the above equation gives

$$\begin{aligned} v_t^{N+1} = &-\frac{1}{2} \lambda_t' \lambda_t - \delta_0^{Ge} - \delta_1^{Ge'} X_t^{Ge} + \theta_{00} + N * \theta_{01} + \theta_1' \Phi X_t \\ &+ \overline{A}_N + \overline{B}_N' \Phi^{Ge} X_t^{Ge} + \overline{D}_N + \overline{E}_N' \Phi X_t \\ &+ \frac{1}{2} \text{Var}_t [(\overline{B}_N' \Sigma^{Ge} - \lambda_t') \varepsilon_{t+1}^{Ge} + (\theta_1' + \overline{E}_N') \Sigma \varepsilon_{t+1}]. \end{aligned} \tag{B.3}$$

Opening only $\text{Var}_t \left[\overline{B}_N' \Sigma^{Ge} - \lambda_t') \varepsilon_{t+1}^{Ge} + (\Theta_1' + \overline{E}_N') \Sigma \varepsilon_{t+1} \right]$, we have

$$\begin{aligned} &\text{Var}_t \left[(\overline{B}_N' \Sigma^{Ge} - \lambda_t') \varepsilon_{t+1}^{Ge} + (\theta_1' + \overline{E}_N') \Sigma \varepsilon_{t+1} \right] \\ &= \text{Var}_t \left\{ \left[(\overline{B}_N' \Sigma^{Ge} - \lambda_t') J + (\theta_1' + \overline{E}_N') \Sigma \right] \varepsilon_{t+1} \right\} \\ &= \lambda_t' \lambda_t - 2 \overline{B}_N' \Sigma^{Ge} \lambda_t + \overline{B}_N' \Sigma^{Ge} \Sigma_N^{Ge'\overline{B}} - 2 \theta_1' \Sigma J' \lambda_t \\ &\quad + 2 \theta_1' \Sigma J' \Sigma_N^{Ge'\overline{B}} - 2 \overline{E}_N' \Sigma J' \lambda_t + 2 \overline{E}_N' \Sigma J' \Sigma_N^{Ge'\overline{B}} \\ &\quad + (\theta_1' + \overline{E}_N') \Sigma \Sigma' (\theta_1' + \overline{E}_N')'. \end{aligned}$$

Substituting into Equation (B.3),

$$v_t^{N+1} = -\frac{1}{2}\lambda_t'\lambda_t - \delta_0^{Ge} - \delta_1^{Ge'}X_t^{Ge} + \theta_{00} + N * \theta_{01} + \theta_1'\Phi X_t + \overline{A}_N$$

$$+ \overline{B}_N'\Phi^{Ge}X_t^{Ge} + \overline{D}_N + \overline{E}_N'\Phi X_t + \frac{1}{2}[\lambda_t'\lambda_t - 2\overline{B}_N'\Sigma^{Ge}\lambda_t$$

$$+ \overline{B}_N'\Sigma^{Ge}\Sigma^{Ge'}\overline{B}_N - 2\theta_1'\Sigma J'\lambda_t + 2\theta_1'\Sigma J'\Sigma^{Ge'}\overline{B}_N - 2\overline{E}_N'\Sigma J'\lambda_t$$

$$+ 2\overline{E}_N'\Sigma J'\Sigma^{Ge'}\overline{B}_N + (\theta_1' + \overline{E}_N')\Sigma\Sigma'(\theta_1' + \overline{E}_N')'].$$

Substituting Equations (A.2) to (A.3) and rearranging the equation above gives $v_t^{N+1} = v_t^{N+1,Ge} + \overline{D}_{N+1} + \overline{E}_{N+1}'X_t$, where $\overline{D}_{N+1}$ and $\overline{E}_{N+1}^{i'}$ are given by Equations (16.9) and (16.10). The proof for $N \geq 2$ is straightforward.

Appendix C   Data: quarterly to monthly frequency

Fiscal balance, debt and GDP monthly data are not available. Monthly data of these variables were constructed from their quarterly observations and from monthly data of some coincident indicators, such as energy consumption, unemployment rate, imports and exports.

Quarterly data consist of general government revenues, general government expenditures, net lending/borrowing and GDP. Monthly data consist of the unemployment rate (UN), industrial production (IP), the consumer price index (CPI), imports and exports (M and X), energy consumption in GWh (EN), and car registrations (CAR).

The transformation method has two steps. In the first step, we run quarterly data regressions:

$$Z_t^q = \alpha + \beta_{IP}IP_t^q + \beta_{UN}UN_t^q + \beta_{CPI}CPI_t^q + \beta_M M_t^q + \beta_X X_t^q + \beta_{EN}EN_t^q$$
$$+ \beta_{CAR}CAR_t^q + \psi_q + \varepsilon_t,$$

where Z is general government net lending/borrowing, total revenues, total expenditure or GDP. The superscript q means quarterly observation data.

In the second step, we make the following quarterly to monthly frequency transformation:

$$Z_t^m = \hat{\alpha} + \hat{\beta}_{IP}IP_t^m + \hat{\beta}_{UN}UN_t^m + \hat{\beta}_{CPI}{}_t^m + \hat{\beta}_M M_t^m + \hat{\beta}_X X_t^m$$
$$+ \hat{\beta}_{EN}EN_t^m + \hat{\beta}_{CAR}CAR_t^m + \psi_m + \varepsilon_t,$$

where the $\hat{\beta}$s are estimates from quarterly data. $\hat{Z}_t^m$ is the variable used in our estimations.

Appendix D   Identification hypothesis

We can rewrite Equation (16.2) in the following structural version:

$$AX_t = \alpha_1 X_{t-1} + Bu_t, \tag{D.1}$$

where A, α_1 and B are $K \times K$ matrices, X_t and u_t are K-dimensional vectors and Var $(u|t) = I$. If A is an invertible matrix, (D.1) can be rewritten as $X_t = A^{-1}\alpha_1 X_{t-1} + A^{-1}Bu_t$, where, in an analogy to Equation (16.2), $A^{-1}\alpha_1 = \Phi$ and $A^{-1}B = \Sigma$. Following Bonomo and Lowenkron (2008), it is assumed that Σ is a lower triangular Cholesky matrix such that $\mathrm{Cov}(\Sigma u_t \Sigma') = \Sigma \Sigma'$. Furthermore, as a consequence of the way they were constructed, it is natural to impose that the principal components of yields and macroeconomic variables have a non-correlated contemporaneous relation. Also, this kind of restriction is a standard practice in term structure models (see Dai and Singleton, 2000; Ang and Piazzesi, 2003; and Joslin, Priebsch and Singleton, 2010, among others). In the estimation of the dynamics of the state equation for Germany, we impose the following restrictions on A and B:

$$A^{Ge} = \begin{pmatrix} 1 & 0 & 0 & 0 & 0 & 0 & 0 & 0 \\ a_{21}^{Ge} & 1 & 0 & 0 & 0 & 0 & 0 & 0 \\ a_{31}^{Ge} & a_{32}^{Ge} & 1 & 0 & 0 & 0 & 0 & 0 \\ a_{41}^{Ge} & a_{42}^{Ge} & a_{43}^{Ge} & 1 & 0 & 0 & 0 & 0 \\ a_{51}^{Ge} & a_{52}^{Ge} & a_{53}^{Ge} & a_{54}^{Ge} & 1 & 0 & 0 & 0 \\ 0 & 0 & 0 & 0 & a_{65}^{Ge} & 1 & 0 & 0 \\ 0 & 0 & 0 & 0 & a_{75}^{Ge} & a_{76}^{Ge} & 1 & 0 \\ 0 & 0 & 0 & 0 & a_{85}^{Ge} & a_{86}^{Ge} & a_{87}^{Ge} & 1 \end{pmatrix}_{8x8},$$

$$B^{Ge} = \begin{pmatrix} b_{11}^{Ge} & 0 & 0 & 0 & 0 & 0 & 0 & 0 \\ 0 & b_{22}^{Ge} & 0 & 0 & 0 & 0 & 0 & 0 \\ 0 & 0 & b_{33}^{Ge} & 0 & 0 & 0 & 0 & 0 \\ 0 & 0 & 0 & b_{44}^{Ge} & 0 & 0 & 0 & 0 \\ 0 & 0 & 0 & 0 & b_{55}^{Ge} & 0 & 0 & 0 \\ 0 & 0 & 0 & 0 & 0 & b_{66}^{Ge} & 0 & 0 \\ 0 & 0 & 0 & 0 & 0 & 0 & b_{77}^{Ge} & 0 \\ 0 & 0 & 0 & 0 & 0 & 0 & 0 & b_{88}^{Ge} \end{pmatrix}_{8x8}.$$

We impose the following restrictions on A and B in the estimation of country i's model:

$$A^i = \begin{pmatrix} A^{Ge} & 0_{8x7} \\ Asp^i & \end{pmatrix}, B^i = \begin{pmatrix} B^{Ge} & 0_{8x7} \\ 0_{7x8} & B^i \end{pmatrix}, \text{ where}$$

$$Asp^i = \begin{pmatrix} a^i_{11} & a^i_{11} & a^i_{11} & a^i_{11} & a^i_{11} & a^i_{11} & a^i_{11} & a^i_{11} & 1 & 0 & 0 & 0 & 0 & 0 & 0 \\ a^i_{11} & a^i_{11} & a^i_{11} & a^i_{11} & a^i_{11} & a^i_{11} & a^i_{11} & a^i_{11} & a^i_{11} & 1 & 0 & 0 & 0 & 0 & 0 \\ a^i_{11} & a^i_{11} & a^i_{11} & a^i_{11} & a^i_{11} & a^i_{11} & a^i_{11} & a^i_{11} & a^i_{11} & a^i_{11} & 1 & 0 & 0 & 0 & 0 \\ a^i_{11} & a^i_{11} & a^i_{11} & a^i_{11} & a^i_{11} & a^i_{11} & a^i_{11} & a^i_{11} & a^i_{11} & a^i_{11} & a^i_{11} & 1 & 0 & 0 & 0 \\ 0 & 0 & 0 & 0 & 0 & 0 & 0 & 0 & 0 & 0 & 0 & 0 & 1 & 0 & 0 \\ 0 & 0 & 0 & 0 & 0 & 0 & 0 & 0 & 0 & 0 & 0 & 0 & a^i_{11} & 1 & 0 \\ 0 & 0 & 0 & 0 & 0 & 0 & 0 & 0 & 0 & 0 & 0 & 0 & a^i_{11} & a^i_{11} & 0 \end{pmatrix}_{7x15}$$

and

$$B^i = \begin{pmatrix} b^i_{11} & 0 & 0 & 0 & 0 & 0 & 0 \\ 0 & b^i_{11} & 0 & 0 & 0 & 0 & 0 \\ 0 & 0 & b^i_{11} & 0 & 0 & 0 & 0 \\ 0 & 0 & 0 & b^i_{11} & 0 & 0 & 0 \\ 0 & 0 & 0 & 0 & b^i_{11} & 0 & 0 \\ 0 & 0 & 0 & 0 & 0 & b^i_{11} & 0 \\ 0 & 0 & 0 & 0 & 0 & 0 & b^i_{11} \end{pmatrix}_{7x7.}$$

The ordering of variables – with the central economy coming first – follows Bonomo and Lowenkron (2008). However, in times of sovereign credit crisis, it is not clear whether the central economy's variables are more exogenous than the variables of the countries that are originating the crisis. Again, we expect this concern is reduced by the inclusion of the Moody's risk indicator in the model for Germany. The correlation between Moody's high yield and yields on bonds of specially longer maturities is large: for 10-year bond yields, it is 0.83 for Italy, 0.79 for Spain and 0.61 for Greece (see scatter-plots in Figure 16.4).

It still remains to discuss our choice regarding ordering of country-specific variables. It is usual to consider activity more exogenous than inflation: Joslin, Priebsch and Singleton (2010) and Perotti (2005) are examples. We follow Favero (2002) and identify fiscal shocks by imposing that the activity and inflation indicators do not contemporaneously react to it. We do not identify non-policy shocks. The fact that our activity indicator is industrial production instead of GDP makes us comfortable about the ordering choice. As noted by Perotti (2005), ordering the fiscal policy instrument after GDP is questionable because government spending is a component of GDP. Therefore, this assumption would impose an implicit assumption of exactly 100 percent crowding out contemporaneously on private GDP. Finally, assuming that the deficit is more exogenous than the debt–GDP ratio seems reasonable, given the definition of these variables.

It is important to stress that the over-identification restrictions on matrices A and Asp (more specifically, the zero restrictions on the lower-left blocks of the matrices) are implications of the method used to find the principal components of yields and spreads: they were estimated from an eigenvalue decomposition of the observed yields (spreads) covariance matrix, orthogonalised with respect to the macroeconomic and risk factors. Therefore, the contemporaneous correlation between macroeconomic variables and these principal components is zero.

Appendix E   Bootstrap procedure

The non-parametric bootstrap procedure follows from Horowitz (2001) and has two steps. In the first step, we estimate the model (the VAR equation (16.2) and the pricing equations (16.3) and (16.12)) and, for each equation, we save the estimated parameters $\hat{\Omega}$ and the vector of residuals u_t. The second step is composed of 400 loops. In the beginning of each loop, we draw a random sample with replacement from the vector of residuals u_t of the same size as u_t, creating u_t^*. Next, using the original regressors, the parameters estimated in the first step $\hat{\Omega}$ and the residuals u_t^*, we construct the new dependent variable vector. We then re-estimate the model using the same regressors and the new set of dependent variables. We save each of the 400 sets of estimated parameters and, based on them, we calculate the mean and standard deviation of the parameters.

There is one difference in the resampling of residuals between the VAR equation (16.2) and the pricing equations (16.3) and (16.11). This bootstrap procedure requires that errors are not autocorrelated. We do not reject the hypothesis (with 95% level of significance) that the pricing errors are autocorrelated of order one in the equations of bonds of longer maturities (it was the case of the 10-year bond for Italy, the 5-, 7-, and 10-year bonds for Spain and the 2-, 3-, 4-, 5-, 7- and 10-year bonds for Greece). For this reason, the bootstrap procedure on the pricing equations has an intermediate step. After the first step, we estimate an AR(16.1) equation for the pricing residuals u_t, $u_t = \alpha + \beta' u_{t-1} + \varepsilon_t$ and save the AR(1) parameters ($\hat{\alpha}$ and $\hat{\beta}$). Then we draw a random sample with replacement from residuals ε_t and create a new time series ε_t^*. The new set of resampled residuals u_t is $u_t^* = \hat{\alpha} + \hat{\beta}' u_{t-1} + \varepsilon_t^*$. This way, if the vector of residual is autocorrelated of order one, our bootstrap procedure is not invalidated. The second step is unchanged.

Appendix F Parameter Estimates

Table 16.3 *Parameter estimates – Germany*

Germany
VAR of Factors
$X_t^{Ge} = \Phi^{Ge} X_{t-1}^{Ge}$
$+ \Sigma^{Ge} \varepsilon_t^{Ge}$

Matrix ϕ^{Ge}

	HY_{t-1}	IP^{Ge}_{t-1}	CPI^{Ge}_{t-1}	Def^{Ge}_{t-1}	Deb^{Ge}_{t-1}	Princ. Comp1$^{Ge}_{t-1}$	Princ. Comp2$^{Ge}_{t-1}$	Princ. Comp3$^{Ge}_{t-1}$
HY_t	0.923***	−0.015	0.058**	−0.022	−0.057	0.004	−0.025	−0.04*
	(0.044)	(0.034)	(0.029)	(0.031)	(0.040)	(0.023)	(0.023)	(0.023)
IP^{Ge}_t	−0.057	0.952***	−0.032	0.024	0.022	0.091***	−0.075***	0.05*
	(0.052)	(0.040)	(0.031)	(0.034)	(0.047)	(0.028)	(0.024)	(0.026)
CPI^{Ge}_t	−0.062	0.12**	0.838***	0.015	−0.035	0.111***	0.058*	0.072**
	(0.062)	(0.048)	(0.040)	(0.044)	(0.055)	(0.033)	(0.030)	(0.032)
Def^{Ge}_t	−0.559***	−0.353***	−0.23**	0.266***	−0.398***	−0.203***	−0.262***	−0.018
	(0.107)	(0.084)	(0.067)	(0.077)	(0.098)	(0.056)	(0.056)	(0.060)
Deb^{Ge}_t	−0.012	−0.053***	−0.005	0.009	0.987***	−0.02*	−0.007	−0.018**
	(0.017)	(0.014)	(0.012)	(0.012)	(0.016)	(0.010)	(0.010)	(0.009)
Princ. Comp1$^{Ge}_t$	−0.192**	−0.104	−0.177***	−0.328***	−0.188**	0.801***	−0.061	−0.156***
	(0.094)	(0.072)	(0.060)	(0.066)	(0.087)	(0.050)	(0.048)	(0.051)
Princ Comp2$^{Ge}_t$	−0.170	−0.109	0.009	−0.384***	−0.083	−0.103*	0.616***	−0.054
	(0.107)	(0.084)	(0.070)	(0.076)	(0.101)	(0.058)	(0.057)	(0.059)
Print Comp$^{Ge}_t$	0.009	−0.042	−0.017	0.010	−0.004	0.136**	−0.031	0.74***
	(0.106)	(0.089)	(0.066)	(0.073)	(0.098)	(0.059)	(0.057)	(0.055)

Matrix Σ^{Ge}

	HY	IP^{Ge}	CPI^{Ge}	Def^{Ge}	Deb^{Ge}	Princ. Comp1^{Ge}	Princ. Comp2^{Ge}	Princ. Comp3^{Ge}
HY	0.269***	—	—	—	—	—	—	—
	(0044)							
IP^{Ge}	0.009	0.307***	—	—	—	—	—	—
	(0.028)	(0.035)						
CPI^{Ge}	0.021	−0.081**	0.353***	—	—	—	—	—
	(0.034)	(0.040)	(0.038)					
Def^{Ge}	−0.191***	−0.024	0.036	0.632***	—	—	—	—
	(0.051)	(0.070)	(0.071)	(0.070)				
Deb^{Ge}	−0.015*	−0.013	0.002	0.020	0.106***	—	—	—
	(0.009)	(0.009)	(0.009)	(0.013)	(0.014)			
Princ. Comp1^{Ge}						0.582***	—	—
						(0.066)		
Princ. Comp2^{Ge}						0.103*	0.672***	—
						(0.054)	(0.037)	
Princ. Comp3^{Ge}						−0.041	0.17***	0.632***
						(0.070)	(0.062)	(0.053)

Vector δ_1^{Ge}

Short Rate Regression

$r_t^{\text{Ge}} = \delta_0^{\text{Ge}} + \delta_1^{\text{Ge}\prime} X_t^{\text{Ge}} + u_t^{\text{Ge}}$

	δ_0^{Ge}	HY_t	IP^{Ge}_t	CPI^{Ge}_t	Def^{Ge}_t	Deb^{Ge}_t	Princ. Comp1$^{\text{Ge}}_t$	Princ. Comp2$^{\text{Ge}}_t$	Princ. Comp3$^{\text{Ge}}_t$
	2.796***	0.108***	0.394***	0.348***	−0.307**	−0.539***	0.421***	0.226***	0.074***
	(0.002)	(0.003)	(0.003)	(0.002)	(0.002)	(0.003)	(0.002)	(0.002)	(0.002)

Table 16.3 (cont.)

Prices of risk λ_0 and λ_1
$\lambda_t{}^{Ge} = \lambda_0{}^{Ge} + \lambda_1{}^{Ge} X_t{}^{Ge}$

				Matrix λ_0 Ge				
	HY_t	$IP^{Ge}{}_t$	$CPI^{Ge}{}_t$	$Def^{Ge}{}_t$	$Deb^{Ge}{}_t$	Princ. Comp1$^{Ge}{}_t$	Princ. Comp2$^{Ge}{}_t$	Princ. Comp3$^{Ge}{}_t$
	3.869	−11.734	−17.574	−7.686	−0.891	1.755	0.260	18.507
	(6.170)	(12.744)	(20.227)	(12.014)	(2.064)	(6.681)	(0.749)	(32.530)
				Diagonal of Matrix λ_t Ge				
	HY_t	$IP^{Ge}{}_t$	$CPI^{Ge}{}_t$	$Def^{Ge}{}_t$	$Deb^{Ge}{}_t$	Princ. Comp1$^{Ge}{}_t$	Princ. Comp2$^{Ge}{}_t$	Princ. Comp3$^{Ge}{}_t$
	−0.120	0.209	0.505	−0.131	0.359	0.078	0.031	1.626
	(0.209)	(0.202)	(0.515)	(0.161)	(0.628)	(0.081)	(0.389)	(0.998)

Standard deviations in parenthesis; *10% significance level, **5% significance level, ***1% significance level

Table 16.4 *Parameter estimates – Italy*

Italy
VAR of Factors
$X^{lt}_t = \mu^{lt} + \Phi^{lt}x^{lt}_{t-1} + \Sigma^{lt}_\varepsilon \varepsilon^{lt}_t$

Matrix Φ^{lt}

	HY$_{t-1}$	IP$^{Ge}_{t-1}$	CPI$^{Ge}_{t-1}$	Def$^{Ge}_{t-1}$	Deb$^{Ge}_{t-1}$	Princ. Comp1$^{Ge}_{t-1}$	Princ. Comp2$^{Ge}_{t-1}$	Princ. Comp3$^{Ge}_{t-1}$	IP$^{lt}_{t-1}$	CPI$^{lt}_{t-1}$	Def$^{lt}_{t-1}$	Deb$^{lt}_{t-1}$	Princ. Comp1$^{lt}_{t-1}$	Princ. Comp2$^{lt}_{t-1}$	Princ. Comp3$^{lt}_{t-1}$
IP$^{lt}_t$	−0.068 (0.062)	0.833*** (0.094)	−0.107** (0.050)	0.043 (0.045)	−0.052 (0.061)	0.1*** (0.032)	−0.101*** (0.030)	0.037 (0.029)	0.121 (0.093)	0.079 (0.055)	0.000 (0.056)	0.179*** (0.053)	−0.071** (0.027)	0.001 (0.028)	−0.064** (0.026)
CPI$^{lt}_t$	−0.089** (0.042)	−0.015 (0.065)	0.106*** (0.037)	0.044 (0.032)	−0.063 (0.041)	0.044* (0.022)	−0.001 (0.019)	0.032 (0.020)	0.058 (0.062)	0.911*** (0.041)	−0.033 (0.038)	0.086** (0.036)	0.003 (0.020)	0.010 (0.019)	−0.003 (0.019)
Def$^{lt}_t$	−0.126 (0.105)	−0.439*** (0.166)	−0.102 (0.084)	0.053 (0.074)	0.375*** (0.094)	−0.146*** (0.049)	−0.109** (0.047)	−0.106** (0.049)	−0.038 (0.150)	0.002 (0.093)	0.015 (0.091)	−0.382*** (0.085)	0.049 (0.051)	−0.17*** (0.046)	−0.088* (0.048)
Deb$^{lt}_t$	0.083 (0.051)	−0.082 (0.088)	−0.035 (0.050)	−0.003 (0.039)	0.023 (0.051)	−0.031 (0.028)	−0.010 (0.026)	−0.007 (0.027)	0.052 (0.084)	−0.081 (0.054)	0.023 (0.052)	0.849*** (0.046)	0.027 (0.026)	−0.009 (0.024)	0.015 (0.025)
Princ. Comp1$^{lt}_t$	0.011 (0.141)	0.086 (0.249)	−0.194 (0.130)	−0.231** (0.107)	0.028 (0.141)	0.037 (0.080)	−0.017 (0.067)	0.125* (0.072)	−0.008 (0.235)	0.114 (0.139)	0.143 (10.133)	−0.035 (0.133)	0.54*** (0.072)	−0.012 (0.068)	−0.065 (0.067)
Princ. Comp2$^{lt}_t$	−0.546*** (0.147)	0.405 (0.268)	0.082 (0.124)	−0.103 (0.112)	−0.220 (0.139)	0.203*** (0.075)	0.023 (0.076)	0.068 (0.075)	−0.805*** (0.241)	0.291* (0.147)	−0.221 (0.143)	0.219* (0.129)	0.064 (0.072)	0.455*** (0.068)	0.019 (0.072)
Princ. Comp3$^{lt}_t$	−0.301* (0.169)	−0.302 (0.277)	−0.027 (0.153)	−0.111 (0.135)	−0.148 (0.168)	0.101 (0.093)	0.059 (0.084)	−0.038 (0.086)	0.039 (0.262)	0.136 (0.162)	−0.013 (0.170)	0.047 (0.155)	0.011 (0.082)	−0.016 (0.085)	0.285*** (0.078)

Table 16.4 (cont.)

Matrix Σ_i^{lt}:

	HY	IP^{Ge}	CPI^{Ge}	Def^{Ge}	Deb^{Ge}	Princ. Comp1^{Ge}	Princ. Comp2^{Ge}	Princ. Comp3^{Ge}	HY	IP^{lt}	CPI^{lt}	Def^{lt}	Deb^{lt}	Princ. Comp1^{lt}	Princ. Comp2^{lt}	Princ. Comp3^{lt}
IP^{lt}	-0.002 (0.025)	0.001 (0.027)	0.001 (0.033)	-0.003 (0.029)	-0.004 (0.077)	-0.001 (0.026)	-0.002 (0.029)	0.003 (0.030)	0.302*** (0.068)	—	—	—	—	—	—	—
CPI^{lt}	-0.002 (0.019)	-0.001 (0.019)	-0.002 (0.022)	0.000 (0.021)	-0.067 (0.091)	0.001 (0.018)	-0.001 (0.022)	0.003 (0.021)	0.012 (0.040)	0.133 (0.106)	—	—	—	—	—	—
Def^{lt}	0.002 (0.038)	-0.001 (0.043)	-0.003 (0.050)	0.002 (0.050)	-0.027 (0.046)	0.001 (0.043)	-0.001 (0.050)	0.000 (0.054)	-0.034 (0.051)	-0.002 (0.046)	0.524*** (0.059)	—	—	—	—	—
Deb^{lt}	0.000 (0.022)	0.001 (0.025)	0.002 (0.027)	0.000 (0.028)	-0.008 (0.024)	-0.001 (0.025)	-0.002 (0.026)	0.000 (0.027)	0.024 (0.027)	0.004 (0.022)	0.025 (0.026)	0.28*** (0.035)	—	—	—	—
Princ. Comp1^{lt}	—	—	—	—	—	—	—	—	—	—	—	—	—	0.804*** (0.093)	—	—
Princ. Comp2^{lt}	—	—	—	—	—	—	—	—	—	—	—	—	—	-0.050 (0.153)	0.796*** (0.088)	—
Princ. Comp3^{lt}	—	—	—	—	—	—	—	—	—	—	—	—	—	0.021 (0.120)	-0.037 (0.115)	0.92*** (0.060)

Short Rate Regression

$$\text{spread}_t^{lt} \equiv \delta_0^{lt} + \delta_1^{lt\prime} X_t^{lt} + u_t^{lt}$$

Vector δ_1^{lt}:

δ_0^{lt}	HY$_t$	IP$^{Ge}_t$	CPI$^{Ge}_t$	Def$^{Ge}_t$	Deb$^{Ge}_t$	Princ. Comp1$^{Ge}_t$	Princ. Comp2$^{Ge}_t$	Princ. Comp3$^{Ge}_t$	IP$^{lt}_t$	CPI$^{lt}_t$	Def$^{lt}_t$	Deb$^{lt}_t$	Princ. Comp1$^{lt}_t$	Princ. Comp2$^{lt}_t$	Princ. Comp3$^{lt}_t$
0.067*** (0.002)	0.082*** (0.004)	0.000 (0.006)	0.000 (0.003)	-0.006** (0.003)	0.139*** (0.004)	-0.029*** (0.002)	0.003 (0.002)	-0.032*** (0.002)	-0.022*** (0.006)	0.04*** (0.004)	-0.02*** (0.004)	0.004 (0.003)	0.045*** (0.002)	0.083*** (0.002)	0.024*** (0.002)

Recovery Intensity

$$\ln(\Phi_t^{lt}) \equiv \Theta_0^{lt} + \theta_1^{lt} X_t^{lt}$$
$$\theta_{00}^{lt} + \theta_1^{lt} X_t^{lt}$$

Vector θ_1^{lt}:

θ_∞^{lt}	θ_{01}^{lt}	HY$_t$	IP$^{Ge}_t$	CPI$^{Ge}_t$	Def$^{Ge}_t$	Deb$^{Ge}_t$	Princ. Comp1$^{Ge}_t$	Princ. Comp2$^{Ge}_t$	Princ. Comp3$^{Ge}_t$	IP$^{lt}_t$	CPI$^{lt}_t$	Def$^{lt}_t$	Deb$^{lt}_t$	Princ. Comp1$^{lt}_t$	Princ. Comp2$^{lt}_t$	Princ. Comp3$^{lt}_t$
0.000 (0.000)	0.028 (0.209)	-0.011 (0.030)	-0.005 (0.033)	-0.005 (0.011)	-0.012 (0.023)	-0.012 (0.009)	0.001 (0.006)	-0.005 (0.017)	-0.008 (0.006)	0.002 (0.019)	-0.001 (0.006)	0.005 (0.025)	0.000 (0.009)	-0.005 (0.004)	-0.001 (0.009)	0.003 (0.007)

Table 16.5 Parameter estimates – Spain

Spain
VAR of Factors
$X^{Sp}_t = \Phi^{Sp} X^{Sp}_{t-1} + \Sigma^{Sp} \varepsilon^{Sp}_t$

Matrix Φ^{Sp}

	HY_{t-1}	Ip^{Ge}_{t-1}	Cpi^{Ge}_{t-1}	Def^{Ge}_{t-1}	Deb^{Ge}_{t-1}	Princ. Comp1 Ge_{t-1}	Princ. Comp2 Ge_{t-1}	Princ. Comp3 Ge_{t-1}	Ip^{Sp}_{t-1}	Cpi^{Sp}_{t-1}	Def^{Sp}_{t-1}	Deb^{Sp}_{t-1}	Princ. Comp1 Sp_{t-1}	Princ. Comp2 Sp_{t-1}	Princ. Comp3 Sp_{t-1}
Ip^{Sp}_t	-0.214*** (0.057)	0.372*** (0.088)	-0.133* (0.068)	-0.039 (0.038)	0.029 (0.066)	0.105*** (0.035)	-0.13*** (0.032)	0.027 (0.033)	0.344*** (0.087)	0.078 (0.073)	-0.123** (0.056)	0.279*** (0.069)	-0.113*** (0.029)	-0.064** (0.027)	0.052* (0.029)
Cpi^{Sp}_t	-0.066 (0.040)	0.161*** (0.060)	0.16*** (0.046)	0.077*** (0.029)	-0.064 (0.046)	0.058** (0.023)	0.042** (0.021)	-0.016 (0.021)	0.054 (0.058)	0.766*** (0.053)	0.114*** (0.039)	0.088* (0.048)	-0.032 (0.020)	-0.032 (0.020)	-0.017 (0.020)
Def^{Sp}_t	0.212** (0.100)	-0.138 (0.141)	0.086 (0.117)	0.086 (0.070)	0.474*** (0.124)	-0.027 (0.056)	0.076 (0.056)	0.148*** (0.053)	-0.258* (0.142)	0.004 (0.124)	0.253*** (0.094)	0.221* (0.124)	0.081 (0.049)	0.023 (0.046)	0.008 (0.051)
Deb^{Sp}_t	0.019 (0.015)	-0.015 (0.020)	-0.012 (0.016)	-0.009 (0.010)	0.010 (0.016)	-0.009 (0.008)	-0.001 (0.008)	0.009 (0.008)	0.001 (0.021)	-0.008 (0.019)	0.018 (0.014)	0.973*** (0.017)	0.010 (0.007)	0.005 (0.007)	-0.002 (0.007)
Princ. Comp1 Sp_t	0.095 (0.153)	0.273 (0.228)	0.178 (0.181)	-0.001 (0.103)	0.214 (0.186)	-0.063 (0.085)	0.062 (0.081)	0.034 (0.081)	-0.198 (0.223)	-0.129 (0.193)	-0.035 (0.144)	0.221 (0.192)	0.418*** (0.074)	-0.208*** (0.073)	-0.115 (0.071)
Princ. Comp2 Sp_t	-0.307** (0.147)	-0.031 (0.201)	-0.120 (0.159)	-0.154 (0.099)	-0.110 (10.183)	0.129 (0.081)	0.065 (0.081)	0.14* (0.080)	-0.140 (0.196)	0.226 (0.192)	0.117 (0.132)	0.101 (0.178)	-0.16** (0.069)	0.473*** (0.071)	-0.088 (0.066)
Princ. Comp3 Sp_t	0.124 (0.140)	-0.49** (0.214)	0.114 (0.171)	0.101 (0.105)	-0.057 (0.175)	0.123 (0.086)	0.032 (0.083)	-0.082 (0.082)	0.694*** (0.217)	0.017 (0.205)	0.23* (0.138)	-0.268 (0.166)	0.091 (0.071)	0.027 (0.076)	0.462*** (0.072)

Table 16.5 (cont.)

Matrix Σ^{Sp}

	HY	$_{Ip}Ge$	$_{CPI}Ge$	$_{Def}Ge$	$_{Deb}Ge$	Princ. Comp$_1$Ge	Princ. Comp$_2$Ge	Princ. Comp$_3$Ge	$_{Ip}Sp$	$_{CPI}Sp$	$_{Def}Sp$	$_{Deb}Sp$	Princ. Comp$_1$Sp	Princ. Comp$_2$Sp	Princ. Comp$_3$Sp
$_{Ip}Sp$	0.001 (0.023)	−0.002 (0.027)	−0.002 (0.032)	0.000 (0.032)	−0.005 (0.047)	0.001 (0.029)	−0.001 (0.030)	0.002 (0.030)	0.315*** (0.020)	—	—	—	—	—	—
$_{CPI}Sp$	−0.003 (0.019)	−0.001 (0.019)	0.001 (0.021)	−0.002 (0.021)	−0.071 (0.091)	0.001 (0.019)	−0.003 (0.021)	0.001 (0.022)	0.039 (0.040)	0.130 (0.108)	—	—	—	—	—
$_{Def}Sp$	−0.001 (0.043)	0.004 (0.044)	0.006 (0.054)	−0.001 (0.053)	−0.022 (0.049)	−0.003 (0.047)	−0.002 (0.053)	−0.002 (0.051)	−0.134** (0.056)	0.011 (0.039)	0.517*** (0.047)	—	—	—	—
$_{Deb}Sp$	0.000 (0.006)	0.000 (0.006)	0.000 (0.008)	0.000 (0.007)	−0.003 (0.007)	0.000 (0.007)	0.000 (0.008)	0.000 (0.008)	0.006 (0.007)	0.001 (0.006)	0.018*** (0.006)	0.075*** (0.005)	—	—	—
Princ. Comp$_1$Sp	—	—	—	—	—	—	—	—	—	—	—	—	0.854*** (0.101)	—	—
Princ. Comp$_2$Sp	—	—	—	—	—	—	—	—	—	—	—	—	0.155 (0.148)	0.778*** (0.094)	—
Princ. Comp$_3$Sp	—	—	—	—	—	—	—	—	—	—	—	—	0.047 (0.137)	0.036 (0.104)	0.805*** (0.056)

Short Rate Regression

Vector δ_1^{Sp}

$spread_t^{Sp} = \delta_0^{Sp} + \delta_1^{Sp'}X^{Sp}_t + u^{Sp}_t$

δ_0^{Sp}	HY_t	$_{Ip}Ge_t$	$_{CPI}Ge_t$	$_{Def}Ge_t$	$_{Deb}Ge_t$	Princ. Comp$_1$Ge$_t$	Princ. Comp$_2$Ge$_t$	Princ. Comp$_3$Ge$_t$	$_{Ip}Sp_t$	$_{CPI}Sp_t$	$_{Def}Sp_t$	$_{Deb}Sp_t$	Princ. Comp$_1$Sp$_t$	Princ. Comp$_2$Sp$_t$	Princ. Comp$_3$Sp$_t$
0.036*** (0.002)	0.061*** (0.005)	0.045*** (0.007)	0.021*** (0.005)	−0.009** (0.003)	0.038*** (0.006)	−0.02*** (0.003)	−0.008*** (0.003)	−0.029*** (0.003)	−0.05*** (0.007)	−0.022*** (0.006)	0.031*** (0.005)	−0.022*** (0.006)	0.046*** (0.003)	0.089*** (0.002)	−0.009*** (0.002)

Recovery Intensity

Vector θ_1^{Sp}

$\ln(\Theta^{Sp})_t = \theta_\infty^{Sp} + \theta_1^{Sp'}X^{Sp}_t$

θ_∞^{Sp}	θ_t^{Sp}	HY_t	$_{Ip}Ge_t$	$_{CPI}Ge_t$	$_{Def}Ge_t$	$_{Deb}Ge_t$	Princ. Comp$_1$Ge$_t$	Princ. Comp$_2$Ge$_t$	Princ. Comp$_3$Ge$_t$	$_{Ip}Sp_t$	$_{CPI}Sp_t$	$_{Def}Sp_t$	$_{Deb}Sp_t$	Princ. Comp$_1$Sp$_t$	Princ. Comp$_2$Sp$_t$	Princ. Comp$_3$Sp$_t$
0.000 (0.004)	−0.016 (0.549)	0.005 (0.027)	−0.009 (0.032)	0.006 (0.034)	0.004 (0.027)	−0.002 (0.027)	0.001 (0.017)	0.004 (0.020)	−0.001 (0.020)	0.017 (0.029)	−0.002 (0.017)	0.009 (0.021)	−0.007 (0.013)	−0.004 (0.023)	−0.004 (0.014)	−0.006 (0.005)

Table 16.6 Parameter estimates – Greece

Greece
VAR of Factors
$X^{Gr}_t = \Phi Gr X^{Gr}_{t-1} + \Sigma^{Gr}_\varepsilon Gr_t$

Matrix Φ^{Gr}

	HY_{t-1}	IP^{Ge}_{t-1}	CPI^{Ge}_{t-1}	Def^{Ge}_{t-1}	Deb^{Ge}_{t-1}	Princ. Comp1 Ge_{t-1}	Princ. Comp2 Ge_{t-1}	Princ. Comp3 Ge_{t-1}	IP^{Gr}_{t-1}	CPI^{Gr}_{t-1}	Def^{Gr}_{t-1}	Deb^{Gr}_{t-1}	Princ. Comp1 Gr_{t-1}	Princ. Comp2 Gr_{t-1}	Princ. Comp3 Gr_{t-1}
IP^{Gr}_t	-0.163 (0.123)	0.271*** (0.095)	-0.080 (0.085)	0.010 (0.077)	-0.119 (0.141)	0.199*** (0.052)	0.245*** (0.060)	-0.024 (0.061)	-0.018 (0.097)	0.206*** (0.092)	-0.013 (0.088)	-0.35*** (0.114)	-0.061 (0.053)	-0.092* (0.053)	0.104* (0.053)
CPI^{Gr}_t	0.221*** (0.083)	0.15** (0.062)	0.132** (0.056)	0.031 (0.050)	-0.261*** (0.095)	0.029 (0.034)	0.041 (0.038)	0.033 (0.038)	-0.056 (0.059)	0.756*** (0.062)	0.038 (0.060)	0.224*** (0.073)	0.050 (0.032)	0.024 (0.035)	0.054 (0.034)
Def^{Gr}_t	0.180 (0.130)	-0.234*** (0.096)	-0.043 (0.090)	-0.153* (0.079)	0.593*** (0.155)	-0.087 (0.059)	-0.070 (0.066)	0.062 (0.065)	0.103 (0.097)	0.059 (0.098)	0.328*** (0.093)	-0.161 (0.120)	0.154*** (0.058)	0.035 (0.057)	-0.036 (0.056)
Deb^{Gr}_t	0.027 (0.037)	-0.088*** (0.030)	0.024 (0.027)	0.014 (0.023)	0.064 (0.046)	-0.053*** (0.016)	0.008 (0.020)	0.034* (0.019)	0.035 (0.030)	-0.059** (0.029)	0.013 (0.028)	0.916*** (0.035)	0.05*** (0.017)	-0.036** (0.016)	-0.038** (0.016)
Princ. Comp1 Gr_t	-0.033 (0.138)	0.231** (0.107)	-0.071 (0.096)	-0.035 (0.080)	-0.184 (0.164)	-0.032 (0.063)	0.062 (0.070)	-0.057 (0.068)	-0.122 (0.107)	0.059 (0.105)	0.236** (0.100)	0.177 (0.139)	0.68*** (0.063)	-0.039 (0.058)	0.006 (0.059)
Princ. Comp2 Gr_t	-0.005 (0.150)	0.020 (0.122)	-0.053 (0.108)	-0.117 (0.091)	0.059 (0.178)	0.029 (0.071)	-0.098 (0.081)	0.143* (0.075)	-0.019 (0.129)	0.121 (0.125)	0.003 (0.115)	0.006 (0.146)	0.010 (0.064)	0.586*** (0.063)	0.163** (0.065)
Princ. Comp3 Gr_t	0.335** (0.165)	0.444*** (0.132)	0.203* (0.120)	0.23** (0.102)	0.096 (0.197)	-0.223*** (0.083)	0.047 (0.080)	-0.225*** (0.082)	0.034 (0.138)	-0.308** (0.122)	-0.057 (0.129)	0.262 (0.161)	0.087 (0.069)	-0.065 (0.072)	0.359*** (0.075)

Table 16.6 (cont.)

Matrix Σ^{Gr}

	HY	IP^{Ge}	Cpi^{Ge}	Def^{Ge}	Deb^{Ge}	Princ. Comp1 Ge	Princ. Comp2 Ge	Princ. Comp3 Ge	IP	Cpi^{Gr}	Def^{Gr}	Deb^{Gr}	Princ. Comp1 Gr	Princ. Comp2 Gr	Princ. Comp3 Gr
IP^{Gr}	-0.002 (0.042)	0.001 (0.048)	0.004 (0.045)	0.002 (0.048)	-0.003 (0.052)	0.001 (0.045)	-0.002 (0.044)	0.003 (0.045)	0.468*** (0.039)	—	—	—	—	—	—
Cpi^{Gr}	0.000 (0.027)	0.000 (0.029)	0.000 (0.033)	-0.001 (0.029)	-0.029 (0.087)	0.000 (0.026)	-0.002 (0.027)	-0.003 (0.030)	-0.031 (0.035)	0.266*** (0.099)	—	—	—	—	—
Def^{Gr}	0.008 (0.042)	0.005 (0.046)	-0.003 (0.048)	0.000 (0.049)	-0.021 (0.050)	0.002 (0.041)	-0.003 (0.049)	0.006 (0.048)	-0.204*** (0.056)	0.054 (0.057)	0.445*** (0.049)	—	—	—	—
Deb^{Gr}	-0.002 (0.013)	0.000 (0.014)	0.000 (0.014)	0.000 (0.015)	-0.001 (0.015)	0.000 (0.013)	0.002 (0.015)	0.000 (0.015)	-0.031 (0.019)	0.003 (0.016)	0.023 (0.014)	0.142*** (0.014)	—	—	—
Princ. Comp1 Gr	—	—	—	—	—	—	—	—	—	—	—	—	0.565*** (0.067)	—	—
Princ. Comp2 Gr	—	—	—	—	—	—	—	—	—	—	—	—	0.021 (0.080)	0.615*** (0.089)	—
Princ. Comp3 Gr	—	—	—	—	—	—	—	—	—	—	—	—	-0.091 (0.089)	0.140 (0.154)	0.62*** (0.079)

Vector δ_1^{Gr}

Short Rate Regression

$$spread^{Gr}_t = \delta^{Gr}_0 + \delta^{Gr}_1{}'X^{Gr}_t + u^{Gr}_t$$

δ_0^{Gr}	HY$_t$	IP$^{Ge}_t$	Cpi$^{Ge}_t$	Def$^{Ge}_t$	Deb$^{Ge}_t$	Princ. Comp1 Ge$_t$	Princ. Comp2 Ge$_t$	Princ. Comp3 Ge$_t$	IP$^{Gr}_t$	Cpi$^{Gr}_t$	Def$^{Gr}_t$	Deb$^{Gr}_t$	Princ. Comp1 Gr	Princ. Comp2 Gr	Princ. Comp3 Gr
0.301*** (0.002)	0.384*** (0.005)	0.253*** (0.004)	0.054*** (0.004)	0.031*** (0.003)	0.298*** (0.006)	-0.205*** (0.002)	0.057*** (0.003)	0.032*** (0.002)	0.001 (0.004)	0.122*** (0.004)	0.166*** (0.004)	0.315*** (0.005)	0.351*** (0.002)	0.137*** (0.002)	-0.029*** (0.002)

Vector δ_1^{Gr}

Recovery Intensity

$$\ln(\theta)^{Gr}_t \equiv \theta^{Gr}_t = \theta^{Gr}_\infty + \theta^{Gr}_1{}'X^{Gr}_t$$

θ_∞^{Gr}	θ_{01}^{Gr}	HY$_t$	IP$^{Ge}_t$	Cpi$^{Ge}_t$	Def$^{Ge}_t$	Deb$^{Ge}_t$	Princ. Comp1 Ge$_t$	Princ. Comp2 Ge$_t$	Princ. Comp3 Ge$_t$	IP$^{Gr}_t$	Cpi$^{Gr}_t$	Def$^{Gr}_t$	Deb$^{Gr}_t$	Princ. Comp1 Gr$_t$	Princ. Comp2 Gr$_t$	Princ. Comp3 Gr$_t$
0.000 (0.001)	-0.009 (1.413)	0.006 (0.104)	-0.003 (0.066)	0.000 (0.049)	-0.002 (0.108)	0.012 (0.084)	-0.002 (0.029)	-0.001 (0.071)	-0.005 (0.044)	0.008 (0.129)	0.002 (0.035)	-0.008 (0.061)	0.000 (0.058)	-0.012 (0.028)	-0.007 (0.029)	-0.010 (0.028)

References

Ang, A. and Piazzesi, M. (2003). A no-arbitrage vector autoregression of term structure dynamics with macroeconomic and latent variables, *Journal of Monetary Economics*, 50, 745–787.

Bernoth, K., von Hagen, J. and Schuknecht, L. (2004). Sovereign risk premiums in the European government bond market, European Central Bank Working Paper, No. 369.

Bonomo, M. and Lowenkron, A. (2008). A term structure model for defautable bonds with macro and latent variables, Working Paper, fftp.econ.puc-rio.br/PDF/seminario/2008/Bonomo_Lowenkron%282007%29.pdf.

Cochrane, J. H. and Piazzesi, M. (2008). Decomposing the yield curve, Working Paper, University of Chicago, Booth School of Business.

Dai, Q. and Singleton, K. (2000). Specification analysis of affine term structure models, *The Journal of Finance*, 55, 1943–1978.

Davison, A. C. and Hinkley, D. V. (1997). *Bootstrap Methods and Their Application*, 10th edition, New York: Cambridge University Press.

Duffee, G. (2011). Information in (and not in) the term structure, *Review of Financial Studies*, 24, 2895–2934.

Duffie, D. and Kan, R. (1996). A yield-factor model of interest rates, *Mathematical Finance*, 6, 379–406.

Duffie, D. and Singleton, K. (1999). Modeling term structures of defaultable bonds, *Review of Financial Studies*, 12, 687–720.

Duffie, D., Pedersen, L. and Singleton, K. (2003). Modeling credit spreads on sovereign debt: a case study of Russian bonds, *The Journal of Finance*, 55, 119–159.

Favero, C. (2002). How do European monetary and fiscal authorities behave?, CEPR Discussion paper, No. 3426.

Georgoutsos, D. A. and Migiakis, P. M. (2010). European sovereign bond spreads: monetary unification, market conditions and financial integration, Bank of Greece Working Paper, No. 115.

Horowitz, J. L. (2001). The Bootstrap, in *Handbook of Econometrics*, Edition 1, Volume 5, Number 5, J.J. Heckman and E.E. Leamer, (eds.), Elsevier.

Joslin, S., Le, A. and Singleton, K. (2011). Why Gaussian macro-finance term structure models are (nearly) unconstrained factor-VARs, *Journal of Financial Economics*, **Vol. 109(3)**, 604–622.

Joslin, S., Priebsch, M. and Singleton, K. (2010). Risk premiums in dynamic term structure models with unspanned macro risks, Graduate School of Business, Stanford University. Working Paper.

Litterman, R. and Scheinkman, J. (1991). Common factors affecting bond returns, *Journal of Fixed Income*, 1, 54–61.

Longstaff, F. A., Pan, J., Pedersen, L. H. and Singleton, K. J. (2011). How sovereign is sovereign credit risk? *American Economic Journal: Macroeconomics*, 3, 75–103.

Pan, J. and Singleton, K. (2008). Default and recovery implicit in the term structure of sovereign CDS spreads, *The Journal of Finance*, 63, 2345–2384.

Perotti, R. (2005). Estimating the effects of fiscal policy in OECD countries, *Proceedings*, Federal Reserve Bank of San Francisco.

Schuknecht, L., von Hagen, J. and Wolswijk, G. (2008). Government risk premiums in the bond market, EMU and Canada, European Central Bank Working Paper, No. 879.

17 Some considerations on debt and interest rates

Luigi Marattin, Paolo Paesani and Simone Salotti

17.1   Introduction

In recent years public debt/GDP ratios have increased considerably in many advanced countries. This is the consequence of three concomitant causes: (i) the Great Recession following the 2007–2009 global financial crisis, (ii) anti-cyclical fiscal measures adopted in response to the crisis, (iii) government transfers to bail out troubled financial institutions. Expansionary monetary policy, operating through conventional and unconventional channels, moderated the impact of fiscal shocks on government refinancing costs. In late 2010, the emergence of unexpectedly large fiscal imbalances in a group of euro area countries shook the confidence of government bond holders. Delays in the response by European authorities aggravated the problem. Interest spreads *vis à vis* Germany increased considerably for many euro area countries. Greece, Portugal and Ireland had to seek international support and are currently grappling with a deep recession which also affects Spain and to a lesser extent Italy.

In view of these developments, the analysis of the linkages among fiscal shocks, public debt and refinancing rates is at the centre of the current debate among economists and policymakers. We contribute to this debate by investigating these linkages for the USA, Germany and Italy, three among the largest issuers of public debt securities in the world.

A large empirical literature is devoted to the study of the relationship between public debt/deficit and interest rates. One branch of this literature, recently summarised by Ang et al. (2008) and Gibson et al. (2010), focuses on term structure models; Chapter 16 by Burity et al. in this book aptly exemplifies this line of research. A parallel branch of the literature builds on multivariate models of observed government bond yields and of their macroeconomic and financial determinants. Our

504

research is coherent with this line of investigation. Half of the 58 studies surveyed by Gale and Orszag (2002) find a positive impact of public debt/deficit on government bond yields; in other cases the evidence is inconclusive (on this see Muscatelli et al., 2004, and Engen and Hubbard, 2004). Reviewed studies differ in terms of model specifications, estimation methods, sample and time periods. As to the impact of shocks to the debt/GDP ratio on interest rates, the main focus of our research, Kinoshita (2006, p. 13) finds that 'a one percentage point increase in the government debt-to-GDP ratio raises real long-term interest rates by about 4–5 basis points (...). The estimates are close to those obtained by Laubach (2003 – *published in 2009*) and Engen and Hubbard (2004), who report about a 3–5 basis points increase in the real interest rate stemming from a one percentage point increase in the government debt-to-GDP ratio using very different frameworks for the United States.' As documented in more detail below, our findings are in line with these results. In general, it should be noted that shocks to the deficit/GDP ratio and shocks to projected variables are found to have a stronger impact on interest rates than shocks affecting the debt/GDP ratio (Thomas and Wu, 2009; Laubach, 2009; Afonso, 2010). There is also some evidence pointing towards asymmetric effects of debt on interest rates when debt rises above a certain threshold (Ardagna et al., 2007).

Investigating the impact of fiscal shocks on refinancing rates is particularly relevant for the assessment of government debt sustainability. For a given primary surplus and a given growth rate, evidence of increasing interest rates, in response to adverse fiscal shocks raising the debt/GDP ratio, might signal problems on the front of governmnent debt sustainability. This may be particularly relevant for countries with a poor record in terms of fiscal discipline, which normally results in a high debt/GDP ratio. The impact of fiscal shocks on interest rates may thus be partly conditional on the country's past government debt path.

Identifying the impact of debt shocks on interest rates requires controlling for possible countervailing forces, including inflation and monetary policy. As government debt increases, for example, inflation expectations might increase in turn, due to monetisation concerns. This may reverberate on: (i) nominal interest rates more or less than proportionally, depending on the weight the central bank attaches to price stability; (ii) its independence from the government; (iii) its concern for government refinancing costs; (iv) term structure effects. A more than proportional response of nominal interest rates to changes in inflation expectations might in turn lead real interest rates to rise. *Ceteris paribus*, this would induce the debt/GDP ratio to further increase.

In this chapter we tackle these issues, investigating the relationship among fiscal shocks, public debt and government bond yields both theoretically and empirically. First, we develop a simple DSGE model to identify the main linkages among the variables of interest. Based on this model, we argue that in the presence of imperfect asset substitutability, observed long-term government bond yields depend not only on the expected path of short-term interest rates, which are influenced by monetary policy, but also on the supply of government bonds. Moreover, we posit that a trade-off exists between fiscal discipline and monetary accommodation of fiscal shocks by the central bank.

Building on our theoretical model and on Paesani et al. (2006), we measure the impact of fiscal shocks on observed government bond yields, in nominal and real terms, and on the slope of the yield curve (long-term minus short-term interest rate). Our empirical analysis is based on the estimation of four-dimensional vector error correction models containing: government debt/GDP ratio, inflation rate (year on year ICP change), short-term interest rate (3 months – money market rate), long-term interest rate (10 years – government bond rate). The variables are chosen on the basis of theoretical *a priori* and are tested to be non-stationary and co-moving. This motivates the choice of the VEC modelling strategy. As discussed in more detail in Section 17.3, we address the problem of structural identification using the common trends methodology (Stock and Watson, 1988; Warne, 1993; Gonzalo and Granger, 1995).

We observe data at a quarterly frequency between 1983 and 2011. Our choice of a long-run perspective reflects the idea that the recent deterioration of fiscal balances in the countries of interest is the latest of a series of analogous episodes which can be analysed within a unified empirical framework.[1] Specific considerations on the present crisis and on its policy implications are introduced in Section 17.5.

Our main results may be summarised as follows. We find that fiscal shocks play an important role in determining the behaviour of nominal interest rates mainly in the case of Italy and Germany. Our estimates suggest that in the USA nominal interest rates do not respond to fiscal shocks. Building on our theoretical *a priori*, we relate this finding to the combination of: (i) perfect asset substitutability and (ii) limited fiscal discipline. As shown in Section 17.2, the latter insulates monetary policy

---

[1] Germany and Italy's participation in the EMU may seem to run counter to this intuition. However, both countries formed part of the same fixed but adjustable exchange rate regime for the best part of the pre-EMU period, with Germany acting as the anchor country. For a different perspective focusing on EMU years only see Bernoth and Erdogan (2011).

decisions and short-term interest rates from changes in the government debt/GDP ratio.[2] In Germany both the short-term and the long-term nominal rate decrease in response to a fiscal shock. As argued below, this response is compatible with the combination of strict fiscal discipline, leaving the central bank leeway to accommodate adverse fiscal shocks, and partial asset substitutability. In Italy the nominal short-term interest rate is not affected by fiscal shocks, whereas the long-term rate increases by 7 basis points after five years. We relate these findings to the combination of poor fiscal discipline and low substitutability between liquid assets and long-term bonds. These estimates are in line with previous results obtained using nominal interest rates (e.g. Friedman, 2005).

Subtracting the impact of a fiscal shock on inflation from the impulse response of the nominal long-term interest rate, we find that, following a 1% increase in the debt/GDP ratio, the real long-term rate rises by 3 basis points in Germany and by 8 points in Italy after five years (yield curve slopes increase by 5 and 7 basis points respectively over the same time horizon). These numbers are in line with previous estimates for European countries (e.g. Baldacci and Kumar, 2010; Chinn and Frankel, 2007; Kinoshita, 2006) as briefly mentioned above. We interpret the finding for Germany as the result of a crowding-out effect, ideally originating in a context characterised by cyclical downturn, falling inflation and deteriorating fiscal conditions. Default risk considerations, reflecting poor fiscal discipline and imperfect asset substitutability, cannot be excluded in the case of Italy. In the USA, the real interest rate declines by 6 basis points as the debt/GDP ratio increases by 1%, while the effect on the slope of the yield curve is close to zero. This finding is not unusual. Possible explanations advanced in the literature include flight-to-quality (Beber et al., 2009) and liquidity effects (Caporale and Williams, 2002). Regarding the latter, Afonso (2010, p. 1438) notes: 'capital markets may also value the increased liquidity associated with the existence of additional outstanding sovereign debt, and a decrease in the long-term yields cannot be discarded'.[3] Based on our theoretical model, the negative response of the real long-term interest rate to a fiscal shock (and the absence of any response of nominal rate

---

[2] As for the short-term interest rate, our findings are in line with those of Perotti (2004) and Mountford and Uhlig (2009). According to Seater (1993) the unresponsiveness of nominal rates to fiscal shocks can be explained in terms of the Ricardian Equivalence.

[3] The evidence supporting positive effects of debt on real interest rates may depend on the utilisation of projected/expected fiscal balances (for example, Laubach, 2009, finds that a 1% expected debt/GDP shock increases real interest rates by 3/4 basis points five years later).

as discussed above) seems to be largely imputable to inflation positively reacting to the fiscal shock.

In the absence of fiscal adjustment, the recent sharp increase in the US government debt/GDP ratio may alter the relationship between fiscal shocks and interest rates in the future. Over the sample period, however, our findings suggest that fiscal shocks do not pose sustainability concerns in the case of the USA. The same seems not to be equally true in the case of the other two countries, especially in the case of Italy. In view of these findings, the introduction of rules requiring structural budget balancing, as was done in Germany in 2009 and later in Italy, might be viewed as an appropriate institutional response.

Based on these considerations, the rest of the chapter is structured as follows. Section 17.2 presents the theoretical model, building on a simplified version of Andrès et al. (2004). Section 17.3 illustrates the empirical model and the identification strategy. Section 17.4 describes the data and reports the main empirical findings, focusing on the impulse response analysis. Section 17.5 explores the policy implications of the analysis and concludes the chapter.

17.2   The theoretical framework

Andrès et al. (2004) construct a dynamic model to study the impact of shocks to the supply of government bonds on long-term interest rates, allowing for imperfect asset substitutability. They are also able to quantify deviations with respect to the predictions based on the term structure expectations hypothesis. Our theoretical framework is based on a simplified version of this model. In particular, we drop features such as consumption habits and risk premium shocks which are not relevant for the purpose of our analysis. Moreover, we model financial frictions in the representative household's budget constraint, rather than treating them as a utility function penalisation. Finally, we replace lump-sum taxation with distortionary tax rates on labour income. As a result, we come up with a term structure equation where the accumulation of government bonds affects the long-term interest rate. In what follows, we detail the behaviour of households, firms and policymakers.

17.2.1 Households

The demand side is characterised by the presence of a representative infinitely lived household whose preferences are defined over a consumption aggregator (C_t), labour effort (N_t) and real-balances (M_t/P_t), defined as nominal money balances M_t divided by the price level P_t, according to the following utility function:

$$U(\bullet) = E_t \sum_{t=0}^{\infty} \beta^t U\left(C_t, N_t, \frac{M_t}{P_t}\right), \qquad (17.1)$$

where E_t denotes the mathematical expectations operator conditional on the time-t information set, and $\beta \in [0, 1]$ is the subjective discount factor. The consumption aggregator C_t is assumed to be a composite good made of a continuum of differentiated goods c_{it} with $i \in [0, 1]$:

$$C_t = \left[\int_0^1 c_{it}^{\frac{\eta-1}{\eta}} \, di\right]^{\frac{\eta}{\eta-1}}, \qquad (17.2)$$

where $\eta > 1$ denotes the intra-temporal elasticity of substitution across differentiated goods.

The period utility function is assumed to be strictly increasing in its first and third argument, strictly decreasing in the second one and strictly concave, according to the following functional form:

$$U\left(C_t, N_t, \frac{M_t}{P_t}\right) = \frac{C_t^{1-\gamma_c} - 1}{1-\gamma_c} - \frac{a_n}{1+\gamma_n} N_t^{1+\gamma_n} + \frac{1}{1-\sigma}\left(\frac{M_t}{P_t}\right)^{1-\sigma}, \qquad (17.3)$$

where $\gamma_c > 0$ is the inter-temporal elasticity of consumption, $\gamma_n > 0$ is the inverse of the Frisch elasticity of labour supply, $a_n > 0$ is a constant indicating the relative disutility of labour and $\sigma > 1$.

The representative household supplies labour on a competitive market, consumes the aggregate good C_t and pays a proportional distortionary tax rate τ_t^w on its labour income. It has access to three types of financial asset: money (M_t), short-term government bills (B_S), and long-term government bonds (B_L). The household's budget constraint in real terms is given by

$$C_t + \frac{M_t}{P_t} + \frac{B_{S,t}}{P_t \, i_{S,t}} + \frac{B_{L,t}}{P_t \, (i_{L,t})^L}(1 + AC_t)$$
$$= (1 - \tau_t^w)\frac{W_t}{P_t}N_t + \frac{B_{S,t-1}}{P_t} + \frac{B_{L,t-L}}{P_t} + \frac{M_{t-1}}{P_t}, \qquad (17.4)$$

where W_t is the nominal wage. Short-term securities $B_{S,t}$ are purchased in period t at the nominal price of $i_{S,t}$, and mature at time $t+1$ when they are redeemed at par. Long-term government bonds $B_{L,t}$ are zero-coupon securities purchased in period t at the nominal price of $i_{L,t}$ and yielding a unit return in period $t+L$ (Sargent, 1987). Hence, $i_{S,t}$ and $i_{L,t}$

indicate the gross nominal interest rate on – respectively – short-term and long-term government securities.

We model imperfect asset substitutability as portfolio quadratic adjustment costs (AC_t), in line with a consolidated literature (Tobin, 1969, 1982; Andrès et al., 2004; Zagaglia, 2009). We assume that agents aim to keep the ratio between liquidity and long-term government bonds constant, whereas short-term bills are treated as substitutes of money.[4] We model this friction using a quadratic cost function, as in Andrès et al. (2004):

$$AC_t = \frac{\phi}{2} \left[\frac{M_t}{B_{L,t}} \frac{\bar{B}_L}{\bar{M}} - 1 \right]^2, \tag{17.5}$$

where $\bar{B}_L/\bar{M} = k$ is the inverse of the steady-state liquidity requirement. Parameter ϕ measures the degree of substitutability between liquid assets and long-term government bonds. In the case of high substitutability ϕ is close to zero. As substitutability declines, ϕ increases. We interpret asset substitutability as directly related to the liquidity and efficiency of the government bond market.

The household chooses the optimal levels of consumption, labour effort, liquidity, and short-term and long-term nominal bond holdings, maximising the intertemporal utility function (17.1) subject to (17.4) and to standard transversality conditions. First order conditions on, respectively, $C_t, N_t, M_t, B_{S,t}$ and $B_{L,t}$ are

$$C_t^{-\gamma_c} = \lambda_t, \tag{17.6}$$

$$\lambda_t (1 - \tau_t^w) \frac{W_t}{P_t} = a_n N_t^{\gamma_n}, \tag{17.7}$$

$$\left(\frac{M_t}{P_t} \right)^{-\sigma} = \lambda_t \left[1 - \frac{\phi k}{(i_{L,t})^L} + \frac{\phi k^2}{(i_{L,t})^L} \frac{M_t}{B_{L,t}} \right] - \frac{\beta P_t \lambda_{t+1}}{P_{t+1}}, \tag{17.8}$$

$$\lambda_t = \beta \frac{P_t \lambda_{t+1}}{P_{t+1}} i_{S,t}, \tag{17.9}$$

$$\frac{\beta^L \lambda_{t+L}}{P_{t+L}} = \frac{\lambda_t}{P_t (i_{L,t})^L} - \frac{\lambda_t}{P_t (i_{L,t})^L} \frac{\phi}{2} \left[\frac{M_t^2}{(B_t^L)^2} \left(\frac{\bar{B}}{\bar{M}} \right)^2 \right]$$

$$+ \frac{\lambda_t}{P_t (i_{L,t})^L} \frac{\phi}{2}. \tag{17.10}$$

---

[4] An alternative – but equivalent – way to view this assumption is to postulate that there is a kind of implicit 'reserve requirement' following the purchases of long-term bonds: as the accumulation of relatively illiquid assets increases (B_L), agents wish to increase liquidity (M) at the same time.

Equations (17.6) and (17.7) are the standard conditions equating the marginal utility of wealth to – respectively – the marginal utility of private consumption and the ratio between the disutility of labour and the net real wage. Equation (17.8) shows that, at the optimum, the marginal utility of holding money must be equal to the marginal utility of consumption augmented by the component depending on the role played by the 'liquidity buffer' in the accumulation of long-term securities. Finally, Equations (17.9) and (17.10) are the two Euler equations for – respectively – short-term and long-term nominal bond holdings. The latter anticipates the role played the relative supply of long-term government bond in determining the long-term nominal interest rate, which is the focus of our empirical investigation.

By combining (17.6) and (17.7) we obtain the standard labour supply curve:

$$(1 - \tau_t^w)\frac{W_t}{P_t} = \frac{a_n N_t^{\gamma_n}}{C_t^{-\gamma_c}} \tag{17.11}$$

according to which households supply labour up to the point where the net real wage equals the marginal rate of substitution between leisure and consumption. By combining (17.6), (17.8) and (17.9) we obtain the money demand schedule:

$$\left(\frac{M_t}{P_t}\right)^{-\sigma} = C_t^{-\gamma_c}\left[1 - \frac{\phi k}{(i_{L,t})^L} + \frac{\phi k^2}{(i_{L,t})^L}\frac{M_t}{B_{L,t}} - \frac{1}{i_{S,t}}\right]. \tag{17.12}$$

Finally, combining (17.9) and (17.10) we obtain a term structure relationship which, when log-linearised, will constitute the theoretical foundation of our empirical analysis.

17.2.2 Firms

The supply side of the model economy is composed of a continuum of identical firms, each producing a variety i (with $i \in [0, 1]$) according to a simple constant returns to scale production function $Y_t = N_t$. We assume a Calvo-style nominal rigidity framework, where in each period a fraction $0 < \alpha < 1$ of goods prices remains fixed, while the remaining $(1 - \alpha)$ are set optimally. Since all firms who get to change their prices face the same problem, the optimal price p_t^* is the same for every optimising firm. As a result, the nominal price index at each time t is a convex combination of the $(1 - \alpha)$ firms who choose p_t^* and the α firms who stick to the previous period price $p_{i,t-1}$:

$$P_t = \left[(1 - \alpha) p_t^{*1-\eta} + \alpha p_{t-1}^{1-\eta} \right]^{\frac{1}{1-\eta}} . \tag{17.13}$$

Firms who are allowed to change their price at time t maximise the present discounted value of future profits. Formally, they solve the following problem:

$$\max_{p_{it}} E_t \left[\sum_{T=t}^{\infty} \alpha^{T-t} \Lambda_{t,T} \Pi \ (p_{it}, P_T, Y_T) \right], \tag{17.14}$$

where:

$\Lambda_{t,T}$ = stochastic discount factor between time t and T;
α^{T-t} = probability that price chosen at time t (that is p_{it}) will still be in place at time T;
$\Pi \ (p_{it}, P_T, Y_T)$ = nominal profits, which depend on the good-i price (p_i), the general price index P and the aggregate demand level Y.

The first order condition of problem (17.14) is:

$$E_t \left\{ \sum_{T=t}^{\infty} \alpha^{T-t} \Lambda_{t,T} \ \frac{\partial \Pi \ (p_{it}, P_T, Y_T)}{\partial p_{it}} \right\} = 0. \tag{17.15}$$

Equations (17.13) and (17.15) represent the supply-side of the model economy.

17.2.3 Policy

The monetary policy's instrument is the short-term interest rate i_t^S, which the central bank sets according to the following Taylor-type rule:

$$\frac{i_{S,t}}{\bar{i}_S} = \left(\frac{\pi_t}{\bar{\pi}} \right)^{\phi_\pi} \left(\frac{Y_t}{\bar{Y}} \right)^{\phi_y}, \tag{17.16}$$

where $\phi_\pi, \phi_y > 0$. Deviations of the monetary policy instrument from its steady-state value $\bar{i}_S$ are justified when inflation and/or output deviate from their own equilibrium values.

Given our choice regarding the modelling of asset prices, the government flow budget constraint in real terms can be expressed as

$$\frac{B_{S,t}}{i_{S,t} P_t} + \frac{B_{L,t}}{i_{L,t} P_t} = \frac{B_{t-1}^S}{P_t} + \frac{B_{t-L}^L}{P_t} + \frac{(G_t - T_t)}{P_t}, \tag{17.17}$$

where G_t is government expenditure and $T_t (= \tau_t^w W_t)$ is tax revenue.

Government expenditure (i.e., the fiscal policy instrument) reacts to deviations of GDP in period t from its steady-state value and in response to deviations of the stock of government debt at time t from its steady-state value:

$$\frac{G_t}{\overline{G}} = \left(\frac{Y_t}{\overline{Y}}\right)^{\gamma_y} \left(\frac{B_t}{\overline{B}}\right)^{-\gamma_b}. \tag{17.18}$$

The parameter γ_y can in principle be greater or lower than zero according to – respectively – a pro-cyclical or countercyclical fiscal policy stance, whereas the parameter γ_b is assumed to be positive for debt convergence reasons. *Ceteris paribus*, a high (low) value of γ_b in absolute terms is indicative of a high (low) degree of fiscal discipline.

17.2.4 Log-linearisation

Log-linearisation of households' optimal conditions (17.6)–(17.10) around the steady-state results in the following set of equations, where the 'hat' indicates the percentage deviations of a given variable from its corresponding steady-state value:

$$\hat{\lambda}_t = -\gamma_c \hat{c}_t, \tag{17.19}$$

$$\hat{\lambda}_t = \gamma_n \hat{n}_t - (1 - \hat{\tau}_t^w)\hat{w}_t + \hat{p}_t, \tag{17.20}$$

$$\hat{m}_t = \Phi + \Lambda \hat{\lambda}_t + \Omega \hat{p}_t + \Gamma \hat{b}_{L,t} + \Psi \left(\hat{\lambda}_{t+1} - \hat{p}_{t+1}\right), \tag{17.21}$$

$$\hat{\lambda}_t = E_t \hat{\lambda}_{t+1} + \hat{i}_{S,t} - E_t \hat{\pi}_{t+1}, \tag{17.22}$$

$$\hat{\lambda}_t = E_t \hat{\lambda}_{t+L} + \phi \left(\hat{m}_t - \hat{b}_{L,t}\right) - E_t \hat{\pi}_{t+L} + L \left(\hat{i}_{L,t}\right)^L, \tag{17.23}$$

where $\Phi, \Omega, \Lambda, \Psi$ and Γ – in Equation (17.21) – are combinations of steady-state values.

Log-linearisation of supply-side conditions (17.13) and (17.15) leads to the standard New Keynesian Phillips curve:

$$\hat{\pi}_t = \beta E_t \hat{\pi}_{t+1} + \Phi \hat{y}_t, \tag{17.24}$$

where Φ is a combination of steady-state variables and structural parameters such as the degree of price rigidity:

$$\Phi = \left[\frac{(1 - \alpha\beta)(1 - \beta)}{\alpha\beta} \left(\frac{\gamma_c Y}{C} + \gamma_n\right)\right].$$

Log-linearisation of policy rules, under the assumption of government expenditure constant and equal to its steady-state value, leads to

$$\hat{i}_{S,t} = \phi_\pi \hat{\pi}_t + \phi_y \hat{y}_t,$$ (17.25)

$$\hat{b}_t = \phi_b \hat{y}_t,$$ (17.26)

where $\phi_b = [\gamma_y/\gamma_b]$ is assumed to be negative to ensure equilibrium determinacy. Coupled with the assumption that γ_b is assumed to be larger than 0, equilibrium determinacy therefore implies anti-cyclical fiscal policy ($\gamma_y < 0$).[5]

Equations (17.19)–(17.26), along with the log-linearisation of households and government's budget constraints, constitute a system of log-linearised difference equations which describe the model economy behaviour outside the steady-state.

By combining (17.22) and (17.23), using the other equilibrium conditions and assuming that deviations of money supply from its steady state coincide with deviation of nominal GDP[6] ($\hat{m}_t = \hat{y}_t$) we obtain

$$\hat{i}_{L,t} = \frac{1}{L} \sum_{j=0}^{L-1} E_t \hat{i}_{S,t+j} + \frac{1}{L} \phi \left(\hat{b}_{L,t} - \hat{y}_t \right).$$ (17.27)

Combining (17.24), (17.25) and (17.26), we obtain the following expression for the short-term interest rate:

$$\hat{i}_{S,t} = \phi_\pi \beta E_t \hat{\pi}_t + \frac{(\phi_\pi \Phi + \phi_y)}{\phi_b} (\hat{b}_t - \hat{y}_t) - \frac{(\phi_\pi \Phi + \phi_y)}{\phi_b} \hat{y}_t.$$ (17.28)

Recalling that $(\phi_\pi \Phi + \phi_y) > 0$ and $\phi_b < 0$, Equation (17.28) implies that, *ceteris paribus*, positive deviations of inflation and GDP from its steady state values and negative deviations of the debt/GDP ratio from their steady state values lead to higher short-term interest rates. As to this latter effect, our interpretation is that a mildly anti-cyclical fiscal policy, mainly focused on debt stabilisation, leaves the central bank leeway to accommodate adverse fiscal shocks occurring in connection with cyclical

---

[5] In Equation (17.26), no distinction is made between short- and long-term securities. Two alternative justifications may be provided for this. Following Andrés et al. (2004), one may assume that the fiscal rule is specified in terms of long-term securities, and short-term debt is used as a residual mean of public financing. Alternatively, we can assume that the optimal composition of debt is determined by the government debt manager on the basis of optimal issuance considerations (cost–risk minimisation) which we take as exogenous.

[6] This assumption, in turn, is consistent with the central bank choosing the short-term interest rate as its monetary policy instrument and with money supply endogenously adjusting to demand which depends on nominal GDP.

downturns.[7] Based on the same argument, a strongly anti-cyclical fiscal policy and poor fiscal discipline tend to insulate monetary policy decisions from changes in the debt/GDP ratio. Finally, pro-cyclical fiscal policy coupled with poor fiscal discipline (positive γ_y, positive ϕ_b) may induce the central bank to react with monetary restriction to positive changes in the debt/GDP ratio.

Equations (17.27) and (17.28) provide the basis of our empirical investigation. When assets are perfect substitutes ($\phi = 0$), the nominal long-term interest rate reacts to term-structure considerations only. In the case of imperfect substitutability ($\phi > 0$), deviations of the government bond/GDP ratio from its steady state affect the long-term nominal interest rate in the same direction. In the case of strict fiscal discipline and ruling out pro-cyclical fiscal policy (low ϕ_b in absolute terms), adverse fiscal shocks are likely to be accompanied by lower short-term interest rates and (possibly) by lower nominal long-term interest rates through term structure effects. Lax fiscal discipline (high ϕ_b in absolute terms) reduces this effect. Pro-cyclical fiscal policy will reverse this effect, leading the central bank to increase (reduce) the short-term interest rate in response to positive (negative) deviations of of the government debt/GDP ratio from its steady-state value.

17.3   The econometric strategy

We empirically investigate the impact of fiscal shocks on nominal and real interest rates in a multivariate framework, focusing on four variables: the long-term interest rate on government bonds i_L (10 years), the money maket rates i_S (3 months), the CPI inflation rate π, the government debt/GDP ratio b. Based on our theoretical a priori as detailed in Section 17.2 above, we believe these variables contain sufficient information to investigate the relations of interest, controlling for inflation and monetary conditions and for dynamic feedback effects. We assume that the variables are driven by four stochastic shocks: a fiscal shock (ξ_t^φ), a nominal shock (ξ_t^v), an inflation shock (ξ_t^θ), and a financial shock (ξ_t^η).

The non-stationarity of the variables and the fact that the two interest rates and inflation co-move suggest that at least two of these shocks have permanent effects. In particular, we posit that cumulated fiscal shocks determine the level of the government debt/GDP ratio in the long-run (fiscal common trend). We also assume that cumulated nominal shocks determine the common long-run component of the other three variables

[7] To the extent that unexpected reduction in the debt/GDP ratio result from higher than expected growth, possibly accompanied by inflation, they are likely to be accompanied by monetary policy restriction.

(nominal common trend). The nature (transitory versus permanent) of the other two shocks (inflation shock and financial shock) is determined on the basis of empirical tests. Our null hypothesis, based on theoretical *a priori*, is that both inflation and financial shocks have transitory effects only. The following VEC model constitutes the basis of our investigation.

$$
\begin{bmatrix} \Delta b_t \\ \Delta \pi_t \\ \Delta i_{S,t} \\ \Delta i_{L,t} \end{bmatrix} = \sum_{i=1}^{m-1} \Gamma_i \begin{bmatrix} \Delta b_{t-i} \\ \Delta \pi_{t-i} \\ \Delta i_{S,t-i} \\ \Delta i_{L,t-i} \end{bmatrix} + \Pi \begin{bmatrix} \Delta b_{t-1} \\ \Delta \pi_{t-1} \\ \Delta i_{S,t-1} \\ \Delta i_{L,t-1} \end{bmatrix} + \Omega \begin{bmatrix} \text{Const} \\ \text{Trend} \\ \text{Seas.d.} \\ \text{I.d.} \end{bmatrix} + \begin{bmatrix} \varepsilon_t^b \\ \varepsilon_t^\pi \\ \varepsilon_t^s \\ \varepsilon_t^l \end{bmatrix},
$$

$$(17.29)$$

where $t = 1983{:}1, \ldots, 2011{:}4$[8] and $\varepsilon_t \sim N_4(0, \Sigma)$.

As discussed above, we expect the rank of Π to be equal to 2, i.e. we expect our estimates to indicate the presence of two cointegrating vectors ($r = 2$). Preliminary cointegration tests (available on request) bear out this assumption. As mentioned in the introduction above, structural model identification is based on the common trends methodology (Warne, 1993; Mosconi, 1998). We chose this route, rather than that leading to the identification of the cointegration space, as we are mainly interested in the impact of fiscal shocks on interest rates rather than on the long-term linkages among the variables. More generally, the common trends methodology is specifically appropriate to investigate the stochastic determinants of a set of co-moving non-stationary variables in a multivariate context.

Omitting the deterministic component, the moving average representation of the model defines the data-generating process as a function of the initial conditions and of the reduced-form shocks ε_t. This is given by

$$
\begin{bmatrix} b_t \\ \pi_t \\ i_{S,t} \\ i_{L,t} \end{bmatrix} = \xi + C \sum_{i=1}^{t} \begin{bmatrix} \varepsilon_i^b \\ \varepsilon_i^\pi \\ \varepsilon_i^s \\ \varepsilon_i^l \end{bmatrix} + C^*(L) \begin{bmatrix} \varepsilon_t^b \\ \varepsilon_t^\pi \\ \varepsilon_t^s \\ \varepsilon_t^l \end{bmatrix},
$$

$$(17.30)$$

where the matrix $C = \beta_\perp \left[\alpha'_\perp (I - \Sigma_i \Gamma_i)^{-1} \beta_\perp \right] \alpha'_\perp$ measures the impact of cumulated shocks to the system, and $C^*(L)$ is an infinite polynomial in the lag operator L. The relationship between reduced-form and structural-form innovations, as detailed above, is assumed to be

---

[8] Our benchmark results refer to the period 1983:1–2009:4 to abstract from the effects of the European sovereign debt crisis, but we also offer additional results based on data up to 2011:4.

$$
\begin{bmatrix} \varepsilon_t^b \\ \varepsilon_t^\pi \\ \varepsilon_t^s \\ \varepsilon_t^l \end{bmatrix} = B \begin{bmatrix} \xi_t^\varphi \\ \xi_t^v \\ \xi_t^\theta \\ \xi_t^\eta \end{bmatrix}, \tag{17.31}
$$

where B is a 4×4 non-singular matrix. The model is in moving average form, and may therefore be rewritten as

$$
\begin{bmatrix} b_t \\ \pi_t \\ i_{S,t} \\ i_{L,t} \end{bmatrix} = \xi + CB \sum_{i=1}^t B^{-1} \begin{bmatrix} \varepsilon_i^b \\ \varepsilon_i^\pi \\ \varepsilon_i^s \\ \varepsilon_i^l \end{bmatrix} + C^*(L)BB^{-1} \begin{bmatrix} \varepsilon_t^b \\ \varepsilon_t^\pi \\ \varepsilon_t^s \\ \varepsilon_t^l \end{bmatrix}
$$

$$
= \xi + \Phi \sum_{i=1}^t \begin{bmatrix} \xi_i^\varphi \\ \xi_i^v \\ \xi_i^\theta \\ \xi_i^\eta \end{bmatrix} + \Phi^*(L) \begin{bmatrix} \xi_t^\varphi \\ \xi_t^v \\ \xi_t^\theta \\ \xi_t^\eta \end{bmatrix}, \tag{17.32}
$$

where matrix Φ contains the permanent component of the model, and the matrix polynomial $\Phi^*(L)$ the cyclical (transitory) component. The assumption of orthonormal structural innovations places $4(4 + 1)/2 = 10$ identification restrictions on B. In order to get exact identification, $4(4 - 1)/2 = 6$ more restrictions are needed. Following Warne (1993), three sources of restriction can be tapped to identify structural shocks: separation of transitory from permanent innovations, long-run effects of permanent innovations, instantaneous impact of both types of innovation.

Since the last two shocks of the model only exert transitory effects on the variables of the system, we set to zero the last two columns of matrix Φ (this gives us two linearly independent restrictions), then by post-multiplying it by matrix U we impose an additional $(4 - r)r = 2$ restrictions on B. Identification of the two permanent shocks requires imposing $(4 - 2)(4 - 2 - 1)/2 = 1$ restrictions either on Φ_l or on the matrix $\Phi_{01}^* = B'_\perp$, which measures the simultaneous impact of permanent innovations. We identify the two permanent shocks by imposing the neutrality assumption that the monetary trend has no long-term impact on the debt/GDP ratio, which we see as determined by fiscal policy and growth (see Equations 17.18 and 17.26). This requires restricting to zero the $(1, 2)$ element of matrix Φ_l. Finally, the identification of the two transitory shocks requires imposing one additional restriction on the matrix $\Phi_{02}^* = BU$ which measures the instantaneous impact of transitory shocks on the variable. Thus, we restrict to zero the simultaneous impact of the inflation shock, i.e. we set to zero element $(2, 1)$ of matrix Φ^*_{02}. The overall number of restrictions $(4 + 1 + 1 = 6)$ plus the ten orthonormality restrictions guarantees the just identification of the structural model.

17.4   Empirical analysis

17.4.1   *The data*

Figure 17.1 shows the debt/GDP ratios (left column) and the nominal 10-year government bond yields (right column) for the three countries which form the object of our analysis: the USA, Germany and Italy. In all three cases, government debt increased relative to GDP over the sample period. Regarding the USA, we can distinguish three phases: a sharp increase during the 1980s, a reduction in the 1990s and a further upward trend at the beginning of the new millennium. The first part can be explained in terms of the Reagan administration's fiscal stance,

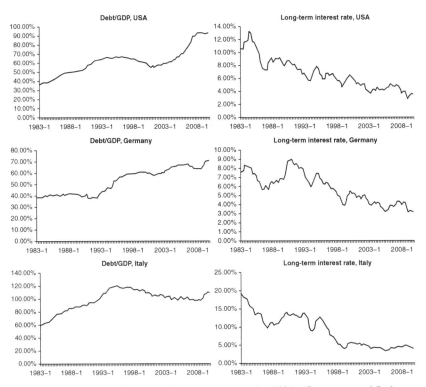

Figure 17.1 Debt and interest rates in the USA, Germany and Italy

which combined tax cuts and increased military spending, along with unwillingness to cut government expenditure in the non-military sectors (Friedman, 2005). This led to a doubling of Federal government debt compared to GDP, rising from 30% to over 60%. The second phase was the result of fiscal consolidation implemented by the Clinton administration during the 1990s in order to tackle the 'twin deficits' issue: the large deterioration in the current account balance accompanied by the sharp increase in public borrowing. The administration believed that reducing fiscal deficit could have improved the US external position that was rapidly deteriorating. Public debt indeed decreased to approximately 50% of GDP at the end of the second term of President Clinton, but external debt did not decrease due to the continuous increase in private sector borrowing. At the beginning of the new millennium the Bush Jr administration restored a fiscal stance similar to that of the 1980s: a combination of tax reduction (especially for higher income taxpayers) and increased military spending (wars in Afghanistan and Iraq). Government debt started to rise again, a trend which was further reinforced by the 2007–2008 financial crisis and the burst of the Great Recession, with pressing needs to increase public expenditure to stimulate the economy and to bail-out the financial system.

Regarding the government debt dynamics of the two European economies in our sample, we can offer the following remarks. German debt had been remarkably low (around 40% of GDP) and stable across the 1980s, as a result of sound public finance and sustained productivity growth. The re-unification at the beginning of the 1990s figured as a proper debt shock, as it led to a strong increase of it in a relatively short amount of time. As a consequence, approaching the end of the 1990s, German public debt stock reached 60% of GDP (Bibow, 2001). Since then, it has remained relatively stable, even though the Great Recession recently triggered a modest upward trend.

In Italy the debt/GDP ratio doubled between 1983 and 1995 reaching 120%, as a result of very poor budget control and political instability (Sartor et al., 1999). In the mid-1990s, the run-up to the euro imposed a more binding fiscal discipline and at the turn of the century public debt had approached 100% of domestic product. However, after the adoption of the common currency the debt/GDP ratio went back on an upward trend – still ongoing – due mostly to very poor GDP growth: over the 2000–2010 decade, the Italian economic growth rate was the lowest in Europe and one of the lowest in the world, mainly due to very weak aggregate productivity growth (Hall et al., 2008).

The dynamics of long-term interest rates are similar in the three countries under analysis, exhibiting a general downward trend reflecting global disinflation with an upward spur between the end of the 1980s and the beginning of the 1990s. However, Italian rates were considerably higher in 1983 – due to higher inflation – so that the decreasing dynamics was much faster. There are several reasons for this generalised downward trend. Monetary policy was on average expansionary during the sample period, so that nominal rates declined, although with irregular patterns. This is consistent with global disinflation (BIS, 2009) and the onset of the Great Moderation (Bernanke, 2004). Moreover, the increased liberalisation of capital flows which occurred during the last twenty years promoted an increase in the supply of global savings, with a negative effect on real rates (Taylor, 2009). Finally, as argued by Faini (2006), decreasing real rates in the 1990s were associated with a general stabilisation of the debt/GDP ratio and a marked improvement of the budget situation in the G7 countries.

17.4.2 *Impulse response analysis*

Based on the empirical model discussed in Section 17.3 above, we firstly calculate the impulse responses of $i_{L,t}$, $i_{S,t}$ and π_t to a 1% debt/GDP increase. Secondly, we subtract the response of π_t and $i_{S,t}$ from that of $i_{L,t}$ to quantify the response of the real interest rate, comprehensive of risk and liquidity premia, and of the slope of the yield curve.[9]

Figure 17.2 shows the impulse responses of the nominal short-term and long-term interest rates, the yield curve slope, and the real long-term interest rate to a fiscal shock leading to a permanent 1% increase in the USA debt/GDP ratio.[10] The dotted lines in the upper panels are 95% confidence bands (Hall, 1989), while in the lower panels there are no confidence bands since the responses result from the subtraction of point estimates of two different responses. According to our estimates, fiscal shocks have a statistically significant positive impact on the short-term nominal interest rate, which disappears after three quarters, and no impact on the long-term interest rate in the USA. Based on our theoretical *a priori*, as synthesised by Equations (17.27) and (17.28), we interpret this finding as indicative of (i) high asset substitutability between short- and long-term securities (low portfolio adjustment costs) and (ii) limited fiscal discipline and moderately anti-cyclical fiscal policy (insulating the short-term interest rate from changes in the government debt/GDP ratio). Finding that a 1% increase in the debt/GDP ratio leads

---

[9] Note that we use observed inflation to ensure consistency with the nominal spot interest rates.

[10] The VEC model includes six lags, a constant, a linear trend, and seven impulse dummies to control for outliers.

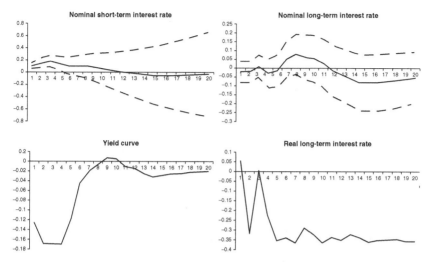

Figure 17.2 Impact of a 1% debt/GDP shock on four different variables, the USA

the real interest rate to fall by 6 basis points after five years, mainly due to inflation increasing in connection with an increasing debt/GDP ratio and pro-cyclical fiscal policy, supports this interpretation.[11] The yield curve results are different from most of the previous empirical evidence, most notably Afonso and Martins (2012). However, these authors adopt an empirical strategy (based on the work of Diebold and Li, 2006, and Diebold et al., 2006) that is hard to reconcile with that of our analysis.

In the case of Germany (see Figure 17.3), both the short-term and the long-term nominal interest rates decline following a 1% increase in the debt/GDP ratio shock.[12] Our theoretical a priori suggest we should relate this pattern to (i) strict fiscal discipline and very moderate anti-cyclical fiscal policy, (ii) low portfolio adjustment costs. The observed behaviour of the real long-term interest rate, that increases by 3 basis points after five years, differs from that of the nominal one mainly due to the response of inflation, which falls more than proportionally vis-à-vis nominal interest rates in the wake of adverse fiscal shocks. As Germany's creditworthiness was never questioned over the course of the observation period, this is consistent with a crowding out effect. Finding that the

---

[11] Other explanations put forth in the literature to explain the documented inverse relationship between government debt/GDP ratio and interest rates in the USA (Gale and Orszag, 2003) include liquidity (Caporale and Williams, 2002) and flight to quality effects (Beber et al., 2009).

[12] The VEC model includes four lags, a constant, a quadratic trend, seasonal dummies, and five impulse dummies to control for outliers.

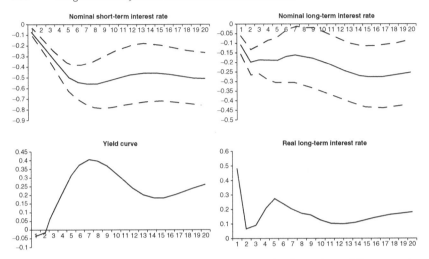

Figure 17.3 Impact of a 1% debt/GDP shock on four different variables, Germany

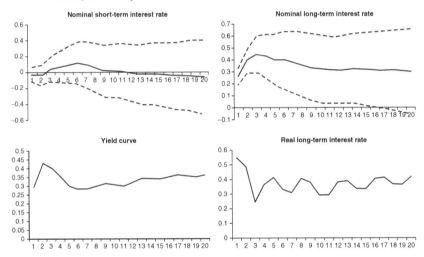

Figure 17.4 Impact of a 1% debt/GDP shock on four different variables, Italy

yield curve increases by 5 basis points over the same time horizon is compatible with this interpretation.

Finally, Figure 17.4 reports the estimated impulse responses for Italy.[13] In this case, while the short-term nominal rate does not respond

---

[13] The VEC model includes five lags, a constant, a quadratic trend, seasonal dummies, and three impulse dummies to control for outliers.

to the fiscal deterioration, both the nominal (and, consequently, the slope of the yield curve) and the real long-term interest rates react positively to the fiscal shock. All these variables increase by around 8 basis points after five years from the shock. Again based on our theoretical *a priori*, we interpret this finding as indicative of (i) limited asset substitutability and high portfolio adjustment costs, (ii) poor fiscal discipline.

17.4.3 Sample extension to test the effects of the crisis

Between 2010 and 2012, the US debt/GDP ratio increased significantly, as a consequence of the Great Recession and of the fiscal measures taken to counter it, rising above 100% in 2012 (it was less than 80% at the end of 2008). Meanwhile, monetary policy has been very accommodating and is projected to remain so in the near future (FED, 2012).Weak growth and high unemployment contributed to restrain inflation and interest rates in spite of fiscal deterioration. Slightly more favourable conditions characterise the German economy. In Germany, the debt/GDP ratio rose to 80%, twelve points more than in 2008. At the same time, long-term interest rates fell as a consequence of foreign capital inflows, monetary policy expansion, and weakening economic conditions at the European level. In Italy, the slow but steady decline in the debt/GDP ratio recorded in the early 2000s has come to an end. Interest rates on government bonds sharply increased, both in absolute terms and *vis-à-vis* German benchmarks, due to international contagion effects, fiscal deterioration and political instability.

As the IMF (2012a, p. 2) reports, 'Worries about the ability of European policymakers to control the euro crisis and worries about the failure to date of US policymakers to agree on a fiscal plan surely play an important role, but one that is hard to nail down.' This is the main reason that led us to exclude 2010 and 2011 from our benchmark estimation in the first place. To test whether the on-going crisis is modifying the transmission mechanism with respect to the pre-crisis period, however, we re-estimated the model over the 1983:1–2011:4 period. Figure 17.5 summarises the main results of this test.

In the USA, we find the decline of the real interest rate (Figure 17.5, top left panel) in response to a fiscal shock permanently increasing the debt/GDP ratio by 1% to be slightly less pronounced when estimates refer to the extend end. The sharp fall in the slope of the yield curve might be related to the expectations of prolonged monetary expansion and weak economic conditions prevailing in the USA. However, in both cases the responses are not quantitatively/economically different from

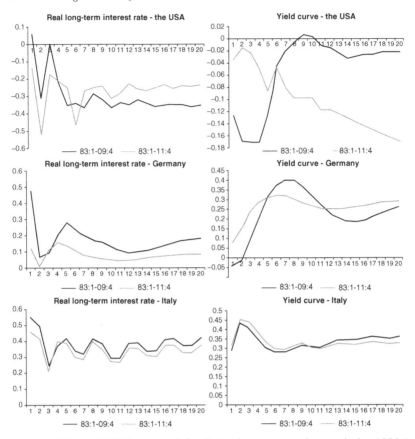

Figure 17.5 Impact of fiscal shocks, comparative analysis: 1983:1–2009:4 vs 1983:1–2011:4

those obtained in the benchmark case. In the case of Germany (middle panels) and Italy (bottom panels), the estimated responses of real interest rates and yield curve slopes to fiscal shocks over the extended sample are both quantitatively and qualitatively very close to those obtained in the benchmark case. We interpret this finding as indicative of the fact that, over the past two years, linkages among the variables of interest have not changed so as to significantly alter the financial impact of fiscal shocks. In the case of Italy, this finding may be justified by the fact that the sample already contained at least one episode similar to the ongoing crisis, i.e. the European Monetary System crisis of 1992.

17.5   Policy implications and concluding remarks

As the IMF noted in September 2011: 'Despite progress in addressing key fiscal weaknesses in many countries, the global fiscal environment remains subject to a high degree of risk' (IMF, 2011, vii). For advanced economies as a group, fiscal deficits are projected to shrink from 7.7% of GDP in 2010 to 5.7% in 2012. In the USA they will change from 10.5 to 8.1% of GDP; in Germany from 4.3 to 0.8%; in Italy from 4.5 to 2.4%. These deficits will increase the burden of already high levels of debt. In 2010 gross government debt relative to GDP was 98.5% in the USA, 83.2% in Germany, and 118.7% in Italy (IMF, 2012b).

This dramatic deterioration in fiscal positions is posing a serious threat to the stability of the world economy. Sustainability-related issues start from fiscal shocks increasing the debt/GDP ratios and lead to rising government securities returns – as government debt is rolled over, governments face higher refinancing costs. Moreover, low growth, possibly favoured by rising real interest rates, has detrimental effects on the sustainability of debt/GDP paths, requiring tougher fiscal adjustments. This chapter focused on the first stage of this vicious circle. Based on a simple theoretical model and focusing on the USA, Germany and Italy, we analysed the relationship between interest rates and the government debt/GDP ratio. This is relevant for the assessment of debt sustainability in the long run, as the real interest rate (minus the growth rate of the economy) determines the endogenous dynamics of the debt/GDP ratio.

Our main results are the following. In line with previous research on European countries (e.g. Baldacci and Kumar, 2010; Chinn and Frankel, 2007; Kinoshita, 2006), we quantify the five-year impact of a 1% increase in debt/GDP to be a 3- and an 8-basis-points increase in – respectively – the German and the Italian real long-term interest rates (yield curves' slopes increase by 5 and 7 basis points respectively). In the case of Germany, we interpret this finding as the result of a crowding-out effect. In the case of Italy default-risk considerations may not be excluded. In the case of the USA, while nominal interest rates do not respond to debt development, the real interest rate decreases by 6 basis points (with an effect which is close to zero on the yield curve) in response to a fiscal shock leading to a permanent 1% increase in the debt/GDP ratio. Flight-to-quality and liquidity effects may both contribute to the explanation of this finding. Additional insights on this point come from the literature on the interaction between monetary and fiscal policy. In particular, Chadha and Nolan (2004) argue that, when the short-term interest rate is the monetary policy instrument, a permanent deficit situation imposes a constraint on monetary policy (taking the form of an upper bound on the interest rate). Our results suggest that such a constraint may have been reached in the USA, but not in Germany and Italy. The similar responses of real interest rates to fiscal shocks for these two countries might be related to their common participation in the European Monetary System (EMS) first and in the European Monetary Union (EMU) afterwards. In the pre-EMU period, national monetary authorities reacted to episodes of pro-cyclical fiscal deterioration by monetary contraction, exacerbating domestic risk premium (Italy, Ciccarone and Gnesutta, 1993) and crowding out effects (Germany). After the start of EMU, increasing fatigue with fiscal discipline (Fatas and Mihov, 2003) and mild pro-cyclicality of fiscal policy (Fatas and Mihov, 2010) combined with bond market integration (reducing portfolio adjustment costs) may have produced similar effects.

Our results offer interesting perspectives on the current macroeconomic situation. Our findings for the USA seem to downplay the case for a generalised fiscal-led increase in real interest rates. The opposite finding for Germany and Italy confirms the relative weakness of European economies, and of the EMU as a whole, in this respect, with a particular concern for Italy where the debt/GDP ratio grew from 70.3% in 1983 to 116.1% in 2009 (reaching a peak of 121.8% in 1994). We derive three main policy implications from our analysis.

First, fiscal fundamentals matter. According to our analysis fiscal shocks seem to pose relatively minor problems in terms of their impact on interest rates and sustainability when occurring in connection with cyclical downturns, as generally observed in the case of the USA. Structural fiscal deterioration, however, as in Germany at the time of re-unification and in Italy in the 1980s, appears to magnify the adverse impact of fiscal shocks on interest rates and through them on sustainability. This supports the introduction, at the national level, of constitutional rules mandating structural budget balancing, with deficits allowed only in response to significant downturns of the economy. Germany adopted such a measure in 2009, Italy in 2012. Achieving sound fiscal positions in good times and complying with the Stability and Growth Pact will be essential for European countries to counter the effects of crises on spreads and risk aversion, as Schuknecht et al. (2010) recently observed. Enhanced multilateral monitoring will also be important in this respect.

Second, the response of government bond rates to fiscal shocks appears to be inversely related to the size of the market and to its international integration. We do not test explicitly this proposition in the present study. However, based on our knowledge of the three bond markets (e.g. Dunne et al., 2006; Caporale et al., 2012) we believe that our analysis points to the following indications. In the US market, the largest and most integrated of the three, fiscal shocks were shown to lead to lower rates. In the German and Italian markets, smaller and relatively segmented during the pre-EMU period, the effect of the shock is positive and significant. With the advent of the common currency, European bond markets became larger, more integrated and more liquid (see Cheung et al., 2005; Laopodis, 2008). This had significant advantages in terms of diminishing interest rates and funding costs, especially for high-debt countries (Marattin et al., 2012). With the outbreak of the European sovereign debt crisis, convergence has come to an end, markets are shrinking and liquidity is at risk. As suggested by our analysis, this can multiply the impact of fiscal shocks on interest rates, putting sustainability in peril, unless liquidity is preserved.

Third, we believe that the adoption of more stringent fiscal rules and credible adjustment plans over time is still the primary condition for permanent stabilisation of the EMU. However, given the current state of the crisis, the temporal mismatch between the beneficial effects of fiscal consolidation and the pressing needs related to the liquidity crisis of some EMU member states (e.g., Spain), EMU institutions might be called upon to take actions in order to preserve liquidity and stabilise the market (European Council, 2012). As recently stated by the ECB president, 'to the extent that the size of sovereign risk premia hampers the functioning of the monetary policy transmission channel, they come within our mandate' (Draghi, 2012). As argued above, strict fiscal discipline and no pro-cyclicality in fiscal policy allow the central bank leeway to accommodate adverse fiscal shocks caused by cyclical downturns contributing to debt sustainability. Poor fiscal discipline and pro-cyclicality of fiscal policy instead make this conjecture very unlikely.

To conclude, our research has interesting implications for the macrofinancial literature. In particular, it seems that asset-pricing models could be improved by addressing the government fiscal position and the uncertainties around public debt issuance.

Appendix: data

USA

The time series used in the empirical analysis are obtained by appropriate transformation of the original dataset. Government debt/GDP ratio $b = B/Y$. The short-term interest rate (spot) $i^S = (S/100)$, the long-term interest rate (spot) $i^L = (L/100)$, inflation $\pi = 4^*\Delta\log(P)$.

Augmented unit root tests are calculated on the variables in levels and first differences. Results are reported in Table 17.2. According to unit

Table 17.1 *USA: quarterly data*

Code	Description	Label
US & WB data	Total government debt	B
IFS..11199B.CZF...	GDP sa	Y
IFS..11164...ZF...	Consumer prices	P
IFS..11160C..ZF...	Treasury bill rate	S
IFS..11161..ZF...	Government bond yield	L

Sources: International Monetary Fund International Financial Statistics, US Bureau of Public Debt, World Bank Quarterly External Debt Statistics.

Table 17.2 *Unit root tests (1983:1–2009:4)*

	Lag	Det	ADF		Lag	Det	ADF
b	5	c	−1.28	Δb	4	$c = 0$	−2.11
π	9	c	−2.48	$\Delta \pi$	8	$c = 0$	−3.98
i^S	1	c, t	−3.35	Δi^S	0	c	−5.49
i^L	1	c, t	−3.79	Δi^L	0	c	−7.78
			10%				5%
ADF	$c = 0$		−1.62				−1.94
ADF	c		−2.57				−2.86
ADF	c, t		−3.13				−3.41

Table 17.3 *Johansen trace cointegration test*

Trace	p-value	H0: $r \leq$
81.67	[0.001]	0
42.86	[0.049]	1
15.48	[0.542]	2
6.89	[0.366]	3

root tests all the variables can be treated as $I(1)$ in levels. The long-term interest rate, however, is borderline stationary.

Germany

The time series used in the empirical analysis are obtained by appropriate transformation of the original dataset. Government debt/GDP ratio $b = B/$(sum of 4 quarters Y), The short-term interest rate (spot)

Table 17.4 *Germany: quarterly data*

Code	Description	Label
Official German data & BIS	Total government debt	B
IFS..13499B.CZF...	GDP sa	Y
IFS..13464.D.ZF... & 13464...ZF...	Consumer prices	P
IFS..13460B..ZF...	Treasury bill rate	S
IFS..13461..ZF...	Government bond yield	L

Sources: International Monetary Fund International Financial Statistics, Bundesbank, Bank for International Settlements.

Table 17.5 *Unit root tests (1983:1–2009:4)*

	Lag	Det	ADF		Lag	Det	ADF
b	4	c, t	-3.13	Δb	3	$c = 0$	-2.01
π	2	c, sd	-3.48	$\Delta \pi$	2	c, sd	-9.79
i^S	1	c	-1.48	Δi^S	0	$c = 0$	-5.40
i^L	4	c	-1.29	Δi^L	3	$c = 0$	-4.98
			10%				5%
ADF	$c = 0$		-1.62				-1.94
ADF	c		-2.57				-2.86
ADF	c, t		-3.13				-3.41

Table 17.6 *Johansen trace cointegration test*

Trace	p-value	H0: $r \leq$
96.13	[0.000]	0
54.78	[0.002]	1
24.65	[0.069]	2
7.90	[0.268]	3

$i^S = (S/100)$, the long-term interest rate (spot) $i^L = (L/100)$, inflation $\pi = 4^* \Delta \log(P)$. Unit root tests reported in Table 17.5 are consistent with treating all the variables as $I(1)$. Note that there is no structural break in 1991 (year of the re-unification) because the series are harmonised (directly by the publishers) by using data for West Germany for the pre-re-unification period, and by splicing growth rates when needed.

Italy

Table 17.7 *Italy: quarterly data*

Code	Description	Label
IFS..136c63..CG... & BdI	Total government debt	B
IFS..13699B.CZF...	GDP sa	Y
IFS..13664...ZF...	Consumer prices	P
IFS..13660B..ZF...	Treasury bill rate	S
IFS..13661..ZF...	Government bond yield	L

Sources: International Monetary Fund International Financial Statistics, Statistical Bulletin Banca d'Italia.

Table 17.8 *Unit root tests (1983:1–2009:4)*

	Lag	Det	ADF		Lag	Det	ADF
b	5	c	−2.43	Δb	4	$c = 0$	−2.28
π	4	c, t, sd	−3.96	$\Delta \pi$	2	c, sd	−9.69
i^S	1	c, t	−2.99	Δi^S	0	c	−8.41
i^L	4	c	−1.59	Δi^L	3	$c = 0$	−5.71
			10%				5%
ADF	$c = 0$		−1.62				−1.94
ADF	c		−2.57				−2.86
ADF	c, t		−3.13				−3.41

Table 17.9 *Johansen trace cointegration test, USA*

Trace	p-value	H0: $r \leq$
76.89	[0.002]	0
43.26	[0.044]	1
18.38	[0.326]	2
3.74	[0.775]	3

The time series used in the empirical analysis are obtained by appropriate transformation of the original dataset. Government debt/GDP ratio $b = B/($sum of 4 quarters $Y)$, The short-term interest rate (spot) $i^S = (S/100)$, the long-term interest rate (spot) $i^L = (L/100)$, inflation $\pi = 4^* \Delta \log(P)$. Augmented unit root tests are calculated on the variables in levels and first differences. Results are reported in Table 17.8. According to unit root tests all the variables can be treated as $I(1)$ in levels. Inflation, however, is borderline stationary (strong trend stationarity).

References

Afonso, A. (2010). Long-term government bond yields and economic forecasts: evidence for the EU. *Applied Economics Letters*, **17**, 1437–1441.

Afonso, A. and Martins, M. M. F. (2012). Level, slope, curvature of the sovereign yield curve, and fiscal behaviour. *Journal of Banking and Finance*, **36**(6), 1789–1807.

Andrès, J., Lopez-Salido, J. D. and Nelson, E. (2004). Tobin's imperfect asset substitution in optimizing general equilibrium. *Journal of Money, Credit and Banking*, **36**(4), 665–690.

Ang, A., Bekaert, G. and Wei, M. (2008). The term structure of real rates and expected inflation. *The Journal of Finance*, **63**(2), 797–849.

Ardagna, S., Caselli, F. and Lane, T. (2007). Fiscal discipline and the cost of public debt service: some estimates for OECD countries. *The B.E. Journal of Macroeconomics*, **7**(1), article 28.

Baldacci, E. and Kumar, M. S. (2010). Fiscal deficits, public debt, and sovereign bond yields. IMF Working Paper 10/184.

Beber, A., Brandt, M. W. and Kavajecz, K. A. (2009). Flight-to-quality or flight-to-liquidity?: Evidence from the Euro-area bond market. *Review of Financial Studies*, **22**(3), 925–957.

Bernanke, B. S. (2004). Remarks by Governor Ben S. Bernanke at the meetings of the Eastern Economic Association, Washington DC, February.

Bernoth, K. and Erdogan, B. (2011). Sovereign bond yield spreads: a time-varying coefficient approach. *Journal of International Money and Finance*, **31**(3), 639–656.

Bibow, J. (2001). On the 'burden' of German unification: the economic consequences of Messrs. Waigel and Tietmeyer. Jerome Levy Economics Working Paper No. 328.

BIS (2009). Another look at global disinflation. BIS Working Paper 283.

Caporale, G. M. and Williams, G. (2002). Long-term nominal interest rates and domestic fundamentals. *Review of Financial Economics*, **11**, 119–130.

Caporale, G., Girardi, A. and Paesani, P. (2012). Quoted spreads and trade imbalances dynamics in the European treasury bond market. *Quarterly Review of Economics and Finance*, **52**, 173–182.

Chadha, J. S. and Nolan, C. (2004). Interest rate bounds and fiscal policy. *Economics Letters*, **84**(1), 9–15.

Cheung, Y. C., de Jong, F. and Rindi, B. (2005). Trading European sovereign bonds: the microstructure of the MTS trading platforms. European Central Bank Working Paper 432.

Chinn, M. and Frankel, J. (2007). Debt and interest rates: the U.S. and the euro area. *Economics Discussion Papers*, 2007-11.

Ciccarone, G. and Gnesutta, C. (1993). *Conflitto di Strategie*. Rome: NIS.

Diebold, F. and Li, C. (2006). Forecasting the term structure of government bond yields. *Journal of Econometrics*, **130**, 337–364.

Diebold, F., Rudebusch, G. and Arouba, B. (2006). The macroeconomy and the yield curve: a dynamic latent factor approach. *Journal of Econometrics*, **131**, 309–338.

Draghi, M. (2012). Global Investment Conference, London, 26 July 2012. www.ecb.eu/press/key/date/2012/html/sp120726.en.html.

Dunne, P. G., Moore, M. and Portes, R. (2006). European government bond markets: transparency, liquidity, efficiency. *CEPR*, May.

Engen, E. M. and Hubbard, G. R. (2004). Federal government debt and interest rates. In *NBER Macroeconomics Annual 2004* (M. Gertler and K. Rogoff, eds.), Cambridge, MA: MIT Press.

European Council (2012). *European Council Conclusions*, 76/12, June.

Faini, R. (2006). Fiscal policy and interest rates in Europe. *Economic Policy*, **21**(47), 443–489.

Fatas, A. and Mihov, I. (2003). On restricting fiscal policy in EMU. *Oxford Review of Economic Policy*, **19**(1), 1419–1447.

Fatas, A. and Mihov, I. (2010). Fiscal policy and the euro. In *Europe and the Euro* (A. Alesina and F. Giavazzi, eds.), Chicago: University of Chicago Press.

FED (2012). *Monetary Policy Release*, March 13.

Friedman, B. M. (2005). Deficits and debt in the short and long run. NBER Working Paper 11630.

Gale, W. and Orszag, P. (2003). The economic effects of long-term fiscal discipline. Working Paper, Tax Policy Center, Urban Institute and Brookings Institution.

Gibson, R., Lhabitant, F. S. and Talay, D. (2010). *Modeling the Term Structure of Interest Rates: A Review of the Literature*. Lausanne: Now Publishers.

Gonzalo, J. and Granger, C. (1995). Estimation of common long-memory components in the cointegrated systems. *Journal of Business and Economics Statistics*, **13**(1), 27–35.

Hall, B. H., Lotti, F. and Mairesse, J. (2008). Innovation and productivity in SMEs: empirical evidence for Italy. NBER Working Paper no. 14594.

Hall, P. (1989). On efficient bootstrap simulation. *Biometrika*, **76**, 613–617.

IMF (2011). Addressing fiscal challenges to reduce economic risks. *IMF Fiscal Monitor*, September.

IMF (2012a). *World Economic Outlook*, October.

IMF (2012b). Balancing fiscal policy risks. *IMF Fiscal Monitor*, April.

Kinoshita, N. (2006). Government debt and long-term interest rates. IMF Working Paper WP/06/03.

Laopodis, N. T. (2008). Government bond market integration within European Union. *International Research Journal of Finance and Economics*, **19**, 56–76.

Laubach, T. (2009). New evidence on the interest rate effects of budget deficits and debt. *Journal of the European Economic Association*, **7**(4), 858–885.

Marattin, L., Paesani, P. and Salotti, S. (2012). Assessing the pre-crisis advantages of the EMU for sovereign debt issuers: a panel VAR analysis. *Rivista di Politica Economica*, **1**(2012), 7–22.

Mosconi, R. (1998). *MALCOLM (Maximum Likelihood COintegration analysis in Linear Models)*. *The theory and practice of cointegration analysis in RATS*. Venezia: Libera Editrice Cafoscarina.

Mountford, A. and Uhlig, H. (2009). What are the effects of fiscal policy shocks? *Journal of Applied Econometrics*, 24(6), 960–992.

Muscatelli, A., Tirelli, P. and Trecroci, C. (2004). Fiscal and monetary policy interactions: empirical evidence and optimal policy using a structural New Keynesian model. *Journal of Macroeconomics*, 26(2), 257–280.

Paesani, P., Strauch, R. and Kremer, M. (2006). Public debt and long-term interest rates. The case of Germany, Italy and the USA. ECB Working Paper 656.

Perotti, R. (2004). Estimating the effects of fiscal policy in OECD countries. IGIER Bocconi Working Paper.

Sargent, T. J. (1987). Dynamic macroeconomic theory, 2nd edition. Cambridge, MA: Harvard University Press.

Sartor, N., Kotlikoff, L. J. and Leibfritz, W. (1999). Generational accounts for Italy. In *Generational Accounting around the World*, (Auerbach, A. J., Kotlikoff, L. J. and Leibfritz, W., eds.), Chicago: University of Chicago Press.

Schuknecht, L., Von Hagen, J. and Wolswijk, G. (2010). Government bond risk premiums in the EU revisited: the impact of the financial crisis. ECB Working Paper 1152.

Seater, J. (1993). Ricardian equivalence. *Journal of Economic Literature*, 31(March), 142–190.

Stock, J. H. and Watson, M. W. (1988). Testing for common trends. *Journal of the American Statistical Association*, 83(December), 1097–1107.

Taylor, J. B. (2009). The financial crisis and the policy responses: an empirical analysis of what went wrong. NBER Working Paper no. 14631.

Thomas, L. B. and Wu, D. (2009). Long-term interest rates and expected future budget deficits: evidence from the term structure. *Applied Economics Letters*, 16(4), 365–368.

Tobin, J. (1969). A general equilibrium approach to monetary theory. *Journal of Money, Credit and Banking*, 1, 15–29.

Tobin, J. (1982). Money and finance in the macroeconomic process. *Journal of Money, Credit and Banking*, 14, 171–204.

Warne, A. (1993). A common trends model: identification, estimation and inference. Papers 555, International Economic Studies.

Zagaglia, P. (2009). What drives the term structure in the Euro area? Evidence from a model with feedback. Mimeo.

Index

Printed in the United States
By Bookmasters